MODERN
SEAMANSHIP

MODERN SEAMANSHIP

DON DODDS

The Lyons Press

Guilford, Connecticut

An imprint of The Globe Pequot Press

The Lyons Press is an imprint of The Globe Pequot Press.

Printed in the United States of America

Design by Catherine Lau Hunt

10 9 8 7 6 5 4 3

Library of Congress Cataloging-in-Publication Data
Dodds, Don.
Modern seamanship / Don Dodds.
p.   cm.
Includes bibliographical references and index.
ISBN 1-58574-528-6
1. Seamanship.   I. Title.
VK541.D617   1995
623.88—dc20   95-17379   CIP

Contents

INTRODUCTION

WHAT IS SEAMANSHIP?

"Seamanship" describes the broad base of knowledge needed to traverse in a safe manner the two-thirds of our planet covered by water. Modern seamanship requires an understanding of the natural world of ocean and sky, and of the unnatural world of electronic and mechanical devices. It requires good judgment and sound decision making.

This book is for those who wish to think for themselves, solving problems by analyzing a situation and deftly using acquired knowledge. It is meant to provide the knowledge necessary to make your own decisions—a rare approach among seamanship texts meant for recreational boaters, which usually offer cookbook solutions that may or may not fit your situation. This book presumes you wish to know why and not just how. If you know why, the how quickly becomes evident.

Although the roots of seamanship are based firmly in the days of belaying pins and creaking yardarms, today's technology has greatly simplified many tasks. Compare traditional celestial navigation with the Global Positioning Systems (GPS), for example. The equipment used in celestial navigation is fragile, the skill and time required to use it considerable, the accuracy of the fix marginal, and the consistency of use irregular due to cloud cover. With GPS, accurate positions can be found by pushing a few buttons on an inexpensive, reliable electronic device.

The dichotomy of technology is that it gives and it takes away. It gives a person extra time to experience many activities in one lifetime by reducing the time necessary for training. Unfortunately, it takes away some of the pride of accomplishment—like painting the Mona Lisa by numbers. Making a landfall using a satellite navigation system is not nearly as rewarding as doing it with a sextant, but it *is* more rewarding than not doing it at all.

The technological solution isn't always the most expedient method. While a $600 GPS receiver will locate you anywhere on the planet, most boating is done in sheltered waters, where a little skill with a $30 handheld compass and a $3 straightedge can locate the boat perfectly well.

Similarly, technology is not necessarily synonymous with convenience. For

1

example, using a computer to keep track of the provisions aboard a boat may sound like a good idea, but it is much more time consuming than the more mundane paper-and-pencil method. The two or three minutes it takes to turn on the computer, boot up the database, search for the item, and delete it from the list every time soup appears on the menu quickly becomes a burden. The cook in the middle of meal preparation vows to boot the computer later. "Later" the soup can is forgotten, and soon the list is no longer valid.

Technology, like water wings, can get the boater literally and figuratively into deep water without knowing how to swim. Any equipment critical to the operation and safety of the boat requires a backup system. The prudent mariner forced to operate in an area subject to frequent fog, for example, might carry two radars, a radar and an individual trained to navigate by compass and run time, or two individuals properly trained in fog navigation.[1]

Modern seamanship is a dynamic subject constantly changing in content. If seamanship is to remain alive and viable in this changing technical world it must itself become more technical. To benefit from technology and use it safely requires a more theoretical understanding of the principles behind the technology. The theoretical approach also has the benefit of extending the value of the knowledge learned today, allowing it to be more readily adapted to future technological changes.

WHY SEAMANSHIP?

The modern boater must deal with the same sea that afflicted the ancient mariner. Modern techniques often supplement rather than replace older methods. "Red sky at night, sailor's delight" is still worth knowing. Local and regional weather broadcasts and weather facsimile charts are still, at best, general information and can change radically in a short time or distance. Solid, fundamental weather skills and valid observations are needed to fill the gaps.

Advances in technology may reduce the skill level needed to participate, but reducing the skill level is not the same thing as going to sea unprepared. While many imprudent boaters have gone to sea knowing little or nothing about seamanship, and have lived and gained notoriety, many more of the unprepared have gone to sea never to return. Going to sea unprepared has been and always will remain a foolhardy undertaking. Even though technology assisted, the safe modern

---

[1] *In the typical mom-and-pop boat it is prudent to have both mom and pop capable seamen. One or the other may fail in a critical situation.*

boater must still acquire a solid background in the many subdisciplines that comprise seamanship.

Safety is an important concept in seamanship, but there is more to it than just carrying the prescribed equipment. In fact, the term "safety equipment" is somewhat of a misnomer, since it implies that by carrying this equipment the boater will be safe. People then tend to rely on this equipment to get them out of situations that good judgment and proper training would have prevented them from ever facing.[2] Ultimately, safe operation of a boat means knowing how to keep out of unsafe situations. To turn a boater into a seaman it is still necessary to observe and understand the subtleties of nature, to practice skills of hand and eye, although aided and abetted by technology, and to apply this knowledge correctly to hold nature's overwhelming forces at bay long enough for ship and master to reach safety.

For example, most sailboats can sail in 40-knot winds; seamanship is the wisdom *not* to sail in 40-knot winds. A seaman does not approach the dock at 5 knots nor sail rail-down into a crowded anchorage. Needless risk of vessel, crew, and passengers is the antithesis of seamanship. Seamanship is as much the development of good judgment as it is good skills. The basis of good judgment is sound knowledge, some of which is technical and some of which is as esoteric as studying sea birds in flight.

And then there's the law. Both national and international law give the skipper of a vessel broad and sweeping powers. The skipper alone is responsible for the safety and security of the vessel, crew, and passengers. These laws assume that the skipper is competent. Thus, the skipper of *any* vessel had better be a competent seaman or have deep pockets, because along with the broad and sweeping authority comes an equally sweeping amount of liability. In other words, connected to that shiny new hull and bright teak trim is a liability for any damage the skipper and his vessel cause, whether by misuse, poor judgment, or just plain ignorance.

Dealers, especially those who sell smaller boats, should impress on the buyer the need for proper training. I have long been a proponent of mandatory boat operator licensing. Boats may go slower than cars, but they are driven in a more complex environment, and the growing numbers of boats have increased loss of life, bodily injury, and property damage alarmingly. An adequate licensing program is an idea whose time has come.

A workable licensing system is already partially in place. The Coast Guard Auxiliary and the Power Squadron teach classes on boating safety, rudimentary sea-

---

[2] John Russell, The Book of Seamanship, first U. S. ed. (New York: Ziff-Davis Publishing Co., 1979), 14.

manship, and maritime law. All that is needed is to require boaters to pass one of these courses before operating a pleasure craft.

Acquiring a seaman's broad base of knowledge and many different skills may seem a formidable task, but remember: very few of the old salts were considered great intellectuals.

Seamanship is a skill that can be greatly improved through reading. So get some deck shoes, a Greek captain's hat, an oiled-wool sweater, and a pipe full of aromatic tobacco, and prepare to get salty. This book is designed to help you acquire the necessary knowledge to deal confidently with the sea. It begins where the introductory sailing books end and concludes where specialty books, like those on racing or cruising, begin. It covers navigation, weather, boat handling, docking, mooring, anchoring, common emergencies, communication, working with rope, and maintenance.

The book can be read from cover to cover, but that really isn't necessary. In my experience, learning is a use-it-or-lose-it proposition. If you use a skill you will retain that skill; any knowledge or skill not used regularly will be forgotten. Since each individual has a need for different information, both in subject and level of detail, this book is designed to be read in parts. Its detailed table of contents and index will allow you to skip around, accessing only what interests you at any given time. You then will better retain the information of immediate importance and can neglect the rest until a new need arises.

You will also find that some of the information given in the book is technical, and explained with mathematics and equations. This information is not here to frighten you, but to provide interested readers with the understanding necessary to make correct decisions concerning a problem with multiple and complex variables. There is no need to read it if you are uninterested in digging deeper into the subject or are willing to accept the author's opinion without proof.

BOATING LAWS, REGULATIONS, AND ETIQUETTE

Maritime law is an important part of seamanship knowledge; however, many of these regulations are in a constant state of flux. Because of this potential for change, any detailed discussion stands a fair chance of being outdated before a book gets into print. Therefore, I will discharge my obligation by briefly describing these laws and recommending that you take a U.S. Coast Guard Auxiliary or U.S. Power Squadron boating safety course to get up-to-date information.

Like many endeavors of humankind, boating has a profusion of laws and regulations, some of them formal and some informal. The formal laws can be broken down into five distinct areas: laws that cover the operation of the vessel; laws that cover the vessel and its equipment; laws that require registration; regulations that concern the environment; and laws dealing with entry into foreign countries. The informal laws are known collectively as common boating etiquette and courtesy.

VESSEL OPERATION

Rules of the Road

The laws governing vessel operation are called the Rules of the Road. They include regulations on passing, overtaking, and crossing the path of other vessels. They also specify the proper location, color, and visibility of lights that must be carried on each type of vessel, and the type, frequency, and duration of audible signals. The laws governing vessels depend on whether the vessel is being operated at sea or inland. Most of the rules are similar; in many instances only the reference numbers differ. Where there are differences, however, they are significant.

The International rules apply in the ocean and in most coastal waters outside established boundaries. These boundaries occur at the entrances to all bays, harbors, and major rivers, as well as along some, but not all, stretches of coastline. These boundaries are described by coastal pilots in terms of prominent features and aids to navigation, and are shown on coastal charts by an appropriately labeled broken magenta line. For all other areas, the Inland rules apply.

In areas where boundaries have not been established, the waters inshore of a line approximately parallel with the shore through the outermost aid to navigation are considered inland waters. If no aids exist in the area, the International rules apply right up to the coastline.

The laws are contained in a pamphlet entitled "Navigation Rules: International–Inland," published by the U.S. Coast Guard (USCG) and available from the Superintendent of Documents (see Appendix A). The rules that concern recreational boaters will be discussed in more detail in Chapter 2, under the section on Collision Avoidance (page 42).

Reckless Handling and Accidents

Reckless operation of a boat that endangers life, limb, or property is forbidden by both local and federal laws and is enforced by the USCG, as well as by local police and sheriff's departments. Breaking these laws is a criminal offense and can subject the offender to large fines or imprisonment. The following are some of the offenses generally considered negligent operation:

> Overloading vessel with persons or freight
> Speeding in a confined area
> Speeding in a posted or swimming area
> Operating under the influence of alcohol or drugs
> Excessive wake
> Operating without proper lights at night
> Unsafe waterskiing practices
> Riding in exposed positions at high speed
> Refusal to correct hazardous conditions[1]

If a boating accident results in loss of life, loss of the vessel, injury causing any person to require medical treatment beyond first aid, or property damage in excess of the state threshold, an accident report must be submitted to the local law enforcement agency or Coast Guard within 10 days of the accident. If a death occurs, the report must be submitted within 48 hours. The Coast Guard has a form for reporting accidents, as do some local law enforcement offices.

Besides the obligation to operate a boat in a safe and accident-free manner, the skipper is also required by law to provide assistance to any person in danger at sea. The failure to meet this obligation could subject the master of the vessel to a fine and/or imprisonment.[2]

[1]*Carl D. Lane*, The Boatman's Manual *(New York: W. W. Norton, 1979), 196.*
[2]Federal Requirements and Safe Tips for Recreational Boaters *(U.S. D.O.T. U.S. Coast Guard, 1 March 92), 6.*

THE VESSEL AND ITS EQUIPMENT

Depending on the size of the boat, these laws require that certain equipment be present aboard. Currently this equipment consists of personal flotation devices, visual distress signals, fire extinguishers, explosion and flame control devices, and sound-producing devices. The regulations also concern marine electrical systems, ventilation requirements, and the process of taking on and storing fuel.

Personal Flotation Devices

All boats must have an approved personal flotation device (PFD) for each person aboard; in addition, boats over 16 feet in length must have at least one Type IV PFD available. The type of the device—indicated by a Roman numeral from I through V—determines the amount of flotation and the weight the device will support. Some PFDs are designed to float an unconscious victim face up; others are designed for use by a conscious victim. Manufacturers are required by law to label their flotation devices with the appropriate Coast Guard designation. See Table 1.1 for a description of PFD characteristics by type.

Table 1.1 Description of Personal Flotation Devices

TYPE	NAME	AREA OF USE	FLOTATION (IN LBS.)	VICTIM'S POSITION	COMMENTS
I	Offshore Life Jacket	All waters	22 and 11	Most unconscious users face up	Delayed rescue
II	Near Shore Life Jacket	Inland Waters	15.5, 11, and 7	Some unconscious users face up	Quick rescue
III	Flotation Aid	Sheltered Waters	15.5, 11, and 7	User must be conscious	Less restrictive for wearer than I or II
IV	Throwable Device	Inland Waters	—	User must be conscious	Immediate rescue
V	Special Use Device	Sheltered Waters	Inflatable	User must be conscious	Must be worn to be acceptable

Visual Distress Signals

Vessels greater than 16 feet in length, operating on open water greater than two miles wide, must be equipped with USCG-approved visual distress signals. Exceptions are made for open, engineless sailboats under 26 feet, manually propelled boats, and boats participating in races or regattas.

Approved visual distress signals may be pyrotechnic devices, flags, or light signals. The pyrotechnic devices are handheld or aerial red flares, red meteors or parachute flares, and handheld or floating orange smoke. All distress flares are red; the white flares are practice flares. The flag distress signal is a 3-foot square orange flag with a black square over a black circle. The U.S. flag flown upside down, extending the arms to the side and waving them up and down, and sounding a fog horn continuously are also recognized as distress signals, but are not counted as approved devices. Approved light signals must automatically flash the international SOS distress signal in Morse code: three short flashes, three long flashes, then three short flashes.

Obviously some of these signals, such as orange smoke and the flag or hand signals, are only of value in daylight, whereas the flashing light is only good at night. Flares are useful both day and night and can be seen from greater distances, but they are expendable, requiring you to carry extras—a minimum of three devices for day and three for night use. Those devices that are useful both day and night serve a dual purpose to fulfill this requirement.

Sound-Producing Devices

The navigation rules require sound signals to be made under certain circumstances. Vessels greater than 12 meters (approximately 40 feet) are required to carry on board a bell and a power whistle or power horn. Boats less than 40 feet are not required to carry sound-producing equipment, but it is a good idea to carry a horn for use in fog or to signal bridge tenders and lockmasters. The use of sound signals as an aid to preventing collision between recreational boats is discussed more fully in Chapter 2.

Fire and Explosion Prevention Equipment

Fire extinguishing equipment is classified by the type of fire it is designed to extinguish. Each extinguisher is designated by a letter and a Roman numeral. The letter designates the class of fire; the numeral designates the size of the extinguisher. Class A fires involve ordinary combustible materials, such as wood, paper, or cloth; these are best extinguished by cooling the burning material. Water is the most common agent used in fighting this type of fire. Class B fires involve flammable petroleum products or greases; oxygen deprivation is the most effective means of combating them. Foam extinguishers commonly are of the Class B type. Class C fires involve electrical equipment; to prevent electrical shock, the extinguishing medium must not conduct electricity. Dry chemical, Halon, and carbon-dioxide extinguishers are commonly used on Class C fires. Extinguishers that use vaporizing-liquid, such as carbontetrachloride and chlorobromomethane, produce highly toxic gases and are not acceptable by the Coast Guard. The regulations outline the number, type, size, and location of the required fire extinguishers.

Boats equipped with inboard gasoline engines must follow additional regulations conerning flame control, ventilation devices, and fueling procedures. Flame arrestors are required on the carburetor of inboard gasoline engines to prevent flames from igniting fumes in the engine compartment. Ventilation regulations concern the type, size, and number of ventilation ducts required for engine compartments, fuel storage areas, and the bilge.

REGISTRATION

All undocumented vessels equipped with propulsion machinery must be registered in the state of principal use. Coast Guard Documented boats may also be subject to state fees. Boaters likely to visit foreign countries other than Canada and Mexico should be aware that Coast Guard Documentation is preferred over state registration by foreign governments.

The regulations specify the size and location of registration numbers and the fee to be paid. Requirements vary depending on the size and type of boat. Failure to register a boat properly can lead to large fines. The owner is also required to notify the registration agency of changes in address or ownership of the vessel, and to inform them if the vessel or the certificate is lost, damaged, destroyed, or stolen.

ENVIRONMENTAL

Environmental regulations are multiplying rapidly. Pollution of the water by oil, fuel, bottom paint, solid waste, and sewage is covered by these laws. Discharge of any oil or fuel that causes a film or sheen upon or discolors the surface of the water, or causes a sludge or emulsion beneath the surface, is prohibited. Violators are subject to a $5,000 penalty.

All vessels over 26 feet in length are required to display a placard stating that it is illegal to discharge oil into U.S. navigable waters. The placard must measure at least 5 by 8 inches, be made of durable material, be fixed in a conspicuous place in the engine area or at the bilge pump control, and adhere to the exact message specified by law.

Marine sanitation devices (MSDs) are required in all recreational boats with installed toilet facilities. These devices are classified as Type I, II, or III. Type I and II devices treat the sewage with disinfectant chemicals or by other means before it is discharged into the water. Type III devices are certified no-discharge appliances. These include recirculation, incineration, and holding tanks. The discharge from these tanks must be emptied into shoreside pumpout stations or at sea beyond the 3-mile limit.

Boats less than 65 feet in length may use a Type I, II, or III MSD. All installed marine sanitation devices must be Coast Guard certified. All Coast Guard certified devices are labeled, except for some holding tanks, which are certified by definition under the regulations.

Regulations also place limitations on the discharge of garbage from vessels. It is illegal to dump plastic trash anywhere in the ocean or in U.S. navigable waters. The discharge of other types of garbage is permitted offshore beyond specified distances as determined by the nature of the garbage (see Table 1.2).

Table 1.2 Waste Discharge Areas	
GARBAGE TYPE	LOCATION
Plastics—includes synthetic ropes, fishing nets, and plastic bags	Prohibited all areas.
Floating dunnage, lining and packing materials	Prohibited less than 25 miles from nearest land.
Food waste, glass, metal, rags, paper and crockery that will not fit through a 1 inch square hole.	Prohibited less than 12 miles from nearest land.
Any waste material	Prohibited less than 3 miles from nearest land.

WHERE TO GO TO KEEP CURRENT

The U.S. Coast Guard Auxiliary offers a free marine examination to all boat owners. This examination includes checking all required equipment and a few optional safety items (see Table 1.3).[3] If the boat passes, it will be issued a decal. The Coast Guard will not board a boat displaying a valid decal to perform a safety inspection unless the vessel is behaving in a suspicious manner. If the boat fails the examination, the owner will be told privately what corrective action needs to be taken to bring the vessel into compliance. No report is ever issued to any law enforcement agency concerning deficiencies.

[3]*U.S. Coast Guard Auxiliary National Board*, Sailing and Seamanship, 2nd ed. (Washington, D.C.: U.S. Coast Guard Auxiliary National Board, Inc.), 6–10.

Table 1.3 Courtesy Marine Examination

ITEM	EXPLANATION
Ship's papers	Verify that ship's papers and FCC Licenses are on board and in order.
Numbering	Verify that registration numbers are located properly, that the lettering is the correct size and type and in a contrasting color.
Sound Producing Devices	Verify the presence of a suitable horn or whistle and bell, if required.
Personal Flotation Devices	Verify that the required number and type of PFDs are on board.
Ventilation	Verify the proper number of cowls and ducts are installed to ventilate fuel engine and bilge areas.
Flame Arrestors	Verify all gasoline engines are equipped with flame arrestors.
Fire Extinguishers	Verify the proper type, number, and size of fire extinguishers are on board, operable and current.
Lights	Inspect the navigation lights for proper type, location and that they are operational.
Fuel Tanks	Verify fuel tanks and lines are free of corrosion and secured properly. Verify fill pipe and plate for permanent tanks fit tightly and are located outside closed compartments.
Carburetor Drip Pan	Verify existence under all updraft carburetors.
Electrical Installation	Verify wiring is in good condition and properly installed. The system must be protected by fuses or manual-resetting circuit breakers. Verify the fuse panels are protected from rain or spray and that batteries are secure and the terminals protected against arcing.
Distress Flares	Verify the presence of the appropriate number and type of visual distress signals are carried on board.
Galley and Stoves	Verify stoves and fuel tanks are properly secured and without leaks, all flammable materials are located away from stoves, no uncommon fuels are being used, shut off valves are accessible, and adequate ventilation is available.
Dewatering Devices	Verify at least one effective manual dewatering device along with any electrical pumps is present.
Alternate Means of Propulsion	Verify vessels less than 16 feet carry a paddle, oars, or extra motor with separate fuel and starting systems.
Anchor System	Verify that a suitable size anchor and the appropriate rode for the vessel and the waters in which it is operating is available.
General Condition	Check the general seaworthiness of the vessel and that the pollution placards are posted properly.

REGULATIONS ON ENTERING FOREIGN PORTS

Regulations for pleasure craft sailing in foreign waters consist of relatively simple entrance and clearance procedures. Permission for entering and leaving a country is obtained from local customs officials. Papers showing ownership and documentation of the boat; a crew list; and valid passports, visas, and immunization records for each person on the crew list are required. It is not necessary for a documented U.S. vessel to clear customs when leaving the United States or its territories, but it is a good idea to secure clearance papers and a Bill of Health from the U.S. Department of Health if entering any foreign country other than Mexico or Canada. Foreign customs agents will want to see papers that clear the vessel from the last port of call; with these papers in proper order, entry will be considerably easier.

It is also prudent to carry several extra copies of all passport photos and the ship's documents. Regulations vary from country to country; on occasion, spare copies may be required by customs or immigration.

Entrance to, and in some cases exit from, foreign countries must be done through specific ports. Upon reaching one of these, the yellow "Q" flag must be raised on the starboard spreader or yardarm of the boat. The captain is the only person who may legally leave the boat until it and its crew have been inspected and cleared by customs and immigration. This means no crewmember may step off the boat onto the dock for any reason, not even to fasten mooring lines. The captain is allowed off the vessel only to secure clearance and must proceed directly with this mission.

When the boat and its crew have cleared customs and immigration, the "Q" flag is replaced by the national ensign or flag of the country being visited. Failure to fly the flag of the host nation properly is not only considered discourteous, but in some nations it is punishable by fine or imprisonment.[4] Flag etiquette is covered in Chapter 7.

Upon leaving a foreign country for any other country except the U.S., be sure to get the proper clearance papers. When reentering the United States, you are again required to enter only at designated ports. An American yacht not carrying merchandise that needs to be inspected or taxed may clear some ports by telephone.

[4]*Lane*, Boatman's Manual, *192*.

ETIQUETTE AND COMMON BOATING CUSTOMS

It isn't the blue blazer that makes a yachtsman, but the observance of common courtesy to fellow boaters.

Boats are small, private spaces—above or below decks—and should not be boarded without permission. If no one is on deck, a sharp rap on the hull will generally attract the attention of someone on board. A simple, "Permission to come aboard?" is all one needs to ask. No one would consider entering someone's home without knocking and being invited in; the same courtesy should be extended on someone's boat.

Rafting presents its own set of problems. When required to raft against another boat, always secure permission first. The process of rafting implies that the people on the outside boat will have to cross over the inside boat or boats to reach the dock. The crossing should be done quietly by way of the foredeck, as few times as possible and at reasonable hours. Parents with children should see that they respect the adjoining yacht.

Boats under power should constantly be aware of their wake, which can damage other vessels and erode sensitive shorelines. On days with little wind, the wake of a boat under power shakes all the wind out of a sailboat's sails and leaves them slamming and banging about for several minutes.

It is proper to reduce as much as possible the discomfort to any boat you pass. This can be done by passing well astern or downwind of the boat, or by slowing down so that the boats' relative speeds are only a few knots different. This is especially important when boats under power pass small craft. The large wakes caused by a speeding powerboat can easily swamp an open boat or canoe.

Many people enjoy boating because it provides peace; preserving this peace is an important element of yachting etiquette. Sailboaters, secure those halyards before you leave your boat. They may not be flapping when you leave, but let a little wind arise and they hammer out a cacophony of clatter, worse than dripping water on the forehead. Consider your neighbors, and remember that sound travels much better over water. Keep the level of conversation and music low, and shut down those generators after dark.

2

BOAT HANDLING

The nomadic propensities of boats can be alarming to beginning operators. Most people learn to handle an automobile before learning to handle a boat, and the automobile is a well-behaved machine by comparison. Its movement is restricted somewhat by the axis of its wheels, and, if the brake is set, it has the attractive property of staying where it is put.

Boats, on the other hand, slip sideways and tend to wander off under the influence of various water and wind forces. The exact direction of this wandering depends on the forces applied. This aberrant behavior generates considerable anxiety in boaters because they have very little control over some of the conditions that cause these forces.

All boats react to the loads applied in a similar manner, but each boat behaves a little differently depending on its shape, trim, speed, and weight; the rudder's shape and position; and the conditions of the environment in which it is operating. General rules can be given to help skippers handle their boats, but the individual boat's handling characteristics and the wide variety of possible conditions that can be encountered require experimentation.

Thus, unfortunately, each skipper must be subjected to a little "ramming and jamming" under the eyes of the assembled neighborhood dock crowd before mastering simple maneuvers. It helps to remember that everybody goes through this phase, and regardless of the number of years of experience handling a given boat, there are natural and manmade conditions that occasionally will lead even the most experienced skipper into an extremely embarrassing situation or worse.

We'll approach the subject of boat handling by presenting some background on the forces that affect a boat's course. Then we'll discuss simple maneuvers like stopping and turning. Once these principles have been digested, more complex maneuvers like docking and collision avoidance will be covered. The chapter then examines advanced boat handling techniques, such as dealing with conditions of limited visibility, current, and heavy weather. Finally, it concludes with some specialized methods used to manage the boat around, under, through, and over bridges, locks, and bars.

FORCES AFFECTING A BOAT'S COURSE

There are many forces generated by water, wind, and machinery that act on a boat. Boats are maneuvered by adjusting only two of those forces: applying power or inducing drag through rudder resistance. To know how and when to adjust power or drag it is helpful to understand the principles behind how all of the forces affect the boat, individually and collectively.

Water Forces

It is convenient to begin with the simplest case, that of water forces only. Water forces are caused by current. Current velocities are generally less than 2 knots, but can be as high as 13 or 14 knots (Nakwakto Rapids, British Columbia, for example). Current velocities of this magnitude make a recreational boat essentially unmanageable and should be avoided.

Since most bodies of water, except for small lakes, have currents, all boats are affected somewhat by this movement. If there is no wind and the engines are off, all boats will drift in the direction of the current. The boat will be stationary relative to the water and is simply carried over the bottom along with the water. The direction and velocity of the boat is essentially the same as the current; technically, however, the air resistance of the boat's superstructure has some small effect.

When the boat is moving under its own power, how much it is affected by the current depends on the boat's velocity and the velocity of the current. The slower the boat is traveling under its own power, the more the current will affect its path. When maneuvering in current it is best to position the boat so that current will take the boat to its destination. If that is not possible and it is necessary to maneuver under the influence of current, then sufficient boat speed must be maintained to overcome the effects of the current. The additional boat speed can make timing critical and boat handling very difficult.

Wind Forces

Wind forces can be important, especially on powerboats with very large superstructures or sailboats with their sails up. The sailboat skipper can control the shape and attitude of the sails to affect the boat's performance. Sail handling is discussed in any good book on sailing. This book is concerned with the wind forces acting on the hull and superstructure, and the discussion is therefore independent of whether the boat is a sailboat or a powerboat.

While it is certainly possible, and maybe sometimes necessary, to maneuver a sailboat in close quarters under sail power, it is best to reduce the unbalancing forces of the wind by dropping sails and maneuvering under power alone. Maneuvering in a confined area solely under sail power is only done on very small boats without auxiliary power, or in an emergency.

The wind forces on the hull are due to the wind pressure acting on the surface area of the hull and superstructure. At any given wind velocity this pressure is constant, but the force is dependent on the area. Because most boats have a larger superstructure forward, the force concentrates forward and pushes the bow downwind. The final attitude the boat assumes varies with each boat. As we will see later, this is dependent on the location of the center of the wind resistance and, since the boat is now being pushed through the water, the center of the water resistance. Because the locations of the two centers of resistance are not normally on the same line, the boat will pivot until they line up with the direction of travel and the center of wind resistance leading the center of water resistance.

Most boats drift sideways to the wind, with the bow 120 to 150 degrees off the wind. In very strong winds, boats with a lot of superstructure and very little aft, or those with small rudders or inadequate keels, require considerable speed in forward gear to overpower the wind forces and bring the bow into the wind. Often these boats will back into the wind; in fact, many times that is the only direction they will go. Boats with a large windage aft, particularly those that have added large spray curtains, may drift with the stern farthest off the wind. Drifting in this manner has some advantage, in that the cockpit and the rudder are protected from the onslaught of the waves and wind. However, sliding rapidly backward down a large wave can damage the rudder.

Mechanical Forces

Machines, unlike water and wind forces, are easy to manipulate; thus humans finally gain some modest amount of control over the maneuvering process. Mechanical forces are generated by simple machines that produce drag, or complex machines, which add a driving force.

Rudder Action

Drag is most commonly, but not always, induced by forcing an appendage, called a **rudder**, into the water moving by the hull. The magnitude of the drag can be adjusted either by increasing the velocity of water striking the rudder or by turning the rudder. Turning the rudder also moves the turning force's line of action outboard. The faster the water passes the rudder, the greater the amount of water deflected by the rudder; and the farther outboard the line of action, the faster the boat will turn.

This makes a boat react somewhat like an automobile, in that the harder the wheel is turned, the sharper the vehicle will turn. There are two major differences, however: First, a car turns from the front of the vehicle, with the rear wheels tracking the front ones. A boat, on the other hand, spins around its center, with the bow and stern moving in opposite directions relative to the centerline of the boat. Thus, a sharp turn to the right pushes the stern left—and into the path of any obstruction that may have prompted the turn.

Second, as noted above, the speed of the water passing the rudder governs the boat's ability to turn. If the boat and the water are moving at the same speed, no water is moving by the rudder, therefore no drag, and the rudder can be put in any position with no effect on the boat. A car rolling downhill can be steered; a boat drifting downcurrent cannot be turned by rudder action.

This relationship produces a common predicament in boat handling. Steering around an object dead ahead means the boat must be moving for the rudder to affect the boat's course. Slow movement means a small turning force and a long distance covered before the boat can turn enough to miss the object. Rapid boat movement produces a larger turning force and a quicker response to the helm, but closes the distance between the boat and the object much quicker. In many instances the only way to miss the object is to increase speed. Now the predicament: If the helmsperson's judgment is off, the impact is much more severe.

Control through Propeller Action

A boat's speed through the water is most easily adjusted with an engine or engines transferring power through the action of a propeller. The thrust or force generated by a propeller depends on its diameter, pitch, type, and the number and shape of blades. The **pitch** of a prop is the maximum distance it could advance during one rotation, usually measured in inches and determined by the angle at which the blades attack the water. Large pitch provides speed, small pitch provides power.

Propellers on recreational boats may be fixed, folding, self-feathering, or adjustable-pitch. Fixed-blade props are the least expensive and therefore the most common. Most powerboats and a few sailboats mount fixed-blade props, with the pitch set to provide a compromise between speed and power. Folding propellers, which are found only on sailboats, have two blades that fold flat parallel to the shaft to reduce drag when sailing. When under power, centrifugal force throws the blades out at right angles to the shaft and provides a driving force. Folding propellers have less power in forward than any other type of propeller and almost no power in reverse. These props and the long, deep keel make sailboats difficult to maneuver under power.

With self-feathering propellers, a small rotation of the shaft in either direction actuates gears that rotate the blades into the proper attitude for propulsion in the desired direction. Thus the blades of a self-feathering prop are better positioned for power in reverse than are those of a fixed-blade prop. When the shaft is not rotating, the force of the water turns the blades parallel to the direction of flow. On sailboats, this reduces drag when sailing.

Adjustable-pitch props are similar to airplane propellers: the engine runs at a constant speed, and the pitch is changed to increase the boat speed or change its direction from forward to reverse. Because the pitch is controlled by the operator, these props can be set to provide maximum power or speed depending on the conditions, while the engine runs at its most efficient RPM. In addition, adjustable-pitch props do not require a conventional gearbox, offsetting some of the additional expense and complexity.

Propellers, no matter the type, affect maneuverability in three ways: thrust, prop wash, and side forces.

Because the propeller in a single-engine boat is usually located on the centerline, the primary effect on turning by thrust is to move the boat through the water so that the rudder can be effective. In boats with twin engines the thrust is aligned off the centerline, and the propeller thrust alone can be a major turning force.

Twin-engine boats have rudders to control the boat underway, but in close quarters manipulating the prop thrust can turn the boat almost in its own length, much like a tracked vehicle. The tightest turn occurs with one engine full astern and the other somewhere between two-thirds and three-quarters full ahead and rudders hard over in the direction of the turn. If the second engine is full ahead, the greater prop efficiency in forward will overpower the reversing prop, and the boat will move forward.

Prop wash, the high-energy water flowing off the prop, is the major turning force in boats with movable shafts, such as outboard motors or sterndrives. It is so effective that most of these boats have no rudder. Instead, the prop wash is directed to move the stern left or right. On single-engine boats with fixed shafts the prop wash plays a minor role. Because the rudders on these boats are mounted aft of the propellers, the prop wash can be deflected by the rudder when the boat is moving forward, thus exerting a turning force on the boat. This turning force is independent of the speed the boat is moving through the water, but is limited to forward gear alone.

Besides developing axial thrust, a turning propeller develops side forces. This unbalanced force is due to the water being under slightly more pressure at the bottom of the prop.[1] This effect, though small, is augmented by the gravitational force assisting the downstroke and resisting the upstroke. The side force depends on the direction of prop rotation. In twin-engine boats this effect is nullified by having one engine rotate right and the other left. Single-engine boats with a single, clockwise-turning prop have a small, unbalanced force that moves the stern to the right and the bow to the left when the boat is in forward gear. In reverse gear the stern moves to the left. This tendency becomes more pronounced when the shaft is sloped; the more the slope, the more the unbalanced force.

When moving forward, a small deflection of the rudder is required to correct this side force. Since the rudder is less efficient in reverse, a larger deflection of the rudder is required to overcome this tendency to back to the port. Some boats are so poorly designed that they will not back to starboard at all.

Combined Effects

So far the discussion has been limited to single forces. Rarely is a boat under the effects of only one force. To understand a little about what happens when forces are applied together, it is necessary to know a little about forces in general. All forces have both a magnitude and a direction. For example, the weight of your body produces a *force* on the chair equal in *magnitude* to your *weight* and acting *downward* in a *vertical direction*. All the forces acting on the boat also have magnitude and direction. The path of the boat depends directly on the combination of these magnitudes and directions.

If the magnitudes and directions of the forces are known, the direction of the boat can be predicted through a form of mathematics called vector analysis. (Things that have both magnitude and direction are called vectors by mathematicians.) Fortunately for nonmathematical types, a boat can be steered by trial and error as well. However, understanding some of the simpler concepts of the complex-sounding mathematics can reduce the number of trials and the severity of errors.

To understand what happens when steering a boat, it is useful to separate all the forces acting on the boat into two groups: those causing or driving the motion, and those resisting the motion. In Figure 2.1, resisting forces are shown with dashed arrows. Next, it is possible to simplify all groups of forces by reducing them down to a single force called a **resultant force**. Therefore there are two resultant forces, one that is a combination of all the driving forces and one that is a combination of all the resistant forces (see Figure 2.2).

The lines of actions of these two resultant forces intersect the longitudinal axis

[1] *Ernest A. Zadig*, The Complete Book of Boating (*Englewood Cliffs, New Jersey: Prentice-Hall, 1972*), 90.

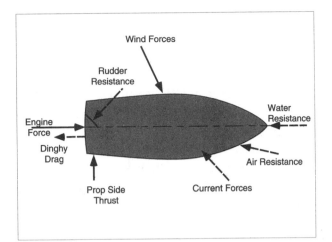

Figure 2.1 Forces Affecting
the Course of a Boat

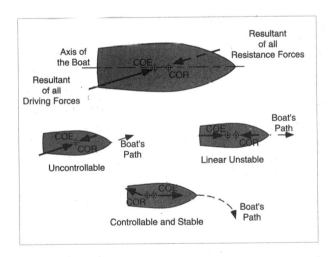

Figure 2.2 Resultant
Forces and Their Position

of the boat at two points called the **center of effort** (COE) and the **center of re-sistance** (COR). The center of effort is the point through which the resultant of all driving forces passes, and the center of resistance is the point through which the resultant of all the resistant forces passes. The relative location of these two points and the magnitude and direction of the two resultant forces affects the attitude of the boat. The drifting boat discussed earlier was at the mercy of these principles. In a boat under the control of an operator the magnitude and direction of these forces are subject to modification. The changes made consciously or unconsciously will affect the handling characteristics of the boat and the direction in which the boat will travel.

It is enlightening to examine the consequences of the various combinations of location and direction of the resultant forces. First, if the COE and the COR are in the same spot, the boat's path will be linear and in the direction of the resultant driving force, but the attitude of the boat will be uncontrollable. Think of a ball drifting in the water pushed along by the wind.

Turning control improves as the COE and COR move farther apart. When the COE is forward of the COR, relative to the direction of travel, a stable condition exists, and any unbalancing forces are automatically dampened by both resultant forces. If the COE is behind the COR, a potentially unstable condition exists. Unfortunately, in most boats traveling in a straight line the COE is behind the COR. If the boat is struck by an unbalancing force, the driving force will tend to unbalance the boat further, and it will broach without helm correction. A similar condition occurs in a rear-wheel drive automobile on ice.

Moving the rudder forces the COR aft of the COE while the rudder is active. However, once the boat is on course again it becomes unstable; therefore in broaching conditions it is best to move the COR as far aft and the COE as far forward as possible. This is why trailing warps, which moves the COR aft, stabilizes the boat and is common practice in a broaching situation. Other common boat-handling practices are based on principles that are just as straightforward.

THE SCIENCE OF STOPPING AND TURNING

A number of design factors affect the manner in which a boat reacts to the natural and mechanical forces during stopping and turning: overall size, weight, weight distribution, configuration of the underbody, and the number of engines.

Large, heavy boats have greater momentum than small, light boats and are harder to stop and turn. The proper trim of a small boat is more easily upset and is much more sensitive to passenger and equipment placement. Very small boats can be steered to a surprising degree by simply shifting the passengers' weight.

The configuration of a boat's underbody affects how quickly it turns and how much it slips sideways. Sailboats with long, deep keels slide sideways very little but are also very difficult to turn. Because of their large lateral plane underwater, they tend to go in one direction, with a turning radius similar to that of an aircraft carrier. In contrast, the shallow planing hull of a small powerboat will skid across the top of the water if turned too sharp.

The number of engines affects how a boat is turned. Twin-engine boats are considerably easier to control than single-engine boats. The most difficult boat to handle has a single engine turning a single propeller through a fixed shaft. Because this is the common configuration for most sailboats and many powerboats, the discussions on boat handling will revolve around this arrangement.

In the end, the steering and stopping process is boat-specific, and each skipper must appraise the forces affecting the boat and the forces available to control it. It is well to remember that in handling a boat, practice does not make perfect. It only improves your chances of success.

Stopping

The one fact that strikes the most terror into the heart of the novice boat handler is that boats don't have brakes. Stopping a boat can be done in only two ways (excluding impact): using an anchor or reversing the engine.

Stopping a boat with an anchor is only for emergencies and doesn't work if the boat is moving faster than a few knots. Excessive speed will cause the anchor to skip over the bottom or plane through the water. If it does catch, the dynamic impact of the boat hitting the end of the anchor rode will generally cause almost as much damage as hitting the obstacle you were trying to avoid. The anchor is still a useful emergency device for arresting the progress of the boat, however, and one should be available for use on relatively short notice.

The usual method for stopping a boat is through engine power. Because the propeller is effectively the boat's brake, the configuration of the propeller determines its efficiency. The best prop for stopping a boat moving forward is either the self-feathering or the adjustable-pitch type. The best prop for stopping a boat moving backward is the fixed-blade type. The folding prop will stop a boat about as well as dragging a foot in the water, regardless of direction. Boats with little reverse thrust should maneuver in reverse in situations that require quick stopping. This way the full power of the greater forward thrust can bring the boat quickly to a dead stop.

Normal Steering

Under usual conditions, steering a boat with a wheel is not more difficult than steering a car. Turn the wheel and the boat turns; the more the wheel is turned, the tighter the turn. Holding a course with either a boat or a car is easiest if wheel actions are kept to a minimum. Do not oversteer. A "loose hand" will let the boat recover from small wanderings on its own.

One difference between boating and driving is that things happen more slowly on the water. Most cars travel at a mile or better per minute; many boats travel a mile in 10 minutes. The appearance of another boat on the horizon does not indicate imminent collision. One of the worst reactions is to alter course too soon only to conclude that collision still appears imminent and then alter course the other way. Conversely, if course and speed are maintained or gradually adjusted, most of these apparent collisions will resolve themselves long before the boats pass.

Normally, steering is so easy that the helmsperson's attention can wander. Inattention can lead a boat into troubled waters, so to speak. One of the most common mistakes of inexperienced helmspersons is cutting corners. New helmspersons quickly learn the lesson about watching the horizon ahead of the boat, and they steer merrily down the middle of the channel. However, when they are required to make a major turn from one channel to another they come to grief. Unlike a car, a boat does not track its bow but turns on its center. This behavior coupled with the practice of steering to a point far forward of the boat takes the novice dangerously close to the shore. Perspective makes the boat appear to be in midchannel, when in fact the boat is approaching shore at an oblique angle (see Figure 2.3).

The best way to prevent this corner cutting when turning is to maintain a constant distance between the shore and the side of the boat rather than trying to center the boat in the channel.

Figure 2.3 Helmsperson's
Perception During Turns

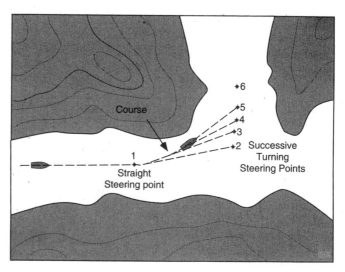

Turning in Close Quarters

When approaching or leaving a pier or dock, the boat must be maneuvered in and around obstacles at slow speeds. And as we have seen, at low boat speed wind and current have a greater effect on the boat's course.

Without the influence of wind and current, a turn to the left in a single-engine boat with a right-hand prop will result in the tightest *continuous* turn because of the side force effects from the propeller. The boat can actually turn more tightly to the right, but it is not a continuous turn. With the boat moving slowly forward with full right rudder, you shift into reverse, and the prop side force kicks the stern to the left. While the boat slows to a stop, the rudder remains full right, then just before sternway begins you quickly turn full left. Continuing in reverse as far as necessary with the rudder left, you then return the rudder to the right while simultaneously applying forward power. The prop wash strikes the rudder and forces the stern to the left even before the boat gathers way. The entire process is repeated as necessary. Some single-engine boats can turn almost on their axis in this manner. Because every boat turns differently, it is best to practice this turning maneuver in open water.

Wind and current make this maneuvering much more challenging. Before attempting a close-quarter maneuver, always check the magnitude and direction of both wind and current. To complicate matters, the boat's motion through the water generates its own wind. This is called **apparent wind**, which can be quite different from true wind and confuse the unwary. It is the wind's true direction and velocity that affects the actions of the boat. The true wind *direction* can be determined by observing wind indicators like a flag on a stationary pole, the drift of smoke, or the wind indicator on the mast of an immobile sailboat. Some indication of the wind's *velocity* can be judged by the wind effects on the water, flags, smoke, trees, or other objects (see Table 8.1 in Chapter 8).

Current is more difficult to judge. Strong currents can be detected by the disturbance of the water surface near a fixed object in the water—a piling or buoy, for instance. Currents of 1 knot or less may not cause enough disturbance to be seen easily, but they are still strong enough to move the boat. These currents can only be detected by observing floating material moving past a stationary object.

Piloting a boat in strong wind and current requires enough boat speed to overpower these forces. The added speed requires better judgment, reduces the time available to make the necessary adjustments, and increases the consequences of mistakes. When presented with these conditions it is best not to fight these forces with the throttle or helm, but to use them to advantage, if possible, by positioning the boat so that the wind and current help take the boat in the desired direction.

If that is not possible, maneuver directly into the current or wind by applying sufficient power to maintain headway, and keep the bow of the boat directly into the eye of the wind or current. When faced with both wind and current, 1 knot of current will have the same effect as 15 to 25 knots of wind. In this instance it is best to maneuver into the stronger effect. For example, in a 5-knot breeze and a 1-knot current, maneuver into the current.

If maneuvering great distances perpendicular to wind or current, it is necessary to crab the boat sideways—angling the boat with the current or wind so that the upstream progress of the boat is offset by the downstream set of the current. The angle of the bow to the wind or current can be regulated with the throttle. If the bow falls off too much, open the throttle.

Reverse

Steering a boat in reverse carries its own set of problems: the prop wash does not strike the rudder, the side thrust of the common right-hand prop pulls the stern to the left, and the rudder is now in "front" of the boat with its leading edge free. Without the prop wash over the rudder, the boat must attain a significant speed before the rudder force is large enough to turn the boat.

Steering in reverse requires more attention, because the water rushing past the leading edge of the rudder can snatch the wheel or tiller out of the helmsperson's hands and slam it violently against its stops. The greater the speed of the boat, the more likely this is to happen, and the more violent the reaction. This is hard on the boat, the rudder, the helmsperson, and the desired course.

Steering the boat in reverse, like steering forward, is simpler if the boat can be kept on course with very little rudder action. It is important to anticipate the turning action of the boat to reduce unnecessary rudder movements. In boats with aft steering locations, however, this requires considerably more concentration, because the short line of sight over the stern doesn't indicate early boat movement. To get this early warning when steering in reverse, turn and watch the bow; as the target gets nearer, shift your attention aft.

Finally, some sailboats with long, deep keels have a strong tendency to back only to port in a long graceful arc. If grace is not your intent, the principles of steering given earlier can be of assistance.

The boat backs to port because the rudder cannot supply enough starboard drag. To correct this, *add* starboard drag. This can be done in many ways, including moving the dinghy to the starboard stern quarter or dragging a bucket off the starboard side. If this added drag is enough to offset the prop side thrust, the boat will pull to the starboard with less than full right rudder, and control will be returned to the helm. Just be careful that the line (use a floating line if possible) on the bucket or dinghy doesn't get swept under the boat and wrapped around the prop.

The bucket trick principle is a good thing to keep in the back of your mind in case of steering failure. If an emergency rudder cannot be rigged, some amount of steering control can be obtained by dragging a bucket or other object behind the boat. Moving the object from side to side will control the direction and degree of the turn.

DOCKING

All boats equipped with engines should be maneuvered around docks under power. Although once common practice, few sailors today are sufficiently skilled to sail a boat into a slip. The inability to apply emergency reverse power to a boat under sail unnecessarily endangers the property of everyone in the marina. Some marinas actually prohibit this practice.

In the broad sense of the word, docking a boat consists of securing to, moving away from, and returning to the dock. Each of these operations has separate nuances, and it is convenient to discuss them in order of ascending difficulty.

Securing the Boat to the Dock

Boats are secured to the dock with line, knots, and splices. (Knots and splices are discussed in Chapter 6.) If securing to a cleat, use a proper cleat hitch or lark's head, depending on which end of the line is secured. Avoid simply dropping an eye splice around the cleat: the eye splice will move, resulting in considerable abrasion damage to the line. When securing a line to a ring, bollard, pile, post, or rail, use a clove hitch or two half hitches. In areas with large tidal ranges, avoid tying the lines to piles or other nonfloating members. If it becomes necessary to tie to these rigid objects, use adequate line length to allow the boat to rise and fall with the tide.

The perfect docking line has only three desirable features: it should be strong, elastic, and indestructible—in other words, nylon line. Nylon is strong, flexible, elastic, and *nearly* indestructible. "Nearly" is emphasized because nylon is very susceptible to chafe. Common methods for protecting against chafe will be discussed later in this section.

Docking lines should not be oversized, because that reduces the line's shock-absorbing properties. Most tables for selecting docking lines recommend inordinately conservative diameters. For example, one table recommends a 1-inch-diameter line for a 64-foot boat. A 65-foot Swan sailboat weighs about 60,000 pounds, however, and the breaking strength of four 1-inch lines is conservatively 100,000 pounds. The four docking lines recommended for securing this boat would be capable of suspending it 100 feet in the air with a safety factor over 1.5.

Realistically, a recreational boat rarely exerts more than 500 pounds of static load on a docking line. It would take a wind of 35 to 40 knots to produce this condition. (See Chapter 4, Table 4.11, Static Loads on Recreational Boats for Various Wind Conditions.) Compare that small load to the 7,500-pound breaking strength of ½-inch nylon line, and the possibility of line failure becomes ridiculously small. Furthermore, at no time is a properly secured boat held by only one line. If the wind is parallel to the dock, two lines are active. If it is perpendicular to the boat away from the dock, all four lines are active. A boat moored with four ½-inch nylon lines has under most conditions a static safety factor against line failure greater than 50. And, more important, they are light enough to stretch under load.

In dynamic conditions where wind, tide, or wave action can cause surging, the ability of the line to stretch with the load is important. Stretching reduces the dynamic loading on the attachment points. Half-inch line will stretch 2.5 times as much as 1-inch line, reducing the dynamic loading significantly. Rubber snubbers can provide the necessary elasticity for larger-diameter line, but they are an unnecessary expense if the lines are the proper size.

Docking lines do not fail in tension when used with the size and type of boat covered in this book; the loads are just too small even in severe conditions. But docking lines *do* fail, and the culprit is abrasion. Abrasion occurs any time dynamic conditions exist. Movement between boat and dock caused by wind and waves in turn causes line movements that abrade the line wherever it contacts an object not moving in concert.

A nylon line will chafe anyplace it comes in contact with rough material or a sharp edge and is subjected to relative motion. Chafe is most severe at the point where a line changes direction. A line can be protected by leading it through a fairlead and attaching adequate chafe protection at all points of contact. The traditional form of chafe protection is a leather patch or a serving of small-diameter cord wrapped around the mooring line. Both of these methods work but are time consuming.

An inexpensive and simple method consists of a 1-foot length of vinyl hose with an inside diameter slightly larger than the outside diameter of the line. The vinyl hose will not damage the line and takes almost unlimited chafe from the hard spot. It also can be positioned easily anywhere on the line—a mixed blessing, since the action of the boat may move the chafe protection away from the spot it protects. Regular inspections are important.

Dock Lines and Their Proper Use

Mooring lines generally have an eye splice on one end and a whipping on the other. The spliced end forms a very tidy attachment, while the free end is necessary to adjust the length of the line depending on the location of the dock cleats. Extra line is coiled either on the boat or the dock. Some boaters have special lines with splices at both ends tailor-made for their home slip, thus eliminating the need to coil.

The length of the mooring lines depends on the length of the boat. Four lines are normally used, two about half the length of the boat and two about two-thirds the length of the boat. Longer mooring lines are rarely needed except when moored to nonfloating docks in areas of extreme tidal range.

The four essential dock lines are the bow line, the stern line, the forward spring line, and the aft spring line (see Figure 2.4). The forward and aft spring lines hold the boat in position; the bow and stern lines keep the boat parallel to the dock. Very small boats can be moored successfully using only two lines by running the bow line forward and the stern line aft at 45 degrees. For larger recreational boats, the extra two lines add security and control. If the lines are laid out as in Figure 2.4 and any one line fails, the vessel remains approximately in its original position.

With the boat secured to the dock, it must now be protected against chafe. In severe conditions this is probably best done by keeping the boat entirely away from the dock, using lines to another finger pier or to an anchor set perpendicular to the dock or to windward. In more moderate situations, fenders and fender boards can be used.

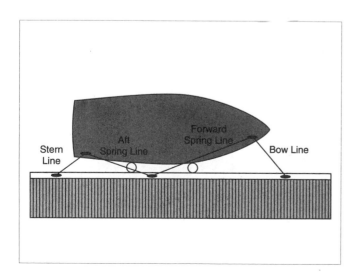

Figure 2.4 Typical Docking Lines

Fenders and Fender Boards

Fenders are air-filled plastic cylinders, spheres, or rectangles attached to the boat with a short length of line to protect the boat from striking the rough, horizontal surfaces of a dock, pier, or float. Fenders come in various diameters from 6 to 24 inches. Larger fenders offer more protection, but they also take up considerable storage space on board. Six fenders are normally considered adequate. Most boats use four fenders on the side toward the pier; the remaining two are used in special cases or when rafting. The center two fenders do most of the work on sailboats because of the boat's shape.

If a boat must lie against a piling or vertical surface, a fender board is useful. A fender board is a 4- to 6-foot-long 2 x 6 plank that can be attached between the fenders and the piling to provide a horizontal surface for the fenders (see Figure 2.5). The board and the fenders must be hung in such a manner that boat movement cannot change the relative position between the board and fenders.

Leaving the Dock

Leaving the dock with little wind or current is relatively simple. Start the engine and let it warm up for a few minutes before leaving; maneuvering around other boats is a poor time for a cold engine to die. Once the engine is warm, remove the docking lines. If there is little wind and current, remove the spring lines first, followed by the bow and finally the stern line. Removing the spring lines affects only the boat's lateral position along the dock. Removing the bow line allows the bow

Figure 2.5 Typical Fender Boards

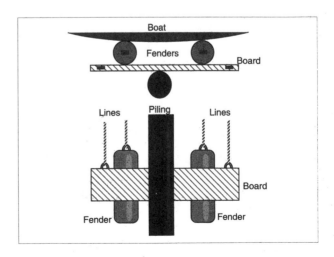

to drift away from the pier so that the boat can be taken away in forward gear. A pull on the stern line by the deckhand on the dock will swing the bow even farther away from the pier and at the same time make it easier to step aboard at the stern. As the deckhand steps aboard, the skipper shifts into forward and the boat moves easily away from the dock. Often this can be done with very little helm movement. If a tight turn is required, remember that the boat rotates on its center: watch that the stern doesn't hit the dock.

As soon as the boat is away from the pier, the deckhand should take up and stow the fenders and mooring lines. Dragging fenders are the badge of a novice.

Returning to the Dock

Returning to the dock is easiest when approaching a dock space several boat lengths long on a windless day with no current. In this situation it is necessary to remember only two things: the boat turns on its center, and a prop in reverse will kick the stern to port on most single-engine boats. The propeller's side thrust can be used to advantage if you approach the dock with the port side to the pier.

Bring the boat in slowly at what appears to most beginners too steep an angle, about 30 degrees. Judge the approach speed by the boat's stopping ability and the velocity needed to maintain steering control. Be careful to check the speed against stationary objects or the speedometer. A common mistake is to underestimate the boat's speed and approach too fast. As the boat approaches the dock, hold course until it appears that the bow will surely strike the dock, then start turning to the right, away from the dock. Remember, the boat turns around its center, not its bow; as the helm is turned the stern will swing inward toward the pier and the bow will swing magically away.

The most common error here is starting the turn too soon. The proper combination of a slow approach and a late turn will bring the bow away from the pier, and the boat will come smartly beam-on to the pier only a foot or so away, where the deckhand can step off the middle of the boat onto the pier and secure the docking lines. The engine can be put briefly into reverse to stop the remaining forward motion, or the deckhand can stop the boat with the forward spring line, and the deed is nicely done.

If the section of available dock is shorter, the process is essentially the same except the boat is put into reverse sooner. In this case reverse power is applied just before the boat is beam-on to the dock. The propeller side thrust will help kick the stern the remaining way into the dockside. If the available space is extremely short, the deckhand leaves the boat as early as possible from the port forward quarter and provides assistance from the dock.

The deckhand positions the docking lines and fenders, assists the docking process with physical force as necessary, and secures the boat properly. The deckhand begins by laying out the proper docking lines and the fenders on the side of the boat chosen by the skipper. The fore-and-aft spring lines should be long enough to reach the center of the boat so that the deckhand can carry both ashore. The boat can be stopped and held in position laterally by securing these two lines to a single cleat if necessary. The bow and stern lines can be left on board and are secured after the spring lines are in place.

The number of fenders and their placement horizontally differs depending on the boat and skipper. Three or four are generally adequate. Their horizontal location can be fixed in position earlier and deployed by the deckhand as the boat approaches the dock. The fenders' vertical location is the responsibility of the deckhand and should be adjusted to match the edge of the dock or pier as soon as it comes into view. The deckhand should then take a position where the dock can be reached most easily. Depending on docking conditions this position can be in the center of the boat or slightly forward; the more extreme the conditions, the farther forward the deckhand.

When the boat is within reach of the dock the deckhand steps ashore. Notice the term *step*, not leap. Leaps are only acceptable in extreme conditions. Leaping and shouting during docking show a certain lack of finesse.

Once on the dock, loop the forward spring line loosely around a handy cleat to help bring the boat to a controlled stop if necessary. Do not tighten any dock line without the permission of the skipper, since prematurely fastening or pulling on a line will affect the boat's course. When the boat is stopped, both spring lines are fastened, followed by the bow and stern lines.

Advanced Docking

Advanced docking consists of leaving and returning to the dock under the influence of wind and current. Advanced docking also includes special techniques, such as mooring Mediterranean style and docking if the engine fails. It is impratical to cover the hundreds of situations an individual can encounter when leaving or returning to a dock under extreme conditions. Each skipper must analyze the situation and apply the general principles of boat handling discussed above and the few special techniques presented below.

Wind and Current

When dealing with wind and current, the first step is to determine their direction and force. This is most easily done when leaving the dock, because the skipper has the advantage of a fixed platform to make the necessary judgments. The individual effects of current can be judged by noting any flow past a nearby piling or the boat itself. If the boat is aligned parallel to the current, the speedometer can be used to indicate the current velocity. Also, since the boat is not moving, the true wind direction and speed can be noted from wind instruments.

In most cases it is not the single effects but the combination of forces that will influence the boat. The easiest way to gauge the combined effect is to note how the boat lies against the pier and which docking lines are slack. The boat will lie on or off the dock, forward or back on its lines, depending on the combination of the wind and current. The strength of the combined force can be judged by gauging the effort required to move the boat against the force by pulling on a dock line, and the speed at which the boat returns to its original position.

Because the true wind and current conditions are more difficult to assess from a moving boat, the arriving skipper has a more challenging task. Current can be estimated by stopping the boat and noting the drift or making a preliminary pass by the slip to note any current effects on pilings or other stationary objects. Now the skipper can plan his departure or arrival to make the best use of these variable forces.

It is best to leave and approach the dock into the current. Good control can be maintained at a much slower boat speed relative to stationary objects, because the speed of the water flowing by the rudder affects the force on the rudder, and likewise the speed of the turn. The boat will react much more rapidly if it and the current are moving in opposite directions. If the boat travels with the current, response will be sluggish.

If the wind is off the dock when leaving, the only concerns are the order in which lines are released and getting the deckhand on board. If the wind is *on* the dock when coming in, its force will assist the skipper in landing the boat. The challenge comes when the wind is on the dock when leaving and off the dock when returning.

If the wind's force is pushing the boat onto the dock when leaving, then the bow must be forced away from the dock to permit a forward exit. If the wind force is light enough, sometimes the deckhand can force the bow away from the dock far enough to permit forward exit. In extreme conditions the stern may drag along the dock, and considerable muscle may be needed to control the boat. In this instance it is preferable to have the strongest person—and the best leaper—handle the dock lines. In extreme situations, it may be necessary to get help. Extra hands can handle multiple lines simultaneously and bring extra muscle power to bear on the problem.

If there isn't enough muscle power to effect the necessary turn, sometimes backing the boat against its stern spring line, or for that matter any line attached to the stern, will force the bow far enough into the wind to leave the dock in forward gear. Lead the line around the dock cleat and back to the boat, taking a couple of turns around a suitably placed cleat on board. This way the line can be let go and retrieved from the boat. A crewmember near the stern can keep the boat off the dock with a judiciously placed fender.

If these methods don't work, the next best alternative is backing the boat away from the dock, which takes advantage of the natural tendency for the bow of most boats to blow downwind. Cast off all lines except the bow, lead the bow line around the cleat, then have the deckhand pull the bow in, forcing the stern out. Back away from the dock until sufficient sea room is available to shift into forward and gain the necessary speed for helm control. I prefer this method, but then my boat is relatively well behaved in reverse gear.

On occasion it may be necessary to force the stern into the wind using engine power. This is basically the same process described above, except that the line remains attached at the bow while the boat is powered forward, with fenders being placed to protect the bow. This will kick the stern away from the pier.

By changing the attachment points and the direction of engine power, the clever skipper can manipulate the boat in surprising ways. For example, attaching the bow line forward and backing, attaching the stern line aft and pulling forward, or attaching a line to the center of the boat and powering either forward or backward into the attached line will bring a boat into the dock. This is useful when returning to the dock against a wind off the dock. However, there are two complications to consider: getting the line ashore to perform this maneuver can be a task; and a single line ashore can limit a boat's maneuverability—and if improperly handled can be more hazard than help. If this is still the method of choice, sometimes the bow can be brought in close enough for a deckhand to get on the dock carrying the line.

Another option is to toss a line to dockside help, which is often available because of the pleasant boating custom of assisting docking vessels. However, it is best for the boat's crew to retain control of the docking process. Be cautious about relying on this aid; poor coordination at the wrong time can turn a controlled approach into chaos. Before tossing a line to helping hands, give clear, concise instructions as to what you intend to do and how the dockside help can assist. Just in case, you might also position a precautionary deckhand to cast off any offending line quickly.

Mediterranean-Style Mooring

Mediterranean-style mooring allows more boats to use a single pier. Each boat lays perpendicular to the pier or quay with the bow or stern held in place by an anchor. It is like a marina without the expense or convenience of finger slips. In areas without the necessary space for the proper anchor scope, mooring buoys or piles may be substituted for the anchor.

A boat can be moored stern to the pier if it can be backed under control. If not, the easiest method is to lay bow to the pier, although it's more difficult to get ashore over the bow and you'll need a larger crew.

To moor bow to the pier, slowly approach perpendicular to the pier, and let go the anchor over the stern or attach a line to the buoy or piling, depending on the existing system. As the boat approaches the pier, let out the stern line until the boat is close enough for a crewmember to step ashore with the bow line. Secure the bow line and haul the boat back away from the pier using the line attached to the anchor, buoy, or piling. The anchor should be positioned to provide the necessary scope for good holding (for more on anchoring see Chapter 4). Under ideal conditions, mooring bow-to requires at least three people, one at the helm, one at the bow, and one to tend the anchor line and keep it from fouling the prop. It can be done with fewer people but is more hazardous.

To moor stern-to the pier, drop the anchor off the bow or attach the bow line to the buoy or piling, and back into the slip. Since a bow line is much less likely to become entangled in the prop, this operation can be done with one less pair of hands. If you're shorthanded the forward line can be left to run out on its own. A single crewperson can then be positioned to step ashore with the docking line, secure it, then reboard and adjust the forward line.

Med-style mooring can be extremely difficult with winds or current parallel to the pier. If space is available the boat can be crabbed into the pier; if not and all else fails, drop the anchor or pick up the buoy, then take the dock line ashore by dinghy. Once both lines are secured the boat can be pulled into position by adjusting the length of the bow and stern lines. It may not be as elegant, but it is certainly effective.

Rafting

On occasion it is necessary or desirable to raft with another boat rather than tie to a pier or a float. Rafting can be done for social reasons or in crowded harbors with more boats than mooring space. Bringing a boat into a raft is very similar to bringing a boat into a dock. If the raft is at anchor, be sure that all forward motion is stopped before securing the boat. Common courtesy requires obtaining permission to raft from the moored boat. If permission is granted, the boats should be staggered so that the rigging of any two adjacent sailboats will not touch when the boats roll.

For social rafting the cockpits are positioned so that passengers and crew can move freely between vessels, cockpit to cockpit. Compulsory rafting in crowded harbors often makes neighbors of complete strangers. Because the cockpit and transoms are part of the living space, under compulsory conditions it is best to confine foot traffic to the bows. Where rafting multiple boats is unlikely, two boats can be rafted bow to stern, which allows more privacy and easier access across the inner boat's bow.

When any boat except the outside one leaves a raft, all boats outside and the boat immediately inside the one that is leaving become involved. Foresight and planning will help keep the process an orderly and friendly one. A great number of lines and fenders will have to be adjusted, so each of the involved boats will need crew available. Discuss departure plans with the other boats to determine whether delaying the inner boat's departure will reduce the confusion. The departing boat should leave in a direction that produces the least disturbance.

NAVIGATIONAL AIDS

Boating has been described as the fine art of getting wet and becoming ill while slowly going nowhere at great expense.[2] In this section we are interested in the latter pursuit. When going nowhere, navigation is less important than navigational aids, or channel markers and lights. In remote waters it may be necessary to rely on charts and the piloting techniques covered in Chapter 3, but in well-traveled areas attention to channel markers and lights alone can keep a boater out of trouble.

On federal waters all markers have a standard shape and appearance, regardless of who maintains them. Waters completely within the boundaries of a state and not subject to federal jurisdiction, however, use an entirely different system of buoys known as the Uniform State Waterway Marking System. This system, roughly compatible with the federal systems, is applicable to only a small number of boaters and is covered in Appendix B.

The federal system discussed here follows the International Association of Lighthouse Authorities (IALA) Guidelines System B, which is also followed throughout much of the world. System B places the red buoy on the right side of the channel when returning from the sea. System A, which places the red buoy on

---

[2]Henry Beard and McKie Roy, *A Sailor's Dictionary* (New York: Workman Publishing, 1981), front cover.

the left side of the channel returning, is used by the nations of northwestern Europe: England, Ireland, France, Norway, Sweden, Poland, and Russia.

Channel Markers

Channel markers consist of buoys, daybeacons, and ranges. All of these devices are intended to keep boats within the designated channel and out of harm's way. The system, however, is designed primarily for large ships, and in some instances small boats have some latitude to hedge on their guidance. Before tempting fate, however, a prudent skipper should have local knowledge or a journeyman's ability to read a chart.

Buoys

Buoys are specially shaped objects anchored to the bottom by a weight and chain. There are four major shapes: conical (point up), called nun buoys; cylindrical, called can buoys; spherical buoys; and skeleton buoys. Nuns and cans are the most common. Spherical buoys mark situations with no lateral significance, such as navy testing areas. Skeleton buoys are constructed of solid plates supported on a float by an open skeleton of structural steel. These buoys commonly carry sound-producing devices, lights, or both, and are used in midchannel or around obstructions. Skeleton-style buoys are listed on charts as lighted buoys. Buoys are attached to their anchors with chain, which can be as long as three times the water depth. Because of this, a buoy's position is always approximate and can wander depending on the action of wind and tide. Always give buoys a wide berth.

A buoy's color, shape, and position are used to indicate the location of the safe channel. Can buoys are painted green, indicate the left side of the channel when returning from the sea or traveling upstream, and are marked with odd numbers. Nun buoys are painted red, indicate the right side of the channel when traveling upstream or returning from the sea (thus the phrase "red right returning"). Nun buoys are designated with an even number. Skeleton buoys can be either red or green to mark either side of the channel. "Upstream" is defined on tidal waters as the direction proceeding from the open sea to port and on the Intracoastal Waterway as proceeding clockwise around the country.

Where the Intracoastal Waterway coincides with major rivers or channels coming in from the sea, these separate systems may conflict. In this instance the proper side to pass the buoy is shown by a small yellow square or triangle painted on the buoy—square for the left of the channel, triangle for the right side. The numbering sequence on buoys generally starts at the downstream end of the channel and increases as the vessel proceeds upstream. The numbers normally follow in sequence, with even on the right and odd on the left. However, some numbers may be skipped if one side of the channel has more buoys than the other.

In some instances buoys mark the middle of the channel, indicating safe water or an obstruction, depending on color scheme. These buoys are not numbered, but they may show a letter. A buoy showing *red and white vertical stripes* (its shape may be either spherical or skeleton) is a midchannel buoy, and indicates safe water on both sides. A buoy with *red and green horizontal bands* marks a midchannel obstruction. If the top band is green, the preferred channel is to the right of the buoy going upstream. If the top band is red, the preferred channel is left of the buoy going upstream. Unlighted buoys may be can-shaped (green over red) or nun-shaped (red over green). Lighted (skeleton-style) buoys indicate preferred channel by the color of the top band alone.

There are also buoys colored either yellow or white. Yellow buoys, which can be any of the usual shapes, are used for special purposes such as indicating separate traffic lanes; this is generally noted on local charts. White buoys are informational buoys, and normally are can-shaped with orange stripes. Informational buoys may indicate speed limits or other special requirements.

Lights make buoys easier to find under conditions of poor visibility. The lights are the same color as the buoy except for midchannel buoys, which show a white light. Horizontally striped buoys show the same color light as the buoy's top stripe, which indicates the preferred channel.

Figure 2.6 Standard Navigational Buoys

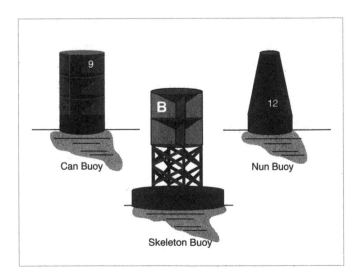

Can Buoy

B

Skeleton Buoy

Nun Buoy

Lights can be fixed or flashing. Flashing lights are distinguished by flashing patterns. A single brief flash at regular intervals is designated **flashing**. A light that is on five times longer than it is off is called an **occulting** light. A light that is on and off for equal periods is called an **isophase** or **equal interval** light. A **quick flashing** light flashes about once a second. **Group flashing** lights flash patterns that are repeated within a designated period of 2.5, 4, 6, or 8 seconds. The designated number of flashes occur in a single group separated by an interval of darkness. **Morse code flashing** lights commonly use an 8-second period to flash a series of dots and dashes representing a letter in Morse code.

Sound is also used to help locate buoys during times of poor visibility. Bells, gongs, whistles, and horns differentiate between buoys within audible range of one another. Bell, gong, and whistle sounds are all produced by the rocking or plunging motion of the buoy in normal sea conditions. Horns are electrically operated, and are used where the sea's motion is unlikely to activate other sound mechanisms.

Daybeacons

Daybeacons are always unlighted, hence their name. Unlike buoys, they are firmly fixed to the bottom by a post or group of posts. Daybeacons may be located on shore or in shallow water. Each has a distinct shape called a **daymark,** and because of this daybeacons are sometimes called **daymarkers.** This is technically incorrect, however; the term daymark here will refer only to the distinctive shape.

Square daymarks are green with an odd number to indicate the left side of the channel. Triangular daymarks are red and have even numbers to indicate the right side of the channel. Daymarks that indicate midchannel obstructions can be square or triangular, with horizontal green and red stripes. The preferred channel is indicated by the shape and the top stripe. Midchannel daymarks are octagonal, with vertical red and white stripes. Midchannel daymarks are not numbered but may be lettered.

Range Markers

While buoys or daymarkers indicate the edges of the channel, range markers indicate the center of the channel. Range markers could be described more accurately as bearing markers, since they indicate bearing not distance. Range markers may be manmade or natural. Manmade markers are common on well-traveled channels, but natural ranges are of tremendous value to boaters in remote areas.

Manmade range markers consist of two markers placed one behind the other so that when lined up they indicate the preferred course. These markers are vertically striped with two of the following contrasting colors: black, white, red, green,

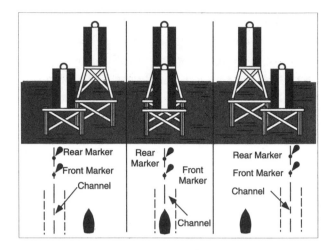

Figure 2.7 Typical Range
Markers

or orange. Figure 2.7 shows how a range marker indicates a boat's position relative to the channel.

Ranges are one of the most accurate ways to position a vessel, and often are used to guide vessels through a narrow channel. Range markers may be lighted to provide guidance at night. Caution should be exercised when following ranges; other traffic using the same range will be on or near a collision course.

The range indicates the preferred lateral position. The upstream or downstream extent of safe water or the usable portion of the range is sometimes designated by other channel markers, always indicated on the area chart by a solid line. Boaters should not travel beyond the usable portion of the range unless strict attention is paid to soundings.

Another form of manmade range indicator is the **directional light**, which consists of a narrow-beam white light flanked by a green light on the left and a red light on the right. If the light shows green the boat is too far to port; if the light shows red the boat is too far to starboard. A steady white light means the boat is on course and in safe water. A variation is a steady white light to indicate the preferred channel and a flashing light to indicate that the boat is off course. The flashing pattern, described in a note on the chart, indicates which side of the true bearing the boat lies. Because the beam emanates from a single source, the width of the indicated preferred path varies in a vee shape, getting smaller as the boat approaches the light. The actual safe path may be considerably different. Directional lights obviously are not as precise as range markers in controlling a boat's lateral position.

Natural ranges consist of a pair of naturally occurring objects that are in alignment when the boat is in the preferred channel. Cruising guides use them extensively, as in this passage: "On Cave Cay Bank there is 7 ft least depth on a line between the white cliffs and the west beach of Lancing Cay." Another might advise to "enter Stockton Harbor aligning the church steeple with the chemical plant's stack." The recreational boater can utilize natural ranges to great advantage. The necessary equipment is a good chart of the area and skill at interpreting what is shown. Chapter 3 discusses this procedure more fully.

Lights

The two main classifications of lights of interest to recreational boaters are **lighthouses** and **minor lights**. Lighthouses are the familiar massive structures of seacoast postcards, while minor lights are mounted on small towers and posts, and are not as powerful. Lighthouses have stronger lights, and are located in critical areas, principally along the seacoast, to mark approaches to important harbors or dangerous offshore shoals and hazards.

Each lighthouse has a different structural shape and shows a light with a distinct color and pattern. The patterns of the lights are similar to lights on buoys, except that lighthouses can show *combinations* of steady and flashing lights simultaneously. The standard colors are red, green, and white. The individual patterns are described on the charts and in the *Light List*.

A light's visible range is marked on the chart, but it obviously depends on the clarity of the atmosphere. Obviously, thick fog will obscure a light inside its visible geographical

The increased candlepower of a lighthouse increases its luminous range when compared with a minor light. Its geographical range depends on the height of the observer's eye and the height of the light, a distance you can calculate using this equation. The actual visible distance given on the chart and in light lists is the distance from the light when the height of the observer's eye (h) above sea level equals zero.

$$D = 1.17 \, (\sqrt{H} = \sqrt{h}\,) \qquad \text{Eq 2.1}$$

Where: D equals the distance in nautical miles,
H equals the height of the light in feet.
h equals the height of the observer's eye.

The visible distance is the sum of the distances derived from the height of the light and the height of the eye of the observer. Note that $\sqrt{H} + \sqrt{h}$ is not equal to $\sqrt{H + h}$.

This distance can indicate how far the boat is from the light when the light is first observed. When the boat is at the light's exact visible distance, the light is obscured in the bottom of wave troughs. If no waves exist, the head can be raised and lowered to obscure the light. This is called **bobbing** a light.

range. In some instances, primary lighthouses can be detected beyond the calculated distance, or given visible horizon, because the light's high candlepower produces loom or sky shine.

Some lights can be seen through 360 degrees; others are limited by natural obstructions, and some are purposely limited in their exposure. On occasion a red light is shown marking an area with dangers to be avoided. The prudent skipper always avoids waters covered by lights showing red sectors.

Minor lights are essentially lighted daymarkers; perhaps they should logically be called nightmarkers. They serve the same purpose as lighted buoys, and follow similar color and pattern conventions. Minor lights may also show a daymark symbol. They generally have a greater geographical range than a lighted buoy because of their greater height above the water. The luminous range of these lights is generally much less than their geographical range.

COLLISION AVOIDANCE

Collision avoidance deals with two specific concerns: identifying when a collision is imminent, and taking the appropriate and necessary action to avoid contact. Although collisions can be avoided by applying the established Rules of the Road, often all that is needed for recreational boaters is a little common sense.

Rules of the Road

A whole body of law and knowledge concerns itself exclusively with keeping two boats from hitting one another. Unfortunately for recreational boaters, these laws were designed long ago to deal with large, difficult-to-maneuver ships. Large oceangoing vessels require several miles to stop and a mile to complete a turn. Small recreational boats, on the other hand, commonly stop in less than 100 feet and can turn 180 degrees in half that distance. Obviously, preventing collisions between two large commercial vessels presents entirely different situations than preventing collisions between two small recreational vessels. If you are interested in reading them, a copy of Navigation Rules, International–Inland (COMDTINST M16672.2A) can be obtained from the U.S. Government Printing Office (see Appendix A).

The Rules of the Road of interest to recreational small boats are based on ommon sense and are few in number—eight to be exact. The first six rules are:

1] A vessel overtaking another from the rear must keep clear of the forward vessel.
2] Give way to all boats approaching on the right side from the beam forward.

3] Boats under power (since they are easier to maneuver) should keep clear of boats operating under sail alone.

4] Stand well clear of working vessels and give them the right of way.

5] Keep the boat under control, travel at a safe speed, and depending on the conditions, keep a safe distance between boats at all times.

6] Be alert, be observant, drive defensively, and never press any supposed right-of-way privileges.

A little contemplation will reveal that these rules are very similar to the laws governing automobile traffic. The first rule is so basic and intuitive that it needs little explanation. Avoiding something directly in front of the boat is the responsibility of the skipper, whether the object is a rock or another boat.

The second rule is very similar to traffic rules for residential side streets, where cars approaching from the right have the right of way.

The third rule, with a little stretching, is similar to cars allowing pedestrians the right of way. Boats under sail are directionally encumbered because they can travel in only 270 of the 360 degrees available to boats under power. Note that a sailboat is considered to be under power if the engine is running, whether the sails are up or down.

The fourth rule is similar to the temporary speed reduction zones and traffic control around highway maintenance areas. On roads, vehicles are forced to pass close to maintenance work in progress, but on waterways, it is rarely necessary for recreational vessels to get near working vessels. Working vessels include commercial fishing boats and tugs as well as those maintaining the waterways.

The fifth rule is very similar to the laws requiring automobiles to adjust speed and position depending on road and traffic conditions, regardless of posted speed limits. A boat's safe speed depends on its ability to stop and turn, prevailing visibility, and traffic conditions. There are on occasion posted speed limits for boaters, but that does not relieve you of the responsibility to reduce speed in congested areas. Unlike automobiles, a boat has a wake. Boats are required to reduce speed if their wakes can cause damage. Note that size is not a factor; a small fast-moving dinghy can cause considerable wake damage.

The sixth rule is drive defensively, with the additional responsibility of maintaining a watch. Boats move very slowly or can be put on autopilot, but all boats not anchored or moored are required to keep an alert watch at all times.

The last two rules necessary for order are based on courtesy and convention.

> **7] Pass with as much distance between boats as possible and in such a manner as to cause minimum disturbance to the boat being passed.**
>
> **8] In all passing situations regardless of direction, make your intentions known as soon as possible. Altering course early will indicate your intentions with a minimum amount of course change.**

Applying the Rules and Using Common Sense

Avoiding collision during regular circumstances first requires the helmsperson to classify nearby boats as recreational boats, large vessels, working vessels, and a few other special traffic types. Each of these classes is treated somewhat differently.

Recreational Traffic

Avoiding collision with recreational traffic involves noting the position of all boats relative to your own course and how these positions change over time. Most boats can be eliminated as possible collision candidates immediately. The remaining questionable boats must be watched closely. Each boat has a destination, distinct or indistinct. In narrow channels this course is generally either up- or downchannel. In large bodies of water the possible courses can be considerably more varied, but each boat's course has a distinct angle with your own. The change in this angle between your course and the rest of this traffic determines whether a potential for collision exists.

To detect a potential collision the helmsperson simply estimates this angle repeatedly. The angle can be estimated by eye or obtained more exactly by sighting over the binnacle compass or a handheld compass (see Chapter 3). Most people make the initial judgments by eye, resorting to the compass only in critical situations. While measuring the angle it is important to hold a steady course.

After a few estimates of angle, three possible conditions can occur: First, the angle between your course and the bearing to the target vessel is becoming smaller, in which case the target boat will pass in front of your boat. Second, the angle between your course and the target boat is becoming larger, which means the boat will pass behind yours. Finally, the angle between your course and the target boat remains constant—the classic "constant angle diminishing range." Collision is imminent unless evasive action is initiated by one or both of the boats.

The actions available are speed up, slow down, turn, or some combination of the three. Boats under sail are limited in their ability to alter speed and change course (see Rule 3 above). Powerboaters can choose whichever action or combination of actions best suits the circumstances. My experience, although statistically insignificant, is that sailboats will opt for a course change while powerboats favor a change in speed. Once the boats have passed, the skippers can resume course and speed.

The action chosen should in all cases provide the greatest clearance between the passing boats and should be done as early as possible. It is, of course, possible to rely on Rule 2 and force the vessel approaching from the right to make the turn necessary to avoid collision. However, the process of identifying a burdened and privileged vessel requires a trust in the other skipper's competence, which may or may not be justified. All of this can be avoided if neither assumes the right of way and each boat turns away from the other. In this case, the turning actions required in most situations are almost instinctive. For example, in Figure 2.8 the natural reflex actions of the two skippers to turn away from the approaching boat will result in a safe passing whether they are approaching from the front or the rear on either side.

The only situation where common sense and turning away from the approaching boat can be confusing is when two boats are approaching exactly head-on. In practice, when recreational boats find themselves in this situation their small size relative to the channel width and their inherent maneuverability resolves the incident into a parallel course rather than an intersecting course long before any real risk of collision occurs.

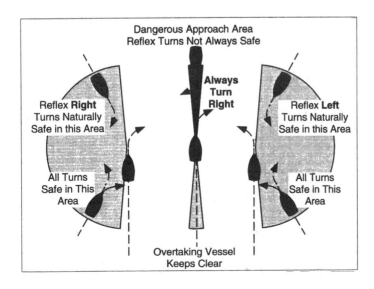

Figure 2.8 Instinctive Turns for Two Boats on Intersecting Paths

Time on the water will show that most recreational traffic is handled by using common sense and general courtesy rather than complicated Rules of the Road. Just remember: The earlier the course change the less extreme it will have to be, and the smaller the opportunity for confusion and compensating actions by the other skipper.

Large Ships

Simple rule: Give large commercial vessels the right of way and a wide berth. They require large distances to turn or stop, and their visibility is restricted. In fact, there is a sizable area immediately in front of these vessels where the helmsperson can see nothing at all. A small boat entering this area is in peril, and the skipper of the larger vessel is in for an upset stomach at best.

Don't expect large commercial vessels to turn or stop to avoid you; they can't. Fortunately these vessels normally follow distinct traffic patterns, especially in confined waters. If in doubt, yield midchannel and head for the relative safety of shallower water. Areas with dense commercial traffic, like Puget Sound, have traffic separation systems with lanes for inbound and outbound traffic separated by an area where traffic is prohibited. In times of heavy traffic and poor visibility recreational vessels should avoid these traffic lanes entirely. If it is necessary to cross them, cross at right angles and with maximum speed.

Large vessels monitor VHF channel 16 and use VHF channel 13 for bridge-to-bridge communication. If the intention of a large commercial vessel is unclear, a call on either frequency should bring an immediate response to clarify intentions and provide an agreement on the appropriate evasive action. (Channel 13 is preferred, because both the call and the conversation can be made without switching channels.) If the name of the large vessel is unknown, a description and location can be used in the call, such as "The cargo vessel southeast of Point Lomax."

Working Vessels

Working vessels that require special traffic considerations include tugs with tows and fishing vessels. Tugs are singled out because they are a definite threat to the safety of recreational boats. Fishing boats, on the other hand, are singled out because recreational boats are a definite threat to them.

Tugs towing a barge are a threat because it is necessary to avoid not only the tug, but the tow and the towline as well. Tow lines are almost impossible to see because they often run a few feet below the surface, but they can snap back above the surface within a few seconds. If you're between tug and tow when this happens (or if the cable snags your keel) you will be swept sideways down the wire toward the onrushing barge. At this point there is very little you can do to avoid disaster.

Whenever you sight a tug, *look for the tow*, whether or not you intend to cross her course. Tugs with tows behind will show two or three vertical white lights, depending on the length of the tow. Since tow lines are almost impossible to see, search for the towed object itself. A barge should be easy to locate, but a log raft, which rises only a foot or so above the surface, is not. Tugs often tow multiple barges; be sure to identify them all. And don't pass too close astern of the last barge; it may be trailing an unused tow line itself, and even without a barge attached the line can do considerable damage.

In open water a tow may lie 1,500 to 1,800 feet behind the tug. In narrow, constricted, or congested areas, the tug will shorten up the towline to 200 to 500 feet. When crossing a tow's course, it is often preferable to cross in front of the tug, in all cases allowing plenty of sea room. A call on Channel 13 will resolve any questions as to the number and location of the tow.

Dealing with fishing boats requires identifying the type of fishing they're doing. Boats that are trolling generally travel slowly, with long poles extending from the sides that trail hooked lines astern. Boats that are trawling, or dragging as it's known in New England, are towing large, deep-running nets far astern on wire cables. Shrimp trawlers may also tow nets from outrigger poles. Avoid passing close astern or following directly behind these boats. Passing in front of them is preferred.

Seiners also drag nets behind them, but unlike draggers the nets are near the surface. Purse seiners set their nets in a large circle to enclose a school of fish, then draw the nets closed. Give the boats a wide berth.

Boats engaged in trap or pot fishing—lobstermen and crabbers for the most part—sometimes move erratically, their attention focused more on picking up their next pot than on approaching pleasure craft. Give pot-fishing boats a wide berth. In addition, the buoys that mark the pot's location can be a significant hazard, as the pot warp can foul props. Some areas of Maine and the Chesapeake Bay seem to have more buoys than water. If you remember that the buoy always lies downtide or downwind of the pot, however, you can avoid trouble: always pass a pot buoy on the downtide side. For more on avoiding buoys, see the section on fouled props in Chapter 5 (page 227).

Fishing boats engaged in gillnetting present a special problem: You must avoid the boat *and* the net itself, which can run hundreds of feet away from the boat in a seemingly random direction—sometimes downwind, downcurrent, or across the channel. The far end of the net is marked with a buoy, and the top of the net is supported by floats. If you spot the buoy on the end of the net, approach it with caution until the line of floats appears. If neither the floats nor the buoy are visible, head directly at the fishing boat until you can see the net. Connecting the right buoy to the right boat can be difficult, especially in large concentrations of gill-netters. It is best to have extra sets of eyes and field glasses to assist.

Special Traffic

Special traffic includes large concentrations of boats engaged in a singular activity such as racing, or individual boats involved in special activities such as diving. If possible, avoid areas where these boats are operating. If this is impossible, show particular consideration for the boats. For example, give racing sailboats the right of way, since avoiding your boat may cause someone to lose a race. Excessive wake adversely affects their performance as well, as does passing close upwind, which disturbs the air flow over their sails. If possible, wait for the fleet to pass or at least until they thin out before crossing the course.

Other boats acting more or less singly whose actions are apparently random and unpredictable—those involved in diving or dredging, for example—should be avoided as well. Boats under power are a definite threat to the life and limb of swimmers, divers, and water skiers. The best course of action is to keep well clear, but if forced to pass close by, reduce speed to less than 2 knots. The high speed and erratic course of water-skiers and jetskis make them difficult to avoid. Be alert and procede with caution. Jetskis, which are often fueled by a lethal mixture of alcohol and testosterone, are particularly hazardous.

LIMITED VISIBILITY

Night Passages

Traveling at night is something every boater should experience. The absolute blackness lit only by stars and the luminescence of the water give the illusion of being suspended in space and time, completely detached from the real world. But as at any other time, traveling at night requires that the boat reach its destination without hitting anything. Fortunately, most well-charted areas are provided with sufficient aids to navigation, such as lighted buoys, lighted ranges, and lighthouses. Before attempting a night cruise the prudent mariner needs to study the area charts to find a route with enough lighted aids to ensure a safe passage.

When selecting the route, consider that you'll be unable to see the shore well enough to judge the channel's length or width or the boat's position in it. Unlit areas of the seacoast are unbelievably dark on moonless nights. Spotlights illuminate very little beyond the boat itself and considerably damage night vision. Under these conditions, don't count on seeing anything but lights. In populated areas, house, street, and other shoreside lights can sometimes be used to indicate channel width, especially if both sides of the channel are lighted.

The easiest operation for the night-time navigator is to sail at or between lights; their different patterns and colors make them readily identifiable, although it is sometimes difficult to tell whether a light is dim and close or bright and far away. Estimating a position between two lights of similar brightness is considerably easier, depending on how close the lights are together. If the lights can be identified, standard navigational techniques discussed in Chapter 3 can be used to establish position.

In narrow, winding, or unfamiliar channels a written plan is helpful. If the course can be described in writing using only lights for positioning, it probably can be run successfully. For example:

> *Pass between the white, flashing 2-second light on Three Tree Point and the yellow, flashing 4-second light on the midchannel buoy. Head between the white, group-flashing 12-second light on Robinson Point and the yellow, quick-flashing light on the midchannel buoy. When these lights are abeam, head between the white, flashing 5-second light on Brown's Point and the yellow, flashing 4-second light on the midchannel buoy. When these lights are abeam, head for the red, flashing 4-second light at the harbor entrance.*

With the addition of compass bearings, night passages become a little more complex, but at the same time more flexible. For example:

> *Pass between the red, flashing 4-second light on Lyle Point and the green, flashing 2.5-second light on Nisqually Flats and head for the green, flashing 4-second light until the red, flashing, 6-second light on Devils Head bears 325° magnetic, then head for that light until the red, flashing 2-second light bears 0° magnetic.*

The compass alone can be used in areas with adequate sea room and no aids. In all cases it is best to plan the passage so that daylight arrives or sufficient lights will be available to verify position before approaching any dangers or areas requiring intricate maneuvering. Arriving at an isolated anchorage on a dark night is considerably different from arriving at a well-lit marina.

A special concern when traveling at night is avoiding unlighted floating objects. On a dark night it is impossible to see these hazards, especially low-floating objects like logs or deadheads. The only defense is good luck.

Fog

Traveling in fog, unlike traveling at night, is not very romantic and should be avoided if possible. However, in certain areas fog is often a fact of life. Moving through fog, like traveling at night, consists of going from one known position to another. The key to navigating unaided by electronics is to make the distance between these points as short as possible. The longer the distance between known points, the greater the possibility for error.

As fog closes in, fix the boat's position accurately using any of the methods discussed in Chapter 3. Then head directly toward lights, buoys, islands, or other landmarks that can be readily identified. Lights and buoys are handy because they are usually numbered for exact identification. In most fog situations, objects will loom up out of the fog a few hundred feet ahead of the boat. With a little planning, you can select points that offer no danger to a maneuverable recreational boat at this distance.

It is best to avoid cross-channel work because of the difficulty estimating the speed of current pushing the boat off course; also, your boat will be running perpendicular to and risking collision with commercial channel traffic. (Dealing with current will be discussed more fully later in this chapter.) If the course is up- and downchannel, the current will only affect arrival time. Time and distance are difficult to estimate accurately, and should be used as secondary indications of position only; avoid using them to make course changes. Change course only at known locations confirmed by visual identification.

When using run time to indicate distance, set the throttle so that the boat's speed is 3, 6, or 12 knots. This will make estimating run times easier, using 0.05, 0.1, and 0.2 nautical miles per minute, respectively. The navigator can then calculate the run time to the next control point, and the helmsperson can be alerted to its arrival. If available, a depth sounder can monitor any radical changes in bottom contours. Depth changes can serve as intermediate points along the course and provide some confidence or concern, depending on whether they are hit or missed.

When running in fog, note all confirmed positions, with the time at that position and the actual courses, on the chart, on a transparent overlay, or in the ship's log. Running in the fog is like building a row of dominos that twists and turns. Each domino depends on the ones immediately ahead of and behind it: Lose one and the run fails. The key to not getting lost in the fog is staying found. This principle applies to any situation with limited visibility, whether or not radar is on board.

Radar

Radar is a great aid during poor visibility, but it is only a tool and not a substitute for good seamanship. The concept of radar's all-seeing eye is far too simplistic. In reality, much of the time small-boat radar is unattended, unobserved, and unnecessary.

Radar can gather considerable data, but most of the time it is easier to get the same information from simpler methods. Realistically, radar has only two limited uses on recreational boats: collision avoidance in fog, and helping guide the boat during times of limited visibility.

Radar's value as an aid to navigation is determined by prevailing visibility, the size of the waterway, and the availability of navigational aids. In the open ocean, radar is valueless as an aid to navigation. In broad, unrestricted, confined waters, or those that are well-lighted, radar's use is limited to fog. At night it is much easier to rely on visual aids, using radar only for occasional confirmation. In waters without lights or navigational aids, radar becomes more important as both the size of the channel and the limit of visibility are reduced. Entering an unfamiliar harbor in near-zero visibility should not be attempted without radar.

Unrestricted Waters in Fog

While navigating broad, unrestricted waterways in the fog, an occasional glance at the radar can confirm the boat's position in the channel and the general outline of the waterway. However, the helmsperson should avoid relying heavily on radar for two reasons. First, in poor visibility, keeping visual watch becomes more difficult and more important, and should be the primary task of the person steering. Second, detailed navigation with radar requires considerable study of the scope and the full attention of a radar operator. If it becomes necessary to navigate using the radar, it is better to assign a second person to that task.

Navigating in the fog with radar is similar to navigating in the fog without radar; it is best to proceed from a known point and constantly update the radar image with chart locations. Once the navigator becomes disoriented it is difficult to reestablish position. Although the operator can get bearings and distances to various objects on the screen, it is practically impossible to identify those objects on the chart in an unfamiliar area.

The most efficient and effective means of relocating the boat is for the radar operator to identify a buoy on the screen and direct the helmsperson to it using relative bearings. When the buoy looms out of the fog, the color and any identifying markings will allow the navigator to find that buoy on the chart. Then, if necessary, a new course can be plotted to return to the intended route.

Restricted Waters

When entering restricted waters, it is possible for the helmsperson to steer while watching the radar scope; however, this splits the helmsperson's attention and at night impairs vision. It is more efficient to have another crewmember operate the radar. This crewmember will have time to direct the helmsperson verbally, identifying important objects on the chart from the radar representation, and do the necessary piloting around dangerous areas.

It is possible to enter some very tight places with the radar on ¼-mile range and this teamwork system. The method requires the helmsperson to assume a course and the radar operator to modify that course by using the heading marker and the electronic bearing line (EBL; see Chapter 9 for more on radar). The necessary course changes are made with simple, relative commands like "left 5 degrees." The helmsperson repeats the command to ensure understanding and then executes it. Once the boat steadies up on its new course the radar operator can reassess the situation and issue further orders as necessary. This leaves the helmsperson free to watch the compass and peer into the gloom for visual clues. The visual information can be passed back to the radar operator to augment what is seen on the screen. Even though this process works well, it is a good idea to practice in good visibility to increase the skills and confidence of the team.

Collision Avoidance

Because avoiding collision depends on observation, it is obviously more difficult to determine another boat's position and course when visibility is limited. Under these conditions, the course of all neighboring boats must be determined through the use of running lights, sound signals, or radar. Once the location and course of the other boats are known, normal collision-avoidance methods are used.

Running Lights

At night the most direct way of detecting the presence of other boats is by observing their running lights. The basic pattern is a white light on the stern, a red light on the left side of the boat, and a green light on the right side of the boat. Any boat operating under engine power is required to show a second white light visible from the front of the boat. Vessels over 164 feet are required to show a third white light forward, behind and higher than the other forward-facing white light. This allows the lights to operate as a lighted range marker: if the two lights line up, you are dead ahead of the vessel. The red and green lights are also designed to tell the observer the attitude of the approaching boat.

Ultimately, however, it makes no difference whether red, green, or white lights are visible; what is important is that there is a boat out there whose course, relative to your own boat, must be determined. The method used to determine the course is the same as that used during the day. Measure the angle or the bearing to the lights and note the changes. If a collision is indicated—constant bearing, diminishing range—alter course. A call on the VHF radio can help eliminate confusion if the boat can be specifically identified.

There are a considerable number of special lights that indicate the size and type of boat and its operation. This information is all supplementary and not re-quired to avoid collision. Interested readers can consult the *Navigation Rules, Interna-tional - Inland*. The only special set of lights you *must* commit to memory, because the consequences of misinterpretation are so severe, is the two or three vertical all-around white masthead lights that signify a tug with a tow. This is worth repeating: Passing between a tug and its tow can be disastrous.

Sound Signals

Bats may do it, but using sound to detect the course of a moving object is be-yond the capability of the human ear. We can at best detect danger heading our way. Fog signals on boats are either bells or horns; bells are used at anchor and horns underway. Neither do much to relieve anxiety. A large vessel's fog horn tells you nothing of its course or speed. And your fog horn will not be heard at all aboard a large vessel underway.

Without radar, the best way to avoid collision in fog is to stay out of shipping channels, travel slowly, sound your fog signal, and be ready for quick evasive ac-tion when other fog signals are heard.

Vessels 40 feet and over anchored in fog outside of designated anchorage ar-eas are supposed to ring their bell at 1-minute intervals, but if I had a dime for every recreational vessel that follows this regulation I couldn't make change for a dollar. But you should be aware that, if another boat collides with yours and you haven't been ringing your bell, you'll be legally at fault. You can play this one by ear, tak-ing into consideration your location and the likelihood of traffic.

Radar

Collision avoidance with radar is a relatively simple process, and the one task where radar proves its worth. Once again, it is best to assign a crewmember to monitor the screen and twiddle the knobs. This task, especially in crowded waters where it is most needed, requires considerable concentration. The process consists of identifying a target on the screen as a moving vessel, determining whether the vessel is on a collision course, and if so recommending evasive action—too much for the helmsperson to handle safely.

It might seem that the radar's maximum range would be most valuable in collision avoidance, but this isn't the case. The most usable range on recreational boats is about 4 miles, only switching up to 8 miles on occasion when activity diminishes, for early warning. Most boats much beyond the 8-mile range will be below the radar's horizon.

If still unconvinced, consider how often, in good visibility, you care about the course of a boat 10 or 12 miles away. True, a large vessel traveling 30 knots can go 8 miles in about 4 minutes; however, most large vessels reduce speed to 15 knots or less in times of poor visibility. Eight or 10 minutes is more than ample time to identify, determine, recommend, and execute proper action. Most small-boat radar operators will find that the 4 or 5 minutes provided by the 4-mile range is adequate, and that this range provides better detail to track the more numerous slower, smaller vessels.

CURRENT

All large bodies of water are subject to water movement or flow induced by wind or gravity, called **currents**. Even though most currents have a vertical component, the direction of current movement of most interest to boaters is principally horizontal. Some currents have steady flow conditions where the horizontal speed, sometimes called **drift**, and the direction, sometimes called **set**, are relatively constant; in others the drift and set continuously change. An overwhelming majority of boaters spend most of their time in currents of less than 2 knots, with only an occasional pass through rapids or tidal races where the velocity is greater.

The types of currents that concern recreational boaters are ocean, river, and tidal currents. Most ocean currents are caused by wind; river and tidal currents are caused by gravity. Density differences can also cause gravity-driven currents. The primary example of this type of current is the strong subsurface current flowing out of the Straits of Gibraltar.

Maneuvering a boat in current requires applying common sense to a general knowledge of current behavior. To get this knowledge it is helpful to look at each different type of current separately.

Ocean Currents

Wind is the primary source of all ocean currents. Wind blowing on the surface of the water in a steady direction for about 12 hours will produce a current.[3] The speed of the current at the surface is about 3.5 percent of the wind speed and decreases with depth.[4] The speed of the current at a specific depth depends on many factors, such as time, wave height, and interlayer mixing. The direction of the ocean current depends on the direction of the wind and the rotation of the earth. The month-to-month location, set, and drift of ocean currents can be found on pilot charts, described in more detail in Chapter 3.

Most recreational boaters rarely encounter ocean currents, but those who do can profit from using them judiciously. Ocean currents are generally less that 2 knots, but because of the considerable time a boat is influenced by these currents, they play a major role in the boat's course and performance. Going with or against a 1-knot current can result in a 50-mile-per-day difference. When compared to the 100- to 150-mile daily run of most recreational vessels, gaining or losing 50 miles per day due to traveling with or against a 1-knot current is significant.

River Currents

The set of a river current is always downstream. The speed of river currents depends on the gradient, or fall, of the channel, the quantity of water flowing, and the cross-sectional area of the channel. Speeds can vary from less than a knot to greater than 13 knots. The velocity of the current also depends on the boat's location in the channel. The frictional forces on the bottom and sides of the channel slow the water down; therefore, the fastest current will be located in the deepest part of the channel. Conversely, the slowest water is found in the shallowest part of the channel. The natural process of erosion and deposition means that fast-moving water in a deep channel tends to pick up silt and scour the channel deeper, whereas in shallow water the flow slows down and deposits the sediment, further decreasing the depth of the water.

In a river channel with straight, parallel sides, the middle of the river is usually deepest and the current flows fastest. When the river channel changes direction,

[3]Nathaniel Bowditch, American Practical Navigator (Washington, D.C.: Defense Mapping Agency, 1984), 815.
[4]William G. Van Dorn, Oceanography and Seamanship (New York: Dodd, Mead & Co., 1974), 105.

momentum influences the current and throws it against the outside bank, scouring and deepening that portion of the channel. The fastest current is generally on the outside of a bend, and a shoal is often found on the inside. River currents can vary considerably depending on the weather or season. The flow in rivers that are controlled by dams can also be subject to considerable variation in flow due to power demand.

Currents in rivers may reach velocities great enough to impede upstream travel of small boats. In any case, upstream travel is generally easier where the current is slower—that is, the edges of straight channels or the inside of bends. When moving upstream, **eddies**, which are circular currents, can be used to advantage. Eddies are local conditions found only where fast-moving water comes in contact with slow-moving water. Some of them are relatively permanent, others very transitory in nature. Because the currents are circular, part of the current runs upstream. Judiciously slipping in and out of these currents can aid upstream progress.

Tidal Currents

Tidal currents, which probably have the greatest effect on recreational boaters, are the flow of water generated by the periodic rise and fall of the water surface due to the gravitational pull of celestial bodies and the rotation of the earth. The principal celestial body is the moon, which provides almost 75 percent of the pull.[5]

The relationship between **tide**, the vertical movement of water, and **tidal current**, the horizontal movement of water, is purely local. In the open ocean and very large bodies of water, the tidal current is essentially rotary, flow rate being almost constant, with the direction changing continuously and passing through all points of the compass during the tidal period. In the open ocean, tidal currents rarely exceed 0.2 to 0.5 knots.[6] In restricted channels such as rivers, straits, and coastal waters, the tidal flow is restricted by the channels, generally flowing upchannel or downchannel as the tide moves from low to high and back.

The current produced by the rising tide is called **flood**, and on a falling tide it is called **ebb**. The period between these two tides when there is no water movement is called **slack**. If the speed of the current passing one point is plotted, the shape of the speed curve varies from day to day and place to place, but it is that of a complex sine curve. Figure 2.9 shows a typical shape for this curve.

[5]*Bowditch*, American Practical Navigator, *789*.
[6]*Van Dorn*, Oceanography and Seamanship, *140*.

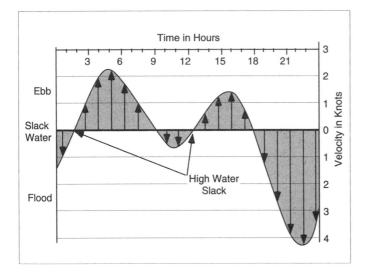

Figure 2.9 Typical Tidal
Current Curve

Some interesting observations can be made from studying this curve. First, maximum ebb and flood occur within a relatively fixed period. Because of the shape of the curve, the velocity of the current remains near maximum ebb or flood for a considerable length of time, but passes through slack very quickly. Theoretically, zero velocity occurs instantaneously. The occurrence of slack and the length of time that no current is present is of great concern to recreational boaters, since some channels are only passable at high-water slack.

The velocity of the current and the time and length of slack water vary considerably throughout the world and from day to day, but depend on the difference between the high and the low tide. The greater this difference, the greater the current, and the shorter the slack period.

It may be concluded, intuitively, that slack water occurs at high or low tide. In some places this is true, but intuition can lead the boater into trouble, because there is no fixed relationship between the time of high and low tides, called **stand**, and the time of slack water. This is especially true in extensive inland waterways or in areas with a constricted entrance. Under these conditions, the times may roughly coincide at the seaward and upper ends of an estuary, but in between the time difference can be considerable, enough in some locations to produce maximum current very close to stand.[7]

Often, rivers, coastal estuaries, and bays are affected by considerable surface runoff or other nontidal flow. This inflow from other sources affects the tidal cur-

[7]*Bowditch*, American Practical Navigator, 812.

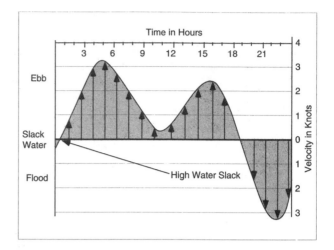

Figure 2.10 Typical Tidal
Current Curve on River
with 1-Knot Flow

rents by shifting the axis away from the direction of the flow. For example, if the tidal current shown in Figure 2.9 were located on a river with a 1-knot current, the current curve would look like Figure 2.10.

Notice that in this instance the inflowing current produces an axis shift, which removes the slack water from the smaller tide. This axis shift results in no flood tide occurring during that period and an increase in the maximum flood velocity. This situation is relatively common, occurring not only in inland waterways, but in the waters of islands surrounded by reefs. In this instance the surplus water comes from waves breaking over the reef and exiting through a restricted channel.

Tidal currents of 5 to 10 knots are not uncommon in atolls that have large areas and very restricted channels. William Van Dorn reported an incident on Takaroa Atoll where one could peer into a vortex 10 to 15 feet deep and see brightly colored reef fish spinning around apparently unconcerned.[8]

It is highly unlikely that the term "unconcerned" would describe an unsuspecting boater caught in the same predicament. Tidal rapids occur in numerous places throughout the world, and they offer considerable danger to boaters. Any restricted channel can cause tidal currents to reach extreme velocities. A large basin with a very small exit channel produces very fast tidal currents. A good example of the conditions that produce extreme tidal currents is Nakwakto rapids in central British Columbia (Figure 2.11). The large volume of water contained in the hundreds of miles of deep channels behind the narrow, restricted opening produces

---

[8]*Van Dorn,* Oceanography and Seamanship, *144.*

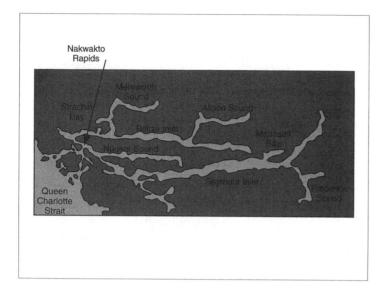

Figure 2.11 Nakwakto
Tidal Rapids

tidal currents that often exceed 13 knots. There is a small island, called Tremble Rock, in the middle of the rapids that literally vibrates when the rapids reach peak velocity.

In any current over 4 knots, whirlpools can develop that make the boat extremely difficult to control; in a 7-knot current these whirlpools are capable of pulling large logs completely underwater and keeping them there for several hundred feet. Any displacement hull caught in a current of greater than 4 knots is in for a wild ride.

Successful maneuvering through tidal rapids requires the recreational boater to have specific information concerning tidal currents, times, and durations of slack water. This information can be found in tidal current tables, sailing directions, coast pilots, tidal current charts, and current diagrams.

Tide and Current Tables

The detailed use of tables, charts, and diagrams is explained quite adequately in their specific publications. All that is needed here are some hints and guidelines.

Most tidal current tables use local standard time; be sure to convert to daylight savings time when appropriate. Because most recreational boating takes place in the summer, this conversion is generally needed. I have made this error more than once. One hour before slack the current is usually less than 2 knots, which can be handled by most boats under power. With a long passage through an inlet, it may be necessary to put in an hour early to pass through the critical area during slack water. On one such occasion I forgot about daylight savings time and entered two

Current tables only give velocity information at maximum and minimum. If it becomes necessary to enter rapids early, the velocity of the current can be calculated at any time other than slack or maximum by using Equation 2.2.

$$V = \sin \left(\frac{90T}{P}\right) V_m \qquad \text{Eq 2.2}$$

Where V is the intermediate velocity of the current in knots

T is the interval in minutes ahead of or behind slack water

P is the interval in minutes between slack and V_m

V_m is the maximum current in knots

P and V_m are taken from the appropriate current table.

For example, if it is necessary to enter an 8.5 knot (V_m) rapid with a period of 4 hours and 20 minutes (P) between slack and maximum velocity 1 hour early (T):

$$V = \sin \left(\frac{90 \times 60}{260}\right) \times 8.5$$

$$V = \sin (20.7°) \times 8.5$$

$$V = 0.3546 \times 8.5 = \underline{3 \text{ knots}}$$

Another useful number concerning tides is the length of time the water velocity remains near zero. As Figure 2.9 illustrates, the velocity is zero only for an instant, but it remains small (less than 1 knot) for a period that depends on the difference between the maximum ebb and flood velocities and the time between these maximum velocities. The greater this velocity difference and the shorter the time span, the less time the tidal current remains near zero. This length of time on *each* side of slack tide can be calculated by rearranging Equation 2.2 to get equation 2.3.

$$T = \arcsin \left(\frac{V \times P}{V_m 90}\right) \qquad \text{Eq 2.3}$$

(continued)

hours early, when the maximum current was more than 8 knots. Fortunately I discovered my error early enough to abort the passage until the current subsided.

Times of slack or near-slack water can be found in Tables 3A and 3B and 4A and 4B of the NOS Tidal Current Tables. These tables require only addition and subtraction, but are not as accurate as the equation method given in the accompanying sidebar. The tables assume that the maximum flood and ebb currents are equal and that the slack occurs midway between the two maximum currents. Tables 4A and 4B also assume that the tidal period is 6 hours and 13 minutes. For a more accurate, precise method of calculating velocity during different tidal stages, see the accompanying sidebar.

Table 3A is essentially a tabulation of the results from equation 2.2. The inherent errors are similar, except that the table is much less precise than the equation. This lack of precision comes from using 20-minute intervals, which can be off plus or minus 10 minutes, and using only one decimal place in the speed factor. The result of this lack of precision for areas where the maximum tidal current velocities are small (< 4 knots) is generally less than ¼ knot and can be ignored. However, for areas where the tidal current maximum velocities are large (> 8 knots), the errors can be as much as 1.25 knots using Table 3A, a significant difference.

Using Table 4 with unequal maximum ebb and flood velocities can produce considerable error if the difference between the velocities is large. Because this error is not on the side of *safety*, Table 4 should not be used when maximum ebb and flood velocities differ substantially. For example, a 1-knot flood and a 7-knot ebb tide would, according to the table, provide a 68-minute slack period. Using equation 2.3, that same slack period is about 30 minutes.

Table 4 also produces unsafe errors for tides with periods between maximum ebb and flood of less than 6 hours, indicating a longer slack period than will actually occur.

Maneuvering in Currents

Handling a boat in current is not difficult. There are three basic situations: parallel to the current, perpendicular to the current, and in tidal races.

Parallel to the Current

The arrival time of a boat traveling parallel to a current will be affected by the current. A 2-knot current will add or subtract significantly to the 6- to 12-knot speed of a typical recreational boat—especially over long distances. Select your time of departure with re-

(Current Tables continued)

Where T is the time in minutes the current remains below V,

   V is the threshold velocity in knots,

   V_m is the tidal velocity in knots

   P is the time in minutes between V_m and slack in minutes.

The total duration of slack is found by adding these two times together. The start and ending hour for slack can be found by subtracting and adding the appropriate time from and to the hour given for slack.

Both equations 2.2 and 2.3 are based on the similarity of tidal current curves to a sine curve and the assumption that slack occurs midway between the maximum tides. For tides with large differences in maximum current this is not the case. Slack occurs much closer to the minimum current than to the maximum current. As a sine curve approaches the minimum or maximum, the value of the velocity changes more slowly. Therefore, the error produced by this assumption is on the side of safety, providing a shorter calculated time than will actually occur.

spect to the tide, and your course with respect to the current's distribution across the channel. For example, when traveling with the current, use the middle of the channel or along the outside edges of bends where the current is strongest. When traveling against the current, favor the edges of the channel and insides of bends where the current is weakest. This strategy will improve arrival time by 10 to 15 percent.

On trips of less than 4 hours in a tidal situation, selecting the time of departure with respect to the tidal currents will increase the effective boat speed as much as 100 percent. For example, a boat making 4 knots over the ground against a 2-knot current would make 8 knots over the ground going with the same 2-knot current. On longer trips, what is gained going with the tide is often lost going against the tide; departure time does not significantly affect arrival time.

Cross-Current

Traveling across a current, a boat will be swept downstream. Normally this is self-correcting. If the helmsperson steers directly for the objective, the course will continuously change as the current moves the boat downstream; eventually the boat reaches an angle with the current so that its velocity upcurrent equals the downstream current's velocity, and the course remains constant. This results in a course with a concave upstream curve.

Several methods are available to calculate the drift of the current and set a direct course to the object by crabbing sideways across the current. In practice these methods require elemental vector analysis, considerable plotting, and knowledge of the current velocity and distribution generally unavailable to recreational boaters. The results produce a concave-curved downstream course, little better than the go-straight-at-it method. For crossing short stretches of current, the correct angle of attack can be estimated with fair accuracy.

Tidal Rapids

Maneuvering in tidal rapids becomes more challenging as the speed of the current increases. On occasion it may be necessary for a boat to pass through areas with currents greater than 2 or 3 knots. Here, it is prudent to determine the time and duration of slack water and the extent of the rapids, and plan the passage. In wide channels, remember that slack water occurs later and for a shorter time in mid-channel than near the edges.

On long rapids, it is better to time the entrance so that the boat enters the rapids against the current, reaches the center at slack, and leaves with the current. In very long rapids the slack period can occur at one end considerably earlier than at the other end. Going with the change, the boat can increase the time it is in slack water. Going against the change, the boat enters the rapids with some current running against it, passes through slack very quickly, and leaves with considerably more current.

If caught in turbulent water, the skipper can move to midstream, where the current and the turbulence are strongest, or choose a path near the edge, where turbulence is less but can cause the boat to strike shore if steering control is lost. Turbulence in a rapid comes from whirlpools and overfalls, both unpleasant if large.

Steering control is almost certain to be lost when running through whirlpools; the boat will yaw and be thrust sideways, and you'll need to allow extra clearance between the boat and other objects, stationary or floating. Steer for the center or slightly to one side of the center of the channel. Most whirlpools, except for the largest, are transitory, appearing and disappearing quite quickly. Whirlpools are very difficult to avoid entirely. A boat caught by one will be spun around but eventually released—though perhaps not in the original or desired direction.

Where **overfalls**, or large standing waves, are present, it is best to avoid them by staying out of midchannel and taking your chances closer to shore. Overfalls result when a fast-moving current strikes slow-moving water. The onrushing water stacks up and forms a stationary breaking wave reinforced by a local surface current running backward against the main current. In a large overfall this backward-running current can lock the boat in position or thrust it backward into the cascading water behind it with disastrous results.

Heavy Weather

What constitutes heavy weather depends on the type and size of boat and the experience of the crew. A small sailboat (20 to 30 feet) can handle considerably more heavy weather than a small powerboat. Large boats (40 to 65 feet) generally fair better than smaller boats. In any given boat, the weather turns heavy when the winds increase a few knots beyond any previously experienced by the crew.

The best defense against heavy weather is avoidance. The careful skipper of a recreational boat rarely need place the boat and crew in jeopardy by operating in inclement weather. It is much safer and certainly more enjoyable to spend another day securely in harbor waiting for better weather. Unfortunately, rarely isn't the same as never. Even a prudent skipper will get caught in a sudden squall or undertake a passage longer than the accuracy of long-term weather predictions.

The major dangers are **pitchpoling** (turning end-over-end), **broaching** (rolling over sideways), and **foundering** (taking on large quantities of water and sinking). Other concerns are keeping the crew on board and free of injury, and handling minor damage from breaking seas.

Preparing for Heavy Weather

Often all one can do when dealing with extreme weather is to prepare the boat and crew and take what comes. The amount of preparation depends on the boat, the crew, the skipper, and the severity of the oncoming storm.

First, *get all information* on the approaching storm that is available on the radio or by using techniques described in Chapter 8 on Weather. Try to determine the wind strength, direction, and the duration of the storm. Write the barometer reading and the time in the log, and update the reading every hour.

Next, *fix the boat's position* on the chart, locate the nearest safe harbor, and calculate a run-time to the harbor. Also, locate the nearest lee shore, and estimate the severity of the wind and the amount the boat will drift downwind. Note the locations of shallow water or adverse currents. Using this information, decide whether the boat should run for protection, try to gain sea room, or continue on course. In making the decision to run for cover, the skipper needs to judge the conditions the boat will encounter at the harbor entrance. See Crossing the Bar at the end of this chapter.

The *crew should prepare* by putting on the proper *warm and waterproof clothing*. Prepare quick snacks. *High-energy foods* like candy and a thermos or two of hot soup are needed to keep the crew efficient. A tired brain makes bad decisions. Any drugs needed to suppress seasickness symptoms should be taken early enough to become effective. Seasickness in a storm is not just uncomfortable but also dangerous, because it reduces the crew's strength when strength is most needed. All too often the boat weathers the storm but the crew perishes from cold, hunger, and exposure.

Any crewmember on deck should wear a safety harness. In a storm-tossed sea without nearby help, anyone lost overboard is lost, unless he can be recovered quickly. Sailboats often run a line fore and aft along the deck to which a safety harness can be attached. Although most powerboat crews spend most of their time in the shelter of the cabin, a crewmember needing to go forward to rig a sea anchor or make emergency repairs needs to be tied off.

The most dangerous time for the crew is immediately after exiting the cabin. Emerging from relative calm into wild motion and fury is startling. If a wave hits before a crewmember adjusts to the force of the wind and the flying spray, they may lose their balance.

The value of *life jackets* is debatable. A life vest's downside is seldom discussed, but the extra bulk makes working awkward and more exhausting. A life preserver may reduce the chances of survival by tiring the crew unnecessarily or upsetting their balance and pitching them overboard. In cold water, death by exposure will come before drowning. These objections do not apply to passengers, or when the loss of the ship becomes imminent. For the crew, staying on board is often the key to survival, and that means relying on safety harnesses, not life jackets.

Survival suits will preserve life for an extended time even in cold water, but they are impossible to work in. If available, survival suits should be positioned where they can be distributed quickly in case the vessel must be abandoned. Any other survival gear, such as extra water and food for the life raft, should also be moved to an accessible location.

Emergency equipment, such as flares, EPIRBS, and the first aid kit, should be located and moved to accessible, secure positions. Rarely used pieces of equipment like drogues, sea anchors, warps, cable cutters, and panels to cover the windows must be located and positioned before sea conditions make rummaging around in the lower reaches of the vessel uncomfortable. All large windows not needed for navigation should be covered early.

The properly dressed and tethered crew should *secure all equipment* on deck. Everything that can be stowed below should be stowed in lockers. Equipment that must be left on deck should be lashed tightly. The force of wind and waves in the center of a severe storm is hard to imagine. Shock cord is woefully inadequate. Larger items should be attached with extra lashings.

All equipment below should likewise be stowed and secured. Locker hatches should be secured both above and below decks. If they come open above-deck, they will lose their contents in the sea and take in water; below, they will empty their contents into the cabin. Heavy flying objects are a hazard to your health.

Secure ports, cowls, and hatches as it becomes necessary. Stale air in the cabin can aggravate seasickness, so allow as much ventilation as possible without endangering the safety of the vessel; large quantities of water can get below through these openings. Check the bilge and the bilge-pump screen to see that they are clean and free of debris. Pump the bilge if necessary. Close all through-hulls not needed. An overturned boat will remain floating as long as air remains inside. Closing the through-hulls will prevent air from leaking out of the cabin.

Powerboats

A powerboat in heavy weather is vulnerable because the high freeboard exposes a large surface area to the force of the wind and seas. Most powerboats also have large windows, which if broken can allow large quantities of water below. Exposed to heavy weather, the powerboat's options are limited to running for cover, defensive course selection, or station keeping.

Running for Cover

A powerboat's main defenses are speed and vigilance. The sooner a storm can be predicted the better the chance the boat can make it to safety. Boat speed limits how far a small powerboat can prudently travel from sheltered conditions. In setting this limit the skipper should be aware that a boat that can do 20 knots in flat water cannot do 20 knots in wind-generated waves, especially if the course is into those waves and the wind.

A boat heading into a rising wind must reduce speed or change course to prevent pounding. If the waves are short and steep the screws may come out of the water as well. Changing course so that the boat is running 45 degrees into the weather extends the boat's path on the wave and reduces pounding, but because the motion is part roll and part pitch, this course is very uncomfortable, and it lengthens the run for cover. Turning downwind reduces the apparent wind by the speed of the boat; the motion is also more comfortable. In most boats with adequate directionaly stability, downwind is the best direction to run for cover.

If the boat's desired course places it beam-to the seas, it may become necessary to tack toward the destination, running first 45 degrees into the wind, then 135 degrees off the wind. The most vulnerable position for a boat in severe conditions is beam-on to the wind and seas; course changes should be made quickly and in the relative shelter of the trough, where the velocity of the water flowing past the rudder is greatest.

Defensive Course Selection

If it becomes necessary to ride out a storm in a powerboat, the major decision is whether to run into the waves or with them. Whether to run into or away from the storm is hotly contested, and depends on the individual vessel, storm, and skipper. The right choice early in the storm, with steep, short seas, may be different later in the same storm when the seas lengthen and flatten.

Running downwind away from the storm decreases the velocity of the wind by the speed of the boat and increases the length of the waves, which in turn reduces the forces the boat and crew must resist. For example, it is possible for a powerboat going 12 knots to run with a 6- or 7-foot wave. This is not necessarily as good an idea as it sounds; the boat will tend to surf down the wave front. When surfing, the water and the boat are moving at the same speed, helm control is reduced, and the tendency to broach is increased. It is better to lose a little distance on the wave and regain helm control.

In this manner, it may be possible to handle very large seas successfully, especially early in a storm when the waves are moving slower or late in the storm when the slope of the wave is more gentle. The general guidelines are, *in short steep seas, slow down and let the waves run under the boat. If the waves are high and long, hold as much speed as possible and run away from them.*

Running downwind increases the chances of pitchpoling, broaching, or being pooped by a following sea, especially early in a storm. In the early stages, the seas have steep faces and sharp crests, and negotiating them safely requires that boat speed be carefully controlled—slow enough so the bow doesn't plunge into the trough or wave ahead, causing the boat to be flipped by the wave coming from behind; yet fast enough to maintain steerage control and avoid broaching or being pooped by a following sea. Slowing a powerboat running downwind may not be easy. The wind force on the superstructure alone will drive it at surprising speeds.

Towing warps, however, should be avoided. Any lines strung out behind may become fouled on the prop with disastrous consequences.

If the skipper cannot control boat speed it may be best to take the more uncomfortable but safer course and power into the wind. This presents the bow, which is better designed to take the force of the storm, to the elements. If the seas have the rounded tops of a mature storm, control is seldom a problem, and running directly into the seas produces a fairly smooth up-and-down motion around the long axis of the boat. In the early part of a storm, when the seas have steep, pointed tops, heading into the wind requires the boat speed to be progressively reduced as conditions worsen. Eventually the boat may be moving so slowly that it is barely maintaining steerage. This is called **station keeping**.

Station Keeping

Station keeping is very similar to heaving-to in a sailboat. Enough power is maintained to keep the boat heading between 50 degrees off and directly into the wind. Just slightly offwind is generally a little more comfortable; the motion is mostly pitch. The more off the wind, the more power that can be applied, but the greater the danger of being caught by a gust and forced broad-on to the wind and waves, increasing the probability of a broach.

Holding the head into the wind by using a drogue, a sea anchor, or trailing warps off the bow may or may not work. I know of no instance of recreational powerboats using this method, but some success has been reported by commercial fishing boats. Certainly a sea anchor will keep the head into the seas and place the bow in a position to split the waves. However, the boat can no longer be powered forward with the engine or it will risk overrunning the lines. This is not a method to consider in a powerboat unless no other options are available.

If warps or sea anchors are to be set it is best to attach them using a harness secured just aft of amidships rather than to the bow. Heavy loads on the bow tend to depress it and increase the possibility of taking green water over the bow. The lines must be protected from chafe and long enough to reach several wave lengths ahead of the boat. The amount of drag is important: the object is to slow and stabilize the boat, not stop it. Too much drag will stop the boat and subject it to the full force of the breaking waves. The boat must be allowed to fall back with the wave to help dissipate the immense force and minimize damage. This necessary backward movement places abnormal loads on the rudder and may damage it.

Changing Tactics

Changing course or removing warps in midstorm is difficult; it will probably be easier to cut the warps loose. Radical course changes that require the vessel to pass beam-to the seas are difficult and dangerous, especially if the crest of a wave hits the boat while it is beam-to. Try to start any turns on the back side of waves. It may not be possible to time the maneuver so that the boat can turn a full 180 degrees before the crest of the next wave hits. The exposure can be reduced by breaking the turn into two segments. First, turn the boat 45 or 50 degrees off the wind and hold this course until a suitable sea approaches. Then, as the crest passes, make the remaining portion of the turn.

Sailboats

A sailboat caught out in open water is much safer than a powerboat. The hull shape, the deep, heavy keel, the lower freeboard, and the smaller openings are all better designed to take the forces of the weather and increase the chances for survival. Because of their construction, sailboats have a few different options than a powerboat in severe conditions, but their essential strategies are still limited to lying a-hull, heaving-to, or running before the storm with or without warps.

As the wind rises, a sailboat progressively shortens sail and maintains course until minimum sail is set—usually around 40 to 50 knots of wind for most sailboats. Winds of this velocity are accompanied by seas that are as dangerous as the winds themselves.

Defensive Course Selection

Once minimum sail is set, the boat can further reduce wind pressure by changing course to alter the apparent wind. The farther off the wind, the less the apparent wind and its accompanying pressure. As the wind increases, eventually the boat is forced to run directly downwind. Running before a storm in a sailboat is very similar to running before a storm in a powerboat, except that it requires at least one person at the helm exposed in the cockpit to the fury of the storm. All the advantages and disadvantages are similar, except that with no turning propeller, towing warps behind the boat to slow its progress is practical. The advice on towing warps given above is applicable here, except that warps attached to the stern will depress the stern and increase the chances of swamping the cockpit; warps should be attached amidships.

Lying a-Hull

Lying a-hull is literally casting your fate to the wind. All sail is stowed, the helm is lashed so the boat turns upwind, and the crew goes below, letting the boat fend for itself. The crew is relatively more comfortable below, where they are warmer and drier. Their only tasks are to hang on, keep the bilge dry, listen to the din, and fight panic. One crewmember should remain dressed for deck duty just in case changing conditions or an emergency require instant attention.

The success of lying a-hull requires sea room, as the boat will drift downwind. If the boat lies with the beam broad to the weather, excessive heeling may expose a considerable portion of the hull's undersides to the force of the waves. If this exposed surface is essentially perpendicular to the waves, such as in a round-bottom or canoe-shaped hull, the waves will slap violently against the bottom. Also, since the helm is lashed upwind, the boat may come beam-on to the seas more and more often, taking large rolls. If these rolls become too frequent or severe it may be more prudent to change tactics. Many boats lying a-hull have suffered 360-degree rolls.

Heaving-To

Heaving-to is the traditional way for sailboats to ride out a gale. It is very similar to lying a-hull, with the addition of setting a small sail and balancing the boat so that it rides closer to the wind than a boat lying ahull. When heading close to the wind, most of the force from the wind and waves is off the boat, and it is surprising how well it will ride the storm. A boat hove-to is much more comfortable below than one lying a-hull. Some of the difficulties encountered when hove-to can be attributed to carrying too little sail rather than too much. There is a limit, however, to what sailcloth and fastenings can take, and again the skipper may be required to change tactics. Lying to a sea anchor off the bow is not recommended for sailboats because of their exposed rudders and the conflicting reports of success.

GETTING UNDER, THROUGH, AND OVER

Because boat handling is now so simple, various manmade objects, such as bridges, overhead power lines, dams, and canals, have been sprinkled around the nation's waterways to keep piloting a challenge. Nature, not to be outdone, forms hazardous areas known as bars. The first two obstructions must be gotten under, the next two through, and the last one over.

Overhead Power Lines

Getting under overhead power lines is rarely a concern for boaters, but the consequences of contacting such a line are severe. The greatest danger is to sailboaters in areas devoid of commercial traffic, which generally keeps these hazards high enough off the water not to be a problem. But on small rivers, lakes, and backwater areas off the beaten path, power lines may be low enough to contact the mast of a sailboat; even small power lines contain enough voltage to send a lethal charge through the rigging. If the area is charted, the maximum vertical safe clearance can often be found on the chart. Remember to consider tidal effects when calculating safe clearances. Small trailerable sailboats need to be aware of low-lying power lines ashore, which can be contacted when raising masts or moving the boat to the launching ramp with the mast up.

Raising the Drawbridge

Bridges are of greatest concern to sailboaters, and generally only in areas where large commercial traffic is absent or infrequent. All bridges have limited horizontal and vertical clearance. Horizontal clearance is of little interest to recreational boaters. Vertical clearance depends on the type of bridge, which may have fixed, lifting, tilting, or rotating spans. These clearances are all noted on charts of the area.

On frequently used waterways, bridges that open are controlled by a bridge operator, who can be contacted by horn signals or VHF radio. Bridge operators usually monitor VHF channel 16 or 13. If horn signals are used, a single blast will indicate the ship's desire to pass under the bridge. The bridge keeper will sometimes acknowledge the request with a single blast, but in any case will generally guide the boat with additional horn signals.

Once acknowledged by the bridge operator, you'll have to wait until he has an opportunity to open the bridge. The boat should remain well away from the structure and in full view of the bridge keeper while waiting. The skipper should be alert to signals from the bridge, and be aware of any current that could force the boat into the structure. Sailboats should use engine power for the added control needed in maneuvering around and through congested areas.

The bridge keeper will normally signal with a horn blast when the boat should start its run toward the bridge. This signal may be earlier than expected, because large bridges do not open all the way for small boats. It is best to make the actual passage under the bridge quickly to provide the minimum disturbance to shoreside traffic. Because the bridge operator's view of the passing boats will be obstructed, the last boat through, as a courtesy, can signal with a horn blast when all boats are clear of the structure.

Locking Through

Locks work by equalizing the water level in the lock with the entrance water level outside the lock. Watertight gates are opened to admit boats, which enter and tie to the sides of the lock. When all boats are properly secured, the gates are closed and the water level is adjusted to the exit level. As the water rises, the mooring lines may or may not need attending. When the water reaches the exit level, the exit gates are opened and the boats leave the lock. When all boats have cleared, the lock is ready to receive traffic in the other direction.

Locking through starts with a call to the lockkeeper on VHF channel 16 or 13. By government regulation, recreational boats receive last priority and are scheduled around the needs of other traffic. Recreational boats can be locked through with commercial vessels only if the commercial vessel's cargo is not hazardous.

When approaching a dam, use caution and check the chart for the proper location of the channel to the lock holding area. Accidentally entering spillways, or turbine intake or discharge areas, can be extremely dangerous for a small vessel. Once reaching the lock holding area, boats must wait for the lockmaster's signal before entering the lock. These signals can be lights, horns, or radio instructions. Light signals are usually similar to traffic lights: red for stop, yellow for standby, and green for enter. Horn signals vary depending on the lock, but are generally posted near the lock entrances.

On receiving the signal to enter the lock, proceed inside and tie the boat to the bollards. This process is similar to any docking process, except that deep locks can produce tricky wind currents.

Locks are equipped with two broad kinds of mooring equipment. Older locks and locks with short lifts have stationary bits and bollards on the upper edge of the lock. This is the most difficult kind of lock for the recreational boater. Most newer locks and those with large lifts have floating bits and bollards. In some locks the space between these tie-off points is so large that a small boat can only use a single tie point. In all cases only two lines are used, one fore and one aft, usually rigged as spring lines.

Fixed Bits and Bollards

Locks with fixed tie-off points generally have a couple of lock attendants, one on each side to assist and direct the placement of boats in the lock. You'll need lines a little longer than twice the lift of the lock; the lines are led around the bollards on the lock's rim and back to the boat. Crewmembers will tend these lines as the boat is raised or lowered, taking in or releasing slack as the boat rises or falls with the water level. If a number of small boats are locking through, they may be asked to raft together.

Movable Bits and Bollards

Movable bits don't require line tending, and locks so equipped may have no attendants to assist in the direction and tying of boats. If the bits are numerous enough, the process is like docking with only bow and stern lines. If a boat must use a single bit, a crewmember positioned amidships secures the lines as fore and aft springs to the single bit. A boat moored in this fashion cannot move forward or aft, but the bow or stern can swing in or out. As the boat rises or falls with the water level, crewmembers stationed at the bow and stern and armed with a boat hook or mop handles keep the boat from swinging into the lock wall.

Lock walls always seem to be rough, dirty, and have strange indentations and projections. Use adequate fenders and remain alert so that your boat doesn't get caught. A snagged boat can sustain considerable damage as the water rises or falls.

There is a small amount of turbulence as the water enters or leaves the chamber, and when the gates are opened. The prop wash from a large commercial vessel can also cause considerable turbulence. Wait for this turbulence to subside, and do not cast off before it is time to leave. Unsecured boats in the back of a lock are particularly susceptible to damage.

Crossing the Bar

A **bar** is a stretch of water at a harbor mouth or entrance that is shallow enough to affect the shape of approaching waves. Not all harbors and inlets have bars. Those that do have different degrees of danger which can vary with time and which are all described in great detail in the appropriate coast pilot. If a coast pilot is not available, a chart of the entrance will provide some information on what to expect, but it is best not to attempt an unknown bar without some knowledge of its nature.

River current and any tidal current present also affects the state of the bar. A current running against waves will increase the steepness of the waves and the frequency of breaking. Shallow harbor mouths with large rivers produce the most dangerous bars.

Crossing a bar is a matter of timing, with the best time being during a calm with no sea running, at or just before high-water slack. The worst time is mid-ebb, with storm winds and waves. Unfortunately, it is in just these extreme conditions that a skipper's thoughts turn to the inviting serenity and safety of a nearby but unfamiliar harbor.

Many bars have a nearby Coast Guard station that can provide up-to-the-minute bar conditions. Contacting the Coast Guard is a prudent choice, because it is practically impossible to judge conditions from the deck of a small boat on the seaward side of a bar; the waves break on the shore side, and by the time the boat is close enough to judge the extent of breaking it may be beyond the point of no return. Any turn to escape will place the boat parallel to the waves, the most vulnerable position to be rolled. Unable to maneuver free, the boat's survival is left to chance.

Leaving the harbor in heavy conditions is not as difficult. The breaking seas are clearly visible, and the skipper can assess the situation and decide whether to cross and, if so, where the easiest path lies. During crossing, the rush of water from breaking waves is running against the boat, making it more maneuverable. Once into the breaking water the boat is committed, however, and returning with a 180-degree turn is no longer an option.

If the decision is made to cross in severe conditions, it is necessary to prepare the boat, select the path with the least amount of breaking, and make the transition as quickly as possible. Prepare the boat by closing all open hatches and ports and securing all lines. If the dinghy cannot be brought aboard, it must be cut adrift. Do not run a difficult bar trailing a dinghy. It will either swamp or run up and ram the boat from behind, and the slack towing line may foul the prop. Without engine power the boat is lost.

To select the proper path, observe the wave trains for several minutes and, like a surfer, try to predict the arrival of the large waves. It is best to cross from the ocean side on a single wave. This is only possible if the boat has enough speed to keep up with the wave. For boats with sufficient speed (10 to 15 knots in flat water), it is best to travel on the back of the second wave, not the first wave that follows the large wave. The large wave carries considerable water that must run back against the wave immediately following. This outflow of water will shorten the following wave and cause it to break earlier than normal.

Adjust boat speed to stay on the back of the wave until it has broken, then pass through it. Slower boats can start immediately after the large wave, as their passage will span several waves. It is almost certain that a slow boat will be overtaken by a breaking wave. With luck, the break will not be large nor occur in midwave, where the turbulence is maximum.

In most cases use maximum power, watch both forward and back, and concentrate on steering to keep the boat perpendicular to the wave fronts. Watch the bow relative to the horizon for any lateral movement, an early indication of the boat turning. Never apply reverse power; it will reduce steering ability.

Because broaching and pitchpoling are the common forms of destruction in crossing a bar, and since towing a sea anchor or drogue reduces the chances of both of these occurrences, the use of these devices has been recommended as an aid to help the crossing, especially for slower boats that cannot cross on a single wave.[9]

[9]Howard L. Andrews and Alexander L. Russel, Basic Boating Piloting and Seamanship, first U.S. ed. (Englewood Cliffs, N. J.: Prentice-Hall, Inc., 1964), 237.

I am not convinced that towing a drogue is a good idea. It is true that it will improve control of the boat, but it is also true that it will slow the boat and hold it in jeopardy for a much longer period, exposing it to more waves and increasing the chances of encountering The Big One. The boat, the skipper, the weather, and the bar all play a part in the decision. If a drogue is used, the line must be several wave lengths long so that the anchor remains in unbroken water to provide drag until the boat passes the area of breaking waves. A sharp knife should be handy to cut the tow line if something goes wrong and it becomes necessary to free the boat. Again, attach the drogue near the center of the boat as recommended in the section on Heavy Weather.

When going out over a bar, the situation is similar, except that the fury lasts longer. The boat is traveling slower against the rush of water from breaking waves and will have to take several waves head-on. The key is to get by the major line of breakers on a small wave and before the next big one hits. Wait in the area where the waves are running up until a big one breaks, then apply maximum power and rush out with the returning water.

3

NAVIGATION

I can say with great pride that, in more than 30 years of sailing, I have always known precisely where I was. In the interest of honesty, however, I'll admit there were a few times when I had doubts about the location of the rest of the world. Navigation is the process by which the individual remains in close personal contact with the rest of the world.

This chapter is about navigation for recreational boaters—a style considerably different than that practiced on commercial and military vessels. Aided by modern electronics and common sense, the average recreational boater has no need for many of the navigator's traditional skills. Thus, we will avoid such nonessential skills as labeling lines of positions and sight reduction, and concentrate on those skills that are truly essential.

Navigation divides generally into two parts, piloting and open-water navigation. **Piloting** is the process of guiding a boat in sight of land, using land forms and navigational aids. **Open-water navigation** covers the skills needed to guide the boat when land is not in sight. Sometimes the term "open water" is dropped and the practice is just referred to as navigation.

To further confuse the issue, there is also the age-old practice of **celestial navigation**, finding one's way by signposts located in the sky. Now, however, a major shift is under way from the use of remote celestial aids—the sun, moon, and stars— to nearby celestial aids—artificial satellites. In this book, "celestial navigation" refers to the traditional practice of using a sextant and astronomical bodies for navigation.

I used to feel that no one should put to sea without knowing celestial navigation; now I feel the same way about the satellite-based Global Positioning System, **GPS**. In my view, no one should put to sea in a small boat without GPS on board. With GPS, the boat's exact, current position can be transferred to permanent memory by touching a single button. And, the boat can return to within as little as 10 meters of where the button was pushed. Try that with a sextant.

Satellite navigation has not yet replaced *all* the navigational equipment on board, nor all the skills of a good navigator, however. Presently, and for the foreseeable future, the recreational boater must know how to use fundamental navigation equipment, such as the compass, charts, dividers, and other basic tools commonly found in the navigator's tool kit.

COMPASS

Probably the most common navigation instrument found aboard modern yachts, the compass has been aboard vessels, almost unchanged, since about the year 1300. Today, however, modern navigational devices are reducing the navigator's reliance on this basic instrument. The ancient Polynesians also made many long and complicated voyages of discovery unaided by the magnetic compass. Instead, they relied on extensive knowledge of such natural signs as the locations of celestial bodies, the movement of waves, and the habits of birds.

A magnetic compass is a simple and ancient machine, and there need be no mystery surrounding its use. The modern marine compass consists of a magnet attached to a circular card that is free to rotate on a horizontal axis and tilt 30 degrees or so to keep the card horizontal. This card usually floats in a housing filled with light oil. The card is divided into degrees, starting at 0 and increasing clockwise to 359 degrees, with the conventional compass points—N, S, E, W—printed on an inner circle. North corresponds to 0 degrees.

The compass card shown in Figure 3.1 is similar to those found aboard most well-equipped recreational boats. It is divided into 5-degree increments, which is adequate for recreational use. Compasses that have cards 8 inches in diameter or larger are generally graduated in 1-degree increments.

Figure 3.1 Typical Compass Card

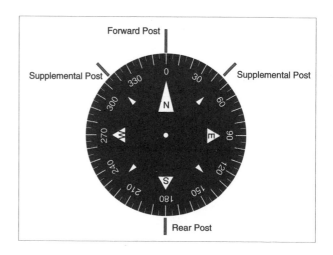

In the center of the card is a small post that corresponds to a large post in the forward edge of the compass and a small post at the rear. The large post forward, the center post, and the aft post form what is called the **axis** of the compass. On some compasses, the forward post is replaced with a line scribed in the bowl, called **a lubber's line**. There are sometimes two or more auxiliary posts at 45 degrees off the compass axis on each side to aid sailboat tacking and steering from an offset position.

The compass works because of magnetism. A region of influence called a **magnetic field** surrounds a magnet. It is useful to visualize the forces in this field as acting along lines, called **magnetic lines of force**. Any magnet that is free to rotate will align itself parallel to these imaginary lines of force, much as a comb aligns hair.

The earth, because of its iron core, produces a weak magnetic field full of these lines of force. A compass needle is a magnet that is free to rotate in this field. Therefore, if the compass is isolated from all other magnetic fields, the magnet in the compass will respond to the earth's weak magnetic field and align itself parallel to the lines of force, pointing always to the earth's magnetic pole. Unfortunately, there are three problems with this neat-sounding package: two are combined under the concept of **magnetic variation**, and the third is called **magnetic deviation**.

Magnetic Variation

First, there is no real magnetic pole, at least not in the same sense as the geographic pole that can be found precisely at a single point on the earth's surface. The magnetic poles are really polar areas, and unlike the geographic poles are not diametrically opposite one another. Further, these polar areas are not coincident with the geographic poles and tend to wander around rather arbitrarily from year to year.

Second, the earth acts as a somewhat irregular magnet, and the lines of force are not the perfect parallel lines one finds surrounding bar magnets. These two difficulties cause the angle between the magnetic lines of force and the geographic poles to vary from place to place on the earth's surface. This angle is called magnetic or compass variation, and it is measured east or west of the true geographic pole. Figure 3.2 shows the lines of equal compass variation, or isogonic lines, on a Mercator projection.

Three things are of interest in this figure: the amount of irregularity in the lines, how slowly the variation changes with distance, and the position of the **agonic**, or zero-variation, line through Europe and Asia. Notice that in most areas frequented by recreational boaters the variation remains relatively constant over distances as large as 100 to 500 miles. The significance of this will become more

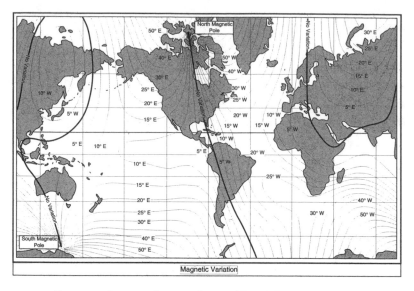

Figure 3.2 Isogonic Lines or Lines of Equal Compass Variation

apparent when we discuss how to use the compass. What makes the position of the agonic line interesting is that it covers a large part of two continents and falls through the cradle of ancient civilization. This fluke of nature is probably responsible for the early use of the compass as a direction-indicating device, because in this area the magic lodestone always pointed to the north star. The usefulness of the magnet's ability to align itself with the earth's magnetic field would have been less apparent in areas where the variation was large or changed more rapidly.

Magnetic Deviation

A compass is seldom free of other magnetic influences, such as ferrous metals and electrical currents in the immediate vicinity. These influences cause the compass needle to deviate from exact alignment with the earth's lines of magnetic force. The resulting error is called **magnetic deviation**. Since most boats contain both ferrous metals and electrical currents, their compasses must be corrected for deviation. The compass deviation in a single location is not constant, but varies depending on the orientation of the compass within the earth's magnetic field; therefore, compass deviation also depends on the boat's course.

The deviation on each course can be measured by **swinging the compass**. This process (described in Appendix C) is not costly, and I would recommend the use of a professional. The result of swinging the compass is a card that shows boat-specific deviations from the magnetic bearings at 45-degree intervals or less. If the deviations are more than a couple of degrees, magnets can be added to the compass to correct and reduce the deviation angles to acceptable limits. All recreational boats should reduce magnetic deviation below 3 degrees.

Most fiberglass, aluminum, and wooden boats have very small magnetic fields, which reduces magnetic deviation for most recreational boats to a nonproblem. The larger concentrations of ferrous metal, the engine and fuel tanks, generally are remote from the compass and have little effect on it. Table 3.1 shows the compass deviation card for my own boat, *Bird of Time*. These uncorrected deviations are typical for fiberglass boats.

Table 3.1 Typical Magnetic Deviation Cards

	DEVIATION	
MAGNETIC COURSE	BIRD OF TIME (FIBERGLASS HULL UNCORRECTED)	STEWBALL (STEEL HULL CORRECTED)
000°	0	0
045°	1° West	1° East
090°	0	0
135°	1° West	1° West
180°	0	0
225°	1° East	0
270°	0	0
315°	1° East	1° West
360°	0	0

This table shows that if I steer my boat on a magnetic bearing of 45 degrees, I am actually steering 1 degree to the West, or 44 degrees; therefore, if I wish to steer due magnetic East, or 45 degrees, I must steer magnetic 46 degrees. One degree deviation would produce an error of about 300 yards in 10 miles; it is almost impossible for a recreational boat to hold a course accurate to 1 degree for that distance.

Compass deviation for steel boats is a more serious problem. An uncorrected compass can be off as much as 25 degrees. Five degrees of deviation can produce an error of close to a mile in 10 miles of run. It is imperative that owners of steel boats have their compasses corrected. If they do, and if the compass is properly compensated, its deviation can become minimal as well. The uncorrected magnetic deviation for *Stewball*, a boat with an all-steel hull, was originally as large as 20 degrees. Its magnetic deviation card, also shown in Table 3.1, is a typical example of the results of good compass correction. Owners of nonferrous boats should consider their use of the boat and the behavior of the compass to determine whether a deviation card is needed.

Compass deviation is not a one-time problem. Large ferrous objects, such as chain, if stored temporarily near the compass, can effectively change the ship's magnetic field. The magnetic deviation of steel boats can change if the boat's location changes significantly. Turning on and off electrical equipment, such as radios or windshield wipers, can also temporarily affect the ship's magnetic field.

Bird of Time's autopilot used to turn her 5 degrees to port every time the refrigerator came on, because the autopilot compass was located too close to the refrigerator's electric line. A large steel belt buckle or a knife in the helmsperson's pocket can temporarily affect the compass reading. Vigilance is the only way to keep such influences from affecting the boat's course.

Compass Course Inaccuracies

When running a compass course, wind, current, magnetic anomalies, compass error, and human error all contribute to inaccuracy. Human interaction can produce course errors of as much as 5 or 10 degrees. The error introduced by the compass is between 2 and 5 degrees. Recall that most compasses used on recreational boats are subdivided into only the nearest 5-degree increment. Steering a compass course of 123 degrees is not practical on a small boat; what that course really means is, keep it somewhere between 120 and 125 degrees.

All boats not traveling directly into or away from the wind or current are subject to leeway. The amount of leeway depends on the boat's underbody and superstructure, the direction of the boat relative to the wind and current, and the relative velocity of the wind, current, and boat. As shown in Chapter 2, the strength and direction of current is highly variable, and its effects can be large.

Without current, leeway for sailboats is from 0 to 5 degrees and remains relatively constant, if the angle of the wind remains constant. Leeway for a powerboat is more difficult to calculate because there is no relationship between boat speed and wind speed. Powerboat leeway can be anything from zero to as much as 20 degrees. While it is true that the faster the boat goes the less the effects of wind on leeway, it is also true that when the wind velocity increases the wave height increases, and in large waves, powerboats must slow down, therefore increasing leeway.

Magnetic anomalies are irregularities in the earth's magnetic field that occur over relatively small areas. These disturbances, called **local attraction** by professional sailors, can be as much as 80 degrees and are commonly 15 to 20 degrees. Warnings of these local disturbances are generally listed on navigational charts.

It should be apparent that the compass is not a precision instrument, especially on small boats with small compasses. Even on large boats, the compass is used almost exclusively for dead reckoning; the actual boat's position must be corrected periodically by other means, the more often the better.

Using a Compass

Most recreational boats normally carry two different types of magnetic compasses, a fixed compass used mostly by the helmsperson, and a smaller handheld compass used mainly by the navigator to take bearings.

The fixed compass is mounted with its axis aligned parallel to the boat's centerline. The compass card will therefore indicate the direction of the boat relative to the earth's magnetic field. This direction, called the **compass bearing**, is read by observing the degree reading adjacent to the forward post or lubber's line.

Identifying the compass bearing of your desired course can be complex or simple. The simplest way to obtain a compass bearing is from a modern navigational instrument, such as loran or GPS. These instruments contain tables of magnetic variation, and the boat's compass deviation information can also be entered into their memory. Input the longitude and latitude of the origin and destination points, and the instrument will make the calculations internally and output compass bearing directly. In many cases, the boat is the origin point, since the instrument already knows that location; one only need enter the destination point to get a course.

The next simplest way to obtain a compass bearing is to start with **a magnetic bearing** taken from the **compass rose** of a chart. The process of getting a magnetic bearing from the chart using a straightedge and the compass rose is described on page 91. Notice that a magnetic bearing is not technically the same as a compass bearing. To change a magnetic bearing into a compass bearing you must add or subtract the boat's compass deviation. However, because the deviation on a properly adjusted compass is less than 2 degrees, you can usually ignore it.

One can be too precise when dealing with compass courses. The physical "law of cancellation" states that if one is equally sloppy on all measurements, the resulting errors will cancel. Most boaters using a properly adjusted compass can rightly ignore deviation corrections and use the magnetic bearing as the compass bearing with no serious consequences. If the compass has deviations larger than 2 or 3 degrees, see Appendix C for the procedure needed to change magnetic bearings into compass bearings.

The most difficult place to obtain a compass bearing is from **a true bearing**, meaning a bearing derived from true rather than magnetic north. The difference between compass and true bearings is the subject of much unnecessary arm waving and head scratching. A whole mystic lore has been developed by traditional navigators to aid in the alteration of compass to true bearings and back.

The process has to do with adding or subtracting variation to true bearings to first get a magnetic bearing, and then adding or subtracting deviation from this magnetic bearing to arrive at a compass bearing. To be precise in determining the compass bearing it sometimes is necessary to add or subtract each of these variables, but always in the proper order, which of course changes depending on the purpose of the transformation. The process is highly confusing and fraught with opportunities to make significant errors.

If you are unconvinced of the complexity, consider that *Chapman's* dedicates 3½ pages to the process[1] The book dutifully recounts such mnemonics as "Can Dead Men Vote Twice," which is supposed to help navigators remember how to make the mystical change from compass with deviation to magnetic with variation to true bearing. A naval officer or tanker captain may need this, but in my view, a recreational boater rarely if ever needs this calculation. Many recreational boaters have crossed oceans without changing a single bearing from true to compass. Nonetheless, see Appendix D for details of converting true to magnetic bearings. This can be useful with small-scale charts lacking a compass rose to provide magnetic north, or those with wide ranges of magnetic variation.

It is helpful to be aware of variation and deviation, but there is a difference between precision and accuracy. Going through the mental gymnastics can make the course more precise but not necessarily more accurate. The happy result of paying little attention to variation and deviation is that using the compass becomes simpler. My advice to the recreational boater is to adjust your compass correctly and forget true bearings, except as a rite of passage.

Steering a Compass Course

Steering a small boat on a compass course is done by bringing the desired compass bearing adjacent to the forward post or lubber's line and holding it there. Unfortunately, boats are steered on open water that has waves, current, and various amounts of wind. The result is that a compass course is never a straight line, regardless of whether it is steered by hand or by machine.

---

[1] *Elbert S. Maloney,* Chapman, Piloting, Seamanship and Small Boat Handling, *60th ed. (New York: The Hearst Corporation, 1991), 348–351.

The motions of the boat may seem random, but human reaction to these motions is not. A helmsperson's errors tend to be additive, sort of like walking through the forest and passing obstructions always on a favorite side, resulting in a pronounced drift to that side in the intended course. The amount of drift differs between individuals and with wave conditions; it may be as much as 1½ miles over a 10-mile course. On a clear day that's not a problem, but in the fog or if the course spans 100 miles it may become serious.

The key to good helmsmanship is to make these oscillations self-canceling and as small as possible. The common practice of experienced small-boat helmspersons when steering a compass course is to alternately over- and understeer the course by a few degrees. Holding a course of plus or minus 5 degrees is adequate if the time spent on the plus side of the course equals the time spent on the minus side of the course.

Obviously, the smaller the oscillations the better the course. To keep the oscillations small it is necessary to keep the helm movements small. A new helmsperson always finds that coming up on the new course is much easier if the new course is very close to the old one. If the course change is large and the wheel or tiller has to move through a large angle, there is a tendency to overshoot the intended course and go into a series of diminishing oscillations that finally bring the boat back on course. To avoid these oscillations it is necessary to anticipate coming on course early and start turning the wheel back amidships *before* the desired course is reached. The greater the angular difference between the original and the final course, the earlier the wheel needs to be returned amidships.

Once on course, it helps to sense the small boat oscillations early and correct with small helm changes. Sensing the movement of the boat using only the 4- to 6-inch line of the compass is much more difficult than using a long-range reference point, similar to the normal process of steering described in Chapter 2. If no fixed point on the horizon is on the intended course, a star or even a cloud can be used as a temporary point. Temporary reference points must be checked periodically against the compass and changed as necessary.

CHARTS

Nowhere is the old saw about pictures and their worth in words more true than when it comes to explaining how to get from place to place. Graphic representations of the earth's surface are excellent ways of representing large amounts of information. With a little practice, one can picture the location of rocks, shoals, various structures, and the shapes of bays and surrounding hills. There is no better or cheaper boat insurance than a good set of charts for the waters in which you expect to operate.

Because they are important and expensive, charts require proper storage, ideally in an area large enough to keep them flat and unfolded. Storing rolled charts in tubes is hard on the charts, hard on the user, and just not feasible for a large number of charts. Storing charts under the bunk pad is all right for short summer cruises, but the number needed for any reasonable bluewater cruise makes for mighty bumpy sleeping.

Before getting into specific chart information it is helpful to recall some of the terms from third-grade geography: **latitude**, **longitude**, **parallels**, **meridians**, **poles**, and **equator**. Now, after all those years, you'll find a real use for these terms. Recall that lines of equal latitude describe parallel circles on the surface of the globe, and that lines of equal longitude describe circles that pass through both poles. (See Figure 3.3.)

What is interesting about meridians, or lines of equal longitude, is that they all pass through the center of the sphere and therefore cut the earth into two equal parts. With a little introspection one can see that the circles formed on the surface of the sphere by the meridians are the greatest possible circles because the diameters of these circles are always equal to the maximum diameter of the sphere; these are called **great circles**.

One interesting property of a great circle is that the shortest distance between two points on a sphere always lies on a great circle. This is a handy property of longitude or meridians. Another handy property is that they are all the same length,

Figure 3.3 Basic Earth
Coordinates

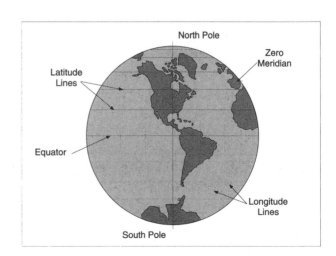

the circumference of the earth. If this circumference is divided into 3,600 equal parts, a unit of measure called the **nautical mile** results. What is not so handy about longitude is that the distance between longitude 10 and 20 at latitude 0 degrees, or the **equator**, is much greater than the distance between the same two lines at latitude 80 degrees.

Parallels, on the other hand, as can be seen from Figure 3.3, are not great circles, except for the equator, and they also do not pass through the center of the earth or both poles. On the other hand, because they are laid out parallel to the equator, the distance between latitude 10 and latitude 20 is the same as the distance between latitude 60 and latitude 70 regardless of longitude. With a little forethought but the same fetish for the number 60, the ancient mapmakers decided to make the distance between degrees of latitude 60 nautical miles. The result is that 1 minute of latitude always equals 1 nautical mile.

Two other geographic concepts are important to navigation: the **zero meridian** and **Mercator projection**. The problem with finding the zero, or prime, meridian was solved arbitrarily by the British declaring that it ran through Greenwich, England. Unlike latitude, which runs from 0 to 90 degrees north and south of the equator, longitude runs from 0 to 180 degrees east and west of Greenwich.

It is difficult to project a double-curved surface like a sphere onto a flat surface. One way of doing it is called the Mercator projection, which projects the surface of the earth onto a cylinder. This cylinder touches the earth only on one diameter, normally the midchart latitude (see Figure 3.4). In this instance one can see that the projection of the longitude lines is relatively simple. They become

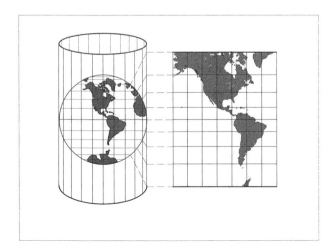

Figure 3.4 Mercator Chart Projection

evenly spaced vertical lines. The latitude lines pose a little more of a problem. These lines can be projected in any number of ways.

Sixteenth-century Flemish geographer Gerardus Mercator decided to expand the latitude using the secant (a geometric name for a straight line that intersects a curve at two or more points) of the latitude, which would have the advantage that the cardinal directions, North, South, East, and West, would run up, down, right, and left, respectively, on the chart, and the angles between all points on the map would be correctly shown. Thus, a constant compass course would be drawn as a straight line on the map. This kind of compass course is known as a **rhumb line**.

The Mercator projection has the disadvantage that the distances in the east and west directions are distorted on the chart, and are only strictly accurate where the projection is tangent to the surface of the earth, normally at the equator. The east and west distances get less accurate the farther one goes north or south of the equator. Since the secant of 90 degrees is infinity, the Mercator projections are of little value in the polar regions. Most Mercator projections do not go beyond 80 degrees of latitude, for this same reason. For more information on Mercator projections and rhumb line sailings, see Appendix D.

The **Lambert projection**, a slight modification of the Mercator projection, projects the surface of the earth onto a cone, rather than a cylinder, that intersects the earth along two lines of latitude or parallels. The surface of the earth is again distorted, so that the change in distance along the parallels is the same as the change in distance along the meridians. A straight-line course on this type of chart is very close to a great circle course. Lambert projections are used more for aeronautical navigation than marine navigation. Older charts of the Great Lakes are Lambert projections, for instance, but the charts most often used by small-boat navigators are all Mercator projections.

Charts are maps of the sea and waterways, and provide information necessary for navigation. Charts indicate the depth of water and the location of shoals, rocks, reefs, and navigable channels. Charts also show the location of harbors, safe anchorages, important landmarks, aids to navigation such as lighthouses, buoys, and range markers, and a great deal of other information. Most major countries produce charts of their local waters as well as of international waters, and require that vessels operating in their waters carry reliable charts. In some countries "reliable" means charts produced only by their own governmental agencies.

The United States, in its usual bureaucratic wisdom, has three different organizations responsible for making charts: the U.S. National Ocean Survey (NOS), a branch of the National Oceanic and Atmospheric Administration (NOAA), which itself is a branch of the Department of Commerce; the Department of Defense Mapping Agency (DOD); and the U. S. Army Corps of Engineers (COE). There is some overlap, but the theoretical difference is that NOS charts are domestic, DOD charts deal with foreign waters and the open ocean, and COE charts are mainly for the Mississippi River and many of its tributaries above New Orleans. This division of labor is not strictly accurate, however, since NOS provides charts on Canadian waters, some open-ocean charts, charts of the Great Lakes, and charts of many other large lakes and rivers as well.

The foreign charts of most interest to U.S. recreational boaters are those produced by the Canadian Hydrographic Service and the British Admiralty. Both agencies provide high-quality charts very similar to U.S. charts.

Reading a U.S. NOS Chart

Even a cursory look at a chart reveals a great deal of information, some text, some graphic, and all important at various times. For convenience, we will break the chart into six areas and discuss each separately: the margin area, the title block, the notes, the compass roses, the land features, and the water features.

Margin Data

The margin data is that information contained near the edges of the chart, including the border and the longitude and latitude scales. The chart's name is found in the lower right-hand corner; its number is found in the lower right and upper and lower left corners.

The name describes the waters covered. For example, the name of the chart might be "Island of Oahu" or "Straits of Juan de Fuca Eastern Part." The number is assigned by geographic area and corresponds to a specific title. For instance, the Hawaiian Island charts all have numbers in the 1900s. Catalogs listing the charts by these numbers are provided free to the public by NOAA. These catalogs also contain maps outlining the areas covered by each chart to assist in locating the chart of choice.

In the upper left and lower right-hand corners of the chart margin is a note indicating whether the chart soundings are in fathoms, feet, or meters. (NOS is in the process of converting all charts to showing depths only in meters.) The depth information is so vital that it is given in the margins and repeated in the title block.

In the lower left corner is the chart's edition number, its publication date, and the date of its last revision, if applicable. Charts are revised at regular intervals. The dates of the most current edition of a chart can be found in a pamphlet called "Dates of Latest Editions," available free from the Distribution Division, National Ocean Survey, National Oceanic and Atmospheric Administration, Rockville, Maryland, 20852.

This information is important to the navigator because natural and artificial changes are occurring constantly, and some may be critical to the safety of the vessel. Changes and matters affecting navigational safety are published weekly by the Defense Mapping Agency, Hydrographic Center. These notices will be sent to any interested party. The local Coast Guard also publishes and broadcasts on VHF notices to mariners that concern the local area. Some of these changes announced by the Coast Guard are both local and temporary and will not be in the Defense Mapping Agency's bulletin.

Information from both of these bulletins can be used to update existing charts; however, this updating process is ongoing and requires considerable effort. Every skipper should be aware of these bulletins and the consequences of ignoring them, and then decide when and how to use the information they contain.

The chart border contains the latitude and longitude scales. These scales normally have three different graduations depending on the area covered. NOAA has a whole set of rules governing the graduations shown on charts of various scales, but the easiest way of determining the value is to locate the numeric values next to the latitude scale and count the major and minor divisions between them.

Title Block

The chart's title block contains much information of interest to the navigator, including the scale of the chart and the latitude where that scale is exactly accurate. The scale is designated by two numbers separated by a colon, for example 1:80,000, or 1 chart inch equals 80,000 inches, or 1 inch equals approximately 1.1 nautical miles.

NOAA produces five classes of charts roughly grouped by scale: Harbor, Small-Craft, Coast, General, and Sailing charts. Harbor charts are published at scales larger (smaller areas and greater detail) than 1:50,000, depending on the size and importance of the harbor and the numbers of existing dangers.

Small-craft charts are published at scales of 1:80,000 and larger (smaller area). They are designed to be used in the limited space of small craft, and come already folded for storage. Small-craft charts are identified by the letters "SC" after the chart numbers.

Coast charts are published at scales from 1:50,000 to 1:100,000. They are intended for coastal navigation and are the charts most commonly used by recreational boaters.

General charts are published at scales from 1:100,000 to 1:600,000. As such they cover large areas and are designed for coastal navigation where the vessel's position can be fixed by landmarks, buoys, and lighthouses. They are also excellent for general planning purposes.

Sailing charts are those with scales smaller than 1:600,000, and are designed for offshore work and coastal approaches. They cover larger areas; for example, chart number 18003 covers the area from Cape Blanco to Cape Flattery on the West Coast, a distance of almost 400 nautical miles at a scale of 1:735,560.

Charts with scales of 1:80,000 or larger (smaller area), where the scale remains for all practical purposes constant throughout the chart area, have, in addition to the text-formatted scale, two sets of graphic scales—one at the top and one at the bottom, and on opposite sides, if possible. The graphic scales are shown in nautical miles and in yards; inland or intracoastal waterway charts often have a third graphic scale showing statue miles. On any chart, one minute of latitude always equals 1 nautical mile.

The horizontal and vertical datums also appear in the title block, with the vertical datum of most interest to mariners. This datum varies and depends on the tides of the area being charted. In areas where the vertical clearance is restricted either above or below the water and these restrictions are very close to the draft and height of your vessel, it is important to understand these chart datums and the difference between them and actual water levels.

By international agreement, the level used as chart datum should be just low enough so that low waters do not go far below the datum. Table 3.2 is a list of the more common datums used on charts, and their meanings. Soundings on the chart are all taken relative to this datum and are shown as positive numbers below this datum.

The other vertical datum of interest is the shoreline plane of reference, which is normally used for heights and elevations. The difference is that height is measured from some high-water datum specified on the chart, and is used to determine bridge and cable clearance. Elevation is always measured from mean sea level. The differences can be as much as 20 feet in areas with very high tides.

The plane of reference most often used for heights is the mean high water datum, which is derived in a manner similar to the mean low water datum. On occasion, however, other clearance datums are used. For example, many lakes and rivers use a special datum; in areas with little tidal fluctuation, mean sea level may be used. The Corps of Engineers maintains a list of clearances for all bridges on U.S. navigable waters. The clearance is often listed both at mean high water and mean low water.

Notes

There are many other notes and tables found on charts. Some refer to special areas on the charts, restricted areas, or areas where travel is prohibited or dangers

Table 3.2 Chart Datums[2]

DATUM	DESCRIPTION
Mean Low Water (MLW)	The average height of all low waters.
Mean Low Water Springs (MLWS) or Low Water Springs	The average level of the low waters that occur at the times of spring tides. Usually used in areas with semidiurnal tides.
Mean Lower Low Water (MLLW)	Usually used along both coasts of the U.S. and in areas of mixed tides. It is the average height of the lower low waters.
Indian Springs Low Water (ISLW)	This datum includes the spring effect of the semidiurnal tides and the tropic effect of the diurnal tides.
Gulf Coast Low Water (GCLW)	Usually used along the Gulf coast of the U.S. where tidal characteristics are complex.
Mean Lower Low Water Springs(MLLWS)	Usually used in areas of mixed tides. It is the average of the two lower low waters on days with spring tides.
Lowest Normal Low Water (LNLW)	This datum approximates the average height of the monthly lowest low waters, discarding any disturbance due to storm surge.
Lowest Low Water (LLW)	This datum is an extremely low datum corresponding to the lowest tide observed.
Mean Sea Level (MSL)	This datum is used in areas where there is little or no tide.
Special Datums	These are datums commonly found in rivers that are affected by tide and runoff, and are referenced to some historical low water. Normal pool level is often used for a datum in reservoirs.

exist. Other points of interest, including anchorages, cables, spoil disposal, and fish trap areas, are explained in the notes as well as shown on the chart. The notes often contain a list of abbreviations used on the chart. Charts that cover small areas often have a table of tidal data showing several stages of the tide, from extreme low water to mean higher high water. Charts covering larger areas often have several nomographs to help the mariner calculate position or speed.

[2]Nathaniel Bowditch, American Practical Navigator (Washington, D.C.: Defense Mapping Agency, 1984), 804–805.

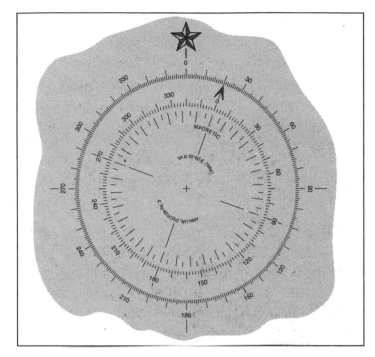

Figure 3.5 A Typical
Compass Rose

Compass Rose

The compass rose, used to determine direction, consists of three concentric circles. The outer circle is accurately subdivided into 360 degrees, zero at true north, parallel to lines of equal longitude. True north is generally indicated by a star, symbolic of the north star. Courses indicated by the degrees of this circle are true bearings.

The middle circle, also divided into degrees, is oriented with its zero pointing toward magnetic north. The symbol for magnetic north is an arrowhead symbolizing the compass arrow.

The innermost circle is divided into 128 points corresponding to the 32 points of the ancient compass. Because there is little call today for a North by Northwest course, except in movie titles, the typical boater can ignore the inner circle. In the center of the rose are some cryptic words that should not be ignored; these deal with variation, abbreviated VAR on the chart.

The number following VAR indicates the difference in degrees between the magnetic and true circles, the magnetic variation in the chart area. E or W indicates whether the differences are east or west of true north, and the date is when the variation was last measured. Variation is shown only to a quarter of a degree. There is also an indication of how much the variation is changing annually and whether it is increasing or decreasing.

Most charts have several compass roses in different locations convenient for plotting. For accurate magnetic bearings, use the compass rose closest to your location on the chart, because the magnetic variation on each compass rose can be different. On some charts covering very large areas, compass variation changes rapidly from place to place, making it difficult to show magnetic variation with a compass rose. On these charts the compass rose is simplified to show only the outer, true bearing circle; isogonic lines are used to show variation. The navigator must take any variation information needed from the isogonic lines and their position and compute magnetic bearings. On these rare occasions, when Dead Men are forced to Vote Twice, see Appendix D.

Graphic Data

Charts rely heavily on graphics, symbols, and abbreviations to convey a lot of information in little space. The standard set of symbols and abbreviations used by NOAA can be found in "Chart No. 1, Nautical Chart Symbols and Abbreviations," a 58-page pamphlet prepared jointly by NOAA and the Department of Defense and distributed by the Department of Commerce. It can be obtained at most locations that sell charts.

Fifty-eight pages of symbols and abbreviations will obviously contain much useful information, and some of only passing interest to the recreational boater— rice paddies and underwater springs, for example. Since everyone should have a copy of Chart 1, I'll cover only those features I feel are most useful, organized into two parts, land and water features.

Land features and characteristics that will assist the navigator are shown on nautical charts in brown, gold, gray, or tan. Details are confined to those near shore or of such prominence as to be seen clearly for some distance offshore. Land features can be subdivided into the shoreline, topography, and other geographical features.

The shoreline or edge between land and water is not always sharply defined, especially on detailed, large-scale charts covering small areas. Between what is always water and always land lies the tidal zone, which is sometimes water and sometimes land. This zone is bounded on one side by mean low water and the other by mean high water. Mean low water is shown as a single row of dots. However, in areas where the tidal zone is very steep or the tidal range very small, the low water line is omitted.

Land areas are delineated from the tidal zones, except in marsh, swamp, or mangrove areas, by a mean high water line, which is derived in a manner similar to the low water datum and is shown by a medium-width single line. In areas of marsh or mangrove the mean high water line is generally obscured by vegetation. In such areas the edge of vegetation (berm line) is used as the shoreline. Shoreline characteristics are represented by the symbols shown in Table 3.3.

SYMBOL	FEATURE
Table 3.3 Common Shoreline Symbols	
	Glacier
	Grass
	Gravel
	Marsh
	Rock or Coral
	Sand
	Trees

Topography is indicated by contours, form lines, hachures, shading, or any combination of these methods. The most useful, contour lines are thin black lines that run across the land portion of the chart. Every point along a contour line is the same number of feet above mean sea level (see Figure 3.6). If the earth were sliced along these lines by a huge bread slicer it would be separated into horizontal slices. The shape of these lines indicates the actual shape of the topography.

The ability to transfer contour lines mentally to actual hill shapes is of great assistance in piloting. Often, unknown islands can be identified by their contour

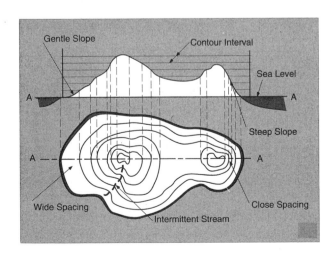

Figure 3.6 Contour Lines

shape. Contour lines can help select an anchorage. For example, an enclosed anchorage may be exposed to prevailing winds funneled through a low-lying valley, which can be readily identified by the shape of the contours.

Contour lines always point upstream on a river or creek and rarely cross one another. Lines spaced far apart indicate a flat surface, close together a steep surface. Contours supply other information as well. If the contours are round, the hill will be round. If they are elongated in one direction, the hill will be long in that direction. If they are far apart on one end and close together on the other, the hill will have a gradual slope on one end and a steep dropoff on the other.

The top of a hill is generally indicated by a dot and its height above sea level. Not all points are labeled with elevation numbers, but elevations of these points can be obtained by using the contour interval.

The contour interval, noted on most charts, is the vertical distance between contours and is always the same on any one chart or map. On extremely flat areas, elevations are sometimes shown on each contour. More often, only every fourth or fifth contour line is labeled with an elevation. Dashed lines, form lines, hachures, and shading are all used to show the general shape of the topography where elevation data is limited.

Form lines are like contour lines but are not continuous. They are drawn only in steeper areas, and like contours trend along the slope at approximately the same elevation, the closer together the steeper the terrain. Unlike contours, however, the actual vertical distance between the lines is not constant.

Hachures are short lines of the same length running down a slope, indicating the approximate location of steep slopes or the summit of a hill or mountain. Steep slopes are divided into cliffs and bluffs. Cliffs are mainly rocky and are good radar reflectors; bluffs are of soil or sand and reflect radar poorly. Bluffs are shown by hachures, cliffs and rocky coasts by vertical lines of different length or a combination of vertical and horizontal lines.

Shading is sometimes used to show topography—the darker the shading, the steeper the slope. When used in conjunction with contour lines, shading gives the chart a three-dimensional effect, which helps the navigator visualize the topography.

Other charted geographic features include manmade objects and landmarks, which are labeled or shown with the symbols in Table 3.4.

Water features of concern to a navigator include the depth of the water, bottom conditions, and hydrographic features.

Depth information is always shown with reference to the chart datum, and is designated by color, shading, figures, and contours. Depth figures are called soundings, normally measured in feet, meters, or fathoms. Eventually all soundings will be in meters to conform to international practice; until that time it is important to check the title block for this information. Some older charts use both feet and fathoms. Fathom readings are used in deep water; in shallow water a fathom figure is accompanied by a subscripted reading in feet. For example, 10 feet of water would be indicated as "1_4" and 3 feet as "0_3."

Table 3.4 Common Geographic Symbols

SYMBOL	FEATURE
⊙	*Accurate Fixed Point*
✈	*Airport*
	Bridge
✝ ■	*Church*
⊖	*Customhouse*
	Dam
	Dock
⚓	*Harbormaster*
⊕	*Health Office*
	Jetty
	Launching Ramp
	Locks
Tower ⊙- - - ⊙ Tower	*Overhead Cables*
	Piers
╫╫╫╫╫╫╫╫╫╫	*Railroads*
	Roads
⚑	*Schools*

Sounding figures appear more frequently where depths change abruptly or irregularly; in areas that are relatively uniform the soundings are spaced farther apart. Thus, the navigator can use the relative spacing of the soundings to judge the irregularity of the bottom. Note, however, that actual depths may be shallower than those charted.

The color of the water area on the chart indicates its depth. On NOS charts, white water is always deep, blue water shallow. How shallow depends on the scale of the chart and the detail covered. Blue can designate water shallower than 1,2,3,5, or 10 fathoms. Depth limits of the blue tint can be obtained by studying the soundings next to the color change. If possible, it is best to avoid blue areas on the chart, regardless of depth. Blue chart areas should be entered cautiously, with strict attention to charted depths.

Olive green indicates areas that are exposed at low water but awash when the tide rises. Bright green indicates that the area has been swept with a cable to ensure that no isolated rocks or wrecks are present; swept water depths are shown in green figures, larger than those used for soundings, and are contained in horizontal brackets.

Fathom line curves are also used to indicate the depth of water. Typically the curves are 1, 2, 3, 5, 6, 10, 20, 30, 40, 50, 100, 500, and 1,000 fathoms. Older charts use different symbols for each fathom line. New charts use solid lines labeled with the depth, similar to land contours. The kind of bottom material and its density are indicated using a system of abbreviations interspersed with the soundings. Because this information is most useful during anchoring, the more common symbols are listed in Table 4.3 in Chapter 4 . A complete list of these abbreviations is given in Section S of Chart 1.

Hydrographic features shown in the water portion of the chart can be subdivided into two broad classifications, those that aid the navigator, like buoys and beacons, and those that are a hazard to navigation, like shoals, rocks, and obstructions.

Buoys, daymarkers or beacons, ranges, and lighthouses are all aids to navigation shown on charts. Each provides substantial information to the navigator about traffic flow and navigational hazards, as discussed in Chapter 2.

Buoys are represented on the chart by a straightforward system, but the explanation of the symbols can be bewildering. The most common symbol for buoys on U.S. charts is a small circle and a diamond emanating from a dot, which indicates the exact location of the buoys. Table 3.5 shows the most common symbols used to represent buoys.

Buoy symbols may be marked with abbreviations to indicate the type, color,

Table 3.5 Common Buoy Symbols

Symbol	Buoy Type
◊	General
◊	Vertical Banded
◊	Horizontal Banded
◊	Diagonally Striped
◊	Checkered
⚓	Mooring or other miscellaneous buoy not covered specifically

and number or letter. For example, can buoys always carry odd numbers, and nun buoys always show even numbers. The common abbreviations are shown in Table 3.6; others can be found in Chart 1.

Can buoys are shown in green, nun buoys in red or magenta. Buoys of other colors, or those on monochrome charts, are designated by a letter (see Table 3.7).

Sound buoys are labeled Bell, Whis, Horn, or Gong, to indicate the type of sound-producing mechanism. Lighted buoys are marked by a magenta circle surrounding the dot marking the buoy's position. An accompanying line of text describes the color and flash pattern of the light. The more common patterns and their abbreviations are given in Table 3.8.

Beacons, unlike buoys, are permanently mounted on shore or on fixed structures in shallow water. Generally unlighted and sometimes referred to as day-markers, their primary use is to indicate channel limits. The symbol for the red or right-side returning beacon is a small magenta equilateral triangle. The symbol for the green beacon is a small green square. A small uncolored rectangle symbolizes any other general beacon. Regardless of whether the chart is colored, the symbol is normally accompanied by letters indicating its color; any text on the beacon is shown in quotation marks on the chart.

Ranges can be indicated by the symbols for beacons, buoys, lights, or any combination thereof. The range is indicated on the chart by a solid line projecting from the outermost range markers, and shows the recommended course. The range line continues beyond its recommended usable range as a dashed line. Boats can

Table 3.6 Typical Letter Designations for Buoy Shapes

LETTER	DESCRIPTION
C	Can or cylindrical buoy
N	Nun or conical buoy
SP	Spherical buoy
S	Pole-shaped buoy
P	Pillar or spindle buoy, which has a broad, low circular base with a narrow pillar rising from its center
Float	Miscellaneous buoys not identified specifically
Tel	Telegraphic cable buoy unless found next to a moorage buoy; then it designates a buoy with telegraphic communication capability
T	Generally found next to moorage buoys and designates a buoy with telephone communication capability
AERO	Generally found next to moorage buoys and designates an aeronautical anchorage buoy used to moor float planes
Deviation	A buoy used to assist the mariner in making compass adjustments

sometimes traverse the water indicated by the dashed portion of the line, but should do so with caution and extra attention to the charted depths.

Lights and **lighthouses** are permanently fixed on shore or on a structure in shallow water. Lights are shown as a black dot with an ice-cream-cone-shaped magenta flare emanating from the dot. The black dot is the fixed position of the light. Fixed lights have the same color and pattern indicators as lighted buoys. As with lighted buoys, lights and lighthouses also are labeled with the characteristics of the light. For example, Gp Fl R(3) 10 sec 85 ft 10M "2" indicates a red (R) group-flashing (Gp Fl) light, 85 feet (85 ft) above the water, flashing three (3) flashes every 10 seconds (10 sec) visible for 10 nautical miles (10M). The numeral two ("2") appears on the side of the light structure.

The remaining hydrological features shown on charts indicate common **dangers to navigation**, such as shoals, rocks, coral, and wrecks. Unlike aids to navigation, the vertical location of a hazard is as important as its horizontal location,

Table 3.7 Typical Letter Designations for Buoy Colors

LETTER	DESCRIPTION
G	A green buoy, usually a can or cylindrical shape
R	A red buoy, usually a nun or conical shape
B	A black buoy (on older charts, cans may be designated as black; all portside cans were painted green in 1983)
W	White
Y	Yellow, commonly used for quarantine buoys
Br	Brown
Gy	Gray
Bu	Blue
Am	Amber
Or	Orange
BW	Black and white

Table 3.8 Common Light Designations

SYMBOL	DESIGNATION
F	Fixed or steady light
Fl	Flashing
Gr Fl	Group Flashing
Mo (A)	Morse Code Flashing; letter flashed in brackets
Q or Qk Fl	Quick Flashing
IQ or Int Qk Fl	Interrupted Quick Flashing
Oc	Occulting

because these dangers can be submerged all or part of the time. The minimum depth of water over the hazard is critical.

Shoals, shallow areas surrounded by deep water, are bordered by a broken line, tinted blue; the depths are shown in the normal manner. A shoal can be mud, sand, gravel, boulders, rock, or coral. Rocks and coral are so dangerous that individual rocks are often charted separately and labeled using a family of symbols: **Rocks** are labeled Rk; **coral** is labeled Co. Because the tidal range is a factor in the exposure of the hazards, the low water and high water datums are important in defining the symbols. To further complicate matters, the standard symbols mean different things depending on where you are. There are four classes of hazards, segregated by depth and ranging from fully submerged through awash to bare (see Table 3.9). Small-scale charts sometimes show individual rocks grouped as a rocky ledge.

Table 3.9 Symbols for Rocks

CHART SYMBOL	DESCRIPTION		
	EAST AND GULF COAST	WEST COAST	GREAT LAKES
3Rk	*Rocks that lie* **more than one foot** *below low water datum*	*Rocks that lie* **more than two feet** *below low water datum*	*Rocks that lie* **more than two feet** *below low water datum*
✳	*Rocks that lie between* **one foot below and one foot above** *low water datum*	*Rocks that lie between* **two feet below and two feet above** *low water datum*	*Rocks that lie between* **two feet below and two feet above** *low water datum*
✳ (2)	*Rocks that lie between* **one foot above** *low* **water datum and one foot above high** *water datum*	*Rocks that lie between* **two feet above** *low* **water datum and two feet above high** *water datum*	*Rocks that lie between* **two feet above** *low* **water datum and four feet above** *low water datum*
⬡(4)	*Rocks that lie* **more than two foot above high** *water datum*	*Rocks that lie* **more than three feet above high** *water datum*	*Rocks that lie* **more than five feet above** *low water datum*

Charted **wrecks** can be stranded or sunken; the former applies when any portion of the hull is above the sounding datum, and the latter when the hull lies entirely below the chart datum. A sunken vessel's masts, however, may still be visible above the datum. A wreck 11 fathoms or deeper is not considered a danger to surface navigation. Wrecks cleared by wire drag are so indicated on the chart by the depth contained in the special bracket symbol for wire dragging. Dangerous wrecks are surrounded by a broken line, and on colored charts tinted blue. Table 3.10 lists some of the common symbols used for wrecks.

Historically, nondangerous wrecks are not plotted outside the 20-fathom curve, except in Alaska. There are, however, a series of wreck charts that show all known nondangerous wrecks for the benefit of anglers.

Miscellaneous dangers to navigation include snags, stumps, pilings, and wells, which are all shown as small circles appropriately labeled. Overfalls, tidal rips, and eddies can also endanger vessels, and are shown with a wavy line or swirl symbols. Miscellaneous obstructions of unknown character are shown surrounded by dots and labeled "Obstr."

Table 3.10 Common Chart Symbols for Wrecks

SYMBOL	DESIGNATION
	Stranded wreck, hull always partially visible
	Sunken wreck, hull always submerged, but masts may be visible
(9)	Wreck over which depth is known
21	Wreck with depth cleared by wire drag
	Sunken wreck not dangerous to surface navigation
Wk 21	Alternate wreck symbol using text abbreviation

Other Types of Charts and Chart Books

There are several other major types of charts: Lake Charts, Inland River Charts, Pilot Charts, and commercial chart books.

Lake Charts cover the Great Lakes and many of the large, navigable lakes and reservoirs throughout the country. Produced by NOS, the COE, or state authorities, they are very similar to the more common coastal charts, although lake charts sometimes employ polyconic, or Lambert, projections rather than Mercator. Lake charts use as many as four different shades of blue to indicate various depths of water—the deeper the blue, the shallower the water. Also, because land features are more important around small lakes, lake charts commonly show distances using statute miles rather than nautical miles.

Most **Inland River Charts** are produced by NOS or the COE. Smaller rivers and rivers not used by commercial oceangoing vessels are generally not charted. Sometimes, however, they are mapped by an agency of the state or local government. The format of these maps varies significantly; commonly, they lack hydrographic detail such as soundings, and often are oriented to fit conveniently on a page rather than being laid out with north at the top of the page.

Commercial chart books are a response to increasing costs of government charts. Most of these books copy NOAA charts photographically and reproduce them in a reduced format. The smaller format, generally 11 by 17 inches or smaller, is easier to handle on small boats with limited space for navigation. The details on these commercial charts vary from exact photographic copies of NOS charts to modified copies that delete some information.

Because it may take a year or more for chart changes to filter down from the government through the publisher to the chandlery shelf, these charts should be used with caution. You'll need to pay more attention to navigational notices published by NOS and the Coast Guard.

PUBLICATIONS

There is a long list of items published by NOS, DOD, the Defense Mapping Agency, the U.S. Coast Guard, and the COE that are useful to the navigator. Each of the various agencies publishes a free catalog listing such items as pilot charts, coastal pilots, tidal current tables, and light lists.

Pilot charts are a compilation of wind, weather, and oceanographic information useful to the navigator in selecting routes across the oceans of the world. The charts cover five areas: the North and South Pacific, the Indian Ocean, and the North and South Atlantic Oceans. They provide a graphical representation of the prevailing winds in 5-degree squares over a specific time period, usually a month. The wind percentages are concentrated on eight points of the compass. Also given is the percentage of calms or light and variable winds. The number of gales is listed for each 5-degree square, along with expected storm tracks for all tropical and extratropical storms.

The direction and velocity of the ocean currents are shown along with the frequency of wave heights above 12 feet. And as the pitchman says, that's not all you get; you get contours showing the percentage of days with visibility less than 2 miles, contours of atmospheric pressure, and contours of the air and sea temperature. But wait, there's more: also included are the minimum, mean, and maximum limits of sea ice. The astute recreational boater will find much of value on these charts when route planning.

Coastal Pilots provide detailed descriptions of the world's harbors and coast-lines. There are nine volumes detailing the coast of the U.S. and its territories, prepared and distributed by NOS. Each major country also publishes pilots for its own coasts. The British publish at least 62 pilots covering the entire world. These books are a great help when approaching an area for the first time or when planning a trip. Coast pilots are a companion to charts, and provide much detail not available on charts.

Light Lists, published by the Coast Guard, and **Tide Tables** and **Tidal Current Tables**, published by NOS and DOD, are often recommended as essential equipment, but except for Tidal Current Tables, few recreational boaters really need to carry them.

Tools

There are several common tools used in navigation in conjunction with the compass and chart to obtain course, bearings, and distances. Most are standard drafting instruments that can be obtained from any stationer. You'll need a few sharp h or 2h soft pencils (hard lead can damage charts), a good eraser, and a small sandpaper block to keep the pencil points sharp. The rest of the equipment consists of scales, parallel rulers, drafting triangles, dividers, a drafting compass, and a protractor.

It is also handy to have an electronic handheld calculator with trig functions, a hand magnifying glass to read very fine print, a small flashlight, a good pair of binoculars, a timer or stopwatch, and some weights to hold down the chart during use. The drafting tools are relatively simple to use, but some descriptions and pointers are helpful before getting into piloting and navigation techniques.

Scales are a draftsman's term for fancy rulers, with more precise divisions. The better ones are triangular in shape, providing six different scales. Since NOAA intends to convert charts to metric, it is handy to have both a metric and a standard inch scale. There is no special technique required to measure the distance between two points; however, one should refrain from using the scale as a straightedge to draw lines. The friction of the pencil will eventually wear the graduations from the edge of the scale, making it difficult to read and inaccurate.

The **parallel ruler** is primarily used to transfer parallel lines, but it can also be used as a straightedge. The principal reason for transferring parallel lines in navigation is to transfer the direction of a charted line to a compass rose and vice versa.

A parallel ruler consists of two rulers attached by two small beams, which are free to rotate. The rotating beams allow the rulers to move apart while remaining parallel. A line is transferred by walking the beams from the original location to the desired location by alternatively moving one ruler, then the other. Firm pressure and a flat surface are required to prevent slippage.

Another form of parallel ruler is constructed using a single ruler supported on its major axis by two identical knurled rollers mounted on a common axle. As long as neither roller slips, the leading edge of the ruler will remain parallel to its original position. This device has the convenience of one-handed operation; however, it does require a clean, flat, firm surface with no obstructions, hard to find on a small boat.

A **triangle** can be used as a straightedge for drawing; coupled with a second triangle, it can be used to transfer parallel lines. Conventionally, one is a 45-degree triangle and the other a 30- to 60-degree triangle. The best triangles are made of transparent plastic, with at least one side longer than 12 inches.

Transferring lines with two triangles is a little tricky but quickly learned. The first triangle is positioned along the line being transferred and held firm. The second is positioned against it, hypotenuse to hypotenuse, held firm, and the first triangle slid along the edge of the second. The line can be transferred any distance by alternating the fixed and moving triangles.

A **drafting compass**, an instrument used to draw a circle, consists of two small metal bars that are hinged at the top and free to move at the bottom. The lower end of one bar holds a pin; the other has a pencil lead. The bars are held apart by a screw device. Cheap, friction-adjusted school compasses are unsuitable for navigational use. Using the screw, the desired distance can be set into the compass for accurate, repeatable measurements. Other uses of a drafting compass are laying off a known distance, constructing perpendicular lines, or bisecting an angle.

A **divider** is very similar to a drafting compass, but with a pin in each leg and no pencil lead. Dividers can be held apart by a screw or by friction. Since dividers are not normally used for geometric construction, the frictional system, which allows easier operation, is preferred.

The dividers' principal use is to measure or transfer distances quickly—for example, transferring the distance between two points on the chart to the latitude scale to determine the distance between the points in nautical miles. If the distance cannot be spanned by the dividers, it must be measured in increments. Set the dividers to a convenient whole number of nautical miles using the chart scale, then step off this distance along the desired line, counting the number of steps. At the end there will be an odd increment; set this into the dividers and transfer that distance to the scale. The total length of the line is the sum of the odd distance and the product of the number of steps times the selected whole number of nautical miles (see Figure 3.7).

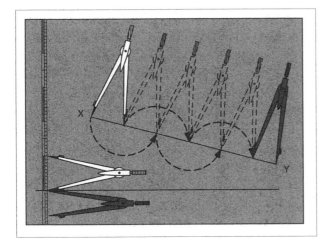

Figure 3.7 Using Dividers to Measure Distance

A **protractor** is a device used to measure the angle between lines on a flat surface, such as a chart. It consists of a graduated 180-degree arc, usually inscribed on transparent plastic. A good protractor has a 6- or 8-inch diameter, is accurately divided, and is graduated with at least 30 second marks. The center of the arc is marked by a hole and two lines intersecting at 90 degrees. An inscribed baseline intersects the 0-degree mark, the center of the arc, and the 180-degree mark. To use a protractor, position the center of the arc over the apex of the angle. Rotate the baseline until it coincides with one of the lines of the angle. Measure the size of the angle by reading where the other leg intersects the graduated arc of the protractor.

PILOTING

Piloting is the art of safely moving a vessel along a desired course by frequently establishing the boat's position with respect to features given on navigational charts and in sailing directions. No other form of navigation requires the continuous alertness, experience, and judgment needed in piloting. The easiest way to find your position is not to lose it in the first place. Every trip starts from a known location. It is a simple matter to leapfrog that known position ahead when the boat changes course, passes a landmark like an island, bay, or point, or enters a new channel. Constantly updating the position will reduce the number of disagreeable surprises.

Updating the boat's position can be done electronically or manually. If it is done entirely electronically, the equipment needs to be sufficiently accurate to ensure avoiding all dangers. This accuracy depends upon the proximity of the danger, the size of the waterway, and the scale of the chart. If it is done manually, partly or solely, the accuracy does not have to be as precise because the awareness of the navigator is involved. The process of manually updating this position is a major part of piloting. Updating the boat's position consists of two basic operations, locating the boat in the water and locating the boat on the chart.

Locating the Boat in the Water

Before you can locate your boat on a chart, you first must know approximately where you are on the water. This is simple if the boat is equipped with electronic navigational equipment that gives the boat's position in latitude and longitude. However, many times this is not the case, and the correct chart must be found by manually matching chart objects to real objects.

Road maps have signposts like "Route 66" or "Ritzville City Limits" that help us find our location. On a chart, the signposts are objects that can be identified on the ground. These fall into two classes, manufactured and natural objects. Manufactured objects are the easiest to identify but are not always available. Natural objects are always around but are not always easily identified.

Manufactured Identifiable Objects

The easiest manufactured objects to use for positioning are navigational aids placed in critical spots for just this purpose. You will recall that many of these aids to navigation—buoys, daymarkers, etc.—are labeled with a number or letter. If you are close enough to identify this number with the unaided eye, you know your location. A good set of field glasses may be helpful in identifying the number or locating the aid.

Lighthouses can be seen for 5 to 10 miles from a small boat. Large towers, bridges, cables, large buildings, and other large manufactured structures can all serve as identifiable objects. Many of these items, if they are shown on the chart, also have a general description to aid in identification.

Natural Identifiable Objects

Natural identifiable objects are the size and shape of the world around us. It is a little more difficult to interpret these signs properly on a chart, because the chart views the world from overhead and the navigator views the world from eye level.

The objects to look for first are prominent features like islands, peaks, points, or bays. If one or two are available, scan the chart for these features. It is most often necessary to locate two or more of these features to confirm position.

If two prominent features can be identified, check their relative position by orienting the chart. Place the chart on a flat surface, point one of the features on the chart toward its location on the ground, and see if the second feature also lines up with its charted position. If it does, you know where you are.

The next step is to verify your position by the relative location of other objects. Check other prominent features to determine if they are forward, behind, in line, or side-by-side the first feature. For example, is the island on the opposite side of the channel from the bay? The number of objects can be important. According to the chart, how many islands should be in view?

Next, you can use the relative location of not-so-obvious objects like streams or rocks, or other techniques like the relative size or height of various objects. It is difficult to tell actual size or height, but relative dimension is easy to use; for example, a channel is three times wider than an island, or peak A is twice as high as peak B. Remember when using widths that the perceived width of an island or channel is not the same as the actual width and depends on the point from which it is being viewed (see Figure 3.8).

The same is true about shape and relative location. The land and seascape can change appearance radically depending on the observer's viewpoint, which is the primary reason these locating techniques are more difficult to use. It is most helpful for the potential navigator to develop the ability to transfer chart features seen from above to actual features seen from eye level, a skill that increases with practice.

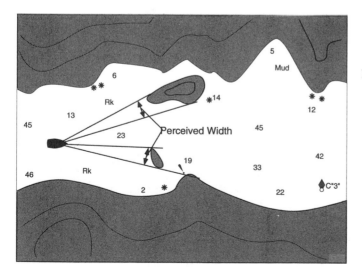

Figure 3.8 The Difference Between Perceived Width and Actual Width

Locating the Boat on a Chart

Once you have located your boat on the water and identified your surroundings, you can locate the boat on the chart—the mainstay of piloting. Think of the surface of the sea as a plane, where it is only necessary to deal with two dimensions. In a two-dimensional system, objects can be located using rectilinear coordinates or polar coordinates. Each method uses a single reference point and two coordinates to locate the object (see Figure 3.9).

Rectilinear coordinates drawn on paper form little rectangles; the primary directions are perpendicular to one another: forward, backward, left and right, or north, south, east, and west. The most common rectilinear coordinates used in navigation are latitude and longitude. The reference point in this system is the intersection of the Greenwich meridian with the equator.

Polar coordinates are not so common in day-to-day living, but are used a great deal in piloting. The two coordinates used in the polar system are the angle from a reference direction and the distance from a reference point to an object. In recreational boating, the reference direction is usually magnetic north; the reference point is either the boat or the sighted object.

Once the references have been selected, the location of the object in polar coordinates is given by two numbers called the **distance** and the **bearing**. One can see immediately how convenient polar coordinates are. You're in the boat, sighting on a known object with a magnetic compass, and you get a bearing directly from the compass. If this bearing is transferred to the chart by drawing a line with the same magnetic bearing through the object sighted, a line of position (LOP) is es-

Figure 3.9 Common
Coordinate Systems

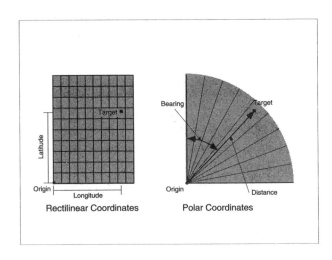

Rectilinear Coordinates   Polar Coordinates

tablished (see Figure 3.10). It is called a line of position because the boat's position is somewhere along that line.

Establishing lines of position is the essence of piloting: identify the object being sighted, take an accurate reading of the magnetic bearing, transfer the magnetic bearing from the compass rose to the object on the chart.

On occasion the navigator can do away with the compass and the parallel rulers by using manufactured or natural bearing markers. For example, if two buoys are exactly in line when viewed from the boat, the boat lies on the line of position drawn through those two buoys on the chart. The same thing can be done with natural objects, such as two points of land, or a combination of natural and manmade markers. Care should be taken in selecting the natural objects to ensure that the exact location of the object can be readily identified. The edge of an island that ends in a steep bluff is easier to identify than one that ends in a flat sand spit, which can vary depending on the state of the tide.

The most advantageous use of natural ranges occurs during gunkholing (exploring interesting, confined, shallow areas), where the boat is maneuvering through shallow water with numerous course changes. Here, the value of natural ranges increases because the distance to the features is small and the course changes so rapid that there is no time to use more elaborate methods. In most instances a line is not even drawn on the chart. The navigator simply passes the information to the helmsperson, for example, "Keep the two rocks lined up until you can see between the two islands on the port side, then turn to the right and line up on the buoy and the point of the island just beyond it."

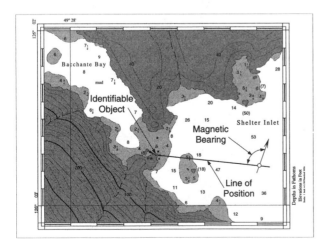

Figure 3.10 A Typical Line of Position

These informal methods will serve for 90 percent of a recreational boater's piloting needs. For the remaining 10 percent it is necessary to use an adaptation of the traditional rigorous piloting methods used by military and commercial vessels. For a recreational boater, piloting skills are used to determine if the vessel is in immediate danger. The historical value of this information is minimal at best. Often there is no need even to mark the chart.

For example, a single LOP can identify a safe zone. To indicate a safe track past a shoal or other danger to navigation, a prominent landmark or feature is identified. The parallel ruler is laid on the chart through the landmark, tangent to the edge of the danger, and then transferred to the compass rose, where the bearing is read without marking the chart. This unmarked line is sometimes called a danger bearing. The lines A-B and C-D in Figure 3.11 are examples of danger bearings.

In Figure 3.11, the bearing of the portside line is 255 degrees magnetic and the starboard-side line is 45 degrees magnetic. As the boat approaches the pass, bearings are taken at intervals from the boat to the identified objects at B and C. If the bearings to the objects remain less than the danger bearings, the boat will miss the rocks in the pass and the shoal water surrounding the small island. This is an excellent way of maneuvering through shallow water, and supplements the use of natural ranges explained earlier.

Multiple Bearings

In some instances, knowing that the boat is somewhere along a line of position may not be enough to ensure safety. You may need to know exactly where

Figure 3.11 A Typical
Danger Bearing

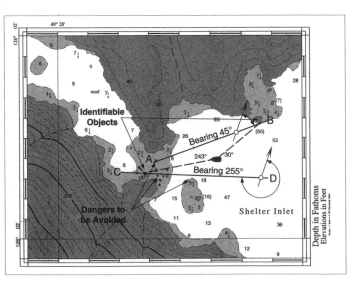

on that line your boat is located. This can be determined in any number of ways. The most obvious is to take a bearing on another object, preferably one that lies 60 to 90 degrees away from the first object. The point at which the second LOP intersects the first LOP is the position of the boat, assuming the navigator made no errors.

This leads us to the First Rule of Navigation: **All Navigators Make Errors**. How much error can be determined by taking a third bearing, again, 60 to 90 degrees from the other two. In practice, it is necessary to take all three bearings as quickly as possible, because a boat traveling 5 or 6 knots will cover 250 feet in 30 seconds. When the third bearing is transferred to the chart, you'll have three lines of position crossing at approximately 60 degrees, usually forming a small triangle. If the triangle is sufficiently small, the position of the boat has been confirmed, and in navigational terminology is considered to be a **fix** (see Figure 3.12).

Distance Measurements

Although taking multiple bearings is the most common way to locate a boat, it is not the only way. Another option is to use one or more distance measurements instead of bearings. Distance can be obtained electronically by using radar or visually with an optical range (distance) finder, or by measuring angles with a sextant. Obtaining distance by radar is the easiest and is discussed later in this chapter.

Some optical rangefinders work on the principle of stereo vision, and others on trigonometric relationships. Those that use stereo optics have two separate lenses that are focused individually on a single target. The horizontal angle be-

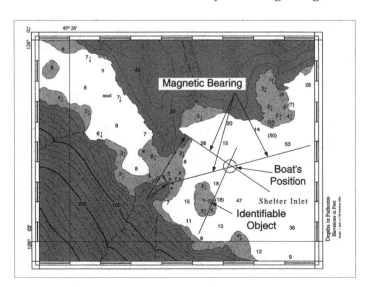

Figure 3.12 A Typical Navigational Fix

tween the lenses and the known distance between the lenses are used internally to calculate the distance to the object; the distance is read directly from the instrument. Since accuracy is dependent upon the baseline distance between the two lenses, these instruments are generally large and bulky.

Rangefinders designed to work on trigonometric relationships require the user to know the height of the target object and to do some simple trigonometric calculations. These devices consist of a graduated reticule in a binocular (see Figure 3.13). The height of the target object in reticule units is read through the binoculars. To obtain the distance, the known height of the target is divided by the number of reticule units and multiplied by a constant, generally 1,000, to get the horizontal distance in the same units as the height. These devices provide distance with about 10 percent accuracy, which improves as the target object approaches, filling the full field of view.

This same principle can be used without the binocular reticule if the vertical angle between the top and the bottom of the target object is known. One way to measure a vertical angle on a boat is with a sextant, which is seldom found aboard most modern recreational boats. However, if a boater feels the need to get vertical and horizontal angles for piloting, an inexpensive plastic sextant (less than $50) can be purchased for this purpose. This is certainly less expensive than an optical rangefinder or radar.

Once the vertical angle is measured the distance from that object is calculated using the basic trigonometric relationship given in Equation 3.1.

Figure 3.13 Typical Optical Rangefinder Reticule

$$D = h / \text{Tan } V \qquad\qquad \textbf{Eq 3.1}$$

Where
D is the distance away from the object in feet,
h is the height of the object in feet, and
V is the measured vertical angle.

Once distance to an object is obtained by any of the methods described above, a circular line of position can now be laid out on the chart with a radius equal to the calculated distance and the identified object as the center (see Figure 3.14).

The boat now lies somewhere along this circular line. This arc can be used as a circular danger distance or can be crossed with any two combinations of arcs or bearing lines to give a fix. Another way to get a circular LOP involves the use of horizontal angles.

Horizontal Angles

A circular line of position can be found by using geometry instead of trigonometry, and horizontal angles found by using the sextant on its side. The use of horizontal angles to get a circular line of position is based on a property of triangles inscribed in a circle: From any two points on the circumference of a circle, the angle between those points and any third point will remain constant as long as the third point remains on the same side of the circle relative to the first two points.

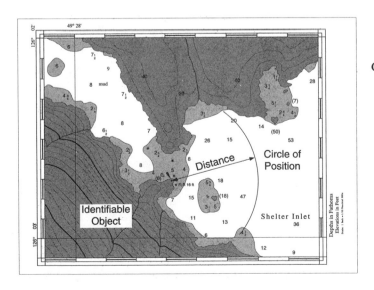

Figure 3.14 A Typical Circular Line of Position

In Figure 3.15 a triangle can be drawn between the three points A, B, and D on the perimeter of the circle. The triangle has the three angles α, β, δ and sides a, b, d. From the laws of sines,

$$a/\text{Sin } \alpha = b/\text{Sin } \beta = d/\text{Sin } \delta \qquad \text{Eq 3.2}$$

and the geometric relationship

$$R = a/2\sin \alpha = b/2\sin \beta = d\sin \delta. \qquad \text{Eq 3.3}$$

From Eq 3.2,

$$\text{Sin } \alpha_1 = a_1 \text{Sin } \beta_1 / b_1$$

and

$$\text{Sin } \alpha_2 = a_2 \text{Sin } \beta_2 / b_2.$$

Therefore, if $\alpha_1 = \alpha_2$, the sine of the angles will be equal. Since $a_1 = a_2$, the condition will be met if the ratios of $\text{Sin } \beta_1 / b_1 = \text{Sin } \beta_2 / b_2$. (Eq 3.3) can be used to show this is true.

$$R = b_1 / 2\text{Sin } \beta_1$$
$$R = b_2 / 2\text{Sin } \beta_2$$

Since the radius is equal,

$$b_1 / 2\text{Sin } \beta_1 = b_2 / 2\text{Sin } \beta_2;$$

or by canceling the 2,

$$b_1 / \text{Sin } \beta_1 = b_2 / \text{Sin } \beta_2.$$

And if this is true, then it is also true that the ratio

$$\text{Sin } \beta_1 / b_1 = \text{Sin } \beta_2 / b_2$$

(continued next page)

That statement may be clear to a geometry professor, but basically it means that in Figure 3.15 the angle β at point B is always equal as long as point B remains on the same side of the line AD. The proof of this point is based on the law of sines (see sidebar).

Because the process involves checking the horizontal angles, it is not necessary to draw a circle to use the danger angle method. It is only necessary to find the danger angle determined by the extreme edge of the charted danger and the two identifiable charted objects.

The identifiable objects are located in the usual manner. To find the point on the danger circle that lies on the extreme outer edge of the danger sometimes requires a little trial and error. If room is available, it may be prudent and expedient to select this point sufficiently far from the actual danger to ensure that the entire danger is contained, leaving a little clear water as a safety factor in case of errors.

To obtain the danger angle, draw lines using a straightedge from the suspected extreme point to the two identifiable charted objects. Using the protractor, measure the angle between these two lines. If the danger is inside the circle, the smallest angle measured will be the danger angle. If the danger is outside the circle, the danger angle is the largest angle measured. If any doubt exists as to whether the point is the extreme point, select another point and repeat the process. Figure 3.17 shows a hypothetical use of two danger angles.

When using danger angles to avoid areas, the navigator takes periodic horizontal angle readings as the boat approaches the danger. In Figure 3.16, if the angles β_1 and β_2 remain smaller than danger angle δ_1 and δ_2, the boat remains in safe water.

As stated earlier, it is not necessary to draw the circles on the chart. However, in the instance shown in Figure 3.17 the passage is so difficult that drawing the circles would eliminate possible errors. The procedure required to draw these circles will be given because the ability to draw a circle enclosing three points on its circumference is also necessary for obtaining a fix using two horizontal angles.

In Figure 3.18, points A and B represent the identifiable objects, and point C is the angle point. In order to draw a circle through these three points, it is necessary to erect perpendicular bisectors to the lines A-C and B-C. These two bisectors will intersect at the center of the circle. To draw the bisectors, place the pin of the compass on the angle point C and scribe a long arc with a radius greater than two-thirds the distance of the largest side, BC. The length of this arc should be almost a semicircle. Using this same radius, move the pin end of the drafting compass to each of the endpoints, A and B, and scribe two arcs such that they intersect the arc drawn from point C in two locations.

If the distances between the points are similar, the center intersection points will be

(continued from previous page)

With a little further thought, it should become apparent from Figure 3.15 that the magnitude of the horizontal angle measured between points A and D from any other point not on the circle but on the same side of the line between A and D as point "B" can be used to determine whether the new point is inside or outside the circle. If the measured angle is smaller than "ß," the point "E" lies outside the circle; if the angle is larger than "ß," then the point "F" lies inside the circle. This property allows navigators to construct a circle that completely encloses or excludes a given danger. Therefore, by keeping a horizontal angle between two points smaller or larger than the danger angle, the hazard can be avoided. This process is a little more involved than danger bearings, but because the circle can completely enclose the danger it is sometimes the preferred method (see Figure 3.16).

close together. Next, using the straightedge, draw a line between the two sets of intersection points (a_1-a_2 and b_1-b_2). These lines are the perpendicular bisectors to sides A-C and B-C of the angle. The point where the two bisectors intersect is the center of the circle. Place the pin end of the compass on that center point and place the pencil end on any of the original points (A, B, or C). The circle drawn with that radius from the center point will intersect all three points.

It is possible, by using this method of constructing circles and two horizontal angles, to obtain a fix. I will admit that it is rare that anybody would want to use two horizontal angles to obtain a fix, but the method has a certain elegance and to my knowledge is not shown in any other texts on piloting.

The method is based on Figure 3.15 and the fact that the angle at B remains constant regardless of the location of the point B on the circle. Therefore, the measured horizontal angle between two identifiable objects will always be the same from any point anywhere on the circle. The fact that the angles at A and D can vary and produce an infinite variety of triangles has no effect. However, since the angle at B is constant, the sum of the angles at A and D must remain constant as well. Therefore, there is always one single isosceles triangle where the angles B and C

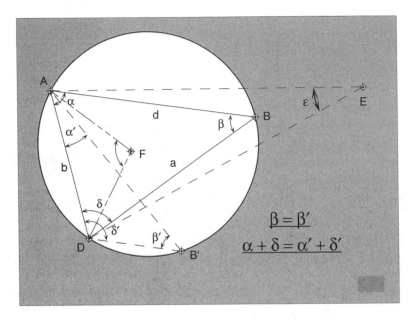

Figure 3.15 Relationship Between Angles and Points on a Circle

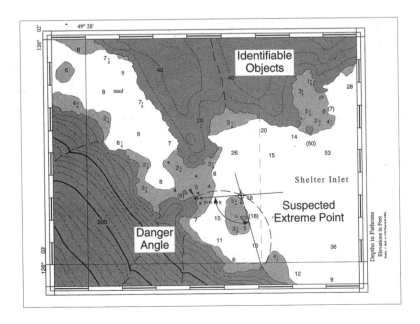

Figure 3.16 A Typical Danger Angle

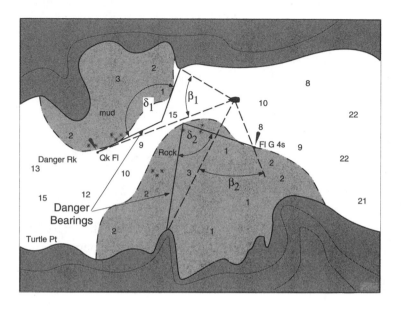

Figure 3.17 A Hypothetical Use of Danger Angles

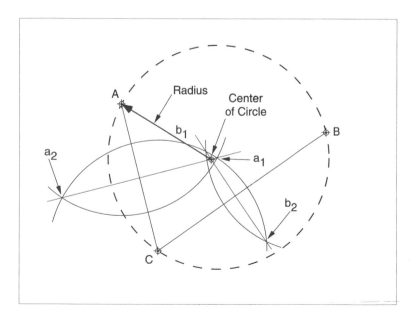

Figure 3.18 Constructing a Circle Using Three Points

are equal to each other. Because the sum of all three angles in a triangle equals 180 degrees, the circle of position can be described by the isosceles triangle with the measured horizontal angle at the apex. To locate the boat it is necessary to construct two of these circles. For example, in Figure 3.19 the horizontal angle measured between identifiable points Y and Z is 32 degrees and between W and X is 46 degrees.

To perform this construction, draw a baseline between the two identifiable points YZ and WX. Select one endpoint and lay off an angle from the baseline at that point with the protractor. The angle is calculated as follows:

$$\text{Angle} = (180° - \text{the measured angle}) / 2 \hspace{2cm} \text{Eq 3.4}$$

Lay off the same angle from the other end of the baseline. The intersection of these two points is the third point of the triangle. Construct the perpendicular bisectors to two of the legs of this triangle and draw the circle that intersects all points as explained earlier. The boat lies somewhere on this circle.

Next, do the same operation with the two other points and the horizontal angle between them. The horizontal angles can have a common point, but it is not required. Since the boat also lies somewhere on this circle, it obviously lies at the point where the two circles intersect.

If four points are used, as in Figure 3.19, there will be two intersection points; judgment is necessary to determine where the boat actually lies. In many cases only

Figure 3.19 Obtaining a Fix Using Two Horizontal Angles

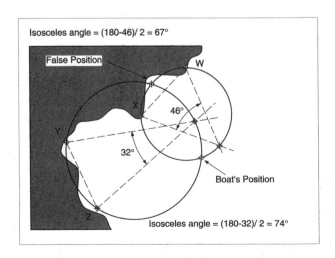

minimal judgment is needed; for example, often the second intersection point lies on land or, as in Figure 3.19, point Y cannot be seen from the false position.

If only three points are used, one of the intersection points will be the common point; because the boat is obviously not on that point, it can be easily eliminated. On occasion, the third point will lie on the circle defined by the first two points. This condition, sometimes called a "revolver," requires a new third point to be selected and another circle drawn.

Running Fixes

A running fix is of little use to a recreational boater. Far less accurate than the usual fix, it is obtained by advancing a single line of position the assumed distance that the boat has moved along its assumed bearing. In reality, both the true distance and the true bearing over the bottom are strongly affected by currents, wind, and the accuracy of the speed and distance measurement. For a recreational boater, the process requires more effort than the accuracy justifies. If the reader is interested in obtaining a running fix, these methods are discussed thoroughly in Bowditch.[3]

ELECTRONIC NAVIGATION

Electronics have become so much a part of the recreational boating scene that almost no boat is without some form of this equipment. The reliability, miniaturization, and accuracy required by the space program has provided the boater with an array of equipment that makes navigation entirely different and in many cases easier and safer than it was 20 or even 10 years ago.

The bewildering array of equipment available leaves the boater with an equally bewildering number of decisions to make. Some of the information needed to make these decisions is contained in Chapter 9. Here we are concerned only with how this equipment is used in navigation. Some of the more common instruments to be discussed here include the depthsounder, radio direction finders (RDF), loran, global positioning systems (GPS), radar, and chart display plotters.

Depth Sounding

Depth sounding is not limited to electronic sensing of depth, which by rights should really be termed echo sounding. In shallow areas, depth can also be obtained by a pole, a lead line, or in clear tropical waters like the Bahamas, by the color of the water over a white sandy bottom (see Table 3.11).

---

[3]*Bowditch, page 296.*

WATER DEPTH	DEPTH
White	1 to 2 feet
Light Green	2 to 3 feet
Blue-Green	4 to 5 feet
Blue	6 to 8 feet
Dark Blue	8 to 10 feet
Dull Black	Greater than 10 feet
Shiny Black	Coral heads—less than 2 feet
Brown	Reef—less than 2 feet

Table 3.11 Water Depth by Color

In navigation, depth information primarily verifies the approximate location of the boat along a line of position. Matching the measured depth with a sounding indicated on the chart can help tell you where you are, and where you are not.

For example, I once ran down the coast of Vancouver Island in the fog on a vessel equipped with only a compass and a depthsounder. This particular coastline is littered with vessels that have come to grief on its rocky shore. To avoid a similar fate, I followed a bearing drawn on the chart that paralleled the coast for 20 miles, tracking my progress along that bearing by noting the major changes in depth. These depth changes matched very accurately the information gathered from run-time and the occasional foghorn heard abeam. When the time came to turn landward the boat's position was known accurately enough to at least avoid tragedy, if not apprehension.

The electronic depthfinder can also be used during gunkholing or in guiding the boat through a narrow, shallow stretch of water, if the sensor is located in the bow. The electronic depthsounder works better than a lead line in this instance because of the continuous readout of depth. In addition, lead lines are restricted to waters shallower than 30 feet and require a crewperson's undivided attention.

When feeling your way in shallow water using a depthsounder, move as slowly as possible while maintaining steering control. By swinging the bow through a small arc, you can sense the trend of the bottom. If the depth reading decreases in one direction and increases in the other, steer the boat toward the deeper water. If the reading remains constant or decreases in both directions, the boat already is in the deepest part of the channel. If that depth is close to the vessel's draft, nothing can be done to ease anxiety, because the sounder cannot predict the depth of water ahead of the boat.

One of the problems with depthsounders or echo sounders is that they occasionally pick up erroneous echoes. Trusting an instrument that can provide erroneous information can sometimes be disquieting. It is a small comfort to know that a rocky bottom is more likely to provide accurate data. Conversely, although readings over soft bottom are more likely to be inaccurate, running aground on soft material, if the boat is going slow enough, may be corrected by simply shifting into reverse.

Radio Navigation Systems

Of the existing navigational systems that rely on radio transmissions to establish the boat's location, the first—and least useful to recreational boaters—is the radio direction finder (**RDF**). Its accuracy is limited, and the units cost as much as inexpensive loran systems, which are far more precise and present information in a more usable form.

The two radio navigation systems of interest to the recreational boater are **Loran-C** and the global position system (**GPS**). Loran relies on shore-based radio wave transmissions, while GPS receives its signals from earth satellites. GPS seems destined to do to loran what loran did to RDF. GPS is easier to use, more accurate, and less susceptible to atmospheric interference, and the small price advantage Loran-C receivers enjoy over GPS sets dwindles daily.

Loran and GPS perform essentially the same navigational functions, providing more information than just position fixes. They both provide position (POS), speed over ground (SOG), course over ground (COG), range (distance) to destination (RNG), bearing to destination (BRG), estimated time of arrival (ETA), time required to get to the destination (TTG), velocity made good (VMG), cross-track error (XTE), and time and date. Most units also include a save-position or man-overboard function and various waypoint and anchor watch alarms. They also generally have an NMEA port (a special plug in the back of the instrument) for communication with other electronic gear such as autopilots, depthsounders, personal computers—almost anything imaginable or marketable.

The effective use of positional data (POS) depends on the scale (precision) of the chart in use. Reliable accuracy with most units currently available is about 100 meters. In other words, the POS on the unit's readout may imply a precise dot on the chart, but that dot is actually a 100-meter circle. This shouldn't be a problem on the small-scale chart used in approaching a coast, but for a detailed large-scale chart used in piloting that coast, the 100-meter circle could place you safely in the channel or high and dry on the seaside golf course. Table 3.12 shows the circle of error for different chart scales using a GPS accurate to 100 meters. Consider GPS sufficiently accurate for use with charts having scales greater than 1:40,000.

Table 3.12 GPS Positional Error	
CHART SCALE	GPS ERROR CIRCLE
1:5,000	
1:10,000	
1:20,000	
1:40,000	
1:80,000	

Comparing speed over the ground (SOG) with the speed through the water provided by the ship's speedometer or log will provide information on tidal and stream currents. The data on course over ground (COG) can be compared to compass data to provide immediate information on actual leeway. Cross-track error and alarms can help the helmsperson stay on the desired course.

The units are also very helpful during trip planning. The user can input individual waypoints on the trip, and the instrument will calculate the course and distance to each intermediate point. Compass deviation and variation data can be stored in these units to calculate the actual compass bearing needed to run a desired course. This is a much easier and more accurate method for calculating bearings between points than hand calculations.

Many units now allow the user to select whether they want the course output as rhumb line or great circle. The ETA and TTG functions help trip-planning under way. And, of course, it is always nice to have the time accurate to a tenth of a second, corrected and updated with every satellite pass.

Radar

Radar is a great help for navigating in fog; it can also be used for piloting, by providing both bearing and distance to targets. If those targets can be identified on the chart as well as on the ground and radar screen, this information can be plotted on the chart, like any other distance and bearing information, and can help determine the boat's position. Any target used will suffer from the distortion problems discussed in Chapter 9, however, and should be used with a great deal of caution. Distortion makes the information inaccurate, and target identification difficult.

Using radar to measure distance to targets is considerably simpler and more accurate than taking bearings to targets. Unless your radar has a north-up display, which requires an external flux-gate compass and is found primarily on large ships, the radar will provide a relative bearing to the target. In the near-ubiquitous head-up display, the boat is at the center of the screen heading up, 0 degrees. If the boat is on any course other than 0 degrees, you must *add* its course to a relative bearing to starboard, subtract it from a target to port. This normally requires a steady helm and some verbal exchange between the helm and the person manipulating the electronic bearing line (EBL).

Measuring distance to radar targets is simpler: you merely move the variable range marker (VRM) to touch the target, and the distance is displayed on a digital readout. Although more accurate than a radar bearing, the distance data does suffer from pulse length errors and range resolution, and can be off as much as 300 feet. (For more on navigating with radar, see Chapter 9.)

Radar beacons make target identification easier. Racon, which provides both bearing and range information, and Ramark, which provides only bearing data, are becoming more common in heavily trafficked areas with difficult navigational challenges. Ramark transmits its unique signal continuously or intermittently depending upon traffic, whereas the racon signal is triggered by a passing ship's radar signal. Both signals show a radial line or a Morse code signal originating from a point just beyond the position of the beacon.

Electronic Chart Displays

As in everything else in the world, the computer is becoming involved in navigation. Electronic chart displays, the next step in this revolution, present a digitized chart on a graphic display. The chart can be zoomed in and out to show greater detail or a larger area depending on the navigator's whim. If the display is connected to a GPS or loran, it will show the boat's position continuously updated, and any waypoints. Some units can be connected to other shipboard instruments as well, allowing the information to be manipulated by the computer and displayed as histograms showing the trend of depth, wind direction and speed, speed over the ground and through the water, etc.

Presently, electronic charts are limited in detail and coverage; many show only the shoreline and navigational aids, and coverage is generally confined to major boating areas. All this is changing rapidly, but the major drawback remains the size of the display. The small display area, typically 5 by 6 inches, requires considerable scrolling and zooming up and down, and limits the amount of available detail. This, too, should change rapidly with recent advances in displays intended for computers.

LIFEBOAT NAVIGATION

Lifeboat navigation is not the same thing as liferaft navigation. Navigation implies that a boat can be steered and that it has some form of power to move it in the desired direction. Liferafts are little more than large flotation devices. The form of lifeboat navigation used depends on the equipment available, which may be anything from a handheld GPS and compass to the navigator's wits. Navigation with a GPS and compass has already been discussed. Because most other forms of lifeboat navigation depend on astronomical bodies, this section will begin with astronomy. It will then cover simple celestial navigation using a sextant and almanac, and progress in steps to navigation with less and less equipment.

Astronomy

Although reliable, inexpensive electronic navigation systems have made "a star to steer her by" less important than it was 10 years ago, almost any form of lifeboat navigation depends on signposts in the sky. Astronomy may not be as important as it once was to the seaman, but a general knowledge of the subject is both helpful and rewarding. Watching the stars whirl overhead is as much a part of a night passage as the motion of the sea. The rewards increase tenfold if the viewing is accompanied by knowledge. For those familiar with the sky, no matter where they are, the night sky always holds a greeting from an old friend.

The possession of this knowledge is also a hedge against emergencies. All that is necessary for emergency navigation is to be able to identify some constellations, all first-magnitude stars, and some second-magnitude stars. This may sound like a tall order, but only about 30 of the 88 constellations and about 40 stars in the entire sky are of interest to the navigator.

Although not many people have trouble identifying 40 or 50 of the states when looking at a map of the U.S., very few can identify 40 or 50 stellar objects. The problem is not with people; it's with the map. I spent years trying to learn the constellations using various maps, to no avail. The problem with identifying constellations is that you must remember what you were looking down at when you are looking up, and vice versa. The result is that, with most books, the user spends most of his time nodding up and down like one of those toy flamingos rather than locating stars.

Finally, I came across a book called *The Stars*, by H. A. Rey.[4] That night in my backyard I was able to identify 10 or 15 constellations. The difference with Rey's book is in the way the author connects the stars in the constellations (see Figure 3.20). They are very easily committed to memory, and the user can spend most of his time looking up searching for the patterns. Many books claim a better and easier way to locate the stars, but the truth is there is no better way than Rey's.

On a clear night, about 2,000 points of light are visible. To deal with this overwhelming array of light, the number of stars must be reduced to a few of interest. With very little additional observation it is immediately apparent that some stars are brighter than others. Navigators deal only with the brightest stars.

The relative brightness of stars is expressed as the star's magnitude. The brightest stars have magnitudes less than 2. There are about 20 of these bright stars in the entire sky. The brightest, Sirius, has a magnitude of negative 1.6. There are

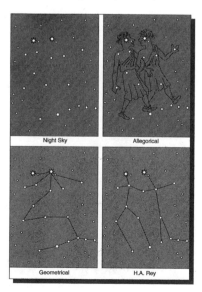

Figure 3.20 Various Ways of Portraying the Constellations

[4]*The Stars, a New Way to See Them* (Boston: Houghton Mifflin Co., 1976).

about 50 second-magnitude stars visible in the entire sky, but only some are important in navigation. Of the 150 or so third-magnitude stars, only one is listed in nautical almanacs. Fourth- and fifth-magnitude stars only clutter the sky.

The 2,000 confusing points of light have now been reduced to about 70, and these can be further reduced by selecting only the second-magnitude stars that are favorably positioned for use as aids to navigation. Before we can do that, however, a few more terms must be defined.

To begin, it is necessary to define an idealized model of what an observer sees looking at the sky. The observer appears to be in the exact center of a celestial globe defined by the dome of the sky overhead and by the horizon in all directions (see Figure 3.21).

Directly above the observer is a point called the zenith. The stars appear on the celestial globe at different heights above the horizon, called altitudes. Because the earth rotates, all the altitudes of the stars appear to change throughout the night and year—all, that is, except one in the northern hemisphere, called the pole star. As long as the observer remains in a single position on the earth, the pole star's altitude remains pretty much constant, because this star is almost directly over the earth's north pole on the axis of the celestial globe. Because the pole star has such a fortuitous position, its **geographic position** (**GP**) is the north pole and its altitude is always fairly close to the observer's latitude—extremely handy for lifeboat navigation. If the observer is located on the equator, the zenith stars are all on the **celestial equator**.

Figure 3.21 The Celestial Globe

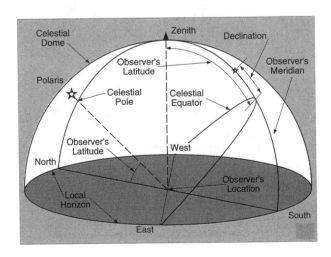

If an imaginary line is drawn through the observer's zenith and the pole star, the observer's celestial **meridian** is defined. This meridian is similar to but not the same as longitude. Remember the difficulty we had in defining the east pole and assigning longitude values. The same problem with celestial meridians has been solved in a more democratic if not better way.

There are three ways to define a meridian, depending on the reference point used. If the angle is measured from the **zero hour circle**, the angle is called the Sidereal Hour Angle (SHA) and is measured west of this circle from 0 to 360 degrees. The zero hour circle is the great circle that runs through the point on the celestial globe where the path of the sun intersects the sidereal equator in the spring of the year (vernal equinox). On occasion this angle is expressed in time units and is called **right ascension**.

If the angular distance is measured from Greenwich, it is called the **Greenwich hour angle** (**GHA**). Finally, if the angular distance is measured from the observer position it is called the **local hour angle** (**LHA**). Both GHA and LHA can be measured as an angle east or west of the reference meridian. *The difference between LHA and GHA is always the longitude.* This is a useful relationship if two of the three quantities are known. All of this may appear confusing—it is—but fortunately the opportunity to use these concepts is limited. Longitude is rarely needed in lifeboat navigation; you should just be aware that these terms exist and can be looked up in the index when needed.

The lifeboat navigator is most often interested in latitude. Latitude is closely related to a star's **declination**—the measure of a star's angular distance from the celestial equator. Although the star's altitude changes throughout the night, its declination remains constant. A star with a declination of 45 degrees north can be found anywhere on the circle 45 degrees north of the celestial equator. However, what is useful to the navigator is that, if a star with declination of 45 degrees passes through the observer's zenith, the observer's latitude is 45 degrees.

The declinations for 28 major stars north of the celestial equator are given in Table 3.13. These stars are also the same ones listed alphabetically and according to sidereal hour angle in the Nautical Almanac.

Notice that only 24 constellations accompany the 28 stars, for a total of 52 objects in the northern hemisphere that are important for navigation. Note also that the southern edge of the great square lies exactly along 15 degrees North declination. The great square is a distinctive square in the sky composed of four bright stars, three in the constellation Pegasus and Alpheratz, the head of Andromeda. The second-magnitude star Markab is the southwest corner of the great square. Remember: when looking down at a star map, west is shown on the *right* of the map.

Table 3.13 Navigational Stars in the Northern Hemisphere

STAR	CONSTELLATION	LOCATION ACCORDING TO REY	DECLINATION
Polaris	*Little Dipper*	*End of the Handle*	N 90
Kohab	*Little Dipper*	*Lip of the Cup*	N 74
Dubhe	*Big Dipper*	*Lip of the Cup*	N 62
Alioth	*Big Dipper*	*3rd Star in Handle*	N 56
Schedar	*α Cassiopeia*	*Bottom of the " W "*	N 56
Eltanin	*α Dragon*	*Nose of the Dragon*	N 51
Mirfak	*α Peruses*	*Chin of Peruses*	N 50
Alkaid	*Big Dipper*	*1st Star in Handle*	N 49
Cappela	*Charioteer*	*Bridge of the Nose*	N 46
Deneb	*Swan*	*Tail of the Swan*	N 45
Vega	*Lyre*	*Can't Miss*	N 39
Elnath	*β Bull (Taurus)*	*End of the Horn*	N 29
Alpheratz	*Andromeda*	*The Head*	N 29
Pollux	*α Twins (Gemini)*	*Head of the Left Twin*	N 28
Alphecca	*α Northern Crown*	*Gemma*	N 27
Hamal	*α Ram (Aries)*	*Neck of the Ram*	N 23
Arcturus	*Herdsman*	*The Hip*	N 19
Aldebaran	*Bull (Taurus)*	*Lower Jaw*	N 16
Denebola	*Lion (Leo)*	*The End of the Tail*	N 15
Markab	*α Pegasus*	*The Rump*	N 15
Rasalhague	*α Serpent Holder*	*The Head*	N 13
Regulus	*α Lion (Leo)*	*End of Fore Foot*	N 12
Enif	*β Pegasus*	*The Top of the head*	N 10
Altair	*Eagle*	*The Eye*	N 09
Betelgeuse	*Orion*	*The Left Shoulder*	N 07
Bellatrix	*Orion*	*The Right Shoulder*	N 06
Procyon	*α Little Dog*	*Can't Miss*	N 05
Menkar	*β Whale*	*The Left side of Tail*	N 04

The star names in bold are brighter than 1.5 magnitude; those shown in italic type are dimmer than 2.5 magnitude. The navigational stars south of the celestial equator are shown in Table 3.14.

This table adds 30 more stars, 27 of which are useful for navigation, and 17 more constellations. This brings the total number of stars for worldwide navigation to 55. It should be noted for observers in the U.S. that not all the southern stars rise above their horizon. This means that the lower 15 or 16 stars, below Shaula, in the cat's eyes, never become visible to an observer in the northern hemisphere above latitude 30 degrees. This reduces the number of items needed to be located by most boaters to about 40 stars and 35 constellations, and will take the navigator almost

STAR	CONSTELLATION	LOCATION ACCORDING TO REY	DECLINATION
Alnilam	Orion	Middle Star in Belt	S 01
Rigel	Orion	Right Foot	S 08
Alphard	α Hydra	2nd Bend in Neck	S 09
Spica	Virgin (Virgo)	The Seat	S 11
Zubenelgenubi	Scales (Libra)	Don't Bother	S 16
Sabik	Serpent Holder	Don't Bother	S 16
Sirius	Big Dog	Can't Miss	S 17
Gienah	Crow	The Eye	S 17
Diphda	α Whale	The Lip of the Whale	S 18
Antares	Scorpion (Scorpio)	The Head	S 26
Nunki	β Archer (Sagittarius)	In the Bow	S 26
Adhara	Big Dog	Upper Rear Legs	S 29
Fomalhaut	Southern Fish	The Nose	S 30
Kaus Australis	α Archer (Sagittarius)	The Neck	S 34
Menkent	Centaur	Top of the head	S 36
Shaula	Scorpion (Scorpio)	Brightest of the Cat's Eyes	S 37
Acamar	β River Eridanuis	Don't Bother	S 40
Ankaa	α Phoenix	Top of the Head	S 42
Suhail	The Ship	Brightest Star in the Sail	S 43
Al Na'ir	The Crane	Where the Neck Joins the Body	S 47
Canopus	The Ship	Bottom Front of Keel	S 53
Achernar	α River Eridanuis	Southern End of the River	S 57
Gacrux	Southern Cross	The Head of The Cross	S 57
Peacock	The Peacock	Top of the Tail	S 57
Avior	The Ship	Foot of the False Cross	S 59
Hadar	β Centauri	Smaller Front Foot	S 60
Rigil Kentauris	α Centauri	Larger Front Foot	S 61
Acrux	Southern Cross	Foot of the Cross	S 63
Atria	Southern Triangle	Southern Corner of the Triangle	S 69
Miaplacidus	The Ship	The Top Front of Keel	S 70

as far south as the southern tip of Africa. The remaining stars are only useful for those sailing the lower southern oceans, and besides, it would be a shame to neglect such famous southern signposts as Alpha Centauri and the Southern Cross.

The other miscellaneous celestial riffraff—the moon and planets—only get in the way of navigation. The moon can cast so much reflected light that it obscures the dimmer navigational stars, and the planets wander through some constellations causing confusion. Most of the planets are brighter than first magnitude, at least part of the time, so they are easily seen and often mistaken for important navigational stars. This confusion can be limited by remembering that the planets only occupy a narrow band, called the **ecliptic**, which runs through the constellations in the zodiac. If the first-magnitude stars in the zodiac constellations (Spica, Aldebaran, Antares, and Regulus) are known to the observer, any other bright object is a planet and, at least for lifeboat navigation, can be ignored.

The amount of this celestial knowledge needed to navigate a lifeboat depends on the equipment available. The more equipment, the less celestial knowledge, but since one never knows what will be available it is always best to plan for the worst. To begin our discussion of the navigation process, we will assume that the following equipment is available: a sextant, an accurate watch, a nautical almanac, a compass, and this book. Then we will cover navigating with less and less equipment available.

Lifeboat Celestial Navigation

With Sextant

With all of the above equipment available, only two celestial bodies—the sun and Polaris—are of interest, and lifeboat celestial navigation is reduced to taking a noon shot and an occasional shot on Polaris with the sextant. Ninety percent of the celestial work on oceangoing yachts with no electronic navigation equipment is confined to the noon sun shot. Certainly this simple, trustworthy practice is good enough for 98 percent of lifeboat navigation.

The sextant consists of a frame in the shape of an arc comprising one-sixth of a full circle. It is this sixth that puts the sex in sextant. The sextant has two mirrors, one affixed to a movable arm and the other to the frame (see Figure 3.22). Using two mirrors halves the actual angle measure, allowing a full 120 degrees to be mea-

Figure 3.22 The Simple Elements of a Sextant

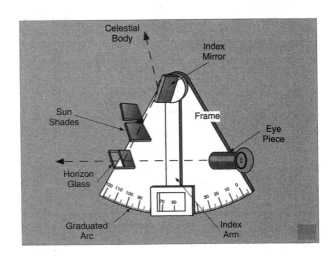

sured on only a 60-degree arc. While this design, attributed to Isaac Newton, makes the device smaller, it also makes it less accurate.[5] Also attached to the frame and aligned with the mirror is a low-power telescope.

Other miscellaneous attachments include a vernier on the moveable arm to improve reading accuracy, and sun shades on the mirror and telescope to keep the user from going blind while looking directly at the sun. The handle on most sextants is positioned for right-hand users.

Two different procedures are used when sighting a celestial body. When the sun is sighted, the user faces the sun and the line of sight is directed at a point on the horizon immediately below the sun. The necessary sun shades are positioned and the index arm is moved upward from the horizon until the reflected image of the sun appears in the frame mirror next to the horizon. This is relatively easy to do because the sun is large, bright, and the only object of its kind in the sky.

The user then sets either the top or the bottom of the sun tangent to the horizon, making fine adjustments to the index arm again while keeping the sextant exactly vertical. To ensure the sextant is vertical at the exact time of the reading, the sextant is rocked through a small vertical angle. During this rocking procedure the sun will trace an arc along the horizon and should just touch the horizon once during the bottom of the arc. At the bottom of the arc the sextant is vertical and the reading is taken.

The entire process requires considerable hand-eye coordination and is not as simple as it sounds, especially while the user is being jostled around in a small boat. To make this more difficult, the vertical angle to the sun keeps changing due to the rotation of the earth and the horizontal angle changes due to the movement of the boat. When the navigator, the sextant, the boat, the sea, the celestial body, and the entire universe are in harmony, the navigator sings out "mark," which means "note the exact time" and signals the completion of this mystical ritual. The vertical angle on the arc indicated by the position of the index is the altitude of the sun; that and the time are the two pieces of raw data necessary to find a position using celestial navigation.

It is of value to practice this procedure indoors first, using the ceiling-wall joint or a chandelier as the celestial body and the floor-wall joint as the horizon. Next, move outdoors on land and, using a distant, relatively flat object as the horizon, find the sun following the procedure described above. When this becomes routine, try sighting a star using the second procedure discussed below.

Sighting a star is much more demanding because stars are much smaller,

[5]W. S. Kals, Stars and Planets (San Francisco: Sierra Club Books, 1990), 204.

they're not too bright, there are many of them, and they all look the same when viewed through a small telescope. Following the method described above provides no assurance that the star of intent is the star actually in the mirror when the procedure is completed. When shooting a star it is much easier to locate the star in the telescope first and then transfer it to the horizon. This works because the horizon is much larger and somewhat easier to identify than the star. Finding the horizon at sea at night is more difficult than one might imagine. On a dark night the sky and water blend together. On a bright night the horizon shows up but the stars disappear. These conflicting problems tend to confine star shots to a short twilight period just before dawn or just after sunset.

To use the second method, the sextant is zeroed and the star is located in the telescope. The navigator next brings the celestial body to the horizon by moving the movable arm and the sextant together in such a manner that the celestial body remains in the mirror. This process is time consuming, because if the star is lost while bringing it down to the horizon it may not be recovered again and the whole process must be repeated. Some people prefer to turn the sextant upside down and move only the index arm, in much the same procedure as used with the sun. Once the horizon is found, with the star still in view, the remaining procedure is the same as the sun shot.

After the two pieces of data have been properly gathered it is necessary to reduce this data to arrive at the boat's position. The method used depends on whether the noon sun or Polaris was taken. (Polaris is the only star used in lifeboat navigation.)

The noon sun shot consists of taking a series of sun shots near local apparent noon to determine the maximum altitude of the sun. Local apparent noon and clock noon are not the same thing. Two or three shots taken three to five minutes apart on either side of local apparent noon is sufficient. It is of course difficult to guess when the sun will reach its maximum altitude, so most of the time you take a few extra shots before noon and only a couple after the maximum altitude occurs.

The next step is to convert local time to Greenwich mean time (GMT) and plot on a piece of graph paper, using any convenient scales, the altitude on the vertical axis against GMT along the horizontal axis. To get GMT from local time it is necessary to know the time zone or the approximate longitude. Since it takes the earth 24 hours to rotate 360 degrees, 15 degrees is turned every hour (360/24). When navigating it is best to leave the watch set to Greenwich time, which avoids these problems but requires observations to get local noon. Draw in the smooth curve connecting these points (see Figure 3.23). Select the GMT and maximum altitude from the peak of this curve. These are the two numbers that will be used to locate the boat's position.

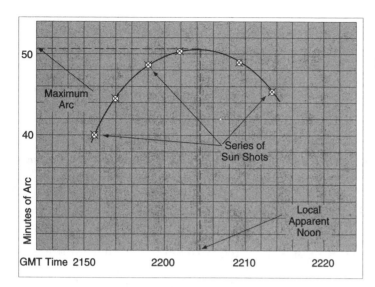

The altitude taken from this graph is known as the sextant altitude (H_s). It must be converted into the observed altitude by adjusting this altitude for instrument error. There are a proliferation of corrections that can be applied, but most are only applicable for very accurate work. Because accurate work is not possible from a small pitching boat in the middle of the ocean, we shall ignore all but the most important. These are **Instrument correction (I)**, **Index correction (IC)**, **Dip (D)**, and **Semi-diameter (SD)**. Instrument correction is due to errors inherent in the instrument and is supplied by the manufacturer; if not supplied, ignore it.

Index error is due to the index mirror and the horizon glass not being parallel when the index arm is set to zero. The amount of error is found by setting the index to zero and directing the view at the horizon. If the mirrors are not parallel the horizon will appear broken. Adjust the index arm until the horizon appears as a single line; the reading on the sextant is the index error. The error is added if the reading is a positive angle (on the arc) and subtracted if the reading is a negative angle (off the arc).

Dip is the term used to indicate the angular difference between the angle of the visible horizon and true horizontal at eye level. It increases as the height of the observer's eye increases. Since much of lifeboat navigation is done close to the surface, it is normally quite small—less than 3 minutes or 3 miles. It can be ignored at the discretion of the navigator without serious consequences. The exact value is given in the first few pages of the Nautical Almanac and can be calculated using the following formula:

$$D = 0.97 \, (h)^{1/2} \qquad\qquad\qquad \text{Eq 3.5}$$

where   D is the dip correction in minutes of arc,
and h is the height of the eye in feet.

The correction for Semi-diameter is necessary only when sighting the sun or the moon. Since lifeboat navigators have no use for the moon beyond esthetics, that leaves only the sun. It is needed because it is easier for the observer to place either the upper or lower edge of the sun on the horizon compared to placing the exact center of the sun on the horizon. The sun's actual Semi-diameter at noon on the middle day is given at the bottom of each page in the Nautical Almanac. If the lower limb (bottom) of the sun was used (placed on the horizon), the correction is added. If the upper limb (top) was used, the correction is subtracted from the sextant reading. However, without the almanac, the correction can be made by observing that the sun's Semi-diameter varies from 15.8 minutes in July to 16.3 minutes in January. Using the average value of 16 minutes, the error is less than a quarter of a mile.

Once all the corrections are made to the sextant reading (H_s), it becomes glorified and is known as the observed altitude (H_o). The next step is to find the angular distance to the zenith (z). This is done by subtracting the observed altitude from 90 degrees.

$$z = 89°59'60'' - H_o \qquad\qquad\qquad \textbf{Eq 3.6}$$

The zenith angle is positive (+) if the observer was looking north to the sun and negative (–) if looking south toward the sun. To find latitude, we need only know the sun's declination. This declination (Dec) is taken from the table in the almanac on the page corresponding to the date of the observation, or it can be estimated from Table 3.15.

The declination to use is found opposite the GMT of the observation. Notice that the almanac only provides declinations every hour. This is because the sun changes declination so slowly that an error of less than a mile is introduced by this simplification. It is possible to interpolate between the two tabulated values if a more accurate number is required. For lifeboat work, interpolating in the almanac is not necessary; however, interpolation in Table 3.15 may be necessary.

If Table 3.15 is used without interpolation, the maximum error is about 24 miles; with straight-line interpolation it can be reduced to about 6 miles. Once the declination is determined, the latitude is then calculated by subtracting alge-

Table 3.15 Declination of the Sun at Noon GMT

DAY	JAN	FEB	MAR	APR	MAY	JUN	JUL	AUG	SEP	OCT	NOV	DEC
1	S 23.0	S 17.0	S 7.5	N 4.6	N 15.2	N 22.1	N 23.1	N 18.0	N 8.2	S 3.3	S 14.5	S 21.8
2	22.9	16.7	7.1	5.0	15.5	22.2	23.0	17.7	7.8	3.7	14.8	22.0
3	22.8	16.4	6.7	5.4	15.8	22.3	22.9	17.4	7.5	4.1	15.1	22.1
4	22.7	16.1	6.3	5.8	16.0	22.5	22.9	17.2	7.1	4.4	15.5	22.3
5	22.6	15.8	6.0	6.2	16.3	22.6	22.8	16.9	6.7	4.8	15.8	22.4
6	S 22.5	S 15.5	S 5.6	N 6.6	N 16.6	N 22.7	N 22.7	N 16.6	N 6.3	S 5.2	S 16.1	S 22.5
7	22.3	15.2	5.2	6.9	16.9	22.8	22.6	16.4	6.0	5.6	16.4	22.6
8	22.2	14.9	4.8	7.3	17.2	23.0	22.4	16.1	5.6	6.0	16.6	22.7
9	22.1	14.6	4.4	7.7	17.4	23.0	22.3	15.8	5.2	6.4	16.9	22.8
10	21.9	14.3	4.0	8.0	17.7	23.1	22.2	15.5	4.8	6.7	17.2	22.9
11	S 21.8	S 13.9	S 3.6	N 8.4	N 17.9	N 23.1	N 22.1	N 15.2	N 4.5	S 7.1	S 17.5	S 23.0
12	21.6	13.6	3.2	8.8	18.2	23.2	21.9	14.9	4.1	7.5	17.8	23.1
13	21.4	13.3	2.8	9.1	18.4	23.2	21.8	14.6	3.7	7.9	18.0	23.2
14	21.3	12.9	2.4	9.5	18.7	23.3	21.6	14.3	3.3	8.2	18.3	23.2
15	21.1	12.6	2.0	9.9	18.9	23.3	21.5	14.0	2.9	8.6	18.6	23.3
16	S 20.9	S 12.2	S 1.6	N 10.2	N 19.2	N 23.4	N 21.3	N 13.7	N 2.5	S 9.0	S 18.8	S 23.3
17	20.7	11.9	1.2	10.6	19.4	23.4	21.2	13.3	2.2	9.3	19.0	23.4
18	20.5	11.5	0.8	10.9	19.6	23.4	21.0	13.0	1.8	9.7	19.3	2.4
19	20.3	11.2	0.5	11.2	19.8	23.4	20.8	12.7	1.4	10.1	19.5	23.4
20	20.1	10.8	0.1	11.6	20.0	23.4	20.6	12.1	1.0	10.4	19.8	23.4
21	S 19.8	S 10.5	N 0.3	N 11.9	N 20.2	N 23.4	N 20.4	N 12.0	N 0.6	S 10.8	S 20.0	S 23.4
22	19.6	10.1	0.7	12.3	20.4	23.4	20.2	11.7	0.2	11.1	20.2	23.4
23	19.4	9.7	1.1	12.6	20.6	23.4	20.0	11.4	S 0.2	11.5	20.4	23.4
24	19.1	9.4	1.5	12.9	20.8	23.4	19.8	11.0	0.6	11.8	20.6	23.4
25	18.9	9.0	1.7	13.3	21.0	23.4	19.6	10.7	1.0	12.2	20.8	23.4
26	S 18.6	S 8.6	N 2.3	N 13.6	N 21.2	N 23.4	N 19.4	N 10.3	S 1.3	S 12.5	S 21.0	S 23.4
27	18.4	8.2	2.7	13.9	21.3	23.3	19.2	10.0	1.7	12.9	21.2	23.3
28	18.1	7.9	3.1	14.2	21.5	23.3	18.9	9.6	2.1	13.2	21.4	23.3
29	17.9	—	3.5	14.5	21.7	23.2	18.7	9.3	2.5	13.5	21.5	23.2
30	17.6	—	3.9	14.9	21.8	23.2	18.4	8.9	2.9	13.9	21.7	23.2
31	S 17.3	—	N 4.3	—	N 22.0	—	N 18.2	N 8.5	—	S 14.2	—	S 23.1

braically this declination (Dec) from the algebraically signed zenith angle (z) found above.

$$\text{Latitude} = \text{Dec} - z \qquad\qquad \textbf{Eq 3.7}$$

If the answer is positive, the latitude is north; if negative, it is south.

To find longitude, the Greenwich hour angle (GHA) corresponding to the hour of the observed sun shot GMT is taken from the Nautical Almanac. To this GHA is added the correction found in the table of increments and corrections in the almanac corresponding to the minutes and seconds of the observed GMT.

If the table is unavailable, the correction can be calculated by changing the number of seconds into a decimal value of minutes by dividing the number of seconds by 60. Add this fraction to the number of minutes and multiply the result by 0.25. The result will be the number of degrees needed to be added to the GHA corresponding to the observed GMT. The fractional portion of this number can be converted back to minutes by multiplying it by 60. The result of these calculations is the GHA of the boat's position. For example, if GMT equals 11 hours, 37 minutes, and 43 seconds and the GHA from the table is 343 59.5, the GHA of the boat is found as follows:

Second portion of the time in minutes equals

$$43/60 = 0.71667;$$

added to the minutes,

$$37 + 0.71667 = 37.71667;$$

multiplied by the conversion factor 0.25,

$$37.71667 * 0.25 = 9.42916.$$

The correction is then 9.42916 degrees. Converting the fractional part back to minutes,

$$0.42916 * 60 = 25.75 \text{ minutes.}$$

Therefore, the GHA is

$$GHA = 343°59.5' + 9°25.75' = 353°25.25'.$$

If the GHA is less than 180 degrees, the longitude is west. If it is greater than 180 degrees, it must be subtracted from 360 degrees; it is then equal to east longitude. The above GHA would indicate a longitude of 6°34.75' East.

Notice that accurate time is only necessary to find *longitude*. Without time it is still possible to find the boat's *latitude* if the tables of declination are available. If both the watch and the tables are unavailable, latitude can still be determined in the northern hemisphere by measuring the altitude of Polaris.

To get latitude from a shot of Polaris, the sextant altitude reading is corrected as described above to find the observed altitude (H_o). This altitude is the approximate latitude of the vessel—approximate because Polaris does not lie directly over the pole, and due to the wobble of the earth on its axis the difference is not constant. Fortunately this error is not large, about 56 minutes or miles. This error can be reduced by observing the position of the stars Alkaid, the outermost star in the handle of the big dipper, and ε Cassiopeia, the star in the dim tip of the "W" (see Figure 3.24).

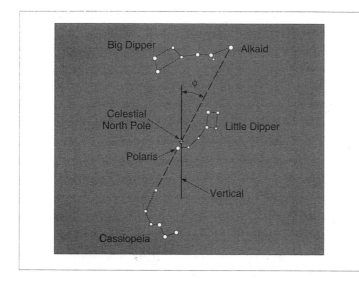

Figure 3.24 Estimating
Altitude Corrections
for Polaris

When a line between these two stars is horizontal no correction is needed; if the line is vertical the correction is 56 minutes. For intermediate corrections (C), the following equation can be used with the estimated angle (ϕ) the imaginary line is off vertical.

$$C = (1 - 0.003\ \phi - 0.00009\ \phi^2)56 \qquad\qquad \text{Eq 3.8}$$

This correction should be added to the observed altitude if Alkaid is on top and subtracted if it is on the bottom. Now, if knowing only latitude seems a bit haphazard when navigating, consider that the entire known world was explored and mapped almost completely without the aid of longitude determinations. Before 1768 no timepiece was accurate enough to estimate longitude with any accuracy.[6] The strategy of the early navigators was to sail north or south until the latitude of the destination was reached, and then sail due east or west depending on the relative location of the ship and the destination. This same method can be used today to navigate a lifeboat very effectively.

Without Sextant

We have seen what can be done without a watch or an almanac; now we will look at what can be done without a sextant. The obvious answer is to build one. With a little patience a 180-degree semicircle can be laid out using a protractor. An

---

[6]*Bowditch, 3.*

example of this type of instrument is shown in Figure 3.25. The larger the circle the more accurate the instrument, but the more difficult it is to use. The best accuracy expected from this instrument is about 30 miles.

For sun sights the instrument is hung from the right-hand pin on the semicircle and weighted so that the 90-degree edge of the arc hangs vertical. The peg in the center will cast a shadow on the sun's altitude. For Polaris shots a weighted string is attached to the center pin and Polaris is sighted between the two pins on the zero side of the arc. The altitude is read opposite the weighted string. This method requires two people for best results, one to sight and one to read.

Using a right angle and a couple of distances, trigonometry can also be used to calculate altitude. For example, if a stick is held vertically at arm's length so that the top of the stick is in line with Polaris and the thumb is moved along the stick until it intersects the horizon, the distance from the top of the stick to the thumb divided by the distance from the eye to the thumb in any convenient units will give the tangent of the angle of latitude.

This method is most accurate in the tropics, where Polaris is low on the horizon, less than 25 degrees. Latitudes of greater value require longer sticks or shorter arms. The accuracy of this method depends on the sighting accuracy and the accuracy of the length measurements, but it can be around 10 miles. The number of ways one can get two distances and a right angle are limited only by the imagination of the navigator and available equipment.

Given no sticks or trig functions, latitude can still be estimated by using zenith stars, a method used by the early Polynesian navigators of the Pacific. Recall that

Figure 3.25 Improvised
Angle Measuring Device

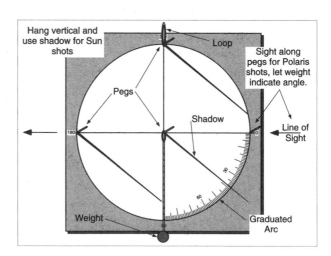

Tables 3.13 and 3.14 listed the declination of 57 stars. If one of those stars is directly overhead, its declination found in this table is the same as the boat's latitude.

Determining whether a star is directly overhead is not a simple matter in a boat. However, with a little practice it can be done with surprising accuracy. David Lewis used this method to navigate from Tahiti to New Zealand, and reported an accuracy in fair weather and with practice of around half a degree.[7] Sighting the zenith star requires lying on one's back and sighting straight up. (A mast or weighted stick can help.) Also, when locating the zenith star it is helpful to steer the boat due north, south, east, or west.

In most locations, one of the listed stars will be within 4 degrees of the boat's zenith. Estimating its distance north or south can be done using coins or fingers. A dime at arm's length is approximately 1.5 degrees wide; so is the little finger. A quarter at arm's length is about 2 degrees wide, as is the thumb.

Estimating angles greater than about 5 degrees introduces additional error. On occasion, Lewis was as much as 125 miles from his estimated position.[8] With these kinds of errors it is necessary to expand the target, especially if the target is a small island. Expanding the target can be done by using several techniques, such as watching clouds, birds, wave patterns, or other indicators of nearby land.

Clouds are transit items constantly forming and dissipating. In the Kiribati (Gilbert) Islands, the islanders have used clouds to expand their targets for centuries. The Kiribatese are not the only islanders in the Pacific to use clouds, but their methods are the most sophisticated. The Kiribatese have observed that clouds move slowly over land and rapidly over the sea. This is due to the difference in the specific heat of land and water. The warmer land generates updrafts that spawn clouds more easily, and the clouds seem to linger because they are constantly being generated. This process results in a V-shaped cloud that points downward toward the island.[9] The clouds drift about but the V appears stationary.

The Kiribatese also have noted that clouds over land are brighter. This apparent brightness depends on a variety of factors, one of which is the size of the water drops forming the cloud. Older clouds form larger drops, and the larger drops darken the cloud.[10] Clouds over islands are newly formed and are much brighter. The underside of clouds also can reflect the presence of large, constant-colored surface areas from a distance of about 15 miles. Lagoons that cover large areas of green water will reflect that green on the undersurface of clouds.

[7]*David Lewis*, We, the Navigators, *first ed. (Honolulu: University of Hawaii Press, 1986), 246.*

[8]*Lewis, 245.*

[9]*Lewis, 175.*

[10]*Charles E. Roth, The Sky Observer's Guidebook (New York: Prentice Hall Press, 1986), 36.*

Cloud reading has a few modern nuances not experienced by the early Kiribatese. In populated areas, city lights at night reflecting off the undersurface of clouds can be seen for 50 or 60 miles. Another modern cloud sign is the jet contrail. Very few portions of the globe are without these telltale cloud streaks. They offer excellent directions in that they are linear and always point toward an airport. Following the contrails, especially if there are several and they are converging, indicates the presence of land; the sharper they converge the closer the land. Between contrails and sky shine it is almost impossible to miss any of the more popular islands of the world.

Jets are not the only flying objects that seek land. Certain birds roost on land and forage at sea. These birds therefore must fly from land in the morning and return toward land at night. The most important of these birds are terns, noddies, boobies, and frigate birds. Large concentrations of these birds indicate that land is nearby. Terns and noddies generally stay within 25 miles of land, whereas boobies and frigate birds range as far as 50 miles.

During the day the birds are busy milling about, absorbed in the business of locating food. Occasionally one may fly back to the nest with a load, but this pattern is too irregular to notice. However, as evening comes on, frigate birds seek elevation, probably to find land by sight, and then set off in a single direction. Boobies fly low and arrow straight, noddies weave in and out through the wave crests, and terns fly about midheight, all following the same path toward land.[11] Although these are all tropical birds, some birds in the temperate zone, such as pelicans and cormorants, exhibit similar behavior. There have been no systematic observations of the northern species on which to base such a conclusion, but it seems reasonable behavior for any bird that feeds at sea and roosts on shore.

Much of this bird lore comes from the experience of the Pacific island navigators. It is also worth noting that these observant individuals use a deep phosphorescence in the water to indicate the presence of land some 80 to 100 miles away. This phenomenon has been reported to occur from 2 to 10 feet down and is composed of streaks, flashes, and momentary glowing plaques of light.[12] The flashes seem to dart out from the direction of the land and in some cases flicker to and fro aligned with the bearing to land. As land gets nearer, the display diminishes, and it finally disappears when the island is in sight. All this sounds a little mystical; however, I have observed a deep luminescence in the sea. At the time I thought it interesting, but I was unaware of this claimed relationship and made no correlation between the flashes and the proximity of land.

[11] *Lewis, 163.*
[12] *Lewis, 208.*

Without a Compass

So far all the discussion has been about locating the boat or the destination, but a major part of finding the destination is the ability to maintain a course. Up to this point that direction has been guided by a compass, which also may or may not be available. Cardinal directions can be located using Polaris and stars that are on the celestial equator, like the star in the belt of Orion farthest from his sword, or the belly star in Virgo. Polaris is always north, and any star on the celestial equator rises due east and sets due west. It is easier to catch the stars as they set because they can be followed for hours before they hit the horizon. Some other points on the celestial equator are the point between the two stars on the lower wing tip of the Eagle, or the eye star in the head of the Water Carrier.

Once due north or east and west have been established a course can be set by steering toward any star on the desired course and allowing for the normal movement of the star from east to west. Those stars closer to the poles move slower. As the star moves away from the desired course the person steering must shift to another star.

Star directions are only good at night. To get direction guidance during the day the only real option is the pattern of waves. There are normally two patterns at sea, wind waves and swell. Wind waves are generated locally and change with the direction of the wind. Swell is generated at a distance, and the bearing of the swell remains relatively constant, sometimes for days and even weeks. On occasion, swell from more than one direction is present. With a little practice the helmsperson can pick out the dominant swell from the rest of the cacophony of waves and steer a constant course relative to this wave pattern, adjusting the course as necessary during the evening hours. Providing the boat can be steered, a determined, educated, and observant navigator can find land again regardless of the amount of equipment on board.

4

ANCHORING

One of boating's major attractions is the feeling of freedom. Swinging on the hook in a secluded cove seems the essence of freedom. Floating free, tethered securely to the earth by a small line, all of your needs met by what is contained in this small capsule. Unhappily, many boaters are robbed of this pleasure by the nagging fear, especially at night, that the boat may not be all that securely attached to the bottom.

The cure for this insomnia is *understanding* anchoring. To select the proper equipment and use it under changing circumstances, it is necessary to understand how anchors work. Humans have been anchoring boats for thousands of years. Yet despite the great body of evolved knowledge that should make it almost foolproof, anchoring has a disturbing rate of failure. Too many boaters rely on rules of thumb: If my boat is 30 feet on the waterline and the bottom is sand and the wind may gust to 30 knots, then *this* is the anchor to use and *this* is how to set it. As is the case with most simple solutions, however, it isn't always that easy. Much of what has been passed down as fact is fallacy. Authorities too often base their findings on a great number of anecdotal uses of an anchor and not on hard theoretical data and thoughtful conclusions. Very few credible laboratory experiments have been performed on anchors. To separate truth from fiction it is necessary to return to theory.

THEORY OF ANCHORING

Gravity Anchors

The simplest form of anchor, the gravity anchor, is used to moor buoys and sometimes boats. Understanding how the gravity anchor works is basic to the understanding of the anchoring process. The holding power of a heavy anchor with no flukes placed on an infinitely strong bottom material such as rock can be described by the classic equation for friction. That is, holding power (Hp) equals the anchor's weight in water (W_w) multiplied by the tangent of the angle of friction (Tan ϕ), or

$$Hp = W_w Tan\ \phi. \qquad\qquad Eq\ 4.1$$

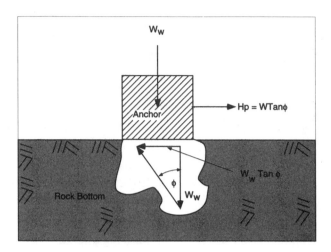

Figure 4.1 Concrete Block Anchor on Rock

The gravity anchor works reasonably well in air, but the anchor's weight in water begins to limit its usefulness when submerged. Since the weight of an object in salt water is 64 pounds less than its weight in air for every cubic foot of material immersed, the weight of a 2-cubic-foot block of concrete is reduced from about 300 pounds in air to about 170 pounds in water.

To evaluate this function further we need the value of the tangent of the angle of friction and the anchor weight. The angle of friction between any two materials is generally considered a constant and depends on the two materials in contact. A typical value for Tan ϕ for a concrete block on rock might be 0.50. Therefore, from Equation 4.1 it can be seen that this anchor would provide about 85 pounds of holding power (170×0.5).

To increase the holding power of this type of anchor, it is necessary to increase either the weight or the tangent of the angle of friction. Since the tangent of friction has rather narrow limits, between zero and one, it is immediately apparent that frictional forces alone require enormous weights to provide practical holding power on unyielding materials.

But suppose the bottom material isn't rock; suppose it's sand. Practical experience shows that it is harder to drag a weight over sand than over rock. While that is true, it isn't the increase in friction that provides the extra resistance. Figure 4.2 shows a heavy block being pulled across a soft bottom material. What happens in this instance is that the block digs into the bottom material on one edge, and the resistance to dragging is increased by the weight of the wedge of bottom material in front of the block (W_s) and the shearing resistance (S_s) of the material along the lower edge of that wedge.

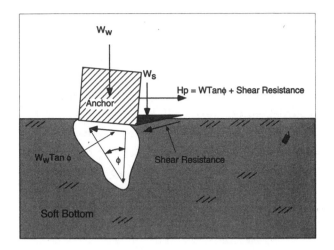

Figure 4.2 Block Anchor
on a Soft Bottom Material

The result is that the holding power (Hp) has been increased by the amount of the shear resistance along the lower surface of the soil wedge. It can be found using the following equation:

$$Hp = W_w Tan\ \phi + W_s S_s A_c \qquad \text{Eq 4.2}$$

where W_w is the weight in water of the submerged block,
            $Tan\ \phi$ is the tangent of the angle of friction,
            W_s is the weight of the soil wedge in water,
            S_s is the shear strength of the soil, and
            A_c is the contact area of the soil wedge.

Now we have a term in the equation that is not dependent upon weight of the anchor, $W_s S_s A_c$. If this term is maximized, the holding power of the anchor can be increased without increasing the anchor weight. To maximize this term it is necessary to increase the weight of the soil wedge being moved in front of the anchor, or to increase the contact area of the soil wedge. Both of these values are to some degree dependent upon the area of the buried portion of the anchor. Carrying this principle further produces a digging anchor.

The Digging Anchor

All digging anchors have a platelike appendage called a fluke that digs into the bottom material. It is this fluke that controls how the anchor digs and supplies most of the digging anchor's holding power. One of the fundamental truths of anchoring is that a 40-pound digging anchor holds more than a 16-pound digging anchor, not because it weighs more, but because the fluke area is larger. The additional weight is only a by-product of the larger fluke area and is of little value once the anchor is buried.

Digging anchors operate by a two-step process—setting and holding; both involve digging. Anchor performance depends on how well the anchor digs into the bottom, but the optimum shape or conditions for setting are not always the optimum shape or conditions for holding. For example, a large fluke area provides optimum holding and a small fluke area provides optimum setting. To select the right anchor for a given set of conditions it is necessary to understand the action of the anchor's fluke during both setting and holding.

The Mechanics of Digging

Anchor digging during setting or holding is a complex transient stage controlled by the soil strength, the forces on the anchor, and the shape of the anchor. Some insight can be obtained by comparing anchor digging to whittling. When whittling, penetrating the wood is a function of the firmness of the wood, the angle of the blade to the wood, and the amount of pressure given to the blade. Balancing these three variables allows the blade to cut a short way into the wood and return to the surface, removing a portion of wood.

Anyone who has whittled also knows that, with the wrong balance of these variables, the blade will skid along the surface or dig deep into the wood. The idea is to vary the force and the angle of the blade to get the desired effect. When anchoring, things are simpler: the idea is always to dig deep into the material. If the tip of the anchor is enlarged as shown in Figure 4.3, it can be seen that three forces interact to control the behavior of the anchor: the force applied to the anchor by the boat, called the **applied anchor force** (A_f); the soil frictional resistance along the soil-anchor fluke interface, called the **fluke frictional resistance** (F_r); and the shear strength of the soil wedge, called the **soil breakout strength** (B_s).

The behavior of an anchor being dragged over the bottom depends on the relative directions and magnitudes of the above forces. Let us first discuss the applied anchor force (A_f). This force is provided during the anchor setting process by the boat's engine pulling back on the anchor, during the holding operation by the forces of the wind and current on the boat, and during recovery by the crew.

The applied anchor force (A_f) can be directed from slightly below the horizontal in use to near vertical during recovery. The optimum direction when anchored is horizontal, or nearly so. Since this force is applied by the anchor rode, a pull below the horizontal is rare, because the boat is always above the anchor. For

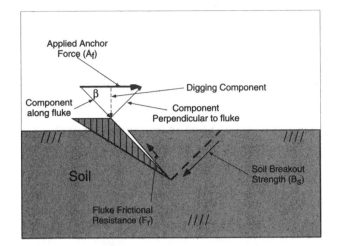

Figure 4.3 Relation of
Forces Involved in
Anchor Digging

the same reason, however, it is possible for the applied anchor force to act on a line above the horizontal during normal use. During retrieval the pull is almost directly upward, which reduces the anchor's holding power to a minimum. It can easily be reasoned that even a slight amount of upward force may be detrimental to the operation of digging during setting and holding.

How much above horizontal before digging is prevented is not known. Some sources state that the pull on the anchor should be less than about 8 degrees above horizontal in order to ensure that the anchor will dig[1,2,3], and one source states that any pull of less than 32 degrees above the horizontal will set the anchor.[4]

By examining three popular anchors and using intuition, a judgment can be made about the accuracy of these claims. If a Danforth, a CQR, and a Bruce anchor are suspended so that their shanks project upward from the horizontal by 8 degrees, the maximum angles the flukes make with the horizontal are about 27, 17, and 2 degrees downward, respectively. From this, it appears that the magic 8-degree angle where digging stops is believable for a Danforth and a CQR, but the Bruce's resulting 2-degree downward fluke angle appears insufficient to support digging.

At 32 degrees of upward pull, the flukes of the CQR and the Bruce both trend upward, by 15 and 30 degrees respectively; the Danforth's residual fluke angle is

[1]*Taylor and Everett, "Looking After Anchoring,"* Practical Boat Owner (*1981*), 6.
[2]*C. F. Chapman,* Piloting, Seamanship and Small Boat Handling (*New York: Hearst Corp., 1972*), 102.
[3]*William G. Van Dorn,* Oceanography and Seamanship (*New York: Dodd, Mead & Co, 1974*), 398.
[4]*Don Bamford,* Anchoring: All Techniques for All Bottoms (*Camden, Maine: Seven Seas Press, 1985*), 39.

only about 3 degrees downward. Common sense tells us that the Bruce and the CQR won't set, and the Danforth (or similar lightweight anchor, known generically worldwide as a Danforth no matter who makes it) is unlikely to dig in. Until better documentation becomes available, we will accept the 8-degree angle as the limiting condition for digging, with a caveat connected to the Bruce.

As it turns out, the 8-degree angle is more important for holding than setting, and will be discussed in greater detail later in this chapter. For the remainder of this discussion we will assume the applied anchor force is directed horizontally and that the bottom is also horizontal. Remember that these conditions can vary, but the principles still apply.

As can be seen from Figure 4.3, a horizontal setting force must be accompanied by a vertical component to force the flukes into the bottom. This is supplied by the inherent downward angle of the flukes on all digging anchors. This downward angle allows the applied anchor force (A_f) to be broken into two components: the component along the fluke, which equals (A_f)cosβ, and the component perpendicular to the fluke, which equals (A_f)sinβ (Figure 4.4).

The magnitude of these two components depends on the angle of the fluke. It can be seen in Figure 4.5 that their values change as the angle changes. The component along the fluke equals the applied anchor force when the fluke angle is zero and then approaches zero as the fluke angle increases. The component perpendicular to the fluke is zero when the fluke angle is zero and increases to equal the applied anchor force when (β) is 90 degrees.

Figure 4.4 Applied Anchor Force Components

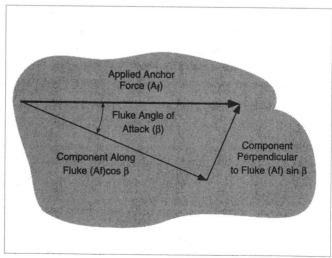

Applied Anchor Force (A$_f$)

Fluke Angle of Attack (β)

Component Along Fluke (Af)cos β

Component Perpendicular to Fluke (Af) sin β

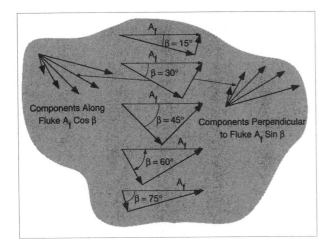

Figure 4.5 Applied Anchor
Force Components

The components perpendicular to the fluke are the forces that tend to break the anchor out of the soil and are directly resisted by the soil breakout strength (B_s). This component could be called the breakout force, and if it exceeds the soil breakout strength the anchor is forced back to the surface. For the anchor to dig, the breakout force must always be less than the breakout strength. Because the component perpendicular to the fluke, the breakout force, is zero when the angle of attack on the soil (β) is zero and increases as angle increases, there is a benefit to keeping the fluke angle small, especially in weak soils where the breakout strength is low. In stronger soils the fluke angle can be considerably steeper.

The other component of the applied anchor force along the fluke directly opposes the soil frictional resistance along the fluke (F_r) (Figure 4.3). This component controls the ease of digging and can be called the digging force. The relationship between digging and fluke angle is not as apparent as the relationship between fluke angle and breakout. In order to make it clearer it is necessary to break this digging force itself into components, one horizontal and one vertical (see Figure 4.6).

The vertical component is of interest here, because it supplies the vertical force necessary to force the anchor into the soil. Figure 4.6 demonstrates that the vertical component of the digging force is zero at zero fluke angle and gets larger as the fluke angle increases until the angle reaches 45 degrees. At fluke angles greater than 45 degrees the vertical component gets smaller again, eventually returning to zero when the fluke angle reaches 90 degrees.

In an ideal material, optimum penetration will occur if both the digging force and its vertical component are maximized. This can be shown mathematically to

Figure 4.6 Components of
the Digging Force

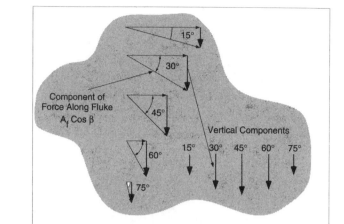

occur when the fluke angle is 30 degrees. As we shall see later, bottom material is seldom an ideal material. The result is that the optimum digging angle can vary one way or the other from 30 degrees. We can make some general conclusions, however.

First, it makes very little sense to have an initial fluke angle greater than 45 degrees. Second, for fluke angles less than 45 degrees, a larger angle transfers more of the applied anchor force into downward motion. Thus, once digging begins the Danforth, with a 37-degree maximum fluke angle, digs faster than the CQR, with a 17-degree fluke angle. A measurement by *L'auto Journal* shows a 16-pound CQR dragging almost twice as far as a 16-pound Danforth before burying.[5]

Third, the steep initial fluke angle is beneficial in penetrating hard materials. This can be illustrated by arranging three common anchors in order of their ability to penetrate hard materials—Fisherman, CQR, Danforth. The initial angle of attack for the fluke is greatest for the Fisherman, least for the Danforth. In situations where penetration is difficult, the Fisherman is the most effective, and the Danforth the least. While it is true that the Danforth can assume a fluke angle of approximately 35 degrees, the initial fluke angle, which controls the onset of digging, is only about 10 degrees.

The Process of Digging

As is apparent from the above discussions, the successful wedding of anchor to bottom depends on the fluke angle and the physical properties of the bottom material, which we'll call soil in the absence of a better term. Three different con-

[5]*Eric C. Hiscock,* Cruising Under Sail *(London: Oxford University Press, 1965), 174.*

ditions can prevent consummation: failure to penetrate, shallow penetration with repeated return to the surface, and deep penetration without breakout.

The first condition, failure to penetrate, occurs if the component along the fluke, digging force $(A_f)\cos\beta$, is less than the frictional resistance of the soil along the fluke:

$$(A_f)\cos\beta < (F_r).$$

The second condition occurs if the digging force is greater that the frictional resistance of the soil along the fluke, and the component perpendicular to the fluke, breakout force $(A_f)\sin\beta$, is also greater than the soil breakout strength:

$$(A_f)\cos\beta > (F_r) \text{ and } (A_f)\sin\beta > (F_r).$$

In this case the anchor will repeatedly break out and gouge a furrow in the bottom.

The anchor will dig into the bottom if the digging force is greater than the fluke frictional resistance and the breakout force is less than the soil breakout strength:

$$(A_f)\cos\beta > (F_r) \text{ and } (A_f)\sin\beta < (F_r).$$

To illustrate this, let's follow a Danforth-type anchor through the digging process. As shown in Figure 4.7, a digging anchor passes through three different stages during anchoring. Initially the anchor lies on the surface, with a small fluke attack angle and a small area of fluke exposed to the soil. The low angle of attack keeps the breakout force small and the digging force large. Because of the small area of the fluke exposed to the soil, the small amount of shear resistance is easily overcome by a large digging force, and the sloping fluke forces the anchor down into the soil.

As digging occurs, more fluke area is exposed to frictional resistance; with the Danforth anchor the fluke angle increases and the point of the anchor moves deeper into the soil. The increase in fluke area exposed to the soil increases the frictional resistance of the soil.

As digging occurs in the Danforth the fluke angle also becomes steeper. As the fluke angle becomes steeper the forces acting on the anchor change. The breakout force increases and the digging force decreases. Also during digging, the point of the anchor is being forced deeper into the soil, increasing the failure path and along with it the breakout strength. This process continues as long as the breakout force

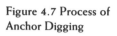

Figure 4.7 Process of
Anchor Digging

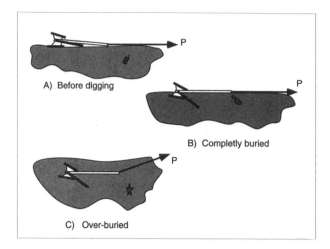

A) Before digging

B) Completly buried

C) Over-buried

is less than the breakout strength, until the digging force along the flukes is equal to the frictional resistance along the flukes. At that point, equilibrium is reached and digging stops. If breakout force exceeds breakout strength the anchor will fail, pull a chunk of soil loose, and return to the surface.

If the anchor holds, how much of the anchor is buried depends on the relationship between the frictional resistance of the bottom material (F_r), the amount of pull on the rode, the applied anchor force (A_f), and the angle (β) and shape of the fluke. By this time the fluke angle, even for the Danforth, is constant, and since the soil's strength at any one location is relatively constant, the only variable is the applied anchor force. Digging will occur again if the applied anchor force increases the digging force ($A_f \cos\beta$) sufficient to overcome the frictional resistance along the fluke (F_r), and if the breakout force ($A_f \sin\beta$) remains less than the soil breakout strength (B_s). This dynamic relationship continues and the anchor rapidly gains holding power until the breakout force exceeds the soil breakout strength (B_s) or the anchor becomes fully buried.

It takes considerable pull to reach this condition. I recall diving on my own anchors to clean the slime from the rodes before leaving an anchorage in the tropics. We had lain for two weeks exposed to 20-knot winds, and neither the 35-pound CQR nor the 20-pound Danforth was fully buried in the loose sandy bottom.

When the anchor is fully buried, any increased pull will overbury the anchor. Because the chain does not dig as well as the anchor, the pull on the anchor shank becomes increasingly upward. This increasing upward pull rotates the flukes upward; digging will eventually stop when the downward component of the digging force is zero. The holding power will still increase to the soil breakout strength (B_s), but the rate of increase diminishes until, at some point, depending on the type of anchor, digging action stops completely. Any further pull either moves the anchor horizontally through the soil or breaks it out.

Since further digging is prevented, the holding power of the anchor is now at its maximum, proportional to the area of the failure plane through the bottom material and the soil breakout strength (B_s) of that bottom material. On occasion, in very soft material, the chain also will bury so that the anchor continues to dig. In this instance the soil provides tremendous anchoring resistance and the anchor itself can be bent or broken.

The second great truth about anchors is now apparent: *The best anchor is the anchor that places the largest fluke area deepest into the bottom material.* Practical application of this truth requires some knowledge about the various strengths and weakness of each component of the anchoring system.

ANCHORING SYSTEM

The anchoring system consists of four separate elements:

1. the boat, including chocks or hawse holes, windlass, bow rollers, Samson post or cleats
2. the rode, including knots, splices, and shackles
3. the anchor
4. the bottom material

Each of these elements plays an important role in the system, with the potential for failure being greatest at the weakest element. Let us begin the discussion of the anchoring system with the element farthest from the boat, the bottom material.

Bottom Material

So far we have only briefly referred to the bottom material, noting that the important properties relative to anchoring are its breakout strength (B_s) and frictional resistance (F_r). The breakout strength and frictional resistance of the soil depend in turn on the soil's weight and shear strength. Because of poor quality control during the creation of the universe, the strengths and weights of bottom materials, from an anchoring point of view, are highly variable and very often the weakest component in the anchoring system. In other words, anchors drag much more frequently than rodes part.

To reduce the occurrence of this most common of failures it is necessary to understand some theory on the strength of bottom material, classifying the material into a few basic groups that share common strength characteristics. Armed with this information and with in-place estimates of the bottom material's holding strength gathered during anchoring, you will have the knowledge you need to choose the proper equipment at a given place and for a particular set of conditions.

Soil has two basic kinds of strength: strength that increases with depth or weight of the soil, and strength that is independent of weight and depth. The first soil strength, common to clean sands, is expressed in terms of the angle of internal friction (tan ϕ), and the second, common to soft clays, is expressed in terms of cohesion (C).

Sands

As we can see from Figure 4.8, the strength of sand increases as the depth increases. The relationship between depth (D) and strength (S) can be written

$$S = D \tan \phi \hspace{4cm} \textbf{Eq 4.3}$$

Tan ϕ depends on the sand's density; the greater the density the higher the value of tan ϕ. The tan ϕ can vary from about 0.4 to 0.9—a very small range, a little greater than a factor of two. The fluke frictional resistance (F_r) is closely related to this strength, and can be expressed as

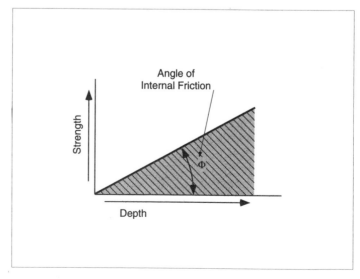

Figure 4.8 Strength of Clean Sand

$$F_r = A_f D \tan \phi \qquad\qquad\qquad \text{Eq 4.4}$$

where A_f is the area of the anchor flukes in contact with the soil and
        D is the depth to the center of the exposed fluke area.

When just the point of the anchor penetrates the soil, both the area exposed to the soil and the depth to its center are very small; therefore, so is the frictional resistance. As the anchor becomes buried, these two variables increase rapidly, as does the frictional resistance to burying.

The holding power of the anchor can be greater than this frictional resistance and, as stated earlier, is proportional to the area of the failure plane through the bottom material and the soil breakout strength (B_s) of that bottom material. The breakout strength (B_s) of an anchor plate embedded in clean, medium-dense sand can be estimated by using the following equation:

$$B_s = \frac{\gamma H^2}{2} K'_p b \qquad\qquad\qquad \text{Eq 4.5[6]}$$

where B_s is the breakout strength of the plate in pounds,
        γ is the unit weight of the soil in pounds per cubic foot,
        H is the depth to the bottom of the plate in feet,
        K'_p is the breakout coefficient from Figure 4.9, and
        b is the width of a square anchor block in feet.

Figure 4.9 is developed for a vertical plate in medium-dense sand with a tan ϕ equal to about 0.6. We can see that this coefficient is dependent upon the depth (H) to the bottom of the plate. As the depth increases the curve is concave upward, and the change in the breakout coefficient value gets larger for each incremental change in depth. For example, if the plate height (h) is 0.5 feet and it is buried 1 foot deep, then the H/h ratio would be 2 and the coefficient would be 7.3. If the same plate was buried 2 feet deep then the H/h ratio would be 4 and the coefficient would be 8.8.

It is worthwhile to note that the breakout strength is more dependent on the width (b) of the flukes and the depth (H) to the bottom of the fluke than on the area of the flukes (bxh). For example, if the area of the plate used above were doubled but its width remained the same, the height would be 1 foot and the depth to the bottom would still be 2 feet. The breakout coefficient would be reduced to 7.3,

[6]G. A. Leonards, Foundation Engineering (New York: McGraw-Hill Book Co., 1962), 467.

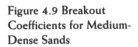

Figure 4.9 Breakout
Coefficients for Medium-
Dense Sands

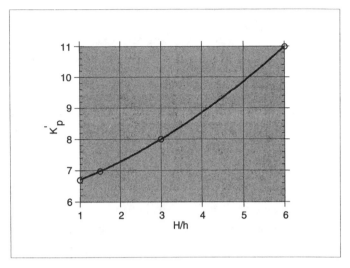

and there would be a net loss in strength. In clean sands it can be seen that the strength of the anchor depends more on getting wide flukes deep into the sand rather than on the overall area of the flukes. This concept of getting a wide surface down deep is exploited by the Bruce anchor.

Using equation 4.5, the holding power or breakout strength of a 1-foot-wide by 1-foot-high plate buried 2 feet deep in soil with a unit weight of 135 pounds per cubic foot is approximately 1,975 pounds:

$$B_s = (135 \times 2^2 \times 7.3 \times 1)/2 = 1,975 \text{ pounds.}$$

Remember that this calculated strength is not necessarily a failure strength for the anchor. Under this load the anchor may continue to dig, which would increase the strength. To illustrate, the area of this plate is approximately the same as the effective fluke area of a 35-pound Danforth. Comparing this load to that given by the manufacturer for this anchor in hard sand (11,000 pounds), a large discrepancy becomes apparent, and it is probable that the anchor would continue to dig. Part of the difference, however, could be due to hard sand being stronger than a clean medium-dense sand. The hard sand used by Danforth for its test may well have contained clay, which could increase the material's strength.

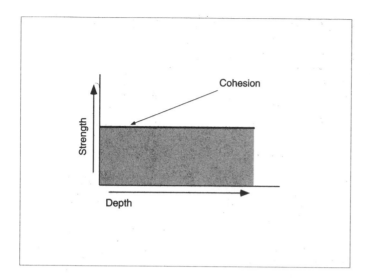

Figure 4.10 Strength of Pure Clay

Clays

The second type of soil strength, cohesion (C), is not dependent on depth; it is constant. This strength can be represented by the rectangle in Figure 4.10.

The strength of pure clays can be expressed rather simply as

$$Strength = Cohesion\ (C) \qquad\qquad Eq\ 4.6$$

The fluke frictional resistance (F_r) in soft clays is related to the cohesion and the area of the fluke exposed to the soil. It can be expressed as

$$F_r = A_f C \qquad\qquad Eq\ 4.7$$

where A_f is the area of the anchor flukes in contact with the soil and
C is the cohesion value of the soil.

It can be seen from this equation that, in pure clays, once the anchor becomes fully buried the fluke frictional resistance is constant regardless of the depth of the anchor. This is why it is easier to bury an anchor completely in pure clay than in sand. The values of cohesion for clay can range from about 50 pounds per square foot for extremely soft marine clays to greater than 4,000 psf for dense, hard clay (see Table 4.1).

MATERIAL	IDENTIFICATION	TYPICAL COHESION (IN PSF)
Very Soft Clay	Fist penetrates several inches easily	40 to 250
Soft Clay	Thumb penetrates several inches easily	250 to 600
Medium Clay	Thumb dents an inch with moderate effort	600 to 900
Firm Clay	Thumb dents an inch with great effort	900 to 1,100
Stiff Clay	Thumb dents less than an inch with great effort	1,100 to 1,900
Very Stiff Clay	Thumbnail dents easily	1,900 to 4,000
Hard Clay	Thumbnail dents with difficulty	> 4,000

Table 4.1 Cohesion Values for Pure Clay

It is apparent that very stiff clays are hard to penetrate and require extremely large setting loads or a very small fluke area. This is why the fisherman anchor with its small fluke area is effective in hard clays. The holding power or breakout strength of the anchor can be calculated using the following equation:

$$B_s = K_c Chb \qquad\qquad\qquad \text{Eq 4.8}[7]$$

where B_s is the breakout strength of the plate in pounds,
K_c is the breakout coefficient from Figure 4.11,
C is the cohesion of the soil in pounds per square foot,
h is the height of the plate in feet, and
b is the width of a square plate in feet.

Figure 4.11 is again developed for a vertical plate and shows the breakout coefficient dependent upon the depth (H) to the bottom of the plate. Unlike sandy soils, here the curve is concave downward or flattening out with depth, eventually reaching a constant value of about 8.5 when H/h equals 10.

With the exception of the Bruce, rarely does an anchor get buried to H/h ratios as great as 10. The Bruce achieves these high ratios not because it gets deeply buried but because the vertical area of its fluke is so very small. In general, however,

[7]Leonards, 468.

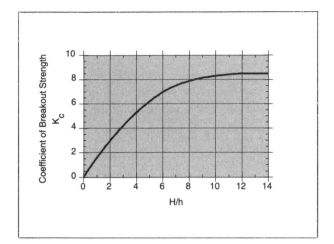

Figure 4.11 Breakout
Coefficients for Pure Clays

it can be seen from the shape of this curve and Equation 4.8 that, in soft clays, the depth of the anchor is not as important as the area (hxb) of the fluke buried. The larger the effective buried area, the greater the holding power of the anchor. This has led some manufacturers to allow the user to vary the maximum fluke angle of the anchor. Increasing the angle by 10 degrees for softer material increases the effective plate area, thereby increasing its holding power.

It is also interesting to note that the difference between the holding power, or breakout strength (B_s), and the fluke frictional resistance (F_r) is the factor (K_c), since the area (A_f) for a rectangular fluke equals (bh). Since (K_c) is always positive in clays, the holding power is always greater than the force required to set the anchor.

Using Equation 4.8, we can see that the holding power of the same anchor used in the sand example above, when set in a pure soft clay with a cohesion value of 400 psf, is calculated to be approximately 1,200 pounds:

$$B_s = 3.0 \times 400 \times 1 \times 1 = 1{,}200 \text{ pounds.}$$

Recalling that the value for cohesion can vary from 40 to 4,000 psf, the example anchor could exhibit holding powers from 120 to 12,000 pounds, depending on the cohesive strength of the clay. Obviously, holding power in clays is extremely variable, a factor of 100 compared with a factor of 2 for sands. This number compares well with the published strength values of the Danforth 20, but this may be coincidence, for the same qualifications apply to these calculations as to the sand calculations.

Soil strength variability also creates a great deal of confusion in determining anchor holding power. Given the right set of conditions, almost any manufacturer can show his anchor to be superior to any other anchor. It is hard to tell from their published data whether the results are valid, since they do not give complete accounts of the testing methods. Don Bamford reports that most manufacturers are reluctant to disclose their testing methods.[8] My own experience with anchor manufacturers is similar. A general rule to follow on evaluating test results is that, if insufficient data is included to duplicate the test and verify the results, the results should be considered questionable.

Mixed Soils

Many soils are neither clean sand nor pure clay but a mixture with both components of strength (see Figure 4.12). The strength can be expressed mathematically as a combination of the two previous strength equations:

$$\text{Strength} = C + D \tan \phi \qquad \qquad \text{Eq 4.9}$$

In a combination bottom material, the $\tan \phi$ value is generally lower than in pure sands, varying from 0.15 to 0.4, and the cohesion values are also more moderate, as shown in Table 4.2.

Figure 4.12 General Soil Strength

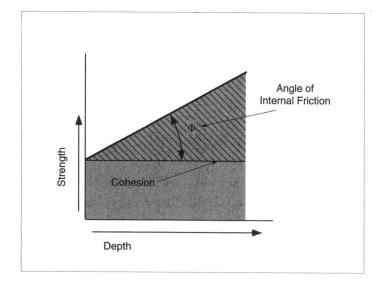

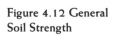

| Table 4.2 Cohesion Values for Common Soils | |
MATERIAL	TYPICAL COHESION (IN PSF)
Mud	50 to 450
Silt	100 to 500
Silty Clay	400 to 800
Sandy Clay	400 to 800
Sandy Silt	600 to 1,000
Dense Sandy Silt	900 to 1,500

Determining Bottom Conditions

Now that we know something about the strength characteristics of various bottom materials, we need to identify them and estimate their holding characteristics before we can anchor with confidence.

The traditional method is to use an "armed" lead—a lead line with a hollow cavity smeared with a sticky material to which the bottom will adhere. The old mariners used tallow; modern substitutes might be shortening or water-pump grease.

Of course, the upscale modern method of determining bottom conditions is to interpret the reflection patterns provided by fishfinders or flashing-light depthsounders. With a little practice one can detect weeds, grass, and hard or soft bottoms. Soft bottoms show a wide, variable bottom line; hard bottoms show a thin, well-defined line; grass and weeds exhibit false echoes above the bottom.

General information can be obtained by examining charts of the area, which are marked with symbols to describe bottom quality and material. A complete list of these symbols is given in Chart No. 1; the most useful are shown in Table 4.3.

Chart symbols are the least accurate source of bottom information, as the strengths of these generic terms—mud, sand, etc.—can vary widely. Nonetheless, the chart and this table can give you a broad, general view of areas worth further investigation as an anchorage. Bottom conditions are grouped under three broad categories: good, average, and poor holding. The subjective strength values help quantify these three broad categories. Some of the terms in this column are values, some are modifiers. The modifiers provide more detail on the bottom conditions and provide more confidence in the strength value. Depending on whether the modifiers are negative or positive, the subjective strength value will decrease or increase. For example, clay is poor to good, soft clay is poor, sticky clay is average, and stiff clay is good.

Table 4.3 Standard Bottom Condition Symbols[9]

NOAA Number	Symbol	Meaning	Subjective Strength Value
2	S	Sand	Average
3	M	Mud or Muddy	Average
4	O	Ooze	Poor to Average
6	Cl, Cy	Clay	Poor to Good
7	G	Gravel	Poor to Average
8	Sn	Shingle	Poor
9	P	Pebbles	Poor
10	St	Stones	Poor
11	Rk, rky	Rock or rocky	Poor
11a	Blds	Boulders	Poor
23	Sh	Shells	Poor to Average
27	K	Kelp	Poor to Average
28	Wd	Seaweed	Poor to Average
28b	Grs	Grass	Poor to Average
39	f, fne	Fine	Positive Modifier
40	c, crse	Course	Negative Modifier
41	so, sft	Soft	Negative Modifier
42	h, hrd	Hard	Positive Modifier
43	stf	Stiff	Positive Modifier
44	sml	Small	Positive Modifier
45	lrg	Large	Negative Modifier
46	stk, sy	Sticky	Positive Modifier
	Si	Silt	Average to Good
	Cb	Cobbles	Poor
	m	Medium	Negative Modifier

As you have probably noticed, no bottom material is classified as good. Good bottom conditions are bottom materials listed as average with a positive modifier—for example *sticky* silt, *hard* sand, and *stiff* clay. The shear strength of the soils in these bottoms can still vary, but most anchors will dig in and hold well in high winds. In hard or stiff material, anchors with low initial fluke angles and flukes with large areas, such as the Danforth, may find the digging difficult. The larger initial fluke angle of the Bruce and CQR can, on occasion, force its way into the bottom

[9]Chart 1. Department of Commerce, NOAA, and Department of Defense, DMA (November 1984), 15.

and get an adequate grip. If the bottom material has high strength, large fluke area is not required to provide good holding. Under good conditions, the smaller flukes and steep initial fluke angle of the fisherman-type anchors, such as the Luke, Northill, or Herreshoff, will often get an adequate grip. Anchors with large flukes provide exceptionally high strength once they get buried, however.

Average bottom conditions are materials listed as average, those listed as poor with a positive modifier, and on occasion a good bottom with a negative modifier. Sand and mud are examples of the first condition; small pebbles or hard shell might be examples of the second condition; and soft silt would be an example of the third. In average conditions, anchors with large flukes hold better. These bottom strengths are suitable for a single anchor in normal wind conditions, but may require multiple anchors for high winds.

Poor bottom conditions are those where digging is extremely difficult or impossible, such as in rock, coral, large gravel, or boulders; and where holding is intermittent or where the bottom is so soft it provides very little breakout strength. It is best to avoid anchoring in these areas unless you're certain of the weather or there are no other alternatives. In soft bottoms, a suitable hold can be maintained in light and sheltered conditions by using an anchor with large flukes.

Anchoring in coral should be avoided, because it is ecologically unsound, illegal in some areas, and the holding power cannot be predicted (this is true of rock as well). If *forced* to anchor in rock and coral, the general practice is to try to hook a crack or crevice in the bottom with a sharp point of the anchor, generally a fisherman-type anchor. Their small, sharp flukes can find a hold in cracks and crevices more easily than the large flukes on digging-type anchors.

The strength and longevity of a hold in rock or coral is tentative at best. A coral head may snap off or, if the direction of pull changes, the anchor may slip out of its crevice. In these conditions, setting two anchors will limit the movement of the boat, spread the load, and provide a backup system. A further complication of anchoring in rock and coral is that the hold may be so good that the anchor becomes difficult to retrieve. Buoying the anchor in rock or coral is a prudent practice. Some boaters use inexpensive grapple or hook-type anchors in coral, leaving the anchor in place rather than breaking the coral to retrieve it.

When anchoring in large gravel and cobbles, fisherman-type anchors with small flukes and steep fluke angles are best; Danforth-type anchors are all but useless in this material. Regardless of the anchor, the hold can be tentative. For example, the anchor may be lodged against a large boulder. An increase in load may push it out of the way, causing a drastic and sudden reduction in holding capacity. A second anchor is wise in this type of bottom.

Bottoms covered with grass, seaweed, or debris can foul the anchor and make digging difficult. Holding can be good, if you can get the anchor to dig down through the vegetation. Extra weight will help force the anchor to the bottom, and a small fluke area and steep fluke attack angle will help it dig in—if the flukes don't foul on the weeds or debris. A fouled anchor must be retrieved and cleared before it will dig properly.

Bottom Testing

The information above will help you select the proper equipment, but you still should actually check the bottom strength where you intend to anchor. Drop the anchor, set it properly, and back down on it to determine how much load the bottom material will take before the anchor drags. If you cannot pull the anchor free, remember that the setting or digging load is always less than the breakout load; the anchor will take a greater load than used during setting. The term "set properly" is very important for this test, and I recommend using the method described later in this chapter under "Anchoring Techniques."

A boat equipped with a variable-pitch or adjustable-pitch three-blade prop can exert large loads on the anchor line; a twin-blade folding prop applies only a minimal load. On my own boat, equipped with an adjustable-pitch prop, I know that when I back down full throttle and the anchor holds, it will take winds in excess of 40 knots to move the anchor.

In conclusion, bottom conditions are a major factor in the strength of the anchoring system and are extremely variable. The prudent mariner has aboard several different kinds and weights of anchors and multiple rodes for use in the various conditions encountered when cruising. The more varied the conditions, the more varied your anchor inventory should be.

Anchors

Selecting the proper anchor inventory for your boat involves sorting through the confusion of claims and opinions read in the literature and heard along the dock. Anchor type is an emotional topic among yachtsmen; every anchor has its champion, albeit rarely supported by scientific data. The problem lies in the number of variables that affect anchor holding power. Each type of anchor operates in a slightly different manner and has different strengths and peculiarities. Anyone looking for the single best anchor for all seasons is doomed to failure. Those who swear by only one anchor type will have occasion to swear at it as well.

Danforth Type

The Danforth-type anchor is well known. There are several different manufacturers, but all models are lightweight and have long, thin, paddle-shaped flukes designed to dig quickly into soft bottom material. Danforth-type anchors have high holding power for their weight and fold flat for storage. The anchor has a low initial fluke angle and considerable fluke area for its weight. Once the fluke begins to penetrate, the fluke angle increases rapidly to about 35 degrees. These characteristics produce an anchor that digs quickly into soft and weaker materials and provides maximum holding power. In very firm bottom material the anchor has difficulty digging, but it will hold well in any bottom that it can penetrate.

The large fluke area can produce very high breakout loads in high-strength soils, and large stresses in the anchor's components. These anchors need to be made of high-strength metal so they won't fail or bend before pulling free of the bottom. The Danforth anchor is widely copied, and some are poorly constructed from inadequate material. Aluminum versions show promise because of aluminum's superior weight-strength ratio compared with steel. A popular version made by Fortress has an adjustable fluke angle, which may provide an increase in holding power on some bottoms.

There have been reports of the flukes of Danforth-type anchors being fouled by shells, boulders, and even the anchor rode. I have had no experience with this, but if it occurs during setting it is readily apparent, and just requires recovering the anchor, unfouling the flukes, and resetting. The only time this could be a real problem is in an emergency, when there is only one chance to set the anchor.

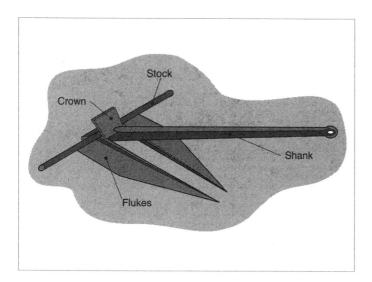

Figure 4.13 The Danforth-type Anchor

Once set, a Danforth-type anchor can fail to reset if turned 180 degrees and pulled free with the flukes held open with stiff mud. Also, the large, flat flukes and the light weight give it a tendency to surf, especially if the boat is under way when the anchor is dropped. If the conditions are right, the anchor may even come back to the surface.[10] This again should only occur during emergencies, when the anchor is dropped while the boat is moving fast.

CQR or Plow

The CQR or plow anchor is also widely known. Shaped like two plowshares welded back to back, the CQR is much heavier than most digging anchors.

Like the Danforth, the CQR produced by Simpson Lawrence is much copied. Most authorities agree with the manufacturer and warn against imitation plow anchors constructed from weak and inferior materials. The CQR's nonvariable flukes have an initial and a maximum fluke angle of about 30 degrees. This suggests that the CQR may dig to less depth than the Danforth type, but the 30-degree initial fluke angle is very near optimum and will penetrate harder bottom materials more easily than Danforth-type anchors. The CQR normally falls on its side, sticks the point of the plow into the bottom, and slowly rolls upright when a horizontal pull is applied to the shank, causing the CQR to dig more slowly than a Danforth in medium to soft bottom material.

Figure 4.14 The CQR Anchor

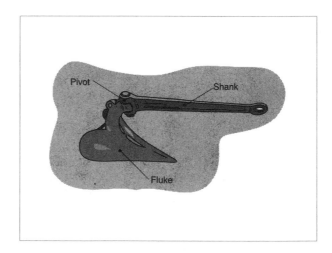

---

[10]Donald M. Street, Jr., *The Ocean Sailing Yacht*, vol. 1 (New York: W. W. Norton & Co., 1973), 290.

With its lower fluke-area-to-weight ratio, a CQR must be heavier than a Danforth to provide the same amount of holding power. This extra weight helps the anchor to penetrate weeds and kelp, and also improves penetration in harder bottom material. Because of its weight, a CQR may dig in conditions where lighter anchors may not.

The CQR's shank is hinged, allowing it to pivot if the direction of pull changes, which tends to keep the anchor buried. The CQR is very unstable in any position that would prevent digging, and is practically immune to fouling, short of impaling a can on the point. It is also easy to store in a bow roller and simple to launch and retrieve.

Bruce

The Bruce anchor, developed by the oil-drilling industry to anchor drilling towers, is light, strong, and, unlike other digging anchors, has no moving parts. Like the CQR, the Bruce can be stored easily in a specially designed bow roller. It is lighter in weight than a CQR of the same relative holding power. Its one-piece construction makes stowage on deck or below decks cumbersome and difficult.

The cupped flukes and rigid shank cause the Bruce to begin digging while on its side. One of the long, sharp flukes attacks the bottom at a very steep angle, approximately 80 degrees, penetrating even relatively hard materials. Once the anchor begins to dig it rolls over and the fluke angle drops rapidly until it is fully buried, with the shank essentially horizontal and the flukes angling down at about 10 degrees. Thus, any further horizontal pull will produce very little digging; the

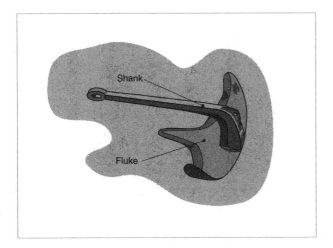

Figure 4.15 The Bruce Anchor

anchor has more fluke area resisting an upward pull than a horizontal pull, which may account for the Bruce's reputation as a short-scope anchor.

The Bruce has a relatively low fluke area perpendicular to the load for its weight, but this doesn't necessarily impair the anchor's holding ability. The Bruce's flukes are long, thin, and cupped, which increases the H/h ratio, in turn increasing the K factors and ultimately increasing the theoretical holding power, especially in sands.

Like the CQR, the Bruce is unstable in any configuration that would prevent digging; it remains buried if the direction of pull changes; and it is extremely difficult to foul, although the cuplike flukes can fill with stiff, sticky clay.

Because the Bruce is such a relative newcomer, it isn't surrounded by a lot of folklore. My experience is that it is sensitive to proper setting techniques, since any upward pull on the rode rapidly reduces the attack angle, but it holds well when set properly.

Fisherman

The fisherman is the generic name for several anchors of similar design, looking more or less like the popular conception of an anchor. All have a stock protruding at right angles to the flukes. The stock turns the anchor into a digging position, but unless it is collapsible, it makes the anchor difficult to stow. The Luke, Nicholson, and Herreshoff anchors are some of the more common makes of this type. The Luke can be disassembled into three major parts, which makes stowing easier.

Figure 4.16 The Fisherman Anchor

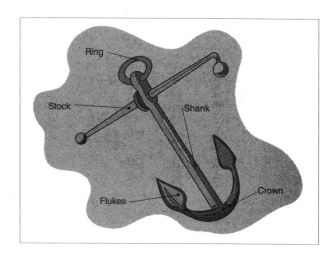

The proper proportions for this anchor are important to its performance. Claude Worth, after experimenting with a variety of these anchors, proposed the following guidelines.

1. **The stock should be the same length as the shank.**
2. **The shank should be more than 1.3 but less than 1.5 times the distance between the tips of the flukes.**
3. **The flukes should make an angle with the shank of about 40 degrees.**[11]

The fluke area on a fisherman is smaller than on other types of anchors, and the initial fluke angle and weight are greater; consequently, this anchor is best used in bottoms that present difficult digging. As these types of bottoms can also have high holding strength, the small flukes provide adequate holding. Because the flukes can be buried deeper than other anchors, the fisherman is often the anchor of choice in cobbles or boulders.

Even when fully buried, one fluke is exposed, presenting the possibility that the rode may foul around the exposed fluke and pull the anchor free. Diamond-shaped flukes, which allow the rode to slide up and off, will reduce the likelihood of fouling.

The fisherman's heavy weight and stock makes it awkward to launch and retrieve. A line tied to the crown of the anchor and secured aboard will reduce its swinging as it is put over the side or pulled aboard, thus preventing many a sprained back and ding in the topsides. When launching, the fisherman should be lowered to the bottom and the rode let out slowly as the boat backs away, so that no extra rode loops around a fluke.

Although a fisherman isn't a true a digging-type anchor, many traditional sailors still prefer them. They certainly hold well if set properly, reportedly with less scope than other anchors, although the reports are vague as to the circumstance and bottom conditions.[12,13]

A number of other anchors are on the market, none with a large following. The Northill, patterned after an ancient anchor used in Malaysia, was adapted for duty as a flying-boat anchor. Its stock is on the lower end of the shank and can be removed or folded flat for storage. The Northill has a high initial fluke angle and a larger fluke area than the fisherman, which increases its holding power in soft materials and decreases its digging capability in hard materials when compared to a

[11]*Eric C. Hiscock,* Cruising Under Sail *(London: Oxford University Press, 1974 edition), 170.*
[12]*Donald M. Street, Jr.,* The Ocean Sailing Yacht, *vol. 2 (New York: W. W. Norton & Co., 1978), 253.*
[13]*Clayton Ewing and Stanley Livingston, Jr.,* Offshore Yachts *(New York: W. W. Norton & Co., 1987), 230.*

fisherman. Other anchors include the wishbone and navy stockless. Few of these anchors are used by recreational boaters.

Rode

The controversy over the ideal anchor rode is simpler, if no less heated, than the one concerned with the ideal anchor. The factions are split between all chain, and nylon with a few fathoms of chain near the anchor. Materials other than chain and nylon are distinctly inferior for small yachts and are not considered here.

The perfect rode would be strong, flexible, elastic, lightweight, inexpensive, chafe-resistant, require low maintenance, and be easy to handle. Too bad it doesn't exist. That leaves you with a choice between two imperfect materials, and it is necessary to understand the advantages and disadvantages of each.

Strength is relative. To judge whether a material is sufficiently strong to serve a purpose, you need to know the maximum load imposed on the material. Once the maximum loads are known, it is a simple matter to refer to a table, such as Table 4.4, to select the proper rode.

Table 4.4 Working Strength in Pounds*					
	CHAIN			NYLON	
SIZE	BB	PROOF	HIGH TEST	BRAIDED	TWISTED
3/16	800	700			
1/4	1,325	1,175			
5/16	1,950	1,750	3,900		750
3/8	2,750	2,450	5,400	1,200	1,100
7/16	3,625	3,250	7,200	1,625	1,475
1/2	4,750	4,250	9,200	2,075	1,875
5/8	5,875	6,900	14,000	3,625	3,050
3/4	10,250	9,125			4,175
7/8					
1					7,350

*For comparison only; strengths vary among manufacturers.

Strength may be expressed in the literature as minimum breaking strength, the load that all samples tested can sustain without failure; and working strength, which includes an adequate margin for safe operation.

The working strength of nylon line and chain is generally one-fourth the minimum breaking strength; for fittings such as shackles, it is one-sixth the minimum breaking strength. *Average* (not minimum) breaking strength may be quoted; this is divided by five to get working strengths. Be careful to understand which strengths are being quoted to stay within safe margins. The breaking strength of nylon depends on its type and whether it is colored; dyed fiber loses about 20 percent of its strength. The nylon values quoted in Table 4.4 are for white Caprolan 2000. All the strengths listed are working strengths.

Chain

As an anchor rode, chain is attractive because it is resistant to abrasion. It can drag over rocks, coral heads—or the bow of your boat—for days with little effect on its integrity, although the same cannot be said for the boat.

Many would include chain's weight as a positive factor. Three hundred feet of chain attached to a 35-pound anchor can be viewed as a long, thin 335-pound anchor. But as we have seen, dead weight and friction alone are an inefficient anchoring system.

The weight of chain creates significant disadvantages. For example, chain is most often stowed high and forward, where its weight adversely affects the pitching moment and significantly degrades windward performance. And an all-chain rode is almost impossible to set from a dinghy. Most boaters who favor all-chain rodes keep a nylon rode handy in case an anchor needs to be rowed into position.

It is interesting to examine the position of a chain rode as wind load increases. With no wind the boat is at point A in Figure 4.17; the anchor chain hangs straight down. As the wind load increases, the boat moves to position B and the chain develops a deep belly, called a catenary curve. As the wind loads become heavier, the belly flattens, which provides elasticity to absorb shock loads from sudden wind gusts or large waves.

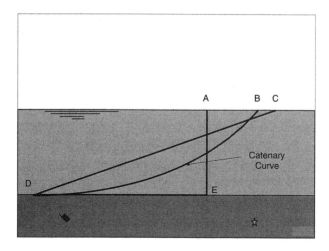

Figure 4.17 Rode Elongation

The distance moved, A-C, is directly dependent upon the depth of the water, A-E. Lengthening the scope only moves the A position farther from the anchor point D without increasing elasticity. Many all-chain buffs may be unpleasantly surprised to find how short the distance A-C can be in shallow water.

William Van Dorn has shown in great mathematical detail that, in order to withstand wind gusts 31 percent above the average, a vessel anchored on all-chain rode must anchor in 360 feet of water on 1,080 feet of chain.[14] If the vessel were moved to only 60 feet of water on 456 feet of chain in the same conditions, it would snub hard enough to damage the bow or jerk the anchor out of the bottom every time a wave with a period longer than 15 seconds and height greater than 5 feet hits the vessel. Adding scope adds no additional elasticity; it only increases the holding power of the anchor, because the pull on the anchor remains horizontal longer.

If we move down to the depths most boaters normally anchor in (15 to 30 feet), things get worse. "The sad truth of the matter is that, at long scope in shallow water, there is very little working stretch while chain still lies on the bottom—and virtually none after it lifts clear. In a sudden wind gust, or very moderate seas, a vessel is apt to come to the end of its tether with a jerk that parts chain or breaks the anchor out.[15]

The bottom line is that anyone relying on the catenary of a chain rode to provide elasticity in critical situations contradicts physics. I wonder how many anchor failures have been due to the wrong rode rather than the wrong anchor.

Chain has disadvantages other than weight. It is difficult to slip if an emergency requires leaving the anchorage quickly. Although chain does not abrade, it rusts and needs frequent examination and regalvanizing. Chain is noisy in use, especially under dynamic conditions. The sound of chain links clanking or dragging on rock produces many sleepless hours. Some skippers, however, have learned to read those sounds, and claim they can detect a dragging anchor by the sound of the chain.

Nylon

The major advantages of nylon rode are its elasticity, cost (one-eighth the cost of comparable-strength chain), and light weight. The minor advantages are that it doesn't corrode, it's relatively easy to clean, and it's easy to retrieve by hand. Its major disadvantages are its difficulty in stowing (it tends to tangle and must be coiled or flaked down) and its tendency to fail by abrasion.

[14] Van Dorn, 410.
[15] Van Dorn, 413.

The natural stretch of nylon provides a positive cushioning effect to both anchor and boat under dynamic loading conditions. This ability to stretch is why most U. S. experts (chain remains popular in Great Britain) feel that nylon is the better anchor rode material. However, not all nylon stretches equally. Figure 4.18 compares some standard nylon line types and their stretch capability. Sta-set is a commercial name for a stiff weave of Dacron and nylon line.

Notice that the stretch is compared relative to percentages of the line's breaking strength. A thick line has a much higher breaking strength than a thin line. One hundred feet of three-strand, ½-inch diameter line will stretch 16 feet when loaded to about 280 pounds; the same load on a ¾-inch diameter line will stretch only about 5 feet. Moral: don't use a nylon rode that is too heavy.

The absolute stretch of nylon is not an exact number; new nylon will stretch about 15 percent more than old nylon. Since the elongation of a nylon rode is dependent upon its length and not on catenary or water depth, it can provide considerably more elongation than chain. Compare two vessels on a 3:1 scope in 33 feet of water, one on old ½-inch-diameter nylon rode, the other on all chain. The catenary of the chain will allow about 5 feet of elongation, the nylon has about 20 feet of maximum stretch. If the scope is changed to 8:1, the useful elongation of the chain remains about 5 feet, but the nylon's ability to elongate has increased to 50 feet. This elasticity reduces peak loads on all parts of the system.

Nylon's low weight means it can be handled without mechanical aids and stowed in more locations. For example, the rode can be stowed high and forward

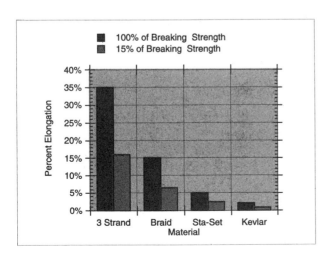

Figure 4.18 Nylon Stretch

without adversely affecting performance. Anchors can easily be set from dinghies, something that needs to be done more often than expected.

The disadvantage of nylon's light weight is that it takes less force to pull the shank of the anchor above horizontal. The tendency to lift can be reduced by adding a small amount of chain near the anchor, however. Four fathoms of chain, for example, would increase that load to 160 pounds before lifting takes place. Since using nylon rode without adding chain is generally considered bad practice, any reference to a nylon rode is assumed to include a chain leader approximately equal to half the boat length. Table 4.5 provides the approximate loads that the various scopes require before the pull on the anchor is above the horizontal.

Table 4.5 Loads Required to Lift Anchor Shank Above Horizontal

Scope	½-in. Nylon in 25 ft.	¼-in. Chain in 25 ft.	½-in. Nylon in 50 ft.	¼-in. Chain in 50 ft.	Max. Angle
7:1	275 lbs.	475 lbs.	415 lbs.	950 lbs.	8°
5:1	185 lbs.	240 lbs.	260 lbs.	475 lbs.	11.5°
4:1	120 lbs.	150 lbs.	170 lbs.	300 lbs.	14°
3:1	90 lbs.	80 lbs.	115 lbs.	160 lbs.	18°

Some interesting conclusions can be found in this table. First, it is important to set the anchor using maximum scope, then shorten up after it is set, especially when using nylon. Chain provides superior setting power, except in shallow water and short scope.

Once the anchor is set we worry about holding. As we have seen, it is important to keep the anchor shank less than 8 degrees above the horizontal. Table 4.6 shows the holding power of nylon and chain rodes in similar conditions. The values in Tables 4.5 and 4.6 were calculated from equations given by William Van Dorn using ¼-inch chain and ½-inch nylon rode with 24 feet of chain.[16]

Table 4.6 Loads Required to Lift Anchor Shank 8° Above Horizontal

Scope	½-in. Nylon in 25 ft.	¼-in. Chain in 25 ft.	½-in. Nylon in 50 ft.	¼-in. Chain in 50 ft.	Max. Angle
7:1	—	—	—	—	8°
5:1	1,950 lbs.	800 lbs.	2,790 lbs.	1,590 lbs.	11.5°
4:1	385 lbs.	320 lbs.	530 lbs.	640 lbs.	14°
3:1	175 lbs.	135 lbs.	230 lbs.	270 lbs.	18°

[16]Van Dorn, 409.

This table does not bear out the old saw about chain's superior holding power on short scope. That statement is only true in deep water.

This superior performance of nylon is due to its elasticity. Contrary to popular belief, the stretch of nylon appears to keep the pull less than 8 degrees above the horizontal better than the catenary of the chain, especially at scopes of 5:1, where nylon doubles the performance of chain. Another way of looking at it is that the elasticity of the nylon actually increases the effective scope. For example, there is enough stretch in a nylon rode at 4:1 to increase the effective scope to 5:1 under load.

The major drawback to nylon rode is chafe where the anchor line passes through the chock to the cleat, and chafe on coral or rock below the water. Chafe can reduce the strength of the line quickly, and the line can part under low loads. Anywhere the anchor line encounters a hard material, chafe can and will occur if there is any relative motion between the two materials. This can be prevented by placing a short piece of plastic hose over the line where it contacts the hard material.

Chafing on rocks, which are geologically distributed and usually avoidable, is less a problem than chafing on coral, which can pop up anywhere that is biologically attractive. Although I prefer to avoid it, when I must anchor in coral areas I try to place the anchors in sand patches, and attach a large (1-foot-diameter) fishing float to the shackle between the nylon line and chain using a small-diameter line longer than the depth of the water—enough to allow all the chain to be on the bottom during setting. The float has no serious effect on the anchor's ultimate holding power, but it does reduce the setting power, and it is important to set the anchor with the float line slack. Take care to see that the rode does not get caught under or on any coral during setting. After the anchor is set, I dinghy out to the float and shorten the small-diameter line enough to haul the end of the chain 7 or 8 feet off the bottom. If there are large or numerous coral heads in the anchor area, I add an extra 24-foot shot of chain to the anchor and pull the end of the chain 15 feet off the bottom.

In these conditions I also believe it is prudent to set two anchors, which prevents the vessel from swinging, regardless of the wind and tide conditions, and in most anchorages keeps the chain clear of any coral heads. I trade off the extra effort required to anchor in this manner against less ecological impact, better performance, more comfort, and independence from mechanical contraptions.

Table 4.7 summarizes the necessary characteristics of anchor rode and compares the performance of the two common materials.

Table 4.7 Anchor Rode Comparison

CHARACTERISTIC	CHAIN	NYLON
Abrasion	+	
Cost		+
Durability	=	=
Ease of Cleaning		+
Effect on Boat Comfort		+
Effect on Boat Performance		+
Elasticity		+
Fittings	+	
Holding in Light Winds	+	
Holding in Heavy Winds		+
Placing Primary Anchor	=	=
Placing Secondary Anchor		+
Quiet		+
Retrievability (without winch)		+
Safety	=	=
Slipping Anchor		+
Stowage of Rode	+	
Total	4	10

A few comments about the selections in this table: The durability of both chain and nylon are considered equal, because chain corrodes, and nylon deteriorates slowly when exposed to sunlight and salt water. The fittings used on chain can be as strong as or stronger than the chain, but the knots and splices used on nylon are at best only 90 percent as strong as the line. If the boat has a winch, the retrievability "+" changes columns. Both rodes are judged equally safe; nylon rode seems to entrap legs, while chain entraps fingers with about equal frequency and severity.

Boat

The last link in the anchor system is the boat and its appurtenant parts, such as the bow roller, winches, and cleats or Samson posts.

Bow Rollers

The bow roller allows the anchor rode to move freely over the bow into or out of the water. It can be designed to stow a CQR or Bruce anchor ready for use. Bow rollers must be strong and firmly attached to the boat with large backing plates, and should be designed to take lateral loads.

The actual roller should be 4 to 6 inches in diameter and grooved to take both chain and line. The groove is necessary to keep the chain from twisting when hauled aboard. Too much twist and the chain will be difficult to stow, or it may jump off the wildcat on the windlass or capstan. The roller should fit snugly into the frame so no line can get caught in the gap. The frame should be such that it has a fair lead for a wide range of rode angles both forward and aft, and all metal parts should be smooth and fair. The cheeks of the roller should be 2 inches high with some means of keeping the rode from jumping out of the roller assembly, especially if a chain rode is used.

Because a cruising vessel often sets two anchors, two rollers mounted side by side provides a better system than passing the second line through a chock. Chocks are adequate for docking lines but do not provide enough protection for anchor lines.

Windlasses and Capstans

Many people feel that anchor windlasses or capstans are like traveler's checks: "Don't go cruising without them." Maybe. I use nylon rode and feel that four of the five anchors I carry can be retrieved by hand. When retrieving the fifth anchor, or any time I need assistance with a snagged anchor, I can run the rode back to a mid-size jib halyard winch on the cabintop. This works for me because of the nylon rode and the handy halyard winch. Every skipper should consider the need for emergency lifting power and devise a scheme that works on his boat.

With an all-chain rode, a windlass is almost mandatory. I say almost because with ¼- to 5⁄16-inch chain, a chain dog or stopper can be used. This device allows the chain to pass in only one direction, back to the boat. During hauling you can take a short break to spit on your hands, summon strength, and let the boat move forward. The steady haul is approximately equal to 1 pound for every foot of water. To get the maximum haul, add the weight of the anchor. In most conditions the maximum load will be about 75 pounds, which drops about 3 pounds per heave until the anchor shank is at the roller.

Depending on individual strength, the use of an anchor much heavier than 45 pounds, even with nylon rode, may require the use of a windlass or capstan. The windlass has a drum mounted on a horizontal axis; the capstan's axis is vertical. The capstan drum axis makes it more tolerant to lines arriving from any horizontal angle, which is handy for kedging off sandbars. The windlass works better with vertical lines and can hoist crewpersons aloft as well.

There are three types of windlass: manual, hydraulic, and electric. The manual is generally cheaper and more reliable, but it is not labor free nor fast. In fact, it takes more energy to raise an anchor with a manual windlass than by hand, due primarily to friction in the windlass mechanism. The value of the windlass is that the energy used is reduced to a more tolerable level and spread out over a longer period of time; what one wins in lower level of effort one loses in longer effort. The windlass should be capable of hauling 25 feet per minute.[17] As the gear gets heavier, the labor gets longer. Eventually the safety of the vessel becomes an issue. A boat with 35 feet of anchor chain dangling down is not the most maneuverable craft, and the skipper with massive ground tackle must look to a power windlass.

The power windlass brings with it several liabilities. First, regardless of the power supply, the engine must be running to retrieve the anchor. Second, the windlass itself must be capable of functioning to retrieve the anchor. These two conditions are not always met. There is a law here similar to the speed and power law for manual winches: as complexity increases, so does vulnerability.

The selection of the power system depends on several factors. While electric systems are the most convenient and the least expensive, hydraulic systems are generally the most reliable and powerful.

An electrical system's batteries must be able to handle the current draw for 5 minutes, even though the engine and alternator are operating. The capacity of the battery bank should be about four times larger than the maximum current draw. The cable necessary to carry the current to the windlass also must be large, since too small a cable may start a fire or cause the windlass to operate improperly. Cable size is dependent upon the amount of current and the distance the current has to travel. Since very few engines or batteries are installed forward and the cable cannot travel in a straight path, the lines to the windlass are long and therefore must be very large, 00 or 000 AWG.

An electric windlass makes good sense on a powerboat with its dry foredeck and massive electrical system. The least likely place for a functioning electric motor would be the foredeck of a small sailboat. There, the clear choice is hydraulic drive.

A hydraulic windlass is easier to install, since hydraulic hose is more flexible than heavy copper cable. The hydraulic windlass is also smaller, lighter, and stronger, and can take more abuse on the foredeck. The major problems include finding a system, cost, and the smell of leaking hydraulic oil. Many people choose to build their own. A small, powerful hydraulic motor can be coupled to the windlass by a clever mechanic. All that is needed to complete the system is a hydraulic pump belted off the engine.

[17]Ross Norgrove, The Cruising Life (Camden, Maine: International Marine Publishing Co., 1980), 165.

Irrespective of type, a windlass must be installed as far aft as possible and through-bolted with the proper backing plates. The aft placement moves the weight of the windlass and the chain aft, which reduces the tendency of the boat to pitch and improves windward performance.[18] The aft placement, however, exposes a considerable portion of the deck to abrasion from the chain and also produces clutter. The deck can be protected by sacrificial strips of wood. Toes have no such luck.

The axis of the windlass should be carefully aligned horizontally and vertically so that the chain feeds into and away from the windlass at the proper angle. The windlass must be mounted so that the chain leads up to it and is in contact with the wildcat for at least 90 degrees so the chain will strip properly. The chain should be stored below or slightly aft of the windlass.[19]

Cleats and Samson Posts

Samson posts and cleats are used to secure the anchor line to the vessel. Samson posts are rarely found on modern boats; to qualify as a real Samson post it must be made from locust or oak and extend through the deck to the stem. The average Samson post will handle loads 100 times those normally imposed; it seems to me this is overkill.

A cleat should be large enough to take two turns of the heaviest line you would expect to handle during anchoring or at dockside. The bolts that attach the cleat to the deck should be large enough to take the maximum expected load and have an adequate backing plate. Table 4.8 lists the strength of stainless steel bolts of various sizes in single shear. By counting the number of bolts and multiplying by the value in this table the strength of the cleat can be found.

Table 4.8 Shear Strength of Stainless Steel Bolts

SIZE (IN INCHES)	STRENGTH (IN POUNDS)
$1/8$	550
$3/16$	1,200
$1/4$	2,200
$5/16$	3,450
$3/8$	5,000
$7/16$	6,750
$1/2$	8,850

[18]*Street, vol. 2, 262.*
[19]*Hiscock (1974), 179.*

The deck where the cleat is attached can fail as well. To check the strength of the deck (S_d), determine the perimeter of the backing plate in inches (P), and multiply that by the thickness of the deck in inches (T). Multiply this area by the tensile strength of the deck material (S_m) in pounds per square inch (listed in Table 4.9):

$$S_d = PTS_m.$$

Eq 4.10

Table 4.9 Shear Strength of Hull Material	
MATERIAL	STRENGTH (IN POUNDS/IN²)
Steel	20,000
Aluminum	15,000
Fiberglass	12,000
Wood (Avg.)	350

For example, if the deck plate is a 2.5-by-3-inch rectangle, the perimeter is 11 inches. If the deck is ¼-inch-thick fiberglass, the failure area is 2.75 inches and the failure strength is 33,000 pounds, or

$$S_d = 11 \times .25 \times 1200 = 33,000 \text{ lbs.}$$

A wood deck would need a larger backing plate. Backing plates are generally not needed for steel or aluminum.

Sentinels and Buoys

A sentinel (a movable weight that can be positioned on the anchor rode using another line) or a buoy is often added to the anchor rode to resist the straightening out of the anchor line under load of wind or current. The sentinel pulls the anchor line down; the buoy pulls it up. As we have seen in Table 4.5, a nylon rode on a 3:1 scope will require 110 pounds of load to bring the pull on the anchor above the horizontal. Add a 25-pound sentinel and it will require approximately 220 pounds of load to do the same. Another way of looking at it is that the 3:1 scope with a sentinel imposes the same loading conditions on the anchor shank as a nylon rode at 5:1 scope without the sentinel.

The addition of a 25-pound sentinel to an all-chain rode is not as effective: about a 60 percent increase in load as compared to 100 percent for nylon. Most of this disparity is due to the placement of the sentinel. Traditionally the sentinel is set at middepth on chain rodes, whereas it is set at the shank of the anchor on nylon rodes. A sentinel only increases the effective scope on an all-chain rode from 3:1 to 4:1. Because of this center placement, as the scope gets larger the effect gets smaller. A sentinel adds very little additional capacity to a chain system above 5:1 scope.

Most boaters who use chain use the sentinel to increase the catenary and prevent snubbing when on short scope in shallow water, rather than to increase their holding power. Many users of chain are unaware that a sentinel increases holding, or believe that the holding of an all-chain rode needs no improvement, or at least not as much as does the apparent elasticity. From the figures in Table 4.5 and 4.6 we can see that this is obviously not the case.

Although the physics of the buoy are more complex, it cannot improve the angle of pull on the anchor as much as the sentinel; however, it does improve the angle of pull on the vessel. If the float is large enough and placed closer to the boat than to the anchor, the almost-horizontal angle of the rode to the bow allows it to rise more easily rather than be pulled down into the wave.[20] This kind of shock-absorbing assistance is generally only necessary with an all-chain anchor system.

Since nylon already has considerable shock-absorbing power, a buoy's greatest advantage on a nylon rode is to protect the rode from abrasion by lifting it free of the bottom. Because a buoy reduces the setting power of the anchor by pulling the chain off the bottom as well, it is best to set the anchor before lifting the chain end. If the buoy is set such that the chain is raised below the scope line, as shown in Figure 4.19, the ultimate holding power of the anchor is unaffected by the buoy.

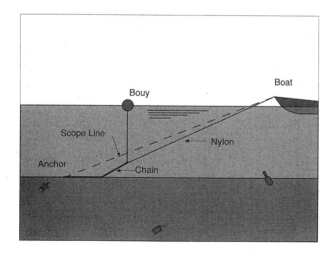

Figure 4.19 Location of Chain End Relative to the Scope Line

[20]Chapman, 107.

Twenty-five feet of chain on a 5:1 scope, for example, would put the nylon about 5 feet above the bottom.

EQUIPMENT SELECTION

There are two methods commonly used to select an anchor system for a specific boat: Use your opinion or someone else's opinion. Using someone else's opinion requires less effort and seems attractive. The expert advice can come from manufacturers or a boating authority. The problem is, these experts do not agree.

Authors of cruising books recommend anchor sizes consistently larger than those suggested by manufacturers. Roth recommends a 75-pound plow for a 46-foot sailboat.[21] His own boat, *Whisper*, a 35-foot sloop with a 9.6-foot beam, was equipped with a 45-pound CQR. The manufacturer recommends a 45- and a 35-pound plow respectively for the same size vessels. Street carries on *Iolaire* a 50-pound Herreshoff, backed up with a 150-pound, three-piece Nevins stowed in the bilge.[22]

There is no doubt as to the quality of nautical judgment and skill possessed by these two men. And while it may be true that manufacturers are trying to sell their products, it is also true that they know a great deal about anchoring in general and their own products specifically, and get no benefits, long or short range, from selling the wrong size anchor. It is hard to discount either source. My opinion is that 80 percent of boaters use too large an anchor. Ninety-nine percent of cruisers use *much too large* an anchor, and rely on a heavy anchor to cover mistakes in anchoring technique. If you are going to use the advice of others, I recommend using the manufacturer's advice coupled with proper anchoring methods.

There is a better way, however. Consider that the experts and manufacturers need to deal with a general audience of unknown skills and that they therefore must err on the side of safety; *you* need only deal with your own boat and skills. The best solution is to rely on your own informed decision. Further, as you will soon see, choosing an anchor system for a specific vessel is not as critical or as difficult as it is made to appear.

You must be prepared for multiple conditions, so the best solution is a multiple-part system that can be put together or taken apart as conditions dictate. During a long cruise you may face winds from dead calm to gale force, current from 0 to 5 knots from multiple directions, waves from 0 to 15 feet, and tides from near

[21]Hal Roth, After 50,000 Miles *(New York: W. W. Norton & Co., 1977), 86.*
[22]*Street, vol. 2, 255.*

0 to 30 feet. Bottom strengths may vary from 100 pounds to several thousand pounds of holding per square foot.

Loads on Anchor Systems

Background on the mechanics of anchoring presented at the beginning of this chapter will assist in the rational selection of an anchoring system. What is missing are the loads imposed by the boat on the anchor. Two classes of loads must be assessed to select an anchor system: static loads and dynamic loads, both of which are produced by the action of the wind on the exposed hull and rigging, and the water on the submerged portion of the hull.

Static loads come from a steady load generated by constant current or wind forces; they are a function of the size and shape of the hull and are simple to analyze. Dynamic loads are generated when the boat changes its velocity either up, down, or horizontally by wave action or wind gusts. They are a function of the weight and motion of the boat that can change in an endless pattern and are relatively unimportant until the wind velocity reaches about 10 knots.

As the wind velocity increases above 10 knots, the dynamic effects of wind gusts and wave actions on a boat become more violent, completely random, extremely complex, and difficult to analyze. Because of this difficulty, we shall neglect detailed discussion of dynamic loads and provide only some basic physics for background. For example, it is important to know that two boats with vastly different weights acted upon by the same dynamic situation can have nearly identical dynamic loads on their anchor systems. This is due to a property called momentum, which is the product of the weight of the boat and its velocity:

$$\text{Momentum} = mv \qquad\qquad \text{Eq 4.11}$$

where   m is the mass of the boat and
         v is the velocity of the boat.

The momentum of two different-weight boats can be the same if neither boat has reached equilibrium, because the heavier boat accelerates slower and therefore is moving at a lower velocity than the lighter boat; what is lost in mass in the light boat is made up in increased velocity, and vice versa. The result is that, in storm conditions, when two boats are constantly changing directions and are in a non-equilibrium condition, the dynamic loads on the anchors can be essentially the same if the forces acting on the boats are the same, regardless of their respective weights. As we shall see, the static forces acting on the boats are a function of their shape, not their weight—much the same as a pound of feathers drops slower than a pound of lead because of its larger surface area.

The dynamic loads on an anchor system are normally handled by increasing the margin of safety on the static calculations. When using an all-chain rode, the static load should be doubled to account for the dynamic loads on the anchor. When 75 percent of the rode is nylon, the safety factor can be reduced to 1.5 because of nylon's flexibility. The static loads are caused by steady wind and current forces and are therefore proportional to the area of the boat exposed to wind and current.

Wind Loads on Anchors

In order to calculate wind loads, it is necessary to deal with C_d, the drag coefficient, and A_e, the equivalent area exposed to the wind. The drag coefficient can vary from .06 to 1.9 depending on the shape of the object and the amount of turbulence in the air.[23] The derivation of this coefficient is beyond the scope of this book. For those interested I suggest reading C.A. Marchaj's *Aero-Hydrodynamics of Sailing*, where the subject is treated in great detail. The equivalent area also varies from a little less than one to two. Given this amount of variability and the error introduced by temperature and pressure change, the correct scientific values are a bit nebulous. This problem is dealt with in the usual practical engineering fashion by making safe simplifying assumptions and hoping the calculated force is as large as or larger than the actual force.

Unfortunately, there seems to be a certain lack of consistency in selecting this value. Bamford[24] selected C_d to be equal to 1.0, which leads to:

$$F = 0.003391 \times A_e \times V^2 \qquad \text{Eq 4.12}$$

where A_e is the equivalent area in square feet and
V is the wind velocity in knots.

Jack West reports that[25]

$$F = 0.004 \times A_e \times V^2 \qquad \text{Eq 4.13}$$

where   V is the wind velocity in mile per hours.

[23]C. A. Marchaj, Aero-Hydrodynamics of Sailing (New York: Dodd, Mead & Co, 1979), 262.
[24]Bamford, 52.
[25]Jack West "Ground Tackle and Anchoring Techniques," Yachting (November 1975), 50.

Since V is expressed in miles per hour, it is necessary to change units and would indicate he favored 1.5643 for the drag coefficient. As if this were not enough in the wild and wacky world of nautical mathematics, William Van Dorn reports the same equation as Jack West, only he indicates the wind velocity in knots.[26] This would result in a C_d of 1.1796. Faced with the lack of precision and this apparent inconsistency in the existing literature, which I strongly suspect has to do with dealing with conversion between dimensional units, the final determination of C_d is left to judgment. Since I feel that West is overconservative, Bamford is underconservative, and I like round numbers, I shall go with Van Dorn and use

$$D = 0.004 \times A_e \times V^2 \qquad \text{Eq 4.14}$$

where A_e is the equivalent area in square feet and
         V is the wind velocity in knots.

Now that C_d has been determined by hand waving and coughing, the somewhat nebulous term, effective area (A_e), is left to resolve. The effective area can be broken into two parts to assist in calculation: the part contributed by the hull, and for sailboats the part contributed by the rigging. The part contributed by the hull depends on the angle the boat lies relative to the wind. Assuming no current, boats in a light wind, boats with two anchors down, and a few well-behaved boats lay at anchor head to wind. In this instance the effective area of the hull is the product of the boat beam and the height above the water of the cabintop or dodger.

When a boat does not lie head to the wind, the effective area is the product of the height of the boat and the length of the boat exposed to the wind. The length of the boat exposed to the wind is the sine of the angle the boat makes with the direction of the wind, times the total boat length. This angle is generally around 30 degrees for sailboats, which are affected more by the current due to their deep keels. Assume the angle to be 30 degrees; the sine of 30 degrees is 0.5, and the effective area becomes the product of ½ the length times the boat height.

The windage area contributed by the mast and rigging of a sailboat can be obtained by multiplying the total length of the mast or masts by 0.5 and the total length of all standing and running rigging by 0.04. The windage due to the rigging is usually about 70 to 100 percent of the head-on boat area.[27] Since all these calculations are inexact, it doesn't pay to make them unduly complicated and time

[26]Van Dorn, 291.
[27]Van Dorn, 293.

consuming. The windage calculations for sailboat rigging are generally handled by increasing the head-on windage area by 100 percent.

Consistent with this practice, the resistance of the boat due to yaw likewise can be simplified to a percentage of the head-on area. The yaw area is about 1.5 times greater than the head-on area. Using these simplifications, the effective area (A_e) of the boat can be reduced to a ratio of the beam of the boat (B) by the height of the cabintop or dodger (H). The total area is then 1 x B x H for head-on area, plus $1 \times B \times H$ for rigging area, plus $0.5 B \times H$ for yaw, or a total of $2.5 \times B \times H$:

$$S = 2.5BH \text{ for sailboats and}$$
$$S = 1.5BH \text{ for powerboats.}$$

The windage load on a sailboat lying to a single anchor can now be found by using the following simplified equation:

$$D = .004 \ (2.5BH) \ V^2 \text{ or}$$

$$D = 0.01 \ BH \ V^2 \qquad\qquad \textbf{Eq 4.15}$$

For powerboats, because they have no rigging, the equation is
$$D = 0.006 \ B \ H \ V^2 \qquad\qquad \textbf{Eq 4.16}$$

It is now a simple matter to calculate the approximate maximum static load on an anchor system due to wind loads. Tables 4.10 and 4.11 are compilations of these loads on sailboats and powerboats respectively over a range of effective areas and wind velocity values. To use the tables, multiple the beam (B) times the height (H) of the boat; the column nearest to this B x H value will be the static anchor loads for the boat. It is interesting to examine the relative values of these loads as the velocity of the wind and effective area of the boat vary.

The first thing to notice is that for low wind velocities, where 90 percent of the anchoring is done, the loads are very low, less than 120 pounds for winds less than 10 knots. Winds in this range have very little dynamic effect, so the total wind loads are essentially the static loads. To get total anchor load it is necessary to add the dynamic loads and water current loads where appropriate.

Current Loads on Anchors
The loads caused by water currents can be calculated by using essentially the

Table 4.10 Static Loads on Sailboats for Various Wind Velocities

WINDS IN KNOTS	LOADS IN POUNDS FOR SAILBOATS WITH B × H										
	50 FT.²	55 FT.²	60 FT.²	65 FT.²	70 FT.²	75 FT.²	80 FT.²	85 FT.²	90 FT.²	95 FT.²	100 FT.²
5	12	14	15	16	18	19	20	21	22	24	25
10	50	55	60	65	70	75	80	85	90	95	100
15	115	125	135	145	160	170	180	190	205	215	225
20	200	220	240	260	280	300	320	340	360	380	400
25	315	345	375	405	440	470	500	530	565	595	625
30	450	495	540	585	630	675	720	765	810	855	900
35	615	675	735	800	860	920	980	1,040	1,105	1,165	1,225
40	800	880	960	1,040	1,120	1,200	1,280	1,360	1,440	1,520	1,600
45	1,015	1,115	1,215	1,320	1,420	1,520	1,620	1,720	1,825	1,925	2,025
50	1,250	1,375	1,500	1,625	1,750	1,875	2,000	2,125	2,250	2,375	2,500
55	1,515	1,665	1,815	1,965	2,120	2,270	2,420	2,570	2,725	2,875	3,025
60	1,800	1,980	2,160	2,340	2,520	2,700	2,880	3,060	3,240	3,420	3,600
65	2,215	2,335	2,535	2,750	2,960	3,170	3,380	3,590	3,805	4,015	4,225
70	2,450	2,695	2,940	3,185	3,430	3,675	3,920	4,165	4,410	4,655	4,900
75	2,815	3,100	3,375	3,660	3,940	4,220	4,500	4,780	5,065	5,315	5,625

Table 4.11 Static Loads on Powerboats for Various Wind Velocities

WINDS IN KNOTS	LOADS IN POUNDS FOR POWERBOATS WITH B × H										
	100 FT.²	110 FT.²	120 FT.²	130 FT.²	140 FT.²	150 FT.²	160 FT.²	170 FT.²	180 FT.²	190 FT.²	200 FT.²
5	15	16	18	20	21	22	24	26	27	28	30
10	60	66	72	78	84	90	96	102	108	114	120
15	135	148	162	176	189	202	216	229	243	256	270
20	240	264	288	312	336	360	384	408	432	456	480
25	375	412	450	488	525	562	600	638	675	712	750
30	540	594	648	702	756	810	864	918	972	1,026	1,080
35	735	808	882	956	1,029	1,103	1,176	1,250	1,323	1,397	1,470
40	960	1,056	1,152	1,248	1,344	1,440	1,536	1,632	1,728	1,824	1,920
45	1,215	1,337	1,458	1,580	1,701	1,823	1,944	2,066	2,187	2,309	2,430
50	1,500	1,650	1,800	1,950	2,100	2,250	2,400	2,550	2,700	2,850	3,000
55	1,815	1,997	2,178	2,360	2,541	2,723	2,904	3,086	3,267	3,449	3,630
60	2,160	2,376	2,592	2,808	3,024	3,240	3,456	3,672	3,888	4,104	4,320
65	2,535	2,789	3,042	3,296	3,549	3,803	4,056	4,310	4,563	4,817	5,070
70	2,940	3,234	3,528	3,822	4,116	4,410	4,704	4,998	5,292	5,586	5,880
75	3,375	3,713	4,050	4,388	4,725	5,063	5,400	5,738	6,075	6,413	6,750

same fluid drag equation given above. It is necessary to use the density of water rather than the density of air, and to change the area to the area of the hull exposed to the drag of the water. Once these changes are made the formula becomes:

$$D = 1.94C_d A_w V^2/2 \qquad\qquad \text{Eq 4.17[28]}$$

where   (D) is the force of the water on the hull in pounds,
(C_d) is a drag coefficient[29],
(A_w) is the area of the wetted surface, and
V is the water velocity in feet per second.

Making the appropriate substitutions to change the velocity to knots, this equation reduces down to

$$D = 0.05 A_w V^2 \text{ (drag in water)} \qquad\qquad \text{Eq 4.18}$$

Because the viscosity of water is much higher than that of air, it is necessary to use a wetted area rather than the vertical projection of the area exposed to the water. This makes getting the correct value for the area more difficult, but it still would be nice if the value could be related to common parameters of the boat, such as draft, beam, and waterline length. A conservative estimate of the wetted area would be the surface area of a prism having the dimension of the beam (B), waterline length (l_{wl}), and draft (D). The area of this prism is equal to

$$A_w = 2l_{wl} (D^2 + B^2/4)^{1/2} \qquad\qquad \text{Eq 4.19}$$

The range in wetted surface area of interest to recreational boaters is from 500 to 1,000 square feet. Very few people would anchor in currents greater than 4 knots, but the range of velocities in Table 4.12 was extended from 0 to about 6 knots to cover other applications.

This table and the preceding tables also should illustrate why it is inadvisable to anchor in currents in excess of 4 knots, which are equivalent to anchoring in 30-knot winds.

[28] John K. Vennard, Elementary Fluid Mechanics (New York: Wiley & Sons, 1954), 340.
[29] Dependent on bottom condition but approximately equal to 0.087.

Table 4.12 Static Loads for Various Current Velocities

CURRENT IN KNOTS	LOADS IN POUNDS FOR GIVEN WETTED AREA					
	400 FT.²	500 FT.²	600 FT.²	700 FT.²	800 FT.²	900 FT.²
0	0	0	0	0	0	0
1	20	25	30	35	40	45
2	80	100	120	140	160	180
3	165	210	250	290	330	370
4	320	400	480	560	640	720
5	500	625	750	875	1,000	1,125
6	720	900	1,080	1,260	1,440	1,620

Anchor Size Relative to Total Load

These tables provide the necessary values to size the various anchor systems needed for boating. To illustrate, suppose it is necessary to size anchors for a 40-foot sailboat equipped with a dodger top 6 feet off the water, with a waterline length of 34 feet, a 12-foot beam, and a 6-foot draft. This boat has an effective bow area of 75 square feet ($12 \times 6 \approx 75$) and a wetted surface area of about 600 square feet [$2 \times 34 (36 + \frac{144}{4})$ ½] ≈ 600.

The primary anchor will be used about 80 percent of the time, in wind conditions of less than 15 knots and in currents of 2 knots or less. The static wind load from Table 4.11 is 170 pounds; with a nylon rode, the dynamic loads will be about 85 pounds. The maximum current load from Table 4.12 is 120 pounds; the total maximum load on this system is the sum of all these loads, or about 375 pounds.

The next anchor to size for this boat will handle 19.9 percent of anchoring situations—wind conditions between 30 and 15 knots. The static load is 675 pounds, and the dynamic load equals 340 pounds with the same 120-pound current load. The total load on this system is less than 1,135 pounds.

The anchor needed for the remaining 0.1 percent of the time is the hurricane holder. At 75 knots, the static load is 4,220 pounds and the dynamic load is another 4,220 pounds; forget the current loads. The total load is then about 8,500 pounds. Anchors or a combination of anchors capable of resisting these three loads—375, 1,135, and 8,500 pounds—will cover any situation you will encounter.

The first thing to note is that these loads are not very large. The second thing to note is that, according to Table 4.6, the load calculated for 15-knot winds is so low that it would not pull a nylon rode above 8 degrees on a 4:1 scope. The anchor load in a 30-knot wind is considerably smaller than most people realize, and is low enough that the anchor shank will not be pulled above 8 degrees with a nylon rode at a 5:1 scope.

Anchor Holding Power

Now that the loads on the anchor system are known, we must select an anchor that will resist those loads in a wide variety of bottom materials. The relationship of anchor holding power to anchor weight shown in Figures 4.20 through 4.23 is from the manufacturer's published data.

Figure 4.20 Danforth Hi-Tensile Anchor in Good Material

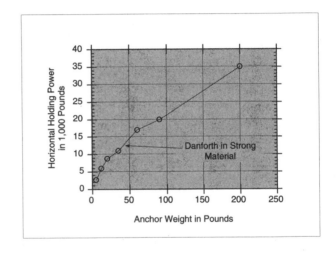

Figure 4.21 Danforth Hi-Tensile Anchor in Weak Material

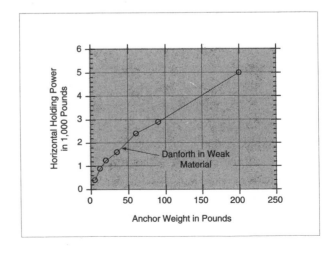

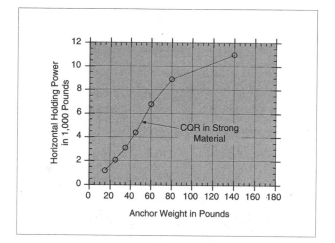

Figure 4.22 CQR Anchor
in Good Material

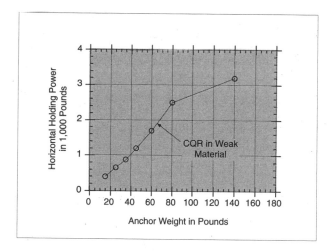

Figure 4.23 CQR Anchor
in Weak Material

The terms "good" and "weak" are nebulous, but then so is anchoring. As we have seen, anchor holding power depends to a great extent on the material in which the anchor is set. These curves are only useful for comparison purposes, and even then they are subjective between different types of anchors. I believe the strengths shown for the good bottom material to be close to the upper limit of the anchors' holding power. The curves given for weak bottom materials are fairly close to what one would expect in soft clay.

To select anchors for our sample boat, I would use the weak bottom material curves for the first two anchors. This would indicate a 5-pound Danforth or a 15-pound CQR for the 80 percent anchor and a 20-pound Danforth or a 45-pound CQR for the 19.9 percent anchor. Trying to select an anchor that will hold under hurricane conditions in soft mud is futile. Far better to run for sea room or, next best, put out tandem anchors. I would choose a 45-pound Danforth for a hurricane anchor and hope for average bottom conditions.

How many 40-foot boats carry a 5-pound anchor, let alone use it 80 percent of the time on a 4:1 scope? Zip! The average weight of anchors on cruising boats, from a recent survey, is shown in Table 4.13.[30]

Table 4.13 Average Anchor Weights

LOA	PLOW	DANFORTH	BRUCE
Over 40 ft.	52 lbs.	65 lbs.	—
Under 40 ft.	45 lbs.	53 lbs.	37 lbs.

With these averages in mind, these conclusions are possible from Tables 4.10 through 4.13:

- The load values are wrong.
- Anchor holding power is way overrated.
- Most boaters use excessively large anchors.

I do not believe the first conclusion, because the mathematics used to derive the data in Table 4.10 is defensible; and from my own experience, I know I can pull my own boat by hand into a 10-knot wind (75 pounds) but not much more. Again from my own experience, these low loads (±170 pounds on each anchor) could explain why, when I dove on the two anchors I used for two weeks under steady 20-knot winds, I found them still unburied.

I have on numerous occasions anchored my 43-foot boat overnight using a 20-pound Danforth. I have pulled on the anchor in reverse under full power using a three-blade reversing-pitch prop with a measured load of about 1,150 pounds. This is consistent with that anchor's published 1,250-pound holding power. I know of others who have used very light anchors

---

[30] *Jimmy Cornell,* World Cruising Survey *(Camden, Maine: International Marine Publishing Co., 1989), 86.*

successfully; for example, a 12-pound Danforth used to anchor a 37-foot Apache.[31]

Many of the cruising people in the survey seemed unaware of how to set anchors properly by backing down the engine.[32] This leads me to believe that the reported incidents of dragging are due more to improper anchoring procedures or using the wrong rode rather than to using an undersized anchor. The larger-than-necessary anchors carried by most cruisers cover a multitude of sins.

It is also interesting to compare the figures in Tables 4.10, 4.11, and 4.12 with those recommended by the American Boat and Yacht Council for horizontal anchor loads (see Table 4.14). The storm anchor load in Table 4.13 for a 40-foot boat is 2,400 pounds—considerably lower than the 8,400 pounds calculated for our example. Comparing this recommendation to the example boat used above would place the storm that this anchor is designed to resist as one with winds less than 45 knots. The question then becomes, what does the ABYC consider to be a storm? Forty-five knots is certainly a storm, but not a very big one, and if you are lying to your storm anchor, you had better know what size storm it is designed to withstand.

Table 4.14 ABYC Horizontal Loads[33]

LENGTH OVERALL	BEAM	STORM ANCHOR	WORKING ANCHOR	LUNCH HOOK
10	4	320	160	40
15	5	500	250	60
20	7	720	360	90
25	8	980	490	125
30	9	1,400	700	175
35	10	1,800	900	225
40	11	2,400	1,200	300
50	13	3,200	1,600	400
60	15	4,000	2,000	500

The ABYC table is simplistic, especially in its lower recommendations. These values are obtained by simply halving the storm load to arrive at the working load and quartering the working load to arrive at the lunch hook value. The working anchor compares favorably with the 19.9 percent anchor designed above for use in 30-knot winds. Again, it depends on how you define working, but I consider the

[31] Robert Bavier, Yachting Magazine, (September 1969).
[32] Cornell, 88.
[33] Chapman, 100.

working anchor to be the one I use daily. In 30 years of anchoring I have anchored very few times in 30-knot winds. But ultimately, each skipper must consider what he or she encounters routinely, and select an anchor accordingly.

The recommended lunch hook compares to the loads encountered by the 80 percent anchor. The term "lunch hook" implies an anchor that is used only rarely, say 20 percent of the time in very light conditions—conditions in which the boat could almost be held by a bait bucket. I prefer to drop the term "lunch hook" altogether and talk in terms of the working anchor (375 pounds), the storm anchor (1,135 pounds), and the hurricane anchor (8,400 pounds).

Unnecessary anchor weight reduces overall boat performance and adds extra effort during anchor handling. In return it provides a certain degree of peace of mind. You may wish to follow current practice and select an oversized anchor, but you should know that there is no scientific basis for your selection. If all of this seems unbelievable, or if you are just curious about the performance of your own boat, the simple experiments in Appendix B will confirm these numbers and produce values to calculate anchor loads especially tailored to your boat.

Rodes

The number and lengths of rodes to have on board depend on the intended cruising area's normal conditions and maximum anchoring depths. A commonly recommended length of rode is three to seven times the water depth for chain, and four to nine for nylon. Our calculations show this is about right for nylon and misleading for chain. Recall that chain's inelasticity indicates it should not be used in waters much less than 50 feet deep unless conditions are settled. Therefore, when waves kick up it is necessary to move the boat to deeper water, which requires a minimum of 385 feet of chain for a boat with 5 feet of freeboard forward.

For nylon, Table 4.6 shows that holding power is not a problem, but Table 4.5 shows that setting loads are very low unless the scope is greater than 7:1. I recommend setting an anchor with nylon rode at 9:1 or 10:1 scope if possible. In 30 feet of water with a 10:1 scope you'll need 350 feet of nylon, with a 5-foot freeboard forward.

When perusing charts to find maximum depth, remember that charted depths are at low tide, and that maximum depth should be calculated at high tide. In many places in the tropics the tides are nil, but in higher latitudes the tides can exceed 20 feet. Using our example and accounting for a 20-foot tide, the maximum feasible anchoring depth would be reduced to 65 feet.

Once you find length, you need to decide on number. Often (in coral for instance), multiple anchors are prudent. With multiple rodes, at least one should be long enough to place the second anchor from the boat. Here again, the key is flexibility. Three nylon rodes of 250 to 350 feet can be used on three different anchors or all on a single line, as needed. Two of these lines can be for the working anchor, but at least one should be a heavier line for storm conditions. A thimble should be spliced into both ends of the lines for easy connection; a splice is stronger than a knot and a shackle more secure. Shackle one end to the anchor chain or another line; shackle the bitter end to an eyebolt securely attached to the boat. It is helpful to have the rode marked every 10 feet to help calculate the amount of scope in use.

Additional chain should be stored in individual lengths of, say, 24 feet; these can be handled easily, stored low and amidships, and shackled together as needed. There is no need to have the entire storm anchor system always ready and stowed forward. The bulk and weight, especially if it is chain, can be prohibitive.

Rational Anchor Selection

There is a school of thought that says get the largest anchor you can handle. I say, why wrestle with a 45-pound anchor when 20 pounds will do the job most of the time. I prefer to go for variety rather than brute size. With several different anchor types and sizes, you have the flexibility to meet any situation.

To illustrate what I mean, on my own 43-foot boat I have a system composed of two ½-inch-diameter, 300-foot-long nylon rodes connected to 4 fathoms of ¼-inch chain for normal anchoring conditions; and two ¾-inch-diameter, 300-foot-long nylon rodes, along with three extra 6-fathom shots of 5/16-inch chain for off-normal conditions. This means I can string together 156 feet of chain and 1,200 feet of nylon before I need to go to the jib sheets and other small bits of line.

The anchors are a 20-, a 35- and a 45-pound Danforth, a 35-pound plow, and a 60-pound Luke. The 20-pound Danforth and the plow are used for normal anchoring and can be backed up by the 35-pound Danforth in heavier winds. The Luke is for difficult conditions in hard bottoms, large gravel, or cobbles where the other anchors will not penetrate. The 45-pound Deep-Set Danforth is the hurricane anchor and could be set in tandem under extreme storm conditions if necessary. Laying the 45-pound Danforth with 48 feet of chain and 300 feet of ¾-inch nylon line, and the 35-pound plow in front of the 35-pound Danforth on another similar rode at 90 degrees will hold in more weather than I would care to face.

ANCHORING TECHNIQUES

Proper anchoring starts with good manners, proceeds with an ordered, coordinated process, and finishes with an in-place test of the complete system to set the anchor properly. Anchors will work without being set or when set improperly, and *may* perform just as well as an anchor properly set. You'll sleep better, however, if you *know* it's properly set.

First a few words on good manners, which are essential because people generally cruise to relax. There is nothing relaxing about a shouting match, even if it's held in a beautiful, secluded spot.

There are very few laws written about anchoring and certainly no anchor patrol to enforce them, so a set of ethical rules have been established by general consent. The basic rule is, the first anchor down is the last anchor to move. As you approach an occupied anchorage, it is your responsibility to anchor your vessel in such a manner that it does not endanger any other vessel currently in the harbor. This rule applies to unoccupied moorings or buoyed anchors as well.

These unwritten laws place three responsibilities on the last boat to enter the anchorage. First, your anchor must not foul the anchor or rode of any system already in place. Second, your vessel must not be in a position to endanger any other vessel in the harbor. Third, if it is impossible to meet the first two conditions, you must leave and find another anchorage—which has significant ramifications. If the next harbor is several miles away the anchor may not go down for several more hours. You can avoid this by proper planning.

Plan to arrive at your anchorage early. How early depends on how many boats are cruising the area, but, in my opinion, anchoring should always be completed before sundown. A considerable portion of the anchoring process is visual, always easier in daylight.

Preparation

Preparing for anchoring begins with selecting the harbor. The harbor should protect the boat from both wind and waves as much as possible. While it is true that wind and waves generally come from the same direction, protection from one is no guarantee of protection from the other. For example, a sandbar or reef can afford protection against waves but leave the vessel exposed to the full force of the wind. Likewise, a small point or island can afford protection from the wind, but you may get considerable roll from the refraction of the waves around the land mass. The anchorage may be protected from wind waves but open to a nasty swell.

Select anchorages by examining charts and sailing directions. The more detailed the chart the better. Look for a harbor that is protected first from the conditions of the day and second from the seasonal conditions. In general, the more enclosed the harbor the better. The shape of the land surrounding the harbor is as important as the shape of the harbor itself. If possible, avoid harbors with deep valleys or high, steep-sided mountains. Deep valleys offer little protection from the wind, and may even funnel it, increasing its velocity. High, steep-sided mountains tend to catch high winds aloft and deflect them down their sides and into the harbor, producing violent squalls.

The suitability of the harbor also depends on the type and configuration of the bottom (see Table 4.3). The bottom material should be of a type that provides the most reliable holding and is free of possible debris and obstructions that can foul your anchor. Avoid areas with submerged cables; snagging one with your anchor can cause a variety of problems, the least of which is recovery of your anchor. You may be legally liable for the interruption of telephone or power to the shore-side residents. If it is power and you have an all-chain rode, you may be in for a rude and life-threatening shock as well.

The configuration of the bottom should afford a large enough area of the proper depth to anchor safely. The maximum area needed is twice the maximum length of the rode plus the length of the boat. This does not necessarily mean that you will anchor with a 7:1 scope, but you should always remember that conditions may change and require maximum scope. In such an emergency you will not want to have a conflict or collision with another vessel, rocks, or a reef.

There are two depths of importance: the depth of the anchor and the minimum depth in your swinging circle. Most people prefer to drop anchor in 15 to 35 feet of water. The selection of depth depends on the area's tides and the amount of anchor rode available. For example, if the boat has 300 feet of rode and the area has 12-foot tides, the maximum anchor depth at low tide should be limited to 30 feet. The formula for maximum preferred anchor depth (A_d) is total rode length (R_l) divided by 7 minus the tidal range (T), or

$$A_d = \frac{R_l}{7} - T \qquad\qquad \text{Eq 4.21}$$

The minimum depth in your potential swinging circle should be several feet greater than your draft to allow for errors in tidal predictions or the depth of a trough due to chop or an inconsiderate wake. I personally attempt to drop the anchor in 25 to 30 feet, although much depends on local conditions; in the Bahamas I have routinely anchored in depths of about 9 feet.

Remember that most charts record some sort of average low water. It is therefore possible to have less water than indicated by the chart at extreme low tides. Also, when you arrive at the harbor the tide may not be at the chart datum; your soundings will be generally greater than the charted low-water depths.

Other minor considerations in the selection of an anchorage concern the comfort of the occupants. For example, some minor considerations might be the beauty of the anchorage, the availability of shoreside attractions or seafood, and the lack of insects, wakes from passing boats, noise, or foul odors.

Once you've selected the anchorage you can select the gear. The bottom conditions dictate the type of anchor, the amount of protection dictates the size of the anchor, and the amount of room dictates the number of anchors. Any large changes to the anchoring system should be made before reaching the harbor.

Approach

Once inside the harbor, drop and secure all sails; a boat under engine power is considerably easier to control than one under sail. As the boat approaches the anchorage area, you will need to gather considerable information visually, best done during a slow, non-wake-producing tour around the desired anchorage. While the skipper cases the anchorage, a crewmember can be making ready the desired equipment. Things you'll need to know include, which way is the wind blowing? Is the desired spot already taken? If so, what is the next best spot? If not, are other boats in the area? If so, how close and what kind of boats? What kind, length, and number of rodes are they using? Are they lying to the current or to the wind? What is the strength of the wind and current? Are the depths satisfactory?

Given this information you can judge where best to drop the anchor. The information on depth is self-evident. The information on other boats is necessary because different boats react differently to conditions. Powerboats tend to be more affected by winds and sailboats more affected by tides, for example.

The kinds of rodes are important because chain rode under light conditions tends to hang straight down, keeping the boat from drifting. The length of rode is harder to assess. One can assume that those with chain rode are using 3:1 or less, because chain fans generally feel that they need less rode. Those using nylon generally have a scope anywhere between 3:1 and 5:1. Some idea of how much scope can be gathered from the angle nylon rodes make with the bow.

A boat with two rodes will not swing nearly as much as a boat with one; therefore, you will need to anchor with two rodes, or in such a manner that when conditions change your boat will swing away from the boat with double rodes. The more crowded the anchorage, the more information the skipper must analyze.

Once you process all the above information, select the optimum position for your boat and signal any changes in equipment to the crewmember on the foredeck. The best spot to drop anchor in a crowded anchorage often may be midway between two vessels or just off their sterns. This way you will not foul their anchors, and when you have reached the end of your scope you will be far away from them. In less crowded anchorages it is best to give other boats as much seclusion as possible.

The crew should have the proper anchor attached to the desired amount of rode, carefully flaked down on deck. Flaked anchor rode is a serious hazard with a reputation for taking along unwary crew when it runs rapidly overboard. Arrange the flaked rode so that it will not tangle any deck hardware or crew. Check all shackles, rig any buoys, and ensure that the bitter end is secured to the vessel. Just prior to deployment, make a final check to see that no lines are over the side and that the dinghy is snubbed close to the boat to prevent stray lines from tangling in the prop during maneuvering.

Deployment

Single Anchor

The simplest situation is the deployment of a single anchor. The skipper approaches the selected spot, moving either upwind or upcurrent depending on which controls the drift of the vessels at anchor. The crewperson readies the anchor by freeing it up and lowering it slightly so that it is above the water surface but free of the bow roller. The vessel proceeds slowly to the desired spot and stops. When the boat is dead in the water the skipper signals the anchor to be lowered and allows the boat to fall slowly back.

The crew on the foredeck, optionally equipped with tough gloves, rapidly pays out enough rode to put the anchor on the bottom. Note that this is not the same as dropping the anchor; rather, it is a controlled release of the anchor rode. This is the most difficult job for the crew; they must see that the anchor gets down quickly, taking care not to release so much rode so that chain piles on top of the anchor, which may prevent proper setting. The crewmember signals that the anchor is on the bottom, and the skipper notes the depth and signals the required rode length for setting; scope is calculated from anchor depth, not water under the boat.

With the anchor on the bottom, as the boat falls back either under the influence of the wind, current, or the engine, the crewmember slowly pays out the anchor rode, perhaps retarding the flow of rode slightly on occasion to straighten the chain and position the anchor. The skipper guides the boat backward in a straight line downwind or downcurrent until the proper amount of rode for setting the anchor is out.

It is here that 95 percent of anchoring problems occur. Partly due to improper backing but mostly due to insufficient scope, the anchor doesn't get set properly. Recall from the discussion of anchoring theory that more scope is needed to facilitate digging than is needed for holding. It is best to set all anchors, regardless of rode type and final scope, at a 9:1 or 10:1 scope, or maximum rode length. As the vessel backs down, the crewmember monitors the amount of rode over the side and secures the rode at the proper length.

The vessel now snubs up against the line and stretches it out to full length. Power is increased slightly to prevent rebound, and the skipper and crew then take a sight on a prominent shoreside feature perpendicular to their current position. The skipper slowly increases the throttle while they both watch the shoreside feature for relative movement. As the anchor digs in under the load the movement will eventually cease. If there is no relative movement under full throttle, your anchor is well set and you can look forward to a night of restful sleep. If the relative movement does not cease, you are dragging the anchor. You may sometimes drag the anchor for several tens of feet before it catches and holds. However, if the movement continues, you need to reset the anchor, set a larger or different type of anchor, or evaluate the expected loads to determine if a lower throttle setting will provide sufficient holding.

Once the anchor sets, the throttle can be slowly returned to zero and the engine turned off. Cutting the throttle too quickly may cause the boat to rebound rapidly in a crowded anchorage and strike a neighboring vessel, particularly if using nylon rode. Generally, with a nylon rode it is not necessary to power forward, as the rebound of the nylon will propel the boat forward, and the excess rode can be recovered to the desired scope for holding by simply taking in slack. Power can be used if necessary, but care should be taken not to overrun the rode and foul the prop.

The desired scope should be enough to provide a good night's sleep. If there is an abundance of room in an uncrowded anchorage that may be 5:1 or 7:1. However, in a small or crowded anchorage it is prudent to reduce the amount of scope as much as possible consistent with good holding. If possible, matching the scope used by others minimizes the possibility of contact.

Double Anchor

Although a secure method, using two anchors is far less common than it should be. Perhaps this is because a boat lying to two anchors stays in one place, while single-anchored boats wander all over the anchorage. This is fine as long as all boats wander together, but let in just one of those double-anchored boats and there goes the neighborhood. Not necessarily true.

In Figure 4.24, most boats in this crowded anchorage are swinging on one hook, sweeping out the circles indicated. The double crosshatched areas show where potential collisions can occur. The double-anchored boat at right takes up no more room, yet is held safely out of any double crosshatched areas. If everyone used two anchors, more boats could use a single anchorage and fewer collisions would occur. I know I would rather my neighbor use two anchors than come dragging down on top of me in the middle of the night.

Double anchors may be placed along or parallel to the direction of the wind or current, or placed perpendicular to or across the direction of the wind or current. Anchors generally are placed parallel to the current to prevent swinging, and across the current to increase holding power due to weak bottoms or severe winds. In either case it is of value to buoy the anchors, which will serve as a good reference to the anchor position during subsequent maneuvers needed to set the second anchor.

Sometimes known as a Bahamas moor, two anchors laid parallel to the wind and current, or a nearby obstruction, can produce great security in tight quarters. To set the anchors without using a dinghy you'll need at least twice as much rode on at least one of the anchors as you intend using when both anchors are set; in other words, if you're in 30 feet of water and you plan to ride to a 6:1 scope, or 180 feet of rode, you'll need 360 feet of rode on at least one of the anchors. Alternatively, you can temporarily shackle the two rodes together, but take care you don't lose the bitter end overboard.

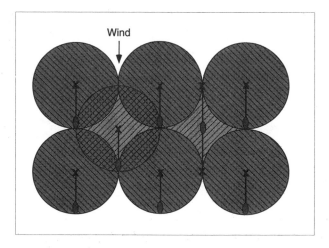

Figure 4.24 Harbor at Maximum Sensible Capacity

Set the first anchor exactly as described above, until the point where you would cut the engine. Instead, pay out rode until twice the finished rode length is over the side and taut, and lower the second anchor. Once it is on the bottom, put the engine in neutral and haul in the first rode until the second rode has reached a 10:1 scope or its maximum extension. The second anchor is now ready to be set.

Because you must be careful to avoid wrapping the first anchor's rode around the prop, many people do not adequately set the second anchor. That's okay if the second anchor is only used to prevent swinging and there is no chance the wind or current will reverse direction and place the primary load on anchor two, but if there is a chance the second anchor may take the load, it can be properly set by walking the rode of the first anchor to the stern of the boat, where a crewmember can keep it clear of the prop. Set the second anchor just as you would a single anchor.

Once the second anchor is set, take up its rode and pay out the first rode until the boat lies midway between the two anchors. Usually, both anchor lines are taken to the bow, which allows the boat to swing to the wind or current and minimizes rolling. However, one of the rodes can contact the hull or keel, or worse, tangle around the other rode or another part of the boat such as the rudder or prop. This can be prevented by letting out a small amount of additional rode, allowing the slack rode to drop below the hull.

Sometimes it is desirable to take the second rode to the stern, generally in sheltered waters with limited room to swing; because this prevents the boat from swinging with the wind or current, it is feasible only where seas or winds from abeam are not expected.

Anchors may be set perpendicular to the current or wind direction in special cases where holding is poor or where storm conditions are expected. Using two rodes keeps the head of the boat into the wind, which reduces wind loads by 20 percent. It also alters the resulting load on the two anchors, depending on the angle between the rodes. Table 4.15 shows the amount of alteration as a function of rode angle.

Above 120 degrees, load reduction rapidly approaches zero. Somewhere between 120 and 150 degrees the load on the double rodes becomes larger than would occur on a single rode. For example, the rode tension at 150 degrees is 1.5 times that of a single rode. The length factor is the distance between the anchors divided by the rode length.

The 178-degree entry is just for illustration purpose and has no practical usage. It can be seen from this table that the Bahamas moor (±178°) places very large loads (23 times greater) on the anchor system if the wind shifts perpendicular to the trend of the anchors and the angle can be held—a remote possibility. A nylon

Angle	Length Factor	Change in Load
178°	–	23.0
150°	2.0	1.5
120°	1.75	.80
90°	1.5	.56
60°	1.0	.46
45°	.75	.43
30°	.5	.41

Table 4.15 Rode Angles

rode subjected to this kind of load would stretch and the angle would decrease; a reduction of only a couple of degrees would reduce the load by half. Chain rode under the same circumstances would probably drag an anchor far enough to reduce the angle the same few degrees. Yet, even at half, the loads are extreme.

In order for the two-anchor system to provide extra security during a storm, the angle between the rodes must remain small. Sixty degrees is a good angle for this purpose. Decreasing the angle below 60 degrees provides very little extra load reduction (0.05 percent), and reduces the ability of the two rodes to keep the boat head-on to the wind.

To set two anchors perpendicular to the current or wind, place the first as described above (using maximum scope if storm conditions are expected), put the engine in neutral, and take in rode until it is at the desired length factor given in Table 4.14. For example, if the desired angle is 90 degrees, the first rode is taken in until its length is 1.5 times as long as the desired length of finished rode.

Put the engine into gear and turn the boat to take an angle of about 60 degrees to the anchor rode; maintaining this angle under low power will slowly rotate the rode about the first anchor. When you reach a point opposite and perpendicular to the wind, let go the second anchor.

At an angle of about 120 degrees from the first rode, slowly back down and away from both anchors until reaching a 10:1 or maximum scope on the second rode, then snub it off and set the anchor. Once it has been properly set, shut down the engine and adjust the two rodes until the desired scope is reached and the angle between the rodes is about 90 degrees.

Setting an Anchor with the Dinghy

Maneuvering in reverse to set the anchors in the normal manner is difficult, and for many boats next to impossible. One way to avoid the embarrassment of wandering all over the anchorage is to place the second anchor with the dinghy. Once the anchor is placed, back down with the boat to set the anchor.

The preferred procedure is to transfer the anchor and nylon rode to the dinghy, taking as much care as possible in stowing the anchor and line to ensure a smooth process. The first thing that goes into the dinghy will be the last thing that comes out. Pass the bitter end of the rode to the crewmember in the dinghy, who firmly secures it. Coil the remaining line neatly on the bottom of the dinghy, in either the bow or the stern, whichever is most convenient. The line is followed by the chain, the anchor, and then any anchor buoy.

The dinghy now moves to the desired anchor position—often not a trivial undertaking. Without the first rode to assist in locating the proper position, the dinghy crew must make the judgment totally by eye. Once at the desired location, remaining there while dropping the anchor can be complicated by wind, current, or chop.

When the proper position is located, put the anchor buoy over the side, followed by the anchor and sufficient rode to reach the bottom. I prefer to do this from a standing or kneeling position over the stern of the dinghy, although, depending on the dinghy, this may not be the most stable situation. With the anchor on the bottom, the next task is to prevent the chain from piling on top of the anchor as you return to the boat.

When using an outboard, I find it easier to lead the line over the bow and to back away from the anchor while applying a small load to the anchor line. With oars it is best to lead the line over the stern and apply load to the line with one foot as you row away from the anchor. Once the chain has stretched out, take the bitter end back to the boat. With the bitter end aboard and secured, back down on the second anchor to set it, shut down the engine, and adjust both rodes to their desired scopes.

Another way to use the dinghy in setting an anchor is to put the anchor and chain in the dinghy first, with the bitter end of the rode remaining attached to the boat. As the dinghy proceeds to the anchor location, line is payed out by a crewmember on board or by the dinghy operator, depending on whether the line is left aboard or put in the dinghy. This common procedure has two faults, however. First, the drag of the trailing anchor line makes travel much more difficult because the weight of the rode pulls the dinghy back toward the boat. Second, when the anchor is launched from the dinghy it does not go straight down, moving instead toward the boat and resulting in the loss of considerable scope—from my experience, generally about 1 to 1.5 times the depth of the water. This method does have the advantage of speed, however, which can be significant if the anchor is to be used as a kedge in case of unintentional grounding. (See Chapter 5.)

Special Cases

Many times while cruising, and especially when gunkholing, a second anchor can be replaced by a line ashore to keep the boat from swinging aground. In several instances I have had two lines ashore and no anchors down. Popular methods in narrow coves are lines tied to a tree, or dropping the anchor behind some rocks on shore.

Less well known is a device called a rock nut, developed for rock climbing (see Figure 4.25). Once set, these small, light devices provide an amazing amount of holding power. I carry several varieties and sizes and have used them successfully on many occasions. They are simply slipped into a crack or crevice in a rock; any pull then jams the rock anchor in place.

Another special case is the use of two anchors on a single rode. Not only will the holding power increase because both anchors will have to drag before the boat moves, but the anchor closest to the boat guarantees that the pull on the anchor farthest from the boat is always horizontal. The advantages of this system leads to its consideration for anchoring in heavy weather.[34] The shank of one anchor is shackled to the crown of the other with a length of chain, which is, if possible, slightly longer than the water depth. This will allow the first anchor to be set properly and brought back aboard without needing to break out the second anchor.

To set the anchors, buoy the first anchor and use the normal procedure to set it, using the extra length of chain and the maximum length of rode. Then retrieve the rode carefully to the point where the chain is shackled to the nylon rode, unshackle the chain from the nylon rode, and attach the chain to the second anchor.

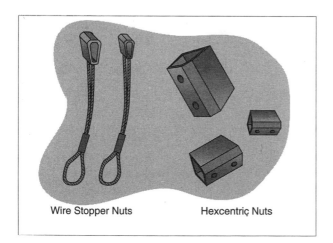

Wire Stopper Nuts   Hexcentric Nuts

Figure 4.25 Rock-Climbing Anchors

[34] *John Mellor, "Proper Anchoring Methods,"* Sail Magazine *(April 1976), 68.*

Reshackle the nylon rode to the chain of the second anchor. Using the buoy as a guide, place the second anchor on the bottom in line with the desired direction of pull and slightly less than the water depth, if possible. Setting the second anchor with maximum rode is best.

It is obvious that during setting both of the anchors will not set completely; the one that digs the fastest will stop the setting of the other. The slow-setting anchor will have to wait until storm loads drag the fast-setting anchor before it can dig enough to develop its full power. As the loads increase, eventually both anchors will reach their ultimate strength. There seems to be no clear argument as to the best arrangement of anchors. I prefer the largest anchor farthest from the boat; this way the forward anchor, even if it is pulled free of the bottom, will still act as a sentinel to keep the remaining rode pulling horizontal on the large anchor.

Retrieval

Retrieving a single anchor begins in most instances by starting the engine and letting it warm up so that when power is needed there is less chance the engine will die at an inappropriate moment.

If the winds are light, the rode can be retrieved slowly. Pacing the retrieval with the forward motion of the boat makes for the least amount of work in getting the rode back aboard. If the winds are not light, then the motor must be used to move the boat toward the anchor, pacing boat speed to the retrieval of the rode.

The helmsperson keeps the boat at the correct speed and heading, directly toward the anchor. The crew on the foredeck can assist this process with hand signals: left, right, slow down, or speed up. The alert helmsperson will anticipate the foredeck crew's needs. Good teamwork on anchor retrieval has prevented many a divorce.

When the rode is vertical the foredeck crew snubs the rode securely. In light conditions, it is time for a second cup of coffee; a short wait will allow the motion of the boat to break the anchor free. The remaining rode and the anchor are then hauled aboard, cleaned, and stowed.

If conditions are not light, the motion of the boat will generally free the anchor much sooner. If this does not occur fast enough to suit you, the engine can be brought into play to help break it out. If this still doesn't free your anchor, chances are it has fouled on an underwater obstruction.

Fouled Anchor Recovery

Recovering a fouled anchor is a combination of foresight, correct tactics, and good luck. If you have had the foresight to attach a stout line to the crown of your anchor, it can be retrieved by hauling on this line. Move the boat to the side of the anchor opposite the original trend of the rode, as far as the length of the buoy line will allow. A pull on the buoy line at this point will pull the anchor backward, out and away from the obstruction.

If you didn't attach a crown line, try brute force. On a sailboat, run the anchor line to your largest winch, which is usually considerably more powerful than most anchor windlasses, and use its added power to haul the mess to the surface. Power-boats, unfortunately, have no such handy device.

The court of last resort is to form a small loop with about 1.5 feet of chain, place it around the anchor rode, and attach it to a stout line. Lower the line down the taut anchor rode and try to slip it over the shank and up to the crown of the fouled anchor. This is sometimes more easily done from the dinghy, where the line can be approached more easily from different directions. If the fishing process is successful, slacken the anchor line and maneuver the boat to the side of the anchor opposite the direction from which it was set. Hauling on the line may now pull the anchor backward and free of the obstruction.

If good luck was not with you, your only recourse is to dive on the anchor. This is easy if scuba gear is present; however, with a mask and snorkel even a moderately skilled free diver can reach an anchor in 25 feet of water by using the rode to assist the descent. It may take a few tries to coordinate the clearing of the ears with the descent, but 5 or 10 seconds on the bottom may be all that it takes to free the anchor. If the anchor is deeper and scuba gear is not present, it is a question of economics: is it cheaper to hire a diver or buy a replacement anchor?

Recovery of Multiple Anchors

Multiple anchors are recovered in essentially the same fashion as a single anchor; the only difference is in selecting the first anchor to recover and maneuvering the rode over the anchor so that the pull on it is vertical enough to break it loose. The first anchor to recover is the one with the least load or the one closest to any obstructions. Remember, once one anchor is up the boat is free to swing on the remaining anchor, and in most instances with additional rode.

To get over the first anchor, the rode on the other anchor must be adjusted. If there is insufficient rode, it may be necessary to retrieve that anchor with the dinghy, normally by pulling the dinghy to the anchor along the rode. As the rode comes in over the transom, the upward force is generally sufficient to break it loose. The anchor is hauled into the dinghy and the crew hauls in the rode, dinghy, and anchor. If for some reason the first anchor cannot be broken loose, the rode can be freed from the boat, coiled neatly, and buoyed. The dinghy can then return to the vessel while it retrieves the remaining anchor. Once this anchor is safely aboard, the boat returns to the buoyed anchor and retrieves it as described above.

MOORING

A mooring is a permanent anchoring system attached to a float. Since the system need not be portable, all of its parts can be oversized. The anchor is often a huge concrete block connected to the surface by oversized chain, which allows scope to be reduced to around 2.5:1, allowing more boats to use less space. The oversized parts lead many people to believe that mooring is more secure than anchoring. It is certainly easier, but it is not necessarily more secure, for two reasons: One, because the system is too large to be hauled conveniently, it remains constantly underwater, rarely inspected and maintained. Oversized components will resist corrosion for a while, but eventually the chain and shackles will fail.

The second and most important reason can be understood by referring back to the first part of this chapter, where the elasticity of short, all-chain systems was discussed. With any kind of sea running, the boat will continually come up hard against its mooring, imposing tremendous forces on all parts of the system. Since every part of the mooring system except the boat is oversized, that's where the failure will be. If forced to lie to a mooring in a major storm unprotected from the seas, adding a couple of hundred feet of nylon line adequately protected from chafe will increase the chances for survival.

Installing a Mooring

When installing a mooring, much of what has been learned about wind and anchors can serve as a guide. Much attention has been paid to the anchor; however, given the variability of the strength of bottom material, what will work in any given situation is still a matter of trial and error. As it turns out, holding power may not be that important. For example, Table 4.11 shows that a 15-knot wind will exert only 200 pounds of load, but Table 2.1 shows that the same 15-knot wind can develop a 5-foot wave. A 5-foot wave on an all-chain rode can make a shallow mooring untenable. In many instances it is not the power of the wind that controls, but the power of the waves.

If an area protected from large waves cannot be found, elasticity must be built into the system if it is to be used during heavy weather. Once the site has been selected, it is possible to perform an anchor load test by setting the boat's normal anchor. If the bottom is soft, it may be best to install a burying-type anchor, such as the mushroom, or something that will sink deep into the mud. If the holding is good, it may be best to use multiple conventional anchors.

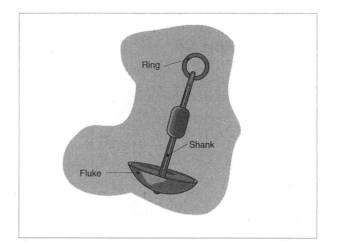

Figure 4.26 A Typical
Mushroom Anchor

The traditional form of private mooring utilizes a mushroom anchor. (See Figure 4.26.) These anchors come in various weights from 125 pounds to 550 pounds, suitable for boats ranging from 25 to 55 feet in length. Mushroom anchors require time to set properly. They must have enough weight to slowly sink into the bottom material and completely bury the circular fluke. The larger the circular fluke and the deeper it is buried, the stronger the anchor and the longer the time required for proper setting. The weaker the bottom material the quicker and deeper the anchor will bury itself. Many yacht clubs that require moorings also provide minimum requirements for the mooring components. These specifications are generally based on local experience and err on the side of safety, since the club has accepted some liability by making the recommendations.

The typical mooring system consists of the mushroom anchor with a heavy chain, ¾ to 1 inch in diameter, running from the anchor to a swivel shackle on the bottom; from the swivel shackle a lighter chain, 7/16 to 9/16 inch in diameter, connects to the mooring buoy. The mooring buoy or float can be of almost any design that will pass the load directly through the buoy to the mooring eye with a rod or chain. The buoy must hold the eye above the water, not damage the hull of a boat that hits the buoy, and be marked in accordance with any federal, state, or local laws.

Sometimes a 10- to 15-foot nylon pendant is attached to the mooring eye of the buoy and the free end to a float or a man-overboard pole. This makes picking up the pendant and attaching the boat to the buoy much easier. I recommend ½-inch line to provide the necessary elasticity, and vigilance to prevent chafing. The pendant is entirely above the water and can be inspected regularly for wear or abrasion.

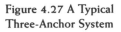

Figure 4.27 A Typical
Three-Anchor System

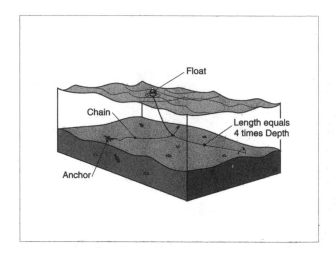

When conventional lightweight anchors are used as a mooring, they are deployed in a radial pattern—three anchors set 120 degrees apart, as shown in Figure 4.27. The advantage of this system is that the distance from the pivot point to the anchor can be increased to four times the water depth for added scope and increased holding power; and since the swivel point remains fixed, the density of moored vessels can be increased. However, since elasticity of a chain system is dependent upon water depth, this added chain does very little to increase the elasticity and hence the ultimate safety of the system.

This system is much more complex to install properly compared to the mushroom anchor, which can just be chucked over the side. To be most effective, the anchors must be laid out and set in the intended pattern, which is not easily done from a boat; each anchor must be temporarily buoyed. Set each anchor in turn from the stern of the boat and pull forward with maximum scope and engine power to dig it in as far as possible. Attach the swivel and light chain to the buoy and set it in its desired location. Set the second and third anchors in a similar manner. The second anchor can be attached to the buoy and the buoy repositioned easily, but the third may require a diver to make the final attachment underwater, or a slightly longer primary chain so that it will reach the swivel. The third anchor should be positioned so that it lies in the direction of the lightest and least frequent winds. This system properly set is much stronger than the traditional mushroom anchor system. There have been reports that two of these systems held the only two boats to survive a hurricane.[35]

[35]Chapman, 255.

Using a Mooring

Using a mooring requires coming alongside the buoy, attaching the mooring line to the buoy and then to the boat. The process is in some ways easier and in some ways more difficult than docking. It is easier in that overrunning the buoy causes much less damage than overrunning a dock. It is more difficult because the buoy is small and is out of the helmsperson's sight at the critical moment. Picking up a buoy without a mooring pendent attached is more difficult.

Approach the buoy heading upwind and upcurrent. As the boat approaches the buoy, the crew must constantly indicate its relative position to the helmsperson. Hand signals for left, right, speed up, slow down, and stop are helpful during this operation. It is not necessary to pick up the buoy over the bow. I prefer to pick it up amidships, where the freeboard is lower, and walk the mooring line forward. It may be easier for powerboats to back into the buoy.

Once the buoy has been captured, the crewperson runs a line from the boat through the eye and back to the boat. This operation must be done quickly, because it is difficult for even a hefty crewperson to hold a boat for more than a few seconds in adverse conditions. Many people capture the buoy with a boathook, and there are commercial devices available for quickly attaching mooring lines to a buoy. I prefer to have the crew attach a 50-foot line to a cleat forward, and as the boat comes to the buoy pass the free end through the ring on the buoy. If they cannot easily reach the buoy, the helmsperson has missed the mark and needs to come around again.

When the line is through the eye, the free end can be walked forward to the bow as the boat falls back on the wind, then secured to the other bow cleat. This continuous line serves two purposes. First, it is easy to cast off, and second, if attached on either side of the bow, the boat will lie to the buoy with much less charging from side to side. If conditions are rough or the boat is to be left unattended, the mooring line should be protected against chafe where it passes through the eye of the buoy, or against any sharp or rough objects on the boat, such as bobstays or chocks.

5

COMMON EMERGENCIES

PLANNING, JUDGMENT, AND PROBABILITY

Almost everyone knows somebody who is accident prone, but is this just bad luck? I don't think so. Most "accidents" are the result of bad planning, poor judgment, or failing to think. Not much can be done about poor judgment, but something can be done about bad planning and failing to think. Few people would fly an airplane without proper training, but a lot of people go boating with no training at all.

Training includes not just the skipper, but the crew as well. For example, consider the traditional "Mom and Pop" boating team (Pop handling the boat and Mom handling the galley). If Pop goes over the side, can Mom handle the boat well enough to come back and get him? Good judgment says that training the crew is good planning.

Once you acquire basic knowledge, you must practice to perfect and retain your skills. Routine operations like docking and sail handling are practiced continually. Nonroutine, safety-oriented practices are a different story. Almost no recreational boater I know has ever performed a fire drill or a man-overboard drill, although we're encouraged to perform them on a regular basis. This clears the conscience of the author or instructor, but does little to help the boater who still finds ways to postpone practicing the drills.

Some things can be done short of an actual drill. Talk is cheap, consumes little time, and attracts little attention. Take a little time to talk about fire on board, people lost overboard, and other common emergencies. It can be done at lunch, over a cocktail, or anytime the crew is gathered and there is a lull in activity. Detailed discussion will encourage each crewmember to think about emergency procedures ahead of time. Thinking fast is a myth. Show me a person who thinks fast and I'll show you a person who has thought the situation through beforehand.

Use incidents of opportunity to practice. For example, many of the skills needed to return and pick up a lost hat are the same as those used for returning and picking up a person who has fallen overboard. After the event, critique the procedure and point out similarities and differences.

A Float Plan

Forethought is very close to but not the same as good planning, which becomes more important as the length of the voyage increases. The length of the trip that requires planning is left to the discretion of the skipper; however, on any extended trip covering a few hundred miles and lasting a week or more, it is a good idea to prepare a float plan. The plan should include a description of the boat—hull type, color, length, registration number, and name—and a list of the radio types and frequencies available. This information is needed by the Coast Guard if a search or rescue operation becomes necessary. Record, too, the name, age, and telephone number of each person aboard, and a person to contact in case of emergency. A form can be made up with this information to save writing it repeatedly. (Figure 5.1.)

The float plan should provide an itinerary with planned departure and arrival times for all destinations. The value of this plan, which should be left with a reliable person, is twofold. First, it provides a guide for those ashore who may need to locate an overdue boat or reach you because of a shoreside emergency. Second, developing the itinerary familiarizes the skipper with the route, forewarns of potential dangers, and provides some control over proposed stops for customs, food, fuel, laundry, and showers, as well as critical slack-water times at tidal rapids or bar crossings.

Figure 5.1 Typical Float Plan

Float Plan

Hull Type ______	Hull Color ______	Hull Material ______	Make ______
Length ______	Boat Name ______	Boat Number ______	Captain ______
Contact ______	Phone number ______	VHF Radio ______	EPRIB PIN ______

Crew and Guests	Phone number	Crew and Guests	Phone number	Crew and Guests	Phone number

Date	Place	Time	Remarks
Sunday August 3	Hole in the Wall	1800 hrs	
Monday August 4	Dent Rapids	0830 hrs	Slack Tide
	Forward Harbor	1700 hrs	
Tuesday August 5			Groceries and Shower

Emergency Equipment

Some emergency equipment, such as fire extinguishers, visual distress signals, and flotation devices, is required by law (see Chapter 1); other equipment is optional. The challenge is to make appropriate selections so you don't find yourself with boatloads of gear that may never be used. A proper assessment depends on the probability of encountering a particular emergency, the severity of the consequences of the emergency, the size of the boat, and the activities and areas in which the boat is to be used. Individual pieces of equipment should be analyzed as to ease of use, required maintenance, and whether each will perform the intended function.

Emergency Use of the Radio

When danger threatens and immediate help is required, the radio can be used to transmit an emergency call. The procedure is to transmit on the calling frequency the word "Mayday" or "Pan-Pan" repeated three times. Mayday is used for life-threatening emergencies *only*, and Pan-Pan for all other grave and imminent emergencies. Either should silence all other radio traffic and give the emergency traffic priority. The procedure for an emergency call is given in Chapter 7.

UNINTENTIONAL GROUNDING

Unintentional grounding can be a nuisance or an emergency, depending on such circumstances as boat speed, firmness of the bottom, sea state, and state of the tide. In flat, calm water with a rising tide, hitting a soft mud bottom when going very slowly is hardly even an inconvenience. The situation can be corrected by simply putting the engine in reverse, backing off the bottom, and altering course. If the boat cannot be backed, you need only look casual while waiting for the tide to rise and the boat to float free.

In more severe situations prompt action is essential. The first thing to assess is whether the hull has been ruptured. If it has, you must control the water flow before attempting to free the boat from the bottom. Handling the flow of water and repairing the leak is covered later in this chapter. Here the concern is with one of the four ways to get off the bottom: use engine power, be pulled off by another boat, kedge off, or float off on an incoming tide. The easiest is backing off and the surest is kedging. If a short burst of reverse power does not free the boat and kedging is a viable option, immediately begin the kedging operation.

Using Engine Power

Because of its simplicity, backing off should always be tried briefly before alternative methods. If waves or wakes are present, apply the power concurrently with the arrival of the wave peak. If a short burst of full power in reverse does not move the boat, cut the engine power and make a more detailed assessment of the situation. Continued use of reverse power, especially in powerboats, may wash silt and sand around the hull, making the situation worse or blocking the engine intake lines. Sailboats, because of their deep keels and the placement of the propeller, are not as prone to this problem.

If you're unable to back off, reduce the boat's draft by jettisoning or repositioning ballast or by relocating crew. A sailboat can sometimes be heeled over sufficiently to free the keel from the bottom by putting the heaviest crewmembers on the boom or the spinnaker pole and swinging them out over the water, or by pulling on a halyard that runs from the top of the mast to a position a couple of mast heights away from the side of the boat. Sails should not be used to heel the boat unless the wind is blowing away from the shallow water, or the boat may be driven farther onto the bank or reef.

Powerboats usually have more draft aft than at the bow. If this is the case it may be possible to transfer enough weight forward to free the stern. If these alternatives fail the boat must be lightened by whatever method is available. Concentrate on heavy gear. Pump fresh water overboard. If the anchor cannot be used as a kedge, buoy it along with its chain, then jettison it. If the water is warm or a dinghy is available, having the crew go over the side can remove 100 to 200 pounds per person. Be careful when using the engine with crewmembers in the water: be sure they are all well clear of the propeller and its wash.

If another short burst in reverse fails to move the boat, it may be possible to turn the boat so that forward gear can be used. Most propellers have considerably more power in forward than in reverse, and any loose material is moved away from the boat rather than under it so the engine can be used continuously. Turning the boat requires that force be applied to the hull from off the boat, generally by kedge or towline. The value of turning a boat has always seemed limited to me. The amount of force required to turn a boat always seems greater than that needed to pull it off backwards.

Pulling off

If you opt for an external pull, the surest method is to pass a line or lines to an anchored sailboat that can use winch power rather than engine power. Being towed off by another recreational boat under engine power is only slightly more likely to work than powering off under your stranded vessel's own power. Recreational props are designed for a combination of speed and power. The faster the boat's top speed the less its pulling power. The general guidelines for towing a boat are described later in this chapter, in the section on towing.

If there is a wind or current broadside to the direction of pull, it may be necessary to attach the towline on the windward side of the boat doing the pulling, or to pull at an angle, in order for that boat to maintain steerage control. If the boat is pulled free, the stored energy in the line may cause the towed boat to surge forward; be careful that the towing line does not become slack and entangle the prop of either vessel.

Kedging

Kedging is the process of moving a boat using an anchor. In addition to the anchor you'll need a dinghy, a suitable length of nylon rode (chain is too heavy to handle from the dinghy), and a winch to apply power to the anchor line. The dinghy is needed to carry the anchor and rode into position. It may be possible in an emergency to swim the anchor into position, using a fender to float the anchor. Sailboats have a distinct advantage over powerboats when kedging due to their large winches for handling sails.

Most people can generate about 2,000 pounds of pull on a large sheet winch and 1,500 pounds on a medium-size winch. If necessary, a second or third anchor can be placed, and 4,000 to 5,000 pounds of pull can be brought to bear on freeing the vessel even without using the engine. If the holding is good, a block and tackle can be put into the system, increasing the pull on each anchor to between 6,000 and 8,000 pounds. If the winches don't pull out, there is a whopping 24,000 pounds available. A typical boat engine and prop will supply only between 1,000 and 2,000 pounds.

An anchor windlass is a poor substitute for a large winch. Windlasses are designed to recover anchor line quickly, and the maximum loads they can sustain are much lower. Unlike winches, which hold the load indefinitely, an electric or hydraulic windlass consumes large amounts of power when sustaining maximum loads. This will eventually damage the windlass.

The first decision involved in kedging is where to put the anchor. This depends on the location of deep water and how badly the engine is needed to assist in freeing the boat. If the engine is not needed, the best direction is normally opposite to the direction the boat was originally traveling, or backward. If the engine is needed, then you must turn the boat to bring the engine thrust in line with the best route to deep water. Turning the boat will require the placement of the anchor

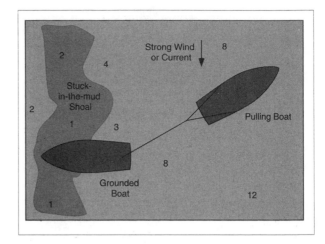

Figure 5.2 Towing a
Grounded Boat

at 90 degrees to the axis of the boat. The turning moment is greatest in this position and drops off with the cosine of the angle. Once the boat has been turned through an angle of approximately 25 degrees, the load on the line drops about 10 percent, and the anchor should be reset perpendicular to the new position of the boat.

When you've chosen the direction, position the anchor by placing it and any short chain portion of the rode in the dinghy. As the dinghy moves away the crew on board the main vessel pays out the nylon line. The anchor is taken as far away from the boat as the rode will allow in the desired direction of the pull and dropped overboard. The finesse with which this is accomplished is not as important as the speed. If the tide is falling and the boat is in an area with a large tide, 1 minute of delay can mean as much as ½ inch less water.

Once the anchor is in place, the crewmember on board takes the anchor rode to a primary winch. To get a fair lead to the winch it may be necessary to pass the bitter end of the rode through some turning blocks. Once the rode is properly rigged the crew can haul on the line while the dinghy returns for the second anchor. Repeat the process until you are satisfied with the results. It is truly amazing the load that can be moved with only a couple of anchors and winches.

Floating Free

If no other alternatives are available and the helmsperson was far-sighted enough to run aground at a time other than maximum high tide, and in an area with no surf, the solution is to let nature float the boat free on the next high tide. The area around the boat should be surveyed and the boat made to heel toward the side that will provide the softest bed. If the choice is about equal, heel the boat toward the shallow water; this will give her less heel. You can make the boat heel in the desired direction by positioning an anchor on that side and snugging up on the line.

Close all hatches to keep water out, stow all loose objects, and lighten the boat using any of the methods described earlier. Large stones and sharp objects should be removed from the area if possible. Depending on the conditions, it may be necessary to place boat cushions, fenders, inflatable dinghy, or whatever padding is available, to reduce damage to the hull from pounding on sharp rocks. If no sharp objects or waves are present, all you need do is secure items in the interior against displacement. Grounded powerboats finally have an advantage over grounded sailboats in that their angle of heel is nowhere near as severe. All that's left to do is to try to look casual. You might as well take advantage of the opportunity and check the through-hulls and bottom paint as they become exposed. Who knows—maybe you can pass it off as an intentional grounding.

If a surf is running the situation is much more serious. Heavy surf can destroy a boat in a few hours. It is important to minimize pounding by keeping the stern or bow pointed into the surf. In light surf it may be possible to set an anchor to keep the boat from turning broadside to the surf. In desperate situations, it may be necessary to flood the boat to stop the pounding. Open a through-hull and flood the interior until the vessel settles down. This will save the integrity of the hull. Once that is done, the salvage operation becomes a major effort. Recover as much equipment as possible, call your insurance company, and hope for a moderation in conditions. If conditions moderate so that pounding is no longer a problem, the boat can be pumped dry and refloated using one of the methods described above.

Once the boat is afloat again, inspect the rudder, check the engine intakes for mud and the bilge for water, and clean up the mess. If the boat hit hard or took any pounding, it may be necessary to go over the side with mask and snorkel to check the rudder, hull, and keel for damage. If the boat has external ballast, be sure the keel bolts were not damaged. Continue to check the bilge for several hours; a leak may be slow in developing.

LEAKS

Good navigation will prevent leaks caused by striking coral heads or rocks or by grounding. Vigilance will prevent leaks caused by striking flotsam and dead-heads (large water-saturated logs that float almost completely submerged).

Leaks caused by equipment failure can be reduced by proper maintenance, most notably of through-hull fittings. These fittings, usually bronze, penetrate the hull, normally for discharging or taking in water. Through-hulls should be backed up with an operational seacock, and the hose attached to the seacock should have double hose clamps. On occasion, through-hulls are used to house instrument sensors, such as paddlewheels for speed indicators or transponders for depth indicators. These should have a plug nearby to replace the instrument if it is damaged or removed.

It is important to inspect through-hulls, valves, and hose connections at each haulout. On the outside check for adequate zincs and any sign of electrolysis; on the inside keep the seacocks in smooth working order and check for hose or hose clamp wear. This is sometimes not an easy task because of their location, but the process reduces the chances that the system will fail and at the same time familiarizes the crew with their location in case they do fail. Through-hull preventive maintenance is discussed more fully in Chapter 10.

The Physics of a Leak

Before dealing with water inflow directly it helps to understand a little of the physics that controls the process. Flow varies with depth (see Figure 5.3). The quantity of water entering a boat through a hole in its hull can be found using the following equation:

$$Q = A \sqrt{2gh} \qquad\qquad \textbf{Eq 5.1}$$

Using this equation, where (g) is the gravitational constant, and assuming the area of flow is generally circular, then the area of flow (A) is equal to the diameter of the hole (D) squared multiplied by pi and divided by four.

$$Q = \frac{\pi D^2 \sqrt{2gh}}{4} \qquad\qquad \textbf{Eq 5.2}$$

or

$$Q = 19.6 \times D^2 \sqrt{h} \qquad\qquad \textbf{Eq 5.3}$$

where   Q is flow in gallons per minute,
D is through-hull diameter in inches, and
h is the depth from the water surface to the through-hull in feet.

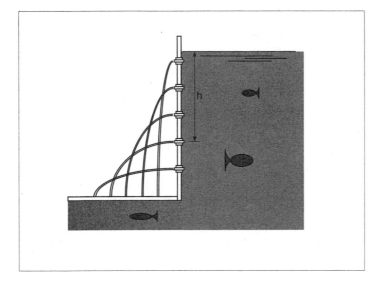

Figure 5.3 Flow Varies
with Depth

Using this equation, we can calculate the consequences of the failure of through-hull fittings. For example, the flow through a 1.5-inch diameter hole 6 inches below the waterline will produce about 31 gallons per minute (gpm). Flow through the same hole 4 feet below the waterline will produce 88 gallons per minute. One can see from this the advantage of locating through-hulls nearer the water surface.

Pumps

Compare this volume with the capacity of the largest bilge pumps commercially available, which can handle about 65 gallons a minute (drawing 20 amps of power)—not enough to handle the inflow from a typical through-hull failure. A modest 3-inch hole 4 feet below the surface will admit a whopping 350 gallons of water per minute into the boat.

Five maximum-capacity bilge pumps could handle this flow, but how long could the batteries or the alternator take the 100-amp draw? And 3 inches isn't much of a hole. Double it to 6 inches and the flow quadruples to 1,400 gallons per minute. A pump of this capacity, with a small gasoline engine, takes up 10 or 12 cubic feet and weighs well over 50 pounds. Most recreational boats do not have the space for a rarely used piece of equipment of this size.

The Coast Guard has larger-capacity pumps that can be dropped in floating containers to boats that need them—if the boat is afloat long enough for them to arrive. For example, a 40-foot boat with 4 feet of freeboard taking on 1,400 gallons a minute will stay afloat less than 10 minutes.

Using the engine cooling water pump to help keep the bilge free of water is often recommended. While this sounds like a good idea, in practice setting up the engine to pump bilge water takes valuable time from the process of locating and stemming the leak. Once the system is operating, additional time is required to keep the intake screen free of debris and monitor the water level. The last thing one needs while trying to fix a leak is an overheated or frozen engine because of insufficient cooling water. Most sailboat engines still only pump about 60 gallons a minute; although large powerboat diesels may pump many times that, few will pump the required 500 to 600 gpm.

The message: Don't depend on pumps to keep a severely damaged boat afloat. Bilge pumps are not meant for damage control; they are a convenience for packing-gland leakage and small spills. If a boat is holed the only way it will stay afloat is if you plug the hole and plug it quickly. Pumps come into play only after the inflow has been reduced to a point where they can handle residual flow.

The Basics of Leak Management

If a leak does develop in the hull you are not necessarily defenseless, nor are you inevitably going to the bottom. Once again, a little forethought and planning will help, so run through in your mind the steps to take when a leak develops in the hull:

- stop the boat
- locate the leak
- stop or slow the flow
- remove and regulate the water with the pumps
- repair the hole

The variables are the leak's size, shape, and location, how soon it is discovered, and the proximity of the boat to shallow water.

Locating the Leak

How the leak is generated determines the method to use in locating it. If the leak begins with no warning—without a sound or impact—it is probably a failed through-hull. If you are alone, locate the leak immediately; if you have crew, start pumping and locating the leak simultaneously. Lift the floorboards to determine the direction from which water is entering the bilge. If you know the direction of flow, you can reduce the number of through-hulls you'll have to check. The amount of flow can give clues to the type of failure. Large flow generally means complete failure of the through-hull or hose. Small flow indicates a crack around the through-hull or a small tear in the hose. If the water level is already too high to determine the direction and quantity of the flow into the boat, check all the through-hulls systematically, starting in the area with the most through-hulls.

If there has been an impact and you know where the boat sustained it, locating the hole is generally easier, as it will be confined to that area. If you don't know the location of the impact, you are faced with a more difficult task than finding a broken through-hull, because any portion of the hull might be leaking. The method used to search for the hole depends on the inflow.

If the flow is small, finding the hole is less urgent and can be accomplished from inside the boat, using essentially the same system as for finding a ruptured through-hull. Try to cut the search area in half with every probe. Lift a center floorboard and determine if the flow is coming from forward or aft, port or starboard. Then cut that area in half again; if there is no flow, the hole is between that point and the previous point. If there is flow, it is beyond that point; if necessary, cut the area in half again. The location process can cause considerable damage to the interior of the boat, since cabinetry that blocks access to the hole must be removed.

If the flow is large, there is little time for trial and error. If the water is clear and warmer than 60 degrees, the hole can be located more easily from the outside with mask and snorkel. If the water is not clear or it is too cold, skip the location process and immediately rig a collision mat, as described on page 224. With luck, by covering a large area blindly you will cover the hole as well. When the initial flow is large, even a partial block will buy time for a better solution.

Controlling the Flow

Once the leak is located the type of failure can be determined. Temporarily stem the flow so the pumps can handle the inflow; then make a more permanent patch. If you have enough crew, assign each member a different task. If alone, remain in position, reducing the flow until the pumps eliminate most of the water, then prepare to go over the side to repair the damage more permanently from the outside. You will need a line to keep the outside repair person attached to the boat, a mask, fins, snorkel, and maybe a wetsuit, depending on water temperature.

The process of stemming the flow and making the temporary repair depends on whether the leak is due to a failed through-hull or a rupture in the hull. A through-hull failure can be handled in several ways, depending on whether the failure is a broken hose or complete or partial loss of the through-hull. If the hose is leaking, closing the seacock should stop the leak. This may not be as simple as it sounds. Most seacocks have short handles; closing them can be difficult, especially if the seacock is large and has an accumulation of barnacles or other growth in the body of the valve. A short piece of pipe slipped over the handle will give you more leverage; it's a good idea to keep one aboard in a handy location. If the seacock will not close even under the additional torque applied by the cheater, wrap duct tape around the hose, with hose clamps over the duct tape on both sides of the hole, to slow the flow and reinforce the hose.

If the entire through-hull is missing, stem the flow with rags, tapered wooden plugs made especially for this purpose, or body parts. It may be necessary to gasket the wooden plug with cloth or rubber if the hole is jagged. Tapered wooden plugs, or for that matter any kind of stopper, are best inserted from the outside, where the water pressure works to force the plug farther into the hole. A good temporary solution is to have a crewmember stand on the hole; the sole of his shoe will cut the flow to almost zero. This will give a diver time to get to the hole from the outside.

If the through-hull is only partially failed and the leak is from a crack around the perimeter of the fitting, it will be difficult to repair. There will be less flow if the through-hull body remains in the hole, so if possible brace the through-hull to keep it in place. Again, put the temporary patch on the outside of the hull.

If the hull is ruptured by impact, stemming the flow of water is even more difficult, because the hole is generally irregular. It may be more convenient to work from the inside, but it is easier to get at the opening from the outside. When attacking the hole from the inside, do not be too quick to knock out bulkheads. If the top edge of the compartment is above the waterline, it may be better to plug the weep holes in a compartment to contain the leak.

If it is impossible to contain the leak in a compartment, form a temporary patch. Depending on the size and shape of the opening, a braced and padded pot, bucket, or board can be used to slow the inflow from the inside, as shown in Figure 5.4. Adjustable boathooks can sometimes be used for the strut.

If the flow is large, time is of the essence. Get the temporary patch in place quickly to determine whether it will slow the flow enough for the pumps to gain control of the inflow, and if not still leave enough time to abandon ship in an orderly manner. For large holes it is faster to control the leak from the outside and use the water pressure to help seal it.

A collision mat—a tarp or a piece of heavy sailcloth with lines attached at the four corners—may be effective in controlling the leak. Sailboats can use a working sail as a collision mat; powerboats can use any tarp or a mat carried especially for this purpose. Start at the end of the boat closest to the hole and pass the two op-

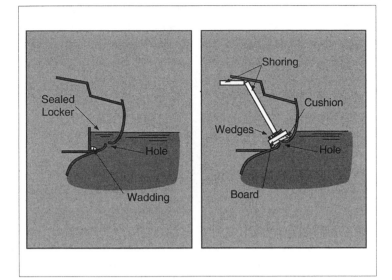

Figure 5.4 Slowing
Inflow Using
Temporary Patches

posite lines on opposite sides of the boat. Slide the mat overboard and use the lines to work it aft along the bottom of the boat until the body of the mat covers the leak. Tie the mat in this position. If a sail is used, attach lines to the head, tack, and clew, and position it with the head of the sail pointing toward the side away from the leak.

Often the cloth, especially if it is modern sailcloth, will slow the flow of the water enough for the pumps to regain control. If the hole is too large or the cloth is too porous to stop enough of the flow, it may be necessary to go over the side and position pillows or cushions over the hole and under the mat. The water pressure, because it is from outside in, will help seal and hold an outside patch in place.

Collision mat deployment is a good addition to the list of drills that should be but never are practiced. Their effectiveness is demonstrated in Figure 5.6, which shows an open through-hull with and without a patch in place.

When the flow is reduced enough for the pumps to gain control, a more permanent repair can be made. Often a satisfactory repair can be made from inside the boat with the aid of quick-setting underwater epoxy.

The puttylike epoxy should be forced through the hole if possible so that the entire hole is filled. The patch can be held by hand or foot for the 5 to 10 minutes required for temporary set. Permanent setting takes 3 to 4 hours, however. It is best to confine the epoxy in a form for the full curing time if possible.

Figure 5.5 Rigging the
Collision Mat

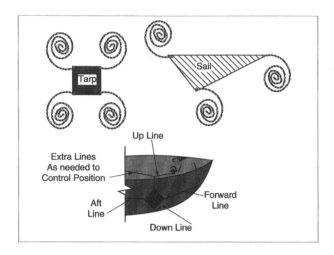

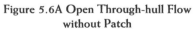

Figure 5.6A Open Through-hull Flow
without Patch

Figure 5.6B Through-hull Flow
with Patch in Place

FOULED PROP

Fouled props as a common emergency are generally more common than emergency. The prop is most often fouled by a line dragging in the water. Although this can occur while docking and lead to a few concerned moments trying to maneuver the boat without power, most of the time this kind of prop fouling causes more embarrassment than harm.

Causes and Avoidance

Lines that foul the prop are sometimes attached to the boat, such as dinghy lines, anchor lines, and, on sailboats, an occasional errant sheet that has slipped over the side. The prop can also pick up lines not attached to the boat, such as crab, shrimp, or lobster pot lines, pendants from a mooring buoy, or even just a floating scrap of line carelessly tossed or lost overboard.

The dinghy line is by far the most frequent line to foul in propellers. Dinghies are normally towed several tens of feet behind the boat. Often the boat is maneuvered in reverse during anchoring or docking. Because the skipper's attention is on maneuvering, a long dinghy line can get washed under the stern and become entangled around the prop, causing the engine to stall and rendering it useless.

If the fouling occurs during docking, the boat is at the mercy of wind, current, and anyone on the dock. Quick action may be necessary to get a line ashore, fend off other boats, or drop a temporary anchor. If prop fouling occurs while anchoring it is not so critical, especially if the anchor is already down. The prop can be freed so casually that even nearby boats may not suspect that the dinghy line was fouled. If the anchor was not dropped before the prop fouled, it is most likely ready for deployment and can be temporarily dropped until the fouling problem is resolved.

To prevent fouling the dinghy line, always take the excess slack out of the line before docking, anchoring, or performing any maneuver that may involve backing. The length of line that can be left free depends on the depth of the propellers. Outboard motors are the easiest to foul, but because they swing up out of the water they are also the easiest to free. On boats where the props are close to the surface it may be necessary to bring the dinghy aboard or snub it tight against the stern, but be aware that a dinghy attached tightly to the boat will affect maneuverability, and that some boats have sufficient power to swamp a dinghy attached in this manner. Another solution is to move the attachment point from the stern of the boat forward, so that the dinghy is still free on its line but rests forward of the stern.

The anchoring line is most often fouled during a serpentine backing maneuver while setting the anchor. The easiest way to prevent this is to back the boat in a straight line directly away from the anchor. It doesn't matter what direction, as long as it is away. Both the helmsperson and the deckhand need to be alert and communicate if the boat does not back straight down when setting the anchor.

Because the helmsperson cannot always see the anchor line, the deckhand needs to indicate the position of the anchor and line. If the boat loops back on the line, the deckhand needs to alert the helmsperson and must recover all slack anchor line. Recovering the line may require the boat to reduce speed. If the line drifts under the stern, do not try to stop the boat; the racing prop will only draw the line into it more easily. Instead, simply shift the engine into neutral until the boat is clear of the line.

It is good practice to drop and furl the sails well before any engine maneuvers so that the sails, lines, and deck are all shipshape. Sailing into a dock or crowded moorage requires that the sails be dropped quickly to stop the boat. It is during this type of hasty operation that the lines are most likely to be dropped into the water. If you suddenly need emergency engine power, a stray sheet will find the prop, and just as suddenly, the desperately needed engine power will not be available.

The lines that are most commonly fouled that are not on the boat are pot lines and mooring pendants. To avoid them, stay well clear of the floats. Mooring buoys often have a small pendant attached to the float that trails downwind or downcurrent from the buoy. Sometimes the end of the line is buoyed with a smaller buoy. It is safest to pass on the upwind side of the main mooring buoy.

Fishing pots, on the other hand, are less consistent. Sometimes the small buoy is on the end of the pendant, sometimes the large buoy occupies that position. The location appears to be purely the whim of the fisherman. Although the fishermen in any one area tend to show some consistency, it is best to pass well away from fishing buoys and never pass between closely spaced buoys.

Scrap line and netting in the water may get fouled around the prop, but rarely stall the engine. They degrade the performance of the prop, however, and may go unnoticed for months.

Freeing the Prop

If the prop becomes entangled, someone is probably going to get wet. If the line is not tightly wrapped, it may be possible to work it free by pulling the line from different angles with the clutch in neutral. This operation is done blind, and you're as likely to succeed as you are to win the lottery. To improve the odds it is necessary to get a look at the mess. If the water is clear, this may be possible using a face mask or a viewing glass from the dinghy. Using visual clues and a boathook, the loops may be worked off the propeller.

If these measures are not successful, it is necessary to go over the side with mask, fins, and snorkel to free the prop by hand. Scuba tanks allow a more leisurely approach to the task. Free diving will require many dives, and it is best to keep them short. Make reconnaissance dives first. Try to determine how tightly the line is wound, whether you'll need a knife, which loops will come off first, and which loop is locking the tangle of line. On each successive dive try to free one loop and determine which loop will be next before resurfacing. This procedure is easier with the clutch in neutral. Methodically work down to the locking loop. Once that is removed the remaining line will drop free.

During the fouling process the line often gets cut in several places. When a free end is encountered, bring it back aboard the boat. This may seem like an unnecessary step, but anyone untangling a fouled anchor line for the first time may instinctively drop the end of a line that is attached to a 40-pound anchor. The fact that the anchor is already on the bottom may occur to him after the fact. If reason does not return before the line drifts down out of reach, the tangled-prop problem escalates to a lost-anchor-and-tangled-prop problem. If the fouled line is a fishing pot it will be needed aboard to repair the line and reattach the buoy once the prop is free.

If the line is tightly wound, it may be necessary to cut it, which can be difficult under water because of the lack of leverage. If it is wound very tight, the coils are stretched and may be difficult to cut with a knife; try a hacksaw. If the process is protracted and the water is cold, it may be necessary to change divers in mid-tangle to prevent hypothermia.

Once the prop is free, rotate it through a complete 360-degree turn to see that it does not strike the hull or rudder. If the fouled line was very tightly wrapped, damage may have occurred to the shaft, strut, stern bearing, or stuffing box. If the prop turns freely, start the engine and cautiously engage the gears. Accelerate slowly while checking for undue vibration. If excess vibration occurs, it may be necessary to tow the boat to a repair yard.

LOSS OF STEERING

Common Causes

Steering failures can be broken into two broad classes, those dealing with failure of the rudder and its attachment and those dealing with failure of another part of the steering system. Common causes include loss or failure of rudder, rudder stock, or pintel; failed tiller; broken cables or hydraulic lines on wheel-steering boats; and a few other miscellaneous problems.

Loose, sloppy steering or abnormal handling can indicate potential problems that may be corrected more easily if addressed before an outright failure occurs. It is good practice to stop the boat as soon as any of these symptoms develops and determine the cause. Once the boat has been stopped, be ready to drop an anchor if necessary to keep the boat from drifting into a critical situation. If the rudder is thrashing about due to wave action, take immediate steps to control it, to prevent further damage to the rudder or boat.

If the problem is not obvious, make a thorough inspection of the steering system. On cable systems inspect the wires and the connection points for breaks or frayed spots, and examine the quadrant and wires to ensure that nothing is interfering with their free movement. On hydraulic systems examine all lines and fittings for breaks or leaks. If the interior inspection does not reveal the cause of the problem, it may be necessary to go over the side with mask, fins, and snorkel to inspect the rudder and its exterior connections.

Once the cause of the problem has been identified it may be possible to repair it at sea. If not, some kind of jury rigging or emergency steering will be necessary to get the boat to a repair facility.

Emergency Steering Systems

Boats with autopilots attached directly to the rudder post can use the autopilot to bypass the steering system. Many wheel-steering boats have an emergency tiller that can be secured atop the rudder post and used to steer the boat if the rudder is intact. However, many of these emergency tillers, especially on larger boats, are woefully inadequate. It is a good idea to try any emergency tiller before you actually need it. It may be necessary to add some mechanical advantage in the form of block and tackle or winches to move the tiller from side to side.

If the rudder stock has been broken, it is sometimes possible to force a U- or V-shaped implement such as a large shackle over the aft end of the rudder (see Figure 5.7). If lines are then attached on each side of the shackle and run forward, tension on the lines will move the rudder, steer the boat, and keep the shackle in place. Those with foresight can drill a ⅝-inch hole near the bottom aft end of the tiller. During a steering emergency a line passed through this hole with stop knots on either side will perform the same function more expeditiously.

Ancient mariners steered their boats with long sweeps or oars. In an emergency this same method can be employed. A large sweep, or steering oar, could be fashioned using a long pole, a flat board, and a fulcrum point. Attach the

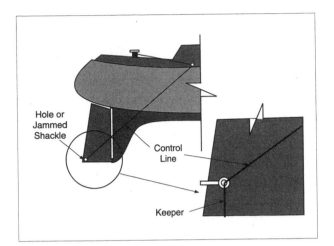

Figure 5.7 Emergency
Rudder Control

emergency steering oar to the stern of the boat so that it can be moved from side to side with suitable leverage to steer the boat; the precise means I leave to your imagination. Sometimes the sweep can be used as a large tiller with a fulcrum in the middle, other times the inboard end can be fixed as the fulcrum and the boat steered using ropes attached to the outer end of the sweep.

If neither of these methods is feasible, recall from Chapter 2 that steering is accomplished by applying an offsetting force. This force can be applied by dragging a bucket, a sail, or any other expendable object. Dragging the object on the left side of the boat will turn the boat to the left, and vice versa. The farther outboard the object is dragged, the faster the boat will turn.

Sailboats can be steered by changing the size, shape, and attack angle of the sails. Recall from Chapter 2 that the position of the driving force and the resisting force control the direction of a turn. Increasing forces on the aft sails and decreasing the force on the headsails tends to turn the boat into the wind. Reversing the process turns the boat away from the wind. A sail set to optimum position has the greatest driving force, one set too close to the wind has the least.

The force on an individual sail can be moved about as well. For example, on a flat sail the force is farther forward than on a full sail. For more information on this process see any good book on sail handling. Steering downwind is easier if a staysail or small jib is trimmed in tight amidships and the main is used for power. The tightly trimmed staysail will keep the boat headed downwind, and the trim can be altered slightly depending on the desired course. Using these principles it is possible to steer for long distances, but don't expect turns to be rapid.

TOWING AND BEING TOWED

When all else fails, there's always being towed. Many people instinctively think towing the primary solution to all emergencies; however, this should always be the last resort. Keep in mind that two boats tied together are much less maneuverable than one, and your disabled boat is now under the control of a foreign crew with unproven skills. Even the Coast Guard occasionally makes errors.

The safest course is to relinquish control only after all other measures fail. Many boaters, even those with single engines, forget that they have auxiliary power at hand in the form of a dinghy and outboard. I have on several occasions pushed a 43-foot sailboat with the dinghy and a 6-horsepower outboard, once when fully cruise-loaded to 40,000 pounds.

Dinghy as Emergency Power

A dinghy with a 5- or 6-horsepower outboard engine lashed to the stern quarter of a 40-foot boat will power her along at 3 or 4 knots in settled weather. In this situation the outboard supplies the power, but the steering is still done from the main boat's helm.

Using the dinghy as emergency power is fairly simple; just be aware that stopping a large boat with an outboard requires more time. Outboards tend to jump out of the water when maximum power is applied in reverse, and the additional drag of the dinghy makes turning to the side away from the dinghy more difficult. Angling the dinghy into the boat by 3 to 5 degrees will reduce this tendency.

To prepare for this maneuver, move the dinghy up on the stern quarter and position it with fenders and springlines as shown in Figure 5.8. The side chosen depends on how the main boat eventually will be positioned against the dock. I prefer to bring my own boat in portside to the pier, so I always position the dinghy on the starboard side. Station a crewmember in the dinghy to regulate the speed and direction of the outboard should additional maneuverability be needed.

This method of towing is generally a flat-water solution. The dinghy motor will not have sufficient power in much of a headwind or a choppy sea. A larger towboat may have sufficient power, but when the waves get larger than a few feet keeping the boats from damaging one another when tied together in this manner is practically impossible.

Being Towed

Being towed is much easier than towing. The responsibility of the towed vessel is to retrieve the towing line, attach it securely to the vessel, protect the line

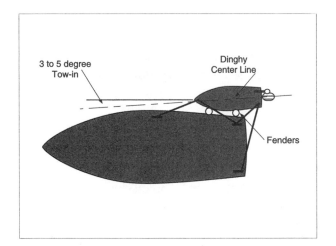

3 to 5 degree
Tow-in

Dinghy
Center Line

Fenders

Figure 5.8 Using the
Dinghy as a Towboat

from chafe, and assign a crewmember to tend the line. The towing line should be attached to a strong bit or cleat sufficiently through-bolted to take the heavy loads. On trailerable boats the eye used to winch the boat onto the trailer is a good attachment point; on sailboats the mast can be used. On boats with inadequate attachment points the safest method is to pass the towing line completely around the hull of the boat. The knot used to fasten the line should be one that can be freed quickly if necessary, like a bowline.

Freeing this line on command is part of the job of the crewmember assigned to tend the towline. He should have a sharp knife available in case the line must be cut free. Safely positioning this crewmember is critical, because very large loads can be generated during the towing effort. If towline parts or a fitting fails under loads of this magnitude, the recoiling line or flying fitting can cause severe if not fatal injury. The line tender in an exposed position is particularly vulnerable.

A small boat being towed should be trimmed down in the stern to provide better handling. The remaining crew and any mobile heavy equipment should be positioned aft.

Towing

Towing a disabled boat is not a simple operation and should not be attempted without careful planning. You must choose the towline; decide how to pass it to the disabled boat and how to attach it to the towboat; determine the length of towline to use; and decide on the general towing procedure.

Line should be of sufficient diameter to handle the load. Braided nylon is often used because of its strength and elasticity. A modest amount of elasticity is helpful in reducing shock loads. Twisted nylon has considerably more stretch than braided nylon, and the added elasticity can be dangerous should it part. Elasticity can be reduced by using oversized lines. Polypropylene lines have too little elasticity and much less strength than nylon, and should be avoided as towlines.

The next responsibility is to get the towing line to the disabled boat. In severe conditions both boats should approach the task with caution; there is little sense in escalating the emergency by imprudent actions on the part of the rescuing boat. It may appear heartless, especially to the skipper of the crippled ship, for the rescue vessel to stand off, but in an extreme situation the rescue vessel's only function may be to pick up survivors. No boat is worth the loss of life.

If the disabled boat cannot be approached close enough to pass the line by throwing, it may be possible to rig a small line attached to a float and tow this line in a loop around the disabled boat. Pull the loop across the bow of the disabled vessel where it can be snagged with a boathook. It is often easier to pass the line using a line smaller than the towline. In this case, polypropylene line is an excellent choice because of its bright color and ability to float. Once the passing line is aboard the disabled vessel the towing line can be pulled aboard.

The towing line should be attached on the towing vessel in a manner similar to that described above, but in addition it should be attached somewhere amidships. Recall from Chapter 2 that a boat turns from the middle. The bow swings in and the stern swings out. A towing line attached at the stern will keep the stern from swinging out and restrict the boat's ability to maneuver.

The towline should be long enough to keep both boats at least a wave length apart. If a sea is running, adjust the length of the towline to keep the line taut. The best length is generally some multiple of the wave length, so that the two boats are on the same part of different waves (see Figure 5.9).

Under normal conditions the towline length is not necessarily a constant distance. In protected waters the line can be shortened up to allow better handling in close quarters.

Power up the towing vessel slowly, keeping in mind that the towed vessel cannot stop. Always tow at a moderate speed, and swing wide around turns. The speed of the tow depends on two factors: the size of the towed boat and the minimum speed needed to maintain control over the towing boat. These speeds are dependent on the waterline length of each of the two vessels. It is possible for a large boat to tow a smaller boat completely under water or swamp it, especially in adverse conditions.

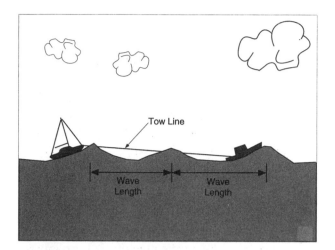

Figure 5.9 Proper Towing
Position When Heavy Seas
Are Running

When approaching the dock or mooring, both skippers should assess the prevailing conditions and agree on an approach. Communication between the two vessels is facilitated by loud hailers or VHF radios. The only remaining judgment call is when the skipper of the disabled vessel should cast off the towline. This decision is generally made by the skipper of the towed boat, who should let the towboat know when they are about to cast off the line by announcing "standby to take in towline." This will alert the towboat so that the load on the line can be reduced and so the cast-off line can be prevented from tangling around the towing boat's prop.

Finally, you should be aware that being a Good Samaritan, especially with regard to towing, carries a certain amount of legal risk in this day and age. Although it's difficult to think of these things in an emergency, if you are accepting a tow from another vessel you should inquire if there will be a charge. The crew of the towed vessel should also stay on board; otherwise the towed vessel could be considered "abandoned" under the laws of the sea, and claimed as salvage. If possible, the towed vessel should pass its own line to the towing vessel; this makes it very clear that you are voluntarily accepting a tow.

FIRE AT SEA

The major sources of fires on board are the galley, the engine room, the fuel lines, the electrical circuits, oil lamps, heaters, and cigarettes. Obviously the best policy is to prevent fire from occurring in the first place. Handle and stow all fuels properly, use proper ventilation, inspect and maintain fuel lines, keep the bilge clean and free of fuel or vapor, and keep flammable material away from open flames (curtains over cooking stoves, for example). Any condition that might cause a fire should be corrected at once.

Small fires often can be controlled by prompt action. Turn off fuel supply lines and jettison burning material if possible. Do not waste the fire suppressant; aim the flow at the base of the fire. Most onboard extinguishers last only 8 to 20 seconds, which means that if yours is a typical recreational vessel with three or four extinguishers, you have about a minute to control the blaze.

Any extensive fire on a small vessel is terminal. Fires that start with an explosion are too large too quickly to fight on a small boat. Take what little time you have to signal Mayday and abandon ship. Once over the side get well clear of the boat, because multiple explosions are probable due to the many fuels kept aboard. In this instance the only possible action, aside from recovering survivors, may to be to tow the burning vessel to a location where it can do little other damage.

If you must approach a burning vessel, do so from the windward side so that the flames, smoke, heat, and burning boat are all blown away from the approaching boat. If the burning boat is unoccupied and must be towed it will be necessary to snag it with a grappling hook or small anchor tossed into the cockpit. Be aware that neither the hook or anchor nor the line can be retrieved. Use a short section of chain to keep the line from burning through prematurely.

PERSON OVERBOARD

Nothing is quite as romantic as standing on a tropical island and watching a boat sail into the sunset. Nothing is quite as traumatic as the same scene without the island. In any but the most moderate conditions, retrieving a person lost overboard is difficult, and the chances for success are uncertain. As with fire, prevention is the key. Toerails, lifelines, and pulpits that are strong and high enough to contain a victim, adequate handholds and grabrails, nonslip, uncluttered deck surfaces, and strong, well-located safety lines and harnesses are the best defense. An adequate safety harness is one that can be slipped into quickly in rough conditions.

When moving about on deck, keep your body weight low and follow the age-old rule of the sea: one hand for yourself and one for the ship. Be aware of special risks like filling a bucket or landing a fish. When filling a bucket from a moving boat, the load on the bucket line can be large and unexpectedly rapid. Keep the decks clean; cluttered decks tend to snag safety lines and restrict movement to such an extent that safety harnesses become difficult to work in and are avoided when they are most needed.

If someone goes over, the chances of survival depend on, in order of importance, the number of people in the crew; visibility; strength of the wind and
condition of the sea; point of sail, on sailboats; temperature of the water; flotation
of the victim; lack of predators; and the crew's ability to haul the victim out of
the water. The first four variables all involve maintaining visual contact with
the victim.

Keeping Contact with the Victim

The most important thing is to maintain visual contact; if you can't see the victim, the probability of rescue is remote. In flat, calm water on a clear, bright day it
is possible to see the head of the victim for a few hundred yards at best. The ability to locate a head in the water when the winds are above 20 knots and the seas
are 6 feet or greater can be limited to tens of yards even on a clear day. It is almost
impossible to express the difficulty of keeping track of an object the size of a
coconut in conditions with winds of 30 knots or better.

In moderately rough conditions it is necessary for both the boat and the victim to be within the same wave trough to see something as small as a head. If the
victim becomes separated from the boat by more than one wave length, it is necessary for both boat and victim to be on the peak of their respective waves at the
same time. The random wave period of ocean seas results in the victim being only
intermittently visible to the boat.

It is easy to see why the next most important factor in retrieval is the number
of people aboard. If a singlehander who is not attached to the boat goes overboard,
his chance of survival is negligible. The two-person crew has a better chance, but
in any but the best conditions (bright sunlight, 5 knots of wind or less, 2-foot seas
or less, with the boat under engine power) a successful recovery is still unlikely
no matter how many pieces of safety gear you have and deploy. When the crew
increases from two to four, the chances of the victim being recovered are increased
by at least a factor of 10. The most important piece of safety gear is extra pairs
of eyes.

The next most important piece of gear is anything that improves the chances
of the victim being seen: personal strobe lights, smoke, handheld flares, whistles,
a man-overboard pole, life rings, or even cockpit cushions—anything that can
be tossed into the water. The problem with the man-overboard pole and life rings
is that they have to be jettisoned to work, and the person doing the jettisoning
must turn his attention from the victim to the equipment. Even when this is done
successfully, the victim must reach the pole or flotation device to be found. Unfortunately, the pole extends high off the water and sometimes can be blown out

of reach. A drogue on the pole will reduce its drift and improve the chances of recovering more than just the pole.

Many GPS and loran units have a man-overboard button that records the latitude and longitude. This feature can aid in getting the boat back to within 300 feet of where the button was pressed. Whether the victim is still in the area is another question.

Throw cushions and life rings are lost as easily as a head; however, sometimes the victim can retrieve one and use it for flotation, or maybe wave it overhead to attract attention. In my opinion, wearing a life jacket while working on board isn't much help. The Coast Guard requires life jackets on board, and certainly if the boat was sinking I would slip into one, but as a precaution against accidentally falling overboard they are of little value. They are bulky and uncomfortable, and may in fact contribute to your falling overboard. As we have seen, flotation is far down the list of important variables. It is more important to stay aboard.

The Victim's Actions

The victim in the water can do a few things to maximize the chances of survival. First, if the engines are running, get clear of the vessel so as not to be struck by the props; there is little to grasp on a high-sided, slick vessel. Next, it is crucial to regain control and fight the overpowering tendency to panic. Contact with the cold water and the vision of the boat sailing away in a limitless sea is overwhelming. Add to this uncertainty as to whether anyone saw you fall overboard, whether you can still be seen, and whether the boat will be able to return and find you, and the tendency to panic is overpowering.

To fight panic and shock it is first necessary to regain control of your breathing. Once that is achieved conserve energy and use controlled actions to attract attention. Waving and shouting may have to be sustained for a long period. Take inventory of any gear or equipment you may be wearing that can improve visibility, provide floatation, add warmth, or defend against shark attack. Remove boots that can fill with water and other equipment that adds only weight. If the water is cold, some judgment must be made as to the effectiveness of clothing to stave off hypothermia. Do whatever is possible to increase the chances of being seen until the boat is out of sight.

If the crew has jettisoned equipment, swim toward it and use it for flotation and location. When the boat returns, watch it carefully, fire smoke or flares, and whistle and wave to indicate position. Conserve energy for the struggle to get back aboard. Resist the temptation to swim toward the boat too early. Only when the boat is close by and the engines have been throttled back should you swim toward the boat or line. A line can be tossed to you or trailed behind the boat on a float and brought to you by a circular motion. Pass the line around your body and tie a bowline. When the knot is completed, signal the crew to haul away.

If a victim cannot tie the knot because of hypothermia or injury, it may be necessary to have a second crewmember enter the water and assist with the rescue. In this case, the crewmember should dress in a wetsuit or suitable clothing and be attached to the boat by a line.

The Crew's Actions

The action of the crew on board depends a great deal on the number of crew available and the conditions encountered. If conditions are moderate to calm and visibility is good, the best course of action is a quick stop or turn and return. For powerboats this is not much of a problem, but for sailboats under sail, it depends on the course, crew, and rig. The prudent skipper should think out the best course of action for his own boat under each of these circumstances.

In an auxiliary-powered sailboat during settled conditions it is always easiest to stop the boat by turning directly into the wind, drop the sails, and approach the victim under power. In sailboats with no auxiliary power one standard procedure is to jibe at once or bear off on a reach and then jibe back. Jibing takes more sail handling than tacking. Sail handling requires that eyes be taken from the victim. When running downwind, jibing makes no sense at all. In any case, stop the boat, locate the victim, then approach upwind and stop the boat slightly to windward. Some people prefer a figure-eight approach, shown in Figure 5.10.

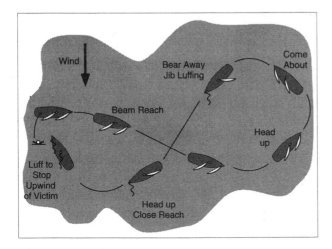

Figure 5.10 Figure-Eight
Approach

Both of these approaches assume ideal conditions. Other points of sail can complicate matters. A sailboat running under spinnaker, for example, can travel considerable distance before the boat can be stopped and turned.

When weather and sea conditions are severe the emphasis should be on keeping the victim in sight. The following procedure assumes a crew larger than three. Several things need to be done immediately. First, at least one person should locate and point to the victim at all times to assist in keeping visual contact. The remaining crew needs to be alerted to the emergency, by yelling "man overboard." Sounding three long blasts on the horn is also acceptable, but it is not as descriptive and may require the watcher to take his eyes off the victim. The first person with the opportunity should push the man-overboard button on the GPS or loran and note the heading of the boat. If the man-overboard pole or life ring can be freed without losing sight of the victim, jettison it.

When you reach the deck, take charge and direct the operation with clear, concise orders—who should watch, who should steer and handle the sails, if necessary. The sails should be dropped quickly without losing control of them. Be sure that all lines are back aboard before starting the engine. This is not a time to be fooling with a fouled prop. In heavy weather it may be best to leave some sail up to steady the vessel; for example, the staysail sheeted flat will reduce roll.

In a situation where the boat is under power and the crewmember falls overboard from the forward part of the boat, the helmsperson should reduce the chances of the victim being hit by the propellers. Immediately cut the throttle, shift into neutral, and turn the boat into the victim to throw the stern away.

Once the boat is under control, if the victim is still in sight it is relatively simple to return, approach, and retrieve him. If visual contact has been lost a search must be instigated. Searching for a lost crewmember takes time. If the boat must return any distance to the position where the accident occurred, all eyes are not needed and a crewmember should be designated to dress in a wetsuit or appropriate clothing for going over the side in case it is necessary to assist the victim in the water. This is also a good time to prepare other equipment—inflate the dinghy or rig lines and tackle to assist in the recovery process.

Search Patterns

If the boat is equipped with a GPS or loran and the man-overboard button has been activated, the equipment will provide distance and bearing to the accident point. The helmsperson merely steers that course with updates as necessary until the boat has returned to its original position. If the boat is not equipped with these devices, a reciprocal compass course must be steered. This method is inferior because it supplies bearing only and does not allow for drift or leeway; considerable judgment must be made as to the distance traveled before the boat was put on the return course.

Even in the best of circumstances, when the boat returns to the exact position of the accident it is unlikely that the victim will still be there. The distance that the victim traveled, however, should be small. Sometimes during daylight, seabirds wheeling above the victim will indicate his presence. If the victim cannot be seen, a standard search pattern must be used.

The purpose of the search pattern is to ensure that all the immediate area surrounding the loss point is covered in a methodical manner. This is not easy in a setting with no visual clues as to location. A man-overboard pole, if one is available, can be used for the center point, but it will soon be lost as the search widens. In any case the course of the boat must be simple so that errors in turning and distance run are minimized and the number of eyes available to scan the water maximized.

The speed of the boat and the distance run depends on the visibility; the faster the speed the more ground is covered, but it is not covered as thoroughly. The boat speed needs to be set at a value such that the victim is located quickly yet not overlooked. If sea conditions are extremely rough and visibility is bad, it may be necessary to slow the boat to search the water adequately. There is value in keeping the engine rpm, and thereby its noise, as low as possible.

There may be several ways to accomplish this. The following example is one of the best for small boats with limited crews. Set the boat speed to a constant value, say about 6 knots. At 6 knots you will travel about 600 feet in 1 minute. Pick a cardinal magnetic direction and head in that direction, away from the center of the search area. After 1 minute, turn 90 degrees to the right and run for 1 minute; then turn 90 degrees to the right again and run for 2 minutes; then turn 90 degrees and run another 2 minutes. After each two turns, increase the run time by 1 minute. This will produce the search pattern shown in Figure 5.11.

This pattern allows new coverage of 300 feet on each side of the boat, with some overlap, and in the first 3 hours will cover an area of about 2 square miles. The number of turns and distance to be run should be recorded as they occur, not left to the helmsperson's memory. After 5 hours the area will have increased to about 4 square miles, or a square area 2 miles on a side. As time goes on, less and less new area is covered and the chance of successfully finding the crewmember diminishes. Obviously, the decision to break off the search is a difficult one that must be based on specific circumstances..

If a loran or GPS system is aboard it is possible to run concentric circles, but this require that someone watch the GPS or loran, which takes a set of eyes away

Figure 5.11 Typical
Search Pattern

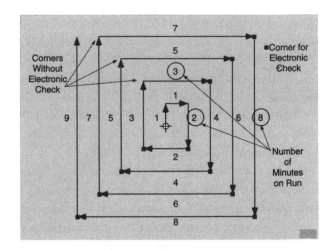

from searching. It is probably better to use the pattern described above, using the electronic navigation system as a corner check on occasion. All corners that bear 45 degrees from the centerpoint can be used for a check. In Figure 5.11, the distance to corners 2, 3, and 4 is approximately 850 feet. The distance to corners 6,7, and 8 is 1,700 feet, the distance to 10, 11, and 12 is 2,250 feet, and so on. The midpoints of the runs can also be used as checks, because the boat will be on a cardinal bearing from the origin; it should be the correct multiple of 600 feet away.

Retrieval Methods

Assuming that contact with the victim has been maintained or that the victim has been relocated, all that remains is the final approach and actual retrieval. The approach should be into the wind, with the boat stopping to windward of the victim. The small slick formed by the boat slipping sideways toward the victim will assist in the retrieval. Also, in this attitude the victim can be brought over the lee gunwale. A sailboat that is hove-to will have its lee gunwale closer to the water. During this process, be aware that turning props are a hazard to those in the water and can also snag a stray line.

As soon as possible, assess the victim's condition. Is he conscious and capable of assisting himself? If so, get a line with a bowline and a float to the victim. The bowline needs to have a bight large enough to contain the person in the water. This can be thrown or towed by the boat in a circle around the victim so that it is pulled across his path. At this point the victim is attached to the boat and has adequate flotation. Before boarding, the victim should shed all unnecessary clothing to lighten the load. If conditions are severe, the crew on board should be tied to the boat before participating in the retrieval.

If the victim is unable to help himself, the tendency is to send someone else into the water. Do not make this decision too quickly even if the crewmember is properly equipped and attached to the boat; this is not necessarily the only solution. It may be possible to get a line around the victim from the dinghy, especially if the dinghy is to be used later in the recovery as described below. It is necessary that adequate muscle power remain on board to get everyone back out of the water.

Do not underestimate this effort. On a pitching, wave-swept small boat the process of getting a crewmember back aboard is bone-jarring hard work. It takes considerable exertion to drag 200 pounds of wet, dead weight over a 3-foot gunwale. Boats with 4 feet of freeboard have considerable room below, but God help anybody trying to get back aboard from the sea.

Victims are generally cold, tired, and unable to provide much assistance. The limited space available along the gunwale makes it difficult for the crew to get a hold on the victim with enough purchase to provide the necessary lift. Even with adrenaline pumping, it is nearly impossible to hoist this weight aboard using arm power alone. In most cases it is essential to be able to assist the victim using a line and some sort of mechanical advantage.

The line attached to the victim can be used along with a halyard and winch, windlass, or block and tackle to hoist him aboard. Sailboats have halyards, booms, and winches to assist in this operation. Powerboats are not as well equipped. Sometimes a small boom for hoisting the dinghy is available; otherwise, use your ingenuity and whatever equipment is at hand.

The simplest device is a permanent boarding ladder mounted over the stern. Ladders mounted along the side of the vessel receive large twisting and shear strains if the boat is moving through the water. In a seaway the boat is always moving, and ladders located anyplace but over the stern are impractical.

In a heavy seaway even boarding over the stern is difficult. The stern, the ladder, and the victim can go through considerable vertical distance, and not always in phase. Being swept under the boat on its downward plunge would leave a lasting impression, so approach the boat with caution, timing arrival for when the boat is near the bottom of its cycle. Make contact with a firm grip, because very shortly the stern will again be high out of the water resulting in both the ladder and the victim taking a beating. Even when using the ladder, the line attached to the victim should be attached to the halyard, and the halyard winch used to assist the victim aboard.

Without an adequate boarding ladder, lines can be looped down along the leeward side of the boat at various levels to provide some foothold so that the legs of the victim can be used in the boarding operation. Separate loops can be put over the side for crewmembers on board to give them better purchase and allow the use of their legs in lifting as well. Again, the line attached to the victim can be taken to the halyard or to the end of the boom, and winch power used to assist the boarding.

There are several other methods that can be used to help retrieve a victim from the water. A partially inflated dinghy can be employed as a halfway house, allowing the victim easy access to the interior of the dinghy, where he can stand and use his legs for boarding. A crewmember in the dinghy can boost from behind. The dinghy should be deflated just enough to allow a lowpoint in the gunwale where the victim can swim aboard easily, but still have enough air for a firm footing.

On a sailboat it is sometimes possible to remove the mainsail from the mast track, leaving it attached to the boom, and lower it into the water with its halyard. The victim then swims into the fold of the sail, and the crew hauls on the halyard so that the rising sail rolls him back aboard. This is also a good method with an unconscious or helpless victim.

Once the victim is back on board he should be treated for shock, exhaustion, and hypothermia. Remove wet clothing and dry the victim thoroughly, place him in a sleeping bag, and give him warm, sweet liquids. Wrapping the sleeping bag in plastic will cause the temperature to rise inside the bag more quickly. Feed warm, light, nourishing food as soon as the victim is able to eat. Finally, when it is all over record the incident in the ship's log as best as can be remembered, in case there is an inquiry. Get opinions and reports from all crewmembers aboard.

HELICOPTER RESCUE

Helicopters are becoming the vehicle of choice on rescue missions. Helicopter rescue requires some understanding of the operation as well as preparation by the crew.

A suitable area must be prepared so that the helicopter can hoist the victim aboard using a cable approximately 60 feet long. The area must be free of overhead obstructions, and loose objects and sails must be secured because the downdraft from the blades exceeds 30 knots.

Powerboats generally have sufficient deck space. On sailboats, because of the mast and rigging, the most favorable area is probably a dinghy towed 100 to 150 feet behind the boat. If the dinghy is used, station a crewmember in it to assist the victim.

Once the area is prepared, try to establish contact with the approaching helicopter on VHF Channel 16 or 2182 kHz to get instructions, relay information, and advise the helicopter of the pickup point so that they can adjust their approach. Once the helicopter has arrived, the noise level will prevent verbal communication.

When the helicopter is sighted, bring the boat onto a steady, slow, comfortable course. It is easiest for the helicopter to approach upwind and from the right side, where the pilot has a better view, so a boat course with the wind on the port bow is preferred. At night, illuminate the mast, rigging, and any other obstructions, as well as the pickup point. Do not shine lights directly at the helicopter.

Pickups are made with a basket for injured individuals or with a harness for those who are functional. Both of these items may contain a considerable charge of static electricity, which must be grounded before it can be handled safely. The easiest way is to allow the basket or loop to touch the water before you touch it. Most helicopter crews will dip the hoisting item into the water before positioning it near the victim.

It may be necessary to unhook the hoisting cable from a stretcher or basket to load the victim. Do not attempt to move the stretcher without unhooking the cable. After unhooking the cable, let it dangle freely. Under no circumstances attach the hoisting cable to the boat. The cable may be difficult to recapture, but tethering the helicopter to the boat severely limits the pilot's control and can cause the helicopter to crash. If the victim is disabled, place him in a life vest and secure him with arms and legs completely inside the basket, then recapture the cable and reattach it to the basket.

If the victim is functional, the standard hoisting sling, a wide nylon strap with a toggle, will be lowered. Place the strap under both arms and snug up the toggle. When all is ready, signal the helicopter to haul away by giving the "thumbs up" signal. Guide the victim or the basket until free of the boat so that neither will swing into any obstructions.

If all crewmembers are abandoning ship, the helicopter pilot might prefer to pick up the crew from the water. In this case he will advise you of the number of people he can hoist at one time. If more than one person is being hoisted at a time, it is a good idea to attach the group together with a short piece of line. Everyone should be in life jackets, and only the number of crew designated by the pilot should be in the water at one time.

A long line should be trailed aft behind the boat with the boat moving slowly forward. Each person or group should wait on deck for those in the water to be recovered and the sling to be relowered before they enter the water. Once in the water each person can quickly work himself aft along the line, keeping contact with the vessel until lifting takes place.

ABANDONING SHIP

Do not abandon ship too early. Even though the life raft is designed to save lives, it does not do this as well as the main boat itself. Stay with the boat as long as possible. When the boat is abandoned, so is a great deal of control over what happens to the crew. In a life raft the survivors no longer have an active part in determining their fate, but must depend on chance, wind, and others for survival. There are many documented cases where people have abandoned ship only to be found dead in their raft with their abandoned boat still floating.

There are only a few reasons to abandon ship. An out-of-control fire or a holed boat with an uncontrollable inflow of water are two situations we have already discussed. Another might be an unsalvageable boat driven hard on a lee shore; however, this obviously is not quite as serious because of the proximity of land. If shore is nearby, before trying to make it unaided, keep in mind that distance over water is often grossly under estimated.

Some books recommend that the survivors stay in the area of the boat because it is easier to see.[1] This does not make sense, because the only common reasons to leave the boat in the first place are fire and a large hole in the hull, and in either case the boat is going to leave the area before the survivors do. *If the boat is not about to sink, it should not be abandoned in the first place.*

Preparations

If the possibility of abandoning ship presents itself, preparations should begin as soon as crewmembers can be freed from the tasks of trying to save the vessel. The life raft and/or dinghy should be made ready for launching.

The necessary equipment should be collected and positioned so that it can be placed in the raft or dinghy, or will float free when the vessel sinks. The necessary equipment in the order of its importance is listed below.

1. water, water catchment equipment, solar stills, or hand-operated desalinators
2. warm, dry, clothing; blankets or sleeping bags
3. food
4. repair kit and pump

[1] *Charles F. Chapman*, Piloting, Seamanship and Small Boat Handling (*New York: The Hearst Corporation, 1991*), 231.

5. bailer and sponge
6. survival gear
7. radio, flares, smoke, and dye
8. survival books

Emergency Equipment

Given that water is necessary for life and that the length of stay in the life raft is indeterminate, take all that is possible to carry. All 5-gallon containers should be filled only 95 percent so that they will float in case they are lost overboard or need to be towed behind the raft. Handy water catchment equipment might consist of a funnel, plastic garbage bags, and resealable plastic bags. A solar still can be as simple as a bucket with clear plastic wrap, as shown in Figure 5.12. Hand-operated desalinators are compact but require human energy to provide water. Without food this necessary energy will soon be lacking. There will come a point where it may be better to conserve the body's limited supply of energy rather than wasting it on producing water.

Warm, dry clothes are vital anywhere but in the tropics. Hypothermia kills quicker than dehydration. The reason warm clothing is second on the list is that many recreational boats are abandoned in warm water. Most good life rafts have double floors and roofs for insulation from the elements, but even then cold is likely to be the major danger.[2] If your raft does not have insulating layers, you will definitely need insulation between your body and the cold ocean water. A wet suit or survival suit, if available, is the best protection.

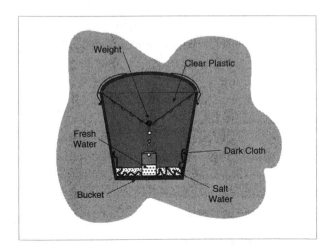

Figure 5.12 Improvised Solar Still

[2] John Chamier, Safety and Seamanship (London: Adlard Coles Limited, 1976), 81.

Concentrate on foods that can be preserved in a wet environment. Almost any food will sustain life, but in a survival situation the high-calorie, high-carbohydrate foods shunned by dieters are best. Salads and vegetables can be passed up for candy and fruit bars or dehydrated fruit. High-protein foods require additional water to digest and pass the generated waste properly without damage to the liver. Two pints of water is the minimum daily requirement if protein is consumed.[3] However, it may be better to eat the protein without the additional water and risk damage to the liver than die of starvation. The body will store the waste for a few days before it causes damage, and the damage is progressive, not instantaneous.

Conserve the emergency rations and try to live off the sea, if water is plentiful. All food from the sea, including fish, turtles, and birds, has a high protein content and requires extra water to assimilate.

Once the body is warm and supplied with water and food, it is necessary to see that the raft remains afloat. The repair kit should contain equipment to patch leaks and keep the inflatable chambers full of air. Partially filled chambers will flex, cause wear, and eventually rupture. Severe chafe can also cause rupture. Be aware that chafe can be caused anywhere contact between the raft and other hard items occur. Some sea creatures also have a propensity for bumping rafts. You may have to ward off turtles, sharks, and other creatures with paddles. It has been reported that trailing a skirt of any material around the edges of the raft to cast a shadow will divert some of these attacks.[4]

The bailer, sponge, and so called "survival gear" begin to make the transition from vital equipment to handy equipment. The bailer and sponge may be necessary to keep the raft afloat but are usually just handy for keeping the living compartment free of salt water and the body free of sores caused by constant immersion. The term "survival gear" includes such items as a sharp knife, a cutting board, a bucket or two, feeding cups or bowls, can opener, pliers, nylon line, resealable plastic bags, compass, fishing equipment, first aid kit, vitamin supplements, paddle, and any other useful small items.

After the gear that improves the chances of survival is aboard, the next most important items are those that increase the chances of rescue. Handheld radios, EPIRBs, flares, smoke, dye, and mirrors all fit this description. The handheld radio should be kept dry and only used if a boat or aircraft is spotted. The EPIRB should be activated immediately. The final items to be put aboard are any charts or books that will supply information pertinent to survival. A portable GPS or other naviga-

[3]E. C. B. and Kenneth Lee, Safety and Survival at Sea (London: W. W. Norton, 1980), 157.
[4]Dougal Robertson, Sea Survival, a Manual (New York: Praeger Publishers, 1975), 28.

tion equipment is only useful if the raft can be steered and propelled.

Launching and Boarding the Raft

When everything is ready and the last hope of saving the vessel has passed, attach a strong safety line to the raft. This safety line must be considerably longer than the line that opens the raft. Next attach the operating cord of the life raft to some strong point on board the boat and throw the raft over the leeward side of the boat. Normally, the action of the raft being thrown overboard will activate the inflation mechanism and the raft will inflate automatically. If not, a sharp pull on the operating cord will release the compressed air into the raft. Launch the dinghy and attach it to the life raft with a short nylon line. The dinghy is a great adjunct to the life raft, supplying extra buoyancy, storage, and living space.

Position the life raft securely alongside the boat and transfer one crewmember to the raft. Transferring crew and materials can be very time consuming and dangerous if weather conditions are severe. In strong winds, life rafts and dinghies can be rolled over unless well weighed down with people or equipment. Most life rafts have a water-filled ballast chamber to reduce this tendency, but any equipment stowed in the dinghy should be tied securely in case the dinghy overturns.

Pass all the assembled equipment into the raft for storage. Once that is accomplished, all but one crewmember should board the raft. If time permits, an audible inventory of all the items abard the life raft should be taken. Any missing item should called out for the last crewmember to locate and pass aboard. It is not pleasant to find yourself free of the boat and unable to return for an item inadvertently left behind. Once all equipment is aboard, loop the nylon safety line around a cleat, pass it aboard the raft so that this line can be released and recovered from inside the raft, and untie all other lines. The last crewmember can then board the raft.

Once all are on board, check the crew for injuries and proper clothing, and pass out seasickness pills. The motion of a life raft is different from the boat's, and the food in the crew's stomach is vital for survival. Even those who are not susceptible to seasickness should take the pills if they are available for a couple of days as a precaution. By that time, the average person will acclimate to the motion.

The crew should be assigned tasks to improve the chances of survival and to keep their minds busy. Monitor the boat to determine the proper time to release the last line. Stay with the vessel as long as it is afloat, because if for some reason it doesn't sink, chances of survival may be better if the crew reboards the boat. Once the vessel sinks, deploy the sea anchor.

Stow and inventory all equipment so it can be found when needed. Cushion any rough edges on the equipment to prevent the raft from chafing. Check the raft and dinghy for leaks and damage, and maintain the correct pressure in the air chambers. The automatic valves blow off pressure because air in the chambers expands due to the sun's heat, and when the raft cools air must be added again to keep the tubes filled to reduce chafing.

Formulate a watch plan and a survival plan. The person on watch must keep alert for ships, planes, and signs of land. Change the watch every 2 hours or less. The survival plan should consider the proximity of land, shipping lanes, currents, and wind patterns, amount of food and water, and the ability to steer the raft. Search-and-rescue operations will center on the last known position of the boat. It is best to try to stay in that area for at least a week if a search is likely, at which time search operations are generally terminated. After a week or if no search is likely it may be best to recover the sea anchor and cast your fate to the winds.

Inventory and ration food and water. Because the time to rescue is indeterminate it is best to minimize all food and water rations. Water should be taken in slow sips. One pint of water per day is considered the minimum. Drinking less will cause the castaways to lose strength quickly. However, it has been reported that people have survived in an active and coherent state for as long as seven days on as little as one-third pint of water per day.[5]

Conserve energy and body heat. Group crew together, keep warm with clothing or blankets, and reduce unnecessary movement to conserve energy and minimize the need for food. Try not to issue food for the first 24 to 48 hours even if food is plentiful. Fasting will reduce the size of the stomach and the survivor's desire for food. Try to restrict eating to one meal a day. Eat slowly and chew thoroughly. Bowels will quickly become constipated and urine dense and difficult to pass. Do not take laxatives. These are normal symptoms for the conditions and should not cause undue alarm.

After the first day there is not much left to do but wait, watch, and try to maintain morale and alertness. Humor and song are helpful in maintaining morale. Create regular routines, and keep bodies clean. Stay out of the sun. If the lifeboat can be steered and propelled, the section on lifeboat navigation in Chapter 3 provides useful information.

[5]Robertson, 63.

6

WORKING WITH ROPE

Selecting, handling, and working with rope is fundamental to good seamanship. A boater's seamanship skills are easily judged by his knots; rank amateurs are often betrayed by the way their boats are made fast to the dock. As knowledge increases, lines are properly coiled, whipped, and spliced. Although there are approximately 1,500 knots, splices, and hitches, the well-educated seaman only needs to know a couple of techniques for whipping a line, 10 or 12 knots and a few splices, and how to coil and put up a line.

TYPES OF ROPE AND THEIR USES

You need to be familiar with the various kinds of rope to select the proper type for each specific task. Once a piece of rope has been assigned a task, it loses the name rope and becomes known by its use, such as halyard or dock line, or just by the generic term, line.

Rope may be made from wire, synthetic fibers, or natural fibers. Wire rope, strong and difficult to handle, is useful mainly for the rigging on sailboats. Natural fibers are susceptible to rot and deterioration. Wet natural fibers shrink upon drying; they may shorten as much as 10 percent, causing a natural fiber rope to exert tremendous force on any fittings to which it is attached. Synthetic fibers were developed to solve these problems, and they have virtually taken over the market.

Synthetic Fibers

The synthetic fibers most commonly used around boats are polyamide, polyester, polypropylene, polyethylene, and aramid. *Polyamide* fiber, the first synthetic fiber to be widely used as rope, is known more commonly as nylon. Nylon rope is very strong, elastic, and resistant to deterioration. It is used mainly as anchor rode, towing line, or mooring lines, where strength and elasticity are important. Nylon is also soft, flexible, and susceptible to wear from abrasion.

The most common of the many brand names for the *polyester* fibers is Dacron. Dacron rope is not quite as strong as nylon, but it is far less elastic and more abrasion resistant. It is used mainly for running rigging on sailboats, principally for sheets, where stretch is undesirable. During the manufacturing process it can be given various finishes that affect its texture, and it may be heat treated, which further reduces its elasticity.

The terms *polypropylene* and *polyethylene* are often used interchangeably. The weakest and least flexible of the synthetic fibers, they are susceptible to deterioration when exposed to sunlight. Stiff and slippery, they are difficult to knot securely—polyethylene more so than polypropylene. Their main advantages are that they are inexpensive and they float. Polypro lines are used on recreational boats mainly for water-ski towlines, crab-trap lines, man-overboard recovery lines, and dinghy painters. To reduce its susceptibility to deterioration in sunlight, thread the poly line through an outer cover of double-braided nylon or Dacron line. A cover of the proper size will protect the line but still allow it to float.

Aramid fiber, commonly known as Kevlar, is very strong and inelastic. Because it is self-abrasive and the stiffest of synthetic lines, it requires larger-diameter sheaves. Kevlar is often combined with a flexible, slippery fiber called Spectra, which improves the rope's performance by reducing internal abrasion. On recreational boats, Kevlar rope is used mainly for halyards.

Wire Fibers

Wire rope can be made from phosphor bronze, uncoated steel, stainless steel, and galvanized steel. Stainless steel wire is strong and resistant to deterioration, and is most commonly used as standing rigging and halyards on sailboats. Galvanized wire is less expensive, more flexible, and does not work-harden as much as stainless, but it needs considerably more maintenance. Galvanized wire has mostly been replaced by stainless or Kevlar ropes.

ROPE CONSTRUCTION

Twisted Rope

How rope is put together significantly affects its strength and elasticity. Rope can be twisted, braided, or double-braided. Natural fiber ropes are generally twisted, although cotton is often braided. Twisted rope is generally more elastic than other ropes, because as the rope is loaded the strands tend to untwist, thereby lengthening the rope. Hanging a heavy weight on a twisted rope so that the weight is free to turn will cause the rope to unlay, reducing its strength considerably. A twisted rope is made up of *fibers*, *yarns*, and *strands* (see Figure 6.1). The fibers in the yarns are twisted in the opposite direction from the yarns in the rope. This opposite twisting balances the internal stresses in the rope and improves its handling and strength characteristics.

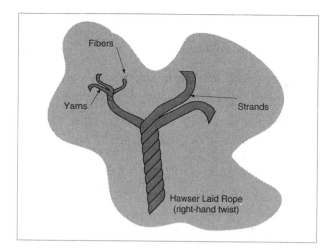

Figure 6.1 Components of Twisted Rope

Rope can be laid up with a clockwise, right-hand lay or a counterclockwise, left-hand lay. Knowing the twist or lay of a rope is important in preventing kinks. By holding the line vertical and observing the direction the strands trend, you can determine whether the rope has a right-hand lay, with the strands trending upward to the right, or a left-hand lay, with the strands trending upward to the left.

Sometimes a fourth strand forms a core around which the other strands are twisted. The center strand reduces stretch. This type of rope laid counterclockwise was once called *shroud laid* rope. When three, four, or more ropes are twisted into a larger rope it is called a *cable*. Wire rope is often twisted in this manner. Since each successive layer is twisted in the opposite direction, and most rope has a right-hand lay, a cable generally has a left-hand lay. Thus, a left-hand laid rope is sometimes called a cable laid rope, and a right-hand laid rope is referred to as plain or *hawser* laid. Cables are commonly used where great strength is needed—in suspension bridges, for example. There is very little call for cables on recreational boats.

Braided Rope

Braided rope is stronger and more resistant to wear and kinking than twisted rope. Like twisted rope, braided rope is made of fibers (or yarns) and strands, but they are laid out slightly differently. Rope can be braided with one, two, three, or four fibers in a strand. In the cover braid of a double-braided rope there are 16, 20, 24, or 32 threads. Half the strands revolve to the right and half to the left. Single-braided ropes are braided with 12 strands.

Figure 6.2 Components of
Braided Rope

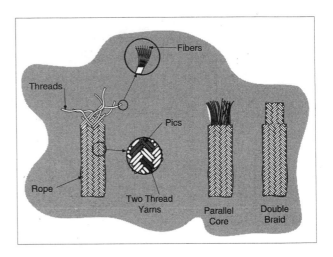

A rope made from eight strands is known as a plaited line. A plaited line is flat, while a braided line is round. Most plaited lines cannot be spliced; they are generally small lines used for flag halyards, sail ties, and other miscellaneous purposes.

Polypropylene ropes are often plaited. The other synthetics are usually doubled-braided, with a braided cover surrounding a braided or straight core, allowing more control over the rope's characteristics; you can select the core for low stretch and the cover for ease of handling, for instance.

Wire Rope

Wire rope is laid up in three general patterns: 7 × 7, 1 × 19, and 7 × 19. The 7 × 7 rope has 7 wires or fibers twisted into a bundle called a strand, and is equivalent to a yarn in natural fiber rope. Six of these strands surround a single strand in the core. The 1 × 19 rope is made up of 18 wires surrounding a single wire core, and should really be called a strand rather than a rope. The 7 × 19 uses six 19-strand bundles surrounding a 19-strand core. The 7 × 19 rope is more flexible because of its smaller strands and is normally used with halyards or running rigging where the line passes over a sheave. The 1 × 19 is more resistant to corrosion and is generally used for standing rigging on sailboats. The 7 × 7 is part fish, part fowl, but is easier to splice than the other wire ropes.

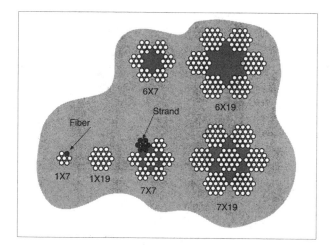

Figure 6.3 Components of
Wire Rope

Rope Properties

The rope properties of importance to boaters are strength, elasticity, and resistance to deterioration and abrasion. The strength of a rope depends on the material in the rope and how it is made. Three-strand twisted rope is not as strong as braided rope, and double-braided rope is not as strong as 12-strand single-braided rope. Figures 6.4 and 6.5 show the relative strength of each of these types of ropes for various materials.

The strengths are shown in pounds per square inch. To get the strength of a specific line in pounds, multiply the strength given on the chart by the area of the rope in square inches. The result is the average breaking strength in pounds. The working load for any given rope is generally one-fifth this strength.

The amount of stretch in a rope also depends on the material and the construction of the rope. The total elongation is divided into three parts: elastic, plastic, and permanent. Elastic elongation is recovered immediately when the load is removed. Plastic elongation is slowly recovered over time after the load has been removed. Permanent elongation is essentially nonrecoverable. The distribution of each type of elongation depends on the applied load. Low loads develop mostly elastic elongation; loading the line near its breaking strength will induce all three types of elongation.

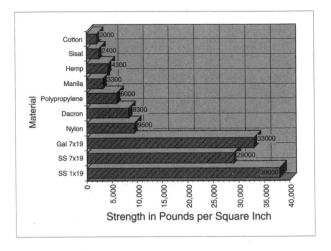

Figure 6.4 Strength of
Twisted Rope

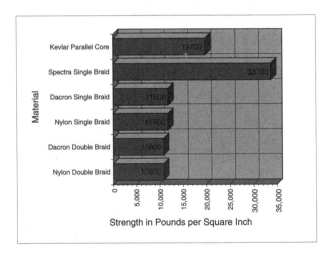

Figure 6.5 Strength of
Braided Rope

Figure 6.6 shows the relative elongation for several common types of materials and rope constructions at 10 and 30 percent of their breaking strength. Since the working load for rope is about 20 percent (one-fifth) of its breaking strength, the larger load would induce considerable nonrecoverable and plastic elongation.

CARE OF ROPE

Rope must be protected from kinks, chafe, dirt, and other conditions that may cause the fibers to deteriorate. Twisted fiber rope, being flexible, can be twisted by

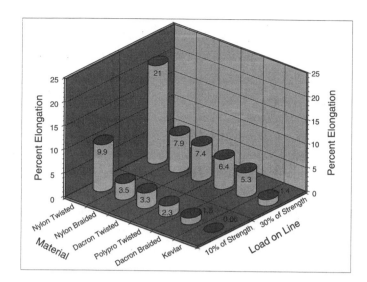

Figure 6.6 Elasticity of Various Rope Materials

rotating one end while the other end remains fixed. How much it can be rotated without damage depends on the rope's length. If the rope is overrotated, a kink will develop; if severe, the kink will reduce the rope's strength. It is much easier to over-rotate a laid rope by twisting it in the direction opposite that of the lay. Braided rope is much less susceptible to kinks than laid rope, but it is still possible to twist it severely enough to develop a kink.

To remove unwanted twist from a rope, start at one end and pull it through a loosely closed hand. This will push most of the twist ahead of the hand, causing the rope's free end to rotate and remove the twist. To remove severe twist, trail the rope over the side of the boat. If the boat is moving, take care to keep it from fouling the prop.

A kink damages rope by bending the fibers through too sharp an angle over a very small radius. The same kind of damage can be caused by leading a rope through a sheave that is too small in diameter. Minimum sheave diameter depends on the fiber material. Table 6.1 lists the minimum sheave diameter for several different materials.

Table 6.1 Proper Sheave Diameter

MATERIAL	SHEAVE DIAMETER
Natural Fibers	6 times line diameter
Dacron Fibers	6 times line diameter
Kevlar	16 times line diameter
7 × 19 stainless wire	20 times line diameter

Chafe and abrasion are the enemies of natural and synthetic fibers. Chafe occurs anytime there is relative motion between the rope and a fixed object. Chafe is most severe on anchor lines and mooring lines where they contact the boat or the dock, but it also can be caused by narrow sheaves or those that have seized and do not turn freely. Protecting docking and anchoring lines from chafe was discussed more fully in those sections.

Chafe generally occurs from the outside, but a rope can abrade from the interior as well. Dirt, sand, and salt crystals can work their way into the body of the rope and wear on the fibers and yarns, eventually cutting individual fibers and weakening the rope. Oil and other chemicals can also weaken rope fibers. Minimize the exposure of rope to these substances, and wash line occasionally in fresh water without detergents.

Salt water and sunlight are a very corrosive team. All lines that can be removed when not in use should be stored in a dry area not exposed to sunlight. Rope that cannot be removed can be protected by worming, parceling, and serving, described later in this chapter.

Coiling

Coiling a line is a simple process. The proper method depends on the type of line. Right-hand or clockwise rope and braided rope should always be put away coiled clockwise. Left-hand rope should be put up coiled counterclockwise. It is assumed in the following discussion that you are dealing with right-hand or braided ropes, since they are the most common; if not, simply substitute the term counterclockwise for clockwise.

Short lines are usually coiled in the hand and longer lines, such as anchor lines, on the deck. A line can be coiled on deck in three ways: a *straight coil*, a *Flemish coil*, or *flaked*, sometimes called faked down.

To make a straight coil on the deck, lay a 180-degree circular turn, called a bight, on the deck in a clockwise direction. Follow this bight with additional bights laid down directly on top of the preceding one until all the line is down. Work any kinks and turns in the line toward the free end. When the coil is finished turn it completely over—this is called *capsizing* the coil. The free end that started the coil will now be on top of the coil, and the line will run free of kinks when pulled from this end.

A Flemish coil is often used for coiling dock lines. Start by making a small, tight circle with the free end of the line. Wind the rest of the line outside this circle in a spiral (see Figure 6.7). The finished coil will lie flat and look like a wound clock spring. A Flemish coil is harder on the line than a straight coil, because the

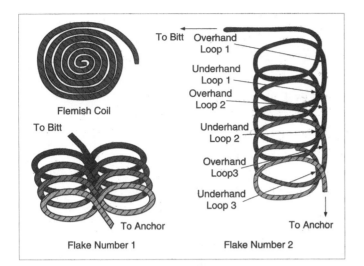

Figure 6.7 Flemish and
Flaked-Down Lines

line picks up more moisture, dirt, and ultraviolet rays. On a teak deck the coil may leave a shadow on certain finishes. The Flemish coil is used more as a decorative than a utilitarian way of putting up a line.

Anchor line is often flaked down so that when the anchor is released the line will run free with no kinks. To flake down a line, coil it in a figure eight pattern or a round coil (see Figure 6.7). To flake the rope in a coil, start at the inboard or secured end and lay down an *overhand* clockwise loop. An overhand loop passes over the rope already down. Follow that loop with an *underhand* loop, one that passes under the line already down. Continue to lay down alternating overhand and underhand loops until the outboard or free end is reached, then attach the outboard end to the anchor. In Figure 6.7, the loops are shown slightly separated for clarity; they can be laid overlapping if space is limited.

Lines can be coiled in the hand using either a straight coil or a *neutral coil*. The line can have two free ends or be attached at one end. Straight and neutral coils look considerably different, but the difference in method is subtle. The straight coil, like its deck counterpart, is a circular coil laid down clockwise. The neutral coil results in the line falling into a more bulky and unsightly coil of figure eights. I personally do not see much use for the neutral coil, and in over 30 years have never needed a neutral-coiled line. It is included here for those who do not share my view.

To straight coil a line with two free ends, place one end in the left hand with the free end facing toward the body and the thumb of the left hand facing away from the body. The free end should hang at least 10 inches below the palm. Grasp the main body of the rope loosely with the right hand, thumb up just beneath the left hand, slide the right hand down the line and away from the left hand, and move the left hand up, until sufficient rope lies between the two hands to form the desired loop size. Grip the line with the right hand and bring the two hands together. Without twisting the line, place it into the left hand so that it runs away from the body. A clockwise loop has now been made, and the line will lay in a flat coil. Continue this operation until the line is completely coiled.

To neutral coil a line with two free ends, place one end in the left hand with the free end facing away from the body. The rest of the process is similar, except as you bring your hands together, pass the line into the left hand so that it runs toward the body. A counterclockwise loop has now been made, and the line will form a figure eight. When the neutral coil is completed, the coil can be folded in half for storage. The folded coil will be circular, with the cross at the bottom.

When coiling a line with only one free end, such as halyards, sheets, and other running rigging lines, start the coil near the secured end. Many people get a neutral coil when coiling this type of line, because they instinctively grasp the line with the left hand so that the thumb points toward the secured end and away from the body. If you want to form a straight coil grasping the line in this manner it is necessary to perform complex gyrations involving twisting the rope or turning in underhand loops. I suspect this gave rise to the neutral coil. However, if you grasp the line with your left hand so that the thumb points along the line toward the free end, then twist your wrist so the thumb points away from the body, a 180-degree turn is put into the line. Now follow the normal coiling directions above, and a straight coil will result.

Braided rope is a little more forgiving than twisted rope, but it too should be coiled clockwise. Once the hand coil is complete, the alternatives are to stand and hold it until the line needs to be used again, or put it up.

Putting Up the Coil

Putting up the coil consists of finishing the coil and stowing the line. If a line is to be used again within a short period, the coil can be laid with the free end down wherever it is convenient. Lines that are used intermittently are stowed hanging on a hook or cleat. To put a loop in the coil for hanging, take one of the coil loops, wrap the single loop around the body of the coil two or three times, then pass the loop of this coil through the middle of the coiled line. Pull tightly on the end of the loop to snug up the coil and provide a protruding loop on which to hang it.

This method works very well if the coil is hung, but if it is stowed flat in a locker the loop will work free and the coil will come undone. For flat stowage, a more secure coil can be formed by wrapping the last part of the line around the coil several times, with each wrap higher than the preceding one. After three or four wraps, reach through the coil and grasp the top wrap and pull it back through the center of the coil, forming a loop. Pass this loop back over the top of the coils and pull on the free end to tighten the coil. The finished coil looks very similar to the one above except that a single line rather than a loop protrudes from the coil.

Another way to finish a coil with a hanging loop is to reach through the coil, grasp one of the loops, and pull it back through the center of the coil. Pass this loop over the top of the coil and back through the center twice; the coil can then be hung on this loop. Lines coiled in this manner cannot be snugged up tightly and come undone very easily.

A temporary method for hanging a coiled halyard is to reach through the coil and grasp the line running from the coil to the cleat, turn in a half hitch, pull the line through the coil, and use the loop thus formed to hang the coiled line. This is not as secure as the methods described above and often results in the halyard falling free prematurely.

To put up a large line or a folded neutral coil it is easiest to tie the bundle with several separate small pieces of line or ties. The bundle should be tied in two to four places depending on its size.

WHIPPING

Whipping is the surest and neatest method to prevent the end of a rope from unraveling. Although synthetic materials can be sealed by heating the ends or cutting them with a hotknife, whipping remains the best end treatment.

There are four traditional methods used to whip lines: common or plain whipping, sailor's whipping, sailmaker's whipping, and needle whipping. The simplest but least effective method is the common whipping; the best and most permanent is the needle whipping.

The equipment needed for whipping consists of a sharp knife, a cutting board, waxed twine, sailmaker's needles, wax, and a palm. A small torch, candle, or other means of melting the ends of synthetic rope is also needed. The amount of twine per whipping depends on the diameter of the rope; use Table 6.2 as a guide.

Table 6.2 Length of Twine Needed for Whipping

ROPE DIAMETER (IN INCHES)	TWINE LENGTH (IN INCHES)
$3/8$	30
$1/2$	36
$5/8$	48
$3/4$	60

To start a common whipping make a ¾-inch loop in the twine. Lay the loop along the rope and take 15 to 20 turns around the rope, against the lay of the rope, and back over the top of the loop. Pull each of the turns of twine as tight as possible and snug them up against the preceding loop. When about ½ inch of the rope is covered, pass the free end of the twine through the upper end of the initial ¾-inch loop. Pull on the other end of the twine, collapsing the initial ¾-inch loop and pulling the free end under the coils into the center of the whip (see Figure 6.8). Snip off the protruding ends.

Begin a sailor's whipping by laying ¾ inch of twine along the rope and making 8 to 10 tight turns against the lay back over the beginning end of the twine. Then take the free end of the twine and lay it along the rope in the other direction, over the turns just put down. Continue by adding another 8 to 10 turns now over both ends of the twine. Pull on the free end now protruding from the middle of the whip until the last loop disappears and is snug against the remaining turns. Cut off the surplus twine where it exits the whipping.

The traditional sailmaker's whipping is only for laid or twisted rope. Unlay the rope for a short way and lay the twine into the strands, as shown in Figure 6.9. Retwist the rope and whip it against the lay in tight turns. Pass the last turn of the free end between the strands, then pass the large loop from the bottom over one of the strands and pull it tight. Finish by knotting the two ends together and clipping the surplus twine.

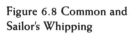

Figure 6.8 Common and Sailor's Whipping

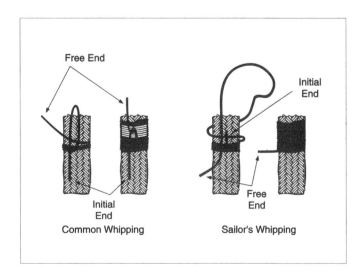

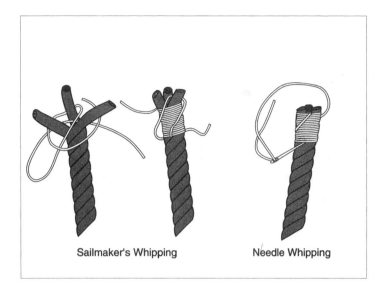

Figure 6.9 Sailmaker's
and Needle Whipping

Sailmaker's Whipping   Needle Whipping

For the needle whipping, you must thread the twine through a needle and knot the end. Start the whipping ¾ inch below the end of the rope. If the rope is stranded, insert the needle between two strands and through one, then pull the knot into the center of the rope. Take 18 or 20 tight turns against the lay and finish by again inserting the needle through one of the strands so that it exits opposite between two strands. Pull the twine tight. Follow this first groove in the rope between the two strands to the beginning end of the whipping. Insert the needle into this groove and exit into a second groove on the opposite side of the line. Pull the twine tight. Follow this second groove to the finished end of the whipping and again pass the needle through this groove and exit into the remaining third groove. Return to the beginning end of the whipping and reinsert the needle in the third groove. Pull tight, and finish the whipping by passing the needle lengthwise through the rope so that it exits the end of the rope. Cut off all surplus twine. If the line is not stranded, space the stitches around the line 120 degrees apart and staggered top and bottom. This is a very secure whipping.

If the rope was not cut with a "hot knife," it is best to finish off synthetic lines by melting the ends with a small torch or candle. Try not to burn the rope or the whipping, which will leave a large, unsightly glob of melted plastic on the end of the line that may make it difficult to pass the line through a block. Natural fiber ropes can be finished by dipping the whipped end into varnish.

KNOTS

Some traditional terms are used when discussing knots (see Figure 6.10). The *bitter end* is the end farthest away, usually already attached securely to the boat. The *standing part* is the middle of the line. The remaining end is called the *free end*, or simply the end.

If the end of a line is taken through a 180-degree turn and led back on itself, it is called a *bight*. If the free end is taken through a 270-degree turn back over the top of the standing part, an *overhand loop* results. If the free end is taken through the same turn but passes under the standing part, an *underhand loop* is made. If the free end is turned 360 degrees and leads off in the direction in which it came, it is called a *round turn*. It is called an overhand or underhand round turn depending on whether the line passes over or under the standing part.

Of the thousands of knots, only about a dozen are of value to recreational boaters. There are three stopper knots used to prevent a line from accidentally running completely through blocks: overhand, figure eight, and stevedore; seven hitches used to tie lines together or to objects: square knot, sheet bend, rolling hitch, cleat hitch, lark's head, clove hitch, and round turn with two half hitches; and two knots commonly used to make nonslipping eyes in rope: bowline and trucker's hitch. There are many ways to tie each of these knots; the following methods were chosen for clarity and simplicity. After you become familiar with these knots, experimentation may provide you with an easier or faster procedure.

Figure 6.10 Knot Nomenclature

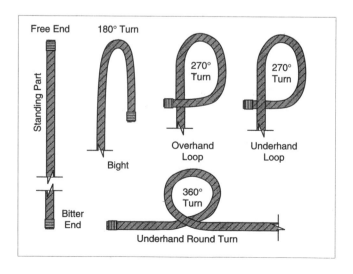

Stopper Knots

The **overhand knot** (see Figure 6.11) is the simplest of the stopper knots. Start with an underhand loop and pass the free end back over the line and through the loop. Pull the ends tight. A sustained large load will tend to force this knot down the line toward the free end and tighten the knot. The overhand knot has two limitations: sufficient load may force the loop completely over the end and untie the knot, and a tightly tied overhand is practically impossible to untie by hand.

The **figure eight knot** (see Figure 6.11) has none of the faults of the overhand knot and makes a larger knob on the end of the rope. Begin with an overhand loop. Pass the end back under the standing part of the line outside the loop, then pass it back both over and through the loop and tighten the knot.

The **stevedore knot** (see Figure 6.11) has even more bulk to stop the line from passing through large openings. It is made like the figure eight, except that before you pass the end back through the loop, make an additional 360-degree round turn around the standing part of the line outside the loop, then pass the end both over and through the loop and tighten the knot.

Hitches

The **square knot** (see Figure 6.12) can be used to tie two ends of a line or two lines of the same diameter together. To make it, pass the right end over the left rope and then back under the left rope, then snug up the lines. This is the familiar beginning to tying a shoelace. For the second half of the knot the ends have changed

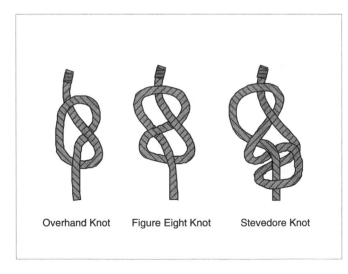

Figure 6.11 Stopper Knots

Overhand Knot   Figure Eight Knot   Stevedore Knot

sides—the right end is now on the left side and vice versa. Take the left end back over the right and tuck it through the loop made by the right line. Pull the knot tight. The finished knot should have both parts of one end of the line either over or under the loop formed by the other end of the line. When ready to untie, you can loosen the square knot slightly by pulling on one free end.

A **sheet bend** (see Figure 6.12) is used to tie two lines of different diameter together or to tie a line to a becket or an eye in a sail. Make a bight in the larger-diameter line and pass the end of the smaller-diameter line up through the bight in the large line (or through the becket or eye), then around and under the bight of the large line and back under itself, forming an overhand loop. The end of the small line does not go back through the bight; pass it out over the edge of the bight in the large line. Tighten the knot securely.

The **rolling hitch** (see Figure 6.12) is used to tie a line to a pole or to the middle of another line. We will describe the knot as being tied to a pole to avoid confusion. Lead the line in at right angles to the pole and take two 360-degree round turns around it. Take a third round turn around the pole on the opposite side of the incoming line from the first two turns, pass the end under this last turn, and tighten the knot. The rolling hitch can also be used to tie a second line to an anchor or to take the load off a line running to a jammed winch. It can be slid up the pole or line, but holds fast if pulled from the bottom, the side with the two round turns.

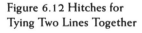

Figure 6.12 Hitches for Tying Two Lines Together

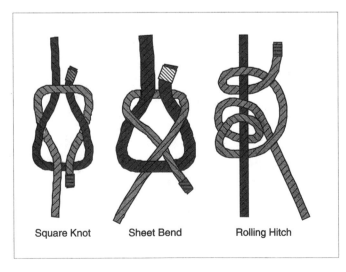

Square Knot   Sheet Bend   Rolling Hitch

The **clove hitch** (see Figure 6.13) is used to tie a line to pole, piling, or bitt. Its ease of adjustment makes it ideal for tying fenders to the lifelines or railings. Use the clove hitch on lines under constant load; intermittent loads tend to loosen the knot, causing it to slip. The clove hitch normally is tied by laying the line over the pole, passing the end 360 degrees around the pole and back over the top of the line. Another 360-degree round turn is taken around the pole and the end passed under this turn.

The knot can also be formed in the hands and slipped over a post, even if both ends are secured. Hold the line in both hands, palms down. Throw a loop into the line with the right hand by flipping the wrist over quickly; the line leading left will be over the line leading right. Hold this loop in your left hand, then form another loop exactly as you did the first, holding it in the right hand. Place the loop in the right hand on top of the loop in the left hand, slip both loops over the post, and pull the ends tight.

The **cleat hitch** (see Figure 6.13) is the knot recreational boaters tie most often. It is also the knot most often tied improperly. As the name implies, it is used to tie a line, such as a halyard or a mooring line, to a cleat. There are eight different "correct" ways to tie a cleat hitch, depending on how the line is led to the cleat, whether the knot is started with a bight or a round turn, and how it is finished. The easiest way to tie a cleat hitch is to pay strict attention to how the line is led to the cleat.

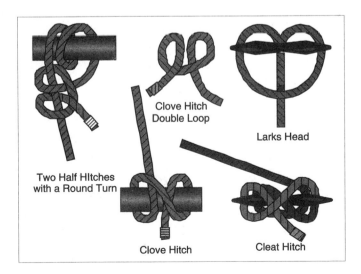

Clove Hitch
Double Loop

Larks Head

Two Half Hitches
with a Round Turn

Clove Hitch

Cleat Hitch

Figure 6.13 Hitches for Tying Lines to Objects

Face the cleat with one horn on the right and one on the left. If the line is coming in essentially parallel to the cleat horns, lead the line to the horn on the far side of the cleat and form a round turn around the base of the cleat, taking the line under both horns. If it is coming into the cleat perpendicular to the horns from behind you, lead the line to either horn and form a round turn around the base of the cleat, again taking the line completely under both horns. Now lead the end up over the top and across the center of the cleat, then down under and around the opposite horn. Take the end back across the top of the cleat and over itself. Finish the knot by turning an underhand loop into the end of the line and slipping it around the horn with the end of the line leading toward your body. When the knot is tied correctly, the two lines going in the same diagonal direction across the top of the cleat are pinned down by the line crossing diagonally in the opposite direction.

The most common mistake is to throw the finishing half hitch in the wrong direction, causing the diagonal line that pins the other two to the cleat to fall along the side of the cleat, where it is not as effective at locking the knot. This most commonly occurs for right handers if the line is coming perpendicular to the cleat from in front of you, because the process of turning in an underhand loop is difficult in this orientation. The same easy flow of the underhand loop can be maintained by taking another half turn around the cleat and passing the line under the opposite horn twice.

If tied correctly, the single underhand loop, or **half hitch**, is sufficient. Using multiple half hitches and crisscrossing the cleat from horn to horn is unsightly, time consuming, and unnecessary. This knot can be started with a round turn instead of a bight; lead the line to the cleat on the near side of the cleat.

The lark's head (see Figure 6.13), used by boaters to tie a mooring line to a cleat, is tied using a line with an eye spliced into the end. The eye is passed through the opening in the base of the cleat and then over the horns of the cleat. This is a more secure way of attaching a line with an eye to a cleat than just looping the eye over the horns. It also reduces chafe.

It has been said that two half hitches will hold the devil. It follows that **two half hitches** with a round turn (360-degree turn; see Figure 6.13) will hold the devil and a couple of my friends. This knot is used in circumstances similar to those described for the clove hitch. Although it cannot be tied in the middle of a line or slipped over a post as easily as the clove hitch, it can be used to tie a line to a ring, an eye, or a grommet. Pass the line around the pole one and one-half times, or 540 degrees. Finish the knot by making two successive overhand loops, half hitches, around the standing part. When properly tied, two half hitches looks like a clove hitch around a line. A variation called the **fisherman's bend** or **anchor bend** is tied by passing the first turn of the clove hitch *under* the round turn. This makes for a very secure knot.

The **trucker's hitch** (see Figure 6.14) is a handy knot for putting a fixed eye several feet from the end of a line. The eye can be used to take additional purchase on the line and cinch down items that need to be tied tightly or battened down. It can be used to tie a dinghy to the boat or car, or to take the slack out of any line that needs to be hauled tight. Form a long loop in the line approximately where the eye is desired, then tie an overhand or figure eight knot with this long loop around the standing part. If you tie the knot properly, you will form an eye that will not slip in the line. Take the free end to the original attachment point and pass it around this ring or bar and back through the fixed eye in the line. Pulling on the end of the line will now put twice the tensioning load on the line.

When all the slack is out of the line, pinch it where it crosses the eye with just the thumb and forefinger holding all the load in the line. A half hitch thrown around the line and snugged up against the eye will hold the load while you add the second half hitch. If you need additional tension, tie a second trucker's hitch in the line.

The **bowline** (see Figure 6.14), the most useful of all seagoing knots, can be used for almost anything and often is. I would estimate that 80 percent of all knots tied aboard a boat are bowlines. It is a very secure knot that can be untied with little effort even after it has been subjected to large loads. The bowline puts a nonslipping eye in a line; this can be used to to tie sheets to sails, to attach a line to a dingy or anything else, or to tie a loop around the body of person who has fallen overboard.

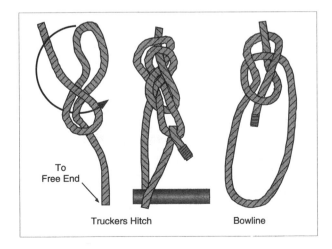

To Free End

Truckers Hitch   Bowline

Figure 6.14 Knots for
Making Loops

To make a nonslipping eye with the bowline, form a small overhand loop in the line about twice the distance from the free end of the rope as the length of the desired eye. Pass the end of the line up through this loop, leaving enough slack to form the fixed eye, around the standing part and back down through the loop. Tighten the knot by holding the end and one side of the loop and pulling on the standing part. The standard phrase used to remember this sequence is that the rabbit (the end of the line) comes out of his hole (the overhand loop), around the tree (the standing part), and back down the hole. The most common error in making a bowline is to start with an underhand loop, in which case the knot will dissolve into a strange figure eight when tightened.

Because the bowline can be used for making a lifesaving eye around your own body, it is worth learning a second method of tying the knot quickly using one hand to hold the rope and the other to tie the knot. Assuming that you are right handed, grasp the line with the left hand about 6 feet from the free end; this will take all load off the last 6 feet of line. Pass the slack end around behind your body and grasp the line about 6 or 8 inches from the end with the right hand, palm up. Lay the right wrist across the top of the line between the body and the left hand. Leave a gap between the body and the wrist. The palm of the right hand is now down and the line forms a closed loop around the body.

Push the right hand down and curl it over and around the line so that the closed right hand is forced back to pass inside the loop next to the body. The palm is now up and a loop is formed around the wrist. Keep this loop loose. The end of the line in the right hand is now leading away from the body parallel with the line coming from the left hand. Pass the end of the line around behind the line coming from the left hand. Flip the end of the line toward the body with the fingers and catch it with the thumb. Change the grip on the end so that the right hand now holds only the very end of the line caught by the thumb. Holding tight to this end, withdraw the right hand from the loop. A bowline has now been tied around the body using only one hand. With a little practice this knot can be made in less than 5 seconds.

SPLICES

When connecting lines or making loops, knots have one very bad feature: they weaken the line. A knot reduces line strength between 50 and 75 percent. For a permanent loop or connection, it is better to use a splice.

It is possible to buy docking lines and anchor lines with eyesplices already installed; however, splicing is a useful skill for customizing boating equipment. For example, many boaters have docking lines with eyesplices on both ends, sized specifically for the slip and boat. These lines are used only in the home slip; standard commercial docking lines are used when visiting other marinas.

There are four basic types of splices: the short splice, the long splice, the eyesplice, and the backsplice. The **short splice** and the **long splice** are used to connect two lines. The short splice joins two ropes and is the easiest to make in a laid line; however, it increases the line's diameter. If the line must pass through a sheave, the diameter must remain constant, making it necessary to use the long splice. The **eyesplice**, the splice most commonly made by recreational boaters, is used to put a permanent loop in a line. The **backsplice** is used instead of whipping to finish the end of a line. Few people backsplice anymore; it not only increases the diameter of the line, but to look finished the splice needs to be whipped anyway. It is included here for the sake of completeness.

The equipment for splicing laid line includes a sharp knife, tape, twine, a cutting board, a felt marking pen, and a hollow or solid fid. The hollow fid helps in getting the strand tucked through the line. The process of forcing one strand under another is called a **tuck**. To make a tuck it is sometimes necessary to twist the line against the lay to open a small gap under one strand into which to push the strand being tucked. Larger lines may require that you use the fid to pry and hold open the strands of the rope.

Splicing technique differs depending on whether the line is laid, single braided, or double braided, and whether the braided line has a straight core or a braided core. The simplest splice to make is a short splice in twisted natural fiber line, but natural fiber rope is no longer used much aboard recreational boats. Twisted synthetic fiber rope is slightly more difficult to work with, because the fibers and strands do not retain their twist and tend to unlay when the rope itself is unlaid. Synthetic fiber is also slightly more slippery than natural fiber. It therefore requires more tucks than natural fiber to make a stable splice.

Since splicing is normally done on a demand basis, not often enough to commit the process to memory, some of the similar procedures are repeated under each splice. The splices are presented in their perceived order of difficulty.

Laid Line

Preparation is the same for all laid line splices. The process described is for synthetic fibers; natural fibers do not require as much line nor the intermediate taping. Measure approximately six line diameters from the end of each line involved, in all splices except the long splice. At this spot whip the line or tape it very tightly. This temporary whipping will prevent the rope from unlaying further than desired and will not allow the strands to loosen beyond this point.

Unlay three or four turns of the line. Tape the ends of each individual strand, starting about 1 inch from the end and winding the tape tightly in the direction the strand is laid. Continue the taping past the end of the strand, then reverse the direction of the taping back to the original point. Taping past the stand end will form a point that will assist in interweaving or tucking the strands. Unlay another three or four turns and tape again partway down each strand. Unlay the rest of the line to the temporary whipping.

Short Splice

Prepare both lines as described above. Next, butt the two whipped ends together, interweaving the separate strands so that the strand of one rope lies alternately between the strands of the other, as shown in Figure 6.15. Working with one rope at a time, undo the whipping on that rope. Now take a loose strand from the other rope and weave it over the strand lying immediately to its left, and under the next strand. This will weave the strands in against the lay of the nonwhipped rope.

When all three strands have been woven in this manner, firmly pull and twist each strand to tighten the lay of the strands while smoothing and tightening the splice. Remember always to twist the strands counterclockwise. These tucks will lock the splice in position. Continue weaving the strands in this manner until five tucks (three for natural fiber rope) have been taken. Twist and pull on the strands after each tuck. When the intermediate tapes on the strands are reached, remove them in turn.

Figure 6.15 Short and Long Splice in Twisted Line

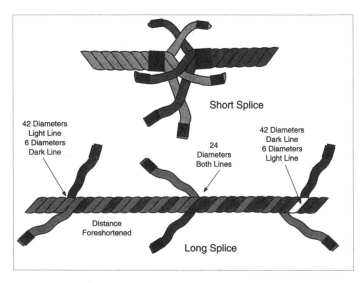

The ends can now be tapered if desired by removing one-third of the fibers from the strand and making another tuck, then removing another third and making the final tuck. Repeat the entire process on the other line. Pull on the completed splice and roll it underfoot to work the strands into the splice before cutting off the remaining strand ends.

Long Splice

In preparing the line for the long splice it is necessary to measure and mark with a felt pen completely around both lines at 6, 24, and 42 diameters from the end. Unlay the ends of both ropes a couple of turns and tape the end of the strands tightly. Unlay both ropes down to the 24-diameter mark, taping the strands lightly every 3 or 4 inches. Marry the lines together in a manner similar to that used for the short splice.

Unlay one strand of the left-hand line back to the mark at 24 diameters. As this strand is being unlaid, place in the space left by its removal the opposing strand from the right-hand line. Remove any intermediate tape before placing the strand in the slot. Cut off and retape the long strand, leaving only about 6 diameters. Repeat the entire process with the right-hand line. Cut off the third strands from both ropes, leaving about 6 diameters, and retape. Now take each pair of strands in succession and tie an overhand knot (or the beginning of a square knot) in the strands. Tuck each strand end twice into the rope, going with the lay, then taper the strand by reducing the fibers as described above and take two more tucks with each strand. Pull on the line and roll the splices to bury the strands. Remove all excess fibers. Properly done, the splice should be difficult to detect and the same diameter as the original line.

Eyesplice

The only difficult part of the eyesplice are the initial tucks. Prepare the line as described for the short splice. Determine the length of the eye and the junction point. Small-diameter eyes are generally made around a thimble to keep them in shape, prevent abrasion, and allow the fibers a longer radius of curvature when loaded. A thimble is a tear-shaped, grooved plastic or metal loop that lines the inside of a small splice. If the eye is to be made around a thimble, place the thimble on the line, position it in its final position, and mark only one strand at the junction point.

If the eye is to be placed in a mooring line, it will not have a thimble and should be made slightly longer than the cleat so that it will fit over it easily. For example, for a 10-inch cleat, measure 22 inches back from the temporary whipping and mark only one strand at the junction point. This strand is designated strand 3. The strand next to it but farther down the line toward the bitter end is strand 2, followed by strand 1 (see Figure 6.16).

Once the junction point is marked, make a loop in the rope around the thimble if one is to be used and bring the unlaid end to the junction point. Hold the loop so the standing part of the line runs away from the body. An unlaid rope can be looked at in only two different configurations. Two of the three strands come off the top of the rope and the third comes from under the rope; or one of the three strands comes off the top and the other two come from underneath. To simplify, a standard configuration will be used in which two strands come off the top of the rope. In this instance, the strand coming from beneath the rope should be the strand farthest back on the line; it should point to the left and is designated strand A in Figure 6.16. The next strand coming off the rope should lead off to the right, and is designated strand C. The last strand should be in the middle pointing straight down the line away from the body; this is strand B.

With the line in the proper position pass strand B under strand 2 from right to left against the lay. Next pass strand A under strand 1. Snug up and twist the strands. Now comes the difficult part: turn the eye over, trace strand 3 around the line, and tuck in strand C under strand 3. Be very careful to pass strand C *against* the lay. The most common mistake is tucking the last strand in the wrong direction or under the wrong strand. The strands should exit the lines in a symmetrical pattern. Take the remaining tucks in normal rotation and finish the splice as described above for the short splice.

Figure 6.16 Eyesplice and Backsplice in Twisted Line

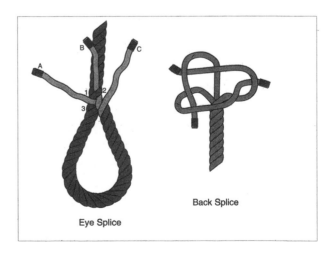

Eye Splice

Back Splice

Backsplice

The trick to the backsplice is in tying the crown knot that begins it. Prepare the line as described above and hold it in the standard configuration described for the beginning of the eyesplice, so that the same strands lead left, center, and right. The strand on the left goes under the center strand and over the right strand. The strand on the right goes over the center strand and under the left strand, through the loop made by the left strand, and exits over the left strand (see Figure 6.16). Snug and twist the strands. The rest of the splice is woven into the rope against the lay as described for the short splice.

Braided Line

A splice in a braided line works on the same principle as the Chinese finger puzzle. When the braided cover is stretched its diameter is reduced and it grips the core of the splice. Splicing braided line is a relatively simple operation; it only becomes difficult in small-diameter lines due to the lack of space. Splicing a 3/16-inch-diameter line is next to impossible. Splices on braided lines are usually eyesplices. The only commonly used method for splicing lines together is the end splice. Large-diameter heavy-duty lines are not normally end spliced.

Braided line can be 8-strand plaited, 12-strand single braided, or double braided with either a braided core or a parallel core. Each of these variations calls for a slightly different splicing technique. Fortunately, the various line manufacturers publish copious literature on splicing their lines. Ask at your chandlery, or write the manufacturer.

Because it is most common, we'll cover eyesplicing generic double-braid line with a braided core. This should cover the needs of the majority of recreational boaters.

The required tools are electrician's tape, a sharp knife, a cutting board, scissors, a felt tip marker, a measuring tape, a crochet hook, a pair of vise grips, and a splicing fid of the proper size. Each diameter of rope requires a different-diameter fid; multipurpose fids are harder to work with than normal fids. It is sometimes easier to use a fid one size smaller than the rope. However, do not use the undersized fid for measurement.

Used line loses some of its elasticity and diameter, which makes splicing difficult. Soaking the section to be spliced in warm fresh water will loosen and lubricate the fibers, making splicing easier.

Eyesplicing Double-Braid Line with Braided Core

The steps involved in splicing double-braid line are marking the line, extracting the core, marking the core, inserting the cover into the core, tapering the cover, inserting the core into the cover, tightening the crossover, tapering the core, burying the tails, and burying the crossover.

To make an eyesplice, tape the end of the line, measure back 21 diameters (one fid length) and mark point A (see Figure 6.17). Form the eye from point A and mark the loop on the line opposite from point A. This is point B. From point B measure 14 diameters and mark the line. This is point D. From point D measure 200 diameters (approximately nine fid lengths) and tie a slip knot. From point A count back toward the end of the line eight pics. Mark these strands. This is point C. Count off five pairs of strands and mark, then count off four pairs of strands and mark. Repeat until the end of the rope is reached.

To extract the core, bend the line sharply at point B and carefully spread the strands apart on the top of the bend to make an opening to the core. Being careful not to distort the strands, pry out the core through this opening. Pull the end of the core totally free and tape. Now slide the cover back toward the slip knot as far as it will go. If there is a marker tape in the rope, cut and remove it. Smooth the cover from the slip knot back over the core and mark the core at the point where it exits from the cover. This is point I. Again slide the cover back toward the slip knot. Measure 7 diameters back from point I and make another mark on the core. This is point II. From this mark, measure another 21 diameters and make a final mark, point III.

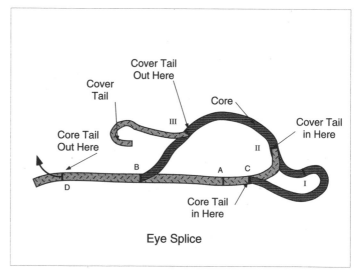

Figure 6.17 Eyesplice in Double-Braided Line

If the splice is to be made around a thimble with ears or a shackle, thread the core through the thimble or shackle at this point. Attach the cover to the fid. Insert the fid into the core at point II, work it down the center of the core, and exit the core at point III. Pull the cover through the core until point A is exposed at point III. Remove the fid and tape the cover end.

Starting at the pair of marked strands on the cover farthest from the taped end, cut each marked strand pair and remove. If the cover tends to bunch up while tapering, hold the cover at point A and smooth toward the end. During this process attach vise grips or tie a loose knot at point A to prevent the cover from disappearing back into the core. Once the cover is tapered, remove the vise grips or knot and pull the cover back out of the core until C is exposed at point II. Reattach the vise grips or tie a knot in the cover tail.

To bury the core, attach the end of the core to the fid. Insert the fid into the cover at point C, pass it through the center of the cover, and exit at point D. If the distance between C and D is longer than a fid length, several passes may be necessary. Go as far as possible and the bring the fid and core out through the cover at some intermediate point. Reinsert the fid and core back into the same opening; repeat until point D is reached. Puckering the cover ahead of the fid and using a smaller fid assists this process.

The next step is to bring points C and II together. Where these two points coincide, called the **crossover point**, the cover goes into the core and the core goes into the cover. To tighten, grasp the crossover point firmly and alternately pull on the exposed cover and core tails, being careful not to pull the cover tail into the core. Continue tightening until the crossover point diameter is approximately equal to the initial rope diameter.

When the crossover is tightened properly the cover can be buried in the core. Untie the knot or remove the vise grips from the cover tail. Hold the line firmly at the crossover and smooth the line from the crossover in both directions. This will cause the tapered cover to slip into the core.

Next, taper and bury the core. To taper the core, mark it where it exits at point D. Pull the core out at D until 14 to 16 diameters of core are exposed between this mark on the core and point D. Cut the core off at the mark, discard the end, and measure back 7 diameters. Tape the core at this spot. Unbraid the core down to the tape and fan out the strands on the cutting board. Cut the strands at a 45-degree angle from the tape to the end. Remove the tape and bury the core tail by holding the crossover point and smoothing the line toward D until the tail disappears and the line between points D and B looks smooth.

The last and most difficult part of the splice is burying the crossover point. Secure the slip knot to something very strong, because this process requires considerable load on the line. Hold the crossover point under tension and slip the bunched-up cover back from the slip knot over the line. Start with light pressure and gradually increase as the eye is approached. Milk the cover over the exposed core, moving the extraction point B toward the crossover point, until the crossover point is buried in the cover beyond point B and point A is opposite point B. Hammering and flexing the throat of the splice may assist in burying the core. In very difficult situations, it may be necessary to move the slip knot farther down the line or attach a line to the crossover point, and to tension the core to reduce its diameter to bury the crossover point completely. The splice can be stitched and whipped if desired.

To lock-stitch the splice, begin six to eight rope diameters from the splice. Using whipping twine, place six or eight large (diameter-length) stitches in the line toward the eye, the return to the starting point with six or eight more stitches. The final step is whipping the throat of the eye using one of the methods described earlier.

Splicing Wire to Rope

Splicing wire to twisted or braided rope is for experts, masochists, and people who hate their fingers. These splices are used mostly for halyards—the wire portion has little stretch under load, and the rope makes the halyard easy to handle. Rope-spliced wire halyards are being replaced by low-stretch Kevlar line in many applications.

The description given here is for splicing double-braided Dacron line and 7 × 19 wire rope.

You'll need a hollow fid, wire cutters, a sharp knife, a cutting board, plastic tape, a marlinspike, 7 × 19 wire rope long enough to reach from the head of the sail to the attachment point on the deck, and braided rope of the proper diameter. Table 6.3 gives the suggested combinations of wire and braided rope.

To begin the splice, taper the wire rope by unlaying one strand about 19 inches back from the end. Cut off about 18 inches of this strand. Unlay a second strand and cut off 15 inches. Unlay the other strands. Cut off 12 inches from the third strand, 9 inches from the fourth strand, 6 inches from the fifth strand, and 3 inches from the sixth strand. Starting 10 inches from the end of the cut-off sixth strand, wrap plastic tape over the tapered wire back to the free end of the wire rope.

Prepare the double-braided line by putting a slip knot about 220 diameters back from the free end. Pull back the cover of the line a couple of feet to expose

Table 6.3 Suggested Rope Diameters (in inches)	
7 X 19 WIRE ROPE	BRAIDED DACRON ROPE
1/8	3/8
5/32	3/8
3/16	7/16
7/32	1/2
1/4	1/2
5/16	5/8
3/8	3/4

the core of the double braid. Cut off about 3 inches of the braided core. Carefully insert the taped wire into the center of the braided core until the taped portion of the wire is buried about 6 inches into the core. Tape the core tightly where the wire rope ends, about 3 inches either side of the end, to keep the wire from poking through the core. Tape the core about 6 inches back from the end, making sure the core is pulled tightly down over the wire. Unweave the core strands and separate them into three equal parts. Tape the ends of these strand bundles together (see Figure 6.18).

Pull the core down the wire to smooth and remove all slack in the core. Insert the hollow fid between the first two strands of wire rope exposed where the core is bundled. Be sure to push the fid away from you in case it slips. Take the bundle of core strands closest to the fid and push the end of the bundled core strands under

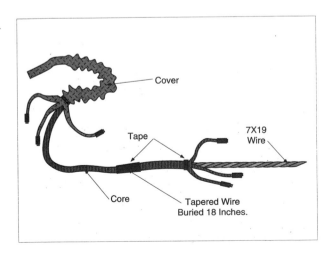

Figure 6.18 Wire-to-Rope Splice for Braided Line

WORMING, PARCELING, SERVING, AND SEIZING

Worming, parceling, and serving (see Figure 6.19) are timeworn techniques used to protect a twisted rope from wear and weather. The durability and low cost of synthetic and wire rope have made these processes largely obsolete, except perhaps for decorative ropework or for traditional-minded boaters.

Worming is the process of laying a small-diameter cord in the grooves between the strands of rope. It makes the rope more circular in cross section and protects the strands from wear. **Parceling** is the process of wrapping fiber tape, traditionally saturated with pine, around the rope in diagonal overlapping turns. It is usually done over worming and protects the rope further from weather and wear. **Serving** is essentially a very long whipping. Like whipping, it consists of winding a small cord tightly and evenly around a rope. Serving can be done on top of parceling for further protection.

Seizing is used to fasten two lines together, and although it too comes down to us from the past, seizing is often used today, particularly to form eyes in braided line for those unable or unwilling to splice it. A seizing is more permanent than a knot but not as permanent as a splice. Seizing can be made in essentially three configurations: clinch, eye, or straight (see Figure 6.20). It is similar to whipping, and is done with small cord in two basic patterns, standard and racked. If both lines are to receive equal load, standard seizing will work. Racked seizing resists slippage better and is therefore preferred when the lines are to be loaded unequally.

(continued next page)

the wire strand, against the lay. Pull and tighten the core strands and remove the fid. Move to the next two wire strands and repeat the process with another core strand bundle. Tuck each core strand bundle five or six times under the wire strands. Cut the bundle ends off flush.

Smooth out the core and the wire rope. Then pull the cover of the braided line back over the top of the core. This may be a tight fit, but get all the slack out of the cover until there are 6 or 7 inches of cover beyond the end of the core wire rope splice. Tape the cover tightly to the wire just beyond the core splice. This is the point where the cover splice will begin. Unlay the cover strands, separate into three bundles, and tape the ends. Insert the fid between the first two strands of wire below the core splice and repeat the splicing procedure described above. Once the first five or six tucks have been taken, taper the cover strands by removing about one-third of the strands for each taper tuck. Cut all loose strands as close to the wire as possible and finish by heating the ends of the braided cover to fuse the synthetic fibers.

TACKLE

A tackle is a combination of pulleys (blocks) and rope. It works because a rope is flexible and bends. Consider Case 1 in Figure 6.21, where a line is simply attached to a fixed bar and a person applies 50 pounds of pull. The reaction in the bar is equal to 50 pounds.

In Case 2, instead of attaching the line to the bar it is bent 180 degrees around the bar and brought back to a second person also pulling 50 pounds. There is still 50 pounds of pull in the rope ends, but there is now 100 pounds of pull on the bar. If the second person is removed and the line is attached to a 50-pound load, the situation is the same. However, if the load and the reaction are reversed, as in the Case 3, the one person applying 50 pounds of pull on the rope can produce 100 pounds of pull on the load.

This increase in pulling power with no apparent increase in effort is called mechanical advantage; in this example, a mechanical advantage of two. This is the principle behind what is commonly called a **parbuckle**, or sometimes a Spanish parbuckle. The parbuckle is a simple tackle that requires no pulleys. The load is the pulley and therefore needs to be roughly cylindrical in shape. A parbuckle requires two lines, as shown in Figure 6.22, not for the added mechanical advantage but to keep the load oriented properly. Tying off one line and pulling on the other line would provide the same force, but the line would have to slide or move around

WORMING, PARCELING, SERVING, AND SEIZING (continued)

To perform a standard seizing, start by tying a clove hitch around one of the lines with the small diameter cord. Position the knot so that it is between the lines. Take enough tight turns around both lines, against the lay, to cover one and one-half to two diameters of the line. The last turn goes around only one line, so that the end of the cord is brought between the lines. To finish and tighten the seizing, take two or three tight turns around it between the two lines, then tie the two ends of the cord together with a square knot positioned so that it is hidden between the lines.

A racked seizing is similar, except the turns around the rope are over one line, between the lines, and under the other, in a figure-eight pattern. If the eye seizing is done around a thimble, start the seizing as close to the thimble as possible.

the load. Two problems are immediately apparent: the object would not roll straight, and considerable friction would occur as the line slid around the load.

Both of these problems can be fixed by adding the recently invented wheel to the system. To avoid patent restrictions the device can be called a pulley (or, nautically speaking, a block). This refinement drastically reduces the friction at the load point. There are many picturesque names for tackles, including whip, double whip, whip-on-whip, Spanish burton, inverted whip-on-whip, gun tackle, luff tackle, watch tackle, handy billy, and inverted double purchase.

Tackle Identification

Most of those tackle names have fallen out of use, but handy billy has become almost a synonym for tackle. Fortunately a much more useful and somewhat less confusing way of referring to a specific type of tackle was developed using the number of pulleys or parts. To make sense of this nomenclature it is necessary to first look at the component of a tackle called a block (pulley). The block is composed of *sheaves*, a *becket*, *cheeks*, a *swivel*, and a *shackle* (see Figure 6.23). The sheaves and the becket are of the greatest interest in this instance because of their involvement in the nomenclature of tackle.

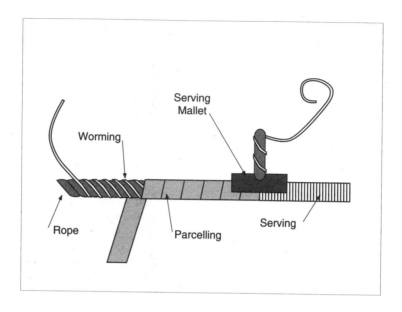

Figure 6.19 Worming, Parceling, and Serving

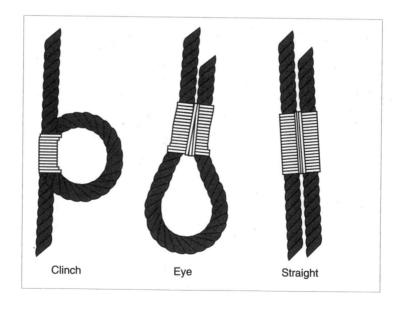

Figure 6.20 Seizing

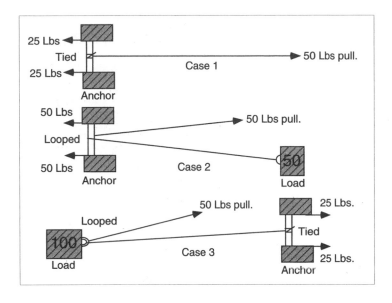

Figure 6.21 The Miracle of Flexibility

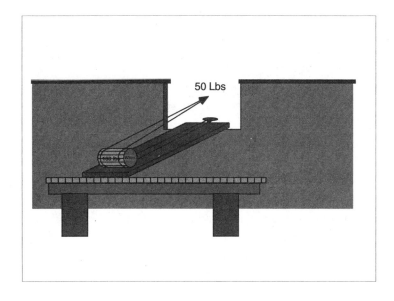

Figure 6.22 Parbuckle

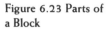

Figure 6.23 Parts of a Block

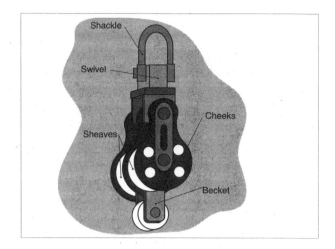

The mechanical advantage of a tackle is directly dependent on the total number of sheaves. Therefore, a tackle can be uniquely described by its total number of sheaves. For example, a tackle with two blocks each containing two sheaves has a total of four sheaves and can be referred to as a four-part tackle.

Details of Operation

The number of sheaves, sometimes called parts, plus the location of the becket, determines the mechanical advantage gained by using the tackle. A two-part tackle can provide a mechanical advantage of two or three, depending on the position of the becket and how it is attached to the load. To bring to bear the greatest mechanical advantage, the block with the becket must be attached to the load. Notice that in Figure 6.24, when the block with the becket is attached to the load, the mechanical advantage is three.

To calculate the mechanical advantage, count the total number of lines attached to the load. Note, however, that if this load was being lifted vertically the pull would be applied upward. Pulling upward is not as effective as pulling down, where the body weight can be utilized in addition to arm strength. The convenience of pull-down is why a tackle is sometimes used in the reverse position with less mechanical advantage.

Before you conclude that something is gained for nothing, consider the principles of work and friction. The apparently magical operation of a pulley depends on a physical principle called work, defined as moving a load through a distance. When using a pulley the load may drop, but the work remains the same.

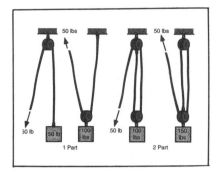 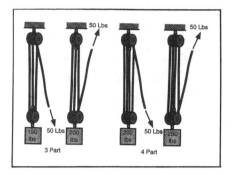

Figure 6.24 Mechanical Advantage of Common Tackles Arrangements

If in the case of a single pulley the rope is attached to the load, as shown in First Situation in Figure 6.25, and the pulling end of the rope is moved a distance of 10 feet, the load will be moved 10 feet. The work is 500 foot-pounds. The mechanical advantage is one, and the amount of pull required is 50 pounds.

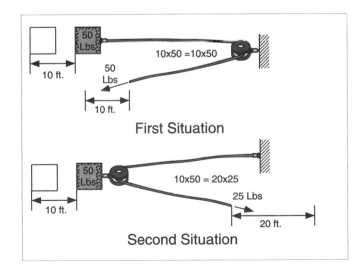

Figure 6.25 Equal Work Principle as Applied to Pulleys

If the pulley is attached to the load, as shown in Second Situation in Figure 6.25, and the load is again moved 10 feet, the pulling end of the rope must move through a distance of 20 feet, 10 feet for each line on the pulley. Even though the load on the pulling end has dropped to 25 pounds, the work is still 500 foot-pounds (25 × 20). This is true for all tackles. The greater the mechanical advantage, the smaller the distance the load will move for any given movement of the pulling end of the rope.

Friction is another reality of tackle systems. We said earlier that a tackle can increase an individual's pulling power with no apparent increase in effort. But note the word "apparent." All sheaves introduce friction losses into the system, but by how much? Estimates range from 20 percent to 5 percent per sheave. My feeling is that, using modern sheaves with good bearings and adequate lubrication, these estimates are conservative and the actual friction may be as small as 2 percent. Still, this adds up, especially in tackles with many parts.

Making up tackle

Putting together a tackle is reasonably straightforward. It consists of using the correct sheave for the desired line and threading the line through the pulleys properly. The diameter, width, and material of the sheave are all important in selecting the proper sheave. The proper diameter, as explained earlier, prevents internal wear of the rope caused by flexing around the pulley. Table 6.1 (page 257) gives the minimum sheave diameter for various rope materials. The width of the sheave is important because, if the rope is too large for the groove in the sheave it will abrade, and if it is too small it may come out of the sheave and jam between the sheaves and the cheeks. The sheave material should be designed for the type of line that will be used. For example, a wire rope should not be taken around a plastic sheave.

Threading the line through the pulleys, called reeving, is straightforward except for six-part tackles. The lines should travel from one block to the other in the most direct route, without contacting other lines. On a six-part tackle it is best to bring the pulling line from the center of the block and reeve the rest of the line as shown in Figure 6.26. Reeved in other manners, six-part blocks tend to twist (capsize) and bind the line.

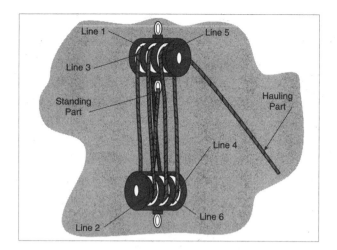

Figure 6.26 Reeving a
Six-Part Tackle

7

COMMUNICATIONS

VISUAL SYSTEMS

Prior to the 1900s, society relied primarily on visual communication systems such as signal flags and semaphore, because people can see farther than they can hear. Although these visual systems are rarely used by recreational boaters, other visual signals have been developed for use when background noise makes auditory signals impracticable—such as when approaching a mooring or putting down an anchor. Hand signals for turn left or right, go forward or reverse, and go fast, go slow, or stop are commonly used and almost instinctively derived by individual skippers and crew.

Flags

Signal Flags

The major use of signal flags for recreational boaters is for decoration. This can be done at random, selecting the flag or pendant (number or repeater flag) that suits the boatowner's color preference, or it can be done in conformance to the U.S. Navy's system. The Navy displays the flags in the following order, beginning at the bow:

> A...B...two...U...J...one...K...E...three...G...H...six...
> I...V...five...F...L...four...D...M...seven...P...O...
> 3rd repeater...R...N...1st repeater...S...T...zero ...
> C...X...nine...W...Q...eight...Z...Y...2nd repeater.

The only signal flag truly of use to recreational boaters is the yellow flag (Q), flown when entering a foreign port to signify the need for customs and immigration clearance.

Other uses of flags are informal, inconsistent in meaning, and confined to local areas. For example, in a few small harbors the "T" flag—red, white, and blue vertical stripes—is used to request a harbor taxi. Some doctors are rumored to fly the "M" flag, meaning a doctor is on board; supposedly this has a reassuring effect on the marina.

Other Flags

Two flags not included in the set of international signal flags but commonly seen are the all-red rectangular flag indicating that a water-skier is down in the water; if used during a sailboat race it indicates a rule infraction, real or imagined. The red rectangular flag with a white diagonal stripe indicates a diver is down. The international signal flag for diver down is the "A" flag, but it is rarely used by recreational divers.

Other flags flown by recreational boats range from the U.S. Yacht Ensign to flags signifying "mother-in-law on board." The U.S. Yacht Ensign was originally restricted to documented yachts of a specific class; however, it can now be flown on any recreational boat in place of the national flag. In foreign waters the U.S. flag is preferred.

The U.S. Power Squadron, the U.S. Coast Guard Auxiliary, and most yacht clubs have club and officer flags, and detailed rules surrounding their use. Generally, the flags can be displayed at the masthead or the port spreader, where the owner's flag or other miscellaneous flags are flown. Very small boats and boats without masts can fly them from the bowstaff if the boat is not in foreign waters.

Flag Etiquette

Improper display of national flags shows disrespect for the country and its people and reflects poorly on the offending boat and crew. There are only a few places to fly a flag on most recreational boats: the masthead, the right and left spreaders, a stern staff or bowstaff, and the leech of the aftermost sail.

The U.S. flag can always be flown from a stern staff, whether the boat is underway or at anchor. Gaff rigged sailboats may fly the U.S. flag from the peak of the aftermost gaff. On sailboats where the boom can strike the stern staff, the U.S. flag is flown two-thirds of the way up the leech of the after sail. Sportfishing boats may fly the flag aft of a tower to keep it clear of fishing lines. A powerboat with a gaff on its signal mast may fly the U.S. flag from the gaff while underway.

The U.S. and foreign flags should be displayed only between the hours of 0800 and sunset. The U.S. flag should be the first flag raised and the last lowered. Traditionally, the U.S. flag is flown at half mast on Memorial Day from 0800 to 1200 hours. Flag size depends on the size of the boat; too small a national flag can show disrespect. The U.S. flag should be about 1 inch on the horizontal dimension for every foot of boat length.

When visiting other nations, it is a courtesy to fly the flag of the host nation once clearance has been received from customs and immigration. Foreign courtesy flags should be about a half inch on the horizontal dimension for every foot of boat length. The proper place for the foreign flag is at the upper starboard spreader.

Since this is also where signal flags in general and the "Q" flag specifically are displayed, the "Q" flag is displayed first and then replaced by the national flag when clearance is obtained. A mastless boat can fly the foreign national flag from the bowstaff. State flags can be flown from the masthead or from the starboard spreader, similar to foreign courtesy flags, when visiting that state. The masthead and the left spreader are generally reserved for miscellaneous flags and pendants.

Audio Amplification

Until the beginning of this century, verbal communication across open water consisted of shouting—nautically speaking, *hailing*—and its effectiveness depended on whether the receiver was up- or downwind, and on the lung power of the hailer. Its limit, however, is generally about 300 feet. This can be increased about three times by an audio amplifier called a *loud hailer*.

The loud hailer is very straightforward in use, and it requires no license. The only difficulty comes from speaking too close to or too loud into the microphone. Used properly, a loud hailer can extend the range of normal speech up to 30 times.

Manufacturers of loud hailers often incorporate related features that are useful for boaters. My own loud hailer is used most often as a foghorn that sounds automatically every 60 seconds. The loudspeaker can be converted into a sensitive listening device, useful when trying to understand other hailing vessels or to find horns, bells, and other sound-producing devices in fog. Most of these units can also be used as engine or security alarms. Many can be rigged to amplify the output from a stereo or other radio, and some incorporate intercom systems.

Radio

Radios are perhaps the most misused device aboard a boat. Many boaters consider it a shipboard telephone. It is not. It is also not a water-based 911 service. A radio can be used without understanding how it works, but proper use requires knowing a significant number of rules and understanding some basic principles.

Basic Principles of Radio

Radio has undergone a tremendous metamorphosis in its short history.

The huge, unpredictable, complicated transmitter and receiver sets of 50 years ago have been replaced by small, compact, reliable, easily operated transceivers. The basic principles remain the same, however; to understand radio it is necessary to know something about frequency, modulation, propagation, power, and modes of operation.

Frequency

Radio wave frequencies occupy the energy wave band between 3,000 and 300,000,000,000 cycles per second. A single cycle per second is called a hertz (Hz) in honor of Heinrich R. Hertz, a pioneer in the study of electromagnetic waves. The metric system of prefixes is used in conjunction with hertz; radio waves occupy the band from 3 kilohertz (kHz) to 300 gigahertz (GHz). This definition of radio waves is somewhat arbitrary. A radio could be made to operate on other frequencies, but these designated frequencies are assigned by international agreement for radio use only. Obviously, a certain amount of arbitrary agreement is necessary, because a single radio set operating on its own frequency is useless.

The broad band of possible radio carrier waves is broken down into several different layers called band plans (see Figure 7.1). Wave length is equal to the speed of the wave divided by the frequency of the wave. Because the speed of radio waves is approximately 300,000,000 meters per second, the band breaks occur approximately at even metric units.

Figure 7.1 Radio Wave Spectrum

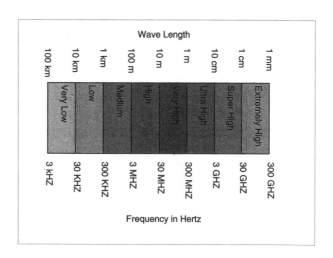

Extremely high frequency (EHF) has a wavelength between 1 cm and 1 mm long; superhigh frequency (SHF) from 1 cm to 10 cm; ultrahigh frequency (UHF) from 10 cm to 1 meter; and so on. The bands of most interest to boaters are the very high frequency (VHF), high-frequency (HF), and a small portion of the medium-frequency (MF) bands. The wavelengths of these bands are between 1 and 10 meters, 10 and 100 meters, and 100 and 1,000 meters respectively.

The VHF band contains four subdivisions of interest to boaters. The bands between 50 and 54 MHz, 144 and 148 MHz, and 220 and 225 MHz are allocated for licensed amateur radio operators (ham) use, and may be used by boaters who are licensed hams. The general marine band is between 156 and 163 MHz, and has been broken down further into channels, which are pretuned on marine VHF radios.

The various channels on the marine VHF band, and their frequency, mode, and type of operation are given in Table 7.1. The three modes of operation are simplex, semiduplex, and duplex. Most marine radios operate in the simplex mode, which requires both stations to receive and transmit on the same frequency. This is the simplest form of operation, but it is impossible to transmit and receive messages concurrently.

Duplex operation uses two frequencies, one for transmission and one for reception. This allows the radio to operate more like a telephone, but requires two antennas, some equipment modification, and takes up more band space. The extra frequencies required for duplex run from 160.65 to 162.075 MHz.

Semiduplex is operation on a duplex channel without all the duplex equipment. Semiduplex offers no improvement in operation over simplex, takes the band space of duplex, and is not used in marine applications.

Channel designations without the letter A are the same in international waters and in the United States. Those prefixed with A are U.S. channel designations only. Because of the large volume of traffic, the U.S. uses the simplex mode on these channels rather than the duplex mode used by the rest of the international community.

Note that the channels open for general recreational use are limited to 68, 69, 71, 72, and 78. The remaining channels can be used only by a recreational boat when it is engaged in the operation assigned to that frequency; for example, calling another vessel on Channel 16, requesting bridge or lock operation on 13, or using the public telephone on the channels designated.

The medium- and high-frequency bands are used by ham radio and the maritime single sideband service. The transmission characteristics of these frequency bands vary significantly from band to band and within each band from hour to

Table 7.1 VHF Channel Assignments

CHANNEL	FREQUENCY	MODE	TYPE OF OPERATION
01	156.05	Duplex	International Public Correspondence and Port Operations
01A	156.05	Simplex	U.S. Port Commercial Operations only
02	156.1	Duplex	International Public Correspondence and Port Operations
02A	156.1	Simplex	U.S. Port Commercial Operations only
03	156.15	Duplex	International Public Correspondence and Port Operations
03A	156.15	Simplex	U.S. Port Commercial Operations only
04	156.2	Duplex	International Public Correspondence and Port Operations
04A	156.2	Simplex	U.S. Port Commercial Operations only
05	156.25	Duplex	International Public Correspondence and Port Operations
05A	156.25	Simplex	U.S. Port Commercial Operations only
06	156.3	Simplex	Mandatory Safety, Ship-to-Ship and Ship-to-Aircraft
07	156.35	Duplex	International Public Correspondence and Port Operations
07A	156.35	Simplex	Commercial, Tugboat Industry
08	156.4	Simplex	Commercial Intership, Ship-to-Aircraft
09	156.45	Simplex	Calling and Hailing for Noncommercial Vessels, Commercial Intership and Ship-to-Shore
10	156.5	Simplex	Commercial, Tugboat Industry and Port Operations
11	156.55	Simplex	Commercial, Port Operations
12	156.6	Simplex	Port Operations, Navigation and Vessel Traffic
13	156.65	Simplex	Bridge-to-Bridge (1 watt of power only), Tugs, Dredges, Bridgetenders and Locktenders
14	156.7	Simplex	Port Operations, Bridgetenders and Locktenders
15	156.75	Simplex	Environmental receive only in U.S., International Ship-to-Shore, Class C EPIRB
16	156.8	Simplex	Calling and Hailing Mandatory Distress, Safety
17	156.85	Simplex	State-Controlled, Ship-to-Shore (1 watt of power only)
18	156.9	Duplex	Port Operations
18A	156.9	Simplex	Commercial, Tugboat Industry, Ship-to-Aircraft
19	156.95	Duplex	Port Operations
19A	156.95	Simplex	Commercial, Ship-to-Shore.
20	157.0	Duplex	Port Operations, Ship-to-Shore only
21	157.05	Duplex	Port Operations
21A	157.05	Simplex	U.S. Government
22	157.1	Duplex	Port Operations
22A	157.1	Simplex	U.S. Coast Guard Vessels and Stations; Coast Guard Information Broadcasts and Rescue Operations
23	157.15	Duplex	Public Correspondence
23A	157.15	Simplex	U.S. Government
24	157.2	Duplex	Public Correspondence (Marine Radio Telephone Operators)
25	157.25	Duplex	Public Correspondence (Marine Radio Telephone Operators)
26	157.3	Duplex	Public Correspondence (Marine Radio Telephone Operators)
27	157.35	Duplex	Public Correspondence (Marine Radio Telephone Operators)
28	157.4	Duplex	Public Correspondence (Marine Radio Telephone Operators)
60	156.025	Duplex	Public Correspondence (Marine Radio Telephone Operators) and Port Operations

Table 7.1 VHF Channel Assignments, continued

Channel	Frequency	Mode	Type of Operation
61	156.075	Duplex	Public Correspondence (Marine Radio Telephone Operators) and Port Operations
62	156.125	Duplex	Public Correspondence (Marine Radio Telephone Operators) and Port Operations
63	156.175	Duplex	Public Correspondence (Marine Radio Telephone Operators) and Port Operations
63A	156.175	Simplex	Vessel Traffic Service
64	156.225	Duplex	Public Correspondence (Marine Radio Telephone Operators) and Port Operations
65	156.275	Duplex	Public Correspondence (Marine Radio Telephone Operators) and Port Operations
65A	156.275	Simplex	Port Operations
66	156.325	Duplex	Public Correspondence (Marine Radio Telephone Operators) and Port Operations
66A	156.325	Simplex	Port Operations
67	156.375	Simplex	Commercial Ship-to-Ship and Ship-to-Aircraft; local rules apply in Puget Sound and the lower Mississippi
68	156.425	Simplex	Noncommercial Ship-to-Ship and Ship-to-Shore
69	156.475	Simplex	Noncommercial Ship-to-Ship and Ship-to-Shore
70	156.525	Simplex	Distress Safety and Calling; Digital Selective Calling only
71	156.575	Simplex	Noncommercial Ship-to-Ship and Ship-to-Shore
72	156.625	Simplex	Noncommercial Ship-to-Ship and Ship-to-Shore
73	156.675	Simplex	Port Operations
74	156..725	Simplex	Port Operations
77	156.875	Simplex	Port Operations (1 Watt of power only)
78	156.925	Duplex	Port Operations
78A	156.925	Simplex	Noncommercial Ship-to-Ship and Ship-to-Shore
79	156.975	Duplex	Port Operations
79A	156.975	Simplex	Commercial, Fishing Industry, Special Local Uses
80	157.025	Duplex	Port Operations
80A	157.025	Simplex	Commercial Fishing Industry, Special Local Uses
81	157.075	Duplex	Port Operations
81A	157.075	Simplex	U.S. Government
82	157.125	Duplex	Public Correspondence (Marine Radio Telephone Operators) and Port Operations
82A	157.125	Simplex	U.S. Government
83	157.175	Duplex	Public Correspondence (Marine Radio Telephone Operators)
83A	157.175	Simplex	U.S. Government
84	157.225	Duplex	Public Correspondence (Marine Radio Telephone Operators)
85	157.275	Duplex	Public Correspondence (Marine Radio Telephone Operators)
86	157.325	Duplex	Public Correspondence (Marine Radio Telephone Operators)
87	157.375	Duplex	Public Correspondence (Marine Radio Telephone Operators)
88	157.425	Duplex	Public Correspondence (Marine Radio Telephone Operators)
88A	157.425	Simplex	Commercial Ship-to-Ship

Table 7.1 VHF Channel Assignments, continued

CHANNEL	FREQUENCY	MODE	TYPE OF OPERATION
WX1	162.55	Receive only	NOAA Weather
WX2	162.4	Receive only	NOAA Weather
WX3	162.475	Receive only	NOAA Weather
WX4	162.425	Receive only	NOAA Weather
WX5	162.45	Receive only	
WX6	162.5	Receive only	
WX7	162.525	Receive only	
WX8	161.65	Receive only	Canadian Weather
WX9	161.775	Receive only	
WX0	163.275	Receive only	

hour, day to day, season to season, and year to year. The MF and HF bands have been subdivided and assigned general uses; these are found in Table 7.2.[1]

The uses shown in Table 7.2 are maritime, ham, aeronautical, and weather stations. The modes of operation are self-explanatory except for radio telegraphy, which consists of digital information such as machine-generated Morse code, Baudot, ASCII, AMTOR, and Packet radio transmissions. The use of these services, as well as fax, requires a radio modem and a printer; except for weather fax transmissions, they are rarely used by recreational boaters.

Modulation

All modes of operation impress information onto the basic radio wave, or *carrier*, in a process called *modulation*. The simplest form of modulation is *carrier wave modulation* (CW), which is just starting and stopping the carrier wave at specific intervals that convey logic. Morse code is the most common form of this modulation; a similar format is used by Baudot, ASCII, AMTOR, and Packet radio. What we most often think of as radio uses an analog form of modulation to carry voice, music, and any audible sounds. There are three basic kinds of analog modulation: amplitude modulation (AM), frequency modulation (FM), and phase modulation (PM). Phase modulation is rarely used in marine radio and will not be discussed.

Amplitude modulation encodes information onto the carrier wave by changing its amplitude in a process called *heterodyning*. Heterodyning works very much like water waves. If two waves of different frequency are introduced into the same system, they interact and produce one wave form by adding the amplitudes algebraically (see Figure 7.2).

[1]*Robert J. Halprin, ed.,* The ARRL Operating Manual, *3rd ed. (Newington, Connecticut: American Radio Relay League, 1987), 1.9–1.20.*

Table 7.2 Medium- and High-Frequency Band Assignments

FREQUENCY BAND IN KHZ	MODE	GENERAL USER
Medium		
9 to 190	Pulse Signals	Radio Navigation
190 to 415	Code	Aeronautical Beacons
415 to 510	Code	Maritime SSB
500	Code	Calling and Distress
530 to 1610	Voice (Receive only)	Commercial Broadcast
1800 to 2000	Code, Voice Radio Telegraphy and Fax	Ham
2000 to 2300	Voice	Maritime SSB
2122	Fax	Weather
2182	Voice	Calling and Distress
2495 to 2505	Voice	WWV, Time Signal
2850 to 3155	Voice	Aeronautical
3400 to 3500	Voice	Aeronautical
High		
3500 to 3750	Code and Radio Telegraphy	Ham
3775 to 4000	Code, Voice and Fax	Ham
4063 to 4438	Voice, Code and Radio Telegraphy	Maritime SSB
4125	Code and Voice	Calling and Distress
4268	Fax	Weather
4298	Fax	Weather
4346.1	Fax	Weather
4650 to 4750	Voice	Aeronautical
4855	Fax	Weather
4955 to 5005	Voice	WWV Time Signal
5450 to 5730	Voice	Aeronautical
6200 to 6525	Voice, Code and Radio Telegraphy	Maritime SSB
6215.5	Voice, Code and Radio Telegraphy	Calling and Distress
6525 to 6775	Voice	Aeronautical
6946	Fax	Weather
7000 to 7150	Code and Radio Telegraphy	Ham
7150 to 7300	Code, Voice and Fax	Ham
8195 to 8815	Voice, Code and Radio Telegraphy	Maritime SSB
8364	Voice, Code and Radio Telegraphy	Calling and Distress
8459	Fax	Weather
8494	Fax	Weather
8644.1	Fax	Weather
8682	Fax	Weather
8815 to 9040	Voice	Aeronautical
9396	Fax	Weather
9982.5	Fax	Weather
9995 to 10005	Voice	WWV Time Signal
10100 to 10150	Code, Radio Telegraphy	Ham
11090	Fax	Weather

FREQUENCY BAND IN KHz	MODE	GENERAL USER
Table 7.2 Medium- and High-Frequency Band Assignments, continued		
High (Continued)		
11175 to 11400	Voice	Aeronautical
12125	Fax	Weather
12230 to 13200	Voice, Code and Radio Telegraphy	Maritime SSB
12730	Fax	Weather
13200 to 13360	Voice	Aeronautical
14000 to 14150	Code, Radio Telegraphy	Ham
14150 to 14350	Code, Voice and Fax	Ham
14826	Fax	Weather
14990 to 15010	Voice	WWV Time Signal
15010 to 15100	Voice	Aeronautical
16135	Fax	Weather
16360 to 17410	Voice, Code and Radio Telegraphy	Maritime SSB
17151.3	Fax	Weather
17408.6	Fax	Weather
17900 to 18030	Voice	Aeronautical
19990 to 20010	Voice	WWV Time Signal
21000 to 21200	Code and Radio Telegraphy	Ham
21200 to 21450	Code, Voice and Fax	Ham
21837	Fax	Weather
21924 to 22000	Voice	Aeronautical
22000 to 22855	Voice, Code and Radio Telegraphy	Maritime SSB
23331.5	Fax	Weather
24890 to 24930	Code and Radio Telegraphy	Ham
24930 to 24990	Code, Voice and Fax	Ham
28300 to 29700	Code, Voice and Fax	Ham
25070 to 25210	Voice, Code and Radio Telegraphy	Maritime SSB
26960 to 27410	Voice	Citizens Band
28000 to 28300	Code, Radio Telegraphy	Ham
28300 to 29700	Code, Voice and Fax	Ham

Two things are apparent in Figure 7.2. First, the amplitude of the resultant wave is changing. The amount of change is controlled by the frequency shift of the impressed wave. For example, if a 2000 kHz signal is mixed with a 2002 kHz signal, a 2 kHz wave is produced. Since sound waves have a frequency between 0.02 and 15 kHz, this wave played through a speaker would then produce a 2 kHz audible tone. By adding frequencies between 0.02 and 15 kHz to the carrier wave, all the audible tones can be reproduced.

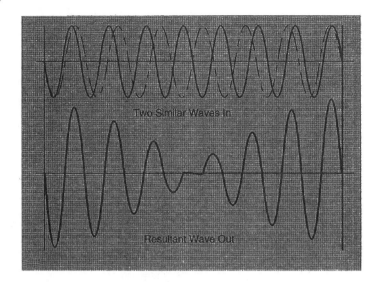

Figure 7.2 Wave
Addition or
Heterodyning

The second thing to notice is that the frequency of the incoming wave now varies between 15 kHz above and below the carrier frequency. Any other radio signal within that band would distort the original signal. This is why, when tuning a radio on the AM band, the sound can be heard on each side of the designated carrier frequency. This spurious signal is called *sideband*. One of these identical mirror-image sidebands exists on each side of the carrier wave. Thus, the closest together that two AM radio stations can operate without interference is 30 or 40 kHz apart—a very inefficient use of the radio spectrum.

Fortunately, it was determined through experimentation that voice can be transmitted successfully by using only the frequencies between 0.2 and 3 kHz.[2] This reduced the spurious signal width to about 6 kHz. Further reduction is possible because the upper and lower sidebands are identical; only one sideband is needed to transmit the information. Further, since all the information is contained in the sidebands, it is not even necessary to send the carrier wave. Thus was born *single sideband radio* (SSB).

The narrower signal width of SSB radio reduces adjacent-station interference, and because no power is wasted in sending the extra sideband and carrier wave, an SSB signal requires less power. Almost all voice transmissions on the medium- and high-frequency radio bands use SSB transmissions. Music, which requires a larger bandwidth, suffers on SSB. The medium-frequency broadcast bands stay with AM transmissions, using both sidebands and the carrier wave.

[2] *Wyland Dale Clift, ed.,* The Radio Amateur's License Manual *(Newington, Connecticut: American Radio Relay League, 1981), 5.19.*

With *frequency modulation* (FM), the other common form used to carry information by radio waves, the amplitude of the carrier wave remains constant; the information is carried by varying its frequency. FM theory is complex and beyond the scope of this book. Because the information is carried by frequency variations, FM receivers can be made insensitive to amplitude change. Most noise, particularly manmade noise, changes the amplitude of a wave, thus the signal-to-noise ratio of FM equipment is markedly improved. FM is used for music and other situations where signal clarity is important.

Unfortunately, the frequency shift needed to carry the necessary information requires a band about five times larger than the maximum audio frequency. With FM music, that may be as large as 75 kHz. FM has been assigned to the VHF radio band, where the large bandwidth is less noticeable. Another disadvantage of FM is that a strong FM signal tends to dominate a weaker signal and exclude it entirely from reception.

Propagation

After information is impressed on a radio wave it must get to its destination, through a process called *propagation*. As energy waves travel they lose strength, depending on the medium they pass through and the distance they travel. If the medium is constant, the strength loss is dependent upon the inverse square of the distance ($1/d^2$). That is, if point "B" lies twice the distance from the transmitter as point "A," the strength of the signal at point "B" will be one-quarter ($1/2^2$) of the strength at "A." However, in real life the medium is not constant. Radio waves travel through the ground, water, and air.

Waves traveling through air are of the most interest in radio transmissions. The wave can travel in three ways: direct propagation, ground wave, and refracted wave. *Direct waves* travel in a direct line of sight between two antennas; this is most common in the VHF spectrum.

Low-frequency waves can travel along the ground following the curvature of the earth for some distance, typically 100 to 200 miles. AM broadcasting uses mostly ground-wave propagation. Short-distance transmissions with high-frequency radios are also possible using ground-wave propagation.

Most long-distance communication relies on refracted radio waves through air that varies in density and composition with altitude. The density and composition of the air affects the strength and speed of the wave and also bends it. The bending caused by density change is not as severe as that caused by ionization. There are four separate bands in the atmosphere that extend from about 30 to 260 miles above the earth, where ionized particles gather in sufficient number to bend radio waves. These four bands are the D layer at 30 to 35 miles, the E layer 60 to 70 miles, the F_1 layer at about 120 to 140 miles, and the F_2 layer between 180 and 210 miles up. These layers are shown in greater detail in Figure 8.1 (page 322).

Ionization is caused by solar radiation striking air molecules. Both the D layer and the E layer, being lower and relatively more dense, contain many molecules of air. Any molecules broken up by solar radiation in these layers are quickly recombined back into a stable configuration by frequent collisions with other particles. Therefore, the amount of ionization in the D and E layers depends directly on the amount of solar radiation: at noon the ionization of the D and E layers is maximum; it becomes almost nonexistent by sunset. As a result, the D layer does little wave bending at any time and the E layer is only effective in bending radio waves around local noon. The less-dense F layers stay ionized throughout the night but still reach their peak at local noon. The upper F layer is almost entirely responsible for all long-distance radio communications.

Streams of ionized particles are generated by the sun during solar storms call sunspots. These particles also get trapped in the F layer, increasing its ionization. Thus, the total level of ionization depends on sunspot activity, which varies from high to low in roughly an 11-year cycle. The more the sunspots the more the waves are bent and the better the propagation. The American Radio Relay League (ARRL) publishes monthly predictions of sunspot activity and propagation conditions.

Bending also depends on the angle at which radio waves strike the layer and are refracted back to earth. This process, called *skip*, may be repeated several times. Figure 7.3 shows the results of ionospheric bending for three different wave angles.

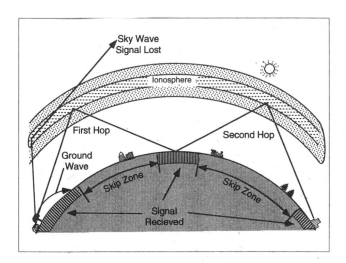

Figure 7.3 Ionospheric Bending of Radio Waves

Most of the propagation of radio waves below 30 MHz occurs through bending sky waves on the first or second skip.

Propagation in the HF radio bands depends on the time of day, the sunspot activity, and the wave frequency. Table 7.3 gives some general propagation guidelines for each subband. The most consistent band for long-distance communication is the 20-meter band, between 16 and 12 MHz.

Bending due to density changes occurs in the troposphere, the earth's atmosphere below about 10 miles. This bending is most useful for VHF waves, especially above 144 MHz, and occurs because the temperature, which normally decreases with an increase in altitude, occasionally becomes inverted. Warm air may overlay colder air and form a sharp boundary. The warm air is less dense, and the radio waves are refracted when passing through this air mass. If a second sharp temperature boundary exists, the radio wave can become trapped between these two boundaries and travel great distances with very little loss in strength. This process is called *tropospheric ducting*. Ducts form more often over water than over land.

Table 7.3 High Frequency Radio Wave Propagation

FREQUENCY	DAYLIGHT HOURS	NIGHT TIME HOURS	SUNSPOT ACTIVITY
2000 kHz	25 to 60 miles	200 to 1,000 miles	Low
4000 kHz	25 to 200 miles	1,000 to 2,000 miles	Low to Medium
8000 kHz	25 to 700 miles	> 500 < 3,000 miles	Medium
12000 kHz	25 to 2,000 miles	> 800 < 4,000 miles	Medium
16000 kHz	25 to 3,000 miles	> 1,000 < 6,000 miles	Medium to High
22000 kHz	25 to 3,000 miles	> 1,000 < 8,000 miles	Medium to High
24000 kHz	25 to 3,000 miles	> 1,000 <12,000 miles	High only
32000 kHz	25 to 3,000 miles	> 1,000 <18,000 miles	High only

Antennas

Wave propagation is also dependent on the type and shape of the antenna. A vertical antenna radiates vertically polarized waves, or waves that are perpendicular to the ground. A horizontal antenna radiates horizontally polarized waves, which are parallel to the ground. A receiving antenna oriented in the same plane as the transmitted signal will yield the greatest signal strength. Longer radio waves (lower frequencies) tend to retain their polarization; shorter VHF waves lose theirs rapidly. Most VHF antennas, especially on boats, are vertical. However, a horizontal VHF antenna has an advantage in that most manmade noise in the VHF marine band is vertically polarized. A horizontal antenna will produce a better signal-to-noise ratio and may improve performance.[3]

The most common antenna used aboard boats is the dipole, a centerfed wire that is electrically one-half the length of the radio wave. The 3-foot whip antenna supplied with most VHF radios is a half-wave dipole. (A half wave for the VHF marine band is about 36 inches.) For optimum performance these simple whip antennas need to be matched to the radio; however, for emergency use any 3-foot wire can be used for an antenna.

How much energy a given antenna system will pick up or radiate is measured in decibels (dB), a logarithmic unit that measures relative volume. Commercially available VHF antennas are advertised as having so much gain over a simple dipole, typically 3, 6, and 9 dB. A 3 dB gain represents an increase in volume at the receiver's speaker of 3 dB over that received by a simple dipole antenna.

A 6 dB antenna does not double the sound produced by a 3 dB antenna, however; it only increases the level by 3 dB. If that volume measured 60 dB, a 3 dB antenna would increase the sound to 63 dB and a 6 dB antenna would increase the sound to 66 dB—not much. For example, consider that the average noise level in a library is around 40 dB, in a typical office about 65 dB.

The easiest way to increase an antenna's output is to increase output power. But, because marine VHF radios are limited by law to 25 watts, the output must be increased by concentrating available horizontal radiation, by suppressing vertical radiation, and by narrowing the emission lobe, the simplest way being to increase the electrical length of the antenna. A 3 dB gain antenna is about 3 feet long, a 6 dB about 8 feet long, and a 9 dB about 19 feet long (the actual length may be shorter than the electrical length).

At first it would seem that concentrating horizontal emissions to provide more effective "talk power" is the way to go, but VHF signals travel are line of sight, traveling in more or less straight lines. The problem is, boats and their attached antennas heel, pitch, and roll. When heeled, higher-gain antennas, with their narrow lobes of emission, actually are less efficient than a standard VHF whip (see Figure 7.4). Antennas with greater than 3 dB gain are not recommended on sailboats.

Since the length of the antenna depends upon the wavelength, HF radios with their longer wavelengths require longer antennas. The most common antenna for HF SSB transmission on sailboats is a random-length wire, often an insulated backstay. The input impedance of the antenna is matched to the transmitter's output impedance by using an antenna tuner. A backstay antenna has a small amount

---

[3]*Clift, 6.34.*

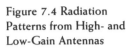

Figure 7.4 Radiation
Patterns from High- and
Low-Gain Antennas

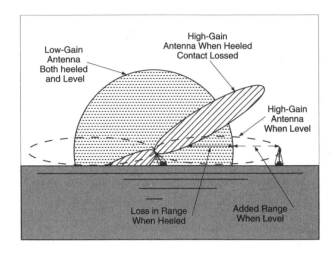

of directionality; transmission and reception are generally best with the backstay
pointed directly at the target station and worst when it is pointed away from
the target. Powerboats without rigging generally install a long whip antenna
(23 feet). This may require an antenna tuner as well, or it may be pretuned by
using internal traps.

Grounding of antennas is important, especially for HF radios, because the
ground acts as the other half of the antenna. A 3-foot VHF needs 3 feet of effective
ground. A 2 MHz SSB radio, however, must supply enough ground to make up for
75 feet of missing antenna. Fortunately, seawater is an ideal ground.

Copper plates in contact with the water or screen imbedded in the hull are the
recommended method of supplying ground to HF radios. The amount of actual surface area necessary to supply this ground is a little obscure. One hundred twenty
square inches is considered ample for shore radios, but three or four times this
amount has been recommended for boats.

Since the design of a proper ground system is so poorly understood, I recommend trial and error. Start with the simplest system and proceed in steps to the
more costly and complex methods. Keel bolts and engine mounts are not considered good grounds.[4] This isn't always so, however; much to the surprise of many radio wizards, my own ham radio thunders out full power grounded to the engine
block—but then I have 15 bronze through-hulls also grounded to the engine block.
I know others who have acquired ample grounds by attaching the ground to the

---

[4]Ed Graves, "Getting on with SSB," Sail (September 1981), 47.

keel bolts. These solutions may not work for all boats, but trying these simple, straightforward methods first might eliminate considerable trouble and cost.

Power

Electrical power (P) is defined as the current (I) in amps multiplied by the potential (E) in volts, and is measured in watts:

$$P = IE$$

Because in a radio the voltage and amperage are constantly changing, the power used by the radio depends on when and where it is measured. The two most common methods are output power at the antenna feed point for VHF radios and peak envelope power (PEP) for SSB radios.

Marine VHF radios are limited by law to 25 watts, with a front panel switch to limit output to 1 watt for short-range communications. On short-range channels used for bridge and lock communications, 1 watt is mandatory. The full 25 watts is sufficient to transmit a usable signal 20 to 30 miles, which is the normal range of a line-of-sight VHF signal. Additional power only interferes with other users.

The power of single sideband radios varies between 50 and 1,150 watts PEP, depending on where the radio is to be used, the type of transmission, and its frequency. Long-distance propagation of high-frequency radio waves depends more on atmospheric conditions and antenna construction than it does on output power. Limits of space and power aboard recreational boats confine an SSB's practical usable PEP power to around 200 watts.

Radio Equipment

Selecting radio equipment requires informed decisions about use, cost, quality, space, and features. While power limits are fixed by law, not all manufacturer-rated power is equal. Some sets produce rated power only when the transmitter is first turned on, rapidly losing power to internal heating of low-cost components. For example, 100-ohm resistors can be designed to handle 1 watt or 5 watts. Either will allow the radio to operate, but the 5-watt resistor will allow it to operate at full power longer because it doesn't heat up as rapidly. Five-watt resistors cost more than 1-watt resistors. Quality in a radio, as in anything else, costs. The cost difference between two radios can indicate the quality of their components.

VHF

The competition in marine VHF radios is fierce in a small market niche proscribed by federal regulations, so a great deal of effort goes into supplying strange features. Keeping abreast of the latest features is almost impossible. The most common features are the number of channels, scanners, dual watch, and memory channels. Some of the more exotic features are built-in loud hailers, intruder alarms, automatic Mayday transmissions, and scramblers.

How many channels does a recreational boater need? A glance at Table 7.1 (page 294) will show the number of channels available; only nine are usable by recreational boaters. Excluding the telephone channels, they are 6, 9, 13, 16, 22A, 68, 69, 71, and 78A. Most recreational use is limited to the latter four channels and four of the weather channels.

A scanner listens to a set number of channels in quick succession. When a signal is detected, the radio stays on that frequency until the traffic stops, then continues its scan. Scanning is of little value for most recreational boaters unless the channels can be user programmed; for instance, scanning the calling channel and one or two other communication channels. Scanning the other 70-odd channels only increases noise pollution. Dual watch is a sort of miniscanner that allows the user to scan two channels alternately, such as the calling channel, 16, and one other.

A handy device on a radio with all VHF channels is a memory channel button, which allows quick switching between the calling and communication channels.

Citizens Band

Unlike VHF, the citizens band (CB) radio is designed for those who just want to chat. Although the Coast Guard on occasion monitors CB Channel 9, the de facto emergency channel, it is not a substitute for VHF because it does not have clearly designated emergency and working frequencies. CB AM transmissions are limited to 4 watts output power, 12 watts peak power for single sideband transmissions. This limits reliable CB range to about 5 to 10 miles.

Ham Radio

Amateur SSB radio is used by many people who cruise because of its ability to communicate over long distances. It is less expensive than commercial marine SSB sets, but requires considerably more technical knowledge to operate. Unlike other types of marine radio, ham radio requires a license attesting to the practical skills and theoretical knowledge of the operator. The ARRL will assist anyone interested in obtaining a ham license; see the section on licensing later in this chapter.

Emergency use of ham radio, however, does not require the possession of a ham license. Even though there are no official frequencies designated as emergency and calling frequencies, 14313 and 7268 kHz are accepted for use as such. In many instances ham radio is more effective in an emergency than marine-band SSB because of the number of hams searching the bands for traffic.

Ham radio has some restrictions; for example, it cannot be used for business transactions. The FCC regulation states that "Third party traffic involving material compensation, either tangible or intangible, direct or indirect, to a third party, a station licensee, a control operator or any other person is *strictly prohibited*."[5]

On the surface, this rule seems quite clear, but it has caused some confusion. Some hams feel that calling another ham and asking him to order parts is not allowed.[6] Other hams feel this is too restrictive an interpretation. For example, a strict interpretation would prevent the popular ham practice of sending QSL postcards to confirm a radio contact, since the post office, a third party, receives compensation for the stamp. The problem is defining "third party." Fortunately, the FCC and the ARRL have defined the term: "The control operator is the first party to the amateur communication and the control operator of the other station (the one you're calling) is the second party. Any other person participating in the communication is a *third* party."[7]

Clearly the only person receiving material compensation is the supplier, and like the post office they are not participating in the conversation and therefore are not a third party according to the FCC's definition. It is to be hoped that this confusion will be cleared up in the near future, since this type of use is of significant value to boaters who are also hams.

Another service of significant use to boating hams are maritime mobile (Mickey Mouse) nets. Any ham operator on a boat making a passage can register on these nets and use their services. The Mickey Mouse net generally operates on 14313 beginning at 1200 Zulu (Greenwich time).

The net begins with a call for emergencies, medical and otherwise. Anyone with an emergency can respond, ham or not, and in many instances speak directly with a physician, who will diagnose over the radio and prescribe treatment. Removing an appendix in the middle of the Pacific using kitchen equipment is not my idea of entertainment, but considering the alternative, a ham radio certainly makes it easier.

After handling any emergencies, the net operator calls all vessels registered on the net one at a time, sequentially. Each vessel gives its current position, course and speed, and local weather conditions. This data is verified and recorded by net con-

---

[5]Communications Act of 1934, *paragraph 97.114(b), U.S. Federal Communications Commission.*
[6]*Donald D. Kavanagh, "Beyond VHF," Yachting (September 1985), 81.*
[7]*Clift, 5.40.*

trol. After the position information is relayed, the vessel is asked for any outgoing traffic, at which time it can request weather advice or data from the net, or place an outgoing call through one of the hundreds of other ham operators who monitor the net. Chances are, one will reside in the area the vessel is calling and will offer assistance for a phone patch to local land lines.

After outgoing traffic, the net operator will ask for incoming traffic. All outgoing and incoming traffic is switched to another frequency and the net operator continues with roll call. A vessel not answering its call generates considerable concern; missing two or more consecutive net calls will trigger emergency procedures. The net's records on the boat and its last position will assist authorities in the search.

After roll call, the net operator will ask for any new vessels who wish to join the net. Any ham operator on a vessel making a passage can respond, whereupon the net operator will switch the calling boat to another frequency, where an assistant will record destination, call sign, vessel type, size and color, number of people on board, next of kin, persons to contact in case of emergency, and other pertinent information. In my book, the maritime mobile net should change its name to the Mighty Mouse net. You may leave your traveler's checks at home, but don't go to sea without ham radio.

Marine Single Sideband

Marine single sideband radios offer the only means of long-distance communication for nonham operators. Marine SSB radios are more complex and costly than roughly comparable ham radios. Because the license requirements are minimal, the radio itself must be essentially foolproof, and provide considerable electronic safeguards to prevent it from being used improperly. The major features of a marine SSB set are the number of bands it can access and the power output. The antennas tend to be more expensive as well.

Although there are no semiofficial nets on marine SSB offering the same services as the ham radio nets, often several boaters get together and establish temporary nets. Marine SSB is monitored by commercial radio telephone services, which are not available on ham SSB.

Emergency Position Indicating Radio Beacons

Emergency Position Indicating Radio Beacons (EPIRBs) are small radio transmitters that send out signals to rescue services in life-threatening emergencies. EPIRBs are divided into two groups. The first group is subdivided into three classes and operates on two frequency bands. The first, 121.5 and 243.0 MHz, contains

Class A units, which can float free and self-activate, and Class B units, which are operated manually. A Class C EPIRB is for inshore local use only, and operates on 156.75 and 156.8 MHz.

The second group of EPIRBs operates on 121.5 and 406 MHz. These units are broken into Categories I and II, again indicating whether they float free and activate automatically. These EPIRBs are more useful than those in the first group in three distinct ways. First, by operating on 406 MHz they can use STARSAT satellites to store the emergency message until it can be relayed to ground stations. Second, the signal is encoded with a personal identification number, which indicates who is in trouble and who to contact. The radio must be registered by the owner to make this service available. Third, the transmitters are more powerful and precise than the other group, which allows the satellite to calculate the position of the emergency with an accuracy of about a mile. Currently, EPIRBs in this group cost about five times as much as those in the first group .

Cellular Telephones and Modems

Cellular telephones are finding their way aboard boats. While the equipment is not expensive, the service charges can be. The range of these units is similar to VHF radios. The major advantage of cellular telephones is the convenience of accessing a land-based telephone system. All the common telephone services such as direct dialing, call waiting, and call forwarding are available. There is no need to monitor a channel for calls; they simply ring in like a telephone, and calls are not missed because the radio is off.

Like regular telephones, cellular phones can use modems to send text and graphics using personal computers. Radio modems are also available; these can receive weather fax maps and charts as well as radio telegraphy, packet radio, AMTOR, Baudot, and ASCII communications.

Legal Requirements

The legal requirements surrounding radio include licensing, station identification, the type of calls that can be made from the station, and the legal rights to the use of the information transmitted. There are requirements for both the equipment and the operator. It is not necessary to keep a copy of the FCC rules aboard the vessel, but the licensee is responsible for knowing them and ensuring that the radio is used in accordance with those rules. The law does require that a copy of all radio licenses be kept aboard, readily available for inspection. They need not be posted in a conspicuous place.

There is no legal requirement to keep a radio log, although it may be wise to note in the ship's log the type and date of any repairs to the radio and who made those repairs. If the equipment malfunctions and violates the rules, this information may mitigate the circumstances. Similarly, notes on any emergency and distress calls involving the licensee's vessel are also kept handy in the ship's log.

Licensing

A valid license must be obtained before the ship's radio is operated. Depending on the circumstance, a license may be needed for both the operator and the equipment. If the radio is to be used entirely within the U.S. and no foreign ports are to be visited, VHF and SSB radios require only a license for the equipment, called a ship's station license. This license allows the radio to be installed and operated by the owner. All repairs must be made under the supervision of a licensed General Class commercial radio operator.

Ship station licenses can be applied for by mail using FCC form 506. Once the application is in the mail the radio can be legally operated if the temporary operating authority (FCC form 506A) is kept with the station records. Each application must be accompanied by a check or money order payable to the FCC for the appropriate fee. Be sure to fill out the form correctly, because errors will cause delays and extra fees if the form is returned to the applicant. It is also a good idea to ask for all the frequencies that may be required—radar, EPIRB, SSB, UHF, etc.

The license, valid for five years, is issued in the name of the owner and a registered or documented vessel. Processing may take time, so begin the renewal process well before the license expires. The license cannot be transferred with either the vessel or the radio. If either the boat or the owner changes, the license is invalid. When the boat is sold, the license must be returned to the FCC for cancellation.

The owner may add to or replace the radio with one that operates on the same frequency band without notifying the FCC. However, if the owner changes his legal name or address, changes the boat's name, or loses a license, the FCC requires a letter of explanation. The letter should include the owner's name, the vessel's name, the station call sign, and a check for any appropriate fee. Adding a transmitter that operates on a frequency not covered by the license requires the ship's license to be modified.

Citizens band and cellular telephones do not require licenses. Amateur radio requires an operator's license. The complexity of the test and the privileges of the license depend on the class of operator license. Currently there are five classes: novice, technician, general, advanced, and extra. The testing and management of the amateur bands is administered by the American Radio Relay League. For information on amateur radio and how to get licensed, write ARRL HQ, 225 Main Street, Newington, CT 06111.

Station Identification

The law requires that the radio station be identified by the FCC-assigned call sign in English at the beginning and end of each transmission. Current practice, however, does not follow this rule very closely. Most operators just identify the station by boat name alone at the beginning and end of each transmission. This has two benefits: it shortens the transmissions on the crowded channels by 15 to 20 percent, which allows another 850 boats to use the calling frequency every day; and the boat name tends to be remembered more easily than a random string of numbers and letters.

The only drawback to using just the boat's name is that it is against the law. The fact that the FCC has not chosen to enforce this rule rigidly in the past does not mean that they will always ignore the violations.

Types of Calls

The type of calls, safety, business, and pleasure, that can be legally made using VHF, SSB, and ham are restricted. Distress and safety calls have the highest priority and can be made on any frequency or radio regardless of license restrictions. The FCC requires that VHF Channel 16 be monitored for emergency calls when the radio is turned on and not in use on other frequencies. On SSB radios, 2182 kHz and 4125 kHz are used as calling and distress frequencies.

Boat operational communication consists of ship-to-ship messages concerning collision avoidance and rendezvous. Ship-to-shore traffic consists of scheduling berthing and repairs, as well as bridge and lock operation. Other business communications are restricted to maritime business only, such as between tug boats or fishing boats. Pleasure boats cannot use VHF or SSB for business transactions except on the marine telephone channels. All business transactions are prohibited on ham radio. Cellular telephone is probably the best choice for business communication.

Pleasure communications consisting of social, personal, and superficial conversations are restricted to marine telephone channels, citizens band radio, cellular telephones, and ham radio. The normal working channels of VHF, other than the telephone channels, are *not* to be used for pleasure communications.

Non-Disclosure

Operators or those monitoring radio traffic need to be aware that certain radio transmissions are protected by law from being monitored. The contents of those monitored by accident are protected from disclosure, in substance or meaning. Additionally, individuals intercepting the message cannot use the contents for their own benefit. This law applies to transmissions not readily accessible, such as cellular telephone, electronic mail, various video/data communications, and scrambled or encrypted transmissions. Messages on ham radio, citizens band radio, and commercial broadcasts are all exempt from this restriction. On VHF and SSB, only the distress and safety traffic are exempt.

Penalties

If the FCC finds that an operator or owner has willfully or repeatedly violated the Communications Act or the FCC Rules, his license may be revoked and he may be fined up to $10,000 and/or imprisoned for as much as two years. The FCC sends citations and warnings by mail. No reply is necessary to a warning notice. A citation must be answered within 10 days to the office issuing it. The answer must explain the incident, describe actions to be taken to prevent a reoccurrence, and be complete with all the pertinent facts without reference to other correspondence.

Besides citations, the FCC has the authority to levy administrative forfeitures of up to $100 for any of 12 specific violations. This statute, which bypasses the overcrowded court system, has some rights of appeal, but only within the FCC. These broad powers, if abused by the FCC, may border on violations of civil liberty.

The most common infractions of rules sited by the FCC involve operating a marine radio on land or without a valid license. These offenses can carry a fine of $8,000 or more for a first offense. Be careful with marine handheld radios. Their portability can get the operator into trouble if they are taken ashore and used on land.

Operation

Correct operation of the radio is based on common sense and courtesy to make the best use of the crowded channels. The radio is like a party telephone line with several thousand users: one user tying up the airwaves prevents thousands of others from using that line. There are two basic rules, be brief and take turns. Calls on a calling frequency must take less than 30 seconds. Calls on a working frequency must not exceed 3 minutes, and any calling vessel must wait 10 minutes before placing another call.

The following procedures are the official ones given by the FCC. However, as stated earlier, an overwhelming majority do not strictly follow the FCC guideline of supplying the call sign after the boat name at the beginning and end of each transmission. Not following these procedures exposes the boater to FCC fines. Presently, the FCC has chosen to ignore these minor infractions unless coupled with a major violation. In truth, call sign violations would be a nightmare to enforce. In the procedures described below, the call signs in parentheses are those most often neglected.

Receiving Calls

Unlike cellular telephones, a radio must be on and tuned to the proper frequency to receive a call. On VHF, Channels 16 and 9 are used for calling frequencies. Other available frequencies can be used if prior arrangements are made. For example, if the boat is expecting a marine telephone call at a certain time that channel can be monitored. Some, but not all, marine operators call on Channel 16. This is a good place to use a dual watch radio.

In the following example, the bold print is the receiving boat, the good ship *Sluggo*, which has its radio on and tuned to Channel 16 or 9.

"Sluggo, Sluggo, Sluggo this is Rock Bottom (WOK 1234), Over."

A crewman picks up the microphone on Sluggo and presses the talk button.

"Rock Bottom this is Sluggo (WNG 4321), Go Ahead."
"Sluggo go to 68 and up."

This gets the two radios off Channel 16 or 9 quickly and sends them to Channel 68 for the information portion of the call. "And up" means that if Channel 68 is busy, go to 69, 71, 72, and 78 until an open channel is found.

"Roger, Rock Bottom, Over."

Channel 16 is now free for the next call, and the two stations tune their radios to Channel 68.

"Sluggo, Sluggo, Sluggo this is Rock Bottom, Over."

"Go ahead, Rock Bottom."

The message from Rock Bottom is now passed to Sluggo as briefly as possible so that no confusion exists. At the end of the conversation the following exchange takes place.

"Roger Rock Bottom this is Sluggo (WNG 4321), Out."
"Rock Bottom (WOK 1234) Clear."

Both radios are again tuned to Channel 16 or 9. Both *Rock Bottom* and *Sluggo* should wait at least 15 minutes before using the radio again unless either is called by a third party.

How to Make a Call

Making a call is only a little more complicated. There are generally four kinds of calls, test calls, ship-to-ship or ship-to-shore, ship-to-marine operator, and distress calls.

Test calls on Channel 16 to Coast Guard stations or open calls are prohibited. Modern radios are reliable, and calls for routine radio checks are not normally necessary. If a test is necessary, select a working frequency with traffic in progress. Wait for the end of the conversation, then call one of the vessels directly and ask for a radio check, using the procedure described below for making a ship-to-ship call.

Ship-to-ship and ship-to-shore calls are similar in construction. The only difference is the working channel chosen. Often shore facilities, such as a marina or repair dock, use a specific channel. The first step is to estimate the distance to the station being called. If it is only a couple of miles or less, set the transmitter power to 1 watt.

If it is a ship-to-shore call and the designated working channel for that station is known, check to see if it is free. If clear, first try calling the shore station on the working channel. If there is no answer, return to Channel 16 or 9 and wait until that channel is free to make the call.

If it is a ship-to-ship call, tune briefly through the working channels to find one that is free. Use this as the working channel when contact is made with the desired boat. Return to 16 to make the call, and listen for 10 or 15 seconds to be sure that no Mayday is in progress. In the following example, the bold print is the procedure for the calling boat.

"Dumpy Bay Marina, Dumpy Bay Marina, this is Rock Bottom (WOK1234), Over."

If there is no reply, wait at least 2 minutes before making another call. If there is no answer, on a busy calling channel wait 15 minutes before calling again. Dumpy Bay may be busy with the cash register. If not, they will answer.

"This is Dumpy Bay Marina, go to Channel 65, Over."

Shore stations will often come back immediately with their working frequency.

"Dumpy Bay, this is Rock Bottom. I do not have Channel 65. How about 72? Over."
"Roger, Rock Bottom."

Now the calling channel is free and the two radios are tuned to the working channel for their traffic.

"Dumpy Bay Marina, this is Rock Bottom, Over."
"Go ahead Rock Bottom."

Shore stations rarely give their call signs except at the beginning or end of the day. Whether this is appropriate procedure is between them and the FCC. The traffic is ended with the final transmissions.

"Dumpy Bay Marina Out."
"Rock Bottom (WOK 1234), Clear."

The working frequency is now clear for other traffic, and both the ship and the shore station return to monitoring calling channels.

To make a call to a marine operator, select the channel with a marine operator nearest to the boat's location. Lists of marine operators are sometimes provided in local marine directories. If not, tune through Channels 24 to 28 and 84 to 87, recording in the back of the ship's log the locations of the stations received. Keep in mind that the shore stations have both more power and higher antennas. A shore station may be heard clearly but be unable to hear the calling station.

Once the marine operator channel has been selected, listen to determine if the channel is being used. If not, pressing the call button on the microphone will active a ring, very much like a normal telephone ring. The marine operator will answer the ring with:

"Malo Vista Marine Operator."

"This is Rock Bottom, WOK 1234, I would like to make a credit card (Collect, Person to Person, etc.) call to 509 683 4421; can I have privacy?"

"Privacy is on Rock Bottom. What is your card number?"

Once the operator signifies that privacy is on, any transmissions from *Rock Bottom* are heard on other radios as a repetitive beep. Privacy only works from the calling station; all radios can hear the land side of the conversation. Do not give your credit card number or any personal information without having privacy turned on. If the station does not have privacy, call collect if possible.

The call is put through, and the remaining operation is much like a landside telephone conversation, except that only one party can talk at a time. The use of Over is optional; much of the time it just gets in the way of the conversation. When the conversation is done, hanging up the land-based telephone will break the connection and alert the marine operator that the call is over. The calling boat should clear the channel by saying,

"Rock Bottom, WOK1234, Clear."

"Out" can be used instead of "clear"; in fact, it is the prescribed term, but clear is used as often.

Distress calls come in three varieties designated by three international emergency signals: Mayday, Pan Pan, and Security. The distress signal Mayday is reserved to indicate that a *life-threatening situation* exists with grave, immediate, and eminent danger that requires immediate *assistance*. Pan Pan is the signal used when the safety of the vessel or crew is in jeopardy but the danger is not life-threatening, grave, or immediate. Most Mayday calls on VHF are really Pan Pan calls—engine failure, minor strandings, etc. Security (pronounced se-cure-i-tay) is used to precede messages about safety and navigation or important weather warnings. Security calls are often used by large commercial vessels entering restricted waterways. Rarely does a recreational boat need to make a security call.

If an emergency occurs, try to remain calm and resolve the crisis without assistance. If assistance is required, turn the radio to Channel 16 and make the call immediately unless a higher-priority emergency call is in progress. The call might go something like this:

"Pan Pan, Pan Pan, Pan Pan, this is Rock Bottom (WOK1234), Rock Bottom (WOK1234), Rock Bottom (WOK1234). Over."

Note that the security code Pan Pan was repeated three times and no information was given other than the boat name and call sign.

"Rock Bottom this is the U.S. Coast Guard. Go to Channel 22, Over."
"Roger, Coast Guard."

Tune to Channel 22 and continue the traffic.

"U.S. Coast Guard this is Rock Bottom."
"Go ahead Rock Bottom."
"We are ¾ mile southeast of Point Flab and have a broken fuel line. The boat is in no immediate danger, with three people aboard and no injuries, but we need assistance."

Notice that the location of the boat, the description of the emergency, and the condition of the crew were given.

"Roger, Rock Bottom. What is the description of your vessel?"

The Coast Guard will prompt for any missing information, such as the boat description. Time can be saved by providing all information on the first call.

"This is Rock Bottom. We are a red, white, and blue 40-foot custom power-boat."
"Roger, Rock Bottom. I will put out a call on 16 for assistance. Stand by on 22. Over."
"Rock Bottom, standing by on 22, Over."
The Coast Guard will make a call for any boats in the area to render assistance. Boats answering the call will be directed to Channel 22 and will call the distressed boat directly or with the aid of the Coast Guard. Once contact is made, the boats involved in the relief operation may be directed to another working channel.

A Mayday call is a much more serious operation, and the entire conversation can take place on Channel 16. It begins similarly to the Pan Pan call, except the emergency information is given immediately without waiting for a reply. In these calls, time is of the essence and the calling vessel may have only enough time to relay the details of the emergency once. Any vessel in the middle of a call that is interrupted by a Mayday call should immediately discontinue the call and copy the Mayday message. A call from a distressed vessel should go as follows:

"Mayday, Mayday, Mayday, this is Rock Bottom (WOK1234), Rock Bottom (WOK1234), Rock Bottom (WOK1234).

Mayday this is Rock Bottom ¾ mile southeast of Point Flab. We have hit a deadhead and are taking on more water than the pumps can handle. There are three persons on board, one with chest pains. The boat will remain afloat for approximately 15 minutes. Rock Bottom is a red, white, and blue 40-foot custom powerboat. Mayday, standing by on 16, Over."

Release the microphone button and listen for a reply. Notice that there are no call signs to waste time and the entire message was given without waiting for an answer. There is no guarantee that time will be available for a second call. If there is no answer and time permits, repeat the entire call.

If a Mayday call is received, copy the message and determine a course and distance to the distressed vessel. If the distressed vessel is near, alter course immediately for it. If the Coast Guard answers and is directing the rescue, wait until they have finished their conversation with the stricken vessel, then call and offer assistance. The following conversations are examples of a vessel receiving a Mayday call.

"U.S. Coast Guard, this is Sluggo. We are a 35-foot sailboat, 1 mile north of Rock Bottom. Our estimated time of arrival is 10 minutes."

"Roger, Sluggo, Stand By."

As an assisting vessel, immediately alter course directly toward the stricken vessel, monitor Channel 16, and maintain radio silence unless called by the Coast Guard or the stricken vessel.

If the stricken vessel is too far away to render assistance physically, it may be possible to render verbal assistance by offering solutions to the problem or relaying the Mayday message. If there are no answers to the Mayday, continue to monitor Channel 16 for several calls from the stricken boat. If there are still no answers from nearby ships or the Coast Guard alter course to the stricken boat; it may be necessary to pick up survivors.

"Rock Bottom, Rock Bottom, Rock Bottom, this is Sluggo, Sluggo, Sluggo (WOK 1234). We have received your Mayday."

"Roger Sluggo. What is your location?"

"We are 15 miles west of your position and it will take about 2.5 hours to reach you. Can we relay your Mayday?"

"Affirmative Sluggo."

At this time ask the stricken vessel for any information not provided in the original transmission regarding the position of the boat, nature of the emergency, number of persons aboard, any injuries, present seaworthiness of the boat, and its description. Then make the relay call, speaking slowly.

"Mayday Relay, Mayday Relay, Mayday Relay, this is Sluggo (WOK 1234) with a Mayday Relay. The ship Rock Bottom is ¾ mile southeast of Point Flab. They have hit a deadhead and are taking on more water than their pumps can handle. There are three persons on board, one with chest pains. The boat will remain afloat for approximately 12 minutes. The Rock Bottom is a red, white, and blue 40-foot custom powerboat. Mayday Relay, this is Sluggo standing by on 16, Over."

As an assisting vessel, stand by and relay any answers to Rock Bottom. If no answers occur within 10 seconds, repeat the message. If a third party answers, it may be necessary to relay calls until contact is established between the two primary boats. If no answer occurs at all, arrangements should be made with the stricken vessel to pick up survivors.

In a true emergency, it is doubtful that the CC will cite the offender for not using the call sign.

Misuses and Abuses

The most serious misuse of the radio is using a Mayday call instead of a Pan Pan call. The most serious abuse of the radio is transmitting over ongoing Mayday traffic. The most common abuse is using Channel 16 for other than distress or calling. Other frequent abuses are calling over someone else's call, especially on 16 or crowded working channels; and long-winded communications in general. Be brief and concise.

THE PHONETIC ALPHABET

The standard phonetic alphabet, used by radio operators worldwide, can be useful where transmissions are garbled or indistinct, to clarify key points through spelling.

Alpha
Bravo
Charlie
Delta
Echo
Foxtrot
Golf
Hotel
India
Juliet
Kilo
Lima
Mike
November
Oscar
Papa
Quebec
Romeo
Sierra
Tango
Uniform
Victor
Whiskey
X-ray
Yankee
Zulu

For example, "Sluggo, this is Rock Bottom, I spell Romeo Oscar Charlie Kilo; Bravo Oscar Tango Tango Oscar Mike, Over."

8

WEATHER

Weather knowledge is especially useful for recreational boaters. Certainly, few people consider being caught out in a small boat in a storm "recreation." However, making good use of weather information is much more than just avoiding storms. Sometimes a change in weather affects safety and sometimes the enjoyment of the boater. The powerboater looks for flat, calm days with seas of glass. The sailor, whose vessel operates in concert with the weather, prefers days with just the right amount of wind, always from behind the boat.

The judicious use of weather reports alone does not assure the boater of favorable weather. Weather forecasts can be wrong, and even correctly reported conditions can change unexpectedly. The inquisitive mariner looks to the skies and relies on his or her own knowledge and experience.

WEATHER ELEMENTS

Long ago the Greeks divided the universe into four elements: earth, water, air, and fire. Earth, water, and air represent the three common states of matter—solid, liquid, and gas—and make a good basis for discussion of weather. (Fire was added as a political expedient to satisfy a powerful religious lobby.)

Solar radiation encountering the air, water, and earth produces effects both random and ordered. These processes cannot be controlled, but they can be understood and predicted using the laws of probability. Solar radiation changes the atmosphere's temperature, its pressure, and the amount of water it contains; each of these changes influences weather. To better understand these changes, we will first examine the atmosphere, the envelope of air surrounding the earth.

The Composition of the Atmosphere

The ocean of gases enclosing the earth is layered and difficult to define boundaries around. The earth's spin bulges the atmosphere at the equator and thins it at the poles. Figure 8.1 shows the general cross section of the atmosphere, with enough artistic license to make the essential facts clear.

Although the entire atmosphere influences the weather, most weather action

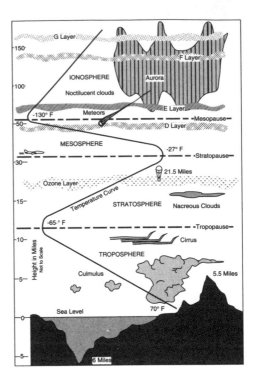

Figure 8.1 Composition of
the Earth's Atmosphere

takes place in the bottom 10 miles of air called the *troposphere*. The highest point on earth, the top of Mount Everest, is about in the middle of the troposphere; about half the mass of the *entire* atmosphere is contained below this point.[1] The troposphere is bounded by the earth on the bottom and the *tropopause* on the top.

The tropopause is defined by a reversal of the temperature gradient. Initially, the temperature gradient is negative: with increasing distance from the surface, the temperature of the atmosphere falls about 1°F for every 300 feet of height. At the tropopause the temperature gradient reverses, and the air temperature begins to rise as height increases. Additional temperature gradient reversals occur at even greater heights and define the *stratopause* and the *mesopause*.

The location and temperature of the tropopause are considerably more variable than the location and temperature of the stratopause and mesopause. The troposphere is about 11 miles thick over the equator, and the temperature falls to about −117°F at the tropopause.[2] With the temperature on the surface at around 80°, this leaves a difference of almost 200°. At the poles the atmosphere is only about 5 miles thick, and the minimum temperature is about −50°F. The *lapse rate*— the rate at which the temperature changes—is essentially the same above about 2 miles. Below 2 miles the temperature of the earth's surface strongly affects the air's temperature, as shown in Figure 8.2.

[1] William G. Van Dorn, Oceanography and Seamanship (New York: Dodd, Mead & Co, 1974), 53.
[2] William J. Kotsch, Weather for the Mariner (Annapolis, Maryland: Naval Institute Press, 1977), 30.

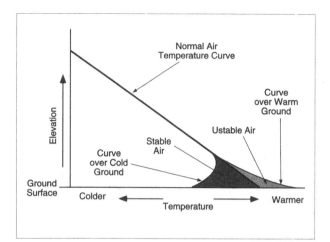

Figure 8.2 Temperature
Distribution near the
Surface

If air with this normal temperature distribution passes over a warm surface that heats the air next to the surface, the temperature distribution looks more like the right-hand curve in Figure 8.2. The overheated air at the surface becomes unstable and rises, producing squalls and showers. This kind of instability is greatest in tropical air; hence the greater violence and frequency of storms in the tropics.

If the air passes over a cold surface, the temperature gradient falls below the normal curve. The air becomes more stable, because heating will only return it to its normal condition. Called *temperature inversion*, this condition is responsible for the stagnant air most noticeable over large industrial areas. Temperature inversion also commonly occurs in the polar regions, where cold dense air hugs the ground in winter, resulting in weeks of stable conditions.

In temperate zones there is a mix of the two conditions. Hot air rises and cold air falls, so air constantly moves up and down like a piston in a great heat engine, transferring huge amounts of energy from place to place. Weather is the visible result of this transference process.

Heat Energy and Temperature

Heat is a measure of the amount of molecular motion in a body. When an object's molecules have no motion, it possesses no heat energy and its temperature is absolute zero. If the molecules are excited, the temperature of the object rises; likewise, if an object is heated the motion of the molecules increases.

Heat is transferred in four ways: radiation, convection, conduction, and change of state. For our purposes, temperature transfer by change of state is important only in regards to water. This is discussed more fully under "Humidity," beginning on page 338.

Radiation transfers heat as an energy wave. Energy waves transfer various amounts of energy depending on their frequency, and all warm bodies radiate a broad band of waves. The infrared wavelength is the most efficient wavelength for transferring heat. Since short-length energy waves move easily through empty space, radiation is an effective means of transferring heat energy over long distances.

When the energy wave encounters matter it excites the molecules of whatever it strikes and increases their motion. For example, the sun heats the atmosphere by radiation. Solar radiation striking the molecules of the atmosphere pushes them around like billiard balls, causing their motion to increase, thus increasing the temperature of the atmosphere.

The denser the material the radiation strikes the more of its energy is transferred to heat. The sun's radiation passes through the atmosphere, where it loses a little energy to heat, but when it reaches the earth's surface all the remaining energy is given up as heat. The earth, a warm body, radiates some of this heat back into the atmosphere. By the same principle, sunlight passing through a large window on a cold day heats a dark stone floor, which in turn radiates heat that warms the room.

Convection is the process of transferring heat by fluid motion. In a fluid, density changes and the action of gravity can move molecules from place to place. The two fluids that affect weather most are water and air.

Convection is the primary way in which heat is transferred in air. Air, like most materials, expands and gets less dense with an increase in temperature. This loss in density causes hot air to rise, taking with it the heat energy it contains. Cooler, more dense air falls to take its place.

Water, unlike most materials, attains its maximum density at about 40°F. Below that temperature water gets less dense, which is why ice floats in water. If ice did not float, most of the earth's water would be tied up as ice at the bottom of the sea. Above 40°F water behaves like most materials, losing density as heat is added. Water's peculiar density reversal is responsible for temperature-driven ocean currents, which transfer heat not only vertically but horizontally, from the equator to the poles.

Conduction is the process by which heat energy is transferred through direct molecular contact. This is more important in solids—the earth, for example—

where the molecules stay in the same relative position and do not travel. The excitation of one molecule excites those immediately surrounding it, and the energy is moved slowly through the solid.

A substance that conducts heat well absorbs heat quickly and gives it up quickly. Aluminum is a good heat conductor. Air is a poor one; it absorbs heat so slowly that it has very little to give up. If prevented from moving (convection), air is a good insulator. In fact, most commercial insulating materials work by trapping air in small, stationary pockets.

Thermal conductivity is a bit like Goldilocks and the three bears. Too much and too little have little effect on weather, but earth and rock thermal conductivity is just right. Earth and rock act as heat capacitors; their capacity is high enough to allow significant amounts of heat energy to be stored during the day, yet low enough that the heat remains near the surface, where it can be released back to the cooler atmosphere at night.

Water again plays a convoluted role. In large quantities water acts more like air, transferring large amounts of heat energy throughout its mass by convection. In small drops, however, convection is limited, and water changes roles; because it has greater conductivity than air, it stores heat in the air mass. Daily temperature fluctuations depend dramatically on the amount of water vapor in the air. Dry air may swing through a daily temperature change of 60 degrees compared with as little as 10 degrees in moist air.

Earth, air, and water, because of their different thermal properties and molecular processes, form the basis for weather by storing and moving heat. The other two major players in this drama are the tilt of the earth's axis, which causes uneven heating and the seasons, and the earth's rotation, which daily distributes solar radiation and influences the path of the winds.

Temperature Effects

It is time to look beyond the molecular toward events on a large scale by examining what takes place as the temperature effects interact. The simplest of these events is the solar cell, generated when dense surface air is heated from beneath by the earth's hot surface. This heated air expands, becomes less dense than the air above it, and rises. As it rises the air pressure surrounding it drops, and it is cooled due to further expansion. When it comes back into density equilibrium, it stops rising and spreads out to replace the cooler, heavier air that has fallen to take the place of surface air. This vertical movement of air on a local scale is most obvious when it drives the land-sea breeze; on a global scale this process produces the prevailing wind belts.

Land-sea breezes are generated along the shoreline of large bodies of water. The temperature differential needed to produce this wind is caused by the difference in the thermal properties of land and water. To understand this process it is helpful to consider the pressure at four locations: points A and B over the land and points X and Y over the water, as shown in Figure 8.3. In the morning the temperature over the land is equal to the temperature over the water, with the pressure at A equal to the pressure at X and the pressure at B equal to the pressure at Y.

Because transferring heat away from the surface by conduction on land is not as efficient as transferring heat by convection in water, the land warms up faster than the water when struck by the sun's radiation. Therefore, the sun's heat remains in the top few feet of earth, but in the water the heat is spread out more uniformly by convection and the surface is cooler.

The air is heated by radiation more over the warm land surface than over the cooler water, causing the air over the land to expand more than the air over the water. The expanding air at point A rises and reduces the pressure below that of the air at point X. This causes air to flow from X to A, reducing the pressure at X, causing the upper air at point Y to fall, reducing the pressure at point Y. The air rising from A to B plus the drop in pressure at Y causes the upper air to flow from point B to point Y, where it is cooled and can be drawn down to repeat the cycle. This process produces a surface wind called a sea breeze. The greater the difference in temperature the greater the pressure gradients and the harder the wind will blow.

Figure 8.3 Generation of a
Land-Sea Breeze

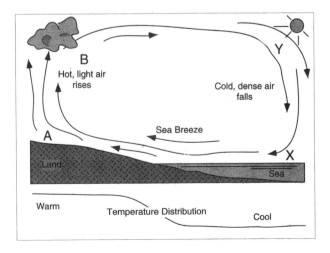

Sea breezes generally occur in the early afternoon and die away by sundown because the driving mechanism, the heat of the sun, and the resulting temperature differential go away. At night the water's surface temperature drops only a few degrees, but the land rapidly loses most of its solar-generated heat. Especially in areas where the water is warm, such as the tropics, a temperature gradient exists in the other direction. Now a wind will develop that blows from the land to the sea; this is called a land breeze. Because the land loses heat rapidly, land breezes are generally weaker than sea breezes, blow for a shorter duration, and are generally gone by sunrise.[3]

Land-sea breezes are local events, do not show up on weather maps, and normally penetrate less than 50 miles inland.[4] These temperature circulation cells are about 130 times longer than they are high. When they develop on a grand scale to their maximum height of 11 miles in the tropics, they extend about 1,500 miles horizontally and produce several distinct bands of winds called prevailing wind belts.

Prevailing wind belts, like land-sea breezes, are generated by uneven heat distribution, but the reason for the uneven heating is related to global temperature differences. These differences are established over long distances because of the tilt of the earth's axis and the angle at which the sun's radiation strikes the surface. The sun's radiation bears down almost vertically along the equator and heats the surface much more than it does even 30 degrees farther north or south. Warm air rises at the equator and moves north or south, where it cools and falls. This sets up three rotating heat cells in each hemisphere. Because these belts are essentially symmetrical, only the northeast quadrant is shown in Figure 8.4.

Coupled with these belts of wind are the semipermanent highs and lows that generate 11 bands of relatively stable winds on the surface of the earth. On a stationary earth, these surface winds would tend to flow either north or south from high to low. However, because the earth rotates, the winds in the northern hemisphere are deflected to the west when flowing south and to the east when flowing north. The result is that the winds actually blow from the northeast or the southwest in the northern hemisphere. In the southern hemisphere the system is a mirror image, and the winds flow from the southeast or the northwest.

Starting at the equator, the first of these belts is called the intertropical convergence (ITC) zone, or doldrums. Because the predominant direction of the airflow over the equator is up, the ITC zone has much atmospheric turbulence,

[3] Jeff Markell, The Sailor's Weather Guide, first ed. (New York: W. W. Norton, 1988), 53.
[4] Peter Johnson, ed. Yachting World Handbook (London: Edward Stanford Limited, 1972), 277.

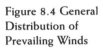

Figure 8.4 General
Distribution of
Prevailing Winds

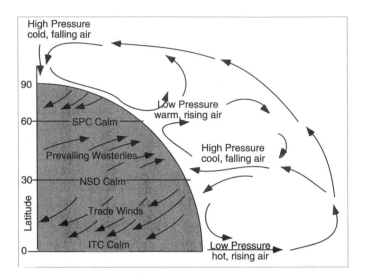

producing long periods of relative calm punctuated by extremely violent winds. Moving either north or south one encounters the steady surface trade winds, which blow predominantly from the northeast in the northern hemisphere, returning cold, dense air to the tropics. The name "trade winds" comes from a time when trading was done by sailing ships, which used these winds to carry them from Europe to the New World.

Above the trades lies the northern subtropical divergence (NSD) zone, or horse latitudes. The airflow in the NSD is predominantly downward, which produces another belt with very little wind. This air is very stable, and very few storms occur in this zone. The term "horse latitudes" comes from the colorful language of the Age of Sail. Ships might be becalmed for weeks at a time in these latitudes. When food and water for the horses ran low, the horses were jettisoned, an occurrence regular enough to make the sight of floating horse carcasses fairly common in these latitudes.

To complete the global picture it is necessary to look at the other temperature extreme, the poles. It is colder at the poles than anywhere else on the globe; hence about 30 degrees north or south of the poles there is an area of relatively warmer air. The presence of this warm air sets up another thermal cell, with the air flowing up at approximately latitude 60, creating a predominant low-pressure area called the subpolar convergence (SPC) zone, and creating the polar divergence zone down at the poles. Due to this unstable air many gales and extratropical storms are generated in this area.

Between these two counterrotating cells—that is, between 30° and 60° latitude—the air flows from the high at 30 to the low at 60 degrees. This airflow forms a band of winds, the *prevailing westerlies*, that flow predominantly from the southwest to the northeast in the northern hemisphere and from the northwest to the southeast in the southern hemisphere. Above the SPC zone, the winds again flow predominantly easterly, but because of their high latitude and cold, ugly weather they did not play a major role in world trade. The recreational boater of today generally can ignore these winds for much the same reason.

The concept of 11 different weather zones is rather simplistic. The zones shift north and south seasonally, their lateral extent changes, and they are affected by the distribution of land and water. To get a more realistic picture of the actual turbulence that produces the earth's weather it is necessary to introduce a concept called a cohesive air mass. Figure 8.4 shows that the general vertical wind flow is also positioned for a horizontal circular flow in a clockwise rotation around the high-pressure NSD belt in the northern hemisphere. This horizontal rotation does occur, and it sets up large cohesive air masses, which develop essentially the same general properties.

Cohesive Air Masses

The conditions conducive to producing a cohesive air mass exist in many places throughout the world. The properties of the air mass depend on where it develops, and each of the six distinct types is named accordingly: Arctic, continental polar, maritime polar, continental tropic, maritime tropic, and equatorial.

Arctic air masses (A) are composed of cold dry air, which is much colder aloft than on the surface. This temperature distribution generally forms over the polar ocean regions, because the heat conducted through the ice from the water below warms the lower air. These air masses are considerably thinner in summer than in winter. Arctic air masses do not affect recreational boaters until the cold, dry air moves south.

Continental polar air (cP) forms over large polar landmasses such as Canada and Siberia. The cold land and permafrost cool the continental polar air mass from below. Thus cP air is clear, dry, and occasionally colder near the ground than aloft. This results in a very stable air mass with little turbulence. Because there is no mixing, in winter cP air can become bitterly cold—60° below zero—increasing stability. Almost all cP air is generated in areas surrounded by mountains, where the cold air is prevented from flowing out of the source area until it has attained considerable height and spills over the edge. Once it breaks out it can move rapidly.

Maritime polar air (mP) is formed over the polar oceans. The air is more humid than cP air, and the vertical temperature gradient is less pronounced because the water is not as cold as the land. The temperature of mP air varies only slightly from summer to winter, from 40° to 60° above zero. This stability leads to steady conditions and good visibility; however, low clouds and fog can develop because of the higher moisture content.

Continental tropical air (cT) is formed only over North Africa and the desert steppes of the Eurasian continent. All other tropical land areas are too small and are influenced by maritime air. Continental tropic air is extremely dry and hot near the surface, and it is unstable. Average daytime temperatures can be quite hot—80° to 120° or more—but nighttime temperatures can plummet due to lack of moisture in the air. Visibility is good, but due to the large temperature swing the lower atmosphere can be unstable, with gusty winds.

Maritime tropical air (mT) is warm, moist, moderately stable, and homogeneous. These air masses carry large amounts of moisture, and thus can distribute heat and energy from place to place not only by moving warm air but by storing the sun's energy in water vapor. Maritime tropical air comes mainly from the trade wind belts over the oceans. Its temperature range is also very stable—around 70° to 85° summer or winter. Due to temperature and high humidity, considerable cloud cover is formed.

Equatorial air (E) is extremely moist and uniform in temperature. Generated in the doldrums, this air is hot, humid, and unstable as it rises through a deep layer. It is the predominant air mass for breeding hurricanes and typhoons.

By definition, all these cohesive air masses must have boundaries. The interior of each air mass is rather uniform; however, conditions at the boundaries are extremely unstable due to the direction of the rotating winds (see Figure 8.5).

Not only is the wind moving in opposite directions at these boundaries, there is also a distinct break in the temperature, humidity, and atmospheric pressure of the air on either side of them. This presents a situation ripe for violent and radical events. As one would expect, most unpleasant weather occurs along these boundaries, called weather **fronts**, a term first introduced during World War I because the conditions on the weather front were analogous to those on the battle front.

Fronts and their Associated Weather

Frontal weather is caused by the interaction of air masses along these boundaries. There are four possible situations at the boundary: no motion, warm air moving into a colder region, cold air moving into a warmer region, and the destruction or decay of the boundary.

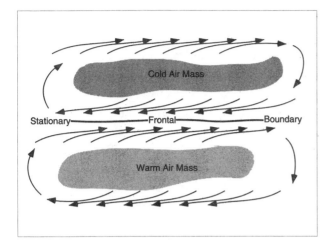

Figure 8.5 Boundary
Conditions Between
Air Masses

The boundary between two air masses at rest is called a **stationary front**. Despite the name, a stationary front is a very transitory condition, at least with respect to time. They last only a few hours before they are changed into moving fronts by the unstable wind along the front. The winds on the pole side of a stationary front tend to blow in a westerly direction, and those on the equator side blow east. Eventually these opposing winds form a ripple in the stationary front and spawn two moving fronts, one cold and one warm. West of the ripple, in the northern hemisphere, the cold air mass begins to move down into the warm air mass, and east of the ripple the warm air mass begins to move up into the cold air (see Figure 8.6).

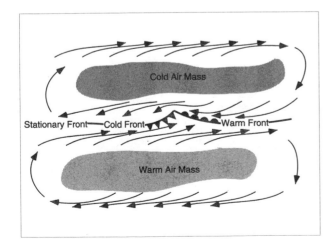

Figure 8.6 The
Destruction of a
Stationary Front

A **cold front** is the edge of a cold air mass moving into a warmer air mass or over ground warmer than the air. As the cold front advances, the dense, cold air plows into the lighter, warmer air in front of it and pushes it up and away. This causes clouds to form and precipitation to occur. The boundary between the cold air and the warm air in the vertical plane typically looks like Figure 8.7.

Because the interaction of the two air masses occurs over a relatively short distance—100 to 150 miles—most unpleasant weather occurs in this local band. Clouds begin to form 100 miles or so ahead of the front. The precipitation associated with the front is equally distributed some 25 to 50 miles either side of it. Showers sometimes precede the frontal cloud band, but more commonly they follow it. The presence of showers depends on the vertical stability of the air mass, the vertical distribution of temperature, and to some extent on the relative temperature of the ground over which the air mass is moving. As discussed earlier, cold air moving over warm ground produces unstable air. A cold front can move at 15 to 30 knots; the faster the front moves, the more unstable the air and the more violent the weather.

Very fast moving cold fronts are sometimes preceded by a violent band of weather called a **squall line**. The squall line, often between 50 and 150 miles ahead of the front, appears as a seething black wall of very low clouds and contains some dangerously high velocity winds. The severity of these storms is accentuated by the rapidity of the change in wind velocity and direction. The wind ahead of the squall moves predominantly upward, leaving a calm belt with little wind. The violent

Figure 8.7 Vertical Cross Section through a Typical Cold Front

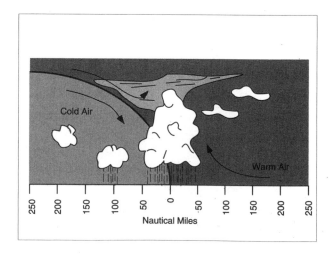

wind in the squall leaves a definite mark on the water, and this line serves as another warning of the approaching conditions.

A **warm front** occurs when a warm air mass moves over colder ground. The warm air is not as dense as the colder, heavier air, and it has a more difficult time displacing it. Warm fronts generally move much more slowly than cold fronts —15 knots or less. The vertical boundary between the two masses typically looks like Figure 8.8.

The warm air cannot plow the cold air out of the way; instead, it tends to force it out from underneath by squeezing it like toothpaste from a tube. A warm front is about three times wider than a cold front, and it can extend as much as 1,000 miles. The cloud system associated with a warm front is a long, gradually changing system that gets progressively lower and denser as the front approaches. Most of the clouds occur ahead of the front. Precipitation begins 200 to 300 miles ahead of the front and ends soon after the front passes.

Because the oncoming warm air is cooled by the ground the lapse rate is reversed, there is no vertical mixing, and the air is stable, producing steady conditions. If the surface air is cooled sufficiently a temperature inversion can occur. Warm-front temperature inversions are notorious for creating stagnant air.

When one front overtakes another the frontal boundary is called an **occluded front**. During this process the warm air between the two fronts is lifted off the ground. The resulting occlusion depends on the relative temperature of the cold air mass moving up from behind and the one the warm front was pushing ahead

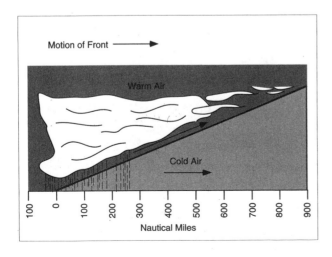

Figure 8.8 Vertical Cross Section through a Typical Warm Front

of it. A typical vertical cross section through each type of occluded front is shown in Figure 8.9.

Occluded fronts contain the worst of both kinds of fronts. The most severe weather in a storm system occurs as the fronts begin to occlude. A warm-front occlusion produces a longer duration of bad weather; a cold-front occlusion is more violent. Once the warm air is forced into the upper atmosphere and dispersed, the lower air mixes and the frontal boundary dissolves, not with a bang but a whimper.

Pressure Effects

As pointed out earlier, global thermal differences produce global thermal cells because of the pressure differences produced by expanding air. Differences in air pressure at sea level are principally caused by thermally induced density changes in the atmosphere. This occurs locally and globally. Globally it results in barometric tides, which produce a twice-daily maximum and minimum pressure. The maximum pressures occur at 1000 and 2200 hours and the minimum at 0200 and 1400 hours local sun time.[5] In an emergency the peak at 1000 hours has been used to estimate longitude in the tropics with an error less than 200 miles.

The warm air in the doldrums is an area of predominantly low pressure, whereas the colder air in the horse latitudes, some 25 to 30 degrees poleward, is an area of predominantly high pressure. While the temperature differences are readily apparent to the human body, the pressure differences are not. Why then bother with air pressure?

Figure 8.9 Vertical Cross Section through a Typical Occluded Front

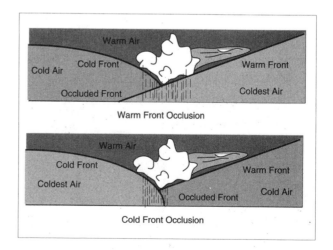

[5] Van Dorn, 53.

As it turns out, "good" weather is always associated with areas of high pressure and "bad" weather with areas of low pressure; but the same cannot be said for areas of cool and warm air. Even though the pressure difference is basically due to the difference in the density of hot and cold air, it is not possible to determine the location of a high- or low-pressure area based on air temperature alone. For example, the area of the highs in the horse latitudes is obviously warmer than the area of the lows in the subtropical convergence zone.

To understand why high-pressure areas always produce good weather and low-pressure areas always produce bad weather, imagine that the surface of the upper atmosphere is composed of hills and valleys of air. The hills produce high pressure, the valleys low. This is not strictly true, because density differences can produce pressure differences without an upper-surface elevation change, but the topographic model simplifies the discussion, particularly if contours of equal pressure called isobars are plotted. These isobars indicate areas of equal atmospheric pressure and allow one to visualize high-pressure areas as mountains and low-pressure areas as sinkholes.

In a perfectly ordered world the pressure would get progressively lower as one moved north or south away from the high-pressure ridge of the horse latitudes toward the low-pressure troughs of the doldrums and the subpolar lows. The isobars would all trend due east and west parallel to the latitude lines. If the earth were not rotating, the winds would blow directly perpendicular down the isobars from high- to low-pressure areas. The velocity of the wind would be dependent on the pressure gradient or slope of the imaginary air surface. The closer together the isobar lines, the steeper this imaginary surface and the greater the wind velocity.

If we move a little closer to reality and allow the earth to rotate, we will see that the wind is deflected to the right of the intuitive path in the northern hemisphere and to the left in the southern hemisphere. The amount of deflection depends on the balance between the pressure gradient (gravitational forces), the frictional forces, and the rotational forces. The result is that near the surface, where the friction is large, the winds are deflected as much as 60 to 75 degrees (see Figure 8.10). The frictional forces are even greater over land than over water; therefore the deflection of the wind is greater over land.

Notice that these effects combine to cause the wind to flow clockwise around a high and counterclockwise around a low in the northern hemisphere. The trends are reversed in the southern hemisphere. (Have you ever thought how much simpler life would be without the southern hemisphere?)

Also, notice that the tidy topography of our simplified model of pressure ridges and troughs takes on circular shapes. Both the high- and low-pressure areas

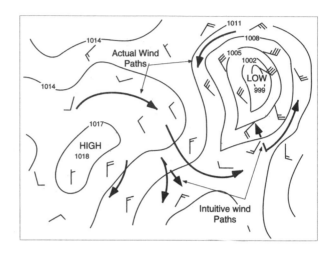

Figure 8.10 Wind
Directions around High-
and Low-Pressure Areas

have some distinct characteristics. The interesting thing is that the high-pressure domes by their very nature are all large objects with relatively flat slopes—one never finds a steep peak of air. Consequently the winds in a high are very light and variable, especially in the center, where they are likely to flow in any direction on the hypothetical flat surface. In the center of the high the skies are always clear and the weather good. Near the edges the wind velocity and the number of clouds increase. Highs can be relatively stable, remaining in one location for weeks. When they do move they rarely exceed 20 knots.

At the other extreme, the low-pressure areas are not really valleys, they are more like sinkholes or whirlpools. The lows form very steep cavities; the lower the pressure, the steeper the sides. Because of these steep gradients low-pressure areas are associated with violent weather, high winds, heavy precipitation, and thick cloud cover. They can appear and disappear in a matter of days. Lows are transitory, moving between 18 and 25 nautical miles a day and rarely stationary for more than a couple of days. They can be extremely hazardous to boaters.

It takes little intuition to conclude that it is best to avoid low-pressure areas and to do one's boating in areas of high pressure. High- and low-pressure areas are developed by several related mechanisms illustrated by two models, the frontal model and the jet stream model.

According to the frontal model, high pressure is developed in the center of an air mass where the air is moving down, and low-pressure areas are developed along the frontal boundaries where air is moving up. The first step in the development of a low was shown in Figure 8.6. This initial ripple is caused by the up-welling of air and the associated reduction in atmospheric pressure.

The reduction of pressure sucks the cold front in and pushes the warm front up and out as the low deepens. The low runs eastward along the front like a wave snapped into a rope. The remaining steps toward a fully developed low are shown in Figure 8.11. The energy contained in the warm air caught between the two cold bodies of air is the fuel for this storm. The onrushing cold front pushes more warm air aloft, and the low deepens until all the warm air between the fronts is exhausted. At that point the front is totally occluded; with the energy gone, the low fills, dissolves, and the storm dissipates.

The jet stream model takes the position that high- and low-pressure areas are developed by the winds aloft. Recall that in an ideal world the isobar lines would be parallel to the latitude lines, producing a situation where the winds aloft would tend to flow in bands also parallel to the lines of latitude due to the lack of frictional forces in the upper atmosphere. In the real world these bands tend to form into fast-moving streams of air called *jet streams*. Again, because life is not ideal, for various reasons such as cold air pushing south, warm air pushing north, these jet streams are deflected into meanders called *Rosby Waves* (see Figure 8.12). The deflected whirls form pockets of cohesive air, with the cold air moving south, where it is warmed and rises, generating a low-pressure area. The warm air masses move north and are cooled, forming high-pressure ridges.

The advantage of the jet stream model is that it provides a mechanism that explains the eastward migration of high- and low-pressure areas. These pressure cells are embedded in the jet stream, which pushes them eastward. The jet stream alternately meanders and straightens, spinning off highs and lows at random intervals.

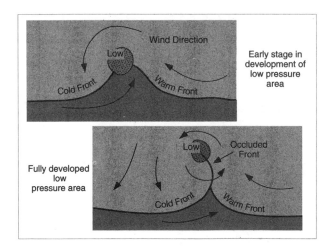

Figure 8.11 The Development of a Low-Pressure Area

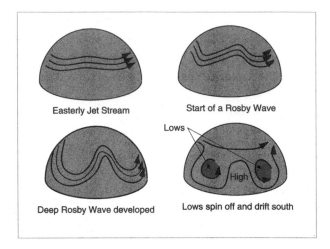

Figure 8.12 High- and Low-Pressure Areas Developed by the Jet Stream

Easterly Jet Stream

Start of a Rosby Wave

Lows

High

Deep Rosby Wave developed

Lows spin off and drift south

By watching the path of the jet stream, you can predict the weather. For example, if the jet stream west of your position is deflected north, a high-pressure cell is forming west of you; expect good weather. Conversely, if the jet stream is deflected south, expect bad weather, and if it is straight, expect change.

Humidity

It ain't the heat it's the humidity. The presence of water vapor in the air significantly alters its properties, affecting both temperature and pressure. Completely dry air is a rarity near the earth's surface. It is only completely dry at high altitude or near the poles where its temperature is below −40°F. Unlike the other gases in the atmosphere, the content of water vapor is extremely variable. Air can contain as much as 4 percent water. This may not seem like much, because air is mostly nitrogen and oxygen, but it amounts to 100 times more water than carbon dioxide. The amount of water in the air is referred to as humidity.

Humidity can be measured as absolute humidity, specific humidity, or relative humidity. Boaters need only deal with *relative humidity*, the ratio of the amount of water in the air divided by the maximum amount of water it can hold. The air's temperature determines the maximum amount of water it can hold; as it becomes warmer, its capacity to hold water vapor increases (see Figure 8.13).

Two properties of water affect the way it influences the atmosphere: its ability to change state readily from gas to liquid to solid, and its large capacity for absorbing and storing heat. While discussing heat transfer, we saw that the daily temperature swing depended on the amount of moisture in the air. Now we will look more closely at this heat transfer process.

The amount of heat energy it takes to raise the temperature of 1 gram of pure water 1° Celsius is 1 calorie. (The term may seem familiar, but the calorie used by nutritionists is really a kilocalorie, or 1,000 calories.) Raising the temperature of 1 gram of dry air 1°C takes only about 0.25 calorie, or about one-quarter the energy required to raise the temperature of water. In other words, the sun's energy is able to heat dry air four times faster than water. Because moist air heats up more slowly, its daily temperature swing is limited.

The other important part water plays in weather is its ability to change state from solid to liquid to gas over a small temperature range (100°C)—which corresponds to the normal range of temperatures in the earth's atmosphere. Thus water is constantly changing state, a process that transfers large amounts of heat energy around the atmosphere, materially influencing the weather.

Recall that adding heat to a substance increases its molecular activity, and taking heat away decreases it. There are two thresholds at which the state of activity in matter causes it to change its form from solid to liquid or liquid to gas. Crossing this threshold requires the addition of sufficient heat energy to overcome the molecular bonding that holds the matter rigid or fluid.

For example, to change water from a liquid to a gas, the surface tension of the liquid must be overcome. The amount of energy needed to do this is called the *heat of vaporization*, which is 539 calories per gram for water. This is significantly more heat energy than is needed to raise the temperature of the water (1 calorie per gram). When heat is added to water the molecules are accelerated, raising the

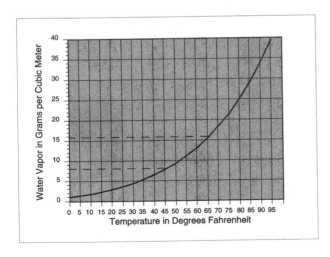

Figure 8.13 Amount of Water in 100 Percent Saturated Air

water temperature. Some of these molecules are accelerated sufficiently to break free of the surface and change state from liquid to gas, or evaporate.

Evaporation is continuous, not a step process. That is, as long as heat is added to water some of the molecules will be accelerated sufficiently to free them from surface tension. Water does not have to boil to evaporate, but it does require the addition of 539 calories of heat per gram. If the water temperature is below boiling, part of the added heat goes into evaporation and part goes into increasing the overall temperature of the water. Once the water reaches 100°C, however, all the additional heat goes into evaporation.

Water evaporating from the skin cools, because heat is taken from the skin to provide the energy necessary for evaporation. The same principle causes the air over water to be cooler. Likewise, because heat is required to turn water from ice to liquid, ice cools. This is called the *heat of fusion*, and requires only 80 calories per gram.

The heat of vaporization and fusion is not lost; it is stored in the water and released again when the vapor returns to a more dense state. When it is released it is called the *heat of condensation* or solidification, but it is still equal to 539 and 80 calories respectively. The significance of this fact in weather is that large amounts of heat are stored during evaporation and melting and liberated during condensation and freezing. For example, falling temperatures are retarded by the heat liberated from moisture in the air freezing into snow or sleet.

Evaporation and Condensation

It is not hard to see that the big number, 539 calories, is involved during evaporation and condensation. A closer look at this process shows that the amount of water actually in the air depends on its availability and temperature. One spot where it is hot and plenty of water is available is over the tropical oceans. Large amounts of heat energy from the sun are stored by evaporation in the tropical atmosphere, where it becomes available to fuel storms. For example, water vapor condensing into clouds or rain provides the enormous amount of destructive energy found in hurricanes.

Condensation occurs when the air becomes 100 percent saturated and can hold no more water. The most common way that this occurs is to cool moist air. Figure 8.13 shows that air that is 50 percent saturated at 65° contains 7.9 grams per cubic meter of water (15.8 x 0.5). If this air were then cooled to 45° it would become 100 percent saturated. Any further reduction in the air's temperature would cause water to be forced out of the air. The temperature at which moist air becomes 100 percent saturated is called the *dew point*. While evaporation goes on almost unnoticed, condensation usually attracts immediate attention. Condensation takes many forms, such as precipitation, clouds, fog, and dew, all of which are of interest to boaters.

Precipitation

Rain, snow, hail, and sleet are all forms of precipitation. If all the moisture in the air were to fall as rain, it would only cover the earth's surface to a depth of about 2 inches[6]—hardly enough to float an ark. On occasion enough falls to obscure long-range visibility, but in general precipitation, even though it may accompany violent weather, is more to be tolerated than feared.

All precipitation is formed in clouds, but all clouds do not form precipitation. Precipitation requires large amounts of moisture in the air, time, and vertical mixing sufficient to allow small drops to coalesce into drops large enough to fall. The extreme vertical mixing that occurs along with cold fronts produces large, heavy drops of water. The precipitation formed during the passage of warm fronts is caused by the thickness of the clouds and the time the water has to collect. Thus, raindrops falling from a warm front generally are smaller. If sufficient moisture, time, or vertical mixing is not present, clouds will form but no precipitation will occur.

Basic Cloud Formations

Clouds are formed as warm, moist air from the surface rises and is cooled by the colder atmosphere aloft. When the air temperature aloft reaches the dew point, condensation takes place and clouds are formed. Because this change of state is temperature sensitive and occurs exactly at dew-point temperature, all clouds have nearly flat bases. As the height of the cloud increases the temperature of the air continues to drop; therefore high clouds are formed mostly of ice particles.

Clouds are useful to boaters because they indicate the moisture content of the air, the temperature of the atmosphere, and the direction of the wind aloft. The various possible combinations of weather conditions produce significantly different types of clouds. From the cloud types and their sequence, boaters can get an indication of the type of weather to expect in the near term.

Cloud names are derived from five terms that roughly describe their appearance. Clouds that are formed with considerable vertical mixing tend to accumulate in piles and are called *cumulus*. Those formed in the presence of high horizontal winds but with very little vertical mixing form long wispy curls and are called *cir-*

[6]*Van Dorn*, 50.

rus. Those without vertical mixing or high horizontal wind form layers, or stratification, and are called *stratus*. The last two terms are modifiers: *nimbus*, meaning rain, and *alto*, meaning high.

These terms are applied to 10 different cloud layers, listed here from high to low: cirrus, cirrostratus, cirrocumulus, altostratus, altocumulus, stratus, stratocumulus, nimbostratus, cumulus, and cumulonimbus. Thus being "on cloud nine" means having spirits as high as a cirrostratus cloud.

Cirrus clouds, the highest clouds, generally are formed above 32,000 feet. They are thin, hairlike, detached wisps formed by ice crystals in very strong horizontal winds from very cold air with little vertical mixing. They form in an air mass that is rising slowly and steadily over a broad front—the exact conditions found ahead of an advancing warm front. They generally appear about 6 to 12 hours ahead of the front.

Because of their hairlike appearance, cirrus clouds are sometimes called "mare's tails." Their linear nature makes them appear to converge to a point on the horizon. Cirrus clouds are sometimes formed in fair, stable weather, but more often they foretell a change, especially if their movement is significantly different from the surface wind direction.

Cirrostratus clouds are the result of cirrus clouds becoming thicker and dropping lower, around 30,000 feet. Cirrostratus clouds form a complete thin veil that hides any vertical structure and turns the sky from blue to almost white. They are not thick enough to obscure the sun or the moon, and often form rings or halos around them. These clouds are the next in sequence to arrive before an approaching warm front; hence the saying "ring around the moon (or sun) brings rain."

Cirrocumulus clouds, the lowest of the upper cloud group, appear at around 28,000 feet as white rippled patches that show definite vertical structure. As the upper air becomes less stable, bands and waves are formed as the air oscillates above and below the dew point, first rising, cooling, and condensing, then dropping, warming, and evaporating again. These alternating bands of light and dark reminded the old seafarers of the stripes on a mackerel, hence the name "mackerel sky." These clouds are too thin to show shadows or obscure the sun. Often they follow the other two cirrus types indicating the definite approach of a warm front.

Altostratus clouds are the highest of the middle-level clouds. They are gray and have a uniform appearance due to lack of vertical mixing. It will be apparent, with a little study of Figure 8.13, that the higher the clouds are formed the less moisture is available to condense. Altostratus clouds form at around 20,000 feet—about the elevation at which sufficient moisture to obscure the sun begins to be present. The sun cannot shine through them, but they pass considerable diffused light that scatters everywhere and in sufficient quantity to hide or disperse shadows. Altostratus clouds are among the most reliable weather indicators. Once they arrive a warm front is almost assured and not far behind. They frequently signal the approach of a storm long before the barometer starts down or the wind picks up. Some precipitation can fall from altostratus clouds, particularly in the middle latitudes (30° to 60°) where the clouds are lower and thus contain more moisture.

Altocumulus clouds are middle-layer clouds, forming at about 1,300 feet. Because of their vertical mixing, well-defined white cloud patches are formed. The highest clouds formed mostly of water droplets, altocumulus clouds are thick enough to cast shadows. They are sometimes compared to a herd of sheep because of their small, elongated, lenticular shape. Altocumulus are distinguished from the other cumulus clouds because they lack vertical development and form at a much higher altitude. They are the only cloud form common to both cold and warm fronts. If they appear first in a clear sky and exhibit vertical structure, they indicate an approaching cold front. Altocumulus clouds with a predominantly horizontal structure preceded by a sequence of steady, lowering cirrus clouds indicate the approach of a warm front.

Stratocumulus clouds are gray, irregular layers of clouds that form rolls that look like dough wrapped around a stick. They are slightly larger and much lower than altocumulus clouds, forming at around 8,000 feet from degenerating cumulus clouds or as part of the series of steady lowering cumulus-type clouds that foretell the approach of a cold front. Stratocumulus clouds rarely produce precipitation. As fair-weather clouds they form at the top of high convection cells, and therefore often disappear at night.

Stratus clouds appear as a low, uniform layer with no definite vertical form and a base at around 3,000 feet. They give the sky a heavy, leaden appearance. Because of the delicate nature of this cloud type, it normally forms in areas with light winds. Stratus clouds that form from static air foretell dull, dreary weather. They can develop as part of the warm front series of clouds or a fog that lifts from the surface. Often when the clouds form from rising fog they are dispersed by the wind and sun. When the wind is stronger and the clouds are part of a series of thickening and lowering clouds, they indicate the imminent approach of a warm front. If the wind becomes too strong, it breaks the uniform cloud layer into parts called *fractostratus*. Little rain falls from stratus clouds—at worst only a light drizzle—because they lack the vertical mixing necessary for heavy rain.

Nimbostratus clouds develop when stratus clouds thicken. These thick, dark clouds are the end product of a warm front and bring steady and prolonged rain that can last several days. Nimbostratus are of little help in weather prediction because the bad weather is already at hand. The wind accompanying nimbostratus clouds can be light or heavy, but is generally steady, with few gusts. Heavy winds can be foretold by the presence of the fractostratus clouds mentioned above. Changes in the weather will be gradual.

Cumulus clouds are everybody's favorite. These small, white, low puffs form at around 4,000 feet, often accompanying warm weather and fair skies. They indicate the top of unstable air or small thermal cells and are typical of mildly unstable air on a summer day or in the trade wind areas. Cumulus clouds are patchy and do not cover the entire sky. On occasion they give the appearance of thickening on the horizon, but that is essentially an illusion created by the viewing angle.

Cumulus clouds have discernible vertical development. They change constantly into interesting and quixotic shapes, giving rise to the pastime of cloud-watching. Nothing is quite as monotonous as a blue sky without a white cloud scudding by.

As long as cumulus clouds remain detached and have minimum vertical development, enjoy; however, if they accumulate and build, they can bring showers or foretell the arrival of a cold front. The arrival of a cold front is foretold by the earlier presence of the higher cumulus series and the gradual, continuous change from cumulus to cumulonimbus as the front approaches. Because cumulus clouds are formed with considerable vertical mixing, the winds that accompany the front are often strong and gusty.

Cumulonimbus clouds are the massive, towering clouds that indicate the imminent arrival of an advancing cold front. They are heavy and very thick, and their density turns them from white to dark gray or black. They are formed where there is considerable turbulence in the atmosphere, with the base at around 1,000 feet and the top at around 45,000 feet. At this height the top is flattened off by the high-velocity upper winds and blown downwind, forming what is often called an anvil top or a thunderhead.

Because cumulonimbus clouds form in the presence of violent updrafts, a large amount of heat energy is transferred from the surface and released in the upper atmosphere, where it can fuel violent weather. Cumulonimbus clouds are associated with high, gusty winds, heavy rain, hail, and lightning. They can form in a few tens of minutes.

Minor and Miscellaneous Clouds

There are a few minor and miscellaneous cloud types that are local in distribution but important because of the violence of the accompanying weather. **Cumulus mammatus** clouds are associated with tornado formation. These low cumulus clouds have round downward projections that resemble breasts, hence the name. Tornadoes rarely affect boaters, but because of their great potential for destruction, it pays to be aware of this cloud form. Waterspouts, similar to tornadoes in appearance, are more related to dust devils and generally do not carry the destructive power of a tornado.

The **morning glory** is a rolling-pin-shaped cloud found in tropical Australia. It can be as long as 100 miles and only 300 to 600 feet thick. Morning glory clouds usually appear at sunrise on the eastern horizon on calm, otherwise cloudless days. They advance like a wave running up the beach, traveling between 30 and 70 miles per hour, often no more than 200 feet off the ground. Morning glory clouds carry with them strong, gusty winds.

Fog

The last of the clouds of interest to boaters, and the only one with which most people come into intimate contact, is fog. Boaters often dread fog almost as much as a gale. However, given the information in Chapters 2 and 3 on navigation in fog, that dread can be reduced to mild annoyance.

Fog occurs when moisture in surface air condenses, becoming visible as very small water drops with insufficient mass to fall or coalesce. These droplets stay suspended in the air and reduce visibility. When visibility is less than 2 miles it is designated poor visibility. When it is less than 0.5 miles it is called fog, and when it is less than 50 yards it is called dense fog.

Knowing how fog is formed and dispersed will help you predict its behavior and choose the appropriate course of action. The common types of fog are advection, upslope, radiation, steam, and precipitation or prefrontal. Fog is dispersed by heating, mixing, or sometimes coalescing.

Advection is the horizontal movement of air. **Advection fog** forms when warm, moist wind blows horizontally over a cold surface. The moving air gives off heat to the underlying cold surface, and the air temperature is reduced below the dew point. This is the type of fog most commonly formed at sea. It often persists for long periods and may be quite dense and extensive. Its density and thickness depend on the temperature difference between the air and water, the amount of moisture present, and the wind. Light winds cause mixing and thicken the advection fog layer. As the wind velocity increases, so does the turbulence. Normally, when the wind velocity is over 15 knots, too much turbulence exists for advection fog to form. On rare occasions, however, this type of fog has persisted in winds of as much as 20 knots.[7]

[7]*Markell, 94.*

Advection fog is common to certain locations and seasons. For example, in the northern hemisphere in summer, advection fog is commonly formed in the North Atlantic, where the Gulf Stream runs into the Labrador current; the Pacific Coast, from California north; and the northern central Pacific along the Aleutian chain, where the cold Bering Sea water meets the warm Japanese current. Due to the large temperature difference, the Aleutian fog has been reported to persist in winds as great as 35 knots.[8]

A form of advection fog called *tropical air fog* can be formed when moist, warm tropical air moves north or south into colder surroundings of higher latitudes. Fog formed in this manner is normally not very dense but covers large areas.

Upslope fog is essentially another form of advection fog. It forms when air moves over land that is steadily increasing in elevation. As you may recall, atmospheric temperature and pressure drop as elevation increases. The average temperature decrease is about 3°F per 1,000 feet of elevation. A modest 3,000-foot rise can reduce the surrounding air temperature by about 10°, which may be sufficient to produce condensation and fog. As there are very few slopes at sea, this fog is encountered most often by inland boaters on upland lakes.

Radiation fog is formed mostly over land or within 10 miles of land at night. The land surface loses heat by radiation rapidly; the cold land then cools the air near the surface. Clear skies, high pressure, and a gentle 2- to 4-knot breeze are required for the formation of radiation fog. The clear skies increase the cooling due to radiation; the breeze mixes the air along the cold surface so that it is cooled sufficiently to reduce its temperature below the dew point. The stronger the wind the more air is mixed and the smaller the temperature drop. If the quantity of air becomes too large, the temperature may not drop sufficiently to produce fog. Winds of 15 knots will create too much turbulence, and radiation fog will not develop. In absolute calm where there is not enough mixing, radiation fog will be patchy, somewhat thicker, and perhaps only waist deep.

Radiation fog ranges between 40 and 100 feet thick and is thickest in low-lying areas because cold air flows downhill. It does not form over water, but it can be blown to sea and can obscure land beacons, shore markings, and harbor entrances. Radiation fog generally dissipates as soon as the sun warms the layer of air sufficiently to raise the temperature above the dew point and absorb the moisture. In most cases it is gone by noon.

Steam fog is formed when the temperature of the water is greater than the temperature of the air over it. The air over the water becomes supersaturated, and

---

[8]*Kotsch, 187.*

any evaporation condenses almost immediately. Steam fog is very shallow and resembles rising columns of steam coming out of the water. It sometimes consolidates into a thick low-lying fog called *Arctic sea smoke*, which obscures the horizon and surface objects but leaves the sky relatively clear.

Precipitation or **frontal fog** is caused by the advance of a warm front. The warm rain falls through the frontal band and into the colder air below. Evaporation from the warm rain increases the humidity of the surrounding colder air. If the water content of the air is increased sufficiently to become 100 percent saturated, fog will condense. This type of fog is generally thin and rather short-lived, lasting only until the front has passed.

WIND

Wind is not really a weather element but is more a result of changes in other weather elements like temperature or pressure. All wind affects boaters, but strong winds can cause considerable damage and as such must command the attention of mariners. Earlier, the causes of winds were discussed; now we will examine how local topographic conditions affect wind and how wind in general behaves during storms.

Topographic Winds
Local topographic conditions alter the flow of wind either horizontally or vertically and change its character, producing three basic types of wind: anabatic, katabatic, and venturi. The first two are due to airflow over horizontal restrictions such as hills and mountains. The latter is due to air flowing through a vertical restriction such as a mountain pass.

An **anabatic** wind is one that is forced to rise because the surface of the earth is rising to form hills or mountains and the wind is blowing up the slope. These winds are usually light, notable exceptions being the khamsin of North Africa, which can reach velocities of 50 knots, the sirocco of the Northern Mediterranean, which can reach 40 knots, and the virazon of Chile, which attains 30 knots.

A **katabatic** wind is one that blows down a slope. Katabatic winds can be quite strong. They are usually formed at night and blow out to sea from high ground on shore. They seem to come out of nowhere and can wreak havoc in an otherwise peaceful anchorage. Katabatic winds are further subdivided into foehn and fall winds, depending on their temperature.

Foehn winds are warm, dry winds that are formed on the lee side of a mountain range because the winds that blow up the windward side cool down and lose moisture. As the moisture condenses, the temperature of the air increases due to the heat of condensation being released into the air. Once across the barrier, the air flows down the other side, being further warmed by compression as it descends. The winds may blow hard enough to endanger small craft anchored or underway near the shore. Locally different names are applied to these winds. Chinook and Santa Ana are a couple from the west coast of North America. Simoom and zonda are names of other foehn winds around the world.

Fall winds are cold winds blowing down an incline, caused by cold air damming up behind a topological barrier. When it suddenly spills over the divide, the heavy cold air rushes down the other side with great force. Although the wind warms slightly during the fall it is still colder than the surrounding air. These winds are often quite violent, sometimes reaching hurricane force. Tehuantepecer, pampero, levanter, mistral, and bora are regional names for a cold fall wind.

The **venturi effect**, caused by the winds being constricted and funneled through a topographical opening, can easily increase wind velocity by 100 percent. The most famous and probably the largest venturi effect is produced where the southern ocean winds are squeezed between the Antarctic continent and the tip of South America, creating the strong, persistent winds rounding the horn. The venturi effect is also responsible for one of the premier windsurfing areas of the world, the Columbia River Gorge near Hood River, Oregon. There the winds are accelerated as they are forced through a small opening in the Cascade mountain range, produced by the river.

Wind Behavior in Storms

Winds are generally the most significant effect of storms, so much so that the severity of the storm is usually cataloged by its wind strength. Before we discuss the effects of storms specifically, it is helpful to understand some characteristics of wind in general.

Wind strength and direction are not constant. Wind strength commonly varies as much as 40 to 50 percent and is generally given as the average wind speed. Wind direction can vary as much as 10 to 20 degrees. In the extremely squally and gusty conditions found in unstable air, these variations can be even larger, and wind speed may be given as an average plus a maximum upper gust value (15 knots gusting to 25). Estimating wind speed from the deck of a small boat is difficult. Speed is often overestimated, because lulls do not noticeably reduce angle of heel or boat speed before the wind rises again.

Wind speeds are usually measured in knots, especially over the water. In the early 1800s, Sir Frances Beaufort, an admiral in the British Royal Navy, developed a system to estimate wind speed based on its visual effects. At the time anemometers were not available. The system recognizes 13 different wind brackets, from calm (Force 0) to hurricane (Force 12). While the system is not very accurate, especially in confined waters, Beaufort was an admiral and people tend to do what admirals say; his system is still around today.

The descriptions in Table 8.1 are slightly different from those commonly given. The response of sailing vessels to various wind speeds on the traditional tables are some two centuries old; I have used the response of modern small sailing vessels.

Table 8.1 Beaufort Wind Speeds

BEAUFORT NUMBER	WIND SPEED	VISUAL CLUES
0	0 to 1 knot	Water surface completely flat. Smoke rises vertically.
1	1 to 3 knots	Small ripples with no apparent direction. Upper branches of trees begin to stir. Sailboats begin to show wake.
2	4 to 6 knots	Small wavelets with definite direction. Flags begin to stir. Sails remain full and boats make average speeds.
3	7 to 10 knots	Waves less than 2 feet, occasional breaks. Flags extend full. Sailboats heel and reach top speeds using light-air sails.
4	11 to 16 knots	Waves 2 to 5 feet, frequent whitecaps. Flags flap. Leaves and paper rise up. Sailboats make top speed under working sails.
5	17 to 21 knots	Waves greater than 4 or 5 feet. Almost all waves have whitecaps with some spray. Flags beat in violent ripples. Trees begin to sway. Birds stay grounded. Sailboats are reefed.
6	22 to 27 knots	Very large waves. Continuous whitecaps. Flags beat violently. Whistling begins in wires. Sailboats are fully reefed.
7	28 to 33 knots	Beginning gale. Foam begins to blow in streaks. Resistance felt in walking into wind. Most sailboats can no longer make course.
8	34 to 40 knots	Spray from the tops of waves is blown downwind. Sailboats hove-to or lying ahull. Branches are blown off trees. Walking is difficult.
9	41 to 47 knots	Estimating wind speed from a small boat is impossible because of gusts and boat motion. Surface structures sustain damage.
10	48 to 55 knots	At sea, visibility impaired. Difficult to look into wind.
11	56 to 63 knots	Impossible to stand. Widespread damage ashore.
12	Above 64 knots	Who cares? At this stage it is difficult to see in any direction.

The average worldwide year-round wind speed taken from pilot charts, excluding the roaring forties, is a little over 12 knots. The distribution of the winds from Force 0 to 8 is shown in Figure 8.14. This figure indicates the percentage of time a world traveler not frequenting the extreme southern latitudes would experience winds of these various strengths. Note that going to sea does not have to mean encountering one gale after another, because the predominant winds are Force 3 and 4. Judicious use of knowledge and information can further minimize the chances of encountering bad weather.

Winds above Force 8 are encountered very rarely, and recreational boaters have the significant advantage of being able to choose time and location to avoid violent weather. For example, don't go boating in the northern latitudes of the northern oceans in the winter. In over 30 years of boating in the inland waters of the Pacific, I have only reefed for high winds once. Passagemaking is a different story, but even then I have spent very few hours in winds over 30 knots. Furthermore, storms and violent weather are not random or instantaneous events. They occur in definite locations at definite times and develop over a period of days in a consistent manner. However, once encountered they do tend to leave a lasting impression leading to a resolve to avoid future encounters.

Winds with velocities greater than about 30 knots are known as a storm. Those who drive around in big boats insist that technically a storm requires winds from 48 to 55 knots, and that winds above 30 knots are called near gales. Anyone caught in a "near gale" in a small boat will settle for the term storm.

Figure 8.14 Worldwide Wind Distribution

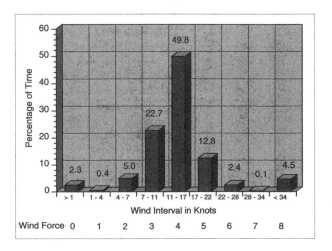

We will examine storms based on how they developed. Storms of concern to boaters fall into three broad categories: thermal storms, gales, and hurricanes. Each has unique features that help in dealing with them successfully.

Thermal Storms

Thermal storms consisting of squalls and thunderstorms are not quite as violent as the other two classifications because they are generally short-lived and cover a small area. Normally they last for minutes rather than hours or days. Unfortunately, because of this short life, they develop rapidly (in about an hour) and are a threat to the unaware or uninformed. Thermal storms always develop in unstable air. Line squalls are a kind of thermal storm.

The difference between a squall and a thunderstorm is minimal. Both most commonly occur in temperate climates on warm summer days late in the afternoon, when the air is in its least stable configuration. The unstable air behind a cold front or in the doldrums is also notorious for thunderstorms and squalls. Large, growing cumulus clouds should be watched for the four noticeable features indicating the development of a thunderstorm: great height, an anvil top, turbulence, and a dark, threatening underside.

To develop the necessary energy for strong winds, the cloud must reach great heights where the water can freeze. The freezing and thawing processes transfer large amounts of heat, causing turbulence, lightning, and the high winds. The turbulence inside a violent thunderstorm is immense, with vertical winds in excess of 50 knots. There is a documented case of an individual forced to parachute into a thunderstorm who was held aloft for nearly two hours, making several round-trips through the tumultuous cloud.[9]

These high clouds take on the shape of cauliflower. When the clouds get high enough the tops extend into the high winds of the upper atmosphere and are blown to the windward, causing the anvil top. The direction of the anvil top is the direction in which the storm will travel (see Figure 8.15).

The lower clouds in front of the storm have considerable shape due to the violent rolling and thermal currents. The dark, threatening area in the lower central portion of the cloud is caused by the thickness of the clouds and the heavy precipitation accompanying the storm, which prevent light from penetrating the cloud. Sometimes this dark area will extend to the surface of the water. The darker the cloud the more violent the weather underneath it.

[9]Van Dorn, 65.

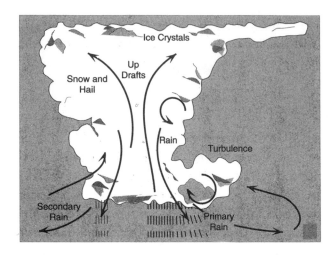

Figure 8.15 Air Currents
and Winds Involved in
Thunderstorms

The Defense: I have spent many hours in the doldrums trying to duck and dodge between these storms, and I am not sure my planning and maneuvering had much effect on the outcome. Being hit was more an inconvenience than a threat. Paying attention to cloud conditions always gave me ample time to take defensive measures such as reducing sail and positioning the boat to take the brunt of the short-lived violence.

The lightning that accompanies thunderstorms is not as much of a threat as one would expect, even though the boat is the highest point on the water. Most strikes are cloud-to-cloud strikes. Most, however, is not the same as all, and there has been a lot of discussion about the need for lightning protection on boats.[10] Although it is true that grounded lightning rods can pass the current safely to the water and protect the boat, it is also true that lightning rods draw more strikes. Lightning is a large amount of electrical energy, and the conductor must be massive. Too small a conductor is much worse than no conductor at all. Lightning strikes the boat because it is trying to get to the water. A good insulator is as much protection as a good conductor, and a poor insulator is better than a poor conductor. In other words, do not protect the boat unless you can do it adequately.

Gales

Gale is the name generally applied to winds above 34 knots that develop outside the tropical regions. Gales are sometimes known as extratropical cyclones or anticyclones; however, not all extratropical cyclones are gales. An extratropical

[10]*Martha R. Hutchison, "Lighting Strikes Twice,"* Yachting *(December 1984), 48.*

cyclone develops whenever a tuck is formed in a stationary front.

A gale will develop out of this storm if the difference between the low pressure developed around the occluded front and the high pressure following closely behind is significant enough to generate intense winds. The indicator of the intensity of the winds is both the depth of the low and the density of the isobars or the abrupt fall of the pressure gradient. The low needed to develop strong winds is around 988 millibars or less.[11] The depth of the low is recorded on weather fax transmissions and announced on many weather radio broadcasts.

Detection: The movement of a gale is generally eastward or northeastward at speeds between 500 and 700 miles per day. These storms generally cover large areas (1,500 miles) and can influence the weather for two days or more, but the heavy winds generally last less than 12 hours in a single location, even though the storm winds may continue for much longer.

The first warnings that a gale may be on the way are the swell from the storm itself and a halo around the sun or moon. This is followed by the arrival of the high cirrus clouds known as mare's tails and the falling of the barometer. By this time the storm is generally a day or less away. As the storm nears, everything increases: the rate at which the barometer falls, the wind, the cloud cover. The direction of the wind shifts counterclockwise (in the northern hemisphere), and the cloud cover thickens to a solid, translucent high sheet of altostratus clouds. This is a good indication that rain will begin in about 4 hours and the center is about 12 hours away.

The clouds continue to thicken and lower. The barometer continues to lower as well. The barometer has been used for centuries to get an indication of wind intensity. The depth of this depression and therefore the intensity of the winds can be estimated by using both the rate at which the pressure drops and the period of the fall. A drop of 10 millibars in 3 hours usually will result in gale-force winds.[12] The rate of fall changes as the storm approaches, with the most rapid drop occurring near the frontal boundary.

Because normal highs are around 1,012 to 1,014 millibars, the total fall to produce a gale is around 30 millibars. If the drop is greater than 50 millibars, hurricane-force winds can be expected. The period of the drop can be estimated by the length of the cloud sequence that foretells the storm's approach. Obviously, a storm that arrives in 6 hours will not produce winds as strong as one that takes 24 hours to arrive with a long, steadily increasing fall of both clouds and barometer. Thus the old weather adage "short forecast, soon past."

[11]*Kotsch*, 170.
[12]*Van Dorn*, 93.

As the storm approaches, the conditions encountered by a small boat depend on its position relative to the storm center. If the boat passes through the occluded portion of the storm or above the latitude of its center, the wind will continue its counterclockwise shift and the rain will continue for about 16 hours. At this time the barometer will begin to rise and the skies will clear. The strongest winds are most commonly on the north and west sides of the storm.

If the boat passes on a latitude below the occluded storm center, it will pass through two frontal systems in close succession. The first rain will be of much shorter duration, followed by a rise in temperature, partial clearing, and a reasonably steady barometer. Then there will be a short burst of squally rain and a drop in temperature when the boat passes the trailing cold front. As the boat passes both frontal systems, the wind direction will change in a clockwise direction (in the northern hemisphere). The seas on the southern side of a gale are often steep and confused because of the violent and sudden wind shift that usually accompanies the passage of the fronts. After the front passes, the seas and wind are no longer in their normal alignment and produce an uncomfortable, dangerous situation where boat handling becomes extremely difficult.

This sequence is one that many people are familiar with, because extratropical storms pass over land continually. The wind at sea, however, will be a little stronger because it is less restricted. Even at that, it is not always the raw ferocity of the wind and waves that are the real dangers in a gale. The genuine threat is the extensive fatigue and disorientation caused by the duration of the storm and the substantially colder wind and water. Defense tactics for handling a gale were given in Chapter 2.

Frequency: Extratropical cyclones develop regularly, but gales are generally winter storms. They exist in summer, but on a much more socially acceptable scale. At certain times and in certain places, 1 out of every 3 anticyclones develops into a gale (off the southern tip of Greenland in January, for example); however, most of the time in the waters surrounding the United States above 35° latitude the number is closer to 1 out of 20. South of that latitude gales become almost nonexistent. Unfortunately, storms do not; they simply change labels from extratropical to tropical.

Tropical Storms

Tropical storms, known regionally as typhoons, cyclones, or hurricanes, are predominantly found over tropical oceans. They are known for the extreme velocity of their winds, commonly in excess of 100 miles per hour and occasionally greater than 200 miles per hour. Tropical storms are also compact. Fine weather can rapidly deteriorate into a major tropical storm.

The Weather Bureau categorizes storms in the tropics as tropical disturbances, tropical storms, and several classes of hurricanes, depending on the wind velocity in the center of the storm. In this book the term tropical storm covers all categories.

Because most people rarely experience winds greater than 60 miles per hour, the power of hurricane-magnitude winds is difficult to imagine. The average hurricane generates 300 to 400 billion kilowatt hours of energy per *day*. Compare this with the combined *yearly* energy output of all U.S. hydroelectric dams of only around 300 billion kilowatt hours.

Fortunately, these storms are normally short-lived; they are born, reach maturity, and die within 7 to 10 days. Seven to 10 days may not seem like such a short time, but the storms do not spend their entire lives in one spot; they have a radius of ± 200 miles and generally move at speeds of 250 or more miles per day. A little arithmetic will show that any one spot normally has to tolerate the violence for only 24 to 36 hours even if the center of the storm passes directly over it.

The Cause: The causes of these engines of destruction are not completely known. What is known is that a hurricane is a very delicately balanced system. A myriad of subtle conditions must exist for it to be born, and the balance between these conditions must be maintained for it to live. Presently, what is understood is that both a high-level and a low-level wind system need to react in such a way as to carry more air away at the high level than is introduced at the low level. Also, the lower air mass must be warm, saturated marine air to provide the huge amount of energy needed to drive the storm. Hurricanes are never born over land.

The rising air releases heat, the moisture in the air condenses and produces rain. The condensation process releases even more heat, which provides the power to drive the hurricane. The hot air ascends rapidly, sucking in more warm air at the bottom to fuel the engine. The high winds aloft carry the exhaust away and the storm intensifies. The magnitude of the storm depends on the amount of heat available and the efficiency of the exhaust system. The hurricane continues until something upsets this balance and causes it to dissipate. The surest way to dissipate a hurricane is by the introduction of cold semitropical air as the storm moves into higher latitudes or the drier air usually found over a landmass. More wind coming in at the bottom than escaping at the top will also cause the disturbance to fill and dissipate.

Frequency: Fortunately, hurricanes are far less numerous than gales and are confined to tropical waters and specific seasons. There are five major hurricane-spawning areas located just north and south of the equator: the North Atlantic (around the Caribbean), the western North Pacific (off the Philippines), the eastern North Pacific (off Mexico), the South Pacific (off Australia), and the tropical Indian Ocean. Table 8.2 gives the mean annual frequencies of hurricanes in these areas.

The probability of most recreational boaters ever encountering a hurricane at sea is remote. It has been calculated than if a boat were to cross the most prolific hurricane system near the Philippines during the worst possible time at a mean speed of 6 knots, the odds of encountering gale-force winds or above would be about 12 to 1.[13] This is about the same odds as being dealt two pair in a game of draw poker. The consequences of not making two pair, however, are considerably less severe than those of being hit with a hurricane. It may be prudent to increase the odds as much as possible. Fortunately that is not hard to do. The chances of encountering a hurricane can be reduced by avoiding breeding grounds and seasons and by taking advantage of hurricane weather forecasting networks.

Defense: For those unlucky enough to encounter a hurricane, the course of action depends on where the boat is located. If at anchor, assess the depth of the water, the holding power of the bottom, and the protection from wind and waves offered by the anchorage. Assess the capabilities of the other skippers and boats in the anchorage to hold position and not blow down on your boat. If the situation seems doubtful or unsuitable, head for the open sea. If conditions are suitable, lay down several anchors, using the longest possible scope. If chain is being used as a rode, be sure the depth is adequate to provide the necessary shock-absorbency (see

Table 8.2 Mean Annual Frequency of Hurricanes[14]

Month	Caribbean	Philippines	Mexico	Australia	Indian Ocean
January	0	0.3	0	0.7	1.3
February	0	0.2	0	1.1	1.1
March	0	0.2	0	1.3	0.8
April	0	0.7	0	0.3	0.5
May	0	0.9	0.3	0	0.5
June	0.3	1.2	0.6	0	0.2
July	0.4	2.7	0.9	0.1	0.1
August	1.5	4.0	2.0	0.1	0
September	2.7	4.1	1.8	0	0.1
October	1.3	3.3	1.0	0	0.4
November	0.3	2.1	0	0.3	0.6
December	0	0.7	0	0.5	0.7
Total	6.5	20.4	6.6	4.4	6.3

[13]Van Dorn, 90.
[14]Nathaniel Bowditch, American Practical Navigator (Washington, D.C.: Defense Mapping Agency, 1984), 935.

Chapter 4). Protect all lines from chafe. Remove and stow below all items that can produce windage or be blown loose. Secure all hatches, ports, and openings.

If tied to a pier or dock, assess the strength and height of the dock against the predicted storm surge. In many tropical ports the normal tidal range is small and the docks are fixed. The additional tidal surge pushed in by the storm is often sufficient to submerge the dock completely. Often in these cases the boat will end up on top of the dock. Assess the capabilities of all nearby boats; again, if unsuitable, head for sea. If suitable, double all docking lines, deploy extra fenders, protect against chafe, remove all equipment from above deck, and secure hatches and ports.

If you are at sea and the direction of the wind is changing in a clockwise manner (veering), your boat is in what is referred to as the dangerous semicircle. It is dangerous because if the easiest course is taken, that of running with the wind astern, the boat will head directly into the worst part of the storm. The course of action under these conditions is to take the wind on the starboard bow as tight as practical and make the best possible speed for as long as possible. Secure or remove all loose gear on deck and batten down hatches and ports. When this course can no longer be held, hove to, go below, hang on, and remember that like all good things, all bad things come to an end.

If at sea and the wind is changing counterclockwise (backing), the boat is in the navigable semicircle. Again, secure or remove all loose gear on deck, batten down hatches and ports. Take the wind on the starboard, stern quarter (135° relative to the wind), and get out of there as fast as possible. Take normal storm defensive actions, described in Chapter 2.

If the wind direction is steady, the velocity is increasing, and the barometer is dropping, the boat is directly in the path of the approaching eye. Take the preparatory actions suggested above and set a course with the wind more toward the stern, say about 160° off the starboard bow. This will push the boat farther out away from the storm until the navigable semicircle can be reached, from which point the course can be altered as described above.

If the wind direction is steady, the velocity is decreasing, and the barometer is rising, the boat is behind the eye with the eye moving away. Take the most comfortable course that keeps the boat moving away from the eye. Most hurricanes move west with a long curve to the north. However, not all hurricanes follow this textbook course, and occasionally they will loop back around on their old course.

Storm Warnings

The old standard system of weather warnings consisting of red triangular and square flags and colored lights has been discontinued by the National Weather Service. One triangular flag was flown for small craft warning, two meant a gale, a single square red flag with a black square in the center meant storm, and two of them indicated a hurricane. The light signals consisted of red over white, white over red, two reds, and a red-white-red three-light combination, which signaled small craft warning, gale, storm, and hurricane respectively.

In truth, both the flags and the lights were poor methods of relaying this information because of their limited range. Yacht clubs and some small countries may still use these systems, but knowing where to look for the flags or lights is always a problem for a visitor. Even after they are located, the vigilance of the flag tender is unknown, and the boater must determine how accurately they indicate upcoming conditions.

PREDICTING THE WEATHER

Eighty years ago the bulk of weather information for recreational boaters came from looking at the sky. Today the same information comes from almost every form of communication: radio, television, newspaper, and telephone. It may seem that the only skill needed to predict the weather is the ability to punch the correct "on" button and listen to a professional report.

Certainly there is truth to that statement. If a weather report is available, it is not in the best interest of the recreational boater to try to predict the weather himself. Weather prediction is for professionals who are trained to do this complicated and difficult task. Depending on how one judges accuracy, their national average is around 60 percent.

If professionals with all their equipment and training make mistakes, what hope is there for an amateur? Those who said "slim to none" are only half right and have made their first error in weather-related matters. The recreational boater's limited knowledge of weather is needed to assess the believability of available professional reports, to adapt the area-wide forecast to account for local and changing conditions, and to deal with areas where accurate professional reports are not available.

The recreational boater should know where to go to get good weather reports, what information is available on weather fax, and how to make the best use of weather map information. The boater should also understand the use of some simple weather instruments to increase the value of the weather reports, and develop a "weather eye" capable of interpreting nature's warning signals: clouds, wind shifts, and wave action.

Weather Reports

The best and most available source of weather reports is the marine VHF radio, which assigns 10 channels to provide continuous weather information. Presently only channels 1 to 4 are being used. Generally speaking, in the coastal waters of the United States and Canada two or three channels can be received at a time. The origin of the broadcast on each channel changes with location of the receiver. There is some overlap on the area covered, but due to the local nature of the VHF radio, the channel with the best reception is normally the one with the most relevant information. In most locations the weather information provided on these channels is of special interest to marine users. For example, more emphasis is given to wind velocity and direction than in normal weather broadcasts. Even though the reports are repeated continuously, they are only updated every 6 hours.

This weather information is broadcast in four different formats. The first is a general weather synopsis, which includes frontal activity within the next 36 hours. The second is a series of weather predictions for 6, 12, and 24 hours, based on the general synopsis for the local area and three longer-range forecasts for inland waters, coastal waters up to 60 miles off the coast, and offshore waters out to 250 miles. The third format lists the current local conditions at various coastal weather stations, including visibility, wind direction and velocity, sea condition, and barometric pressure. The final format is directed at agriculture and deals more with frost and precipitation conditions.

For those without access to VHF radio, most large population areas also have a prerecorded telephone weather report similar to the first VHF format. Weather reports can also be found on local television and in newspapers. While these have the advantage of visual aids, such as simplified weather maps, they are less detailed. Television reports must serve a broader audience and therefore have less specialized information of interest to boaters. Newspapers can provide considerably more detail than the other reporting methods, but are only updated every 24 hours.

Weather broadcasts available on HF radio are generally not continuous. The National Weather Service publishes a book entitled *Selected Worldwide Marine Weather Broadcasts* (see Appendix A). It lists frequencies, broadcast times, and geographic areas covered, and is especially useful for those wishing to venture beyond the limits of U.S. and Canadian VHF broadcasts. It also lists the same information on worldwide weather facsimile broadcasts.

Weather Fax

Weather fax can provide a wealth of information, but more knowledge is required to interpret and get the maximum use from this information. Fax transmissions provide satellite imagery, surface and upper-air analysis and prognosis, sea temperature, wave height, sea ice maps, jet stream location, and ocean-current maps. Most of this information is directed at commercial and military shipping.

The value of all this information to a recreational boater is limited. When going for an afternoon sail or even a cruise in sheltered water, it certainly is not necessary to receive daily weather fax transmission. Its only real use is for offshore work, and then only for the short term. The accuracy of weather predictions drops off considerably after about three days. Weather fax is used extensively by ocean-racing yachts to divine the best route to the finish line, but on a passage of longer than three or four days in a recreational boat, once committed, there is little one can do but brace oneself and take general precautions.

For example, when leaving the Straits of Juan de Fuca heading into the South Pacific, the weather fax charts are of great value. They allow one to make predictions as to when the high will be well enough established to provide a following wind and deflect incoming anticyclones. The boat can sit in harbor scanning the faxes until conditions are right. Once it leaves, three days later the boat will be far enough south that most storms will cross behind it.

On the other hand, when leaving Kauai going north the information is useless because the weather for the first 3 days is produced by the fairly consistent trade wind belt. Weather fax information gathered before leaving will not help you guess what will happen to the North Pacific High when it is reached 7 to 10 days later.

The equipment necessary to receive weather fax information comes in self-contained and modular units. The self-contained units are easier to use and more compact. They consist of a special HF pretuned receiver, a fax modem, and a printer. The modular units consist of a computer, a printer, an HF receiver, and a modem. Because more and more boats are equipped with computers, printers, and HF receivers for other reasons, the addition of a modem can be a less expensive choice. The modular units require more skill and time to operate but can be used for other applications. The radio modem is not generally marketed through marine outlets; it may be necessary to research the amateur radio market to find this equipment.

The frequency of the broadcasts and station for each geographical area are given in Tables 8.3 through 8.7. The schedules for these broadcasts and the broadcast type can be obtained from each station and are also listed in several publications.[15,16,17] Once a day each station transmits its latest schedule, including time and type of broadcast.

[15]U.S. Department of Commerce, Selected Worldwide Marine Weather Broadcasts (Washington, D.C.).
[16]Meteorological Facsimile Broadcasts, pub. no. 9, vol. D. (New York: Unipub, Inc. Reprint.)
[17]Worldwide Marine Radio Facsimile (Westborough, Massachusetts: Alden Electronics).

Table 8.3 Facsimile Broadcasts in the North Pacific Area

STATION	FREQUENCIES IN KILOHERTZ	AREAS COVERED
Esquimalt, BC, Canada	4268, 6968, 12125	North Pacific and the North Polar Region
San Francisco, CA, U.S.	4346, 8682, 12730, 17151	Eastern North and South Pacific
La Jolla, CA, U.S.	8646, 17410.5	Pacific Ocean north of latitude 5°S and south of latitude 30°N; east of longitude 140°W
Honolulu, HI, U.S. (Navy)	2122, 4855, 8494, 9396, 14826, 21837	North Pacific Ocean
Honolulu, HI, U.S.	9982.5, 11090, 13627.5, 16135, 23331.5	Pacific Ocean north of latitude 25°S and south of latitude 40°N; east of longitude 160°E and west of longitude 140°W
Kodiak, AK, U.S.	4296, 8457	Gulf of Alaska and Bering Sea
Guam, Mariana Islands	3377.5, 4975, 7645, 10255, 10966, 13807.5, 18620, 22865, 23880	Western North Pacific and Eastern Indian Ocean
Khabarovsk, former USSR	4516.7, 7475, 9230, 14737, 19275	Western North Pacific
Tokyo, Japan	3622.5, 7305, 9970, 13597, 18220, 22770	Western North Pacific
Peking, ROC	5525, 8120, 10115, 12110, 14365, 18235	Western North Pacific and Eastern China Sea
Bangkok, Thailand	6765, 7395, 17520	North of latitude 30°S and south of latitude 50°N; east of longitude 45°E and west of longitude 160°E

Types of Charts and Their Uses

Each of these stations broadcasts some or all the following charts: surface weather, upper air, wave height, sea temperature, ice charts, and satellite imagery. Some of the stations also broadcast special charts used mostly for research and special interest groups. The first three types of charts are broadcast in three formats: analysis, prognosis, and extended forecast. *Analysis charts* show the data recorded within the last few hours. *Prognosis charts* indicate patterns 12 to 36 hours in the future. *Extended forecasts* provide information on the patterns expected within 2 to 5 days.

Surface weather maps show isobars, locations of high- and low-pressure areas along with their direction and speed of travel, location of fronts, and wind speed and direction. These charts are the primary tool for understanding the present weather, locating good and bad weather areas, and route planning.

Upper-air maps (500 millibars) show wind speed and direction, temperatures, and atmospheric moisture at an altitude of about 18,400 feet above the earth. The contour lines are the height in meters at which the pressure is 500 millibars. These

Table 8.4 Facsimile Broadcasts in the North Atlantic Areas

STATION	FREQUENCIES IN KILOHERTZ	AREAS COVERED
Frobisher Bay, Northwest Terr., Canada	3253, 7710, 15644	Hudson Strait, Hudson Bay, East Coast Baffin Is., Foxe Basin, Lancaster Sound, Queen Elizabeth Is.
Halifax, N.S. Canada	4271, 6330, 9890, 13510,	Western North Atlantic
Boston, MA, U.S.	3389,7530,8502,12750	North Atlantic north of latitude 35°N and west of longitude 60°W
Brentwood, NY, U.S.	9290, 9389.5, 11035, 17436.5	Western, North Atlantic
Norfolk, VA, U.S. (Navy)	4875, 8080, 10965, 16410, 20015	North Atlantic
Mobile, AL, U.S.	6852, 9157.5, 11145	Gulf of Mexico
Bracknell, England	3289.5, 4610, 4782, 8040, 9207, 11086.5, 14436, 14582	Eastern North Atlantic
Northwood, England	2813.85, 3436.85, 4247.85, 6436.35, 8494.85, 12741.85, 16938.85	Eastern North Atlantic
Norrkoping, Sweden	119.85, 4037.5, 6901, 8077.5	Eastern North Atlantic and the Baltic Sea
Helsinki, Finland	83.1, 8018	Baltic Sea
Copenhagen, Denmark	5850, 9360, 13855, 17510	North Atlantic, Greenland, and North Sea
Moscow, Russia	2815, 5355, 7750, 10980, 15950	Eastern North Atlantic
Offenbach, Germany	1342	Eastern North Atlantic and the Mediterranean Sea
Hamburg, Germany	3855, 7880, 13657	Eastern North Atlantic
Paris, France	131.8, 4047.5, 8185, 12305	North Atlantic and the Mediterranean Sea
Dakar, Senegal	7587.5, 13667.5, 19750	Eastern Tropical Atlantic

Table 8.5 Facsimile Broadcasts in the Southern Ocean Areas

STATION	FREQUENCIES IN KILOHERTZ	AREAS COVERED
Darwin, Australia	5755, 7535, 10555, 15615, 18060	North of latitude 25°S and south of latitude 25°N and east of longitude 75°E and west of longitude 180°
Canberra, Australia	5100, 11030,13920, 19690	South of latitude 10°N between longitude 70°E and 150°W
Wellington, New Zealand	5805, 9410, 13550, 16220	Between latitude 30°N and 60°S and longitude 140°E and 120°W
Nairobi, Kenya	10115, 22867	Indian Ocean
Tehran, Iran	8715	Black Sea, Caspian Sea, Arabian Sea, Red Sea, Eastern Mediterranean Sea
New Delhi, India	7405, 14842, 18227	Between latitude 45°N and 25°S and longitude 30°E and 125°W

Table 8.6 Facsimile Broadcasts in the Southern Atlantic Areas

STATION	FREQUENCIES IN KILOHERTZ	AREAS COVERED
Rio de Janeiro, Brazil	8291.1, 12025	South Atlantic
Brasilia, Brazil	10225, 18030	Between latitude 15°N and 35°S and longitude 85°W and 10°W
Buenos Aires, Argentina	5185, 10720, 18093	Between latitude 4°N and 48°S and longitude 12°E and 132°W
Pretoria, South Africa	4014, 7508, 13773, 18238	South Atlantic east of longitude 40°W; Indian Ocean west of longitude 80°E
Reunion—Saint Denis	8176, 16335	Antarctic Ocean
Orcades (Summer)	2422.5, 8818, 8195, 11147	South of latitude 5°S between l longitude 20°W and 90°W
Orcades (Winter)	2422.5, 4250, 6454, 9984	South of latitude 50°S between longitude 20°W and 90°W

Table 8.7 Facsimile Broadcasts in the Mediterranean Areas

STATION	FREQUENCIES IN KILOHERTZ	AREAS COVERED
Rota, Spain	7417, 9875	Eastern North Atlantic and Mediterranean
Madrid, Spain	3650, 6918.5, 10205	Eastern North Atlantic and Mediterranean
Athens, Greece	5206, 8100, 12903	Eastern North Atlantic and Mediterranean
Monsanto, Portugal	4235, 8526, 13002	North Atlantic and Western Mediterranean
Rome, Italy	477.5, 8146.6, 13600	North Atlantic, Mediterranean, Black, and Caspian Seas
Beograd, Yugoslavia	3520, 5800	Mediterranean Sea
Sofia, Bulgaria	5093	Eastern North Atlantic, North, Baltic, Mediterranean, Black, and Caspian Seas
Ankara, Turkey	3377, 6790	Mediterranean Sea
Cairo, Egypt	4526, 10123	Mediterranean and Red Seas

charts are useful because surface pressure systems and fronts tend to be steered by these upper-air highs, lows, and winds, providing information to base estimates as to where these systems will go next.

Wave height charts show contours of equal wave heights and are taken from shipboard reports. *Sea temperature charts* show contours of sea surface temperature and can be used to predict fog and locate the limits of warm or cold currents. Ice charts show the location, thickness, and type of sea ice and the location of any known icebergs. Under normal conditions, recreational boats can make very little practical use of any of these charts.

Satellite imagery comes in three basic varieties: visual, infrared, and radar. The visual picture displays cloud cover and areas of fog. The types and extent of the clouds provide information on the weather beneath them. Infrared pictures show cold and warm areas, which help to locate warm and cold bodies of air and water. Radar images show areas of dense precipitation. Again, this level of detail is only of use to a recreational boater in a limited number of special cases.

Reading a Weather Map

Because weather always travels generally eastward or northeastward propelled by the jet stream and the position of the upper-level highs and lows, it follows that tomorrow's weather here will be similar to yesterday's weather there. Weather maps are a way to determine what the weather was like "there" yesterday so today's weather "here" can be predicted. A weather map is a pictorial representation of key weather information concerning: atmospheric pressure, temperature, wind direction and force, cloud cover, and up to 20 other pertinent bits of data.

The most accessible weather maps are published in newspapers. Although the popular press does not always follow a standard weather map format, the features of greatest use to recreational boaters—isobars, frontal boundaries, wind arrows, and some details on precipitation—generally do appear, sometimes in abbreviated form.

The most helpful feature is the **isobars**. These lines of equal pressure, discussed earlier, show the high- and low-pressure areas and the gradients between them. The word high or low or a large capital H or L or, even better, a single number designating the maximum or minimum atmospheric pressure is sometimes found in the center of each air mass. The air masses are rarely labeled as continental or maritime, etc., but these characteristics can be inferred from their location. Given this information, you can apply the knowledge obtained earlier in the chapter to predict what conditions may be encountered.

Frontal boundaries are shown with heavy symbolic lines. The conventional symbols are shown in Figure 8.16. On occasion the cold front symbol is shown as triangular rather than circular arcs. In color presentations, the warm front symbol is shown in red, the cold front in blue, the occluded front, because it is one front on top of another, in purple, and the stationary front in alternating red and blue.

Weather bureau wind symbols are shown as wind arrows pointing in the direction the wind is blowing. The number of feathers or half feathers indicates the

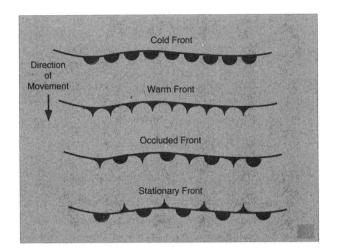

wind speed. Each half feather is 5 knots. A triangle indicates 50 knots. Generally the wind speed is indicated in knots; however, on occasion the statute miles per hour or the Beaufort scale may be used, so check the notes and legend for details. The standard symbols and their meanings are shown in Table 8.8.

Precipitation symbols are shaded or crosshatched with a descriptive word nearby. Precipitation is also designated by station symbols, a composite of 170 different characters and signs describing the weather occurring at specific locations. The detail of the information is considerably beyond the needs of the recreational boater.

The Weather Eye

Mother Nature's weather map can be read just as easily as the weather bureau's—and Mom's map is constantly updated. It consists of reading the clouds, the change in wind patterns, and barometric pressure. For example, a wind shift in a clockwise direction around the compass is **veering**. A veering wind often foretells improving weather. When the shift is counterclockwise, the wind is said to be **backing**. A backing wind often foretells worsening conditions. Wind pattern changes, however, are of little value in areas with significant topographic features; wind is easily deflected by mountains and channeled by valleys. For example, in the Inland Passage of the Pacific Northwest, the wind only blows in two directions, upchannel and down, regardless of the direction reported by the weatherman.

The approach of a front and its accompanying bad weather can be foretold by the changing sequence of clouds. This information can be used to judge the length

Table 8.8 Weather Map Wind Symbols

SYMBOL	WIND SPEED IN KNOTS	SYMBOL	WIND SPEED IN KNOTS
	Calm (less than 2.5 knots. Variable Direction)		40 Knots (37.5 knots or greater but less than 42.5 knots.)
	Calm (Less than 2.5 knots. Constant Direction.)		45 Knots (42.5 knots or greater but less than 47.5 knots.)
	5 Knots (2.5 knots or greater but less than 7.5 knots.)		50 Knots (47.5 knots or greater but less than 52.5 knots.)
	10 Knots (7.5 knots or greater but less than 12.5 knots.)		55 Knots (52.5 knots or greater but less than 57.5 knots.)
	15 Knots (12.5 knots or greater but less than 17.5 knots.)		60 Knots (57.5 knots or greater but less than 62.5 knots.)
	20 Knots (17.5 knots or greater but less than 22.5 knots.)		65 Knots (57.5 knots or greater but less than 62.5 knots.)
	25 Knots (22.5 knots or greater but less than 27.5 knots.)		70 Knots (67.5 knots or greater but less than 72.5 knots.)
	30 Knots (27.5 knots or greater but less than 32.5 knots.)		75 Knots (72.5 knots or greater but less than 77.5 knots.)
	35 Knots (32.5 knots or greater but less than 37.5 knots.)		100 Knots (97.5 knots or greater but less than 102.5 knots.)

of the storm and whether the winds will be steady or gusting. Cirrus, cirrostratus, altostratus, stratus, and nimbostratus clouds indicate the prolonged rain associated with a warm front. The cumulus sequence is not quite as dependable, but the change from altocumulus to stratocumulus to cumulus and finally to nimbocumulus signals a cold front. How fast the cloud sequence changes indicates how quickly bad weather will arrive.

Barometer movement also gives clues to the upcoming weather. Recall that an approaching storm will always cause the barometer to fall. The reverse, however, is not always true. That is, every falling barometer does not indicate a storm. The barometer goes up and down continually. The trend is only one of the indicators. The other two are the rate at which it moves and the distance it moves. Rapid movement of the barometer—defined as .06 inches of mercury per hour or more—indicates rapid change in weather. As discussed earlier, a large drop indicates a large storm.

A few simple rules for using these indicators are given below. Keep in mind that predicting the weather using these rules is a gross oversimplification and that errors will occur. Otherwise, why would we need the weather bureau? During the predicting process, remember that a single indicator is not as convincing as multiple indicators. Also, you can modify these general rules to make them more accurate for your area.

Fair weather will generally continue for a few days if the sky is clear of clouds, the barometer is high and steady or rising slightly, and the wind is out of the west or northwest.

A change from **fair to foul** weather is coming if the number of clouds increases and they lower with time, the barometer is falling, and the wind backs from west to southeast and increases in velocity.

Foul weather will generally continue if the clouds are low, thick, and dark, the barometer is low and steady, and the wind is from the northeast to the east.

Change from **foul to fair** weather occurs when the clouds dissipate, the barometer rises, and the wind veers east to southeast.

Reading the waves

Waves can also be used to foretell weather. Because high wind generates waves and waves often travel faster than the storm, waves can bring information as to the distance and general strength of the winds. As waves move away from the storm they become gradually longer and

---

THE WISDOM OF THE ANCIENT MARINERS

A great many weather sayings have been developed over the years, some truer than others.

Red sky at night,
   Sailors delight.
Red sky in the morning,
   Sailors take warning.

This rhyme is based on the color of the sun as seen through dry air. Dry air to the west at sunset indicates that fair weather will prevail. Dry air to the east has no bearing on the weather to the west, and just completes the rhyme.

Rainbow to windward,
   Foul falls the day.
Rainbow to the leeward,
   Damp runs away.

If moisture-laden air is to the windward it will be blown down on the observer. Conversely, if it is to the leeward it will be blown away from the observer. However, the appearance of a rainbow also depends on the position of the sun relative to the observer. The sun must be behind the observer, so in the afternoon the rainbows would all be to the east and in the morning all to the west. Because most foul weather comes from the west, this could be modernized into:

Rainbow in the morning,
   Sailors take warning.
Rainbow in the afternoon
   brings rain once in a blue moon.

I never said I was a poet; you have to give me some credit for not taking the easy way out by using night and delight.

Mackerel skies and mare's tails
   Make tall ships carry small sails.
When a halo rings the moon or sun
   The rain will come upon the run.

(continued next page)

**THE WISDOM OF
THE ANCIENT MARINERS (continued)**
These sayings are based on the thin cirrus to cirrostratus cloud sequence that precedes a warm front. The first is a direct reference to the cloud shapes themselves; the second refers to the effects of the cloud cover. These thin clouds do not obscure the sun or moon, but cause a ring of reflected light to appear around the celestial body; the higher and thinner the cloud band the larger the ring. Because the clouds both thicken and lower as the storm approaches, the size of the ring can be used as a rough estimate of the storm's arrival. The National Weather Service has verified that sun halos predict rain about 75 percent of the time; moon halos are only about 65 percent accurate.[18]

Sounds traveling far and wide,

A stormy day will betide.

Birds sit before a storm.

Distant shores loom up nearer before rain. These sayings are based on the effects of dropping air pressure that precedes a low-pressure cell. Because the pressure is less, the density of the air is less, which may make flying more difficult for birds. However, sound actually travels slower in a less-dense material. To protect the honor of old wives and salty sea dogs, there has been some speculation that cloud cover reflects sound. Whether the difference can be perceived by the human ear is hard to say, but generally speaking, if the cloud cover is low and dense enough to reflect

(continued next page)

lower. It is mathematically possible to estimate the distance, travel time, and intensity of the wind from the height and period of the swells, but the assumptions made and the difficulty in getting accurate data from a small boat make the calculations meaningless.

Some useful information can be obtained, however. Long, high swells indicate the presence of a storm in the direction from which the waves arrive. These swells may be from a storm that has passed, one that will come nowhere near, or one that is heading toward the boat. The swells from a storm heading toward the boat will be out of the west or southwest. If these swells get larger and the period shorter, the storm is getting nearer. Table 8.9 can be used to estimate conditions where the disturbance is from winds greater than 30 knots, within the accuracy of the shipboard estimates.

A few examples: If a 5-foot swell is timed at 12 seconds there is a probability that a storm with winds greater than 30 knots will arrive in less than 2 days (45 hours). For a given wave period, as the wave height increases the distance to the disturbance decreases. If the wave height is the same but the period is greater, the velocity of the wind producing the waves is higher and the disturbance farther away. Suppose the wave height is 8 feet and the period 14 seconds. The storm would be a little more than 2 days (60 hours) away, with winds greater than 40 knots.

Obviously, this table does not contain all the possible combinations of swell height and period that can occur. Swells with a period less than about 12 seconds offer too many different possibilities to be useful for onboard prediction. Swells less

---

[18]Charles F. Chapman, Piloting, Seamanship and Small Boat Handling, 75th anniversary ed. (New York: The Hearst Corporation, 1991), 333.

Table 8.9 Storm Location from Swell Parameters

WAVE HEIGHT IN FEET	APPROXIMATE TIME TO STORM IN HOURS	
	12-SECOND WAVE PERIOD	15-SECOND WAVE PERIOD
10	35	55
7 to 8	40	60
5	45	65
2 to 3	50	70

than 2.5 feet in height are caused by winds too light to be interesting. Other swells that fall outside the limits of this table are from disturbances that are either too close or too far away. Storms that are within 24 hours can generally be tracked by better means, storms further than 72 hours away can be ignored.

THE WISDOM OF
THE ANCIENT MARINERS (continued)
sound, it is already raining. There is no reason less-dense air would magnify distant objects. Air clarity may make objects appear closer, but clean air more often follows a storm than precedes one. In summation, the first two are questionable and the third is highly doubtful.

Smoke curls downward means a storm. Smoke curling downward reflects a temperature inversion. Temperature inversions sometimes accompany bad weather, but not always. Los Angles is not exactly a rain forest.

Most of the rest make good rhymes
But little sense and
Bad prophets of the times.

9

SELECTED ELECTRONIC EQUIPMENT

Of the wide universe of electronic equipment, this chapter covers only the basics for the most common gear found on recreational boats: depthsounding equipment, autopilots, loran, GPS, and radar. For more detailed coverage, see dedicated books on the subject, such as *Boatowner's Guide to Marine Electronics* (International Marine, 1993).

DEPTHSOUNDERS

How much water is under the keel is always of interest to boaters, particularly those with large boats. Echo sounders are more than just a replacement for a lead line; they produce continuous depth readings considerably beyond a lead line's limits. The earliest, simplest, and cheapest models of depthsounders are rotating flashers. These old standards have been replaced by digital units and chart recorders, or fish finders. Chart recorders may use a stylus and paper, but are now almost all some form of LCD (liquid crystal display) or CRT (cathode ray tube) display.

Some fish-finder units have multiple transponders to provide information at greater depth, or to provide information ahead or to the side. Some units approach the capability of sonar, the underwater cousin of radar.

How Depthsounders Work

All depthsounders operate on the same basic principle. An ultrasonic pulse produced by a transducer located in the bottom of the boat passes through the water and is reflected back to the boat by any material more dense than the preceding layer the pulse traveled through. Materials returning an echo may be a denser layer of water, a fish, or the bottom. If the pulse travels through multiple layers of progressively denser material, more than one reflection is returned. This is most readily seen on LCD chart displays. The amount and thickness of layers penetrated is a factor of power and frequency. Any layer less dense than preceding layers is invisible to the unit.

Depth is calculated by measuring the time between the emission of the ultrasonic pulse and its return echo. To make this calculation it is necessary to assume that the speed of the pulse is approximately equal to the velocity of sound in cold, fresh water (normally assumed to be 4,800 feet per second). This assumption, while not true in salt water, errs on the side of safety. A good signal will produce a depth with an accuracy of about ± 5 percent—in 30 feet of water an error of about ± 1.5 feet.

As the beam passes through the various materials, energy is absorbed. The more energy available at the source the farther the beam will penetrate. Thirty watts is normal for small recreational boats, especially for sailboats that must run the instruments off their batteries. A 30-watt transponder will draw about 2.5 amps when the pulse is being sent. Fortunately, the pulse rate, sometimes called the sampling rate, is anywhere from 1 to 50 readings per second. This means that the average power consumption of the transponder is between 0.04 and 2.0 amps respectively. Obviously, a higher sampling rate uses more power.

The value of a high sampling rate is accuracy. All units occasionally produce a spurious reading. Units that sample rapidly can analyze more data for a better representation of the bottom depth. The sampling rate depends on depth. Obviously, it is pointless for the unit to send out more pulses than can be returned. In 500 feet of water the signal returns in about 0.2 seconds. This means that a sampling rate of about 5 pulses per second is all that is useful.

Inexpensive units use a fixed sampling rate that is appropriate for the maximum usable depth. Better units vary the sampling rate depending on water depth. This is of significant value in shallow water, where 50 or more pulses can be analyzed before the display is updated. Units with very low power consumption numbers use low-power transducers and low sampling rates; both sacrifice performance.

It is difficult to obtain the sampling rate for most transducers. Manufacturer's representatives commonly confuse display update with sampling rate. The display update rate is how often the unit's processor sends information to the display. Most displays are updated at least every second. On many units this rate can be varied by the operator. In rough conditions the unit may take as long as 15 seconds to average data before it updates. This reduces the scatter of data but does not increase sampling rate. Display update rate is important along with sampling rate when gunkholing. For example, a boat traveling 1.5 knots will cover about 3 feet in 1 second or 45 feet in 15 seconds, which is a long time to travel blind in very shallow water.

The frequency of most transducers is generally between 50 and 200 kHz. Higher frequency gives better resolution at the cost of penetration. Most recreational boaters are concerned about depths less than 300 feet and good resolution in shallow water. Therefore, a 200 kHz transducer, which can record depths in the range of 300 to 500 feet, is generally adequate. Depths beyond 500 feet require lower-frequency transducers. A 50-kHz transducer will reach depths around 1,300 feet.

Beam width is also important. The signal travels through the water in the approximate shape of a cone. The edge of the cone is defined as the point where the signal strength is 50 percent of that in the center of the beam. The angle at the apex of the cone is called the beam width, which varies from about 8 to 60 degrees. At any given power rate, narrow beams provide greater penetration and resolution, wide beams provide more coverage; this reduces the chances of missing an important bottom detail, and also reduces the false reading from boat motion, rolling or heeling. A 20-degree beam width covers a bottom area about one-third as wide as the depth (2 [tan 20/2] = 0.33).

Transducers can be mounted in five ways: low profile, flush, high speed, in-hull, and transom mount. The first three mounts all require a hole through the hull. On the low-profile mount, a small flange extends beyond the hull surface. The flush-mounted transducer is countersunk into the hull and the flange is flush with the hull surface. High-speed transducers have a large, boat-shaped foot that protrudes through the hull; it is designed to reduce turbulence around the sensor on fast boats. Transom-mounted transducers attach to the transom with a metal flange. If the cable is led to the display on the exterior of the boat, it is unnecessary to drill a hole in the boat. Transom-mounted transducers are generally used on boats with outdrives; the propeller turbulence on other boats affects their operation.

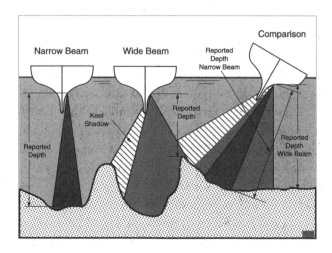

Figure 9.1 Effects of Depthsounder Beam Width

The in-hull transducer is mounted on the inside surface of the hull. It does not require a hole but does require that the hull be of a single material with acoustic properties close to those of water. *Solid* fiberglass hulls are about the only type that can use in-hull mounts. Wooden and aluminum boats or fiberglass boats with balsa and foam cores must use other mounting arrangements. An in-hull mount reduces the depth range by about 20 percent. Some resolution will also be lost.

The velocity of the wave pulse is not the only source of erroneous readings. Turbulence from the propellers in reverse or passing through the wake of another boat causes strong echoes. Submerged floating debris, seaweed, dense or turbid layers of water, air bubbles, the boat itself, and fish all produce echoes. How this multitude of echoes is processed depends on the type of display.

Digital units do not flood the user with information. Rather, they are designed to analyze all this information and select only one number, the unit's best guess at which signal actually represents the bottom. Each manufacturer uses a slightly different algorithm to choose the ordained reading. Usually it involves some or all of the following techniques: rejecting all signals below a certain strength, averaging multiple readings, excluding extreme readings that vary from the sample average by more than a set limit, and weighting the readings according to their signal strength. The more data the unit can analyze the higher the probability that the number it reports will accurately reflect the depth.

Units that use some form of graphic display are often called fish finders. Even though many of these units also display the bottom depth digitally, the algorithms used to calculate this depth are much less sophisticated. The digital display allows the user to reject any digital information that does not agree with the graphical data. Spurious readings returned from floating debris, fish, or seaweed can be easily identified from the true bottom profile.

Some of those spurious readings are important to the boater. Often the bottom is composed of multiple layers of material that become more dense with depth. These layers will show up on a graphic display. Soft mud, overlying sand, and overlying rock can all be seen, and the depths of the mud and sand estimated. This information can be helpful when selecting a site to anchor. The profile of the bottom over which the boat has passed indicates trends that are useful in locating the boat. Many fish finders also display surface water temperature. This feature is designed to help locate fish, but when compared with air temperature, surface water temperature also indicates the likelihood of fog (see Chapter 8).

The final concerns when selecting a depthsounder are the total power consumption of the unit and the features desired. Some of the features include shallow and deepwater alarms, temperature and speed transducers, the ability to interface with other navigational equipment, the type of display, and multiple-screen viewing. Power consumption varies with the unit's complexity. Digital displays are less confusing, but the various graphical representations provide a wealth of information. These units present a constantly changing display of the bottom as the boat moves through the water. The display can be frozen for more detailed study. Displays often use color or other coding methods to indicate the strength of the returning signal. Some displays need to be shaded from direct sunlight for the best viewing.

Installation

Installation of the equipment is relatively simple. The best location for the transducer is forward on a flat run of the hull, with nothing forward of the transducer to cause turbulence. The slope of the transducer's base should be less than 15 degrees. On sailboats it is best to mount the transducer ahead of the keel and within 2 feet of the centerline. If mounted beside the keel, the keel will block the transmission of ultrasonic waves and hide the true bottom readings on one side of the boat. On planing powerboats the transducer must be located far enough aft to remain in solid water and far enough forward to avoid turbulence from the propellers.

Finally, the selected location should be easily reached from inside the boat in case the unit needs to be replaced or the through-hull fails. Avoid transducers that are an integral part of the through-hull, because transducer repair will require the replacement of the entire through-hull, which must be forcibly knocked out of the hull.

On all except in-hull mounted units, the exposed surface of the transducer must make good contact with the water. Biological growth will reduce performance, but so will heavy coatings of bottom paint. A single thin coating of conventional antifouling paint is recommended. Another advantage of the removable transducer is that if the boat will not be used for several months the transducer can be replaced by a plug, limiting its exposure to performance-inhibiting biological growth.

The slope of the hull is not as critical in selecting a location for an in-hull mount as it is for a through-hull mount, because the transducer can be mounted vertically rather than perpendicular to the hull. In-hull mountings require minimum hull thickness and a transducer tuned to the hull for best results. It is necessary to ensure that the wave reflected from the interior surface of the boat is in phase with the wave being emitted from the transducer. It is best to test the selected location and the transducer position before final installation to minimize problems with repair and replacement.

Petroleum jelly or silicone grease can be used to hold the transducer in place for the testing. If a stable depth is indicated, back off on the gain control until the reading becomes unstable to see how much reserve gain is available. Compare this gain setting with the transducer hung over the side. This will give an approximation of the signal loss at the chosen location. If this test is suitable, check the location underway at different speeds before the final bonding. If the unit operates satisfactorily, clean the surface of the transducer and the hull to remove grease, paint, and any surface coatings. Sand the surface of the hull and the face of the transducer with 400-grit sandpaper.

Cement the transducer to the hull with epoxy or polyester resin. Soft silicone sealer does not make a good bonding agent here, although it (or modeling clay) can be used to make a temporary form to control the resin while it hardens. Twist the transducer as you push it into the resin to help force out air bubbles. There should be a minimum amount of epoxy between the hull and the transducer face. Clamp or load the transducer to force it firmly into the epoxy until it dries.

The resistance of the cable from the transducer to the display is taken into account when the unit calculates depth. Cutting the cable alters this resistance, and prevents proper calibration of the unit. Although most units have some depth-calibration capability, it may not be sufficient; it is best to coil excess cable and secure it away from bilge water.

Displays can be mounted almost anywhere convenient. Many displays are waterproof and can be mounted outside; others are merely water-resistant and should be mounted in a protected location. If mounted outside, be sure the display is readable in direct sunlight; some LCD units are not. If the display is to be mounted next to the compass, check to ensure that it does not generate an electrical or magnetic field that will affect the compass reading.

Once installed the sounder will need calibration, since the transducer is located neither at the surface nor in the deepest part of the boat. Most units have a transducer offset control which allows the operator to select whether the unit measures depth below the keel (a negative setting), or from the surface (a positive setting). Both systems have their advantages and depend on the skipper's preference. It is best to stick with one system, because changing it can cause confusion. Once the zero offset has been determined, the depth of water can be measured with a pole or a lead line and the unit calibrated.

AUTOPILOTS

While most people merely use their depthsounders or GPS, they often have a personal relationship with their autopilots, giving them names like Otto or Hal and treating them as pets. Watching from the comparative warmth of the companionway while the little fellow works in a cold rain, it is difficult not to feel some rapport.

Autopilots do much to relieve the boredom and fatigue of steering and can often accomplish the task better than most helmspersons. They never get tired or inattentive, and they save fuel and time by steering the best possible course. Without doubt, a strong, reliable autopilot is a most useful piece of electronic equipment aboard any boat.

Just as assuredly, the most worthless piece of gear on a boat is a weak or unreliable autopilot. Unfortunately, autopilots have external moving parts that must pass through an otherwise watertight case; this can allow water to enter and wreak havoc on the internal electronics. This is especially true for cockpit-mounted autopilots.

Quality and power are related to price; paying too little for an autopilot is worse than paying too much. Steering a boat in flat calm water is far different from steering the same boat in difficult conditions. Many people buy an undersized autopilot, rationalizing that it will only be used in good weather. The fact is, it is in bad weather that most people do not wish to steer; the undersized autopilot is forced to handle the boat in conditions far beyond its capabilities.

How Autopilots Work

Autopilots are composed of various sensors, a processor or control unit, and a drive unit. They work by constantly comparing the actual heading to the desired heading and adjusting the course of the vessel to match this heading. Any corrections required are assessed by the control unit, and specific instructions are given to a drive unit attached to the boat's steering mechanism.

Sensors

The heading is sensed by an integral or remotely mounted magnetic or electronic fluxgate compass. Units that use a standard compass and photoelectric sensing are subject to more error and are not as reliable as fluxgate models. The actual compass course is compared to the desired course dialed into the machine by the operator, and commands are sent to the drive unit that activates the rudder. The smarter the autopilot the better it steers. An autopilot's IQ depends on the amount of information it can process.

In addition to the angle between the desired and actual course, better autopilots sense the time off course, the rate that the boat is turning, the position of the rudder, the pressure on the rudder, and the rate at which the rudder is changing position. Information from other electronics such as wind direction or navigational equipment does not necessarily help an autopilot steer better, but does allow the unit to hold course better. For example, being coupled to an electronic navigation system will allow the autopilot to adjust for leeway and current.

Sailboaters sometimes prefer to set a course relative to the wind. This would appear to be a relatively simple task for an autopilot, which need only sense the direction of the wind and compare the course with the wind direction instead of the compass. Unfortunately, very few hold a satisfactory course operating in this manner. First, the wind coming off the sails makes it difficult to get an accurate wind direction; on most sailboats that means the sensor must be mounted forward or atop the mast.

But the real problem is caused by the autopilot's quick response time. On a sailboat, the sensor reads the apparent wind, which changes direction with changes in boat course and velocity as well as with changes in wind velocity and direction. Recall from Chapter 8 that true wind direction normally moves through 10 or 20 degrees and changes velocity as much as 50 percent of the average velocity. These constantly changing parameters send a steady stream of course corrections to the drive unit. The autopilot dutifully responds to each of these commands, which results in the boat wandering all over the place.

The need to steer sailboats by the wind is probably based on the historical development of wind-vane steering before autopilots. The truth is, there is no need or real advantage to steering by the wind. If the boat is steered by the compass, the person on watch is made aware of wind shift by fluttering sails and can adjust for optimum performance. If the boat is steered by the wind, the boat may be miles off course before the watch becomes aware of the course change. Steering with the wind may provide optimum speed, but not the optimum course unless the watch is attentive. Steering by compass provides the optimum course but not the optimum speed unless the watch is attentive. People who prefer wind sensors must care less about where they're going than about getting there fast.

Processor and Control Unit

There are three methods for processing the data. The simplest is called *hunting*. The processor unit constantly sends out course corrections, causing the drive unit to change the rudder position continuously searching for the correct course. This consumes large amounts of power and steers a zigzag around the desired course.

The second method is called the *proportional deadband*. An error band on either side of the desired course, called a deadband, is set by the operator, and as long as the course remains within this deadband no rudder corrections are made. When the course varies outside this deadband a correction proportional to the heading error is made. Thus, the system doesn't operate continuously, which reduces power demand and wear.

The third method is called the *proportional rate* method. With this system there is no deadband, and the amount of rudder movement is determined by the rate of heading change. Thus, the amount and speed of rudder movement is dependent on whether the boat is moving quickly or just slowly drifting off course. This system more closely duplicates the performance of an experienced helmsperson.

Most autopilots need adjustments of trim, yaw, rudder ratio, and time delay. Some of these adjustments are made automatically, others manually. Trim control is necessary to account for weather helm on sailboats, and allows the drive unit to locate the rudder in the balanced position rather than the center position when the autopilot is on course. Then, as course changes are needed, the rudder's position will vary on either side of this trimmed position. On sailboats this null position varies with course and wind velocity changes. On single-engine powerboats the helm adjustment is needed to offset engine torque.

Yaw control, sometimes called sea-state control, adjusts the width of the deadband on either side of the desired course in which the autopilot remains inactive. On any course other than directly into and away from the waves or seas, the boat will yaw first one way and then the other as the swell passes underneath it. The boat may rotate as much as 10 degrees before returning essentially to its original course. If the yaw control is set too low the autopilot will try to correct for these turns by helm movement, first one way and then the other. The result of the autopilot's effort has little effect on the boat's course and wastes considerable power. In heavy seas, this control can be set to allow maximum swing when heading into the wind, but can be tightened up to reduce the possibility of broaching when the course is off the wind.

The rudder ratio control is boat dependent; once set it is left alone. This control tells the autopilot the amount of rudder movement required to produce a given turn. The time-delay setting is similar to the deadband or yaw control discussed above. Instead of allowing the boat to swing through a larger angle, it allows the boat to be off course for a longer time before the autopilot acts to correct the course.

Most sophisticated units apply counter rudder as the boat comes back on course to prevent the boat swinging past the set course. Also, many models analyze the characteristics of the boat and sea state and memorize the rudder motions. This function allows the autopilot to get a feel for the helm, better anticipate the boat's motion, and steer a much truer course, especially if leeway is present.

Drive Units

Drive units come in three general categories: those that attach to a tiller, those that attach to a wheel, and rudderpost units mounted below decks. Both tiller and wheel units are mounted in the cockpit of sailboats, where they are exposed to considerably more weather than rudderpost units. Tiller units are push-pull models, designed for small sailboats. They are relatively easy to install, require little power, and are inexpensive; often they can be removed for security by detaching them from the tiller. Most of these units are about 18 inches long, but can be lengthened by using extension rods. The more-or-less standard 10 inches of stroke allows approximately 15 degrees of rudder change either side of center.

Wheel models are rotary units that attach directly to the steering wheel. Generally belt driven and in sailboats exposed to the weather, they use little power but are relatively slow acting. Unlike linear units, they can turn the rudder from lock to lock. These units are detached by moving the motor mount away from the drive belt.

Inboard models, including those that work with hydraulic steering, are all installed below decks. These units are much more robust and are used mostly by powerboats and sailboats that need a serious autopilot. The linear units attach directly to the rudderpost; therefore they need more power and must be disengaged from the steering system by a mechanical or electrical clutch. Depending on where they are mounted, the rudder movement is restricted to between 15 and 30 degrees each side of center. All other factors being equal, linear drive units are more efficient than hydraulic drive units.

Selecting an Autopilot

Selecting the proper size autopilot depends on the force needed to turn the boat, which depends directly on the size of the rudder and the speed of the boat moving through the water, which is in turn loosely dependent on the weight or displacement of the boat. Unfortunately, most manufacturers recommend autopilots based on boat displacement. To size an autopilot properly it is necessary first to know either the turning force or the steering force and the difference between the two.

Turning force is the force on the rudder needed to turn the boat. *Steering force* is the force the helmsperson needs to steer the boat. This is different from turning force because steering mechanisms include some sort of mechanical advantage, depending on how the boat is steered. In small sailboats, steering force is applied by a lever called a tiller. The longer the tiller the greater the mechanical advantage, but the farther the tiller end must be moved to effect a turn. On boats with wheel steering the mechanical advantage is provided by a combination of gears and levers. The force needed to steer gets smaller as the wheel gets larger or the number of rotations increases.

An autopilot attached to a wheel or tiller can make use of the mechanical advantage afforded by the steering system; less power is needed because it is dealing with the smaller steering force, but response time is sacrificed. If it is attached directly to the rudderpost, response time is increased, but the autopilot must supply more force to overcome the larger turning force.

Units that attach directly to the wheel supply between 50 and 80 foot-pounds of torque (T); the equivalent steering force (F_s) on a steering wheel of radius (r) can be calculated by the following equation:

$$F_s = T/r.$$ **Eq 9.1**

For example, equivalent steering force provided at the wheel rim of a 30-inch wheel by the smaller unit would be:

$$F_s = 50/1.25 = 40 \text{ pounds.}$$

To select the proper size wheel autopilot it is necessary to estimate or measure the maximum force needed to turn the wheel with the rudder hard over while the boat is going top speed. This force seldom exceeds 75 or 80 pounds; it can be measured by attaching an appropriately sized fish scale to the outer rim of the wheel. Getting an accurate number is not as easy as it would appear, because a sudden high-speed turn on some boats is dangerous, and a slow turn reduces speed because the rudder acts as a brake. Several trials should be made in both directions; the maximum force (F_m) measured should be the one used for selecting the unit. Because it is not practical to install a unit that must work at its maximum, apply a safety factor (S_f) of at least two to this number. The torque (T) needed can be found by rearranging Equation 9.1 as follows:

$$T = F_m S_f r$$ **Eq 9.2**

The thrust of linear units varies from 80 to over 1,000 pounds. Where that force is applied determines the amount of torque available to turn the rudder. Most linear units extend between 10 and 18 inches and are mounted between 18 and 24 inches from the rudderpost. This means that when the linear drive unit is attached directly to the rudderpost it produces from 120 to 2,000 foot-pounds of torque. Arriving at the amount of thrust the autopilot needs to steer a tiller-controlled boat is relatively simple, and can be estimated or measured. In either case, be sure the estimate or measurement is taken at the point where the unit is to be mounted, not at the end of the tiller.

Linear units to be installed below decks on wheel-steered boats present a more difficult case and cannot be estimated as easily. It is necessary to go from steering force to turning force and then back to force on the autopilot. First, measure the wheel steering force as described above for wheel units and count the number of turns from lock to lock (N_L). If the rudder moves through roughly 90 degrees, the mechanical advantage (M_a) of the wheel can be calculated approximately by the following formula:

$$M_a = 4 \times N_L \times r,$$
Eq 9.3

where   r is the radius of the wheel in feet.

If the rudder turns through 60, 45, or only 30 degrees, replace the 4 with 6, 8, and 12 respectively. To get the exact mechanical advantage, replace 4N by the total angular displacement of the wheel divided by the angular displacement of the rudder ($900°/90° = 10$). The turning force is then equal to the mechanical advantage (M_a) multiplied by the maximum measured wheel steering force. To calculate the thrust required by the linear unit it is necessary to know where the unit will be mounted—the position of the unit relative to the rudderpost controls, the response angle of the rudder, the thrust needed by the unit, and how close to maximum capacity the unit will have to work. Recall that most linear units are mounted between 18 and 24 inches from the rudderpost and extend between 10 and 18 inches. This combination of dimensions means drive units are only capable of turning the rudder 15 to 30 degrees, rather than the normal 40 to 45 degrees each side of center (see Figure 9.2).

Obviously, there are many times when a rudder must be turned more than 15 degrees; then, autopilots with smaller response angles will not function well. The response angle (ø) of the autopilot can be calculated by Equation 9.4.

$$\text{Tan } ø = S_o/2A,$$
Eq 9.4

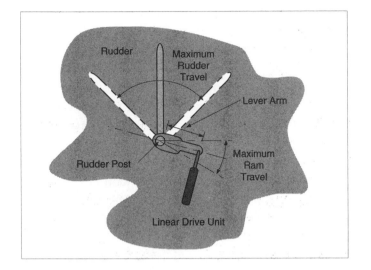

Figure 9.2 Torque
Available from Typical
Linear Drive Unit

where S_o is the operation stroke in inches and
         A is the distance from the center of the rudderpost to the attachment point in inches.

While it is true that the closer the drive unit is mounted to the rudderpost the greater response angle and the better the unit will control the boat's course in extreme conditions, it is also true that the closer the drive unit is mounted to the rudderpost the more thrust will be required by the autopilot to move the rudder. Remember, the strength (S) of these units is measured in pounds of thrust, not torque. To change thrust into torque a lever arm (A) is required. The lever arm in this case is the distance the drive unit is mounted away from the center of the rudderpost. The thrust needed by the autopilot can be found using Equation 9.5.

$$S = F_m \times M_a \times S_f / A,$$ Eq 9.5

where   A is the lever arm in feet.

The safety factor (S_f) depends on how hard the unit must work. Because the greater the rudder angle the greater the turning force, drive units that have larger response angles will work closer to the measured maximum steering force. Therefore, the safety factor depends on the response angle, and varies from 1 to 1.5 as the response angle varies from 15 to 30 degrees.

Another feature important in selecting an autopilot is the response time of the unit, or how fast it will turn the rudder from lock to lock. This depends on the load on the rudder. It is generally reported as no-load, or with a standard load between 50 and 100 pounds. The 50-pound response time is generally about 1.45 times the no-load response. When comparing different units, be sure rudder loads are similar.

The time required to travel the full extension on a linear unit varies from 4 to 15 seconds, on wheel units from 22 to 91 seconds. A boat traveling 6 knots will cover about 50 feet in 5 seconds. A human helmsperson can turn the rudder from lock to lock in under 3 seconds and a tiller in less than a second. The necessity for this type of crash turn depends on the conditions; the more extreme the conditions the more advantageous is rapid response time. For example, handling a boat in broaching conditions requires rapid response, a Sunday afternoon cruise on flat water does not. Before selecting a response time, it is a good idea to time a few lock-to-lock turns at various speeds to get a feel for how the boat will respond to a 15-second or 91-second turn.

The final consideration is power consumption, especially for sailboats where the unit may need to run on battery power for considerable time. Power consumption, or input power, is measured in watts or amperage at a specified voltage, and is related to output power by efficiency and duty cycle. The efficiency factor is commonly between 0.5 and 0.8. Because the output power depends on the combination of force (pounds) generated by the unit, where it is applied (feet), and how fast the unit will respond (seconds), it is physically impossible for a low amperage unit to provide high-output torque and fast response time. However, all is not lost, because total power consumption also depends on the amount of time the unit is actually operating, or the duty cycle.

Because of this dependence on duty cycle, power consumption (or input power) is commonly reported in two different formats: standby power, which is the minimum power draw, or some sort of duty cycle power. Standby by power is less important than duty cycle power. When comparing units, be sure that the duty cycle and voltage are similar. If the voltage is different, remember that power is equal to voltage multiplied by amperage ($P = IE$). If the duty cycles are different, they can both be converted to 100 percent duty for comparison by dividing the duty power (or amperage) by the duty cycle (percentage).

The actual duty cycle on any given boat will vary depending on the manufacturer, nature, and the boater. When the drive unit is operating, the current draw varies between 0.5 and 5 amps, but the total input power depends on how often the drive unit operates. Operation time can be reduced by making the unit smarter, mild weather, and efficient boat operation.

Not much can be done about the weather, but the boater can do several things to reduce the duty cycle. For example, a sailboat is difficult to steer because it is poorly designed, poorly tuned, or poorly sailed. In all these cases the autopilot will be required to operate continuously to adjust the course. Provided the boat is well designed, the duty cycle can be reduced by getting a smart unit, tuning the rig properly, and setting the sails so that the boat almost steers itself. Most good books on sailing discuss sail balance to attain maximum performance or speed. Adjusting the sails to steer the boat uses the same principles but with a different result. Generally speaking, a balanced boat sails slightly below optimum speed.

Installation

Before installing any unit, select a calm, windless day and make a few powered runs in opposite directions. Mark the center helm position traveling in each direction. If there is any difference between these two marks, split the difference. This mark will indicate the operational center helm position. Retain this mark for use in aligning the drive.

Compass Unit

Proper compass installation requires a little planning. Ideally, the compass unit should be installed low in the boat, along the centerline, midway between the bow and stern. This is the most stable and best reference position from which to sense the boat's movements. Most compasses are gimbaled either internally or externally to rotate at least 45 degrees. If not, provisions should be made to allow for this movement. And, like any compass, the unit should be at least 3 feet away from magnetic metals and all motors and current carrying wires to reduce deviation. Remember that another compass is also a magnetic source.

The problem of autopilot deviation is relatively common. My own boat tended to veer off to port whenever the refrigerator kicked on. Rerouting the refrigerator power cable fixed the problem. Movable magnetic objects can also cause problems. Two friends cruising together, one in a fiberglass boat and the other with a steel hull, found that the glass boat's autopilot would home in on the steel boat whenever the boats got within 50 feet of each other.

Control Unit

Control units, like the brains of any outfit, are best located where they are out of harsh weather and have fresh, cool breezes to dissipate the heat they generate. Even though most units are sealed to prevent moisture intrusion, it is best to locate them away from active splash areas. Do not mount the unit in a closed compartment or in a compartment with other sources of heat. Some units are sensitive to voltage surge, the most common offender being the starter motor. Be sure that the control unit's wiring is isolated from surge sources.

Drive Unit

Tiller control units are relatively easy to install. They are mounted in the cockpit of a sailboat about 18 inches away from the rudderpost and perpendicular to the tiller in its center position. The push-rod end is attached to the tiller and held in position by gravity. The base end of the unit must be attached to a point with enough strength to take the maximum thrust. Although extension rods can be purchased for the push rod, those who service these units do not recommend extending it by more than 8 inches. Installation takes around one hour.

To mount a **wheel control unit**, the drive wheel is clamped to the steering wheel, and the motor is attached either to the pedestal or the inside of the cockpit, whichever is more convenient. In most instances the pedestal mount is preferred, and special brackets can be obtained for this purpose. The pedestal mount keeps the belt, which drives the wheel, from obstructing the helmsperson's path to the wheel. Installation takes about two hours.

Inboard units are often installed by professionals. The unit needs to be located in an area free of obstructions. Although storage space is limited on small boats, storing things in the locker with the autopilot drive should be avoided. Rough sea conditions can dislodge equipment and block movement of the piston, which will probably damage both the offending piece of gear and the drive unit.

Turning loads are considerably larger than those of other drive units, and the attachment points must be strong enough to handle these heavy loads repeatedly. Linear drive units have a small amount of lateral movement toward the rudderpost when operating. If they contact anything, extreme bending stress will be placed on the drive unit, causing it to fail.

Because these units need considerable power, especially on sailboats where efficiency is important, the current loss in the wire should be kept below 1 percent. Table 9.1 gives the wire sizes needed for various lengths and loads to achieve this end.

Table 9.1 Wire Size for One Percent Loss

	MAXIMUM LOAD								
WATTS	1.3	6.4	13	26	64	130	260	640	1,300
AMPS	0.1	0.5	1	2	5	10	20	50	100
10 feet of run	24	24	20	18	14	10	8	4	1
15 feet of run	24	22	18	16	12	8	6	2	0
20 feet of run	24	20	18	14	10	8	4	1	*
30 feet of run	24	18	16	12	8	6	2	0	*
50 feet of run	24	16	14	10	6	4	1	*	*

LORAN

There are basically two types of electronic navigation systems of interest to recreational boaters, loran (long range aid to navigation) and GPS (the Global Positioning System). In my opinion, loran will soon be replaced by the more accurate and user-friendly GPS. Loran is included here because the publication of this book overlaps its demise.

Loran operates on 100 kilohertz, using radio waves transmitted from a master station and two to four slave sources to fix a position. Designed to provide excellent location in a zone from the coast to about 50 miles offshore the usable signal often exceeds these minimum distances. Loran units constantly receive signals and constantly update the vessel's position. The equipment is capable of locating a position within 300 feet. If it is used to relocate a point it has occupied before, its accuracy is even better; as little as 60 feet has been reported.

How Loran Works

Loran works on a pulsed radio wave, and assumes that the speed of the radio wave is everywhere constant. To obtain a position, the loran locks onto a master and two or more slave signals. It uses a very accurate time source to calculate the differences in arrival time of the radio wave pulses from each of these stations. Knowing the location of the stations, the unit is able to calculate its distance from each station and triangulate its position. The frequency of the pulses and the time are controlled by reference to Atomic standards. If any of this sensitive equipment loses its calibration, a coded message is sent to warn the operator of possible error.

Using the time differences between the transmissions from various stations, the loran receiver calculates latitude and longitude. It is important to remember that the device thinks in time differences and converts this raw data to latitude and longitude. Error can be introduced during the conversion process because the time of day and the season of the year can affect the wave's position. Further, there are differences between the actual wave propagation and the mathematical algorithm used for this conversion.

These differences are particularly large when the waves travel over land. Errors are introduced by conductivity of the soil, fluctuations in the earth's magnetic field, magnetic anomalies, and features of the terrain. The more rugged the terrain the more error introduced. So while loran is accurate offshore, once the vessel puts land between it and the sending station, accuracy diminishes. In the mountainous regions of the Pacific Northwest's Inland Passage, from Seattle to Skagway, I have recorded latitude and longitude positions that were off as much as 30 miles.

If an accurate navigational fix from loran is needed, it is best to use *time differences*. Using TDs, rather than latitude and longitude, eliminates the use of the algorithm and all its related errors. To use this method the boater must know the actual time and difference readings of the destination. Using charts with these differences overprinted is not much better than using the algorithm in the instrument, because the overprinted values are calculated using the same algorithm.

The best way to determine the actual time difference readings is to occupy the destination and record the reading. Obviously, this has some limitations. If you don't know where you are (using loran for a positional fix) or where you are going (finding a new destination), you obviously won't know the time difference readings and will have to rely on the latitude and longitude output. Loran's greatest value is in returning to a previous position.

Presently, the fundamental problem with loran is that its area of use is limited to open water within 300 or 400 miles of a loran transmitter. Because the loran net is not worldwide, and even in areas where it is present the stations may be inland, it is generally usable in local areas within 200 miles of shore.

Installation

The performance of a loran system is strongly influenced by its installation. The antenna, a large, six-foot whip, should be installed in clear air away from any metal objects. This is difficult for sailboaters unless they want to remove the mast and rigging or put the antenna on top of the mast. These solutions are unacceptable to most sailboaters, so their signals will always be degraded to some extent.

Because the unit is essentially a very accurate radio receiver it is essential that both receiver and antenna coupler be grounded properly. It is also important to eliminate interference from other equipment on board, such as engine ignition systems, alternators, TV sets, fluorescent lights, and many other appliances. Turning on one fluorescent light can cause the loran to lose its fix. It is possible to filter some of this interference, but the only way to eliminate it is to remove the offending equipment.

GPS AND SATNAV

The other common system of radio navigation is satellite navigation (satnav) or the system that replaced it, the Global Positioning System (GPS). GPS is superior to any of the previous methods, and will eventually make those systems obsolete.

How GPS Works

The GPS system operates with 21 satellites in six orbits around the earth, using the Doppler shift in the incoming signal to determine position to an accuracy within 300 feet 95 percent of the time. The system uses two frequencies, 1227.6 and 1575.42 MHz. The signals are coded in two formats, *coarse/acquisition* (C/A) and *precision* (P); the precision code is currently only available to the military.

Presently, the government only allows civilians access to C/A signals that have been degraded in accuracy to around 100 meters by a couple of processes called *selective availability* and *antispoofing*. The general accuracy of the fix depends on the number of satellites the receiver is tracking. The Department of Defense (DOD), which currently operates these satellites, can turn them off as they see fit.[1] In times of national emergency, as defined by DOD, they will turn off satellites and degrade the accuracy of the fix. Until the government becomes less paranoid, GPS users must use some caution when considering the accuracy of their fix. Without degradation, those same signals would allow accuracy of 20 meters or less.

Fortunately, what one branch of DOD (the Air Force) puts asunder is easily put back together again by another branch (the Coast Guard). An accurately located station receives the satellite data and compares its known position with the GPS-derived position, then calculates the positional error scrambled into the signal. This correction factor can then be transmitted to any nearby GPS systems with a properly tuned receiver, which can then apply those same corrections to its scrambled data, thereby improving the accuracy of its fix.

This procedure, called the Differential Global Positioning System (DGPS), reduces the error to between 5 and 10 meters (±15 to 30 feet). Even though the differential signals are available to the general public, not all areas have ground-based beacons, nor can all GPS units use these signals to improve their accuracy. It is a fairly safe bet, though, that without government intervention the differential stations will sprout like weeds, and all GPS will be DGPS within a very short time.

With the demise of the cold war the federal government may eventually allow civilians access to both codes. The implementation of the full GPS, with its capability of establishing a position within 1/2 inch (using post processing and a number of fixes averaged over time), will cause a revolution in the chart and mapping industry. Present accuracy standards for NOAA charts are shown in Table 9.2. As can be seen, charts with a scale smaller (larger number) than 1:100,000 are less accurate than the present capabilities of standard GPS. Charts above 1:20,000 are less accurate than standard Differential GPS, and all charts are at least 250 times less accurate than units used by the military.

[1]*Captain Bill Brogdon, "GPS: When is it Most Accurate?" Yachting (January 1993), 41.*

Table 9.2 Chart Accuracy	
CHART SCALE	ABSOLUTE ACCURACY
1:300,000	825 feet (240 meters)
1:200,000	550 feet (160 meters)
1:100,000	275 feet (80 meters)
1:80,000	220 feet (64 meters)
1:40,000	110 feet (32 meters)
1:20,000	33 feet (10 meters)
1:10,000	17 feet (5 meters)
1:5,000	8 feet (2.5 meters)

Standard GPS receivers track satellites in two basic configurations: one tracks several satellites at a time using multiple receivers, and the other uses a multiplex technology and a single receiver. Multiplex receivers have only one channel and must receive all the information on the same channel sequentially. These receivers are less expensive, slower, and smaller. Multichannel receivers receive data on more than one channel simultaneously. They are more sensitive and update the data more rapidly. In both configurations, receiver and antenna are very small and use very little power.

Many units are portable and virtually waterproof. Portable units are just as accurate as base units and can be removed from the boat for security or taken on board a liferaft if necessary. Liferaft operation must be intermittent to protect battery life (about 10 hours continuous use). Operating the unit for 10 minutes a day could provide as much as 60 days of positioning.

Installation

GPS installation is extraordinarily simple. Portable models can be slipped into your shirt pocket. In fact, there's no reason to install a fixed unit unless it is to be interfaced with other equipment or you want a larger display. Many portable units come with a mounting kit that allows them to be connected to any NMEA cable, an external antenna, and the ship's batteries. Mounting fixed units is also relatively simple, because the antenna and ground requirements are minimal.

RADAR

As seen in Chapters 2 and 3, radar can be used to help guide the boat in poor visibility, or to obtain distances and bearings to objects. Small-boat radar is handy and useful, but it is not foolproof. The whirling radar antenna may appeal to the captain's vanity, but much of the time the radar goes unattended and unobserved, the whirling antenna serving only to bombard the brains of those on board with high-energy microwaves.

How Radar Works

To understand the limitations and applications of this instrument it is first necessary to understand how it works. Radar, in its simplest sense, consists of a radio wave generator that sends a very strong, short pulse of energy; the circuitry to amplify a very weak returning signal; an antenna to send the original pulse and to catch the return echo; an accurate timing device to reduce the data; and a display. Recall from the discussion of depthsounders that the frequency of a wave is related to penetration and resolution. This relationship is true for all radiation.

The frequency of radio waves is three or four orders of magnitude greater than light waves. Thus, radar penetrates fog where light fails. But the resolution of the longer radar waves is considerably less than light. Radar generally operates on three bands: the S band, with a wavelength of about 10 centimeters (3,000 MHz), the X band, around 3 centimeters (10,000 MHz), and the Q band, about 10 millimeters (30,000 MHz).

A radar with a frequency of about 3,000 MHz (S band) gets excellent penetration and will penetrate rain and snow, whereas increasing the frequency to 10,000 MHz (X Band) will cause rain and snow to show on the screen. The ultrahigh Q band gives excellent definition, but only over short distances. Most small-ship radar operates on the X band, where it gets moderate penetration but without the sharp resolution of light waves (see Figure 9.3).

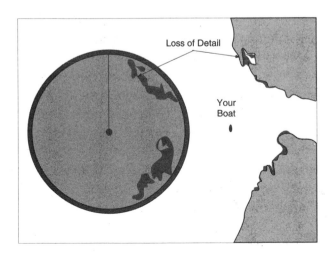

Figure 9.3 Effects of Low Frequency on Radar Resolution

The radar beam width, both in the horizontal and vertical planes, also plays a role in resolution. The narrower the beam the easier the unit can resolve and separate two small, adjacent objects. The beam width is dependent on the frequency and the dimensions of the antenna. Narrower beam widths are obtained using higher frequencies, and for a given frequency, the larger the antenna the narrower the beam. The characteristics of the beam also strongly affect the minimum and maximum range of the unit.

Most people infer that maximum range is synonymous with a better unit. This may be true for the military, but it is not true for a small, easy to maneuver recreational boat. Something 24 miles away offers much less danger than something 24 yards away. Minimum range can be a better measure of small-boat radar. Often, radar is most valuable for small boats when the unit is set on the ¼-mile range.[2]

Range is a function of frequency, beam width, peak power, pulse length, pulse repetition rate, antenna rotation rate, receiver sensitivity, curvature of the earth, target characteristics, weather, and the position of the operator's lower jaw. Not much can be done about the last four variables, but frequency and beam width have already been discussed in earlier chapters.

Increasing peak power is an inefficient method of increasing range, because power and range follow the inverse square law, which states that doubling the power will only increase the range by one-quarter. Changing pulse length, pulse rate, and antenna rotation to increase the range degrades the sensitivity of the unit. Some signal degradation is acceptable, so most recreational units change the pulse rate and length depending on the range setting on the receiver; however, the antenna rotation remains constant.

The remaining component of radar of interest to the recreational boater is the display unit. Most modern sets now come with a raster-scan or liquid crystal display (LCD) rather than the older cathode ray tube (CRT). Raster-scan is a digital process displayed on a computer-type TV screen or a CRT. Because of the processing, this type of display can be seen clearly in direct sunlight and eliminates the need for the hood to shield the unit from external light sources. Raster-scan displays can also be color coded or brightness coded to show stronger signals, thereby relaying more information to the user. LCD models draw less power than CRT models, but suffer in resolving detail.

All the displays use a *Plan Position Indicator* (PPI) type of display. This view more closely represents what the navigator would see when looking at a chart or from an airplane than what is seen when looking at the actual ground from deck level.

[2]*Chuck Husick, "Radar Antenna Location,"* Ocean Navigator (*November 1992*), 49.

Although the display provides a chartlike representation when a landmass is being scanned, the image painted by the sweep is not a very true representation of the shoreline, for several reasons. Some, such as frequency of the signal, have already been discussed. Other factors, such as range resolution, bearing resolution, and some qualities of the target, make interpretation difficult.

Range resolution is similar to bearing resolution; the reflected signal from two targets, one behind the other, can merge into one signal if the targets are too close together. Range resolution is a function of pulse length. A 0.5 microsecond pulse will cover about 500 feet. The receiver can separate targets that are about half this distance, or 250 feet. Anything closer together than this will appear as one target. If the pulse is 0.15 microseconds, the resolution is about 75 feet.

Bearing resolution has to do with the beam width. All targets are widened by the effective horizontal beam width. If the beam width is 6 degrees, two targets that are 1 mile off will appear as one if they are closer together than 500 feet. At 2 miles the targets must be separated by 1,000 feet; at 24 miles a 6-degree beam width will merge objects that are almost 2.5 miles apart. This can make interpretation of the display difficult. For example, if the navigator is trying to locate a bay it may appear on the display as shown in Figure 9.4 until the boat is close enough to reduce the beam-width error. Also, the beam width is more of a problem if the target is not perpendicular to the beam as is the case with the vessels located at point C.

The target has a strong affect on what the display produces. Its position, roughness, and material all influence the amount of signal returned. Metal, rock,

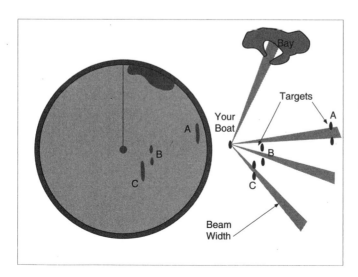

Figure 9.4 Effects of Beam Width on Radar Resolution

and soil reflect better than vegetation, wood, and plastic. Vertical surfaces reflect better than angled surfaces. The closer the angle is to horizontal, the more the object becomes invisible to radar. Rough surfaces reflect better than smooth surfaces unless the surface is exactly perpendicular to the beam.

If this isn't enough to make interpretation of radar interesting, consider the occurrence of multiple echoes, side-lobe echoes, and indirect echoes. Multiple echoes occur when a strong echo is returned from short range. A second or third echo may be observed at multiples of the original target's range. Side-lobe echoes occur when the target is in a position to reflect energy received from the side lobes of the beam. False echoes from side-lobe or multiple echoes are apparent because the echo is in front of or behind the true echo or in a semicircle on the same range, respectively. These errors can sometimes be eliminated or reduced by proper adjustment of the display.

Indirect echoes are received from another radar source or from a reflection of your own beam off a strong radar reflector hitting a target and then returning to the receiver. Indirect echoes appear at the same range as the true object but on the bearing of the reflecting surface. The movements of the false target are normally erratic. If the reflected signal is off your vessel, the false echo will appear on the display aligned with the 0° or 180° bearing mark.

Another unwanted echo occurrence, which is relatively uncommon but worth mentioning because of the concern it can cause, is the reflection from an overhead power cable. The display will show this feature as a single blip, always at right angles to the cable. As the boat approaches the cable the display shows a blip closing on a steady bearing. No amount of evasive action, save course reversal, will alter the apparent collision.

Radar Installation

Proper installation of the display and the antenna is important to the use of the instrument. Many displays are waterproof and can be positioned in full view of the helmsperson, but this is not as important as it may seem; as shown earlier, the correct interpretation of the display requires considerable concentration and attention to detail not easily performed by an active helmsperson. The best use of the radar is to have a full-time observer verbally relaying any necessary instructions to the helmsperson.

Having the radar below, rather than on deck (on a sailboat) also allows the crew the luxury of staying below out of inclement weather and letting the autopilot steer the boat, popping up on rare occasion to see if the radar has missed anything.

Antenna location strongly affects the set's performance.[3] The distance a radar can see is directly dependent on the height of the antenna. This distance can be calculated by rearranging the formula used to calculate lighthouse visibility (see Equation 2.1 in Chapter 2).

$$D = 1.2 \sqrt{H} \qquad\qquad \text{Eq 9.6}$$

where   D is the distance in miles to the object
and   h is the height in feet above the surface.

From the equation it can be seen that, to see an object on the surface using 24-mile radar, the antenna would have to be mounted 420 feet above the surface:

$$H = (24/1.17)^2 = 420 \text{ feet.}$$

Very few recreational boats have the capability of mounting the antenna at this height, thereby reducing the need for a 24-mile radar. Consider that not all targets are surface targets, but have some height themselves. Suppose the target is 50 feet high, which would include most large ships. Performing the necessary math shows that the antenna would have to be mounted 180 feet high, still much too high for most recreational vessels.

$$D = 1.17 = 8.3 \text{ miles;}$$
$$24 - 8.3 = 15.7 \text{ miles;}$$
$$H = (15.7/1.17)^2 = 180 \text{ feet.}$$

Let's approach the problem from the other side. Using a 12-foot-high antenna, common for powerboat antennas, how high must the target be to be seen 24 miles away? This height works out to be about 275 feet. While it is true that the most common objects of this height are landmasses, it is also true that these heights are usually reached some distance inland from the shore. Because it is the shore that is of interest and not the mountains, 24-mile radar is still of little use to a recreational boater.

As pointed out earlier, *minimum distance* is more important for small-boat radar. The height of the antenna above the water also affects the minimum distance that an object on the surface can be detected. The beam width of most radar antennas is about 25 degrees. This would give a 12.5 degree downward angle to the beam

[3]*Husick,* 48.

from its mounted position. The minimum distance can be calculated using the following formula:

$$d = h/0.22, \qquad\qquad Eq\ 9.7$$

where   d is the minimum distance in feet,
            h is the height of the antenna in feet, and
            0.22 is the tangent of half the angle of vertical beam width.

Most objects can be visually picked up at 100 to 150 feet, corresponding to an antenna height of between 22 and 33 feet. This means the practical limit on antenna height is below about 35 feet. Recall that the pulse width of the radar at close range corresponds to a distance of about 75 feet; nothing can be seen closer than that width, so mountings of less than 16.5 feet are of no value in picking up short-range targets.

The remaining considerations in locating an antenna concern ship's motion and frying the brain. Obviously, motion on a small boat becomes more extreme as the antenna rises above the deck. A roll through 30 degrees will move an antenna mounted 20 feet above the deck through a distance of about 10 feet. This amount of movement produces an error dependent on the resolution. At about 200 feet, a 10-foot target can be resolved by a 6-degree beam. For targets closer than about 600 feet this amount of movement is about one-third of the target width and therefore negligible.

Recall that microwave ovens used to be called radar ranges. Radar can cook your brains. The fact that the full-rated power is on for only short bursts does not eliminate the risk to persons near the radar antenna. It is recommended that humans remain at least 8 feet horizontally from the dome.[4]

Three things should be pointed out about this recommendation. First, 8 feet is not an absolute number; some damage occurs beyond this range. Second, damage of this type is additive; that is, a small dosage of radiation over a long period of time is as damaging as a large dose for a short period of time. Third, due to the beam width, the full power of the unit extends 2 feet below the unit 8 feet away. This means that to minimize the risk you should mount the dome as high as possible and use the radar only when absolutely necessary.

Remember that radar manufacturers, salesmen, and installers may not be as concerned about the long-term effects on your brain as they are on the short-term effects on their purse. One final note: radar emissions are especially damaging to

---

[4]*Husick, 52.*

eye tissue. Looking closely at an operating radar antenna is clearly not a good idea, and dome-mounted units give no indication that they are operating.

I recommend that the antenna be mounted between 16 and 32 feet above the water and at least 12 feet above any deck level. This means that the maximum usable range for most small-boat radar is between 8 and 12 miles; extra money spent on 24-mile radar is wasted. The final consideration is that the antenna should be mounted to minimize obstructions to the radar beam itself. Obstructions produce blind spots. The most common obstruction for a sailboat is the mast. Unfortunately, on a sailboat the choices are forward or aft of the mast. It seems preferable to me to have the blind spot behind the boat rather than forward.

10

MAINTENANCE

The truth is, even for so-called low maintenance hulls, a large portion of boat usage is maintenance. Consider that a boat spends most of its life in a rather hostile environment exposed to solar radiation and corrosive salt water. Hulls take a constant beating from the elements and marine organisms. Engines, sails, and rigging require attention to keep them in working order so that they respond properly on demand. As boaters demand more comfort, internal systems such as batteries and plumbing add to the maintenance tasks.

A simple way to minimize frustration and maximize success is to approach a job with the right tools. The tools needed to maintain a recreational boat properly are numerous, varied, and depend on the boat, the task, and the person using them. Certainly there is no need for a caulking iron on a fiberglass hull.

There is a certain amount of risk involved in recommending tools, since some items may sound handy but will never be used. The sidebar is a guide for the owner of an average fiberglass boat. Specific problems and tastes will add to this list.

HULL AND TOPSIDES

The maintenance-free hull may be a myth, but there are still degrees of maintenance; fiberglass requires the least, aluminum, steel, and wood need progressively more. Regardless of hull material, boat maintenance ranges from just keeping the boat functional to keeping the boat in yacht fashion. Keeping the topsides functional requires inspection and cleaning of the lifelines, stanchions, pulpit, stern rail, grabrails, chocks, cleats, ventilators, ports, and hatches. Keeping the hull functional requires inspection and cleaning of through-hull fittings, propeller, rudder fittings, zincs, and any keel fittings. Keeping both the hull and topsides attractive requires washing, polishing, and painting.

Functional topside maintenance is normally done on an annual basis. Corrosion most often occurs on lifelines at the fittings. Cables with heavy corrosion should be replaced. Pelican hooks and turnbuckles should be oiled after cleaning and inspection. Finally, the tension in each cable should be adjusted to eliminate excessive play.

TOOLS

General	50-foot tape
Hammers	trouble light
claw or ball peen	wire brushes
Screwdrivers	magnets
battery operated	Exacto knife
flat head	tape
Phillips heads	chisels
jeweler's screwdrivers	rasps
Drill and bits	files
⅜-inch drill	C-clamps
wood bits	For the Hull
steel twist bits	buckets
hole saws	brushes
right-angle drilling attachment	mops
countersinks	sponges
Saws	Mechanical
sabersaw	socket wrenches
hacksaw	open-end wrenches
keyhole saw	adjustable wrenches
coping saw	Allen wrenches
Miscellaneous tools	strap wrench
12-foot carpenter's tape	pliers

Stanchions, pulpit, and stern rail deck fittings should be inspected to see that there is no play or give and that they are all tight and free of corrosion. Inspect the bolts at the base of the stanchions for dry or cracked bedding compound. If necessary, remove the bolts, clean out the old bedding material, apply fresh bedding material, and replace the bolts.

Inspect the chocks to see that all surfaces are smooth and free of sharp edges that will damage mooring or anchor lines. Check the cleats to see that they are securely fastened and bedded properly.

The ventilators need to be removed, cleaned, and any moving parts oiled. Opening hatches and ports should be cleaned and the rubber gasket treated with vinyl or rubber conditioner, which restore the natural oils lost to exposure to sun and water. Glass or Lexan can be cleaned and polished, but be careful that the cleaning product is compatible with these sensitive surfaces.

Functional hull maintenance should be performed each time the boat is hauled. The through-hull fittings should be inspected for wear and deterioration. Through-hulls should be bronze or plastic and have a ball valve attached directly to the hull fitting. Plastic through-hulls should not be used on wood hulls; a wooden hull can swell sufficiently to shatter a plastic through-hull. Ball valves are best because the closing mechanism is not as easily fouled as a gate valve and they require only a 90-degree turn to close. Examine the surface of all bronze fittings. If the surface appears reddish, the fitting is losing zinc through electrolysis. This loss, caused by inadequate cathodic protection, weakens the bronze and may cause the fitting to fail. Grounding the through-hulls and relocating or increasing the size of the zinc anodes will help reduce this loss. In extreme cases the fitting may have to be replaced.

Green encrustation on bronze valves does not weaken the fitting, but it should be cleaned away because it builds up and may prevent the valve from closing properly. All valves have a tendency to freeze up. If the valve has a grease plug, remove the plug and lubricate the barrel; if not, grease the valve from the outside and oil the action from inside. After lubrication, work the handle several times to ensure proper functioning. Finally, inspect the hose clamps for corrosion and the hose for weak spots and wear.

Bronze through-hulls on aluminum boats are particularly troublesome. If possible, remove and replace with aluminum or plastic. If not, they should be well insulated from the hull by a rubber gasket and well coated with sealant. Check the hull surrounding the fitting to ensure the aluminum is not corroding.

Feathering, folding, and adjustable-pitch props need to be disassembled and lubricated. The propeller should be pushed from side to side to check the Cutless bearing or stern glands. If the play is greater than $\frac{1}{16}$ inch, the shaft should be removed, checked for wear, and repacked. If the propeller is pitting, the size and number of sacrificial zincs should be increased.

When repacking the stuffing box, cut the packing into lengths sufficient to cover one circumference of the shaft. Place three of these rings around the shaft so that the butt joints of the packing are staggered. Do not wind the packing around the shaft in a continuous spiral (see Figure 10.1).

Swing the rudder back and forth to check for binding or rubbing. Binding may indicate a bent rudder or other potential failure, especially if the rudder has been hit. Continue the inspection until the cause is located and repaired. The steering system can be checked by locking the wheel or tiller and pushing on the trailing

---

TOOLS (continued)

Mechanical (continued)
- slip-joint pliers
- vise grips
- files
- tin snips
- tap and die set
- thread chasers
- easy out
- cold chisel
- feeler gauges
- center punch
- caliper

Plumbing
- pipe wrenches
- tube cutter
- flaring tool

Electrical
- wire strippers
- wire cutters
- needlenose pliers
- 25-foot snake
- multimeter

- soldering irons
- propane torch
- hydrometer
- forceps

Painting
- masks
- eye protection
- rubber gloves
- head sock
- surgical gloves
- orbital sanders
- disc sander
- screen sander
- putty knife
- paint scraper

Rigging
- bosun box
- sharp knife
- cable cutters
- swaging tools
- grommet tool
- pop-riveting gun

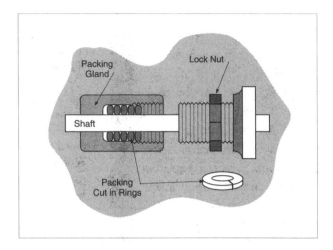

Figure 10.1 Packing a Stuffing Box

edge of the rudder. Excessive play indicates that the steering system needs inspection. Check all bolts that hold the system to the boat, all cables to be sure they are tight, and any wires for corrosion and wear. Stainless steel wires can work-harden and lose strength. Lubricate all pulleys and turning points.

Check and tighten the bolts on all couplings. Use a chemical fixer on bolts that are to remain permanently tight and an antiseizing lubricant on those that need to be removed periodically. Antiseizing is especially important where the bolts are of a different material than the object being bolted. This occurs most often where aluminum is bolted with stainless steel bolts. It is best to match the fastener material with the material being fastened, but in cases where aluminum is being attached to stainless or vice versa, choose the fastener material to match the threaded material and insulate the dissimilar materials.

MANUALS AND GUARANTEES
Every piece of gear, from autopilots to winches, comes with manuals. File them on board along with the guarantees and receipts. Small plastic (not metal) file boxes that take standard file folders make excellent shipboard filing systems.

On hydraulic systems, check the pipes and joints for leaks. Check the seals on the rams for wear. Any air in the system will cause erratic action and should be bled from the high point in the system.

Finally, check the rudder for leaks. This may sound a little like the proverbial snipe hunt, but most rudders on glass boats are made using a foam core surrounding a steel skeleton covered with an outer layer of fiberglass. If the rudder leaks, the steel skeleton can rust away, causing the rudder to lose its structural strength.

The easiest way to check for leaks is to inspect the rudder after it has dried. Leaks will show up as small wet spots as the internal water continues to weep from the hole. Water inside the rudder can come from a break in the laminate seams, bolt holes where the rudderpost enters or exits the rudder, the original hole itself, or an as yet undetected hole. These leaks are not necessarily a problem unless the water is rust stained or there is a rust stain on the rudder, which may indicate that the steel framework inside the rudder is deteriorating. If this is the case, it will be necessary to enlarge the opening, drain the water from the rudder, inspect and repair the framework, and locate and patch the leak.

Inspect external keels bolted to the hull to see that the keel is tight to the hull and that the keel bolts are in good condition. If there is any rust around the joint, remove and inspect the bolts. If the diameter of any bolt has been reduced by 10 percent or more, seek the advice of a professional to determine whether they need to be replaced. Remove any rust and prime the bolts with a good rust inhibitor. Before reattaching the keel, wire-brush and paint the top surface with at least three coats of paint. Reattach the keel with copious amounts of sealant. If the joint looks good and the keel has been in place for several years, the keel can be x-rayed or a single bolt drawn to check on general bolt condition and allay any nagging fears of losing a keel.

Cleaning and Polishing

Maintaining the appearance of the boat is a large part of hull maintenance, and consists of cleaning, polishing, and painting. Cleaning the surface is important whether it is gelcoat, paint, or even polyurethane; all are strongly affected by industrial pollutants, solar radiation, and corrosive liquids. Many marinas are located in industrial areas or near airports where heavy concentrations of industrial gasses or jet fuel dissolve the oils in the finish, and many areas away from industry are affected by acid rain. The sulfuric acid formed will etch the finish of the boat and create small pits unless it is removed periodically. Bird droppings contain uric acid, and although it is a milder acid, it lands in greater concentration and if not removed will etch the surface.

Surfaces should be cleaned with a biodegradable, pH-balanced cleaner. It is best not to use household detergents or dishwashing liquids. Even though Joy, renowned in the boating world for producing suds in salt water, is biodegradable, it is not pH balanced and will strip the oils from the boat's finish, accelerating oxidation and discoloration. Just because a product is biodegradable does not necessarily mean that it will not harm the boat's finish.

Harsh cleaners do have their place on board, to remove stubborn dirt or stains. I have found that Soft Scrub is about the only thing that will remove teak oil stains from the boat's finish. If it is necessary to use harsh cleaners, the area where they were used should be rewashed with milder, pH-balanced soap and water to remove any residue left by the strong cleaners. When rinsing the boat, remove the nozzle from the hose so that the water sheets over the surface rather than beating hard against it. This will result in better rinsing action and less spotting.

Applying polish to the finish provides three benefits: it returns some of the natural oils to the finish; it seals the surface, preventing further loss of these natural oils; and it provides a sacrificial barrier for attack by acid and oxidation agents. There are two ways to determine if the surface needs to be polished. First, water will bead up on an adequately polished surface. When it no longer beads it is time to repolish. Second, if the surface is no longer protected by polish, it will squeak when a cloth rag over the index finger is twisted on the surface.

It is debatable whether there is any difference except price between boat polish and car polish. Often a good car polish will work. If the surface is deeply oxidized, a heavy-duty cleaner should be used first, followed by a reconditioner to put back some of the oils and chemicals that have been leeched out of the finish. An abundance of products are on the market; some experimentation is needed to find the system that suits you best.

Surface Finishing

Surface finishing is a better term than painting for two reasons. First, not all surface coatings are paint, and second, the actual application of the surface coating is anticlimactic. All the real work and the quality of the final product depends on surface preparation. Before dealing with the process of surface finishing, it is helpful to know a little about the coatings and the application equipment.

Coatings

Finishing a surface introduces the boater to the bewildering world of chemistry. Part of the bewilderment is caused by patent laws, which do not protect chemical inventions adequately. Consequently, the formulas for most finishing products are protected only by secrecy, and manufacturers are reluctant to talk openly about the exact composition of their products. Surface finishes are composed of some or all of the following ingredients: oils, resins, solvents, pigments, and dryers. These can be separated into three broad classes.

Varnishes are composed of a solution of oils, natural or synthetic resin, a solvent, and some stabilizing chemicals. The oil is commonly linseed and the solvent is turpentine, but other oils and solvents can be used. The characteristics of the varnish depend on the mixture of oil and resins. As the resin content is increased the product changes from a penetrating oil to what is termed a short varnish. In general, the more resin the less the product penetrates and the harder the resulting finish. Other chemicals and the manner in which they are mixed also affect in a minor way the attributes of the end product.

Paints and **enamels** are composed primarily of varnish plus a pigment for color. The resin can be alkyd, vinyl, acrylic, phenolic, or any of the epoxy or polyurethane resins. The type of solvent, sometimes referred to as a base, used in paints and enamels varies widely, from turpentine to water. Some paints use alcohols, esters, acetates, ketones, or mineral spirits for a base. This is the solvent used to thin the paint and clean up spills and equipment. By the way, try to avoid using solvents to clean paint off your skin unless it is a water-based product. Most of these solvents are extremely harsh and may force some of the chemicals deeper into the skin.

The word "paint" covers a wide variety of sins. There are bottom paints, topside paints, undercoats, primers, and sealers. Modern painting technology sometimes requires systems of coatings that augment and reinforce each other to produce the desired end product. The undercoat is designed to adhere to the surface, the primer is often used to prevent corrosion, and sealers are placed on porous surfaces to reduce absorption of the other finishes.

Topside paints are very smooth, hard, glossy coatings. The best are formulated to have enough surface tension to smooth out brush strokes. Alkyd enamels dry fast, are easy to apply, least expensive, come in the most colors, and are more forgiving of amateur application. They do not adhere well to fiberglass and are not particularly durable. Two-part polyurethanes provide a very high gloss and a durable, hard finish, but are toxic and difficult to apply. One-part polyurethane paints are easier to apply than two-part paints at the cost of some durability.

Bottom paints contain an additive toxicant to kill marine organisms. U. S. government regulations ban the use of almost anything except copper, molybdenum, and lead. The paints differ in how they release their biocides. Some use modified epoxy, ablative polymers, or vinyl. Some paints are soft and slough off; others are very hard, smooth, can be polished, and are used for racing hulls. Table 10.1 lists the attributes of each of these general classes of bottom paint. Paints that have poor out-of-water storage should be launched wet, those with good out-of-water storage capability should be launched dry. Local conditions also play an important part in selecting the best bottom paint. If the boat is to be used in one area, obtain local opinions before making a final selection.

Table 10.1 Bottom Paint Attributes					
	EPOXIES	POLYMERS	VINYL BASED	RACING PAINTS	SLOUGHING
Boat Speed (Over 10 Knots)	Good	Good	Good	Good	Poor
Price (1 = high, 5 = low)	2	1	3	4	5
Longevity	Good	Good	Good	Fair	Fair
Durability	Good	Good	Good	Good	Poor
Friction	Medium	Medium	Low	Low	High
Out-of-Water Storage	Poor	Good	Fair	Fair	Poor

Lacquer is a combination of resin and solvent, with or without pigment. Lacquers differ from ordinary paints in that they are solutions and not mixtures, and they dry by evaporation, not oxidation. Lacquers dry extremely fast, sometimes too fast for brush application. They produce a high gloss and an elastic surface, but are rarely used on the exterior of a boat. Most lacquers are highly flammable and require good ventilation.

Application Equipment

Coatings can be applied with brushes, rollers, or by spraying. Brushes are most often used. The best brushes are made with hog bristles, and have tapered rather than square ends. These brushes are very expensive and need proper care. Some brushes made with synthetic bristles also provide a good finished product. Cheap, throwaway brushes made from inexpensive bristles or foam can be used in many applications where the coating is tolerant or does not need to be decorative. For example, a foam brush might be used to apply teak oil to brightwork.

Rollers are useful for covering large areas with paint quickly, most often for bottom paint and some low-gloss topside paints. Power painters, both the roller and spray types, also speed up painting because they need not be dipped. Standard paint spraying equipment is generally too expensive for regular boating use; however, for small quantities, any good paint store will load any sprayable paint product into an aerosol can. This is particularly useful for touchup of topside paints. An artist's airbrush can also be used for paint touchup. I know of one cruising couple who used this method and bottled air, rather than a compressor, to touch up the topside paint on their aluminum hull on a regular basis.

Application Procedure

As pointed out earlier, the universal truth about painting is that the results are only as good as the surface preparation. This is especially true for dark colors. Consequently, we'll concentrate on surface preparation here, followed by a few brief tips on application.

Before beginning it is helpful to assemble the needed tools and don the necessary safety equipment (masks, gloves, etc.). You will be subjected to some very toxic substances, ranging from airborne particles produced by sanding and surface preparation to fumes and potential direct contact of the substances with skin and eyes. More than any other maintenance tasks around a boat, these jobs require protective clothing.

Preparation of a surface for painting requires removing incompatible coatings, repairing and smoothing the surface, and masking areas not to be painted. Often, removing some of the hardware and fixtures will make the work considerably easier and eliminate some masking. Before removing hardware, consider that most hardware on a boat is installed in bedding compound; removing it will require rebedding. This may be an advantage if the bedding compound is old and leaking; however, there is a great deal of wisdom in the saying "if it ain't broke don't fix it."

Removing Existing Surface Coatings: Sanding is the most common method of removing old paint and corrosion, but sandblasting, wire brushes, heat guns, chemical paint removers, and wax strippers all have their particular applications.

Sandblasting is often thought of as a means of preparing large, difficult surfaces; however, it is quite useful for small, difficult items as well. For example, sandblasting propane tanks is a fast, simple, and economical way of preparing the surface for painting. Most sandblasting businesses have an area where small items are routinely cleaned. Because a minimum fee is charged for sandblasting small objects, cleaning one propane tank often costs the same as cleaning three or four. Gather your neighbors' tanks and share the fee.

A heat gun is much better than a blowtorch for removing unwanted coatings. With a heat gun there is no open flame, and the amount of heat applied to the surface can be controlled much better, eliminating fires and scorched surfaces. Once the surface coat is loosened it can be scraped away with a paint scraper.

Chemical paint removers also loosen the bond of the surface coat so that it can be scraped away; however, because these chemicals are very toxic and boatyards in general are coming under more pressure to handle toxic waste properly, they are losing popularity. This environmental pressure is transferred to the boatowner by the yard in the form of a larger bill or a barrel of toxic waste that the owner must dispose of properly.

On a new fiberglass hull surface, wax or other coatings used to assist the release of the hull from the mold must be removed before painting. Even on hulls where the old paint is in good condition, any waxes and polishes used to protect the paint surface must be completely removed before painting. Commercial dewaxers are better than solvents because they do not evaporate as fast and will hold more of the wax in suspension. Rags need to be changed often to keep from reapplying wax trapped in an overused rag.

Once all the old surface coating has been removed, the exposed surface must be lightly sanded and washed thoroughly to provide a clean, rough surface for the primer. The proper primer depends on the hull material. Fiberglass hulls need to be primed to provide adhesion for the covering coatings. Wood needs to be sealed against the weather. Steel and aluminum should be etched before priming to reduce corrosion and electrolysis.

Surfacers: Once the surface has been primed, it is necessary to fill all scratches, dents, and other imperfections with surfacing compound. A surfacing or fairing compound is a relatively thick coating that contains a large amount of easily sandable filler. When the coating is sanded down, the peaks and valleys are filled and a smooth, level surface is available for painting. Two-part epoxy fillers are extremely durable and can be used to fill fairly large imperfections. Epoxy coatings are also used on fiberglass hulls as a water barrier against gelcoat blisters caused by osmosis. Make sure that the fillers, surfacing compounds, and any caulking used are compatible with the surface and the coatings that will follow. All filled spots need to be sanded smooth and feathered into the existing hull surface.

Sanding is one of the most universal and least inspirational chores involved in boat maintenance. Sanding can be used to remove surface coatings, to smooth the final surface before applying the coatings, or between coatings to provide bonding and additional smoothing.

Almost any type of surface can be sanded to prepare it for painting. On wood surfaces, sand with the grain, and on flat surfaces, use a block to keep the surface flat. On fiberglass and metal surfaces, which have no grain, be careful that the grit is fine enough not to produce visible surface scratching.

Sanders: A disc sander is used for initial sanding of large areas and for rough sanding because it removes large amounts of material fast, but it can leave circular scratch marks in the finish. A belt sander removes material very fast and does not leave circular scratch marks, but if handled carelessly it can quickly and deeply gouge the surface. The orbital sander, the most commonly used, is slower but more forgiving of operator error. The block sander is used for small areas and final touchup.

Sandpaper is made from different abrasives and comes in various degrees of roughness, called grits, which range from around 30, very coarse, to 600, very fine. The coarser the paper, the more material it removes and the deeper the scratches on the finished surface. Often the surface is sanded using several different grits, starting with the coarse and finishing with the finer grit. Final sanding for sensitive surfaces is usually done with 200 grit or finer.

The abrasive coatings are flint, aluminum oxide, or silicon carbide. Flint paper, the common household variety, is the least expensive, but the grit is softer and does not cut as well as the other two coatings. Aluminum oxide paper is a little more expensive, but it lasts longer and cuts better. Silicon carbide sandpaper, the most expensive and the most abrasive, is often designed with a special glue to be used wet or dry. Wet sanding, often used for the final sanding with very fine grits, not only produces a more consistent finish but also increases the life of the paper. Very fine grits tend to load up with residue quickly, which prevents the abrasive from cutting. Wet sanding washes away the residue.

When using coarse grit this residue problem requires that you change papers often to keep removing material. A relatively new product, the sanding screen, developed for use by wallboard finishers, is made from silicon carbide or aluminum oxide and can be used wet or dry. The large holes in the screen keep it free of residue. The roughness of the screen has more to do with the screen material than with the mesh size. Screens are manufactured in sizes roughly equivalent to sandpaper grits from 100 to 200, and outlast sandpaper 10 to 1.

Once sanding is complete the surface is ready for a final cleaning to remove any residue. A thorough cleaning is especially important when varnishing. Any dust left in the immediate area will somehow find its way to the drying surface.

Masking: When the surface is clean any adjacent surfaces and hardware not to be painted should be masked with tape and masking paper. Masking paper covers large areas and is held down with tape. Tape is used for small areas and for producing sharp edges between different painted surfaces. There is an abundance of tape on the market, all with different characteristics and uses.

Choosing the proper tape for the project depends on how long the tape will be on the surface and how sharp a line is needed. When left in place for long periods, some tapes deteriorate in the sunlight and are very difficult to remove or leave a residue. Some tapes allow small amounts of paint to seep under the edges and produce ragged lines. Plastic-backed tapes stretch more than paper-backed tapes. Table 10.2 lists some of these tapes and their recommended uses. The numbers refer to the 3M company designation.

Table 10.2 Masking Tape Qualities

3M No.	BACKING	COLOR	LINE QUALITY	EXPOSURE	RELATIVE COST*	COMMENT
233	Crepe Paper	Tan	Average	1 day	3	Noncritical uses
2040	Crepe Paper	Tan	Poor	1 day	2	Inexpensive
2050	Crepe Paper	Tan	Poor	1 day	1	Least expensive
2070	Flat Paper	White	Good	1 day	5	Delicate finishes
218	Plastic	Green	Excellent	5 days	6	Sensitive color separation
256	Flat Paper	Light Green	Good	5 days	8	Long straight lines
225	Crepe Paper	Silver	Poor	1 Month	7	Moderate duration
226	Crepe Paper	Black	Poor	3 Months	10	Paint stripping
481	Plastic	Black	Average	2 years	9	Boat storage
2090	Crepe Paper	Blue	Average	7 days	4	Multipurpose
346	Plastic	Black	Average	180 days	n/a	Heavy-duty wear

*The numbers indicate relative cost; 1 is the least expensive, 10 the most expensive.

After the surface is properly prepared, the coating itself requires preparation. Surface coatings that are mixtures, such as paint, should be stirred or vibrated vigorously to mix the ingredients thoroughly. This is especially true for bottom paints that contain heavy metals like lead and copper, which tend to separate and settle to the bottom. Many paint outlets have vibrators that shake paint. Shaking the can thoroughly mixes the ingredients but at the same time introduces bubbles into the mixture. Products with a high viscosity, like high-gloss paint, hold the small bubbles in suspension. These bubbles will mar the finished surface. High-gloss paints should be stirred, not shaken. Surface coatings that are solutions do not need to be mixed. Varnish should never be stirred or shaken.

Most surface coatings are strained at the factory. However, on sensitive jobs, professional painters re-strain them before applying. This is especially important when using products from a partially empty can. Bottom paints are the exception to this rule and need not be strained. Onsite straining is not a major event, since it is never a good idea to paint directly from the original container, which exposes all the paint to oxidation and drying. Instead, pour 2 or 3 inches of paint into a small paper container, enough to wet about a third of the brush, and tightly seal the original can. Pouring the paint through a strainer adds very little time to the operation. Inexpensive paper funnels with strainers are available for this purpose.

Application

The actual application of the surface coating depends to some extent on the job. The most common painting tasks involve the bottom and the brightwork. Painting the topsides is a major undertaking and beyond the scope of this book.

Bottom painting is a very forgiving task, since it is hidden from view and any brush marks or other imperfections will go unnoticed. Surface area not covered by paint, commonly called holidays, however, will be found quickly by marine plants and animals. The key to applying bottom paint is to get it on quickly and copiously. How quickly depends on yard cost, how copiously depends on paint cost.

Surface preparation depends on the hull material and whether the paint is going on over old paint or on a surface that has never been painted before. Painting over an old painted surface with the same type of bottom paint requires a thorough cleaning to remove all dirt and marine organisms, a general roughing up of the surface to improve bonding, and masking the line between the bottom paint and the topside paint. Painting over an old surface with a different paint depends on the compatibility of the two paints. If they are incompatible, all the old paint must be removed. The can will list incompatible coatings. Painting over a new surface requires cleaning with a dewaxing agent, light sanding to roughen the surface, and priming with a suitable primer designed for the hull material.

Bottom paint should be applied straight from the can without thinning. Most people apply the paint with a roller because of its ability to cover large surfaces quickly. This painting is relatively straightforward, requiring no special techniques, but gravity produces three small but annoying problems. First, gravity requires the heavy paint to be stirred often. Second, because the boat must always rest on something, there is always a small area under that something which does not get covered by paint; those areas are generally part of the bottom of the keel and under the pads used to brace the boat. How these small areas get painted depends on the type of paint being applied. Third, gravity, speed, and the roller's tendency to spray paint will polka-dot the painter, a special problem for eyeglass wearers. Wear a hat.

Paints designed to go into the water wet generally get one coat; the support spots are painted just before the boat is launched. For paints that need drying before launching, the boat must be moved slightly in the cradle or the shoring repositioned. Do not reposition shoring yourself; this is the responsibility of the yard, and mistakes can be costly.

Be sure that everything that will be exposed to the water gets covered. Painting the inside of a centerboard trunk requires ingenuity; some owners wrap a rag around a thin stick. Painting the prop is questionable, since the rapid motion quickly removes the paint. If you choose this option, be sure that the paint is compatible with the propeller metal. Electrolysis between the metals in the paint and the prop may cause damage to the propeller. Some boaters report that water-pump grease or STP fuel additive slows down prop fouling.

Unlike bottom paint, **brightwork**, the other never-ending task of boat maintenance, is always visible. There are three broad schools of thought on how to treat the brightwork or teak trim on a recreational boat: varnish, oil, or nothing. The protection and the results of the first two methods can be essentially the same. Varnish lasts longer than oil treatment, however. A good varnish job will last 9 to 12 months, but an oil finish must be treated every 4 to 6 months. Oiling teak is a much easier and more forgiving task; it is also more economical: a quart of good teak oil runs about one-third the cost of a quart of good varnish. The character of the oil finish is also more flexible; it can have the deep gloss commonly associated with varnish, or it can be left matte.

Doing nothing is the easiest on the person doing the maintenance but the hardest on the wood. As teak dries out, it turns from a deep golden to a dirty silver color. Many people cruising the tropics let their teak go silver for several reasons. First, tropical weather is very hard on teak finishes; second, the sun heats a treated teak surface sufficiently to cause a severe burn to unprotected skin; and finally, the tropics are not a pleasant place to work in the sun.

Untreated decks are not necessarily maintenance free; they need vigorous scrubbing or holystoning to keep in proper shape. *Holystoning*, the traditional form of treating bare teak decks, is really a form of wet sanding. Because it removes the surface layer of dried-out wood, the deck needs to be thick and will eventually have to be replaced. Left unprotected for long, the wood will eventually dry out and need to be replaced. Be wary of buying a boat with untreated brightwork; the owner may be equally lackadaisical about performing other maintenance.

Like any surface, teak must be made clean and smooth in preparation for coating. Sanding, the traditional way to prepare teak, cleans, removes old surface coatings, and smoothes the surface. Use 60-grit sandpaper for difficult spots, and follow with 100-grit. Newly exposed teak is bright gold, but the sun oxidizes it very quickly. A freshly exposed surface partially covered will leave a spot after being exposed to bright sun for less than an hour. It is best to treat the exposed surface as soon as possible to keep the light golden color.

I cannot recommend commercial teak cleaners. They are hard on the teak, hard on the boat, and hard on the environment. The chemicals dissolve the softer parts of the wood along with the dirt and old finish. They also oxidize paint or gelcoat and are toxic. Fortunately, they are also expensive, which limits their use. Any good household abrasive cleaner with bleach, such as Comet, and a scrub brush will clean gray, dirty, oxidized teak back to a rich gold color with just a few minutes and a little effort.

How much effort depends on the original condition of the teak. I find it easier to prepare unfinished teak or finishes that just need touching up by using a household cleaner. When touching up, the problem with sanding is that the whole surface must be taken down evenly, and it is difficult to feather the edges. Using household cleaner, just the area that has deteriorated can be cleaned, and feathering is much easier. This is especially useful if the teak has been dented by a falling object. A paste made from the cleaner, forced into the depression and allowed to set for a few minutes, will return the discolored teak to its original gold. Sanding, however, is still the best procedure for surfaces that need a large portion of old finish removed.

Once the surface has been prepared, wipe it down thoroughly and immediately apply the finish. Regardless of the type of finish, three to seven coats are needed for proper protection. Like dancing, oiling and varnishing techniques are seemingly endless in variety. There are some basic steps, but then each individual seems to find different tricks that work for them.

Basic oiling techniques vary depending on the desired gloss. For a matte finish, apply three coats with a rag, allow to set for 15 minutes, and wipe the excess with a clean cloth. Allow 8 to 24 hours between coats. This procedure should be repeated every two or three months.

For a high-gloss oil finish, apply with a foam brush and do not wipe off the excess. Let dry 8 to 24 hours and apply five to seven coats. After the third coat the surface will develop a deep gloss. A light sanding between coats with 200- or 600-grit paper will produce a very fine, smooth coating with a deep gloss indistinguishable from varnish. An additional one or two coats needs to be applied every four to six months, preceded by a washing and a light sanding where necessary.

Generally speaking, it takes about half the time to oil that it does to varnish; however, it is necessary to oil about twice as often. The amount of work is roughly the same; oiling is more forgiving and has fewer frustrations, but there is no accounting for taste.

Varnishing is a practice for the thorough and patient. First, it is important to choose a warm day that is not too damp, free of wind and flying insects. Applying varnish over a damp surface will discolor it, while wind will distribute dust and debris on the surface, marring the finish Since insects prefer to fly on windless days, it takes a little imagination to calculate the probability of finding the perfect day for varnishing.

Here are some tips on varnishing.

1. Don't. But if you must. . . .
2. Do not stir or shake varnish; this will create air bubbles that are difficult to remove and will mar the finished surface.
3. Don't use varnish out of the original can. Pour what you need into another container and cover the original container immediately. Small disposable paper containers work well, as does a varnishing cup, which has a lip to remove the excess varnish from the brush. Dragging the brush on the sides of the container will remove excess varnish, but will also produce a run of varnish down the outside of the can. Eventually there is varnish on the brush handle, on both hands, on the end of your nose, in your hair, and in all sorts of other awkward places.
4. Strain all varnish before using regardless of whether it is new or old.
5. Use only good-quality (expensive) brushes. A short bristle will spread the varnish quicker.
6. Be sure all bristles are completely wet with varnish before applying. A partially saturated brush will leave the Dreaded Air Bubbles.
7. Avoid applying varnish during the heat of the day or in hot sun. Under these conditions it may dry too rapidly and show brush strokes.
8. Reserve the (expensive) brush for varnishing only. Clean the brush thoroughly after each use. If a varnishing cup is used, it must be thoroughly cleaned as well.
9. Do not varnish in a cool shaded area and then move the surface into the bright sun to dry. Expansion of air trapped in the wood will cause the Dreaded Bubbles.
10. Dilute the first coat of varnish with thinner, about half and half, so that it penetrates deeper into the wood surface.
11. For deep gloss on coats 4 through 7, brush on a light coat of thinner immediately before applying the varnish. This softens the old finish and improves the bond.

**Figure 10.2
Varnishing Cup**

R IGGING

The primary source of propulsion on a sailboat is the rig. Isn't it strange that most nonracing sailors tune their engine before they tune their rig? Rigging is certainly much simpler than an engine; it has no moving parts. It is composed of stays, the wires that run fore and aft, the shrouds, which run athwartships, and the mast. Briefly, the shrouds keep the mast from falling over sideways. They are generally very lightly loaded, and when under sail, the windward shrouds carry the entire wind load, leaving the leeward shrouds completely loose and without load. The stays keep the mast from falling over forward or backward. The load on the stays is considerably higher than on the shrouds because the headsails are attached to the forestay, and to keep the proper sail shape the forestay must not sag.

The stays, shrouds, and mast work together to transfer the wind loads from the sails into forward motion of the boat.

Tuning the Rig

The step-by-step process of tuning a rig begins by assuming that the mast is properly stepped and all shrouds are loose but not slack. Next, it is necessary to center the mast between the port and starboard gunwales, and to ensure the mast is parallel to the major plane of the keel. Then, the attitude of the mast fore and aft is adjusted. The next step is to see that the mast is straight and true in both the fore-and-aft and athwartships planes. Finally, the shrouds and stays are tensioned to ensure that the mast stays in place and functions as intended.

Getting the Mast Parallel to the Keel

The process of getting the mast parallel to the keel requires using some accurate and stable reference. This can be done in two different ways, depending on the situation. The short method assumes the boat is well built and can be balanced on her lines. The second method takes longer but makes no assumptions as to the quality of the craftsmanship.

The short method begins by observing the boat's designed waterline, the horizontal plane on which the boat is intended to float; it is often scribed into the hull by the builder. A painted line is not necessarily the designed waterline, so look for a scribed line. While the actual water may be above or below this line, the amount above or below should be the same at the bow and stern, and port and starboard amidships. If the boat is only slightly off its designed lines, temporarily positioning heavy objects along the deck will correct the misalignment. If the boat is considerably out of balance, she will not sail well, and heavy equipment and gear should be permanently repositioned until the water level is a constant distance above or below the scribed line.

Keep in mind that the position of a 200-pound rigging expert can affect balance, particularly on small boats and especially if the expert is positioned near the extremes of the boat. Fore-and-aft balance is more important than athwartships balance, which is harder to maintain because of the short base length.

Assuming that the boat is properly built and the hull is presently balanced on its waterlines, the vertical plane and the plane of the major axis of the keel are now parallel. Gravity can assist the process of positioning the mast. The jib or main halyards can be used as plumb bobs by adding weights and allowing them to hang from their respective mast-top sheaves. Select whichever weighted halyard hangs free of the mast; this line is now a true vertical line hanging directly down from the sheave. If the masthead sheave is in the center of the mast, the weighted halyard will indicate the desired position of the center of the mast. Normally, on an untuned mast the weighted halyard will lie either port or starboard of the centerline.

When reading the location of the halyard take particular care that all crew are exactly on the fore-and aft-centerline of the boat, because the athwartships balance is easy to disturb. Now adjust the port and starboard upper shrouds, tightening one side while loosening the other until the halyard falls directly along the center of the mast. Always adjust the shrouds in pairs, loosening one and tightening its opposite. Also during this process, be sure that all lower shrouds remain loose. Once the mast is plumb the shrouds should be snug but not tight.

If the boat cannot be balanced on her lines, then geometry must be used to get the mast in the plane of the keel. The best way to do this is to locate two points that are equidistant from the center of the boat in both the fore-and-aft and athwartships planes. There are several ways of doing this; the following method assumes that the head, backstay, and mast are all on the longitudinal axis of the keel. If they are not, you are in a world of hurt, and tuning the rig will probably not help anyway.

Tape two pieces of paper to the deck slightly aft of the mast in approximately the same position near each gunwale. Mark a spot on the backstay using tape or a marking pen. Be sure the spot has a clear line of sight to both pieces of paper. Repeat the process on the forestay. Now, using a measuring tape or a light line and a pen, swing an arc from the spot on the backstay across both pieces of paper. Be sure the length of the line to the arc is the same on each paper. Repeat the process from the point marked on the forestay. The length of the line from the forestay should be adjusted so that the forestay arc scribed by the pen will intersect the arc already on the paper drawn from the backstay. Using the same length, scribe a similar arc on the other paper.

At this point you should have two intersection points that are equidistant from the longitudinal axis of the boat and on a line perpendicular to that axis, which is just what is needed to plumb the mast in the athwartships direction. Select the main halyard and determine if this halyard exits the masthead in the center of the mast. If not, adjust the intersection points on the deck to compensate for this error; that is, if the halyard exits ½-inch port of center, move the marks on the deck ½-inch to port.

The next step is to find the intersection point closest to the top of the mast. To do this bring the halyard to either point, so that the end of the halyard just barely touches the point, and tie it off or stopper it down. Now move the halyard to the opposite point. If it does not reach the point, this point is the farthest from the masthead and you are ready to begin adjusting the mast. If the halyard is too long, the top of the mast is closer to this point and you need to readjust the halyard so that it just touches this point and tie it off again.

To adjust the position of the mast once the halyard length is established, return to the point farthest from the mast top and adjust the two upper shrouds, tightening one and loosening the other to move the top of the mast port or starboard as necessary until approximately half the distance from the bottom of the halyard to the point is recovered. Again, find the point closest to the top of the mast and repeat the process until the tied-off halyard just touches both points. At this time the mast is exactly where it should be and the upper shrouds can be adjusted snug but not tight.

Plumbing the Mast Fore and Aft

Next, adjust the position of the mast in the fore-and-aft direction. The tilt of the mast in the major plane of the boat is called *rake*. Some boats, particularly older schooners and ketches, rake the masts aft. When the mast is raked aft a lightly loaded sail will tend to swing inboard and lose drive. Raking the mast also moves the center of effort in the direction of the rake; forward moves the center of effort forward, aft moves the center of effort aft—the same concept used to maneuver windsurfers.

For sailboats, however, the consensus is that the best rake is no rake at all.[1] To assist in getting the mast vertical, use both a weighted jib and main halyard, because the mast will impede the movement of one of the halyards. The mast must be adjusted until both of the weighted halyards just touch the mast. Too much lean forward and the jib halyard will move away from the mast; too much lean aft and the main halyard will move away from the mast. The weights can be moved fore and aft by tightening or loosening the forestay and backstay. Again, always adjust the stays in pairs by loosening one a specific number of turns and tightening the other the same number of turns. When both halyards just touch the mast it is vertical. At this point the fore- and backstays should be snug but not tight.

Now, by gravity or geometry, the top of the mast has been adjusted to its proper position. It is a good idea to mark permanently the two points athwartships on the deck to expedite future tuning. To do this, use the main halyard and a center punch or cold chisel. Take the halyard to the port or starboard shroud chainplate and adjust its length so that it just touches the plate surface. Tie the halyard off and move to the opposite chainplate. If the halyard just touches the top of this plate somewhere, mark that spot with the center punch or cold chisel. Return to the first chainplate and mark it in a similar manner where the halyard just touches the plate.

Straightening the Mast

Once the mast is plumb, the next step is to see that it is straight. Place your head close to the mast and sight up the mainsail track; the track should be straight from top to bottom unless one of the intermediate shrouds is pulling it out of line. Sight up the side of the mast to see that it is straight fore and aft as well. Loosen and tighten all the intermediate shrouds until the mast is straight.

At this point, the rig tuning process drifts from science into the occult. The process involves much squinting up the sail track to see that the mast remains straight, alternating with small rotations of the turnbuckles. Tightening is again always done in pairs, and in some cases pairs of pairs if you have both fore and aft lower shrouds. Remember that this is an interactive process. Tightening one shroud

---

[1] Juan Baader, The Sailing Yacht (New York: W. W. Norton & Co. Inc., 1974), 101.

pulls the mast toward the shroud at the attachment point but pushes the mast away at the spreader, if the shroud passes over one.

Tensioning the Shrouds

The purpose of all this behavior, I am told, is to tension the shrouds properly. But what, you may ask, is the proper tension for a shroud? You might as well ask a mute witchdoctor, for the rigger will just tug on the shrouds and say righteously, "about that much." It seems that no one knows for sure, even though it is possible to buy a device to test the proper tension in a shroud, complete with a table of desired values. The truth is, almost any answer is the right answer for a particular boat.

The recommended procedure for tuning shrouds is to tune them moderately tight at the dock and then finish the tuning job while sailing. Pick a day with moderate conditions that will heel the boat to about 30 degrees. Then, while on one tack, tighten the loose, leeward shroud to remove about half the slack from the cables. Count the revolutions made on each of the turnbuckles. Turn the boat onto the opposite tack and tighten the new lee shrouds the same number of turns.

If this does not remove all the slack, continue tightening these shrouds until half the slack is removed, again counting the revolutions of the turnbuckles. Turn the boat onto the original tack and tighten the original lee shrouds the same number of revolutions. Repeat this process until in your judgment, based on current sailing conditions, all the shrouds have the proper tension to prevent adverse dynamic loading when they are lee shrouds during any sailing conditions you are likely to

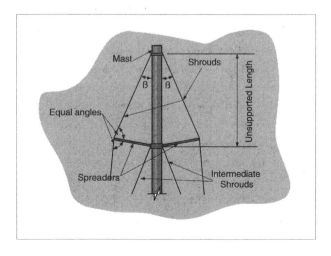

Figure 10.3 Typical Shroud Components at the Masthead

encounter. If that statement means something to you, you're well on your way to conversing with the mute witchdoctor. So much for the easy part; now we will tackle the stays.

Tensioning the Stays

Contrary to popular belief, the backstay is always the windward stay and the forestay is always the leeward stay. I am sure you have all heard about the alert helmsman who saved his rig by turning downwind when the headstay failed. The force from the wind on the sails is always in the forward direction, otherwise boats would sail backward. As long as the sails are drawing, the boat is going forward, or at worst slipping sideways through the water; therefore the resultant wind force on the sails and the rig has to be forward regardless of what sails are flying. Of course, if the sails are not drawing, as when the boat is headed directly into the wind, all bets are off and the backstay can become the leeward stay.

I know of numerous headstay failures where the mast stayed in the boat and a jib halyard was used as a temporary headstay. One individual sailed for thousands of miles in this condition. It may have been a credit to his seamanship, but it was undoubtedly a credit to the physics of the situation as well. Therefore, I repeat: under normal sailing conditions, the headstay is always the leeward stay; only when the boat is dead into the wind and the sails are flogging is there any wind loading in the headstay, and that is relatively minor. However, if you lose the headstay and turn directly into the wind, the loads are probably sufficient to bring the mast down.

Another difference between shrouds and stays is that the angles between the stays and the mast are not equal; the headstay angle is usually smaller. This smaller angle produces a higher stress in the headstay for any given tuning load. This may lead one to believe that a backstay smaller than the headstay can be used, but not so. As wind load increases, the stress in the backstay increases while the stress in the headstay decreases, similar to the conditions described for the leeward shroud. The maximum load in the headstay is just the tuning load, while the backstay's maximum load is the tuning load plus about half the wind load. Rarely does the wind load exceed one-quarter the optimum tuning load, so the maximum load on the backstay is approximately 115 percent of the tuning load.

The headstay, unlike shrouds and the backstay, also has the function of holding the leading edge of the jib in the proper shape for maximum performance. Windward performance of the boat is profoundly affected by the shape of this leading edge. As the tension in the stay is reduced the sag increases, which reduces the windward performance.

The result is that the jib performs most efficiently in light winds, and as the wind increases the efficiency of the sail drops off. Therefore, it is important to get the stay as tight as possible to maximize upwind performance.

In conclusion, one can say that shroud tension should be as low as possible and stay tension as high as possible, but both depend on wind strength. And, since tension in the stays can get quite high, it is a good idea to relax the tension in the rig if the boat is not going to be used for an extended period.

Sails

Periodically inspect the sail's seams for broken threads. Look over the main body of the sail for chafe from spreaders or shrouds. Check and oil the jib hanks. Check any battens for breakage and the batten pockets for tears. Besides these periodic inspections, sail maintenance consists of proper storage and damage prevention.

Sails should be stored off-season dry and folded in their sailbags. Not only is this easier on the sail, but it takes up considerably less room. Fold the sails slightly differently each time so that a permanent crease does not develop. Spinnakers can be loosely stuffed in a large bag. Avoid storing spinnakers wet for any length of time, as the dark colors may bleed into the lighter ones.

Sails can best be dried by going sailing, or if the wind is from the right direction the sails can be raised while tied to the dock as long as the sail does not flog and remains in its normally loaded position. If this is not possible, spread the sail out flat on a large area; avoid letting it flap in the wind.

Direct sunlight, chafe, abrasion, flexing, high temperature, dirt, mildew, and accidents all damage sails. Direct sunlight is extremely hard on Dacron and nylon sails and will eventually end the life of most modern sails. Covering the sails immediately after each use will add years to their life.

Chafe can be reduced by constant vigilance. Check the boat for cotter pins, fittings, burrs, screw heads, or anything sharp that may come in contact with a sail. Remove or cover these sharp areas with tape. Check the front of the mast, and any shrouds and stays. Sanded nonskid foredecks can cause damage to a sail rubbed or dragged over the deck.

Dirt on a sail acts like dirt in a fiber line: the sharp particles chafe the individual fibers. Because washing is almost as hard on sailcloth as dirt, it is best to *keep* sails clean rather than washing them after they are dirty. The easiest way to keep them clean is to keep the decks clean. For example, dirt left on deck from retrieving a muddy anchor rode is soon transferred to the headsail. It is best to wash down the foredeck before taking the sails from their bags. If a good hosing will not clean dirty sails, don't put them in a washing machine; soak them in warm water and mild detergent. If it is necessary to scrub the dirtiest areas, do so gently with a soft sponge. Scrubbing may do more harm to the sail than the original dirt.

Flexing of a sailcloth fiber produces an action similar to multiple bending of a wire. Rapid and repeated bending in the same spot will break a wire, and will also break sailcloth fibers. Flapping, flogging, and fluttering will degrade sailcloth at an extremely rapid rate.

Synthetic fibers are all sensitive to high temperatures; that is why the ends of rope can be sealed with heat. Storing sails in places subjected to high temperatures, like the trunk of a car parked in the hot sun, may fuse the sail's synthetic fibers.

Under the heading of accidents comes damage due to operator error, like flying a sail in too heavy a wind for the cloth. This generally happens to light-air sails like spinnakers and genoas, and is dependent on the weight of the sailcloth, the weight of the boat, and the point of sail. Damage can range from tearing the sail or seams to permanently stretching the cloth and destroying the sail's aerodynamic shape. A very broad guideline is to fly the heaviest sail that will fill. If a light sail is up and the wind increases, douse a sail made from ½-ounce cloth at 10 knots apparent, and one made from ¾-ounce cloth at 15 knots apparent.

The other common misfortune to befall mainsails is shaking out a reef and forgetting to untie the reefing pendants, which almost guarantees a rip along the reef points. There are no foolproof methods for avoiding this error, except maybe using roller reefing. Training may help, as may use of brightly colored reefing pendants.

ENGINE

The maintenance requirements for diesel and gasoline engines are very much alike. The major difference involves the gas engine's electrical system. Outboard motors can be removed for maintenance and storage, which is a distinct advantage because most marine engines are located in the most difficult position possible for maintenance. Not only is it difficult to reach some parts, in some instances it isn't even possible to see the part. This is especially true on sailboats.

Other than these difficulties, marine engine maintenance is similar to automobile engine maintenance. Routine maintenance consists of checking the cooling system, the lubrication system, the fuel system, and, on gasoline engines, the ignition system. It is a good idea to start and run the engine until it reaches normal running temperature every 30 to 60 days to keep all the systems operating correctly.

Cooling System

Engines are cooled by air, sea water, or a combination of fresh and sea water. Probably the most common is the combination of fresh water and sea water. This system circulates fresh water or engine coolant through the engine and then through a heat exchanger, which is cooled by circulating sea water. This keeps corrosive sea water from direct contact with the engine. Engine coolant or antifreeze not only protects the engine coolant from freezing, it also protects against corrosion and raises the boiling point.

Before the engine is started, verify that the seacock that supplies salt water to the cooling system is open, and check the level of the coolant in the heat exchanger. After the engine is started, verify that cooling water is flowing from the exhaust system. Annually, check the concentration of the coolant. It should be kept above 25 percent, and in areas where the ambient temperature drops below 10°, the percentage of coolant should be increased according to the coolant manufacturer's recommendations. Periodically, the engine cooling system should be completely flushed and new coolant installed. The sea water intake is equipped with a filter, which should be inspected and cleaned every 100 hours of engine operation.

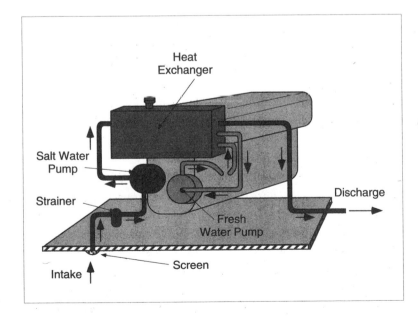

Figure 10.4
Common Engine
Cooling System

Lubrication System

Before each start, check the level of engine oil and add oil if necessary. After every 100 hours of operation, or if the engine is left unused for several months, drain and replace the engine oil, change the oil filter, and replace the filter gaskets. Do not overtighten the new filter. The transmission oil should be changed every 400 hours of operation, or annually if the boat is left unattended or the engine is not operated for long periods.

Changing oil in most marine engines is not as simple a job as changing oil in the family car. Getting to the drain plug is next to impossible, let alone catching the drain oil and removing it. As a consequence, most marine engines are equipped with a sump pump to extract the engine oil. Skippers of boats that are not so equipped generally list it as their top priority after attempting their first oil change.

Some of these pumps are better than others, but it is always easier to pump warm oil. I find that a short hose clamped to the end of the pump and running to a narrow-mouth jug keeps the oil contained. Pumping into a pan or pail tends to induce splashing and may allow the unrestrained hose to wander about squirting oil at random.

Fuel System

Fuel, especially diesel fuel, must be kept clean. There are generally two fuel filters attached to marine engines. Many skippers install a third or even a fourth fuel filter in the line. Fuel filters should be changed every 400 hours. Once a year, fuel tanks should be inspected, cleaned, and drained of water if necessary. Water enters fuel from many sources; even the most careful boatowner will have water collect in the fuel tanks from condensation. Keeping the fuel tanks topped off reduces the amount of condensation but does not eliminate it entirely.

Water in the fuel promotes the growth of a fungus that lives in the interface between the fuel oil and water. The result is a thick black film of slime that clogs filters and fuel lines. Growth is promoted by stagnation and warm temperatures.

Test kits are available that will determine the presence of fungus; however, in extreme cases the eyes and nose will indicate the problem. Contaminated fuel is dark and smells like rotten eggs. If the tank becomes badly fouled, a fungicide designed to treat fuel oil should be added to the tank. The tank should then be drained, thoroughly cleaned, and the contaminated fuel disposed of properly. Fungicide kills the fungus but does not dissolve the slime mats; without proper cleaning a small fortune can be spent on fuel filters. Low levels of infestation can be controlled by the normal addition of small amounts of fungicide or water dispersants and regular filter changes.

Most fuel systems also have an air intake filter. Fortunately, most boats spend limited time in dusty areas, and the air filters rarely get dirty. They should be checked every decade or two and replaced or cleaned if dirty.

Electrical Systems

Electrical systems consist of the starter, the alternator, and on gasoline engines the ignition system. The starter motor needs no routine maintenance beyond occasional inspection of the electrical connections, which must be clean and tight. The connections can be sprayed with a silicone sealer to protect them from moisture.

The alternator or generator belts should be checked for proper tension. On a correctly tensioned belt, the longest run should depress about ⅜ inch. The rear bushing on a generator should be lubricated with a few drops of 30-weight oil every 100 hours or so.

Gasoline ignition systems require that the spark plugs and, if so equipped, distributor points be checked for wear and replaced if necessary. Dirty or damaged plugs can indicate engine trouble such as improper fuel mixture, worn piston rings, or defective cooling. Spark plugs should be cleaned or replaced and the gap checked according to manufacturer's recommendations before tightening. Check the spark plug wires for breaks and corrosion.

All terminals in the distributor cap should be checked for wear and any dirt and oil should be removed. On engines without electronic ignition, the rotor tip and breaker points should be cleaned with a fingernail file or sandpaper if they show any grayish deposit. Check to see that the point gap meets the manufacturer's requirements. To set the correct gap, remove the rotor by simply lifting it off the top of the distributor shaft. Then crank the engine until the rotating cam has opened up the gap to its fullest extent. Consult the engine manual for the correct gap. Loosen the mounting screw and open the points wider than the thickness of the correct feeler blade. Insert the blade into the gap and set the gap back until the points just touch the blade on both sides. Tighten the mounting screw and test the gap by slipping the blade between the points again. Lightly oil the wick inside the distributor shaft and replace the rotor. Replace the distributor cap. Electronic ignition systems are not user maintainable.

Visual Inspection

A thorough periodic visual examination of the engine for oil, water, and dirt will reveal many pending failures. Oil or water spots indicate a leak; the cause should be determined and corrected. Inspect all hoses for leaks and to ensure that the hose clamps are securely fastened. Check that all wires and hoses near the engine do not contact the engine where vibration and heat can damage them.

BATTERIES

As more electronic devices are added to boats the importance of the batteries increases. Battery maintenance is relatively simple, consisting of good ventilation, keeping the electrolyte at the proper level, and keeping the terminals free of corrosion.

Good ventilation is needed to keep the batteries cool and free of explosive gases. During charging both hydrogen and oxygen are created in the battery cells. These two gases are the same used to power most space vehicles, so unless the object is to place the boat into orbit, good ventilation is necessary to keep concentrations below that necessary for detonation.

The water level in the batteries should be kept above the plate level. The batteries will be damaged if the plates are exposed. The loss of water is related to the charging rate; the higher the rate, the more often the water level should be checked. Checking the water level every 30 to 60 days is usually adequate. If the water level is low, add *distilled* water; tap water contains minerals that will damage the battery's plates. Be careful not to overfill and spill water or battery acid. Spilled battery acid will damage the wires and connectors as well as clothing and many other materials it contacts.

The battery terminals should be cleaned when they become corroded. Use a wire brush, a round file, or sandpaper. Vaseline or grease will slow the growth of new corrosion. It is a good idea to check all cells with a hydrometer annually. A hydrometer checks the charge by determining the concentration of the battery acid. If the cell acid concentration gets low enough, the cell is lost and will not hold a charge again. This is generally indicated by a red area on the hydrometer. A single red cell in a battery renders the entire battery useless. A single bad battery in a bank of batteries severely degrades the entire bank's ability to hold a charge. So for the want of a cell the bank is lost, so to speak.

WATER SYSTEMS

There are usually three different water systems on board a recreational boat: fresh water, bilge water, and waste water. Some boats also add a fourth system, which supplies sea water to the galley for cleaning. Maintaining the various systems consists of the occasional treatment of tanks, water lines, and pumps.

Tanks and Lines

Water tanks and lines need to be kept clean and sterile. The most common way for tanks and lines to become contaminated is through the introduction of contaminated water. A household water filter designed to be installed under the sink can, with a little ingenuity, be rigged into the hose line used to bring shore water aboard and into the tanks. This will keep most contaminants out of the water, but not bacteria. A heavy dose of chlorine bleach can be used to sterilize the tanks and hoses, but questionable water should be treated with *iodine*, not bleach. *Bleach and chlorine do not kill waterborne parasites.*

Do not drink water directly from even remote mountain streams. The parasite Giardia, carried by wild animals, has reached even the most isolated areas and high latitudes. If you drink untreated water you risk infection, nausea, abdominal cramps, and diarrhea.

On occasion, water tanks need to be drained, inspected, and cleaned. Water tanks that have picked up an odor or taste can be refreshed by dissolving baking soda in water, pouring the solution into the tank, and letting it stand for several days. A 1-pound box will treat about 25 gallons of water. Following this procedure, flush out the tank with clean water and add about an ounce of white wine per gallon. This treatment will rid the tank of even heavy chlorine or iodine taste.

Pumps

Annually, electrical connections should be checked on all the various electrical pumps. Quarterly, the automatic bilge switch should be checked to see that it is in proper working order and the bilge pump checked to see that it has not lost its prime. Any parts that will accept lubrication should be lubricated. The screen over the intake end of all bilge and sump pumps should be clean and free of debris. Bilge pumps can be cleaned while cleaning the bilge itself by letting some of the soapy water stay in the pump for a few minutes. Rinse the bilge and the pump with copious amounts of water, then lubricate the pump by pumping through some water-soluble oil.

Heads

Most problems with marine heads are due to operator error. The wise skipper thoroughly instructs all neophytes before letting them use the facilities. Routine maintenance consists of repacking the packing gland on the pump piston rod, oiling the piston, and removing the buildup on the inside of the discharge hose.

Marine heads are much more delicate than their shoreside cousins. Corrosive liquids, including chemicals designed to clean drains, should not be pumped through them. Use only soap and water to clean the bowl, and after each cleaning pump some vegetable oil through the pump to relubricate the piston.

Every five or six years, depending on the temperature of the water and the frequency of use, the outlet hose should be stripped from the head and cleaned. A very hard crystalline growth collects inside the hose, which eventually restricts the flow enough to cause a stoppage. Cleaning the growth from the hose is a messy job, but nowhere near as messy as cleaning a blockage of the normal impediment that travels the hose. The growth is brittle and can be removed by pounding the outside of the hose to break it into small pieces, which are then rinsed away.

Somehow this doesn't seem to be a good subject on which to close a book. I thought about adding a chapter on selecting a hull, or one on selection of mechanical equipment. Then I thought about one on the layout of interior space, another on cruising rigs, and another on cruising budgets. I ended up with so many chapters that I decided to write another book. The result is that this one will have to end here, and the reader will have to wait for my next book, on a thinking man's approach to bluewater cruising.

A

USEFUL PUBLICATIONS

Many of the publications on this list can be found at local bookstores, chandleries, or chart stores. Publishers' addresses are listed following the table in case you cannot find the documents you need locally.

Table A.1 Useful Publications

TITLE	SUBJECT	PUBLISHER
American Practical Navigator, vol. 1 (Bowditch)	*Navigation*	*DOD*
American Practical Navigator, vol. 2 (Bowditch)	*Navigation*	*DOD*
Boater's Source Directory	*General*	*Boat/U.S.*
Catalog of Maps and Charts (9 volumes)	*Navigation*	*DOD*
1. United States and Canada		
2. Central and South America and Antarctic		
3. Western Europe, Iceland, Greenland, and the Arctic		
4. Scandinavia, Baltic, and USSR		
5. Western Africa and the Mediterranean		
6. Indian Ocean		
7. Australia, Indonesia, and New Zealand		
8. Oceania		
9. East Asia		
Catalog of Maps and Charts (5 volumes)	*Navigation*	*NOS*
1. Atlantic and Gulf Coast including Puerto Rico and Virgin Islands		
2. Pacific Coast including Hawaii, Guam, and Samoa Islands		
3. Alaska		
4. Great Lakes		
5. Bathymetric Maps and Special Purpose Charts		
Chart No. 1 Nautical Chart Symbols and Abbreviations	*Navigation*	*NOS*
Coast Pilots (9 volumes)	*Navigation*	*NOS*
No. 1 Eastport to Cape Cod		
No. 2 Cape Cod to Sandy Hook		
No. 3 Sandy Hook to Cape Henry		
No. 4 Cape Henry to Key West		
No. 5 Gulf of Mexico, Puerto Rico, and Virgin Islands		
No. 6 Great Lakes and St. Lawrence River		
No. 7 California, Oregon, Washington, and Hawaii		
No. 8 Dixon Entrance to Cape Spencer		
No. 9 Cape Spencer to Beaufort Sea		

Table A.) Useful Publications (Continued)

TITLE	SUBJECT	PUBLISHER

Current Tables
    Atlantic Coast of North America
    Pacific Coast of North America and Asia
	Navigation	NOS

Dates of Latest Editions (charts)	Navigation	NOS
Federal Requirements for Recreational Boats	Legal	USCG
Field Guides	Nature	Audubon
Handbook of Magnetic Compass Adjustment and Compensation	Navigation	DOD
Heavy Weather Guide	Weather	USNI

Light and Fog Signal Lists (6 volumes)
  1. Greenland, East Coast South and Central America, Mexico, Canada, and West Indies
  2. West Coast South and Central America, Mexico, Canada, Australia, and Islands of the Pacific
  3. West Coast of Europe and Africa, Mediterranean Sea, Black Sea, and Azovskoye More
  4. British Isles, English Channel, and North Sea
  5. Norway, Iceland, and Arctic Ocean
  6. Baltic Sea, Kattegat Belts and Sound, and Gulf of Bothnia
	Navigation	DOD

Light Lists (U.S. only; 5 volumes)
  1. Atlantic Coast Maine to South Carolina
  2. Atlantic and Gulf Coast South Carolina to Rio Grande
  3. Great Lakes
  4. Mississippi River
  5. Pacific Coast and Islands
	Navigation	U.S. Print

Magnetic Variation Chart of the World	Navigation	DOD
Marine Fouling and its Prevention	Weather	USNI
Nautical Almanac	Navigation	U.S. Print
Nautical Almanac	Navigation	NOS
Navigational Rules	Legal	U.S. Print
Notice to Mariners	Safety	USCG
Notice to Mariners	Safety	DOD

Table A.1 Useful Publications (Continued)		
TITLE	SUBJECT	PUBLISHER

Pilot Charts (4 sets of charts)
  1. Central American Waters and South Atlantic
  2. South Pacific and Indian Ocean
  3. Northern North Atlantic
  4. North Pacific
	Navigation	DOD

Radar Navigation Manual	Navigation	DOD
Safety Standards for Backyard Boat Builders	Safety	USCG

Sailing Directions (12 volumes)
  1. Greenland and Iceland
  2. Latin America and Antarctica
  3. Scandinavia and Northern USSR
  4. Western Africa
  5. Australia and Southwest Pacific and Northeast
  6. Central and South Pacific
  7. Mediterranean
  8. North Atlantic Ocean
  9. North Pacific Ocean
  10. Southwest Pacific Ocean
  11. Indian Ocean
  12. North Sea and Baltic Sea
	Navigation	DOD

Science and the Sea	Oceanography	DOD
Selected Worldwide Marine Weather Broadcasts	Weather	U.S. Print
The Radio Amateur's License Manual	Radio	ARRL
The Ship's Medicine Chest and First Aid at Sea	Safety	U.S. Print

Tidal Current Charts
  Boston Harbor
  Charleston S.C. Harbor
  Long Island Sound and Block Island Sound
  Narragansett Bay
  Narragansett Bay to Nantucket Sound
  New York Harbor
  Puget Sound, Northern Part
  Puget Sound, Southern Part
  San Francisco Bay
  Upper Chesapeake Bay
  Tampa Bay
	Navigation	NOS

Tune in the World	Radio	ARRL
World Port Index	Navigation	DOD

Table 8.2 Publishers

ABBREVIATION	ADDRESS/PHONE
ARRL	American Radio Relay League 225 Main Street Newington, CT 06111
Boat/U.S.	The Source Boat/U.S. Foundation 880 S. Picket Street Alexandria, VA 22304
USCG	Commandant U.S. Coast Guard Headquarters Washington, D.C. 20593-0001 (800) 368-5647
DOD	Defense Mapping Agency Hydrographic/Topographic Center Attn.: DDCP Washington, D.C. 20315-0020 (800) 826-0342
Audubon	National Audubon Society 950 Third Avenue New York, NY 10022
NOS	Distribution Branch (N/CG33) National Ocean Services Riverdale, Maryland 20737-1199 (301) 436-6990
USNI	U.S. Naval Institute Annapolis, MD
U.S. Print	Superintendent of Documents U.S. Government Printing Office Washington, DC 20402 (202) 783-3238

UNIFORM STATE WATERWAYS MARKING SYSTEM

The waters that lie completely within a state's boundaries are subject to that state's authority. The Uniform State Waterways Marking System (USWMS) was developed to mark these waterways. There are essentially three types of markers: channel markers, informational or regulatory markers, and moorage buoys.

CHANNEL MARKERS

Under the USWMS, a channel buoy is normally cylindrical or can-shaped but can be any other convenient shape. A buoy's color conveys more meaning than its shape. In well-defined channels the buoys are solid colored; red marks the right side of the channel facing upstream, black or green marks the left side. In areas where the channel is indistinct or where hazards may be approached from more than one direction, buoys are white with a colored band around the top. A red horizontal top band indicates that the channel lies south or west of the buoy. A black or green horizontal top band indicates that the channel lies north or east of the buoy. A white buoy with vertical red stripes indicates that the obstruction lies between the buoy and the nearest shore. Solid or striped daymarkers may be used instead of buoys.

If the aids are numbered, the even numbers are on the all-red or red-topped buoys. Left-side channel buoys have odd numbers. The numbers get larger as they progress upstream.

Channel buoys may be lighted; if so, they will have one of three configurations: flashing, quick flashing, or occulting. Red and green lights are used on red and black buoys, respectively. All other lighted buoys show white lights.

INFORMATIONAL OR REGULATORY MARKERS

State informational markers are distinguished by their international-orange border and white background. Each of the markers or buoys shows a distinct shape, recognizable from a distance, that conveys the purpose and type of message or information found on the buoy or marker (see Table B.1).

	Table B.1 USWMS Informational Markers	
SHAPE	TYPE	TYPICAL MESSAGES
SNAG	*Diamond indicates danger*	*Rock, Snag, Dredge, Ferry Cable*
RAPIDS	*Diamond with red cross indicates danger, keep away*	*Swim Area, Dam, Waterfall, Rapids, Domestic Water*
5 MPH	*Circle indicates controlled area*	*Speed Limit, No Fishing, No Skiing, No Swimming, No Prop Boats, Skin Divers Only, No Wake*
MARINA	*Square indicates general information*	*Place names, distances, services*

MOORAGE BUOYS

State mooring buoys are white with a horizontal blue stripe around the middle of the buoy. They may show lights. Some state mooring buoys are for use by state agencies and carry markings to indicate ownership (Fish and Game, for example).

CONSTRUCTING A COMPASS DEVIATION TABLE

This is not about compass adjustment. The compass is a delicately balanced instrument that does not take kindly to people muddling about in its innards. Compass adjustment involves among other things the determination of six coefficients and solving several equations, and is best done by professionals. If you are inclined to pursue the art of compass adjustment, practice on a cheap compass and read Chapter 7 in Bowditch.[1]

Fortunately, compass deviation on most fiberglass, wooden, or aluminum recreational boats is quite low and often may not require adjustment. What is required is a table showing the residual compass deviation on each intercardinal direction. As discussed in Chapter 3, this table is helpful for proper boat handling. The four methods given differ slightly depending on the equipment available.

This process seems simple, but several frequently recommended methods do not work due to subtle pitfalls. Heading at a single point and running known courses between buoys both suffer from leeway induced by wind or current. Run-

Figure C.1 Invalid
Compass Data Due
to Leeway Error

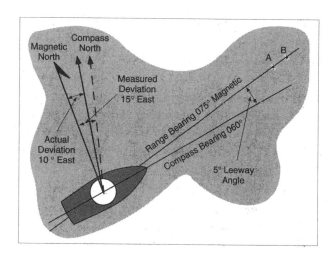

---

[1] *Nathaniel Bowditch*, American Practical Navigator, *vol. 1 (Washington, D.C.: Defense Mapping Agency, 1984),*
201–269.

ning a known course between two points also suffers because it is difficult to keep the boat on the line. Using the ship's compass, another method often recommended, is impractical because the compass lacks sighting posts and is graduated in 5-degree increments—not fine enough for an accurate elevation card. And using temporary buoys made of plastic milk bottles, a method recommended by a popular seamanship text, suffers both from leeway and from littering.

Fortunately, there are several acceptable methods for constructing a deviation table that avoid all these problems. The four methods described below use a pelorus, an azimuth ring, a hand bearing compass, or a GPS. The pelorus and azimuth ring are traditional methods often used by professional compass adjusters. Although the equipment is not normally found on recreational boats, these methods provide a background for the other methods as well as a basis on which to judge the value of a professionally generated deviation table. The hand bearing compass and GPS methods use equipment commonly found aboard recreational boats.

Preparation

First, survey the environment of the compass and remove any stray movable magnetic influences that may affect the compass reading. This includes tools and electrical devices, as well as any metal objects on the helmsperson and adjuster, such as belt buckles, pocket knives, keys, and clothing that retains static electricity like nylon. Have the certified nonmagnetic helmsperson observe the compass needle while a second crewmember switches on and off all electrical equipment—running lights, pumps, refrigerator, etc. Note the direction and amount of any deflection.

The compass should be checked for bubbles and that it is securely fastened to the binnacle with no play. If bubbles are found, have them removed by a reputable compass repair shop. The lubbers line should be checked to be sure it is on or parallel with the boat's longitudinal axis. Prepare a worksheet similar to the one shown in Figure C.2. If the pelorus method will not be used, delete or ignore the row for Pelorus data.

Next, select a location on a chart where two prominent, fixed landmarks form a known bearing in a large, open, sheltered area with light traffic. Avoid using buoys, which may be shifted by tide, wind, and accidents from their charted position. If the true bearing between the two landmarks is given, it must be converted to magnetic bearing by adding the west variation or subtracting the east variation given on the chart. (See Appendix D for greater detail.) If no bearing is given, it must be measured as accurately as possible. Use the magnetic compass rose closest to the two landmarks. Repeat the measurement until the subsequent readings agree. Record the magnetic bearing on the worksheet.

Compass Deviation Worksheet

Boat Name _____ Date _____

Range Line Bearing (β_r) _____ Page __1__ of __3__

Intercardinal Direction **North**   Average Deviation _____

Pelorus Reading (P_s)										
Magnetic Bearing										
Compass Bearing										
Deviation										

Intercardinal Direction **Northeast**   Average Deviation _____

Pelorus Reading (P_s)										
Magnetic Bearing										
Compass Bearing										
Deviation										

Intercardinal Direction **East**   Average Deviation _____

Pelorus Reading (P_s)										
Magnetic Bearing										
Compass Bearing										
Deviation										

Figure C.2
Compass
Deviation
Worksheet

A large area must be selected because the boat must make repeated passes, crossing the line of bearing from all directions. Other boat traffic should be light enough so that it will not be necessary to alter course during a compass run. The area should be free of wind and current that may produce excessive waves or heeling. Remember that the purpose of this exercise is to determine compass errors as small as a single degree. Leeway caused by current and wind may make the procedure more difficult but will not invalidate the results if the correct procedure is followed.

Swinging Ship Using a Pelorus

A pelorus is the device used most often by professional compass adjusters to determine deviation. It looks very similar to a compass, with a stationary card divided into 360 degrees, but it has no magnetic properties. It has a rotating sighting arm with front and back sight through which accurate relative bearings can be taken. The instrument is set up so that the axis of the pelorus is parallel to the boat's axis, with 0 degrees forward.

Once the boat is in the selected area, a series of short, slow runs are made across the selected range line on the eight intercardinal magnetic bearings (000, 045, 090, 135, 180, 225, 270, 315). As the boat approaches the range line, the pelorus operator alerts the helmsperson, who steadies the boat on the selected course. As the boat passes through the range line, the pelorus operator sights down the range and calls "mark." The helmsperson then reads the magnetic bearing from the compass. The magnetic bearing and the angle from the pelorus are recorded on the data sheet. Five to 10 passes are made on the same course, and the actual deviation is calculated from the average of these readings.

Normally, the opposite courses are run alternately, that is, a pass running north and then a pass running south. It is not necessary to be exactly on the desired course when the boat passes over the bearing line, because it is the difference between the pelorus reading and the compass reading that is used for the calculations. However, the boat's course should be as close as possible to the desired course to minimize errors from other sources.

Because the readings are taken instantaneously as the boat crosses the range, any leeway can be ignored. The data is reduced by first calculating the boat's actual magnetic bearing (β_m) from the pelorus reading (P_r) and the magnetic bearing (β_r) of the range line, using Equation C.1.

$$\beta_m = \beta_r - P_r \qquad\qquad \text{Eq C.1}$$

The compass deviation $(D_\emptyset)$ on that intercardinal course is calculated from the compass reading (β_c) and the calculated magnetic bearing (β_b), using Equation C.2. for each set of data.

$$D_\emptyset = \beta_c - \beta_m \qquad\qquad \text{Eq C.2}$$

The final deviation is the average of all the deviations rounded to the nearest degree. This produces an east deviation that is negative and a west deviation that is positive. This is the same sign convention used to change a magnetic bearing into a compass bearing. That is, if the compass deviation is 1 degree west, to change a 50-degree magnetic bearing into a compass bearing the 1 degree must be added and the boat's course set to 51 degrees compass. Once again, for more detail see Appendix D.

Swinging Ship Using an Azimuth Ring

An azimuth ring can take a variety of forms, but consists of a ring that fits snugly over the ship's compass. A pair of movable sighting vanes and a mirror are attached to the circle. As the boat crosses the range, the targets are sighted through the vanes and the bearing is read off the compass card through the mirror. This reading is entered into the compass bearing row on the data sheet.

The procedure and the data reduction are essentially the same as the pelorus method, except that the range line bearing is entered into the magnetic bearing row on the data sheet. The deviation is calculated using equation C.2.

Swinging ship with this equipment has three distinct disadvantages over the pelorus method. First, the ship's compass is only divided into 5-degree increments, which means that the actual course must be estimated. Second, the helmsperson and the person using the azimuth ring are fighting over the same space. Finally, the azimuth ring must fit tightly over the compass bowl or the accuracy of the bearings will suffer.

Swinging Ship Using a Hand Bearing Compass

This method takes advantage of the availability of a good hand bearing compass and the fact that deviation is a function of compass environment. The boat is taken to an environment where magnetic influences are negligible; for example, a vacant slip with no large metal objects or power lines nearby. It is necessary to have access to at least two sides of the boat, but the ideal situation is a U-shaped slip where the base of the U is larger than the boat's length. See Figure C.3.

The boat is positioned in the slip with its longitudinal axis parallel to one of the intercardinal directions and held in this position by taut docking lines. With the boat held in this position, the bearing on the ship's compass (β_c) is compared to the magnetic bearing of the boat's longitudinal axis taken from the dock with the hand bearing compass (β_h). It is not necessary to use the data sheet with this procedure. The deviation is calculated by subtracting the two bearings as shown in Equation C.3

$$D_\emptyset = \beta_c - \beta_h$$ **Eq C.3**

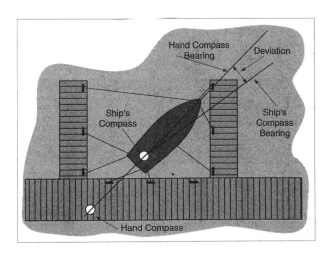

Figure C.3 Swinging Ship
with a Hand Bearing
Compass

This produces the usual sign convention, with an east deviation that is negative and a west that is positive. The docking lines are shifted so that the longitudinal axis of the boat is shifted to a different intercardinal direction, and the process is repeated until the boat has been positioned on all eight compass points. Again, the boat does not need to be set exactly on the intercardinal direction, because it is the *difference* between the compass readings that is important. The boat's position should be as close as possible to the desired direction, aligned on an even 5 degree increment, and the two courses read simultaneously to minimize errors.

Swinging Ship Using the GPS

This method takes advantage of the accuracy of the global positioning system, which without differential or selective availability is about 300 feet. The angular accuracy required to swing ship is about 1 degree. The combination of these conditions requires that the boat be about 2 miles from the designated sighting point. The selected sighting point should be prominent enough to be easily seen from a distance of 2 miles, approachable within 20 feet, and located in the center of a large body of water such that a circle with a 2-mile radius can negotiated without running aground. If a single point cannot be found that fits these requirements, use two or three points. A fixed mark is preferred but a buoy can be used, even though they wander somewhat; the angular error introduced by this wandering is made insignificant by the distance the boat is away from the buoy when the data is actually gathered.

The first step is to approach the mark and record its position in the GPS. This reduces the error in the GPS and any error contained in the charted position. Then take the boat on any intercardinal direction away from the buoy a distance of 2 miles. The process of gathering the data is best performed with three people: one to read the magnetic bearing on the GPS, one to read the compass, and one to steer. When the GPS indicates that the boat is more than 2 miles away from the sighting point, turn 180° and head back toward the point on the reciprocal of the original intercardinal direction. When the boat is heading directly back at the buoy, the helmsperson calls "mark," and the other two people read the compass heading and the GPS heading. The GPS reading is entered into the magnetic bearing row and the compass heading into the compass bearing row on the data sheet.

Repeat this process 5 to 10 times and average the results. The readings must be taken instantaneously and when the helmsperson is heading exactly at the sighting point to avoid leeway error. It is again not necessary for the boat to be exactly on the intercardinal bearings.

The boat is then moved around the 2-mile circle until the GPS indicates that the sighting point bears in a different intercardinal direction from the boat. The data-gathering process is repeated here and at each intercardinal point around the perimeter of the circle. The data is reduced by calculating the deviation for each set of GPS (β_g) and compass bearings (β_c) using Equation C.4. The final deviation for that intercardinal direction is the average of all the deviations to the nearest degree.

$$D_\emptyset = \beta_c - \beta_g \qquad\qquad\text{Eq C.4}$$

The results have the usual east-west sign convention. If GPS has differential correction or the government turns off selective availability, the circle radius can be reduced to a quarter mile.

Conclusions

A table, similar to Table 3.1 in Chapter 3, should be made listing the deviation for each of the eight cardinal directions and stored in the navigation area. If the deviations are greater than 2 or 3 degrees, the compass should be adjusted. The compass deviation should be checked every few years, and steel-hulled craft should check the deviation table if they move to a new location where the compass variation changes more than 5 degrees.

D

DISTANCE AND BEARINGS CALCULATIONS

It is *possible* that a recreational boater will need to calculate the distance and bearing between two points on the earth. However, the probability of this occurring is about the same as the probability that it may become necessary to calculate the same two factors on Mars. Fortunately, in either case, any of the following four methods will work: graphically, by plotting the points on a chart and measuring the desired values; electronically, by inputting the coordinates into an electronic navigation instrument as waypoints; by using a programmable navigational calculator; or by hand calculation using methods traditionally known as *sailings*. That term should indicate how long ago these methods were in vogue. The first three methods need no instructions, so this appendix will concentrate on sailings.

SAILINGS

On a flat plane, the shortest distance between two points is a straight line. On a globe this is not the case, however; there are two ways to go at any given destination: straight at it or the shortest distance. A linear course straight at the destination is called a *rhumb line*, and allows the navigator to hold a single course on a globe from the beginning to the end of the voyage. The shortest distance between two points is called a *great circle* course. The problem is, on great circle courses the bearing changes constantly.

The differences between the distance traveled by the two methods become larger as the course trends more to the east and west, the latitude increases, and the distance between the two end points gets larger. Because the differences between rhumb line and great circle courses are small if the distances involved are very small, most great circle courses are run as a sequence of short rhumb line courses. However, present technology allows them to be run directly using an autopilot connected to the GPS.

There are many ways to calculate the distances and bearings needed for each of these courses. Only three are given here: middle latitude sailings and Mercator sailings, which both give rhumb line courses, and the sight reduction method for the great circle course. For others, see Bowditch.[1]

---

[1] *Nathaniel Bowditch*, American Practical Navigator, *vol. 2 (Washington, D.C.: Defense Mapping Agency, 1984)*, 575–620.

Middle Latitude Sailings

The middle latitude method assumes that the surface of the earth is a plane and is only accurate for distances less than a few hundred miles. The method involves standard trigonometric equations and rectangular coordinate geometry.

In Figure D.1, two points Start and Finish are shown with the coordinates of 45°36'22" N, 125°51'17" W and 46°16'38" N, 124°12'52" W respectively.

In order to calculate the distance and bearing between these two points by using the middle latitude sailing method, it is first necessary to get the distance between the two points in the north-south direction (D_{ns}) and in the east-west direction (D_{ew}). The actual distance (D) between the two points is then calculated by using the Pythagorean theorem, and the bearing (β) by using standard trigonometric relationships.

North-South Distance

The north-south distance (D_{ns}) in nautical miles is the difference between the latitudes of the two points in minutes:

$$D_{ns} = Lat_1 - Lat_2 \text{ or } Lat_2 - Lat_1 \qquad \textbf{Eq D.1}$$

$$Lat_2 - Lat_1 = \begin{array}{ccc} 46° & 16' & 38" \\ \underline{45} & \underline{36} & \underline{22} \end{array}$$

Note: The order in which the latitude of the points is subtracted is unimportant when determining the difference between the latitudes. Converting 1 degree into minutes and performing the subtraction gives:

$$Lat_2 - Lat_1 = \begin{array}{ccc} 45° & 76' & 38" \\ \underline{45} & \underline{36} & \underline{22} \\ & 40 & 16 \end{array}$$

It is convenient to convert 16 seconds back into a fractional part of a minute because of the equivalence of minutes of latitude and nautical miles, as follows:

$$16"/60" = 0.267' \text{ or (nautical miles), and}$$

$$(D_{ns}) = 40 + 0.267 = 40.27 \text{ nautical miles.}$$

Therefore, the north-south distance is 40.27 nautical miles.

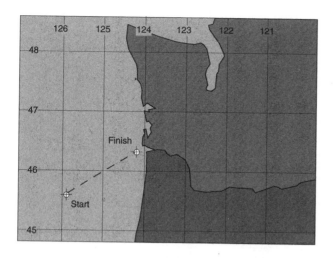

**Figure D.1 Rhumb Line
Sailing Problem**

East-West Distance

Because latitude lines converge as they move away from the equator, the distance between the two points in the east-west direction (D_{ew}) is dependent on the latitude of the two points. The east-west distance between any two points on the same latitude is equal to

$$D_{ew} = (Long_1 - Long_2) \cos Lat \qquad \text{Eq D.2}$$

However, in most instances the two points are not on the same latitude, and some sort of mathematical trickery must be used. The type of trickery varies from simple and inaccurate to accurate and complex, and in general gives its name to the sailing methods. Since this method is called the middle latitude method, it follows that the average latitude (Lat_{ave}) of the two points will be used. This is the simple but inaccurate method. However, if the points are within a few hundred miles of one another, the loss of accuracy is negligible. Using the middle latitude method yields the following equation for east and west distance:

$$D_{ew} = (Long_1 - Long_2) \cos Lat_{ave} \qquad \text{Eq D.3}$$

Applying this equation to the example problem, it is necessary to first calculate the difference in longitude:

$$(\text{Long}_1 - \text{Long}_2) = \quad 125° \quad 51' \quad 17''$$
$$\underline{124 \quad 12 \quad 52}$$

Again, convert 1 minute to seconds:

$$(\text{Long}_1 - \text{Long}_2) = \quad 125° \quad 50' \quad 77''$$
$$\underline{124 \quad 12 \quad 52}$$
$$1 \quad 38 \quad 25$$

and convert the degrees and seconds into minutes so the calculations can be done in nautical miles:

$$(\text{Long}_1 - \text{Long}_2) = 60 + 38 + 25/60 = 98.417 \text{ minutes of longitude.}$$

There are several ways to calculate the average of a number, for example $(\text{Lat}_2 + \text{Lat}_1)/2$. All of the methods apply to average latitude, select whichever you desire. The method given here was chosen because $(\text{Lat}_2 - \text{Lat}_1)$ has already been calculated and is known.

$$\text{Lat}_{ave} = (\text{Lat}_2 - \text{Lat}_1)/2 + \text{Lat}_1 \qquad\qquad \textbf{Eq D.4}$$

$$\text{Lat}_{ave} = (40'16'')/2 + 45°36'22''$$

$$= 20'08'' + 45°36'22'' = 45°56'30''$$

or, again converting to nautical miles,

$$\text{Lat}_{ave} = 45 + (56 + 30/60)/60 = 45 + (56.5)/60 = 45.941 \text{ degrees.}$$

Once the angle is found, the cosine of the angle can be obtained by using a scientific hand calculator or a standard trig table. The calculator manual or any introductory book on trigonometry will explain the respective procedures. The easiest and most accurate method to use is the scientific calculator, which will show the cosine to be equal to

$$\cos 45.941° = 0.695399738.$$

Now that the average latitude has been calculated, the east-west distance (D_{ew}) can be found using Equation D.3, as follows:

$$D_{ew} = (Long_1 - Long_2) \cos Lat_{ave}$$

$$D_{ew} = (98.417) \cos 45.941° = 98.417 \times 0.695399738$$

$$D_{ew} = 68.44 \text{ nautical miles.}$$

Once the two coordinate distances are calculated, the final distance (D) and bearing (β) are found by using the Pythagorean theorem and fundamental trigonometric functions:

$$D = \sqrt{D_{ew}^2 + D_{ns}^2} \qquad\qquad \text{Eq D.5}$$

$$D = \sqrt{68.44^2 + 40.27^2} = \sqrt{4684.03 + 1621.67} = \sqrt{6305.7}$$

$$= \underline{79.41 \text{ nautical miles}}$$

Bearing

To calculate the bearing it is necessary to first calculate an intermediate angle ($\emptyset$), and then by inspection calculate the bearing (β):

$$\emptyset = \arctan (D_{ew} / D_{ns}). \qquad\qquad \text{Eq D.6}$$

The arctangent, or the angle whose tangent is equal to the calculated number, can again be found by using either a trig table or a scientific calculator. The scientific calculator is again the simplest and most accurate method.

$$\emptyset = \arctan (D_{ew}/D_{ns}) = \arctan (68.44/40.27)$$

$$= \arctan (1.699528185) = 59.52 \text{ degrees.}$$

Notice that the angle $\emptyset$ is not a bearing. A bearing is an angle relative to a reference point, and as yet $\emptyset$ has no reference point. To derive bearing from this angle it is necessary to know the direction of travel and set the reference point. If the reference point is true north, the proper equation used to calculate bearing depending on the direction of travel is given in Table D.1

Table D.1 Bearing Equations	
DIRECTION	EQUATION
North and East	$\beta = \emptyset$
South and East	$\beta = 180° - \emptyset$
South and West	$\beta = 180° + \emptyset$
North and West	$\beta = 360° - \emptyset$

In the example problem, because the boat is traveling north and east, the bearing is equal to the angle $\emptyset$.

$$\beta = 59.52 \text{ or } \pm 60° \text{ true.}$$

Summary

To summarize the above exercise, Distance is equal to

$$D = \sqrt{((\text{Long}_1 - \text{Long}_2) \cos (\text{Lat}_{ave}))^2 + (\text{Lat}_1 - \text{Lat}^2)^2} \quad \textbf{Eq D.7}$$

Bearing is calculated from Table D.1, and the angle $\emptyset$ is found using this equation:

$$\emptyset = \arctan [(\text{Long}_1 - \text{Long}_2) \cos \text{Lat}_{ave} / (\text{Lat}_2 - \text{Lat}_1)] \quad \textbf{Eq D.8}$$

where Long_1, Long_2, Lat_1 and Lat_2, are all in minutes and Lat_{ave} is in degrees.

Mercator Sailings

The Mercator method assumes that the surface of the earth is transformed into a plane mathematically using Mercator's equations of transformation. This method is a little more involved because it requires the use of meridional parts. The basic equations are very similar, but the angle between the course line and the latitude lines ($\emptyset$) is calculated first. Once this angle is known the distance can be easily calculated using standard trigonometric relationships:

$$\emptyset = \arctan(\text{Long}_1 - \text{Long}_2/m) \qquad\qquad \textbf{Eq D.9}$$

where   m is the difference between the meridional parts (M) at each
latitude and is expressed in minutes, or

$$m = (M_1 - M_2) \text{ in minutes} \qquad\qquad \textbf{Eq D.10}$$

Recall that on a Mercator projection the degrees of latitude are shown progressively longer than the degrees of longitude as the distance from the equator increases. The meridional parts are the number of minutes of equatorial latitude that are added between the higher latitude lines in order to keep the angle relationship true and construct the projection (see Figure D.2).

The number of meridional parts can be found in tables[2] or can be calculated using the following formula:[3]

$$M = 7915.704468 \text{ Log tan}(45 + \text{Lat}/2) - 23.0133633 \text{ Sin (Lat)}$$
$$- 0.051353 \sin^3(\text{Lat}) - 0.000206 \sin^5(\text{Lat}) - \cdots. \qquad \textbf{Eq D.11}$$

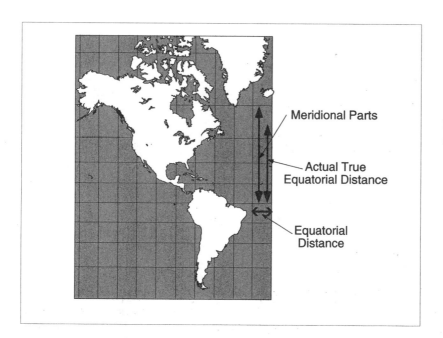

Meridional Parts

Actual True
Equatorial Distance

Equatorial
Distance

Figure D.2
Meridional
Parts

[2]*Bowditch, 115–123.*
[3]*Bowditch, 5.*

For the accuracy required by recreational boaters only the first two terms of this equation are needed. For example, calculating the number of meridional parts for the same problem shown in Figure D.1 produces

$$M_1 = 7915.704468 \text{ Log tan } (45 + 45.606/2) - 23.0133633 \text{ Sin } (45.606)$$

$$M_1 = 7915.704468 \text{ Log tan } (67.803) - 23.0133633 \text{ Sin } (45.606)$$

$$M_1 = 7915.704468 \text{ Log } (2.4507988) - 23.0133633(.7145494)$$

$$M_1 = 7915.704468 \ (.38930766) - 16.444$$

$$M_1 = 3081.644 - 16.444 = 3065.20.$$

Similarly, M_2 equals

$$M_2 = 3139.550 - 16.731 = 3122.819$$

From Equation D.9, the difference between meridional parts (m) equals

$$m = M_1 - M_2 = 3065.2 - 3122.819 = 57.619$$

The angle Ø from Equation D.8 then equals

$$\text{Ø} = \text{arctan } (Long_1 - Long_2/m)$$

$$= \text{arctan } ((125°51'17'' - 124°12'52'')/57.619)$$

$$= \text{arctan } (98.417/57.619) = \text{arctan } (1.70806505)$$

$$\text{Ø} = 59.65 \text{ degrees.}$$

This compares with the mid-latitude method's angle of 59.52°. In this instance the 0.13-degree difference in course certainly cannot be steered by a recreational boater. The bearing is calculated from this angle in a manner similar to that discussed above using Table D.1:

$$\underline{\beta = 59.65 \text{ or } \pm 60° \text{ true.}}$$

The distance is calculated through the trigonometric relationship using the following formula:

$$D = (Lat_1 - Lat_2)\,sec\emptyset \qquad\qquad Eq\ D.12$$

where $Lat_1 - Lat_2$ are in minutes or nautical miles. If your calculator or trig tables do not contain secants, recall that $(sec\emptyset)$ is equal to $1/cos\emptyset$.

$$D = (45°36'22'' - 46°16'38'')\,sec\ 59.65$$

$$D = (2736.3667 - 2776.6333)1.97909723$$

$$\underline{D = (40.2667)1.97909723 = 79.69\ nautical\ miles.}$$

Compared with the middle latitude method of 79.41 miles, the error in the middle latitude method is about a quarter of a mile. This error is not significant under normal conditions where the final position can be corrected visually, but is certainly much larger than that found in the GPS.

Great Circle Sailings
There are several different methods used to calculate great circle sailings, all based upon spherical trigonometry. The one given here is derived from sight reduction formulas.[4]

$$D = arc\ cosine\ (sin\ (Lat_1)\ sin\ (Lat_2)$$
$$+ cos\ (Lat_1)\ cos\ (Lat_2)\ cos\ (Long_1 - Long_2)) \qquad Eq\ D.13$$

$$\emptyset = arctan\ (sin(Long_1 - Long_2)/(cos\ (Lat_1)\ tan\ (Lat_2)$$
$$- sin\ (Lat_1)\ cos\ (Long_1 - Long_2)) \qquad\qquad Eq\ D.14$$

The sign convention observed with this set of equations is that if the latitude direction (north or south) of the destination differs from that of the point of departure, then the latitude of the destination is treated as a negative angle. This only occurs if the course crosses the equator. The sine and tangent of negative angles change the sign of the trig function itself. The cosine of a negative angle is still positive. If the course passes over longitude 0° or 180°, the longitudinal difference

---

[4]*Bowditch, 612.*

(Long$_1$ – Long$_2$) can be seen to be equal to the sum of the two longitudes (Long$_1$ + Long$_2$) or (180 – Long$_1$ + 180 – Long$_2$) respectively (see Figure D.3).

To demonstrate this method, assume a point of departure at latitude 52°47'02" N longitude 130°05'42" W and a destination of latitude 41°35'12" N longitude 149°23'23" E. From E D.12, the distance equals

$$D = \text{arc cosine } ((\sin (\text{Lat}_1) \sin (\text{Lat}_2)$$
$$+ \cos (\text{Lat}_1) \cos (\text{Lat}_2) \cos (\text{Long}_1 - \text{Long}_2))$$

$$D = \text{arc cosine } ((\sin (52°47'02") \sin (41°35'12")$$
$$+ \cos (52°47'02") \cos (41°35'12") \cos (\text{Long}_1 - \text{Long}_2)).$$

Because the course passes over longitude 180°, the angular difference between the two longitudes is the sum of the each longitude subtracted from 180°:

$$\text{Long}_1 - \text{Long}_2 = 180° - \text{Long}_1 + 180° - \text{Long}_2$$

$$\text{Long}_1 - \text{Long}_2 = 180° - 130°05'42" + 180° - 149°23'23"$$

$$\text{Long}_1 - \text{Long}_2 = 49°54'18" + 30°36'37"$$

$$\text{Long}_1 - \text{Long}_2 = 80°30'55";$$

Figure D.3 Sign
Convention Used for
Great Circle Calculations

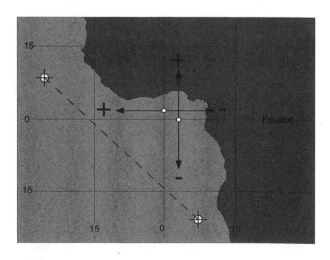

therefore,

$$D = \text{arc cosine} \, ((\sin (52°47'02'') \sin (41°35'12'')$$
$$+ \cos (52°47'02'') \cos (41°35'12'') \cos (80°30'55''))$$

$$D = \text{arc cosine} \, (0.79635988 \times 0.66375217)$$
$$+ (0.60482307 \times 0.74795257 \times 0.16478461)$$

$$D = \text{arc cosin} \, (0.52858560 + 0.07454509) = \text{arc cosin}$$
$$(0.60313069 \,)$$

$$\underline{D = 52.9055° \text{ or } 3174\,.33 \text{ nautical miles.}}$$

The intermediate angle calculated from Equation D.13 equals

$$\emptyset = \text{arctan} \, (\sin (\text{Long}_1 - \text{Long}_2)/(\cos (\text{Lat}_1) \tan (\text{Lat}_2)$$
$$- \sin (\text{Lat}_1) \cos (\text{Long}_1 - \text{Long}_2))$$

$$\emptyset = \text{arctan} \, (\sin (80°30'55'')/(\cos (52°47'02'') \tan (41°35'12'')$$
$$- \sin (52°47'02'') \cos (80°30'55''))$$

$$\emptyset = \text{arctan} \, (0.98632958/(0.60482307 \times 0.88742548 - 0.79635988$$
$$\times 0.16478461))$$

$$\emptyset = \text{arctan} \, (0.98632958/(0.53673541 - 0.13122785))$$

$$\emptyset = \text{arctan} \, (0.98632958/0.40550755)$$

$$\emptyset = \text{arctan} \, (2.43233343)$$

$$\emptyset = 67.65107155° = 67°39'03.85' \_ 68°$$

Because the boat is heading south and west, the bearing from Table D.1 is equal to

$$\underline{\beta = 180° + 68° = 248° \text{ True.}}$$

Summary

It is informative to calculate and compare the distances and bearings for this example problem using each of the various methods. The results are shown in Table D.2.

SAILING METHOD	DISTANCE	BEARING
Middle Latitude	3283.25	270°
Mercator	3344.99	258°
Great Circle	3174.33	248°

Table D.2 Comparison of Results

Comparing the middle latitude and the Mercator rhumb line sailings, we can see that the error caused by using the simpler middle latitude method for large distances is now some 40 miles. This demonstrates why this method should not be used for large distances. Comparing the Mercator rhumb line and the Great Circle methods shows that the great circle path will save about 170 miles distance and about two days in time in exchange for the extra trouble of daily course changes.

CONVERTING TRUE BEARINGS TO COMPASS BEARINGS

Recall that a bearing is an angle relative to a reference point. A true bearing's reference point is true north. A magnetic bearing's reference point is magnetic north. A compass bearing's reference point is the ship's compass.

It is possible to commit these processes to memory by a rational method or by memorizing several silly mnemonic phrases. But because the average recreational boater will rarely need this procedure, the best way is just to remember to look it up in this book.

True to Magnetic

The difference between a true and a magnetic bearing is the compass variation at a particular location. As discussed in Chapter 3, this difference changes as the location of the compass changes, because true north and magnetic north are not in the same spot. To convert a true bearing to a magnetic bearing it is necessary to know the compass variation for the area in which the compass is located. This is generally given on the chart of the area.

The procedure differs depending upon whether the variation is east or west. To convert true bearing (β) to magnetic bearing, if the variation (V) is west, then

$$\beta \text{ Magnetic} = \beta \text{ true} + V. \qquad \text{Eq D.15}$$

If the variation is east,

$$\beta \text{ Magnetic} = \beta \text{ true} - V. \qquad\qquad \text{Eq D.16}$$

If there is any need to convert compass bearing to true, simply perform the necessary algebra on these equations.

Magnetic to Compass

The difference between magnetic and compass bearings is the compass deviation. As discussed in Chapter 3, deviation depends on the location of the compass in the boat's magnetic fields. In most cases this deviation can be reduced to a degree or so by a compass adjuster and then ignored. However, for those too cheap to have their compass corrected properly, converting a magnetic bearing to a compass bearing requires that the compass deviation for each 45 degrees be known (see Appendix C).

The conversion process also depends upon whether the deviation is east or west. To convert magnetic bearing (β) to compass bearing, if the deviation (d) is west, then

$$\beta \text{ compass} = \beta \text{ magnetic} + d.$$

If the deviation is east,

$$\beta \text{ Compass} = \beta \text{ magnetic} - d.$$

True to Compass

To go from true to compass bearing, there are several different possible equations depending on the directions of the variation and deviation. Rather than list all the possible equations needed for a single-step process, I suggest you use the above two steps in the correct sequence, true to magnetic to compass or, heaven forbid, compass to magnetic to true. If a single equation is desired, it is necessary to assume that clockwise angles or east angles are positive and west angles are negative; then the following single relationship can be written:

$$\beta \text{ True} = \beta \text{ Compass} + V + d. \qquad\qquad \text{Eq D.17}$$

This yields

$$\beta \text{ Compass} = \beta \text{ true} - V - d. \qquad\qquad \text{Eq D.18}$$

Equation D.15 will be used most often and will give the same results as the two-step process if you remember that $- (-\text{ value})$ is a $+$ value.

E

MEASURING ANCHOR HOLDING POWER

This appendix describes a series of tests that allows the normal anchor setting procedure to become a useful test of anchor holding power, specific to the boat, anchor, and bottom conditions. This information will allow you to predict the performance of the anchor in various wind conditions. The results are summarized in two tables, one for the wind loads on the anchor and the other for the engine's load on the anchor, which can be converted into anchor strength.

EQUIPMENT

You'll need the following equipment:

1. A tachometer on the engine
2. A wind velocity indicator
3. A scale for measuring tension in a line
4. One long 1/2-diameter line (± 50 feet)
5. Two short 1/4-inch lines (± 5 feet)
6. A four-part tackle
7. A notebook and pencil
8. An immovable object (piling or large bit on a pier)

Except for the scale, all of this equipment is more than likely already aboard the boat. Getting the proper scale can be difficult. The most accurate device is a dynamometer or crane scale. These devices are expensive, but in large metropolitan areas it is possible to rent them from firms specializing in selling, repairing, and calibrating scales. The crane scale should have a capacity of about 500 pounds and should read to the nearest pound.

If you cannot obtain a dynamometer, a high-quality fishing scale can be used. These scales should have a capacity greater than 100 pounds. Avoid inexpensive scales, because the springs will not return to zero after being loaded to their maximum rating, making them extremely inaccurate.

The low capacity of these scales combined with the high loads expected during the testing may require the use of a four-part tackle. This combination is a bit more cumbersome and not quite as accurate as the dynamometer. I shall assume the worst and describe the experimental procedure using the fish scale.

DATA GATHERING

Engine Loads

The first step is to find the relationship between engine RPM and the pull the boat can develop in reverse. On a windless day, attach the boat to the immovable object using the long line. The immovable object must be strong enough to take the full load of the engine without moving. The area around the object should be free and clear of any obstructions to allow your boat to move in any direction while tethered to the object by only the single long line.

Here we will assume that the immovable object is a piling, although it doesn't have to be. Bring the other end of the long line over the bow and attach this line to the scale. Using one of the short lines, attach the scale to a secure cleat, bit, or mast on the boat. Note that the four-part tackle is not used until the engine loads are close to the maximum scale capacity. The scale must be in a position where it can be easily read during the test.

At this point, the boat should be attached to the piling from the bow by a single tether consisting of two lines separated by the scale, as shown in Figure E.1. Station a crewmember at the throttle, where he can read the tachometer, and another crewmember where he can read the scale. The crewmember at the scale

Figure E.1 Attaching the Scale to the Boat and Piling

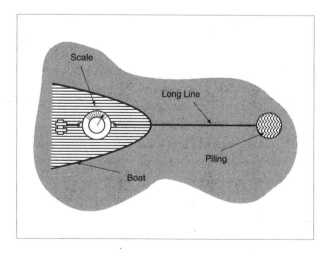

should be equipped with the notebook and pencil. You are now ready to begin the test.

The crewmember at the helm throttles back the engine to minimum RPM and puts the boat in reverse. The boat will pull away from the piling and slowly put load on the line. During this loading process the crewmember on the scale should continually monitor it to ensure that it is not loaded above its capacity. If it nears its capacity, the person on the throttle should immediately be informed so that the test can be halted and the four-part tackle inserted into the system. If the scale is not overloaded, eventually the boat will come to equilibrium, and the load on the line will be steady or reasonably so, varying by only a few pounds.

The crewmember on the scale then records that load and RPM. The rest of the data is gathered in a similar manner by increasing the boat's RPM in steps and recording the resulting loads on the scale after each step. Ten steps in RPM will probably be adequate. Once maximum RPM is reached, reduce the RPM in similar steps and again record the loads. The loads and RPM values should be similar going up and down; if they are not, repeat the process another time and use the average values.

If during loading it appears that the load will be too large for the scale, take the engine out of gear and rig the four-part tackle. This is very likely to occur sometime during the test. When this occurs, remove the scale from the tether system and replace it with the tackle. Secure the tailing line of the tackle to one end of the scale and attach the other end of the scale to a cleat with the second short line, as shown in Figure E.2. Continue the test as above, except that now the scale readings must be multiplied by the number of parts in the tackle, in this case four.

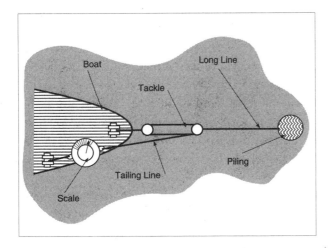

Figure E.2 Attaching the Scale Using the Tackle

It may seem simpler to rig the tackle initially, but with the tackle in, the load is measured to the nearest 4 pounds instead of the nearest pound. During the initial part of the test, where the loads are light, the 4 pounds may be as much as 20 percent of the load, but once the load reaches about 100 pounds the error is only 4 percent.

If during this experiment the maximum load is only about one-third of scale capacity, the scale will have sufficient capacity to repeat the process in forward gear. This information can be used to obtain the anchor load due to current drag. In most instances, current loads are small and can be ignored, but if sufficient scale capacity is available this information is useful and might as well be gathered. Also, in severe weather where holding power of the anchor is important, it may be advisable to set the anchor in forward gear, where more power can be applied.

As mentioned earlier, it is best to perform this experiment on a windless day. If this can't be done or the wind picks up during the test, orient the boat so that the pull on the line is either directly into or away from the wind. It will then be necessary to note the wind velocity and direction at each step of RPM. With this information the loads on the line caused by the wind can be subtracted or added to the loads caused by the engine.

Wind Loads

The next step is to gather information to derive the relationship between the wind velocity and the drag on the boat. Obviously, it is necessary to choose a day when the wind is blowing, preferably about 10 knots with few gusts. The loads due to the wind are obtained in a manner similar to that used above, except that in this case the loads will generally be lighter and it is only necessary to get the loads with the bow attached to the piling. Because these loads should be less than 100 pounds, the boat can be connected to the piling without the four-part tackle.

For this test the engine is off; a little more patience is required because the wind and the load on the line will both be continually changing. Pick a nominal wind velocity, and then get 5 to 10 load and velocity measurements as close to that velocity as possible. Record the instantaneous wind velocity and load. During this process the boat may not lie head to the wind and may change its position constantly. If this is the case you will want to get the maximum loads as the boat moves back and forth. This will generally be when the boat presents the maximum amount of beam to the wind.

If the wind velocity varies sufficiently during the test, pick another nominal velocity significantly higher or lower than the first velocity and get an additional 5 to 10 readings around that velocity. One velocity is sufficient, but two or more are desirable because they will allow the results to be checked.

DATA REDUCTION

Wind Data

Once the field testing is completed, the next step is to reduce the wind velocity data and plot a wind velocity anchor load curve for your boat. You will recall from Chapter 4 that the drag on the anchor line can be obtained from equation E.1:

$$D = 0.004 \times S \times V^2 \qquad\qquad \text{Eq E.1}$$

where   D = Drag or anchor load,
S = Effective area of your boat, and
V = Wind velocity.

What is unknown in this equation is your specific boat's effective area (S). In Chapter 4 we gave several methods for estimating that effective area. The data obtained from the wind field testing can now be used to obtain an exact effective area for your boat.

To make Equation E.1 more useful for this purpose, it can be rearranged to

$$S = 250 \times D/V^2 \qquad\qquad \text{Eq E.2}$$

Where   D = the average drag measured in the experiment, and
V = the average wind velocity relative to that drag.

To solve for S, select the data set from one nominal wind velocity and calculate the average velocity and load from this data. This can be done by adding all the velocities together and dividing by the number of velocities. Do the same with the load measurements. This will provide the average wind velocity (V) and the average drag (D) to be used in Equation E.2. Substitute these values in the equation and solve for the effective area (S) by multiplying the average drag value by 250 and dividing by the average velocity squared.

If you have data from more than one nominal wind velocity, use the average values of load and velocity for each different nominal value and solve for separate effective areas, then average the effective area values to get a final effective area value.

Once the effective area is found for one wind velocity, theoretically it is the same for all wind velocities, and the drag equation, Equation E.1, can be used to solve for the corresponding loads. These loads can be used in predicting the strength of your anchor. Table E.1 can be used to simplify this process. The numbers in the second column are 0.004 multiplied by the wind velocity squared. To obtain the anchor loads in column three for each corresponding wind velocity, multiply your boat's effective area by the factor in column two and write that value in column three.

Table E.1 Custom Anchor Loads		
WIND VELOCITY IN KNOTS	FACTOR	ANCHOR LOAD IN POUNDS
5	0.1	
10	0.4	
15	0.9	
20	1.6	
25	2.5	
30	3.6	
35	4.9	
40	6.4	
45	8.1	
50	10	
55	12.1	
60	14.4	
65	16.9	
70	19.6	
75	22.5	

The data can be kept in table form or plotted as a curve. The table provides more accurate values for specific wind velocities, but loads for wind velocities not shown in the table are easier to obtain from a curve. If the curve format is used, it is best to make two plots using two different scales, one for 0 to 30 knots of wind and another for 0 to 75 knots of wind. Figure E.3 is an example of a curve for a boat whose effective area (Aa) is 100 for velocities below 30 knots.

The second curve should be plotted to show information for higher wind velocities, as shown in Figure E.4. Using the higher-velocity curve alone obscures detail in the lower-velocity portion of the curve.

Since these curves are plotted using an effective area of 100, the values from these curves can also be used to find the wind loads on your boat. To do this it is

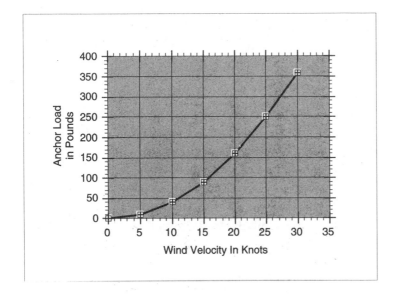

Figure E.3 Anchor
Loads for
Light Winds

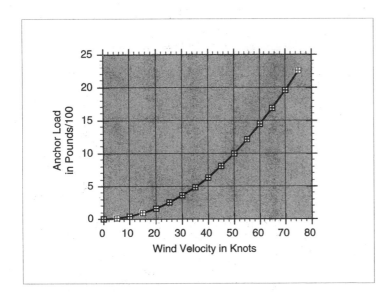

Figure E.4 Full Wind
Load Curve

necessary to multiply corresponding values obtained from these curves by the effective windage area (S) of your boat and then divide the result by 100. Using any of the resulting tables and curves, the line loads on the anchor now can be easily forecast for any expected wind.

Engine Data

The next step is to reduce the engine load data and plot a ship's power curve as shown in Figure E.5, relating the engine RPM to the amount of pull registered by the dynamometer. It is easiest to plot this curve if a table is made listing the load and RPM. The load in this table should be the average of all the readings recorded at each specific RPM. If the wind was blowing during the testing period, the force due to the wind can be estimated by using your curve corresponding to Figure E.3. Depending upon the direction of the wind, the load due to that wind velocity can be added (wind blowing in the direction of the pull) or subtracted (wind against the direction of the pull).

The reverse curve is the most useful and should be plotted alone to maximize the accuracy of the values taken from the curve. If forward gear data is available, plot it on a second curve or a separate axis to preserve this accuracy.

Figure E.5 Ship's Power Curve

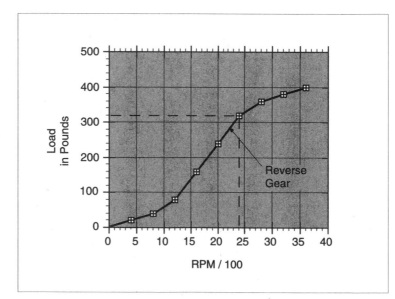

Composite Curve Construction

The final step in reducing the data requires the use of the tables and curves constructed above to produce a composite curve. First, a fourth column, RPM in reverse, is added to Table E.1 so that it looks like Table E.2. Enter in this new column the RPM in reverse taken from the ship's power curve, corresponding to the load shown in column three of the table. For example, if the anchor load is 310 pounds, the corresponding RPM in reverse from Figure E.5 would be 2400.

WIND VELOCITY IN KNOTS	FACTOR	ANCHOR LOAD IN POUNDS	RPM IN REVERSE
Table E.2 Custom Anchor Loads			
5	0.1		
10	0.4		
15	0.9		
20	1.6		
25	2.5		
30	3.6		
35	4.9	310	2400

From the first and last columns in this table, you can develop a wind-anchor capacity curve that is boat specific (see Figure E.6). Using this wind-anchor capacity curve the holding conditions can now be checked during the normal anchor setting procedure established in Chapter 4, with the additional step of noting the maximum RPM, or the RPM that caused the anchor to drag.

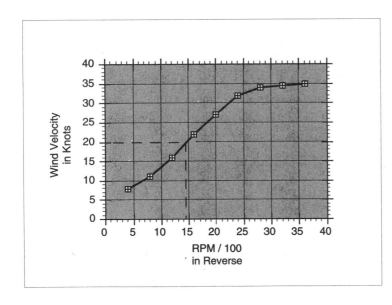

Figure E.6 Wind-Anchor Capacity Curve

Using this RPM and entering the above constructed wind-anchor capacity curve, the minimum wind velocity your anchor will sustain without pulling can be found. If this wind velocity is greater than any possible wind that might occur during the anchoring period, the boat is secure. If not, reset your anchor, use a different anchor, or post an anchor watch. For example, if you expect a 20-knot wind, the RPM in reverse during setting of the anchor should be greater than 1450 RPM. The farther above 1450 RPM, the more soundly the skipper will sleep.

Make a couple of copies of this curve and put them in plastic sheet protectors. Stow one on the boat for use and the other one in a safe place in case the first one gets tattered or lost. The loads calculated do not reflect any load due to wave action or current drag. Under normal conditions, both of these values are negligible because areas with current and wave action are generally avoided when selecting an anchoring position.

LOADS DUE TO CURRENT

If current loads are of interest and data on the ship's power curve for forward gear is available, you can perform one more test. Again, pick a day without wind and an area without current or waves. Ideally, there should be a measured mile available.

Run the measured mile in two directions 180 degrees apart and at 10 different engine RPMs, ranging from idle to maximum in about 10 steps. Record the RPM, the apparent wind velocity, and the time required to run each mile in both directions on a form similar to that shown in Table E.3. Repeat this process a few times for each given RPM. While collecting this data, be sure that the boat reaches a steady speed at each of the selected RPMs before entering the measured mile.

It is the speed of the boat through the water that is important. This can be obtained from knotmeters, but is not as accurate as timing a measured mile in both directions and averaging the time to eliminate current effects. Speed values obtained from loran or GPS readings are of little value since they record speed over the ground.

Data Reduction
To reduce the data, construct a table similar to Table E.4. The first column in the table contains the average boat velocity, calculated by dividing the average time value taken from the data sheet by 60. If the distance run was other than a measured mile, multiply this average time value by the length of the course run in nautical miles to get velocity. The second column is the average RPM taken from the data sheet.

Table E.3 Field Data for Current Testing

RPM	TIME BACK IN MINUTES	TIME OUT IN MINUTES	AVERAGE TIME IN MINUTES	WIND VELOCITY IN KNOTS
Average				

Table E.4 Custom Current Loads

1. BOAT VELOCITY IN KNOTS	2. RPM	3. FORWARD LOAD IN POUNDS	4. WIND VELOCITY	5. WIND LOAD IN POUNDS	6. CURRENT LOAD IN POUNDS

Figure E.7 Current Loads

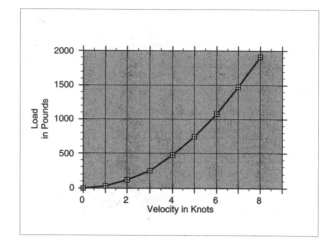

In column three, enter the load value obtained from a curve similar to Figure E.5, only plotted using the forward gear data, corresponding to the listed RPM in column two. In column four, enter the average apparent wind velocity taken from the data sheet corresponding to each of the average RPMs and boat speeds. Using Equation E.1, the boat's effective area, and each of the average apparent wind velocities, calculate the wind drag and enter that in column five. The current load in column six is the load in column three minus the load in column five. A curve can be plotted from the data in columns one and six.

The resulting curve, similar to Figure E.7, will show the loads on the boat due to water moving past it. These loads will be the same regardless of whether the boat is moving and the water is stationary or the boat is stationary and the water is moving.

If you are anchoring in a location where the current is more than 1 knot, the loads from the current should be added to the wind loads to get the total load the anchor must withstand. Using Figure E.7 and the ship's power curve in forward gear, the additional strength required by the anchor system can be estimated.

These current loads will of course change as the boat's bottom becomes fouled with marine growth. If the boat becomes badly fouled, you may wish to get more realistic values by rerunning the current experiment. This will also give you a graphic demonstration of the boat's loss of efficiency due to fouling.

Glossary

ABACK	When a sail is pushed back by the wind, intentionally or unintentionally. In either case the boat's forward motion is reduced.
ABAFT	A relative direction toward the stern of the boat, *e.g.*, The wind is **abaft** the beam.
ABEAM	A relative direction toward the sides of the boat, usually a point at right angles to the centerline and equidistant between the bow and stern.
ABOUT	Changing from one tack to the other, *e.g.*, come **about**.
ADRIFT	Loose, not on moorings or under power.
ADVECTION FOG	Fog caused when the movement of moist air over a colder surface reduces the air temperature below the dew point.
AFTERGUY	The line that runs aft from the spinnaker pole.
AGONIC LINE	An imaginary line joining all points with no magnetic variation and where true and magnetic north lie in exactly the same direction.
AGROUND	Touching the bottom in shallow water.
AHULL	When a vessel with all sails furled is driven by the wind at the angle naturally assumed by the vessel, usually beam-on to the wind.
ALEE	A relative direction on the side of an object away from the wind, *e.g.*, hard **alee**.
ALOFT	A relative direction above the deck.
ALTOCUMULUS	A middle-layer globular cloud type.
ALTOSTRATUS	A middle-layer flat, layered cloud type.
AMIDSHIPS	Halfway between the ends or sides of the boat. Also a helm order to steer straight ahead, *e.g.*, rudder **amidships**.
ANABATIC WIND	Any wind blowing up a slope.
ANALOG	Relating to or being a device in which data are represented by a continuous function, rather than discretely measurable physical quantities, *e.g.*, an **analog** computer.
ANCHOR LIGHT	A white light visible for 2 miles from all directions, shown at night from high above the deck.
ANCHOR RODE	A line, chain, or combination of line and chain that attaches the anchor to the boat.

ANEMOMETER	An instrument used to measure wind velocity.
ANTICYCLONE	A weather system, characterized by good weather, in which the winds rotate clockwise in the northern hemisphere and counterclockwise in the southern hemisphere.
APPARENT NOON	The instant the upper edge of the sun is at its highest position in the sky at the reference location.
APPARENT SHORELINE	A line drawn on a chart where the shoreline is obscured by marsh, mangrove, or other marine vegetation but would appear to a navigator on site as the visible shoreline.
APPARENT WIND	The vector combination of the true wind velocity and the wind developed by the velocity of the boat. The wind one feels when riding on the boat.
ASPECT RATIO	The relationship between the horizontal and vertical dimensions of an object, often used in conjunction with a sail or a keel.
ASSIGNED FREQUENCY	The center of the radio frequency band assigned to an individual station.
ASTERN	A relative direction behind the boat.
ASTROLABE	A medieval instrument, now replaced by the sextant, that was once used to determine the altitude of the sun and other celestial bodies.
ATHWARTSHIPS	The direction perpendicular to the longitudinal axis of the boat.
ATTENUATION	The decrease in wave strength with distance from the origin due to natural or artificial phenomena.
AUDIO FREQUENCY	An energy wave frequency within the audible range between about 20 and 20,000 cycles per second.
AUTOPILOT	An electronic device used to steer a boat.
AWASH	Just breaking the surface of the water, *e.g.*, the rock is **awash**.
AZIMUTH	A horizontal angle measured from a specific reference point, commonly magnetic or true north.
BACK	A change in wind direction that is counterclockwise in the northern hemisphere and clockwise in the southern hemisphere.
BACKSPLICE	A method for weaving rope strands back into the rope to keep the line from unraveling.
BACKSTAY	A cable or rod used to support the mast along the longitudinal axis of the boat running from the top of the mast toward the back of the boat.
BAGGYWRINKLE	Material used to protect sails from chafing on the shrouds.
BAIL	1. A U-shaped fitting, usually on a spar, to which blocks are attached. 2. To dip water from a boat.
BALLAST	Any heavy material placed inside or outside a vessel to lower the center of gravity.

BALLOONER	A large, light foresail.
BANK	Any shallow area having sufficient water to navigate, as opposed to a reef or shoal.
BAR	A shallow area, specifically across the mouth of a river or harbor.
BARBER HAULER	A system of lines and pulleys to adjust the athwartships sheeting angle of the headsails.
BARE POLES	Masts with no sails set.
BATTEN	A thin, narrow strip of wood or plastic used to stiffen the leech of a sail, once flat, now commonly round.
BATTEN DOWN	To fasten securely.
BEAM	1. The widest part of a vessel. 2. A relative direction at right angles to the longitudinal axis of the boat, *e.g.*, a **beam** sea or a **beam reach**.
BEAM REACH	The point of sail with the wind at a right angle to the boat.
BEARING	The direction in which an object lies, usually expressed relative to compass, magnetic, or true north.
BEAR OFF	To turn the boat away from the wind.
BEATING	Sailing as close to the wind as possible to gain distance in a windward direction.
BECKET	A small metal loop on the end of a block, to which a rope can be attached.
BELAY	To fasten a line, generally with a knot.
BENCHMARK	A fixed physical object used as a reference for a vertical datum.
BERGIE BIT	A large piece of floating glacier (about the size of a small house), generally showing between 3 and 15 feet of ice above the water.
BERTH	1. A shipboard bunk. 2. A place alongside a dock, pier, quay, or float to which a boat is tied.
BIGHT	1. The middle portion of a line, particularly when it forms a loop. 2. An indentation or small bay in a body of water.
BILGE	The interior of the boat beneath the floorboards.
BILL	A narrow promontory or peninsula of land.
BIMINI TOP	A sun awning spread over the cockpit, generally used in the tropics for shade.
BINNACLE	The vertical stand that houses the compass.
BIOLUMINESCENCE	The light produced by living organisms, sometimes triggered by physical stimulation.

BITTER END	The inboard end of a line or chain, particularly the end of the anchor rode farthest from the anchor.
BLANKET	To block the wind from reaching an object, usually a sail or a boat. To sail close upwind of another sailboat and block its wind.
BLINK	A colored glare on the underside of extensive cloud banks, generally caused by snow, ice, or atolls. The color may be white, yellowish white, or blue-green.
BLOCK	A wooden or metal case containing one or more pulleys and having a hook, eye, or strap by which the block can be secured.
BOBBING	The practice of raising and lowering eye level when a navigational light is first sighted to determine if the observer is at the geographic range of the light.
BOBSTAY	The cable or chain between the end of the bowsprit and the stem of the boat, used to hold the bowsprit down against the forces of the forestay.
BOLLARD	A strong post on a pier, wharf, or quay where mooring lines are attached.
BOLTROPE	Reinforcing rope sewn into the luff of a sail.
BONE	The white water that tends to pile up in front of a boat when she is fully under way, *e.g.*, having a **bone** in her teeth.
BOOM	1. The horizontal spar attached to the bottom of a sail and the mast. 2. A floating barrier used to shelter a harbor area.
BOOM GALLOWS	A support for the boom that has one or more recesses laterally across the width of the boat.
BOOTTOP	A painted stripe at the waterline of the boat used to separate the bottom from the topside paint.
BOSUN'S CHAIR	A swinglike seat rigged to haul a crewmember aloft.
BOW	The front of the boat.
BOW LINE	A docking line leading from the bow of the boat to prevent the bow from drifting away from the dock.
BOWLINE	The most common knot used to make a fixed loop in a line.
BOWSPRIT	A spar extending forward from the bow of the boat.
BRACKISH	A mixture of fresh and salt water.
BREEZE	Any wind with a velocity between 4 and 27 knots. Subdivided into light, gentle, moderate, fresh, and strong.
BRIDGE	The area, usually on a powerboat, from which the boat is controlled. On large commercial ships this control area is commonly on an elevated structure (a **bridge**) over the weather deck.
BRIGHTWORK	Wood trim on a vessel that is varnished or oiled.

Broach	Uncontrolled rounding up into the wind placing the beam to the seas when the boat is running downwind. Can be followed by a knockdown.
Broad reach	Sailing with the wind aft of the beam, but not dead astern.
Bulkhead	A vertical partition separating compartments of a vessel.
Bungee cord	Cord with an elastic center, a woven cloth cover, and hooks on each end.
Buoy	An anchored float used to mark a position on the water for navigational purposes or for mooring.
Burgee	Generally, a swallow-tailed flag. Specifically, a flag indicating membership in a yacht club.
By the lee	Sailing downwind with the wind on the same side of the boat as the boom.
Cable laid	An uncommon method of twisting ropes together in a left-handed direction. Usually done for large-diameter lines using regular right-hand rope for strands.
Cable length	One-tenth of a nautical mile, approximately 607 feet; close but not equal to 100 fathoms.
Camber	The concave shape of a sail or deck.
Capstan	A revolving cylinder on a vertical axis around which line or chain can be wound. Usually used to recover anchor rode.
Cardinal points	The four principle compass directions: north, south, east, and west.
Carrier wave	The unmodulated portion of a radio transmission.
Cartography	The art and science of making charts and maps.
Catamaran	A boat with two hulls side by side.
Catboat	A simple sailboat driven only by the mainsail.
Catenary	The curve formed by a cable supported only at its ends.
Cat's-paw	Patches of ripples on the surface of the water caused by a puff of light wind.
Cavitation	Air bubbles generated in a liquid by the formation of a partial vacuum.
Celestial navigation	Fixing position using astronomical bodies and time.
Centerboard	A movable board that adds lateral resistance to a sailboat by rotating downward from a slot in the keel.
Center of buoyancy	The point in a body floating in a liquid where the sum of all buoyant forces can be considered to act. The location coincides with the center of gravity of the displaced liquid.
Center of effort	The point in a body where the sum of all the driving forces can be considered to act.

CENTER OF GRAVITY	The point in a body where its entire weight can be considered to be located.
CENTER OF LATERAL RESISTANCE	The point on the longitudinal plane of a boat where all hydrodynamic forces can be considered to act.
CHAFING GEAR	Any material, such as cloth wrapping or tubing, used to protect sails or line from abrasion.
CHAINPLATE	Fittings to which shrouds or stays are attached.
CHARLIE NOBLE	A chimney cap on a boat that restricts the flow of water and wind back into the stove.
CHART	A map used for navigation that shows water depth.
CHEEK BLOCK	A turning block fixed to the deck or the side of a spar.
CHOCK	A fitting through which anchor or mooring lines are led. Usually shaped to reduce abrasion.
CHRONOMETER	A very accurate timepiece, often set to Greenwich time.
CIRROCUMULUS	A high, globular cloud form.
CIRROSTRATUS	A high, thin, layered cloud form
CIRRUS	The highest of all cloud forms; its shape is light and fibrous.
CIVIL TWILIGHT	The period of incomplete darkness when the sun is fully below the horizon but its center is less than 6 degrees below the horizon.
CLAW OFF	Sailing to windward away from a lee shore.
CLEAT	A fitting for securing a line, usually shaped with two horns.
CLEW	The point of the sail where the leech and foot intersect. On headsails or squaresails, the point at which the sheets are attached.
CLOSE-HAULED	Sailing as close to the wind as possible. The sails are trimmed (hauled) into the wind as close as possible, hence the term.
CLOSE REACH	The point of sail between a beam reach and close-hauled.
CLOSE-WINDED	Able to go to the windward with optimum efficiency.
CLOVE HITCH	A knot generally tied around a vertical or horizontal post.
CLUB-FOOTED HEADSAIL	A headsail that has a spar attached to its foot.
COAMING	A low wall around the cockpit.
COAXIAL CABLE	A transmission cable composed of two concentric conductors insulated from each other to suppress spurious radiation.
COCKED HAT	The triangle formed by three bearings when drawn on a chart. The size of the triangle indicates the quality of the bearings. The vessel is considered to be, but is not necessarily, located within the triangle.
COLLISION BEARING	A bearing between two boats that remains constant while the distance between the boat decreases.

COME ABOUT	To change direction relative to the wind by passing the bow through the eye of the wind.
COMPANIONWAY	The opening and stairs leading from the deck or cockpit to the interior of the boat.
COMPASS BEARING	The bearing of an object relative to compass north. This type of bearing includes both variation and deviation.
CRINGLE	An external eye in a sail through which a line can be passed.
CROWN	The part of an anchor where the arms join the shank.
CUMULONIMBUS	A dense, towering cloud form with a low base, associated with thunderstorms.
CUMULUS	A light, fluffy white cloud form associated with clear weather.
CUNNINGHAM	A line that controls tension along the luff of a sail; invented by racing sailor Briggs Cunningham.
CUTTER	A fore-and-aft-rigged sailboat with one mast and two headsails.
CYCLONE	A weather system, characterized by bad weather, in which the winds rotate counterclockwise in the northern hemisphere and clockwise in the southern hemisphere.
DAGGERBOARD	A retractable keel that moves vertically rather than swinging.
DANGER ANGLE	An angle between two points and the boat that indicates the limits of safe approach to an offlying danger.
DANGER BEARING	A bearing from a fixed object that marks the limits of a safe approach to an offlying danger.
DANGEROUS SEMICIRCLE	The half of a hurricane where the velocity of the rotating wind is increased by the forward motion of the storm. The direction of the wind in this semicircle also tends to force a sailing vessel into the path of the storm. With reference to the storm's path, the dangerous semicircle is the right half of the storm in the northern hemisphere and the left half in the southern hemisphere.
DAVIT	A small inverted L-shaped structure used to hoist dinghies or anchors.
DAYBEACON	An unlighted navigational aid composed of a distinct geometric shape, called a *daymark*, attached to a supporting structure, commonly a *single pile* or *dolphin*.
DEADHEAD	A large, barely floating log or tree. Deadheads commonly float near vertical in the water, are difficult to see, and are dangerous if struck by small craft.
DEADLIGHT	1. A small porthole that admits light but cannot be opened. 2. An unbreakable cover for a porthole.
DEADWOOD	The portion of the keel between the hull and the ballast.

DEAD RECKONING	Estimating a boat's position by taking into account the boat's speed, the course steered, and the drift caused by wind and current.
DECKSWEEPER	A headsail with a foot flush with the deck.
DECLINATION	The angular distance north or south of the celestial equator.
DEGAUSSING	The process of neutralizing the effects of a vessel's magnetic field using suitably arranged electric coils.
DEMODULATION	The process by which a radio receiver recovers information impressed by the transmitter during modulation.
DEPARTURE	The east and west distance between two meridians, usually expressed in nautical miles.
DEPRESSION	An area of low barometric pressure, usually associated with poor weather.
DERELICT	Any large floating object that constitutes a menace to navigation.
DEVIATION	Compass error caused by local magnetic fields that surround and move with the compasses.
DEW POINT	The temperature to which air must be cooled at constant pressure to reach 100 percent saturation.
DIAPHONE	A two-toned sound-producing device driven by compressed air, used on navigational aids. The air is generally compressed by wave action.
DINGHY	A small open boat.
DIPOLE	A straight, centerfed, one-half wavelength antenna.
DISPLACEMENT	The weight of a boat.
DIURNAL	Recurring approximately once daily, *e.g.*, **diurnal** tides.
DOCUMENTATION	A federal license or registration of a boat.
DODGER	A collapsible canvas windbreak or spray shield at the forward end of the cockpit.
DOLDRUMS	An approximately 10-degree-wide weather belt near the equator where the air pressure is low and the predominant air movement is vertically upward, resulting in calms and numerous squalls.
DOPPLER SHIFT	An apparent change in the frequency of waves, as of sound or light, occurring when the source and observer are in motion relative to each other, with the frequency increasing when the source and observer approach each other and decreasing when they move apart.
DOUBLE BRAID	Synthetic fiber rope with a braided core and cover.
DOUBLE-ENDER	A boat pointed on both ends.
DOUSE	To lower a sail.
DOWNHAUL	A line that pulls down on a spar or the tack of a sail to tighten its luff.

DOWNWIND	Going in the same direction that the wind is blowing.
DRAFT	1. The distance between the waterline and the lowest part of the boat. 2. The amount of curvature in a sail.
DRAG	Air or water resistance caused by shape.
DRIFT	1. To move by action of wind or current. 2. The speed of a current. 3. The distance a craft is moved by wind or current.
DRIFTER	A large, very lightweight headsail used in light winds.
DROGUE	A device to increase drag and slow a boat, commonly a truncated canvas cone attached at the stern.
DRYDOCK	A place where the water surrounding a moored boat can be removed for maintenance or repair.
EASE	1. To slacken or relieve tension on a line. 2. To reduce the pull on the helm.
EASTING	The ancient practice of sailing due east to reach a landfall.
EBB TIDE	The falling or outgoing tide.
ECHO SOUNDING	The determination of distance by measuring the time interval between emission of a sonic or ultrasonic signal and the return of its echo.
ECLIPTIC	The apparent annual path of the sun among the stars.
EDDY	A circular movement of water in a horizontal plane, part of which runs contrary to the main flow of the stream.
ELECTROLYSIS	The destruction of dissimilar metals through the action of electrical current and salt water.
EPIRB	Emergency Position Indicating Radio Beacon; a small portable radio used by search-and-rescue services.
EPHEMERUS	A periodically published tabulation of the positions of celestial bodies and other data of interest to navigators.
EQUINOX	One of the two times the sun crosses the celestial equator.
ETA	Estimated Time of Arrival.
ESTUARY	An embayment where fresh water is mixed with salt water.
EVEN KEEL	When a boat is not listing or heeling to either side, nor down in the bow or stern, she is said to be on an **even keel**.
EYE OF THE WIND	The direction from which the wind is blowing.
EYESPLICE	A permanent loop splice in the end of a line.
FAIRLEAD	A fitting through which a line is passed so that it leads at the proper angle and without chafe.

FAIRWAY	The main thoroughfare used by ship traffic in a harbor or channel.
FAKE DOWN	To lay a line on deck in overlapping coils so that it will run out without kinking.
FALL OFF	To bear away from the wind.
FATHOM	A nautical measure of length or depth equivalent to 6 feet.
FEATHER	To turn an object so that it presents the least resistance to wind or water.
FENDER	A cushion used to prevent contact between the hull and another object.
FETCH	The distance wind blows over open water.
FID	A cylindrical tool, hollow on one end and with a smooth point on the other, used for splicing line.
FIDDLE BLOCK	A block with two sheaves in the same plane, one larger than the other. A fiddle block will not twist line, as will a block with sheaves mounted side by side.
FISHERMAN ANCHOR	An anchor with small flukes used to penetrate very hard surfaces.
FITTING	A piece of boat hardware.
FIX	An accurate ship's position determined by the intersection of two or more lines of position and without reference to any former position.
FLAKE DOWN	To arrange a rope in figure eights on a flat surface so that it will run free without kinking.
FLINDERS BAR	A bar of soft unmagnetized iron placed vertically near a magnetic compass to counteract deviation.
FLOOD TIDE	The rising or incoming tide.
FLOTSAM	Floating articles thrown or washed overboard from a vessel in distress.
FLUKE	The flat, pointed part of an anchor that digs into the bottom.
FLY	The horizontal length of a flag.
FOEHN	A warm, dry wind blowing down a slope.
FOLLOWING SEA	A sea that comes from the behind the boat.
FOOT	The bottom of a sail.
FOREGUY	The line that runs forward from the spinnaker pole.
FOREPEAK	The extreme forward compartment in a boat.
FOREREACH	To make headway when hove to.
FORESTAY	A cable or rod used to support the mast along the longitudinal axis of the boat, running from the mast to the front of the boat. The forwardmost support on which the jib or genoa is set.

FORETRIANGLE	The area bounded by the mast, the foredeck, and the forestay.
FORM LINE	Broken lines on a chart resembling contour lines but representing no actual elevation. Used where elevation data is inadequate for contours to show the general shape of the topography.
FOUNDER	The process of filling with water and sinking.
FRAPPING	The process of tightening a lashing by passing turns of line around the lashing perpendicular to the main lashing.
FREEBOARD	The vertical distance between the waterline and the lowest point on the deck.
FURL	To completely gather and secure a sail.
GAFF	A spar used to support the top of a gaff sail.
GAIN	The ratio of output to input voltage, current, or power.
GALLEY	A boat's kitchen.
GANGWAY	An opening in the lifelines to facilitate boarding.
GELCOAT	The smooth outer skin of a fiberglass boat.
GENOA	A large jib whose clew overlaps the mast.
GEODETIC SURVEY	A survey that takes into account the shape and size of the earth.
GIMBAL	A device hinged in two planes, designed to keep things level on a boat.
GNOMONIC CHART	A type of chart where great circle courses are represented by straight lines.
GOLLIWOBBLER	A billowing staysail that extends from the masthead to the deck overlapping the mainsail on a schooner-rigged vessel. Usually sheeted to the end of the boom.
GOOSENECK	The fitting securing the forward end of the boom to the mast.
GRABRAILS	Railings placed at various points about a boat to be grasped for balance.
GRADIENT	The rate of rise or fall of a quantity against horizontal distance, expressed as a ratio or percentage.
GRAPPLE	A many-clawed hook used for retrieving articles lost overboard in shallow water.
GREAT CIRCLE	The intersection between the surface of a sphere and a plane passing through its center. The shortest distance between two points on the surface of a sphere always lies on a great circle.
GREEN FLASH	A brilliant green coloring of the atmosphere above the sun as it appears at sunrise or disappears at sunset. It is due to the refraction of the atmosphere and requires a clear, distinct horizon. Occurs most often in the tropics.
GREENWICH	Refers to the Greenwich observatory in England, which is used as a universal basis for navigation and time.

GROMMET	A small metal ring set into sails or canvas.
GROUND SWELL	A long undulation of ocean water caused by a distant storm.
GROUND TACKLE	A collective term for the anchor and all its associated gear.
GROUNDWAVE	The portion of a radio wave that travels along the surface of the earth.
GUNKHOLING	Exploring small, shallow waterways in a recreational boat.
GUNWALE	The upper edge of the boat's sides.
HALYARD	A wire or rope used to hoist a sail or a flag.
HANDY BILLY	A four-part tackle used around boats for miscellaneous jobs.
HANGING LOCKER	A closet on a boat where clothes are hung on hangers.
HANK	A snap hook that secures the jib luff to the headstay.
HARD OVER	To place the rudder in its most extreme position.
HATCH	A cover over an opening in the deck.
HAWSEPIPE	A tube through which anchor chain can run to the stowage locker.
HEAD	A ship's bathroom.
HEADBOARD	The reinforcement in the head of a sail.
HEADER	A wind shift that forces the boat to bear away from the wind.
HEADSAIL	Any sail set forward of the forwardmost mast.
HEADSTAY	A cable or rod used to support the mast along the longitudinal axis of the boat, running from the mast to the front of the boat. The forwardmost support on which the jib or genoa is set.
HEAVE-TO (HOVE-TO)	To lash the helm to leeward with the jib backed so that the vessel lies almost stationary.
HEAVY WEATHER	Rough seas and strong winds, usually gale force and above.
HEEL	To tilt the boat, usually due to wind pressure, but also because of weight distribution.
HEELING ERROR	The compass error caused by the boat heeling.
HELM	The wheel or tiller that steers the boat.
HIGH CUT	Descriptive term used for a jib whose clew is high off the deck.
HIKE	To lean over the windward rail to counter the heeling forces of the wind on the sails.
HITCH	A knot used to attach a line to an object.
HOIST	The length of the vertical edge of a flag.
HOLDING GROUND	The bottom of a harbor in which the anchor is set.
HOLIDAY	A spot left accidentally unpainted.

HORSE LATITUDES	An approximately 10-degree-wide weather belt found near Latitude 30 where the air pressure is high and the predominant air movement is vertically downward, resulting in calms.
HYFIELD LEVER	A quick tensioning device for cables.
IN IRONS	When a vessel attempts to come about and does not have sufficient power to carry her through the eye of the wind. The boat tends to hang in irons and will not head off on either tack.
INTERPOLATION	The process of determining intermediate values between given values in a table assuming a simplified rate of change, usually linear.
INTERTROPICAL CONVERGENCE ZONE (ITC)	An approximately 10-degree-wide weather belt near the equator where the air pressure is low and the predominant air movement is vertically upward, resulting in calms and numerous squalls. See also **doldrums**.
IONOSPHERE	The region of the atmosphere extending from about 40 to 250 miles above the earth's surface.
ISOBARS	Lines connecting points of equal atmospheric pressure.
ISOGONIC LINES	Lines connecting points of equal compass variation.
JAM CLEAT	A serrated, tapered trough that holds a line. The harder the rope is pulled the deeper it goes into the trough and the tighter the grip.
JETTY	A structure built in the water to restrain or direct currents and to protect a harbor mouth or entrance from silting.
JIB	A sail carried on the forestay.
JIBE	Altering course to bring a following wind from one side of the mainsail to the other.
JIFFY REEFING	A quick method of reefing a mainsail employing permanently reeved tack and clew lines.
JUMPER STRUT	A strut that stiffens the mast in a fore and aft plane.
JURY RIG	An improvised replacement for damaged gear, usually the rigging.
KATABATIC WIND	Any wind blowing down an incline.
KEDGE	Generally, to use anchors to move the boat. Specifically, to use an anchor and winches aboard the boat to drag a grounded boat back into deep water.
KELP	A type of seaweed that grows on rocks.
KEEL	An appendage on the bottom of a boat that supplies lateral area to counteract the wind forces pushing the boat sideways. If weighted, the keel acts as a counterbalance to reduce heeling.
KETCH	A two-masted, fore-and-aft-rigged vessel, with the aftermost mast smaller and stepped forward of the rudderpost.
KNOCKDOWN	The roll of a boat through an angle greater than 60 degrees.

KNOT	A measure of boat speed equal to 1 nautical mile (6076.11549 feet, commonly rounded off to 6,080 feet) per hour or 1.15 statute miles per hour.
LAID LINE	Rope made up of strands twisted around each other.
LAMINAR FLOW	Smooth air- or water flow over a surface.
LAND BREEZE	A wind blowing from the shore to the water.
LANDFALL	Returning to the land after making an ocean passage.
LANDMARK	An object on shore that can be helpful in locating the position of the boat.
LANYARD	A short, small-diameter line.
LAPSE RATE	The rate of temperature decrease with increase in height above the earth's surface.
LATERAL RESISTANCE	The resistance of the hull to being driven sideways through the water.
LATITUDE	The distance north or south of the equator expressed in degrees, minutes, and seconds of arc. A minute of latitude is a constant distance equal to 1 nautical mile.
LAY	The direction in which the strands of a rope are twisted.
LAZARETTE	A storage area in the immediate stern or bow of the boat.
LAZYJACKS	Lines that lead from the mast to the boom to confine the mainsail when it is lowered.
LEADLINE	A lead weight on a marked line used to measure the depth of water shallower than about 36 feet.
LEE	An area sheltered from the wind.
LEEBOARD	An external form of retractable keel fitted to the side of a vessel to increase lateral resistance.
LEE HELM	The tendency for a boat to turn away from the wind. Neither desirable nor efficient; can be caused by carrying too much sail forward.
LEE SHORE	Land onto which the wind can blow a boat. To escape, the boat must sail toward the wind.
LEEWAY	Slipping sideways away from the wind.
LEECH	The after edge of a sail; spinnakers and squaresails have two leeches.
LIFELINE	A coated wire, supported by posts called *stanchions*, that encircles the deck to help keep the crew from falling overboard.
LIFT	A wind shift that allows the boat to head more to windward.
LIGHT AIR	Wind less than about 8 knots.
LIMB	The circular outer edge of a celestial body, *e.g.*, the upper **limb** of the sun.

LIMBER HOLES	Holes in bulkheads beneath the floorboards to enable water to run down to the sump of the bilge pump.
LINE	Rope or cordage used aboard a boat.
LINE OF POSITION	A compass bearing drawn on a chart through a known position, the boat being located somewhere along this line.
LINE SQUALL	A short-lived linear area of violent winds and weather.
LIST	The lean of a boat to one side.
LOBE	A portion of an antenna radiation pattern.
LOCAL ATTRACTION	An anomaly of the earth's magnetic field confined to a relatively small area that produces a compass error.
LOCK	An elevator for boats, composed of a channel that can be closed off by gates and its water level raised or lowered, thereby raising or lowering a boat.
LOCKER	A boat's cupboard.
LOG	A written record of shipboard activities.
LONG SPLICE	A splice joining two ropes in such a manner that the splice is no thicker than the original rope.
LONGITUDE	The distance east or west of Greenwich, England, expressed in degrees, minutes, and seconds of arc. A minute of longitude is *not* a constant distance. Its length depends on the latitude.
LOOM	A visible glow in the sky seen before the light source can be seen.
LOOSE-FOOTED SAIL	A sail not attached to a spar.
LUBBER'S LINE	The mark on the compass that indicates the direction in which the vessel is pointing.
LUFF	The forward edge of a sail.
LUFFING	The fluttering of the forward edge of a sail indicating that the wind is striking both sides of the sail.
LUNCH HOOK	A small anchor used for short stops in good weather.
MACKEREL SKY	An area of the sky that contains rounded and isolated cirrocumulus or altocumulus clouds, which resembles the pattern of scales on a mackerel. A harbinger of changing weather.
MAGNETIC BEARING	The bearing of an object relative to magnetic north, therefore a bearing only corrected for variation.
MAKE FAST	To secure.
MANILA	A natural rope fiber.
MARCONI RIG	An alternative name for the Bermuda rig, which has triangular rather than quadrilateral sails.

MARINA	A boat basin equipped with docks, slips, and facilities for small boats.
MARE'S TAILS	Wisps of cirrus clouds, often foretelling a change in the weather.
MARLINSPIKE	A pointed tool used to pry open knots.
MAST BEND	Curvature in the mast produced by the wind or the stays.
MAST PARTNERS	Reinforcing at the deck to handle the stress imposed by the mast.
MASTSTEP	The fitting that supports and positions the bottom of the mast.
MAYDAY	The prefix to a distress call. See also **Pan Pan**.
MERCATOR	The standard type of chart projection.
MERIDIAN	A line of longitude.
MIZZENMAST	The small mast in the back of a ketch or yawl.
MODULATION	The instantaneous variation of some characteristic of a radio carrier wave.
MONKEY'S FIST	A large knot on the end of a heaving line to give it weight to make the line carry farther.
MONOHULL	A single-hulled vessel.
MOORING	A permanently placed anchor with a pendant and buoy to which a boat can be secured.
MOUSING	A length of light line or wire that secures a pin in a shackle or a hook so that it cannot open accidentally.
MULTIHULL	A boat with more than one hull, as in trimaran or catamaran.
NAUTICAL MILE	The unit of distance used on water, equal to 1 minute of latitude or about 6,080 feet.
NAUTICAL TWILIGHT	The time of incomplete darkness beginning when the center of the sun is 12 degrees below the celestial horizon. At nautical twilight it is generally too dark to accurately locate the horizon with a sextant.
NAVIGABLE SEMICIRCLE	The half of a hurricane where the velocity of the wind is decreased because the storm's rotary motion is diminished by the motion of the storm itself. The direction of the wind in this semicircle allows a sailing vessel to navigate away from the path of the storm. With reference to the storm's path, the navigable semicircle is the left half in the northern hemisphere and the right half in the southern hemisphere.
NAVIGABLE WATERS	Waters used as routes for commerce.
NAVIGATIONAL AIDS	Technically, the tools of navigation, *e.g.*, dividers, parallel rulers, etc. The term is commonly confused with *Aids to Navigation*, which are devices external to the ship that assist in navigation, such as buoys, daymarks, etc.
NAVIGATION LIGHTS	The lights aboard a boat used to identify it and to indicate its position and course to other boats.

NEAP TIDES	Small tides occurring when the gravity of the moon and sun are working against one another.
NIMBOSTRATUS	A dark, low, thick, layered cloud form associated with the arrival of a warm front. The precipitation from nimbostratus clouds is long and steady.
NIMBUS	The term for a rain cloud, used only in conjunction with other descriptive terms. See **nimbostratus**.
NOMOGRAPH	A diagram to scale showing the relationship between several variables such that any one variable can be obtained graphically if the others are known.
NOTCH FILTER	An electronic device designed to attenuate or reject a specific frequency, with a well-defined delineation at each end of the desired band.
OCCLUDED FRONT	A composite of two frontal systems, one overtaking the other. This is the condition commonly found in the later stages of a low-pressure disturbance.
OCCULTING	A flashing light that is lit for longer periods than it is unlit.
OFF THE WIND	Sailing with the wind coming from behind the beam.
OILSKINS	Waterproof apparel used aboard a boat in bad weather. Old term for foul-weather gear.
OMNIDIRECTIONAL	Refers to a property that is equally effective in all directions.
ON THE WIND	Sailing with the wind coming from forward of the beam.
ONE-DESIGN	An organized class of identical racing boats.
ONE-OFF	A custom boat of unique design. Only one hull of that design made.
OUTDRIVE	The portion of an inboard/outboard motor that lies outside the hull and contains the drive shaft, gears, and propeller.
OUTHAUL	A device for pulling the clew of a sail outward on a spar.
OUTRIGGER	The small float attached by arms to the main hull, used to reduce the probability of the main hull capsizing.
OVERFALL	A circular movement of water in a vertical plane. The upper portion of the water is running against the main flow of the stream. Overfalls are caused by a fast current rushing into slow-moving water.
OVERHANG	That part of the vessel that projects beyond the waterline either fore or aft.
OVERLAP	The extension of the clew of a headsail behind the luff of the mainsail.
PADEYE	A metal loop to which blocks and shackles are secured.
PAINTER	The bow line of a small boat.

PALM	A leather band worn across the palm of the hand, used to push a needle through heavy sailcloth.
PAN PAN	A prefix to a distress message not concerning events leading to immediate loss of life or vessel. See also **Mayday**.
PARACHUTE	A spinnaker.
PARALLEL RULER	Two rulers connected by small bars that transfer a line from one position to another while retaining the original bearing of the line.
PARBUCKLE	A means of moving a cylindrical object by passing an anchored line around the object and hauling on the free end. The parbuckle increases the force on the object to twice the force exerted on the line.
PASSAGE	Crossing an open body of water beyond the sight of land. Usually a voyage longer than 24 hours.
PAY OUT	To let out in a controlled manner.
PELICAN HOOK	A hinged hook held closed by a sliding collar.
PELORUS	An instrument used to obtain relative bearings that resembles a compass without magnetic properties.
PENDANT	A short length of cable used to connect two objects.
PIER	A platform on posts or piles that projects perpendicular from shore.
PINCH	To sail too close to the wind for optimum performance.
PITCHING	Fore-and-aft oscillations of a hull.
PITCHPOLE	To turn at least 180 degrees around the athwartships axis of the boat; to somersault end over end.
PLANING HULL	A hull that, at speed, generates lift and reduces the drag on the hull.
POINT	Eleven and one quarter degrees, *e.g.*, four **points** (45 degrees) off the starboard bow.
POOPED	A boat is pooped when a wave breaks over its stern.
PORT	The left side of a boat looking forward.
PORTHOLE	A boat window.
PREVAILING WESTERLIES	The zone of winds that blow predominantly westward above the horse latitudes or high-pressure zone.
PREVENTER	A line that restrains a spar from accidental movement.
PRIME MERIDIAN	The meridian of longitude zero passing through Greenwich, England.
PROTRACTOR	A semicircular instrument for measuring and constructing angles, commonly used in navigation.
PULPIT	A guardrail around the bow of a boat.
PURCHASE	A device, such as a tackle or lever, used to increase lifting power by mechanical advantage.

PUSHPIT	A guardrail around the stern of a boat.
QUADRANT	A quarter of a circle.
QUARTERING SEAS	Seas coming on a boat from the side aft of amidships.
QUAY	A solid structure built parallel along the shore that provides berthing to ships.
RACE	An especially strong, turbulent current.
RACON	A transponder navigational beacon that, when triggered by a passing ship's radar, sends a transmission that provides the range and bearing to the beacon.
RADIAN	An angular unit equal to $180°/\pi$.
RADIATION FOG	Fog commonly found over land.
RAFT UP	To tie two or more boats side by side on a single mooring.
RAKE	Tilt of the mast either forward or backward.
RAMARK	A radar beacon that continuously transmits a signal appearing as a radial line on radar screens.
RANGE	1. A line of position formed by two fixed objects. 2. The distance to an object.
RATING	The results of a measurement formula that establishes a boat's racing handicap.
RATLINES	Rope, wooden, or metal rungs lashed between the shrouds to assist the crew in going aloft.
REACH	1. To sailing with the wind coming over the side of the boat. The general point of sail between beating and running. 2. A comparatively straight channel.
REACHER	A lightweight, high-clewed headsail or a flat spinnaker used for reaching.
RECIPROCAL	A quantity equal to the quotient of 1 divided by the number, *e.g.*,the **reciprocal** of 2 is ½ or 0.5.
RECIPROCAL BEARING	A bearing 180 degrees opposite the original bearing.
REEF	1. To decrease a sail's size. 2. A shoal composed of rock or coral.
REEVE	To thread a line through a system of pulleys, blocks, eyes, or fairleads.
REFRACTION	The angular change in direction of an energy wave when it passes from one medium into another having a different propagation speed.
RESOLUTION	The ability to separate two objects at a distance.
RESULTANT	A single vector that is the equivalent of a set of vectors.

RHUMB LINE	A line crossing all meridians at the same angle. A straight line on most flat charts. It is not the shortest distance between two points on the earth's surface. The trace on a globe actually spirals toward the pole.
RIGGING	The gear used to support and adjust the sails, including standing rigging and running rigging.
RIGHT ASCENSION	The angular distance of a celestial body or point on the celestial sphere, measured eastward from the vernal equinox along the celestial equator to the hour circle of the body or point. It can be expressed in degrees or hours.
ROACH	The sail area aft of an imaginary line running between the head and the clew of a sail.
RODE	The system of line, chain, or a combination of both that attaches the anchor to the boat.
ROLL	The oscillation motion of a boat around its longitudinal axis.
ROLLER FURLING	A system for rolling up a sail on its luff.
ROLLER REEFING	A system for reducing the area of a sail by rolling it around a boom.
ROUND UP	The action of a boat turning into the wind.
RUDDER	An underwater appendage used to steer the boat.
RUN	A point of sail with the wind directly over the stern.
RUNNING BACKSTAYS	Backstays that must be set up and tensioned every time the boat changes tack.
RUNNING LIGHTS	Lights required to be shown on boats when underway between sundown and sunup.
RUNNING RIGGING	All the gear aboard the boat that is used to hoist or change the location or shape of sails.
SAFETY HARNESS	A harness worn on the upper body and attached to the boat with a tether to prevent a crewmember lost overboard from becoming separated from the boat.
SAILING DIRECTIONS	A book containing descriptions and details of coastal waters and harbors.
SAIL STOPS	Short lines or straps used to secure a furled or doused sail.
SAMSON POST	A strong post fastened to structural members of the boat to enable it to take large loads.
SATELLITE NAVIGATION	Fixing position using radio transmissions from earth-orbiting satellites.
SCHOONER	A two-masted, fore-and-aft-rigged vessel, with the foremast smaller.
SCOPE	The ratio of the length of anchor rode to the depth of water at the anchor position plus freeboard.
SCUD	Shreds of small detached clouds that move rapidly before the wind. Likewise, the process of running before the wind or a storm.

SCULL	To propel a boat by swinging one oar in a figure-eight motion.
SCUPPER	A deck or cockpit drain.
SCUTTLE	To intentionally sink a boat by opening a seacock.
SCREW	The propeller.
SEA	A local wind-generated wave, *e.g.*, A 3-foot **sea** was running.
SEA ANCHOR	A device attached to the bow to keep the head of a boat into the wind.
SEA BREEZE	A wind blowing from the sea to the land.
SEACOCK	A valve to control the flow of seawater into the boat.
SEA ROOM	A sufficient distance from the shore or other hazard to allow the boat to maneuver safely.
SECANT	1. A line that intersects a curve at two or more points. 2. One divided by the cosine of an angle (1/cos).
SECURITY	Prefix to a message concerning navigational safety.
SEICHE	A stationary wave usually caused by strong winds or changes in barometric pressure. Normally found in lakes and enclosed bodies of water, but can occur occasionally in the open ocean.
SEIZING	Binding two ropes or two parts of the same rope together using light line.
SEMIDIURNAL	Having a period approximately equal to one-half day, *e.g.*, The predominant tide of the world is **semidiurnal**.
SENTINEL	A sliding weight used on an anchor rode to increase the shock-absorbing properties of the rode by increasing the catenary.
SET	1. The direction in which a current flows. 2. The action of hoisting sails.
SEXTANT	An instrument used to measure angles, as between the horizon and a celestial body.
SHACKLE	A U-shaped connector with a pin or bolt across the open end.
SHEAR PIN	A device used to fasten an outboard motor's propeller to the shaft, designed to break when the propeller strikes a solid object and minimize damage.
SHEAVE	The roller in a block or pulley.
SHEET	The primary line controlling the position of a sail's longitudinal axis.
SHOAL	Shallow water.
SHOCK CORD	Stretchy cord with an elastic center and a woven cloth cover.
SHORT SPLICE	A fast method of splicing two twisted lines together. Increases diameter at the splice.

SHROUD	A cable that supports the mast in the athwartships direction.
SIDE LOBE	Any radiation lobe from an antenna other than the main lobe.
SIDEREAL	Of or pertaining to the stars.
SINGLE SIDEBAND (SSB)	Radio transmission in which the frequencies produced by the process of modulation on one side of the carrier are suppressed and not transmitted.
SKEG	A small fixed fin attached to the hull in front of the rudder.
SKIP DISTANCE	The distance between a transmitting antenna and a refracted radio wave's return to earth.
SLACK WATER	A short period at the turn of the tide when there is no tidal current.
SLATTING	Rolling in a calm with the sails slapping back and forth noisily against the mast and rigging.
SLICK	The comparatively smooth water to windward of a boat drifting to leeward.
SLOT	The area between the aft portion of the genoa and the leeward side of the mainsail.
SLOOP	A single-masted, fore-and-aft-rigged sailing vessel, normally flying only one headsail.
SNATCH BLOCK	A block with an opening in one side of the shell so that the block may be inserted in the middle of the line.
SNUB	1. To halt a motion abruptly. 2. To wrap a line around a winch, bitt, or cleat to stop it from running out.
SOLSTICE	The time when the sun is at its farthest point north or south of the equator.
SOUND	To measure the depth of water.
SPAR	A general term for a pole regardless of its function or orientation, *e.g.,* mast, boom, and gaff.
SPINNAKER	A large, light, balloon-shaped sail used off the wind.
SPITFIRE JIB	A small, heavy storm jib.
SPLICE	To join two lines together by interweaving the individual strands.
SPOIL AREA	The area designated for depositing dredged material. Spoil areas should be avoided because their depth changes constantly.
SPREADER	An athwartships strut holding the shrouds out from the mast.
SPRING LINE	A line used in docking to prevent the boat from moving forward or backward.
SPRING TIDES	Large tides occurring when the gravity of the moon and sun are working together.

SQUALL	A sudden violent wind often accompanied by rain.
STANCHIONS	Metal posts supporting lifelines.
STAND	The state of the tide at high or low water when there is no detectable change in height of the water.
STANDING RIGGING	The permanent cables or rods that support the mast, not normally handled during sailing.
STARBOARD	The right side of the boat facing forward.
STATUTE MILE	A unit of distance measurement on land, and commonly on lakes and rivers, equal to 5,280 feet.
STAY	A cable or rod that supports a mast in the longitudinal plane of the boat.
STAYSAIL	A small jib set on a stay behind the forestay.
STEEP-TO	A synonym for precipitous, *e.g.*, The shore was **steep-to**.
STEM	1. The forward edge of the bow. 2. To make progress against, *e.g.*, to **stem** the current.
STEP	1. The part of the boat that contains the base of the mast. 2. The process of raising the mast.
STERN	The aftermost part of the hull.
STERN LINE	A docking line leading from the stern to prevent it from drifting away from the dock.
STOCK	Anchor part that lies on a plane perpendicular to the anchor shank and positions the flukes for digging.
STOPPER KNOT	A knot used on the end of a rope to prevent it from passing accidentally through an eye, block, or fitting.
STOW	To put an item away on a boat.
STRATOCUMULUS	A round, vertical cloud form, highest of the cumulus series.
STRATOSPHERE	The atmospheric layer directly above the troposhere.
STRATUS	A low cloud form resembling fog but not attached to the surface.
STUFFING BOX	A through-hull fitting for the drive shaft or the rudderpost that contains flexible packing to slow water inflow.
SUBLIMATION	The process of passing directly from solid to gas without changing into liquid.
SUNRISE	When the upper rim of the sun is just visible on eastern the horizon.
SUNSET	When the upper rim of the sun is just visible on the western horizon.
SURGE	The rhythmic forward and backward motion of a vessel.
SWAGE	A method of attaching a fitting to a cable using great pressure.

SWAMP	To fill with water.
SWEEP	A long oar.
SWELL	Long waves created by distant winds.
TACHOMETER	An instrument the indicates the revolutions per minute of the engine.
TACK	1. The forward lower corner of a sail. 2. To change course by passing the eye of the wind over the bow.
TACKLE	A combination of blocks and line used to increase mechanical advantage.
TACK CLOTH	A slightly sticky cloth used to pick up dust from a surface before painting or varnishing.
TAFFRAIL	The rail across or around the stern of a boat.
TAIL	To take up the slack on a line coming off a winch.
TANG	A metal strap on the mast to which stays or a block is secured.
TANGENT	A straight line touching a curve in only one place.
TELLTALE	A piece of yarn, string, or ribbon attached to a shroud or sail to indicate the direction of the apparent wind.
TENDER	1. A small boat used as a dinghy 2. A boat that heels easily.
THIMBLE	A metal or plastic liner in a rope eye to protect the rope from chafe.
THROUGH-HULL	A flanged, threaded fitting inserted into a hole through the boat hull, used to pass water or house instruments.
TILLER	A bar or handle attached to the rudder and used to turn the boat.
TOERAIL	The low, raised part of the gunwale.
TOPOGRAPHY	The configuration of the earth's surface.
TOPPING LIFT	A line that holds up a horizontal spar.
TOPSIDES	The portion of the hull above the waterline.
TRADE WINDS	The belt of winds blowing predominantly eastward, situated between the low pressure in the doldrums and the high pressure in the horse latitudes.
TRANSDUCER	A device that converts one type of energy to another, *e.g.*, The depth-sounder **transducer** changes electrical energy to sonic energy.
TRAVELER	An athwartships running track with a sliding car connected to the main sheet.
TRIM	To set a sail.
TRIMARAN	A multihulled boat with three hulls.

TROPICS	The area between the sun's northernmost and southernmost declination, which is the tropic of Cancer and the tropic of Capricorn.
TROPOSPHERE	The portion of the earth's atmosphere extending from the surface to the point where the temperature stops falling with an increase in altitude.
TRUE BEARING	A bearing relative to true north.
TRUE WIND	The wind's direction and strength as felt by a stationary object.
TSUNAMI	A long-period sea wave produced by an earthquake or volcanic eruption. Tsunamis can cause considerable damage near shore but are generally unnoticed at sea.
TUNE	To adjust the standing rigging.
TURNBUCKLE	A threaded fitting that, when turned, shortens or lengthens a cable.
TURTLE	A device to contain a spinnaker before it is set.
TWIST	A fall off or curvature of the sail's leech.
TWO-BLOCK	The position of a tackle when two opposing blocks touch, thereby preventing any further closing of the tackle.
UNDER WAY	The condition of a vessel under controlled motion.
UNIVERSAL TIME	Time as determined from the apparent diurnal motion of a fictitious mean sun moving along the celestial equator at an average rate. Universal time is dependent on the place where it is measured. Universal time is the same as Greenwich time.
UNSTABLE AIR	Air that is warmer than the air above it.
UPWELLING	The flow of water from depth toward the surface.
UPWIND	A direction relative to the wind. Toward the direction from which the wind is blowing.
VANE STEERING	A method of making a sailboat steer itself by using the action of the wind.
VANG	A device used to pull down on the boom and tighten the leech of a sail.
VAPOR PRESSURE	The pressure exerted by a vapor in equilibrium with its solid or liquid phase.
VARIATION	The angle between true north and magnetic north.
VECTOR	A quantity having both direction and magnitude, *e.g.*, wind velocity.
VEER	A clockwise shift of the wind.
VERNIER	A short auxiliary scale situated alongside the graduated scale of an instrument, used to determine the fractional parts of the smallest division of the main scale.
WAKE	Moving waves generated by the motion of a boat through the water.

WARP	To move a boat by using lines alone.
WATCH	A segment of the crew assigned responsiblity for the safety of the boat for a set time period.
WATERLINE	The intersection of the vessel's hull and the surface of the water.
WAYPOINT	An intermediate reference point on a vessel's intended course.
WEARING SHIP	Going from one tack to the other by turning the boat's stern through the wind.
WEATHER HELM	The tendency for a boat to turn into the wind.
WEIGH	To lift the anchor off the bottom.
WESTING	The ancient practice of sailing due west to reach a landfall.
WETTED SURFACE	The area of the hull and its appendages that is covered with water.
WHARF	A structure for ships to moor against.
WHIP	To bind the end of a rope with twine to prevent it from unraveling.
WHISKER POLE	A spar similar to a spinnaker pole used to hold out the clew of a jib when sailing wing-and-wing.
WILDCAT	The cogged wheel on a windlass or capstan that pulls on the chain.
WILLIWAW	A violent gust of wind.
WINCH	A geared drum turned by a handle and used to pull halyards, sheets, and other lines.
WIND GRADIENT	The variation in wind velocity at different heights above the water.
WINDLASS	A revolving cylinder on a horizontal axis around which line or chain can be wound. Usually used to recover anchor rode.
WINDMILLING	The free turning of the prop when the engine is not running due to the motion of the boat through the water.
WINDWARD	Upwind or into the wind.
WING-AND-WING	Sailing downwind with the jib poled out on one side and the main on the other side of the boat.
WIRE DRAG	A supplementary sounding operation that consists of towing a buoy wire at a prescribed depth to ensure the discovery of all obstructions.
WISHBONE	A spar in two halves, between which the sail is hoisted.
YARN	Fibers of a twisted rope that form a strand.
YAW	The twisting motion of a vessel in a horizontal plane.
YAWL	A two-masted fore-and-aft-rigged boat, with the smaller mast aft of the waterline or rudderpost.
ZULU TIME	Greenwich mean time.

INDEX

Note: *n* following a page number refers to a footnote; *t* refers to a table.